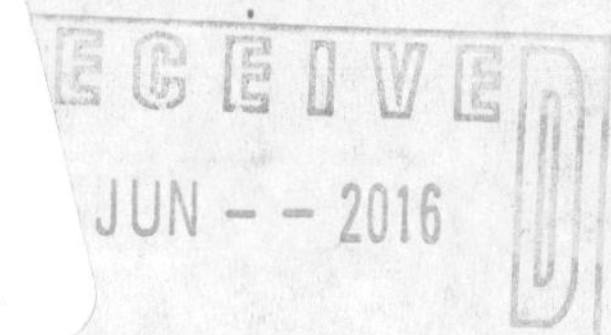


# Camping Northern California

*Middle McCloud Falls near Fowlers Campground in the Shasta-Trinity National Forest. Photo by Bubba Seuss*

## Help Us Keep This Guide Up to Date

Every effort has been made by the author and editors to make this guide as accurate and useful as possible. However, many things can change after a guide is published—trails are rerouted, regulations change, techniques evolve, facilities come under new management, etc.

We would love to hear from you concerning your experiences with this guide and how you feel it could be improved and kept up to date. While we may not be able to respond to all comments and suggestions, we'll take them to heart and we'll also make certain to share them with the author. Please send your comments and suggestions to the following address:


FalconGuides
Reader Response/Editorial Department
246 Goose Lane
Guilford, CT 06437


Or you may e-mail us at:


editorial@falcon.com


**Thanks for your input, and happy travels!**

# Camping Northern California

**Linda Parker Hamilton**

GUILFORD, CONNECTICUT
HELENA, MONTANA

To Doug, Ben & Max
For all the adventures
And all the love!

An imprint of Rowman & Littlefield

Falcon and FalconGuides are registered trademarks and Make Adventure Your Story is a trademark of Rowman & Littlefield.
Distributed by NATIONAL BOOK NETWORK



All photos by Linda Parker Hamilton unless otherwise noted.

Maps by Alena Pearce © Rowman & Littlefield



British Library Cataloguing-in-Publication Information available
Library of Congress Cataloging-in-Publication Data available

ISBN 978-1-4930-0000-5
ISBN 978-1-4930-2529-9 (e-book)

∞™ The paper used in this publication meets the minimum requirements of American National Standard for Information Sciences—Permanence of Paper for Printed Library Materials, ANSI/NISO Z39.48-1992.

# Contents

# Acknowledgments

Many people assisted me in the writing of this book. They are too numerous to mention individually, but I would be remiss if I did not at least acknowledge the organizations they represented. I am indebted to the many rangers and administrative personnel of the national, state, and county parks of California who provided information and offered me assistance, as well as the folks at PG&E Recreation, BLM, and more.

I would like to tip my hat to the many volunteers who are donating their time and energy in our national, state, and county parks and forests. Staffing information desks, assisting with outdoor programs, building and maintaining trails, protecting and adding space to our parklands, serving as campground hosts, and performing other tasks, these dedicated folks, many of them senior citizens and young people, provide many services and perform many jobs that would not otherwise get done. Much gratitude goes to fellow Falcon author Bubba Seuss (*Hiking California's Mount Shasta Region* and *Hiking California's Wine Country*) for his thoughtful fact-checking and suggestions. The book is more beautiful thanks to the folks who contributed photos from their outdoor adventures. And a big thank-you to Imee Curiel and Katie Benoit Cardoso and the rest of the staff at Falcon for their encouragement, patience, and great assistance in getting this book into your hands.

# Introduction

## Welcome to California

Welcome to California, the Golden State, the most populous state in the Union and the third largest geographically. By far the richest state in terms of gross product, California is more appropriately compared to nations than to other states. In this context, California is the seventh-largest "nation" in the world, its gross product exceeded only by that of the United States, Great Britain, Russia, Germany, France, and Japan.

Driving this economic dynamo is agriculture, where California's output far exceeds that of any other state. If the Midwest is the breadbasket of the United States, California is its fruit and vegetable basket, leading the nation in production of grapes, tomatoes, lettuce, and a host of other orchard and vegetable crops. In manufacturing, mineral extraction, and fishing, California ranks among the top four states. With Hollywood and Silicon Valley, California sets trends in entertainment and leads the way in technology.

Geographically, the state resembles a giant water trough. The coast ranges on the west and the Sierra Nevada to the east serve as sides to the trough, while the Central Valley runs north–south through its bottom. Both the highest and lowest points in the contiguous forty-eight states are found in California less than 100 miles apart. Mount Whitney soars to 14,495 feet, while Death Valley plunges to 282 feet below sea level.

The climate of California is as diverse as its landscape. The high reaches of the Sierra Nevada experience arctic winter temperatures, while the southeastern deserts bake in summer's heat. However, in the main, the state has dry summers and rainy winters, with regional variations. The coast from the Oregon border to just north of Los Angeles has cool summers and mild winters. South of Los Angeles, coastal residents enjoy some of the most pleasant year-round temperatures found anywhere. In the Central Valley a continental climate prevails, with hot summers and cool winters, and the mountainous regions are noted for short summers and cold winters.

The 500-some tribes of indigenous people in California, speaking around one hundred distinct languages, thrived for nearly 20,000 years on the abundant resources of the land. Spanish navigator Juan Rodriguez Cabrillo was the first known European to sight California, in 1542. But it was not until 1769 that Franciscan friar Junípero Serra established the first mission at San Diego. Additional missions and the opening of an overland supply route from Mexico spurred colonization from the south, and following Mexico's independence from Spain in 1821, American settlers began to arrive from the east. In 1846 a group of American settlers proclaimed the establishment of the California Republic, and in May of that year the United States declared war on Mexico. In the peace treaty that followed, Mexico ceded California to the United States, paving the way for California to become the thirty-first state in 1850.

*The California poppy is the official state flower.*

With its diverse landscape, its relatively mild climate, and its magnificent scenery, California is a paradise for outdoor and sports enthusiasts. The state contains 27 national parks and monuments, over 500 state and county parks, 20 million acres of national forests, and numerous other recreational lands under federal, state, and local jurisdiction. There are more than 1,200 public campgrounds accessible by car. Stretching from the northern mountains to the southern deserts, they range from primitive sites for tents or self-contained RVs to plush resorts with pools, spas, tennis courts, and even golf courses. What they have in common is that they all provide a memorable outdoor experience.

## Camping in Northern California

Northern California has a campground for everyone. In addition to hundreds of standard family campgrounds, there are campgrounds designed for hikers, bikers, equestrians, boaters, anglers, and off-road-vehicle drivers.

This book describes more than 700 campgrounds accessible by conventional vehicles and managed by public agencies in Northern California. Together, the following agencies administer more than 95 percent of all the public campgrounds in the state.

The National Park Service (NPS) manages campgrounds in all eight North California national parks; in Lava Beds, Devils Postpile, and Pinnacles National Monuments; and in Point Reyes and Whiskeytown-Shasta-Trinity National Recreation Areas. Two made *Sunset* magazine's West's Best Camping list: Summit Lake South Campground in Lassen Volcanic National Park and Pinnacles National Park. Some NPS campgrounds accept reservations, some require them, and others are available only on a first-come, first-served basis. This information is provided in the individual campground entries. NPS campgrounds do not have hookups. Most charge a fee, but some more remote sites with minimum facilities are free.

The USDA Forest Service manages by far the largest number of campgrounds in Northern California. They are found in all thirteen national forests: Six Rivers, Klamath, Modoc, Shasta-Trinity, Lassen, Mendocino, Plumas, Tahoe, Eldorado, Toiyabe, Stanislaus, Inyo, and Sierra. *Sunset* magazine has listed seven of these forest service campgrounds among the top campgrounds in the western United States: Mary Smith at Lewiston Lake in Shasta-Trinity, Highland Lakes Campground in Stanislaus National Forest, Minaret Falls and Saddlebag Lake in Inyo, Woods Lake and Wrights Lake in Eldorado, and Summerdale Campground in Sierra. Although most forest service campsites are available on a first-come, first-served basis, reservations are accepted at the more popular locations, some of which have hookups. Most developed forest service campgrounds charge a fee, and many are operated by concessionaires. At many undeveloped sites, no fee is charged.

In the national forests you needn't restrict your stay to established campgrounds. You may camp anywhere unless specifically prohibited from doing so, as long as your campsite is at least 100 feet from bodies of water, trails, and roadsides. Check with the nearest forest service office or ranger station, where personnel can recommend the best areas for such open camping. These are generally referred to as dispersed sites—pristine and quiet places accessible on park and forest roads. Bring clean drinking water. It is important to have a minimal impact, leaving the site as clean and natural as you found it.

A campfire permit is required outside developed campgrounds, even to cook with a camp stove or charcoal brazier. The permit is free at forest service facilities.

The California Department of Parks and Recreation manages campgrounds in some of the most scenic and recreational areas of the state. *Sunset* magazine includes nine of these areas in its West's Best Camping list: Big Basin Redwoods, D. L. Bliss, Jedediah Smith Redwoods, Russian Gulch, Gerstle Cove in Salt Point, Butano, Henry W. Coe, Samuel P. Taylor, and New Brighton Beach. Many state park campgrounds accept reservations, and during the summer months you'll most likely need them, especially on weekends or holidays. Many state park campgrounds offer hookups; of those that do not, many have flush toilets and hot showers. All state park campgrounds charge a fee.

Individual counties offer first-rate campgrounds in scenic areas that are often off the beaten path and sometimes overlooked by the traveling hordes of summer. If

*Campers in Northern California have a wealth of diversity from which to choose—from campgrounds sprawled across sunny coastal beaches to those tucked amid alpine splendor with views like this one of Mount Shasta. Photo by Bubba Seuss*

you are inclined to pass over county campgrounds, Big Lagoon in Humboldt made *Sunset*'s list. About half of all county campgrounds accept reservations, and about half (not necessarily the same half) have hookups. All charge a fee.

The Bureau of Land Management administers campgrounds in the coast ranges, Cascades, and Sierra Nevada. BLM campgrounds do not accept reservations, and none have hookups. About half the campgrounds charge a fee; undeveloped campgrounds are usually free. You can find many dispersed campsites on BLM land too.

The US Army Corps of Engineers has constructed a series of dams throughout California, and many of the reservoirs created by these dams offer a full range of water sports. The Corps has constructed campgrounds at most of these reservoirs; some have hookups. Corps campgrounds offer amenities, including flush toilets and showers. Some campgrounds accept reservations; other sites are available on a first-come, first-served basis. Fees are charged at all locations.

Special districts and municipalities also manage campgrounds throughout the state. Special district facilities are similar to Corps sites in that they are usually associated with water reclamation projects, such as lakes. Cities and townships also manage campgrounds, normally in connection with a nearby point of interest or within a park. Most have hookups and accept reservations; all charge fees.

## Travel Tips

**Reservations.** If you are traveling in summer, on holidays, or on weekends, it is a good idea to make reservations wherever it is possible to do so—especially for longer stays. Beach, national park, state park, and many other campgrounds fill quickly during these periods, and campers who arrive late may find no vacancies.

**Discounts.** Many public campgrounds offer discounts to senior citizens. The National Park Service, USDA Forest Service, Bureau of Land Management, and US Army Corps of Engineers offer discounts to campers holding Golden Age Passports, and California state parks and recreation areas offer discounts to campers 62 years of age and older. The NPS offers free entry to parks (not campgrounds) for fourth graders and their families as well. Check online for other discounts.

**Pets.** In almost all public and private campgrounds where pets are permitted, they must be confined or leashed. In county, state, and national parks, pets are normally not permitted on hiking trails or beaches. In national forests pets are prohibited on some trails. Public campgrounds often charge additional fees for pets.

**Wheelchair access.** Many public campgrounds have wheelchair-accessible facilities, including restrooms. These campgrounds are indicated on the quick-reference tables in this book. Some have wheelchair-accessible trails. Because many public jurisdictions are making efforts to upgrade the accessibility of existing facilities, you should contact individual campgrounds for the latest information.

**Fishing and hunting licenses.** Licenses are required in California for both saltwater and freshwater fishing. You can purchase an annual license for residents or nonresidents or a license for one, two, or ten days. There are significant discounts for low-income seniors and Native Americans and disabled and recovering military veterans.

To be eligible for a hunting license in California, you must take an approved hunter safety course, present a hunter safety certificate from another state or Canadian province, or present a valid hunting license from another state or province.

**Rules of the road.** The speed limit on rural interstate highways is 65 miles per hour unless otherwise posted. Elsewhere, speed limits are as posted. Right turns at red lights are permitted after stopping unless posted otherwise. At least two people must be riding in a vehicle to use car-pool lanes. All passengers must wear seatbelts. Children up to 8 years of age or under 4 feet 9 inches in height must be in a child-restraint safety seat. Automobile liability insurance is mandatory.

**Maps.** Although it is possible to find most of the campgrounds in this book by using the maps and directions furnished with the entries, additional maps are required to find some of the more remote ones. For those who want more detail, try the DeLorme Mapping Company's *Northern California Atlas and Gazetteer,* available in most large bookstores. For camping in the national forests, the appropriate forest service map is essential to locate the more remote campgrounds and is an invaluable guide, particularly if you intend to hike or explore by car, horseback, or bicycle.

*In many areas of Northern California under an elevation of 5,000 feet in areas of open sunlight, poison oak may be present in the underbrush. The rule goes: "Leaves of three, let it be." If you don't touch it, you can admire its beautiful red color in the fall.*

Maps are available at forest service visitor centers and most ranger stations. You can also order them from the USDA Forest Service by mail (630 Sansome St., San Francisco 94111). Maps for each of the thirteen national forests in Northern California are available for a small cost. A word of warning, though: Campground information on forest service maps is not always up to date. This is particularly true with regard to fee status and availability of water. Some district offices have published separate pamphlets that update campground information. Finally, a good state road map is an excellent tool for getting an overall picture of an area and for finding nearby points of interest, and an up-to-date GPS navigator in your car can help you get there.

**Rules for RVs.** Passengers are not permitted to ride in trailers but may ride in fifth-wheelers if there is a way to communicate with the driver. Trailer brakes and safety chains are required for trailers weighing over 1,500 pounds; power-brake systems require breakaway switches. The maximum width for RVs driving on California roads is 102 inches, and the maximum combined length for two or three vehicles is 65 feet. Propane cylinders must be turned off while your vehicle is in motion. RVs are required to carry a fire extinguisher.

**Off-season travel.** One of the best times to travel in Northern California is the fall. After Labor Day, students and teachers go back to school and campgrounds are less crowded, as are beaches, hiking trails, and other points of interest. Travel is more enjoyable without the hassle of bucking large crowds on the road and at tourist attractions. Spring can also be an excellent time to hit the road, although the weather is not always as favorable. Snow may linger in the mountains, closing roads to certain campgrounds and scenic areas, and spring runoff can cause landslides, road blockages, and muddy conditions. However, spring is the greenest time of year in California and the best time to view waterfalls.

**Avoiding the crowds.** Unless you simply must have your TV or microwave, go to the more remote places, those without hookups and with minimal amenities. You will have more privacy, better scenery, more room between sites, and a better chance to see wildlife. This is particularly true for self-contained RVers, who do not need to rely on hookups.

**Ocean access.** The waters of the Pacific off the Northern California coast are cold and often have undertows. Look for signs at beaches for more information. Proceed with caution if wading or swimming, and heed the adage: Never turn your back on the ocean.

# How to Use This Guide

For the purposes of this book, we have defined Northern California as extending from the Oregon border to the southern borders of Santa Cruz, Santa Clara, Merced, Madera, and Mono Counties. For purposes of tourism and travel, the California Division of Tourism has divided the state into twelve tour regions. Of these, four fall completely within the borders of Northern California and two lie partially inside its boundary. We have grouped campgrounds using these same tour regions, usually in the order of their location along or near major highways.

This book is written primarily for campers who want to drive to campgrounds in conventional, two-wheel-drive vehicles. Thus, the campgrounds listed here vary from plush, amenity-rich locations to wilderness sites with no facilities except scenery and solitude. But there are also hundreds of backcountry and trailside campgrounds that are accessible only to hikers and backpackers, and many of the campgrounds described here serve as excellent base camps from which to reach them. For information about these backcountry sites, consult offices and publications of the forest service, national and state parks, BLM, and similar organizations. While this book focuses on family campgrounds, if there is a group campground adjacent or nearby, it will be mentioned in the campground description. In the national forests, the minimum number of people for group campsites can be as few as one person. If you don't mind the cost, booking one of these assures your family space to run.

For each of the six tour regions covered in *Camping Northern California*, the following information is provided:

- A map of the tour region, as well as maps of smaller areas within the regions.
- A table listing all the campgrounds in the region and their most important attributes.
- A brief overview of the region and, in some cases, of areas within the region.
- A description of each of the public campgrounds within the region.

**Maps of the tour regions.** With the exception of the San Francisco Bay Area and the Central Valley, each of the six tour regions covered in this book has been divided into smaller areas. The regional maps indicate the boundaries of these areas. Each area map shows the location of the campgrounds located within it, with the number on the map corresponding to the number of the campground description within the text.

The maps in this book are not drawn to scale, and campground locations are approximate. However, by using the maps and the instructions in the "Finding the campground" section of each campground description, you should have no difficulty reaching most of the sites. You may need additional maps to find some of the more-remote campgrounds, as noted previously.

**Quick-reference tables.** For quick reference, a table at the beginning of each section lists all the campgrounds in the area and highlights their most important attributes. If you are looking for specific amenities, such as fishing or wheelchair-accessibility, you can use these tables to narrow your selection of campgrounds.

**Overview.** Highlights and points of interest within the tour region are discussed briefly here. Overviews of smaller areas within the region are also included.

**Campground descriptions.** Each campground description is numbered to correspond with the campground's location on the map. For each campground, the following information is provided:

- **Location.** This is the name of a city or town near the campground, the distance in miles from that city to the campground, and the general direction of travel to reach it.
- **GPS coordinates.** The coordinates of the campground or check-in site for the campground.
- **Sites.** This information provides the number of campsites available and whether tents, RVs, or both are allowed. It also indicates whether hookups are available.
- **Facilities.** This describes the facilities and amenities provided, including any recreational facilities available at the campground. For wheelchair accessibility, please refer to the quick-reference tables and contact the campground management or reservation system for the number of sites and other details.
- **Water.** Some public campgrounds do not provide drinking water, and this fact is indicated in this section. But a "no drinking water" notation does not necessarily mean there is no water at the site. Nonpotable water may be available at the campground or from a nearby stream or lake. In either case, the water should be filtered, boiled, or otherwise treated before use.
- **Fee per night.** This is given as a rating. If a campground charges different fees for different sites, the rating includes the highest fee (not including group campground rates, unless noted). Sites that accept reservations usually charge a reservation fee. (***Note:*** Fees are subject to change.)

  None
  $ = Under $20
  $$ = $20 to $29
  $$$ = $30 to $39
  $$$$ = $40 and over

**Reservations.** Many public campgrounds do not accept reservations. For those that do, information about obtaining reservations is provided. If the "Fee per night" section does not mention reservations, the campground does not accept them. In this case, they are first come, first served. Often campgrounds that take reservations will reserve a couple sites for walk-ins.

- **Management.** The authority managing the campground is identified here, along with contact information. As indicated earlier, more than 95 percent of the public

*From full hookup RV sites to hike & bike sites, you'll find the amenities and type of experience you are looking for in Northern California's diverse and abundant campgrounds.*

campgrounds in this book are controlled by one of the following entities: national, state, or county parks; USDA Forest Service; BLM; US Army Corps of Engineers; or various municipal and regional water authorities. The number listed is specific to the ranger district or concessionaire managing the site at the time of writing.

- **Activities.** Recreational activities that can take place at or from the campground are listed here. For example, swimming may be possible at a lakeside campground, hiking trails may be within walking distance of a campground, or boats may be launched from a campground boat launch.
- **Finding the campground.** Detailed instructions are furnished for driving to the campground from the nearest city, town, or major highway. Although it is possible to find most of the campgrounds in this book using these directions and the corresponding map, the task will be easier with the help of forest service maps and/or a good state road map, as well as an up-to-date GPS navigator.
- **About the campground.** This is the information that differentiates this particular campground from others or highlights special features. For example, if a campground is located on the water (ocean, lake, river, or stream), that fact is noted. Also in this section, you will learn the campground's elevation, stay limits, and open season. Many campgrounds are open year-round; others are seasonal. The opening and closing dates can change depending on weather conditions.

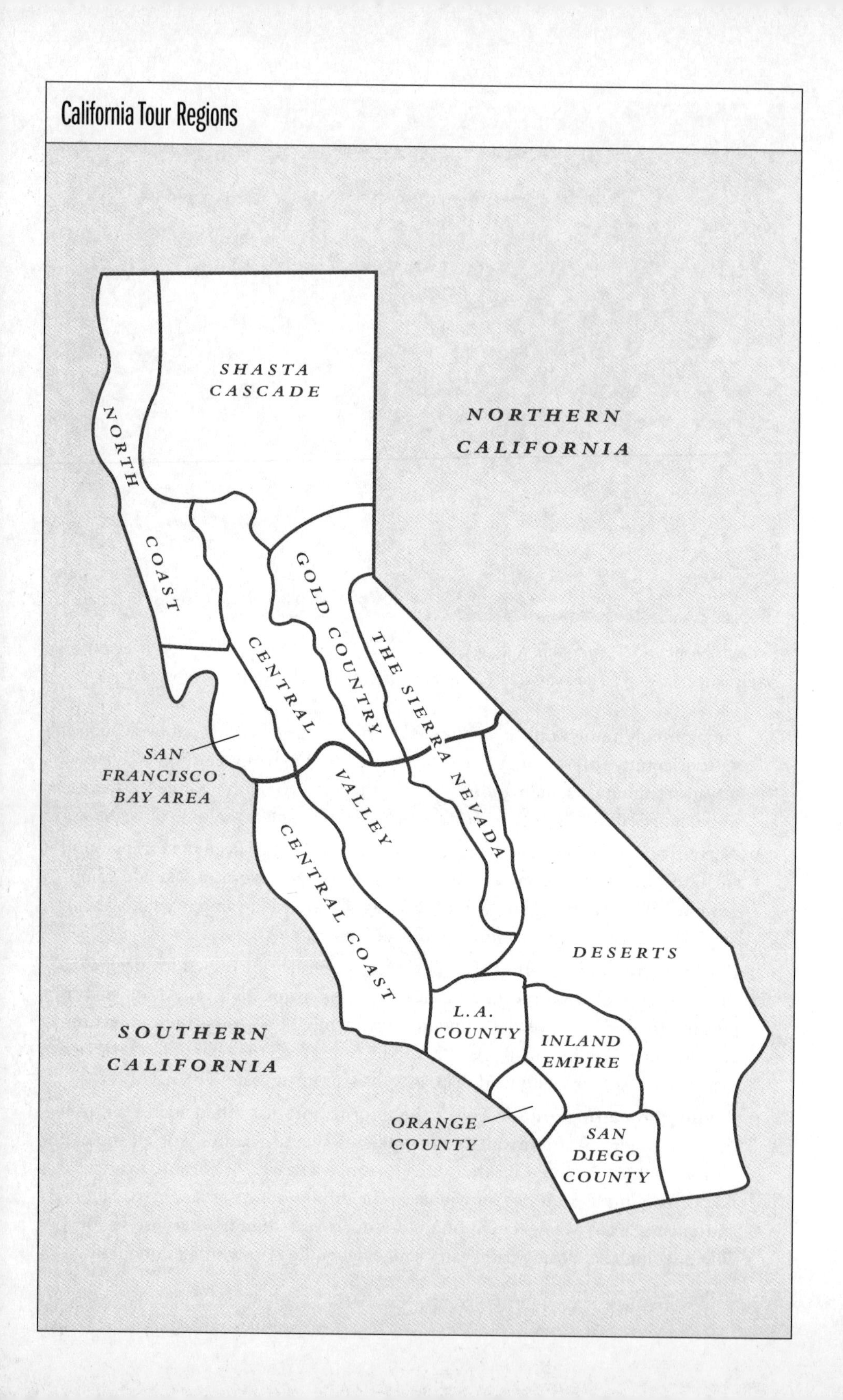
California Tour Regions
SHASTA CASCADE
NORTHERN CALIFORNIA
NORTH COAST
GOLD COUNTRY
THE SIERRA NEVADA
CENTRAL VALLEY
SAN FRANCISCO BAY AREA
CENTRAL COAST
DESERTS
L.A. COUNTY
INLAND EMPIRE
SOUTHERN CALIFORNIA
ORANGE COUNTY
SAN DIEGO COUNTY

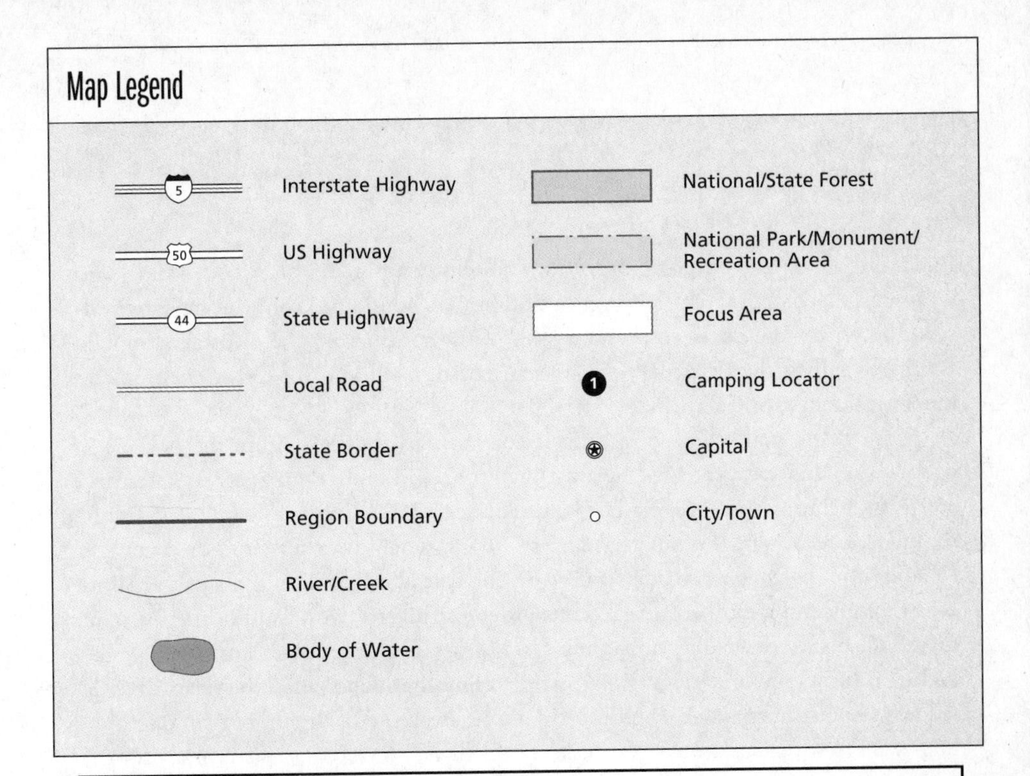


## KEY TO ABBREVIATIONS

I have tried to minimize the use of abbreviations in this book. The few that have crept in are shown below, as well as some that may be encountered on maps or in other travel references.

- **AAA:** American Automobile Association
- **ATV:** All-terrain vehicle
- **BLM:** Bureau of Land Management
- **FR:** Forest Service Road. These letters precede numbers, as in FR 18S03, and designate roads in national forests maintained by the USDA Forest Service. They always appear on forest service maps, but the roads themselves may not always be signed.
- **NPS:** National Park Service
- **OHV:** Off-highway vehicle. This usually refers to a campground or a trail for the primary use of those who wish to drive trail motorcycles, all-terrain vehicles, four-wheel-drive vehicles, and snowmobiles. It does not include mountain bikes. In some publications the abbreviation ORV (off-road vehicle) may be used instead.
- **PG&E:** Pacific Gas and Electric Company
- **SRA:** State Recreation Area
- **SVRA:** State Vehicle Recreation Area (for use of off-highway vehicles)

# North Coast

Extending from the Oregon border to the southern borders of Sonoma and Napa Counties, the North Coast is a region of dramatic contrasts. From the majestic redwood forests of the north to the vineyards of the south, from the Coastal Mountain Range inland to the rugged Pacific Ocean coastline, the North Coast encompasses much of the best of California.

Most of the state's surviving ancient coastal redwoods lie within the borders of this region. They are protected by a national park and more than a dozen state parks and groves. From the Oregon border to Bodega Bay, almost 400 miles of Pacific shoreline lure beachgoers, anglers, surfers, divers, whale watchers, and drivers eager to enjoy the spectacular coastal scenery. To the east, the 2 million acres of the Smith River and Mendocino National Forests provide a diverse woodland home for more than 300 species of wildlife, including black bears, deer, mountain lions, bald eagles, and wild turkeys. World-renowned vineyards line the Napa Valley, the heart of California's wine country. Only slightly less famous are some of the more than one hundred wineries that line the Russian River north of Santa Rosa in Sonoma County; both Mendocino and Lake Counties also produce fine wines.

The temperature of the North Coast varies relatively little and is moderate year-round. However, precipitation varies considerably with the seasons. Over most of the area, more than 90 percent of the annual rainfall occurs from October through April. Rainfall is fairly heavy in the north, averaging 65 inches annually in Del Norte County. Precipitation decreases as you move southward, averaging 38 inches in Humboldt and Mendocino Counties and 30 inches in Sonoma County. Coastal areas are subject to morning fog. Average temperatures range from 42°F to 57°F in winter, 46°F to 60°F in spring, 51°F to 65°F in summer, and 45°F to 64°F in autumn. The average percentage of sunny days declines from a high of 55 percent in spring to 54 percent in summer, 49 percent in fall, and 43 percent in winter.

This guide divides the North Coast into three areas: Redwood Empire, Mendocino, and Sonoma-Napa.

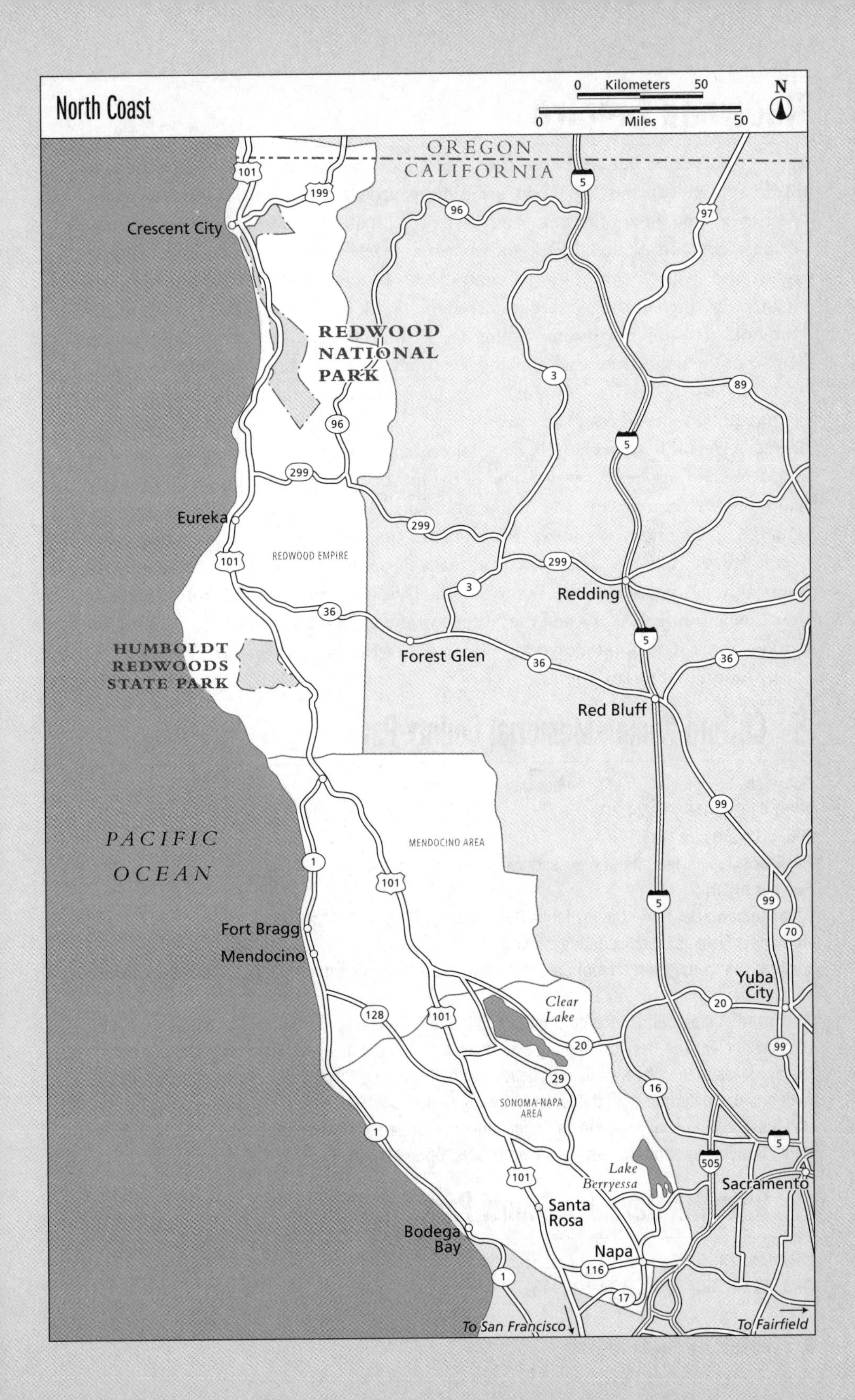
North Coast
0 Kilometers 50
0 Miles 50
N
OREGON
CALIFORNIA
Crescent City
REDWOOD
NATIONAL
PARK
Eureka
REDWOOD EMPIRE
HUMBOLDT
REDWOODS
STATE PARK
Forest Glen
Redding
Red Bluff
PACIFIC
OCEAN
MENDOCINO AREA
Fort Bragg
Mendocino
Clear
Lake
Yuba
City
SONOMA-NAPA
AREA
Lake
Berryessa
Sacramento
Santa
Rosa
Bodega
Bay
Napa
To San Francisco
To Fairfield
101
199
96
5
97
3
89
299
36
1
128
20
29
16
505
99
70
116
17

# Redwood Empire

Sparsely populated but with a great natural endowment of beaches, forests, and fish-filled rivers and streams, the Redwood Empire attracts sports enthusiasts of all stripes. Overshadowing all are the huge and ancient coastal redwoods, which are preserved within Redwood National Park and almost a dozen state parks and groves. But the region also boasts many miles of sandy ocean beaches and hosts California's Lost Coast, created when rugged terrain forced the builders of scenic CA 1 to turn inland. Humboldt Bay offers saltwater fishing for salmon, halibut, and perch, while inland lie two of the nation's best salmon and steelhead rivers, the Smith and the Klamath.

In the east, Six Rivers National Forest encompasses nearly 1 million acres of forest and 1,500 miles of rivers and streams, including 366 miles of designated Wild and Scenic Rivers. These beckon anglers, rafters, kayakers, and swimmers. You can find world-class fishing here, as well as one of the most barrier-free fishing locations in the nation. Hikers, equestrians, and mountain bikers have hundreds of miles of trails and mining and logging roads to explore. The road-bound tourist can enjoy Smith River Scenic Byway (US 199) as it twists and turns through a granite gorge created by the Smith River. A portion of the Trinity Scenic Byway travels eastward from Blue Lake near Eureka along CA 299, and the Avenue of the Giants brings motorists among the world's largest remaining redwoods. The towns of Eureka and Ferndale are noted for their beautiful Victorian homes.

## 1 Clifford Kamph Memorial County Park

**Location:** 18 miles north of Crescent City
**GPS:** 41.973458 / -124.203478
**Sites:** 12 sites for tents
**Facilities:** Tables, fire pits with grills, drinking water, flush toilets
**Fee per night:** $
**Management:** Del Norte County Parks Department, (707) 464-7230
**Activities:** Fishing, beachcombing, surfing
**Finding the campground:** From Crescent City, drive 21 miles north on US 101. Entrance is to the west.
**About the campground:** Located 3 miles south of the Oregon border, campsites are on an open bluff overlooking the Pacific, requiring a short walk from the parking lot. The park offers one of the few accesses to the often-windswept beach north of Crescent City. Private homes bordering the park detract somewhat from the isolated feeling of the coastline. Anglers try for lingcod, cabezon, and rockfish but usually have to settle for surfperch. Surfers camp here and drive down US 101 to South Beach. Elevation 48 feet. Stay limit 5 days. Open all year.

## 2 Ruby Van Deventer County Park

**Location:** 13 miles northeast of Crescent City
**GPS:** 41.851654100 / -124.121046100

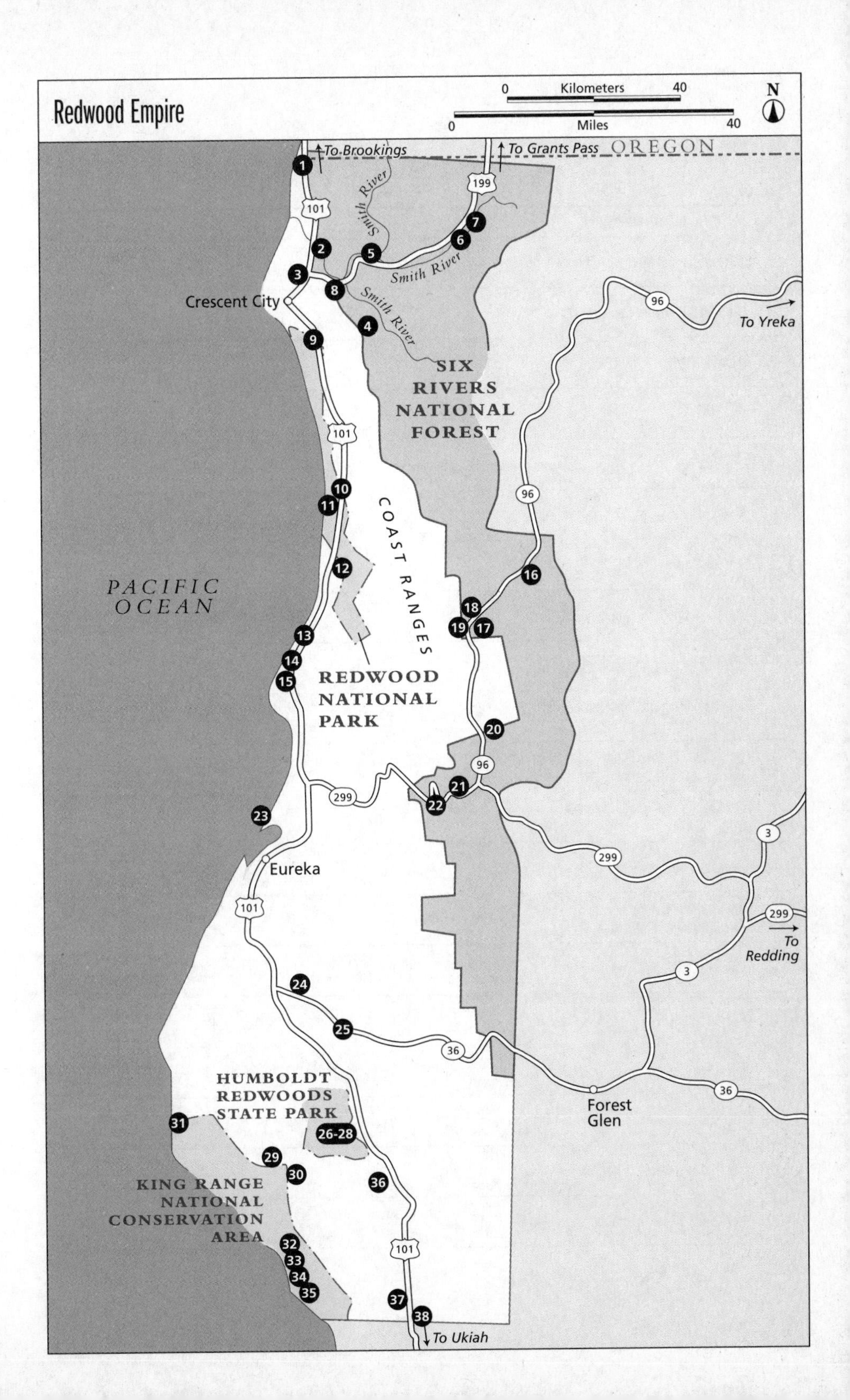

Redwood Empire
0 Kilometers 40
0 Miles 40
N
To Brookings
To Grants Pass
OREGON
Smith River
Smith River
Smith River
Crescent City
To Yreka
SIX RIVERS NATIONAL FOREST
COAST RANGES
PACIFIC OCEAN
REDWOOD NATIONAL PARK
Eureka
To Redding
HUMBOLDT REDWOODS STATE PARK
Forest Glen
KING RANGE NATIONAL CONSERVATION AREA
To Ukiah

| | Name | Group Sites | RV Sites | Max. RV Length | Hookups | Toilets | Showers | Drinking Water | Dump Station | Pets | Wheelchair | Recreation | Fee(s) | Season | Can Reserve |
|---|---|---|---|---|---|---|---|---|---|---|---|---|---|---|---|
| | **REDWOOD EMPIRE** | | | | | | | | | | | | | | |
| 1 | Clifford Kamph Memorial County Park | | | | | F | | * | | * | | F | $ | Year-round | |
| 2 | Ruby Van Deventer County Park | | | | | F | | * | | * | | FSB | $ | Year-round | |
| 3 | Florence Keller County Park | | * | 32 | 1 | F | | * | | * | | HFB | $-$$ | Year-round | |
| 4 | Big Flat | | * | 32 | | V | | | | * | | H | $ | May-Oct | |
| 5 | Panther Flat | | * | 45 | | F | * | * | | * | | SBHF | $$$ | Year-round | * |
| 6 | Grassy Flat | | * | 40 | | V | | | | * | * | FBS | $ | June-Sept | * |
| 7 | Patrick Creek | | * | | | F | | * | | * | * | FS | $ | June-Sept | * |
| 8 | Jedediah Smith Redwoods State Park | | * | 36 | | F | * | * | * | * | * | HFSB | $$$ | Year-round | * |
| 9 | Del Norte Coast Redwoods State Park | | * | 31 | | F | * | * | * | * | * | HF | $$$ | May-Dec | * |
| 10 | Elk Prairie (Prairie Creek Redwoods State Park) | | * | 27 | | F | * | * | * | * | * | HF | $$$ | Year-round | * |
| 11 | Gold Bluffs Beach (Prairie Creek Redwoods State Park ) | | | | | F | * | * | | * | * | HF | $$$ | Year-round | * |
| 12 | Dry Lagoon (Humboldt Lagoons State Park) | | | | | P | | | | * | | HBF | $ | Year-round | |
| 13 | Big Lagoon County Park | | * | | | F | | * | | * | * | BSF | $$ | Year-round | |
| 14 | Agate, Abalone & Penn Creek (Patrick's Point State Park) | * | * | 31 | | F | * | * | | * | * | HF | $$$$ | Year-round | * |
| 15 | Clam Beach County Park | | * | | | V | | * | | * | * | F | $$ | Year-round | |
| 16 | Pearch Creek | | * | 40 | | V | | * | | * | | HFS | $ | May-Nov | |
| 17 | E-Ne-Nuck | | * | 30 | | V | | * | | * | | F | $ | June-Oct | |
| 18 | Fish Lake | | * | 28 | | V | | * | | * | | FSBH | $ | May-Oct | * |
| 19 | Aikens Creek West | | * | 35 | | P | | | | * | | FSBH | None | Year-round | |
| 20 | Tish Tang | | * | 28 | | V | | | | * | | FSB | $ | June-Oct | |

|  | Name | Group Sites | RV Sites | Max. RV Length | Hookups | Toilets | Showers | Drinking Water | Dump Station | Pets | Wheelchair | Recreation | Fee(s) | Season | Can Reserve |
|---|---|---|---|---|---|---|---|---|---|---|---|---|---|---|---|
| 21 | Boise Creek |  | * | 35 |  | V |  | * |  | * | * | HFS | $ | May–Oct |  |
| 22 | East Fork |  | * | 20 |  | V |  |  |  | * | * | HF | $ | May–Oct |  |
| 23 | Samoa Boat Launch County Park |  | * |  |  | F | * | * |  | * | * | SFBLO | $$ | Year-round |  |
| 24 | Swimmer's Delight (Van Duzen County Park) | * | * |  | E | F | * | * |  | * | * | FSB | $$ | Year-round |  |
| 25 | Grizzly Creek Redwoods State Park |  | * | 30 |  | F | * | * |  | * | * | HSF | $$$ | Year-round | * |
| 26 | Burlington (Humboldt Redwoods State Park) |  | * | 36 |  | F | * | * | * | * | * | HSF | $$$ | Year-round | * |
| 27 | Hidden Springs (Humboldt Redwoods State Park) | * | * | 36 |  | F | * | * |  | * | * | HSF | $$$ | May–Oct | * |
| 28 | Albee Creek (Humboldt Redwoods State Park) | * | * | 36 |  | F | * | * |  | * | * | HM | $$$ | May–Sept | * |
| 29 | A. W. Way County Park |  | * |  |  | F | * | * |  | * | * | HFS | $$ | Year-round |  |
| 30 | Honeydew Creek (King Range National Conservation Area) |  | * |  |  | V |  |  |  | * | * |  | $ | Year-round |  |
| 31 | Mattole Beach (King Range National Conservation Area) |  | * |  |  | P |  |  |  | * |  | HF | $ | Year-round |  |
| 32 | Nadelos (King Range National Conservation Area) | * |  |  |  | V |  | * |  | * | * | H | $ | Year-round |  |
| 33 | Wailaki (King Range National Conservation Area ) |  | * |  |  | V |  | * |  | * | * | H | $ | Year-round |  |
| 34 | Tolkan (King Range National Conservation Area) |  | * |  |  | V |  | * |  | * | * | H | $ | Year-round |  |
| 35 | Horse Mountain (King Range National Conservation Area) |  | * |  |  | P |  | * |  | * |  | H | $ | Year-round |  |
| 36 | Benbow Lake State Recreation Area |  | * | 30 | E | F | * | * | * | * | * | SBFL | $$$–$$$$ | Year-round | * |
| 37 | Huckleberry & Madrone (Richardson Grove State Park) |  | * | 30 |  | F | * | * | * | * | * | HSF | $$$ | Year-round | * |
| 38 | Oak Flat (Richardson Grove State Park) |  | * | 30 |  | F | * | * |  | * | * | HSF | $$$$ | June–Sept | * |

Toilets: F=flush V=vault P=pit C=chemical; Fee: $=Under $20 $$=$20–$29 $$$=$30–$39 $$$$ $40 or more; Recreation: H=hiking S=swimming F=fishing B=boating L=boat launch O=off-highway driving R=horseback riding, M=mountain biking Hookups: W=water E=electric S=sewer

**Sites:** 18 sites for tents (parking lot for RVs)
**Facilities:** Tables, grills, drinking water, flush toilets
**Fee per night:** $
**Management:** Del Norte County Parks Department, (707) 464-7230
**Activities:** Swimming, kayaking, seasonal fishing
**Finding the campground:** From the intersection of US 101 and US 199 (about 5 miles northeast of Crescent City), drive east on US 199 for 4.3 miles; turn north onto CA 197 (North Bank Road), and drive 4 miles.
**About the campground:** The campground is situated in a beautiful and usually quiet stand of redwood trees on the banks of the Smith River, the only river system without any dam in California. Access to the Smith River is only 50 yards away, offering swimming, kayaking, and seasonal trout and salmon fishing. It's also a good camp for cyclists touring on US 101. Stay limit 5 days. Open all year.

## 3 Florence Keller County Park

**Location:** 3 miles north of Crescent City
**GPS:** 41.808700600 / -124.151537400
**Sites:** 50 sites for tents and RVs (up to 32 feet), including 1 with full hookup
**Facilities:** Tables, fire pits with grills, drinking water, flush toilets
**Fee per night:** $, full-hookup site: $$
**Management:** Del Norte County Parks Department, (707) 464-7230
**Activities:** Hiking, fishing, kayaking, picnicking, horseshoes, volleyball, playground
**Finding the campground:** From the intersection of US 101 and US 199 (about 5 miles northeast of Crescent City), drive north on US 101 for 0.5 mile. Turn west onto Elk Valley Crossroad and then south onto Cunningham Lane to the park entrance.
**About the campground:** Campsites are tucked in a majestic stand of redwood trees with a small fern-lined creek running through it. There are hiking trails through several parts of the forest, one of which is wheelchair accessible. Lake Earl, about 5 miles away, is the largest coastal lagoon in California. It provides great birding, fishing for cutthroat trout, and light kayaking. It is also popular with local duck hunters. With Crescent City only 3 miles away, you can enjoy its amenities while camping, including a nine-hole golf course and drive-in theater. Limit 5 days. Open all year.

## 4 Big Flat

**Location:** 25 miles southeast of Crescent City
**GPS:** 41.686450 / -123.912778
**Sites:** 23 sites for tents and RVs up to 32 feet long
**Facilities:** Tables, fire rings, vault toilets; no drinking water
**Fee per night:** $
**Management:** Six Rivers National Forest, (707) 442-1721
**Activities:** Hiking
**Finding the campground:** From Crescent City, go north on US 101 and US 199 and continue east on US 199. Turn east onto South Fork Road (CR 427). Turn north onto French Hill Road (CR 405). Turn northwest into the Big Flat Campground entrance. The last 0.5 mile is maintained dirt road.
**About the campground:** Located on the banks of Hurdygurdy Creek, the campground is small and quiet, semi-open with pole pines shading some sites. Shrubs and grass fill in between sites. Hiking

trails explore the surrounding ridges and streambeds. An "all access trail" leads north from the campground 2 miles to Fox Flat. At several South Fork River access points within 0.5 mile you can fish and swim. Elevation 685 feet. Stay limit 14 days. Open mid-May through October.

## 5 Panther Flat

**Location:** 20 miles northeast of Crescent City
**GPS:** 41.84306 / -123.93056
**Sites:** 39 sites for tents and RVs up to 45 feet long
**Facilities:** Tables, grills, drinking water, showers, flush toilets
**Fee per night:** $$$; reservations: (877) 444-6777 or recreation.gov
**Management:** Six Rivers National Forest, (707) 442-1721
**Activities:** Swimming, rafting, sunbathing, hiking, biking, fishing
**Finding the campground:** From the intersection of US 101 and US 199 (about 5 miles northeast of Crescent City), take US 199 east for 16 miles to the campground.
**About the campground:** Set in a mature forest of Douglas fir, cedar, and Pacific madrone trees, Panther Flat Campground is steps away from the Smith River. Anglers can find challenging seasonal fishing for salmon, steelhead, and cutthroat trout. There are no trailheads in the campground, but there are many within 10 miles of the site. A botanical trail to a unique *Darlingtonia californica* (California pitcher plant) bog is just 1 mile away. Stoney Creek Trail, which follows the creek to its junction with the North Fork of the Smith River, begins about 2 miles west of the campground, near Gasquet. A free hiking guide to this and other trails in the area is available by calling Six Rivers National Forest (see Management). Stay limit 14 days. Open all year.

## 6 Grassy Flat

**Location:** 23 miles northeast of Crescent City
**GPS:** 41.85639 / -123.88889
**Sites:** 19 sites for tents and RVs up to 40 feet long
**Facilities:** Tables, fire rings with grills, vault toilets; no drinking water
**Fee per night:** $; reservations: (877) 444-6777 or recreation.gov
**Management:** Six Rivers National Forest, (707) 442-1721
**Activities:** Fishing, kayaking, swimming
**Finding the campground:** From the intersection of US 101 and US 199 (about 5 miles northeast of Crescent City), take US 199 east for 18 miles to Grassy Flat Campground.
**About the campground:** Grassy Flat sits in a Douglas fir forest on the banks of the Smith River. In wetter months, kayakers enjoy the Smith's whitewater. Check the town of Gasquet's website for seasonal events in the area. Stay limit 14 days. Open mid-June through early September.

## 7 Patrick Creek

**Location:** 30 miles northeast of Crescent City
**GPS:** 41.87194 / -123.84667
**Sites:** 13 sites for tents and RVs
**Facilities:** Tables, fire rings, drinking water, flush toilets

**Fee per night:** $; reservations: (877) 444-6777 or recreation.gov
**Management:** Six Rivers National Forest, (707) 442-1721
**Activities:** Fishing, swimming, visitor center
**Finding the campground:** From the intersection of US 101 and US 199 (about 5 miles northeast of Crescent City), travel east on US 199 for 22 miles to the campground.
**About the campground:** Located in a grove of tall Douglas firs at the confluence of Patrick Creek and the Middle Fork of the Smith River, the campground features rock walls, steps, and facilities built by the Civilian Conservation Corps in the 1930s. Large steelhead are caught here, but only by expert anglers. And like nearby Grassy Flat Campground (6), it is closed during the best fishing season. Elevation 848 feet. Stay limit 14 days. Open mid-June to early-September.

## 8 Jedediah Smith Redwoods State Park

**Location:** 9 miles northeast of Crescent City
**GPS:** 41.7975941 / -124.0841888
**Sites:** 67 sites for tents and RVs up to 36 feet long
**Facilities:** Tables, fire rings, food lockers, drinking water, showers, flush toilets, dump station
**Fee per night:** $$$; reservations: (800) 444-7275 or reserveamerica.com
**Management:** California Department of Parks and Recreation, (707) 465-7335
**Activities:** Hiking, fishing, swimming, boating, nature programs, geocaching
**Finding the campground:** From the intersection of US 101 and US 199 (about 5 miles northeast of Crescent City), drive east on US 199 for 4 miles.
**About the campground:** Campsites are beautifully situated within an old-growth redwood forest and along the banks of the Smith River in this state park that dates back to 1929. Several trails in the 10,000-acre park lead from the campground, including a short walk to Stout Grove via a summer bridge over the river. Longer hikes include the Mill Creek and Hatton-Hiouchi Trails. No dogs are allowed on trails. Salmon fishing takes place in the fall in the Smith River, followed by steelhead in winter. Kayaking, canoeing, and rafting are also popular on the free-flowing Smith. Howland Hill Road provides a 7-mile auto tour through some of the less-visited sections of the park. It is a narrow, gravel road, not recommended for trailers or large RVs. Elevation 160 feet. Stay limit 30 days. Open all year.

## 9 Del Norte Coast Redwoods State Park

**Location:** 7 miles south of Crescent City
**GPS:** 41.6708 / -124.1172
**Sites:** 129 sites for tents and RVs up to 31 feet long
**Facilities:** Tables, fire rings, drinking water, showers, flush toilets, dump station
**Fee per night:** $$$; reservations: (800) 444-7275 or reserveamerica.com
**Management:** California Department of Parks and Recreation, (707) 464-6101
**Activities:** Hiking, fishing, windsurfing, beach play, geocaching, interpretive programs
**Finding the campground:** From Crescent City, drive south on US 101 for 7 miles and turn east onto the campground road. The camp is 2 miles east of the highway.
**About the campground:** Located in a mixed forest of mostly redwoods, the campground is deeply shaded, and sites are well spaced in several loops. An excellent 6-mile loop hike through ancient and second-growth redwood stands is possible directly from the campground by combining the

Mill Creek, Hobbs Wall, and Saddler Skyline Trails. The popular Damnation Creek Trail begins about 3 miles south of the campground highway turnoff. This 5-mile round-trip leads through a redwood and Sitka spruce forest, dropping 1,000 feet to the ocean. No dogs are allowed on trails. For fun outings, head south 9 miles to the Trees of Mystery or north 9 miles to the Battery Point Lighthouse. Elevation 1,023 feet. Stay limit 30 days. Open mid-May through December.

## 10 Elk Prairie (Prairie Creek Redwoods State Park)

**Location:** 5 miles north of Orick
**GPS:** 41.3075896 / -124.0235309
**Sites:** 66 sites for tents and RVs up to 27 feet long
**Facilities:** Tables, fire rings, drinking water, showers, flush toilets, dump station, museum, visitor center
**Fee per night:** $$$; reservations: (800) 444-7275 or reserveamerica.com
**Management:** California Department of Parks and Recreation, (707) 488-2039
**Activities:** Hiking, biking, birding, beachcombing, nature study, fishing
**Finding the campground:** From Orick, drive north on US 101 for 5 miles. Take exit 753 for Newton B Drury Scenic Parkway and turn northwest onto the parkway. The visitor center and Elk Prairie Campground are located at the southern end of the parkway.
**About the campground:** Elk Prairie is aptly named, as a herd of Roosevelt elk is almost always in residence, grazing in a large field between the campground and the highway. Revelation Trail (0.3 mile), which begins behind the visitor center, is designed to afford blind and wheelchair-bound people an opportunity to experience the redwood forest. Two trails lead from the campground to the coast: The James Irvine Trail (4.2 miles) leads to Fern Canyon; the Miner's Ridge Trail (3.9 miles) leads to Gold Bluffs Beach. They can be combined with the connecting 1-mile-long Clintonia Trail to form a loop. Some 260 species of birds can be found within the state park. Elevation 1,458 feet. Stay limit 30 days. Open all year.

## 11 Gold Bluffs Beach (Prairie Creek Redwoods State Park)

**Location:** 7 miles north of Orick
**GPS:** 41.3075896 / -124.0235309
**Sites:** 24 sites for tents only
**Facilities:** Tables, fire rings, drinking water, solar showers, flush toilets
**Fee per night:** $$$; reservations: (800) 444-7275 or reserveamerica.com
**Management:** California Department of Parks and Recreation, (707) 488-2171
**Activities:** Hiking, biking, birding, beachcombing, nature study, fishing
**Finding the campground:** From Orick, drive north on US 101 for 3 miles. Turn west onto Davison Road, and drive 4 miles to the campground. No trailers or vehicles wider than 7 feet are permitted on Davison Road.
**About the campground:** Gold Bluffs is an undeniably beautiful location: a wide, windswept, deserted beach backed by sandstone bluffs and forested hills. The beach got its name in 1851 from a gold rush that did not pan out. About 1.5 miles away, along the Coastal Trail, the Fern Canyon Loop follows a stream through a narrow canyon lined with ferns. Because of its prehistoric ambience, this was a filming location for *The Lost World: Jurassic Park*, BBC's *Walking with Dinosaurs*, and IMAX's *Dinosaurs Alive!* Elevation 1,459 feet. Stay limit 30 days. Open all year.

## REDWOOD NATIONAL AND STATE PARKS

One hundred fifty years ago, redwoods covered 2 million acres of coastal Northern California. Since then, intense logging has reduced this vast forest to no more than 300,000 acres, one-third of which are protected in Redwood National and State Parks. The park complex consists of a partnership of federal and state lands, the state making the major contribution with three state parks in the northern portion of the complex. Redwood National Park proper encompasses the southern section of the complex and includes the Tall Trees and Lady Bird Johnson Groves.

The coastal redwood is the tallest living thing on Earth. Many trees stand taller than the Statue of Liberty and weigh up to 500 tons. The world's tallest tree, found in Tall Trees Grove, measured 367.8 feet when it was discovered in 1963. Incongruously, these trees sprout from a seed no larger than a tomato seed. Redwoods grow only along a narrow coastal strip of Northern California and southern Oregon. They can live up to 2,000 years.

The parks' woodlands and meadows host a variety of wildlife, including elk, black-tailed deer, black bears, mountain lions, and smaller animals such as coyotes, foxes, and the North American beaver. Their streams shelter steelhead, cutthroat trout, and chinook salmon. The park complex also includes many miles of coastline, some of it pristine and accessible only by trail.

More than 270 separate groves of redwoods are preserved in 14,000-acre Prairie Creek Redwoods State Park, including many fine old-growth specimens. Seventy-five miles of trails help you visit them and also provide access to miles of wild, rugged coastline. The Newton B. Drury Scenic Parkway provides a 9-mile auto tour through the park, with pullouts along the route to attractions such as Big Tree, and with opportunities to hike on several short trails or segments.

## 12 Dry Lagoon (Humboldt Lagoons State Park)

**Location:** 13 miles north of Trinidad
**GPS:** 41.2305556 / -124.1027778
**Sites:** 6 sites for tents
**Facilities:** Tables, fire rings, pit toilet; no drinking water
**Fee per night:** $
**Management:** California State Parks, North Coast Redwood Division, (707) 677-3570
**Activities:** Hiking, boating, birding, whale watching, fishing, berry picking (seasonal), visitor center
**Finding the campground:** From Trinidad, drive north 13 miles on US 101 to the entrance to the campground parking lot, halfway between mileposts 114 and 115. From the parking lot, it is about a 500-foot walk to the campground.
**About the campground:** This wetland preserve consists of three lagoons, said to be the largest lagoon system in North America. Dry Lagoon is a wooded, usually secluded campground because

of the walk in. As of this writing, Dry Lagoon had been closed due to budget issues, with a plan to reopen in summer 2016. Call before going. The site is close to beach access and to trout fishing at Stone Lagoon to the north and Big Lagoon to the south. It offers access to many trails, including a nature trail and 3-mile segment of the Coastal Trail. Wildlife is often abundant, as are wildflowers in spring. There are also 6 year-round campsites at Ryan's Cove (Stone Lagoon), reachable only by boat. Dress for fog in summer. Elevation 314 feet. Stay limit 15 days. Open all year.

## 13 Big Lagoon County Park

**Location:** 10 miles north of Trinidad
**GPS:** 41.1631649 / -124.1315627
**Sites:** 25 sites for tents and RVs
**Facilities:** Tables, fire rings, drinking water, flush toilets
**Fee per night:** $$
**Management:** Humboldt County Parks Department, (707) 445-7651
**Activities:** Swimming, boating, fishing, hunting (seasonal)
**Finding the campground:** From Trinidad, drive north 8 miles on US 101. Turn west onto Big Lagoon Park Road and drive 2 miles.
**About the campground:** Despite the narrowness of the spit that separates it from the ocean, Big Lagoon contains freshwater, and steelhead and rainbow trout fishing is popular, if only sometimes rewarding. Duck hunting is popular in winter. Firewood is sold, and beach fires are permitted. Except for campsites situated along the lagoon, most sites lack privacy. The boat ramp allows entry into Big Lagoon. Elevation 32 feet. Stay limit 7 days. Open all year.

## 14 Agate, Abalone & Penn Creek (Patrick's Point State Park)

**Location:** 6 miles north of Trinidad
**GPS:** 41.1380822 / -124.1501037
**Sites:** 121 sites for tents and RVs up to 31 feet long in 3 separate campgrounds less than 0.5 mile apart, including 2 group sites
**Facilities:** Tables, fire rings, drinking water, showers, flush toilets, visitor center
**Fee per night:** $$$$; reservations (summer only): (800) 444-7275 or reserveamerica.com
**Management:** California Department of Parks and Recreation, (707) 677-3750
**Activities:** Hiking, fishing, surfing, Sumeg Village Day (Aug)
**Finding the campground:** From Trinidad, drive 5 miles north on US 101. Turn west at the Patrick's Point exit and drive 0.5 mile.
**About the campground:** Patrick's Point encompasses a dramatic coastline of offshore rocks, sea stacks, secluded beaches, and tidepools. All three campgrounds offer large and shaded sites, most protected from the wind. Agate Beach is one of Northern California's most beautiful beaches, reached by a 0.3-mile walk from Agate Campground. The best way to see the park is by hiking the Rim Trail and its six spurs, which descend to coves and tidepools and climb to vistas and lookouts. The park also includes a replica of a Yurok Indian village, "Sumeg," which is well worth a visit. There are two group sites available. Elevation 314 feet. Stay limit 15 days June through September. Only Agate campground is open all year, with a 30-day limit October through May.

## 15 Clam Beach County Park

**Location:** 3.5 miles north of McKinleyville
**GPS:** 41.006964 / -124.1126503
**Sites:** 18 sites; large parking lot with space for 9 RVs, plus 9 sites for tents in a sandy dunes area
**Facilities:** Tables and fire rings at tent sites only; drinking water, vault toilets
**Fee per night:** $$
**Management:** Humboldt County Parks Department, (707) 445-7652
**Activities:** Fishing, beachcombing, clamming
**Finding the campground:** From McKinleyville, drive north 3.5 miles on US 101. Take the Clam Beach exit, and drive west 2 blocks.
**About the campground:** Situated on a wide, long beach, the campground is exposed to windy conditions. It is noted as an excellent clamming spot, particularly at the north end of the beach at minus low tides. Fishing is fair, with perch the usual catch. Stay limit 3 days. Open all year.

## 16 Pearch Creek

**Location:** 2 miles northeast of Orleans
**GPS:** 41.3090156 / -123.5208922
**Sites:** 10 sites for tents or RVs up to 40 feet long
**Facilities:** Tables, fire rings, drinking water, vault toilets
**Fee per night:** $
**Management:** Six Rivers National Forest, (530) 627-3291
**Activities:** Hiking, biking, swimming, fishing, birding
**Finding the campground:** From Orleans, drive 2 miles northeast on CA 96.
**About the campground:** The campground is located on the banks of Pearch Creek, about 0.25 mile from where it enters the Klamath River. Steelhead fishing can be good in the fall. A short drive away, both the Klamath and Salmon Rivers are popular destinations for whitewater rafting, swimming, and kayaking. Stay limit 14 days. Open mid-May through mid-November.

## 17 E-Ne-Nuck

**Location:** 5 miles southwest of Orleans
**GPS:** 41.233953 / -123.660178
**Sites:** 11 sites for tents and RVs up to 30 feet long
**Facilities:** Tables, fire rings, drinking water, vault toilets
**Fee per night:** $
**Management:** Six Rivers National Forest, (530) 627-3291
**Activities:** Fishing
**Finding the campground:** From Orleans, drive 5 miles southwest on CA 96.
**About the campground:** E-Ne-Nuck is situated on the banks of the Klamath River, near great fishing holes and nearby streams offering excellent steelhead fishing, especially in the fall. Elevation 403 feet. Stay limit 14 days. Open June through October.

## 18 Fish Lake

**Location:** 10 miles north of Weitchpec
**GPS:** 41.26417 / -123.68444
**Sites:** 24 sites for tents and RVs (up to 28 feet)
**Facilities:** Tables, fire rings, drinking water, vault toilets
**Fee per night:** $; reservations: (800) 444-7275 or reserveamerica.com
**Management:** Six Rivers National Forest, (530) 627-3291
**Activities:** Fishing, swimming, boating, hiking, berry picking (seasonal)
**Finding the campground:** From Weitchpec, at the intersection of CA 169 and CA 96, drive north about 4 miles on CA 96. Turn west onto Buff Creek Trail Road, and drive about 5 miles.
**About the campground:** Somewhat secluded and shaded campsites lie among Douglas fir and cedar trees on the lake's west side. There are trailheads in the campground for Blue Lake, Red Lake, and Fish Lake Trails. Canoeing and other nonmotorized boating is popular on this lily pad–speckled lake (boat ramp less than 1 mile away). Trout, bluegill, and bass are here for anglers. The elevation is 1,780 feet. Stay limit 14 days. Open mid-May through mid-October.

## 19 Aikens Creek West

**Location:** 5 miles northwest of Weitchpec
**GPS:** 41.228918 / -123.654428
**Sites:** Open camping for tents and RVs up to 35 feet long
**Facilities:** Tables, fire rings, pit toilets; no drinking water
**Fee per night:** None
**Management:** Six Rivers National Forest, (707) 442-1721
**Activities:** Fishing, swimming, kayaking, biking, hiking
**Finding the campground:** From the intersection of CA 169 and CA 96 in Weitchpec, drive northwest 5 miles on CA 96.
**About the campground:** Across the highway from the banks of the Klamath River, the campground provides a good put-in for kayaks and rafts, and excellent steelhead fishing in the fall. Check out your surroundings with a hike on the Bluff Creek Trail. Stay limit 14 days. Open all year.

## 20 Tish Tang

**Location:** 8 miles north of the community of Willow Creek
**GPS:** 41.0226622 / -123.6383184
**Sites:** 40 sites for tents and RVs up to 28 feet long and one group site
**Facilities:** Tables, fire rings, vault toilets; no drinking water
**Fee per night:** $
**Management:** Hoopa Tribal Forestry Office, (530) 625-4284
**Activities:** Fishing, swimming, river rafting
**Finding the campground:** From the intersection of CA 299 and CA 96 in Willow Creek, drive north on CA 96 for 8 miles.
**About the campground:** Located on a bend of the Klamath River on the Hoopa Valley Tribal Reservation, a large, flat gravel beach provides access to good kayaking in spring, swimming in summer, and steelhead fishing in fall and winter. Elevation 442 feet. No stay limit. Open June through October.

## 21 Boise Creek

**Location:** 2 miles west of the community of Willow Creek
**GPS:** 40.94472 / -123.65833
**Sites:** 17 sites for tents and RVs up to 35 feet long
**Facilities:** Tables, fire rings, drinking water, vault toilets
**Fee per night:** $
**Management:** Six Rivers National Forest, (530) 629-2118
**Activities:** Hiking, fishing, swimming
**Finding the campground:** From Willow Creek, drive 2 miles west on CA 299.
**About the campground:** The campground is set above Boise Creek, and an about 0.5-mile trail leads down to its banks. There you might discover a swimming hole and ample native plants and wildlife. Fishing for salmon in the fall and steelhead in winter takes place along the Trinity River, beginning about 2 miles from the camp. Stay limit 14 days. Open mid-May through mid-October.

## 22 East Fork

**Location:** 6 miles southwest of the community of Willow Creek
**GPS:** 40.904650 / -123.706055
**Sites:** 10 sites for tents and RVs up to 20 feet long
**Facilities:** Tables, fire rings, vault toilets; no drinking water
**Fee per night:** $
**Management:** Six Rivers National Forest, (530) 629-2118
**Activities:** Hiking, fishing
**Finding the campground:** From Willow Creek, drive southwest on CA 299 for 6 miles.
**About the campground:** Campsites are fairly private, nestled in a thick understory of ferns and a middle-story of young deciduous trees. When water is flowing, you can hear Willow Creek gurgling by from any site. The only RV-friendly sites are 1 and 2, near the entrance. There are walk-in sites by the creek. Fishing is fair for native trout. Stay limit 14 days. Open May through mid-October.

## 23 Samoa Boat Launch County Park

**Location:** 7 miles northwest of Eureka
**GPS:** 40.7628936 / -124.2281628
**Sites:** 25 sites for tents and RVs
**Facilities:** Tables, fire rings, drinking water, flush toilets, showers, boat ramp
**Fee per night:** $$
**Management:** Humboldt County Parks Department, (707) 445-7651
**Activities:** Swimming, fishing, boating, clamming, birding, OHV driving
**Finding the campground:** From the intersection of US 101 and CA 255 in Eureka, drive 2 miles northwest on CA 255. Turn south onto New Navy Base Road, and drive 5 miles.
**About the campground:** The park is situated on Humboldt Bay at the south end of the Samoa Peninsula. The Samoa Dunes Recreation Area, operated by the BLM, is just south of the campground. It has an OHV driving area, as well as a hiking trail through a protected wetland that is closed to vehicles. Perch and halibut are the main catches in the bay, with some salmon taken

during the fall run. The Samoa Cookhouse and Museum, 5 miles north on New Navy Base Road, is known for its family-style service, large portions, and reasonable prices. It is well worth a visit if you have a large appetite. Elevation 3 feet. Stay limit 7 days. Open all year.

## 24 Swimmer's Delight (Van Duzen County Park)

**Location:** 33 miles southeast of Eureka
**GPS:** 40.4890925 / -123.9707721
**Sites:** 30 sites for tents and RVs
**Facilities:** Tables, fire rings, drinking water, flush toilets, showers, electric hookups
**Fee per night:** $$
**Management:** Humboldt County Parks Department, (707) 445-7651
**Activities:** Fishing, swimming, rafting, paddling
**Finding the campground:** From the intersection of CA 255 and US 101 in Eureka, drive south on US 101 for 21 miles. Turn east onto CA 36 and drive 12 miles.
**About the campground:** The park features virgin redwood groves and is situated on the Van Duzen River, with popular swimming holes and seasonally good fishing for salmon and steelhead. Check regulations carefully, as the river is subject to closures and restrictions. The Van Duzen offers good rafting and paddling in spring; one popular course is the 6-mile downstream run (Grizzly Creek Run) to Grizzly Creek Redwoods State Park. Pamplin Grove Campground is available for large groups. Elevation 403 feet. Stay limit 10 days. Open all year.

## 25 Grizzly Creek Redwoods State Park

**Location:** 38 miles southeast of Eureka
**GPS:** 40.4863927 / -123.9062698
**Sites:** 26 sites for tents and RVs up to 30 feet long
**Facilities:** Tables, fire rings, drinking water, flush toilets, showers, visitor center
**Fee per night:** $$$; reservations: (800) 444-7275 or reserveamerica.com
**Management:** California Department of Parks and Recreation, (707) 777-3683
**Activities:** Hiking, swimming, fishing
**Finding the campground:** From the intersection of CA 255 and US 101 in Eureka, drive south on US 101 for 21 miles. Turn east onto CA 36, and drive 17 miles.
**About the campground:** Situated near the confluence of Grizzly Creek and the Van Duzen River, the campground is only minutes from several fine redwood groves. In one of them, George Lucas filmed scenes for *Return of the Jedi*. One of the most dramatic stands is Cheatham Grove (4 miles west of camp), which has a 1-mile-long trail to explore. Two other groves are within easy walking distance of the campground. Enjoy campfire programs on the weekend. Elevation 446 feet. Stay limit 15 days June through September; 30 days October through May. Open all year.

## 26 Burlington (Humboldt Redwoods State Park)

**Location:** 51 miles south of Eureka
**GPS:** 40.3090294 / -123.9094834
**Sites:** 57 sites for tents and RVs up to 36 feet long

**Facilities:** Tables, fire rings, drinking water, flush toilets, showers, dump station
**Fee per night:** $$$; reservations: (800) 444-7275 or reserveamerica.com
**Management:** California Department of Parks and Recreation, (707) 946-1811
**Activities:** Hiking, fishing, swimming
**Finding the campground:** From Eureka, drive south 50 miles on US 101 to the Weott-Newton Road exit, which is signed for the visitor center. The campground is adjacent to the visitor center.
**About the campground:** This campground is situated in a relatively open grove of second-growth redwoods, with stumps of the old-growth trees scattered throughout. It is sobering to compare the size of these giant stumps with the newer trees. A short trail leads from the campground to the Eel River for swimming and fishing. A summer bridge across the river allows access to extensive hiking trails. Stay limit 15 days June through September; 30 days October through May. Open all year.

## 27 Hidden Springs (Humboldt Redwoods State Park)

**Location:** 56 miles south of Eureka
**GPS:** 40.276383 / -123.8649687
**Sites:** 154 sites for tents and RVs up to 36 feet long
**Facilities:** Tables, fire rings, drinking water, flush toilets, showers
**Fee per night:** $$$; reservations: (800) 444-7275 or reserveamerica.com
**Management:** California Department of Parks and Recreation, (707) 943-3177
**Activities:** Hiking, fishing, swimming
**Finding the campground:** From the visitor center, 1.3 miles south of Weott, drive south 5 miles on Avenue of the Giants.

### HUMBOLDT REDWOODS STATE PARK

This largest of the state's redwood parks encompasses 53,000 acres, 17,000 of which are covered with old-growth coast redwoods. Rockefeller Forest, in the northeast section of the park, is the world's largest coast redwood grove. The average age of redwoods in the park ranges from 500 to 1,200 years; the oldest known tree is more than 2,000 years old. Many trees are more than 300 feet high, and some top 360 feet. More than 100 miles of hiking, mountain biking, and equestrian trails traverse the park's many groves of ancient trees. An inexpensive trail guide describes fifty of the more popular trails. It is available at the visitor center, located just off US 101 on Avenue of the Giants, 1.3 miles south of the small town of Weott.

A feature of the park is Avenue of the Giants, a 32-mile scenic auto tour, with a series of stops at points of interest along the route where you may park and enjoy short walks. The South Fork of the Eel River flows through the park, offering fishing and swimming. Fishing for salmon and steelhead is permitted during fall and winter. You may fish for squawfish at any time. The park offers developed family camps, horse camps, a group camp, and environmental and hike and bike sites—some 250 campsites in all.

*The stately redwoods in Rockefeller Forest, Humboldt Redwoods State Park.*

**About the campground:** Situated on a hillside in a mixed forest, this campground has a short trail that leads to the Eel River, where you can fish or soak in a swimming hole. Another trail, accessible from campsites 133 and 75, leads to Williams Grove via a footbridge. Elevation 446 feet. Stay limit 15 days. Open mid-May through mid-October. For group camping in Humboldt Redwoods, check out Williams Grove Group Camp at humboldtredwoods.org.

## 28 Albee Creek (Humboldt Redwoods State Park)

**Location:** 56 miles south of Eureka
**GPS:** 40.3386027 / -123.9594789
**Sites:** 40 sites for tents and RVs up to 36 feet long
**Facilities:** Tables, fire rings, drinking water, flush toilets, showers
**Fee per night:** $$$; reservations: (800) 444-7275 or reserveamerica.com
**Management:** California Department of Parks and Recreation, (707) 946-2472
**Activities:** Hiking, mountain biking
**Finding the campground:** From the visitor center, 1.3 miles south of Weott, drive north 4 miles on Avenue of the Giants. Turn onto Mattole Road and drive 5 miles.

**About the campground:** Situated on the grounds of an old homestead, campsites are either shaded by second-growth redwoods or sprawled across open meadows. Hiking and mountain biking trails are easily accessible from the campground, and Rockefeller Forest is only a short hike away. Elevation 528 feet. Stay limit 15 days. Open May through September. For equestrian and group camping, check out Cuneo Creek Horse Camp in Humboldt Redwoods State Park.

## 29 A.W. Way County Park

**Location:** 35 miles south of Ferndale
**GPS:** 40.2683312 / -124.2304979
**Sites:** 30 sites for tents and RVs
**Facilities:** Tables, fire rings, drinking water, flush toilets, shower, playground
**Fee per night:** $$
**Management:** Humboldt County Parks Department, (707) 445-7652
**Activities:** Fishing, swimming, hiking, playground
**Finding the campground:** From Fortuna, drive south 22 miles on US 101. Turn west onto Mattole Road and drive 22 miles.
**About the campground:** The park is situated on the bank of the Mattole River with partially shaded, mostly sunny sites. The campground is a good alternative for those who would like to explore the Mattole portion of the King Range National Conservation Area (31) but would like more amenities than offered by the BLM campgrounds there. The Mattole offers good salmon and steelhead fishing mid-November through February. Stay limit 10 days. Open all year.

## 30 Honeydew Creek (King Range National Conservation Area)

**Location:** 41 miles south of Fortuna
**GPS:** 40.227612 / -124.110748
**Sites:** 5 sites for tents and small RVs
**Facilities:** Tables, fire rings, vault toilets; no drinking water
**Fee per night:** $
**Management:** Bureau of Land Management, (707) 986-5400
**Activities:** Riparian wildlife viewing
**Finding the campground:** From Fortuna, drive south 22 miles on US 101. Take exit 663 for South Fork/Honeydew and follow signs to Honeydew. Turn south onto Wilder Ridge Road toward Ettersburg and continue 1 mile to the campground.
**About the campground:** This is an isolated, primitive campground near a pretty creek. The road gets crooked, steep, and narrow for RVs. Elevation 500 feet. Stay limit 14 days. Open all year.

## 31 Mattole Beach (King Range National Conservation Area)

**Location:** 55 miles south of Fortuna
**GPS:** 40.2891854 / -124.3558244
**Sites:** 14 sites for tents and RVs
**Facilities:** Tables, fire rings, pit toilets; no drinking water
**Fee per night:** $

## KING RANGE NATIONAL CONSERVATION AREA

Encompassing some 68,000 acres of Northern California's "Lost Coast," the conservation area extends 35 miles from the Mattole River to Whale Gulch Creek and up to 6 miles inland from the Pacific Ocean. The King Range rises from sea level to more than 4,000 feet in less than 3 miles, creating a spectacular meeting of land and sea, isolated beaches, mountain streams, and virgin forests. The area enjoys a mild but wet climate (between 100 and 200 inches of rainfall annually) and frequent dense morning fog.

The King Range contains over 80 miles of hiking trails spanning from the Pacific shore to its windy peaks. Three major trails run generally north to south through the region. The longest, the Lost Coast Trail, follows the shoreline from Mattole Campground south for 24 miles to Black Sand Beach. Combining with the Chemise Mountain Trail, it continues (inland) from Hidden Valley to Whale Gulch Creek (8 miles) and on into the Sinkyone Wilderness. The King Crest Trail System provides 16 miles of hiking and equestrian trails along the main coastal ridge north of Shelter Cove, with excellent views of the ocean and the Mattole River Valley. Signage may be minimal on trails. Shore fishing may yield perch and cod, and salmon and steelhead are taken by boaters near Shelter Cove, where boat launch facilities and rentals are available. The Mattole River is open to salmon and steelhead fishing from mid-November through February. Mountain bikers can ride the 14-mile Paradise Royale loop and the Tolkan Terrain Park. Some 30 more miles of environmentally friendly trails are in the works, making the King Range a mountain biking destination. There are short seasons for deer and elk hunting. On the coast, surfing, abalone diving, and beachcombing are options on the wild stretch of Lost Coast shoreline.

Roads to and within the area are a combination of pavement, gravel, and dirt. Many are steep, winding, and narrow; some are impassable during wet weather. It may feel like the Lost Coast as you discover each site. Large trailers and RVs are not recommended. Six vehicle-accessible public campgrounds are located in the conservation area. Facilities are minimal to preserve the rustic surroundings. Bring cash for pay stations.

**Management:** Bureau of Land Management, (707) 986-5400

**Activities:** Hiking, fishing

**Finding the campground:** From Fortuna, drive south 22 miles on US 101. Take exit 663 for South Fork/Honeydew and drive 28 miles toward Honeydew\Petrolia. Turn west onto Lighthouse Road (before Petrolia) and continue 5 miles to the campground.

**About the campground:** This campground is situated on an isolated beach at the mouth of the Mattole River. Though starkly beautiful, it can also be cold and windy. The Lost Coast Trail begins here and runs south 24 miles to Black Sands Beach. A good introduction to the trail is a 6-mile round-trip hike to the abandoned Punta Gorda Lighthouse. Perch fishing can be good at the mouth of the river. Elevation 22 feet. Stay limit 14 days. Open all year.

## 32 Nadelos (King Range National Conservation Area)

**Location:** 63 miles south of Fortuna
**GPS:** 40.0209772 / -124.0061394
**Sites:** 8 sites for tents
**Facilities:** Tables, fire rings, drinking water, vault toilets
**Fee per night:** $
**Management:** Bureau of Land Management, (707) 986-5400
**Activities:** Hiking
**Finding the campground:** From Fortuna, drive south 45 miles on US 101 to Redway. Turn west onto Briceland/Shelter Cove Road and drive 16.5 miles. Turn south onto Chemise Mountain Road and drive 1 mile.
**About the campground:** A trail leaves camp and leads to the summit of Chemise Mountain (2,598 feet), and the southern section of the Lost Coast Trail passes by en route to the Sinkyone Wilderness. Groups may reserve the entire campground. Call BLM for fee and reservation. Elevation 1,850 feet. Stay limit 14 days. Open all year.

## 33 Wailaki (King Range National Conservation Area)

**Location:** 64 miles south of Fortuna
**GPS:** 40.0181994 / -124.0028058
**Sites:** 13 sites for tents and RVs
**Facilities:** Tables, fire rings, drinking water, vault toilets
**Fee per night:** $
**Management:** Bureau of Land Management, (707) 986-5400
**Activities:** Hiking
**Finding the campground:** From Fortuna, drive south 45 miles on US 101 to Redway. Turn right west onto Briceland/Shelter Cove Road and drive 16.5 miles. Turn south onto Chemise Mountain Road and drive 1.5 miles.
**About the campground:** Both Wailaki and Nadelos are adjacent to the South Fork of Bear Creek and can access the Chemise Mountain Trail—at 1.5 miles with an 800-foot climb, one of the easier hikes in the King Range. Elevation 1,900 feet. Stay limit 14 days. Open all year.

## 34 Tolkan (King Range National Conservation Area)

**Location:** 66 miles south of Fortuna
**GPS:** 40.083476 / -124.0578109
**Sites:** 9 sites for tents and RVs
**Facilities:** Tables, fire rings, drinking water, vault toilets
**Fee per night:** $
**Management:** Bureau of Land Management, (707) 986-5400
**Activities:** Hiking, biking

**Finding the campground:** From Fortuna, drive south 45 miles on US 101 to Redway. Turn west onto Briceland/Shelter Cove Road and drive 17 miles. Turn north onto Kings Peak (Horse Mountain) Road and drive 3.5 miles.
**About the campground:** It is easy access from Tolkan to the fun and scenic Paradise Royale Mountain Bike Trail and Tolkan Terrain Park, making this campground popular with mountain bikers. The King Crest Trailhead is 4 miles north of the camp. Elevation 1,840 feet. Stay limit 14 days. Open all year.

## 35 Horse Mountain (King Range National Conservation Area)

**Location:** 68 miles south of Fortuna
**GPS:** 40.1056978 / -124.0664234
**Sites:** 9 sites for tents and RVs
**Facilities:** Tables, fire rings, drinking water, pit toilets
**Fee per night:** $
**Management:** Bureau of Land Management, (707) 986-5400
**Activities:** Hiking
**Finding the campground:** From Fortuna, drive south 45 miles on US 101 to Redway, west 22 miles on Briceland/Shelter Cove Road, then 6.5 miles north on King Peak Road.
**About the campground:** The King Crest Trailhead is 2 miles north of the camp. Also at this trailhead is the beginning of the 3-mile Buck Creek Trail, which leads to the coast. Elevation 2,000 feet. Stay limit 14 days. Open all year.

## 36 Benbow Lake State Recreation Area

**Location:** 4 miles south of Garberville
**GPS:** 40.0621721 / -123.793346
**Sites:** 75 sites for tents and RVs up to 30 feet long
**Facilities:** Tables, fire rings, drinking water, flush toilets, showers, dump station, boat ramp and rentals, electric hookups
**Fee per night:** $$$–$$$$; reservations: (800) 444-7275 or reserveamerica.com
**Management:** California Department of Parks and Recreation, (707) 923-3238 (summer); (707) 947-3318 (winter)
**Activities:** Swimming, boating, fishing, hiking
**Finding the campground:** From Garberville, drive 2 miles south on US 101. Take the Benbow Drive exit and drive east 1.5 miles.
**About the campground:** Campers at Benbow enjoy hiking, swimming, nonmotorized boating, and picnicking year-round, and salmon and steelhead fishing during winter. The Thrap Mill Trail starts from campsite 57, rising into the redwoods and can be looped with the Pioneer Trail for peak-top views. Reservations required Memorial Day weekend to Labor Day weekend. Campground may be closed during extreme drought years. Elevation 890 feet. Stay limit 14 days. Open all year.

## 37 Huckleberry & Madrone (Richardson Grove State Park)

**Location:** 7 miles south of Garberville
**GPS:** 40.0212255 / -123.7937682

## RICHARDSON GROVE STATE PARK

This park covers 1,500 acres and protects an old-growth redwood forest. Many of the trees are over 300 feet tall and more than 1,000 years old. A visitor center and a nature trail featuring a walk-through tree are located near the park entrance. Longer trails lead to the most prominent groves, and the South Fork of the Eel River bisects the park from north to south, providing good swimming holes in summer and salmon and steelhead fishing in late fall and winter.

**Sites:** 76 sites for tents and RVs up to 30 feet long
**Facilities:** Tables, fire rings, drinking water, flush toilets, showers, dump station, store
**Fee per night:** $$$; reservations: (800) 444-7275 or reserveamerica.com
**Management:** California Department of Parks and Recreation, (707) 247-3318
**Activities:** Hiking, swimming, fishing
**Finding the campground:** From Garberville, drive south on US Highway 101 for 7 miles.
**About the campground:** Huckleberry is near the park visitor center on the west side of US 101, only a short walk away from the South Fork of the Eel River. The Woodland Loop Trail (1.3 miles) leads from Huckleberry through a mixed forest, and the 2-mile Toumey Trail (accessed by a footbridge over the river) visits an impressive redwood grove and extends southward to Oak Flat. The Tan Oaks Spring–Durphy Creek–Lookout Point Loop Trail (4.6 miles) can be accessed between campsites 58 and 60 in Madrone. It offers a 1,200-foot climb through a forest of large trees, including redwoods, Douglas firs, and tanoaks. Enjoy nature trails from the visitor center. Four cabins are also available to rent. Elevation 610 feet. Stay limit 30 days. Open all year.

## 38 Oak Flat (Richardson Grove State Park)

**Location:** 7 miles south of Garberville
**GPS:** 40.01598 / -123.7883592
**Sites:** 94 sites for tents and RVs up to 30 feet long
**Facilities:** Tables, fire rings, drinking water, flush toilets, showers
**Fee per night:** $$$$; reservations: (800) 444-7275 or reserveamerica.com
**Management:** California Department of Parks and Recreation, (707) 247-3318
**Activities:** Hiking, swimming, fishing
**Finding the campground:** From Garberville, drive south for 7 miles on US Highway 101.
**About the campground:** Situated 0.5 mile from the park visitor center on the east side of US 101, Oak Flat offers easy access to the South Fork of the Eel River. The Toumey and Settlers Trail are close by. Elevation 530 feet. Stay limit 15 days. Open June through September.

# Mendocino Area

The Mendocino area offers some of the most dramatic coastal scenery found anywhere. While much of the area is private and inaccessible, much more is open to the public as marvelous state and county parks and public beaches. The towns in this area are as varied and scenic as the coast itself. The entire town of Mendocino, which was founded by New England whalers, is on the National Register of Historic Places.

Inland, a major wine-producing region centers around Ukiah, which has over thirty tasting rooms within its city limits. To the east, the Mendocino National Forest offers a million acres of trails, rivers, streams, and lakes for outdoor enjoyment. If you really want to get away from it all, check out some of the dispersed campgrounds in the Mendocino National Forest, such as Atchison or Sugar Spring.

*If you're looking for an in-town adventure while camping and touring the Mendocino area, stop into the unique Pacific coast town of Mendocino to stroll on ocean bluffs, take in the sights of historic buildings, and enjoy some great food and shopping.*

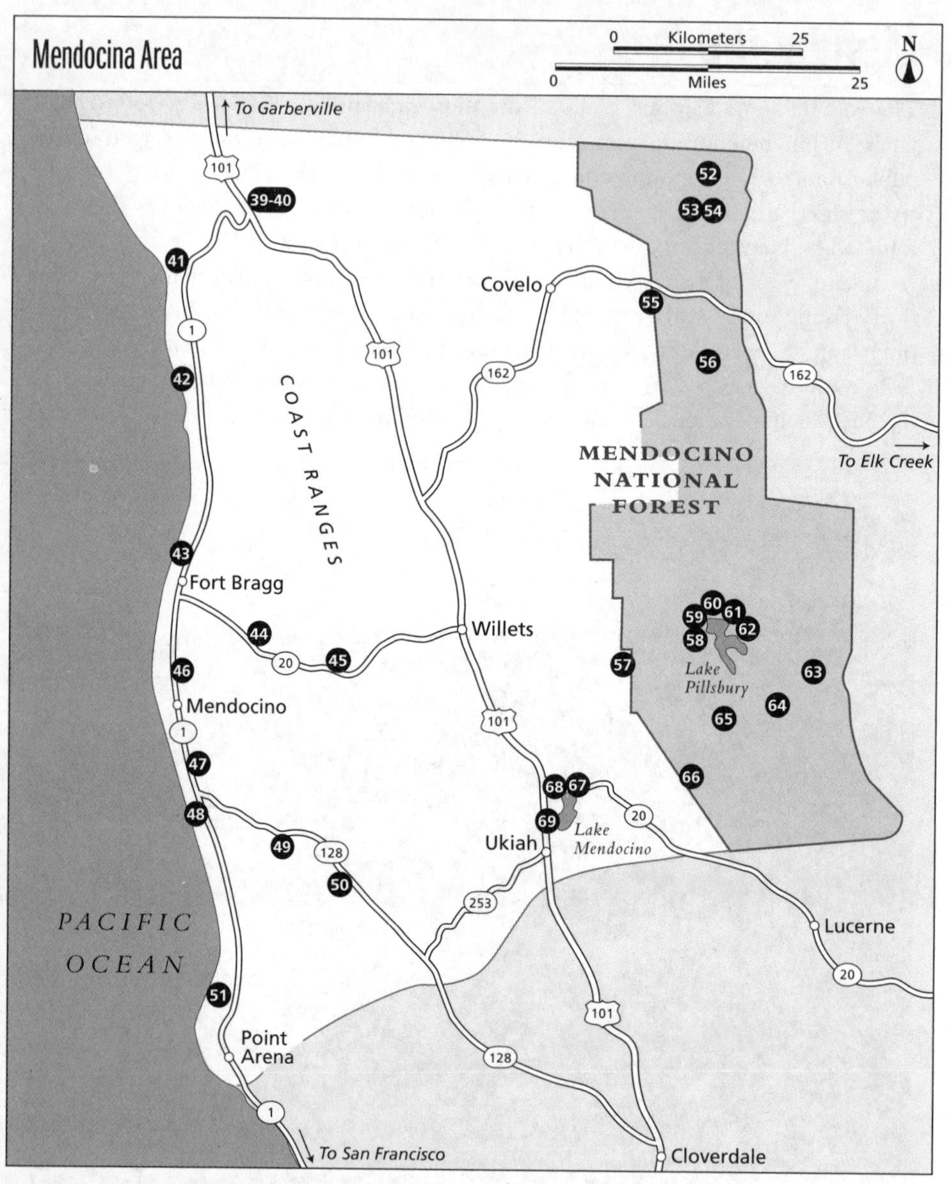


# 39 Hickey and Rock Creek (Standish-Hickey State Recreation Area)

**Location:** 22 miles south of Garberville
**GPS:** 39.8774712 / -123.7375985
**Sites:** 99 sites for tents and RVs up to 27 feet long
**Facilities:** Tables, fire rings, drinking water, flush toilets, showers
**Fee per night:** $$$; reservations: (800) 444-7275 or reserveamerica.com

|  | Name | Group Sites | RV Sites | Max. RV Length | Hookups | Toilets | Showers | Drinking Water | Dump Station | Pets | Wheelchair | Recreation | Fee(s) | Season | Can Reserve |
|---|---|---|---|---|---|---|---|---|---|---|---|---|---|---|---|
|  | **MENDOCINO AREA** |  |  |  |  |  |  |  |  |  |  |  |  |  |  |
| 39 | Hickey and Rock Creek (Standish-Hickey State Recreation Area) |  | * | 27 |  | F | * | * |  | * | * | HSF | $$$ | Year-round | * |
| 40 | Redwood (Standish-Hickey State Recreation Area) |  |  |  |  | F | * | * |  | * | * | HSF | $$$ | Memorial Day to Labor Day | * |
| 41 | Usal (Sinkyone Wilderness State Park) |  |  |  |  | V |  |  |  | * |  | HF | $$ | Year-round |  |
| 42 | *Howard Creek, Westport-Union Landing State Beach* |  | * |  |  | V |  | * |  | * | * | HF | $$ | Year-round |  |
| 43 | MacKerricher State Park |  | * | 35 |  | F | * | * | * | * | * | FHRB | $$$ | Year-round | * |
| 44 | Camp One Area (Jackson Demonstration State Forest) | * | * | small |  | P |  |  |  | * |  | HSRM | $ | Memorial Day to Labor Day |  |
| 45 | Camp 20 Area (Jackson Demonstration State Forest) |  | * | small |  | P |  |  |  | * |  | HSRM | $ | Memorial Day to Labor Day |  |
| 46 | Russian Gulch State Park | * | * | 24 |  | F | * | * |  | * | * | FHSM | $$$ | Mar-Sept | * |
| 47 | Van Damme State Park | * | * | 35 |  | F | * | * | * | * | * | FHSBM | $$$ | Year-round | * |
| 48 | Navarro Beach (Navarro River Redwoods State Park) |  | * | 30 |  | C |  |  |  | * | * | FSB | $$ | Year-round |  |
| 49 | Paul M. Dimmick Wayside (Navarro River Redwoods State Park) |  | * | 30 |  | V |  | * |  | * | * | FSBH | $$ | Year-round |  |
| 50 | Hendy Woods State Park |  | * | 35 |  | F | * | * | * | * | * | HBSM | $$$$ | Year-round | * |
| 51 | Manchester State Beach | * | * | 30 |  | P |  | * |  | * | * | HF | $$$ | Year-round | * |
| 52 | Hammerhorn Lake |  | * | 16 |  | V |  | * |  | * | * | FHBL | $ | May-Nov |  |
| 53 | Howard Meadows |  | * | 16 |  | V |  |  |  | * |  | FHBS | None | Apr-Nov |  |
| 54 | Little Doe |  | * |  |  | V |  |  |  | * | * |  | None | May-Nov |  |
| 55 | Eel River |  | * | 35 |  | V |  | * |  | * | * | F | $ | Mar-Nov |  |
| 56 | Plaskett Meadows (Plaskett Lake Recreational Area) | * | * | 26 |  | V |  | * |  | * | * | FHB | $ | Jun-Oct |  |
| 57 | Trout Creek |  | * | small |  | V |  | * |  | * | * | FSB | $ | May-Oct | * |
| 58 | Fuller Grove (Lake Pillsbury Recreation Area) | * | * | 22 |  | V |  | * |  | * | * | FSBH | $ | Apr-Sept | group only |
| 59 | Pogie Point (Lake Pillsbury Recreation Area) |  |  |  |  | V |  | * |  | * | * | FSBHRL | $ | May-Sept |  |

| | Name | Group Sites | RV Sites | Max. RV Length | Hookups | Toilets | Showers | Drinking Water | Dump Station | Pets | Wheelchair | Recreation | Fee(s) | Season | Can Reserve |
|---|---|---|---|---|---|---|---|---|---|---|---|---|---|---|---|
| 60 | Navy Camp (Lake Pillsbury Recreation Area) | | * | 22 | | V | | * | | * | * | FSBHR | $ | Apr-Sept | |
| 61 | Oak Flat (Lake Pillsbury Recreation Area) | | * | | | V | | | | * | | FSBHR | None | Year-round | |
| 62 | Sunset Point (Lake Pillsbury Recreation Area) | | * | | | V | | * | | * | * | FSBHR | $ | Apr-Sept | |
| 63 | Lower Nye | | * | | | V | | | | * | | H | None | Year-round | |
| 64 | Bear Creek (Upper Lake Recreation Area) | | * | | | V | | | | * | | FH | None | Year-round | |
| 65 | Deer Valley (Upper Lake Recreation Area) | | * | | | V | | | | * | | OM | $ | Year-round | |
| 66 | Middle Creek (Upper Lake Recreation Area) | * | * | | | V | | * | | * | | OR | $ | Year-round | |
| 67 | Bushay (Lake Mendocino ) | * | * | 40 | E | F | * | * | * | * | * | SFBHR | $$$ | May-Sept | * |
| 68 | Kyen (Lake Mendocino) | | * | 35 | | F | * | * | * | * | * | SFBHL | $$$ | Year-round | * |
| 69 | Che-Kaka (Lake Mendocino) | * | * | 35 | | V | | * | | * | * | SFBH | $$ | Apr-Sept | * |

Toilets: F=flush V=vault P=pit C=chemical; Fee: $=Under $20 $$=$20–$29 $$$=$30–$39 $$$$ $40 or more; Recreation: H=hiking S=swimming F=fishing B=boating L=boat launch O=off-highway driving R=horseback riding, M=mountain biking Hookups: W=water E=electric S=sewer

**Management:** California Department of Parks and Recreation, (707) 925-6482
**Activities:** Hiking, swimming, fishing
**Finding the campground:** From Garberville, drive south 22 miles on US 101.
**About the campground:** This 1,070-acre park, bisected by the highway and the South Fork of the Eel River, consists mainly of a mixed forest, with second-growth redwoods and some small pockets of old-growth trees, including Douglas fir. These are the two main campgrounds offering RV access, set against steep bluffs. A trail leads from the picnic area south of the campgrounds to a good swimming hole, and here a summer bridge provides access to the 2.1-mile Big Tree Loop and the Miles Standish Tree. The 1.7-mile Taber Nature Trail begins just across the highway from Hickey. Fishing in the river is for salmon and steelhead in late fall and winter. Elevation 1,000 feet. Stay limit 30 days. At least one campground is open all year.

## 40 Redwood (Standish-Hickey State Recreation Area)

**Location:** 22 miles south of Garberville
**GPS:** 39.8774712 / -123.7375985
**Sites:** 53 sites for tents
**Facilities:** Tables, fire rings, drinking water, flush toilets, showers

**Fee per night:** $$$; reservations: (800) 444-7275 or reserveamerica.com
**Management:** California Department of Parks and Recreation, (707) 925-6482
**Activities:** Hiking, swimming, fishing
**Finding the campground:** From Garberville, drive south 22 miles on US 101.
**About the campground:** This campground is situated in an attractive spot on the bank of the Eel River and is accessible via a temporary summer bridge. The Big Tree Loop (2.1 miles) and the Lookout Point Trail (3.5 miles) are convenient to the campground. Take the Big Tree Trail to see the tallest redwood in the park, the 225-foot Captain Miles Standish Tree, which is also more than 1,200 years old. Elevation 1,000 feet. Stay limit 15 days. Open Memorial Day through Labor Day.

## 41 Usal (Sinkyone Wilderness State Park)

**Location:** 20 miles southwest of Leggett
**GPS:** 39.8345958 / -123.8441892
**Sites:** 15 sites for tents
**Facilities:** Tables, fire rings, vault toilets; no drinking water
**Fee per night:** $$
**Management:** California Department of Parks and Recreation, (707) 986-7711
**Activities:** Hiking, fishing
**Finding the campground:** From the intersection of US 101 and CA 1 at Leggett, drive southwest 14 miles on CA 1. Turn north onto CR 431 (Usal Road) and drive 6 miles. The road is not advised for large vehicles.
**About the campground:** The campground is near an isolated black-sand beach at the south end of the 7,000-acre Sinkyone Wilderness on Northern California's "Lost Coast." (See the sidebar on King Range National Conservation Area, page 25, for more information about the area.) The Lost Coast Trail runs north and south at the campground. There is a barn for sheltered camping. Sinkyone also offers a couple primitive walk-in, tent-only campgrounds. Elevation 50 feet. Stay limit 14 days. Open all year.

## 42 Howard Creek (Westport–Union Landing State Beach)

**Location:** 18 miles north of Fort Bragg
**GPS:** 39.6753856 / -123.7907399
**Sites:** 86 sites for tents and RVs
**Facilities:** Tables, fire rings, drinking water, vault toilets
**Fee per night:** $$
**Management:** California Department of Parks and Recreation, (707) 964-4406
**Activities:** Fishing, hiking, whale watching
**Finding the campground:** From Fort Bragg, drive north on CA 1 for 17 miles to the town of Westport. The park has several entrances between 1 and 3 miles north of the town.
**About the campground:** The park is divided into four segments of bluff and beach, separated by creek gulches, extending along a 3-mile stretch of coastline. There are three campgrounds, all above the beach on the open, almost treeless bluffs, with stairs and trails down to the narrow, surf-swept beaches. Offshore rocks and islands, wave-pounded cliffs, and distant mountains provide a dramatic setting and excellent ocean and mountain views. The park is a good place to whale watch from November through January. Elevation 30 feet. Stay limit 15 days. Open all year.

## 43 MacKerricher State Park

**Location:** 3 miles north of Fort Bragg
**GPS:** 39.4884818 / -123.7975628
**Sites:** 114 sites for tents and RVs up 35 feet long
**Facilities:** Tables, fire rings, drinking water, flush toilets, showers, dump station, boat ramp
**Fee per night:** $$$; reservations: (800) 444-7275 or reserveamerica.com
**Management:** California Department of Parks and Recreation, (707) 964-9112
**Activities:** Fishing, hiking, horseback riding, biking, boating, whale watching, birding
**Finding the campground:** From Fort Bragg, drive north 3 miles on CA 1.
**About the campground:** MacKerricher's 1,600 acres contain an 8-mile-long, wide, sandy beach; a coastal forest; a 13-acre freshwater lake; a boardwalk leading to a promontory for viewing whales and sea lions; hiking/jogging trails; and a shoreline equestrian trail. The spacious campground is spread over several loops, shaded by coastal pines and adjacent to the beach. Cleone Lake, near the campground, contains a resident population of bluegill, bass, and bullhead and is stocked annually with rainbow trout. It offers great birding too, with 90 species living here or visiting the tidal lagoon. Horses may be rented just outside the park. Groceries and services exist in nearby Cleone. Elevation 30 feet. Stay limit 30 days. Open all year.

## 44 Camp One Area (Jackson Demonstration State Forest)

**Location:** 7 miles southeast of Fort Bragg
**GPS:** 39.3686565 / -123.6571721
**Sites:** 20 tent and small RV sites in 19 campgrounds, including equestrian sites
**Facilities:** Picnic tables, fire rings, pit toilets; no drinking water
**Fee per night:** $ (Iron Ranger is located at the Camp One Host site location.)
**Management:** Jackson Demonstration State Forest, (707) 964-5674
**Activities:** Hiking, swimming, mountain biking, horseback riding, hunting
**Finding the campground:** From Fort Bragg, drive south 1.3 miles on CA 1. Turn east onto CA 20 and drive 5.7 miles. Turn east onto JDSF 350 and drive 1.5 miles to the day-use area.
**About the campground:** Established in 1849, Jackson is a working forest (over 48,000 acres) with the goal of demonstrating sustained timber production while maintaining soil, water, scenic, wildlife, and recreational values. Timber production has been continuous in the forest since the 1850s. The campgrounds are located along the North Fork of the South Fork of the Noyo River. To help find them, purchase a map of the forest at the Cal Fire office in Fort Bragg or print one from the calfire.ca.gov website. The road is narrow and bumpy, with sharp curves. A series of trails lead through this isolated redwood and fir forest, including one to 50-foot-high Chamberlain Creek Falls, in a virgin old-growth redwood grove. Fishing is not permitted in the forest. Tilley Campground is available for groups by reservation. Stay limit 14 days. Open Memorial Day to Labor Day.

## 45 Camp 20 Area (Jackson Demonstration State Forest)

**Location:** 18 miles southeast of Fort Bragg
**GPS:** 39.353275 / -123.5562988
**Sites:** 22 tent and small RV sites in 3 campgrounds; equestrian camp with 8 sites

**Facilities:** Picnic tables, fire rings, pit toilets; no drinking water
**Fee per night:** $ (Iron Rangers are located at Dunlap and Big River)
**Management:** Jackson Demonstration State Forest, (707) 964-5674
**Activities:** Hiking, swimming, mountain biking, horseback riding, hunting
**Finding the campground:** From Fort Bragg, drive south 1.3 miles on CA 1. Turn east onto CA 20 and drive about 17 miles. Turn north and drive 300 yards to mile marker 17.
**About the campground:** The campground is located near Chamberlin Creek. Off-road bike enthusiasts enjoy the picturesque, often-challenging trails in the redwoods of Jackson State Forest. Elevation 373 feet. Stay limit 14 days. Open Memorial Day to Labor Day.

## 46 Russian Gulch State Park

**Location:** 2 miles north of Mendocino
**GPS:** 39.3304705 / -123.8019631
**Sites:** 26 sites for tents and RVs up to 24 feet long; 1 group site for tents only
**Facilities:** Tables, fire rings, drinking water, flush toilets, showers
**Fee per night:** $$$; reservations: (800) 444-7275 or reserveamerica.com
**Management:** California Department of Parks and Recreation, (707) 937-0497 (seasonal kiosk) or (707) 937-5804
**Activities:** Fishing, hiking, mountain biking, swimming, scuba diving
**Finding the campground:** From Mendocino, drive north 2 miles on CA 1.
**About the campground:** The park includes both coastal sections and an inland forest of second-growth redwoods, alder, and western hemlock. The campground is located along a pretty, wooded stretch of Russian Gulch Creek, close to the shore. A protecting cove shelters an attractive beach, and trails lead north and south along the coast to the Punch Bowl—a blowhole and collapsed sea cave. Inland, another trail through heavily forested Russian Gulch makes a 6-mile round-trip to 36-foot Russian Gulch Falls, accessible partway by mountain bike. Elevation 85 feet. Stay limit 30 days. Open March to September.

## 47 Van Damme State Park

**Location:** 3 miles south of Mendocino
**GPS:** 39.274726 / -123.7890774
**Sites:** 69 sites for tents and RVs up to 35 feet long; 1 group site
**Facilities:** Tables, fire rings, drinking water, flush toilets, showers, dump station
**Fee per night:** $$$; reservations: (800) 444-7275 or reserveamerica.com
**Management:** California Department of Parks and Recreation, (707) 937-5804
**Activities:** Fishing, hiking, swimming, mountain biking, boating, scuba diving
**Finding the campground:** From Mendocino, drive 3 miles south on CA 1.
**About the campground:** The park contains both coastal and inland sections, including an attractive beach on a scenic coastal bay, a 10-mile round-trip trail through a fern-lined canyon, and a boardwalk through a pygmy pine grove and cypress trees. The campground is well laid out and nicely wooded, with a stream running through the lower level and mixed wooded and open meadow sites at its upper level. Elevation 48 feet. Stay limit 30 days. Open all year.

*There are both open, grassy sites and wooded sites at Van Damme State Park, with an inviting ocean beach directly across CA 1.*

## 48 Navarro Beach (Navarro River Redwoods State Park)

**Location:** 50 miles west of Ukiah
**GPS:** 39.1922175 / -123.758261
**Sites:** 10 sites for tents and RVs up to 30 feet long
**Facilities:** Tables, fire rings, chemical toilets; no drinking water
**Fee per night:** $$
**Management:** California Department of Parks and Recreation, (707) 937-5804
**Activities:** Kayaking, canoeing, fishing, swimming
**Finding the campground:** On the coast near the intersection of CA 1 and CA 128.
**About the campground:** Situated on the beach, just south of the bridge across the Navarro River, you can fall asleep to the sound of the ocean and enjoy riparian recreation and wildlife too. Visit Captain Fletcher's Inn, an establishment operating in the 1860s. Stay limit 15 days. Open all year.

## 49 Paul M. Dimmick Wayside (Navarro River Redwoods State Park)

**Location:** 42 miles west of Ukiah
**GPS:** 39.1578747 / -123.6368991
**Sites:** 28 sites for tents and RVs up to 30 feet long
**Facilities:** Tables, fire rings, drinking water (summer only), vault toilets
**Fee per night:** $$

**Management:** California Department of Parks and Recreation, (707) 937-5804
**Activities:** Kayaking, canoeing, hiking, fishing, swimming
**Finding the campground:** From the intersection of US 101 and CA 253 in Ukiah, drive southwest on CA 253 for 16 miles. Turn north onto CA 128 and drive about 26 miles.
**About the campground:** Closed at the time this book was written, this gem of a campground is projected to reopen in late 2016. This narrow, 674-acre park follows the Navarro River (and CA 128) from the ocean to a point about 12 miles inland. The forest is mainly second-growth redwoods, with huge stumps attesting to the logging of former giants. The 11-mile Navarro River Redwoods Car Tour along CA 128 has turnouts for exploring short sections of the forest. The river provides steelhead fishing in winter. Elevation 200 feet. Stay limit 15 days. Open all year.

## 50 Hendy Woods State Park

**Location:** 28 miles west of Ukiah
**GPS:** 39.0677549 / -123.4635768
**Sites:** 92 sites for tents and RVs up to 35 feet long; 3 cabins and hike & bike sites
**Facilities:** Tables, fire rings, drinking water, flush toilets, showers, dump station
**Fee per night:** $$$$; reservations (peak season only): (800) 444-7275 or reserveamerica.com.
**Management:** California Department of Parks and Recreation, (707) 937-5804
**Activities:** Hiking, kayaking, canoeing, mountain biking, swimming
**Finding the campground:** From the intersection of US 101 and CA 253 in Ukiah, drive southwest on CA 253 for 16 miles. Turn north onto CA 128 and drive about 12 miles.
**About the campground:** The park protects 128 acres of virgin and second-growth redwoods in several groves. Providing fine views of the trees are excellent short trails, including the Gentle Giants All Access Trail (1.5-mile loop) and the Hermit Hut Trail. Kayaking and canoeing in the Navarro River are best in winter and spring. Fishing is not permitted in the river within the park. The Husch Vineyards and Navarro Vineyards are located along the highway, within a few miles of the campground. They offer tours, tasting, sales, and picnicking. Elevation 320 feet. Stay limit 15 days mid-May through September, 30 days off-peak season. Open all year.

## 51 Manchester State Beach

**Location:** 28 miles south of Mendocino
**GPS:** 38.9808237 / -123.6989866
**Sites:** 41 sites for tents and RVs up to 30 feet long
**Facilities:** Tables, fire rings, drinking water, pit toilets
**Fee per night:** $$$; reservations (peak season only): (800) 444-7275 or reserveamerica.com
**Management:** California Department of Parks and Recreation, (707) 937-5804
**Activities:** Fishing, hiking, birding, scuba diving
**Finding the campground:** From Mendocino, drive south 28 miles on CA 1 (2 miles north of Point Arena). Three separate roads lead to different sections of the park. The campground entrance is Kinney Road, and it is signed.
**About the campground:** The park's 760 acres comprise a 5-mile-long gentle sand beach backed by grass-covered dunes with grasslands inland. Two creeks, a pretty lagoon, and a saltwater marsh complete the picture. The area can be windy, especially in summer. Located on a wide, attractive, grassy plateau with some trees, the campground has an excellent view of mountains to the west,

but no view of the ocean. A trail leads to the beach, about 10 minutes away. Shore casting is reputedly good along the beach all year, and Bush and Alder Creeks offer steelhead runs in winter. A 5-mile loop trail, beginning near the campground, offers a fine sampling of the park. There are environmental campsites a 1.1-mile walk from the park entrance and a group site (maximum 40 people). Elevation 52 feet. Stay limit 15 days. Open all year.

## 52 Hammerhorn Lake

**Location:** 31 miles northeast of Covelo
**GPS:** 39.9487482 / -122.9913859
**Sites:** 9 sites for tents and RVs up to 16 feet long
**Facilities:** Tables, fire rings, stoves, drinking water, vault toilets, small boat ramp, fishing piers
**Fee per night:** $
**Management:** Mendocino National Forest, (530) 934-3316
**Activities:** Fishing, hiking, boating
**Finding the campground:** From Covelo, drive east 13 miles on CA 162 to Eel River Work Center. Turn north onto FR M1 (Indian Dick Road) and drive 18 miles.
**About the campground:** The campground is situated in a mixed-conifer forest on the shore of a 5-acre lake. Hammerhorn is stocked annually with rainbow trout, which makes for good fishing in early summer. No motorized boats are allowed on the lake. The Smoke House Trail begins 2 miles northeast of the campground and leads north into the Yolla Bolly–Middle Eel Wilderness. Elevation 3,500 feet. Stay limit 14 days. Open May to November.

## 53 Howard Meadows

**Location:** 29 miles northeast of Covelo
**GPS:** 39.878 / -122.99
**Sites:** 6 sites for tents and RVs up to 16 feet long
**Facilities:** Tables, fire rings, vault toilets, small boat ramp; no drinking water
**Fee per night:** None
**Management:** Mendocino National Forest, (530) 934-3316
**Activities:** Fishing, hiking, boating, swimming
**Finding the campground:** From Covelo, drive east 13 miles on CA 162 to Eel River Work Center. Turn north onto FR M1 (Indian Dick Road) and drive 12 miles. Turn west onto FR 23N37 and drive about 3 miles. The access road is unimproved, so a vehicle with good clearance is recommended.
**About the campground:** The campground is situated in a mixed-conifer forest with a large meadow. The campground is a short walk to 12-acre Howard Lake, which is often stocked with trout. No motors are allowed on the lake, which is good for swimming. Elevation 3,700 feet. Stay limit 14 days. Open April to November.

## 54 Little Doe

**Location:** 25 miles northeast of Covelo
**GPS:** 39.8945983 / -122.9880631
**Sites:** 13 sites for tents and RVs
**Facilities:** Tables, fire rings, stoves, vault toilets; no drinking water

**Fee per night:** None
**Management:** Mendocino National Forest, (530) 934-3316
**Activities:** Fishing and hiking nearby
**Finding the campground:** From Covelo, drive east 13 miles on CA 162 to Eel River Work Center. Turn north onto FR M1 (Indian Dick Road) and drive 12 miles.
**About the campground:** Little Doe is situated in a mixed-conifer forest about 2.4 miles from Howard Lake. Elevation 3,600 feet. Stay limit 14 days. Open mid-May to mid-November.

## 55 Eel River

**Location:** 13 miles east of Covelo
**GPS:** 39.8243211 / -123.0855645
**Sites:** 16 sites for tents and RVs up to 35 feet long
**Facilities:** Tables, stoves, drinking water, vault toilets
**Fee per night:** $
**Management:** Mendocino National Forest, (530) 934-3316
**Activities:** Fishing
**Finding the campground:** From Covelo, drive east 13 miles on CA 162.
**About the campground:** The camp is adjacent to the Eel River Work Center and has good river access. Elevation 1,500 feet. Stay limit 14 days. Open March to November.

## 56 Plaskett Meadows (Plaskett Lakes Recreation Area)

**Location:** 28 miles southeast of Covelo
**GPS:** 39.728513 / -122.845772
**Sites:** 31 sites for tents and RVs up to 26 feet long
**Facilities:** Tables, fire rings, drinking water, vault toilets
**Fee per night:** $
**Management:** Mendocino National Forest, (530) 963-3128
**Activities:** Fishing, boating, hiking
**Finding the campground:** From Covelo, drive east 13 miles on CA 162 to Eel River Work Center. Turn southeast onto FR M7 and drive 15 miles.
**About the campground:** Situated in an area of mixed pine and fir, the campground is adjacent to two small lakes, one 3 acres, the other 4 acres. No motorized boats are allowed. Swimming is not recommended. Fishing for up to 12-inch rainbow trout can be good in early summer. For group camping, check out the Masterson Group Camp (reservation required). Elevation 6,000 feet. Stay limit 14 days. Open June to October.

## 57 Trout Creek

**Location:** 25 miles northeast of Ukiah
**GPS:** 39.3744068 / -123.0672165
**Sites:** 13 sites for tents and small RVs; 3 walk-ins
**Facilities:** Tables, fire rings, drinking water, vault toilets
**Fee per night:** $; reservations: (707) 743-1513 or http://recreation.pge.com
**Management:** PG&E, (530) 386-5164

**Activities:** Fishing, swimming, birding, river rafting

**Finding the campground:** From Ukiah, drive north 6 miles on US 101; turn right (east) onto CA 20 and drive 5 miles. Turn north onto CR 240 (Potter Valley–Lake Pillsbury Road) and drive 14 miles (2 miles past the Eel River bridge).

**About the campground:** The campground is situated near the confluence of Trout Creek and Eel River. Trout Creek offers fair fishing for small native trout. Elevation 1,500 feet. Stay limit 14 days. Open May through October.

## 58 Fuller Grove (Lake Pillsbury Recreation Area)

**Location:** 38 miles northeast of Ukiah

**GPS:** 39.436244 / -122.96975

**Sites:** 23 sites for tents and RVs up to 22 feet long, including 6 doubles and 1 group site

**Facilities:** Tables, fire rings, drinking water, vault toilets, boat ramp

**Fee per night:** $; reservations (for group site only): (707) 743-1513 or http://recreation.pge.com

**Management:** PG&E, (707) 743-1513

**Activities:** Fishing, swimming, boating, waterskiing, hiking, birding, horseback riding

**Finding the campground:** From Ukiah, drive 6 miles north on US 101; turn right (east) onto CA 20 and drive 5 miles. Turn north onto CR 240 (Potter Valley–Lake Pillsbury Road) and drive 26 miles northwest to the Eel River information kiosk at Lake Pillsbury. Continue north around the lake for 1.5 miles.

**About the campground:** Lake Pillsbury is the largest lake in the Mendocino National forest with 31 miles of shore lined with meadows, several beaches, and stands of oaks and conifers. It is stocked annually with rainbow trout, and the lake also contains bluegill, sunfish, salmon, steelhead, and black bass. The water level goes down in the fall. Elevation 1,800 feet. Stay limit 14 days. Open mid-April through mid-September.

## 59 Pogie Point (Lake Pillsbury Recreation Area)

**Location:** 39 miles northeast of Ukiah

**GPS:** 39.4426599 / -122.9688902

**Sites:** 44 sites for tents

**Facilities:** Tables, fire rings, grills, drinking water, vault toilets, boat ramp

**Fee per night:** $

**Management:** PG&E, (707) 743-1513

**Activities:** Fishing, swimming, boating, waterskiing, hiking, horseback riding

**Finding the campground:** From Ukiah, drive 6 miles north on US 101; turn right (east) onto CA 20 and drive 5 miles. Turn north onto CR 240 (Potter Valley–Lake Pillsbury Road) and drive 26 miles northwest to the Eel River information kiosk at Lake Pillsbury. Continue north around the lake for 1.5 miles. Adjacent to Fuller Grove Campground (58).

**About the campground:** The campground is situated in an attractive cove on the northwest shore of the Lake Pillsbury, but with no lake views. The campground will accommodate RVs, but it seems better suited for tent campers. Enjoy the 4-mile Lakeshore Trail for hiking or horseback riding. Elevation 1,800 feet. Stay limit 14 days. Open mid-May through mid-September.

## 60 Navy Camp (Lake Pillsbury Recreation Area)

**Location:** 40 miles northeast of Ukiah
**GPS:** 39.442989 / -122.957839
**Sites:** 20 sites for tents and RVs up to 22 feet long
**Facilities:** Tables, fire rings, drinking water, vault toilets; boat ramp 0.5 mile south
**Fee per night:** $
**Management:** PG&E, (530) 386-5164 or (707) 275-2361
**Activities:** Fishing, swimming, boating, waterskiing, hiking, horseback riding
**Finding the campground:** From Ukiah, drive 6 miles north on US 101; turn right (east) onto CA 20, and drive 5 miles. Turn north onto CR 240 (Potter Valley–Lake Pillsbury Road) and drive 26 miles northwest to the Eel River information kiosk at Lake Pillsbury. Continue north around the lake for 3.5 miles.
**About the campground:** Located on the north shore of the lake, Navy Camp is a quiet, sunny campground with a little shade from scattered oaks. Elevation 1,800 feet. Stay limit 14 days. Open mid-April through mid-September.

## 61 Oak Flat (Lake Pillsbury Recreation Area)

**Location:** 40 miles northeast of Ukiah
**GPS:** 39.4429377 / -122.9533341
**Sites:** 12 sites for tents and RVs; overflow dispersed sites
**Facilities:** Tables, grills, vault toilets; no drinking water; boat ramp 1 mile southeast
**Fee per night:** None
**Management:** Mendocino National Forest, (530) 824-5196
**Activities:** Fishing, swimming, boating, waterskiing, hiking, horseback riding
**Finding the campground:** From Ukiah, drive 6 miles north on US 101; turn right (east) onto CA 20 and drive 5 miles. Turn north onto CR 240 (Potter Valley–Lake Pillsbury Road) and drive 26 miles northwest to the Eel River information kiosk at Lake Pillsbury. Continue north around the lake for 3.5 miles. Oak Flat is just past Navy Camp (60).
**About the campground:** This campground is used as an overflow area for Sunset Point on weekends when other campgrounds are full. Large, informal sites are well shaded by oaks. There is poison oak present in the area. Elevation 1,850 feet. Stay limit 14 days. Open all year.

## 62 Sunset Point (Lake Pillsbury Recreation Area)

**Location:** 42 miles northeast of Ukiah
**GPS:** 39.437928 / -122.940233
**Sites:** 53 sites for tents and RVs, including 14 doubles
**Facilities:** Tables, fire rings, drinking water (except in winter), vault toilets; boat ramp nearby
**Fee per night:** $
**Management:** PG&E, (707) 743-1513
**Activities:** Fishing, swimming, boating, waterskiing, hiking, biking, horseback riding
**Finding the campground:** From Ukiah, drive 6 miles north on US 101; turn right (east) onto CA 20 and drive 5 miles. Turn north onto CR 240 (Potter Valley–Lake Pillsbury Road) and drive 26

miles to the Eel River information kiosk at Lake Pillsbury. Continue north around the lake for 5 miles.
**About the campground:** The campground is situated in an attractive stand of Douglas fir on the north shore of the lake. Some sites in manzanita are more open; some sites have a lake view. There is a nature loop trail directly across from the campground for hikers, bikers, and equestrians. Elevation 1,850 feet. Stay limit 14 days. Open mid-April through mid-September.

## 63 Lower Nye

**Location:** 38 miles north of the community of Upper Lake
**GPS:** 39.443215 / -122.8255523
**Sites:** 6 sites for tents and RVs
**Facilities:** Tables, fire rings, vault toilets; no drinking water
**Fee per night:** None
**Management:** Mendocino National Forest, (530) 934-3316
**Activities:** Hiking
**Finding the campground:** From Upper Lake, drive north 17 miles on CR 301 (FR M1); turn right (east) onto FR 18N01 and drive 7 miles. Turn north onto FR 18N04 and drive 14 miles. ***Note:*** Must ford three creeks to access the campground, dry in summer. Please call the national forest for winter road conditions.
**About the campground:** Situated on the northwest border of the Snow Mountain Wilderness, this dispersed campground is used primarily by backpackers. Elevation 3,300 feet. Stay limit 14 days. Open all year.

## 64 Bear Creek (Upper Lake Recreation Area)

**Location:** 25 miles north of the community of Upper Lake
**GPS:** 39.322663 / -122.8369394
**Sites:** 16 sites for tents and RVs
**Facilities:** Tables, fire rings, vault toilets; no drinking water
**Fee per night:** None
**Management:** Mendocino National Forest, (530) 934-3316
**Activities:** Fishing, hiking, backpacking
**Finding the campground:** From Upper Lake, drive 17 miles north on CR 301 (FR M1); turn right (east) onto FR 18N01 and drive 8 miles. ***Note:*** Must ford three creeks to access the campground, dry in summer. Please call the national forest for winter road conditions.
**About the campground:** Situated near the confluence of two small creeks. Elevation 2,000 feet. Stay limit 14 days. Open all year.

## 65 Deer Valley (Upper Lake Recreation Area)

**Location:** 16 miles north of the community of Upper Lake
**GPS:** 39.2659982 / -122.88444
**Sites:** 13 sites for tents and RVs
**Facilities:** Tables, fire rings, vault toilets; no drinking water
**Fee per night:** $

**Management:** Mendocino National Forest, (707) 275-2361
**Activities:** OHV driving, mountain biking
**Finding the campground:** From Upper Lake, drive 12 miles north on CR 301 (FR M-1) and then 4 miles east on FR 16N01. ***Note:*** Please call the national forest for winter road conditions.
**About the campground:** The campground affords access to OHV trails. Elevation 3,700 feet. Stay limit 14 days. Open all year.

## 66 Middle Creek (Upper Lake Recreation Area)

**Location:** 8 miles north of the community of Upper Lake
**GPS:** 39.2529435 / -122.9511086
**Sites:** 23 sites for tents and RVs, including 2 for small groups
**Facilities:** Tables, fire rings, stoves, drinking water, vault toilets
**Fee per night:** $
**Management:** Mendocino National Forest, (530) 934-3316
**Activities:** Fishing, OHV driving, horseback riding
**Finding the campground:** From Upper Lake, drive 8 miles north on CR 301 (FR M1).
**About the campground:** The campground is situated near the confluence of the East and West Forks of Middle Creek, with an OHV and equestrian staging area (not set up for equestrian camping). Elevation 2,000 feet. Stay limit 14 days. Open all year.

## 67 Bushay (Lake Mendocino)

**Location:** 8 miles northeast of Ukiah
**GPS:** 39.2307877 / -123.1642939
**Sites:** 134 individual sites for tents and RVs up to 40 feet long; 1 electric hookup; 3 group sites for up to 120 people each
**Facilities:** Tables, fire rings, drinking water, flush toilets, showers, playground, horse staging area, dump station; boat ramp 2 miles west
**Fee per night:** $$$; reservations: (800) 444-7275 or reserveamerica.com
**Management:** US Army Corps of Engineers, (707) 467-4200
**Activities:** Swimming, fishing, boating, waterskiing, hiking, horseback riding
**Finding the campground:** From Ukiah, drive north on US 101 about 5 miles. Take the CA 20 exit and drive east about 3 miles. Just after you see Lake Mendocino to the south, you will cross a tall bridge. Turn northwest onto Vista del Lago Road.
**About the campground:** Lake Mendocino offers all kinds of on-the-water fun. Fifteen miles of hiking and biking trails take you through the grassy hills of Coyote Valley with its groves of oak, manzanita, and pine, as well as a 700-acre wilderness area for wildlife viewing. Fish for large- and smallmouth bass, stripers, crappie, bluegill, and catfish. Boat-in camping is also available. Elevation 850 feet. Stay limit 14 days (with extensions available). Open May through September.

## 68 Kyen (Lake Mendocino)

**Location:** 8 miles northeast of Ukiah
**GPS:** 39.2359152 / -123.1770581
**Sites:** 102 sites for tents and RVs up to 35 feet long

**Facilities:** Tables, fire rings, drinking water, flush toilets, showers, dump station, boat ramp
**Fee per night:** $$$; reservations: (800) 444-7275 or reserveamerica.com
**Management:** US Army Corps of Engineers, (707) 467-4200
**Activities:** Swimming, fishing, boating, waterskiing, hiking
**Finding the campground:** From Ukiah, drive north on US 101 about 6 miles; take the CA 20 exit and drive east about 1.5 miles. Turn south onto Marina Drive and drive 0.5 mile.
**About the campground:** The 3-mile Shakota Trail begins at the Pomo Cultural Center within the campground and offers beautiful views of the lake. See Bushay (67) and Chekaka Campground (69) for area information. Open all year.

## 69 CheKaKa (Lake Mendocino)

**Location:** 4 miles northeast of Ukiah
**GPS:** 39.202669 / -123.186949
**Sites:** 17 sites for tents and RVs up to 35 feet long; 1 group site
**Facilities:** Tables, fire rings, drinking water, vault toilets, playground, boat ramp
**Fee per night:** $$; reservations: (800) 444-7275 or reserveamerica.com
**Management:** US Army Corps of Engineers, (707) 467-4200
**Activities:** Swimming, fishing, boating, waterskiing, hiking
**Finding the campground:** From Ukiah, drive north on US 101 about 2 miles; take the Lake Mendocino Drive exit and drive east about 2 miles.
**About the campground:** Lake Mendocino provides 1,822 acres for virtually all water sports. You can launch your boat from one of two six-lane boat ramps located at either end of the lake, and sailing is popular. Boat slips and boat rentals are available near the north end of the marina. The lake is subject to water drawdowns during summer and fall. Enjoy wine tasting at several wineries near the lake. CheKaKa is at the north end of the dam near the park office, within walking distance of the lake and dam. The city of Ukiah is only 15 minutes away for further excursions. Elevation 787 feet. Stay limit 14 days. Open April through September.

# Sonoma-Napa Area

The vineyards of the Sonoma-Napa area are world famous. Many of California's premium wines are born in Napa Valley, and tours of the wineries here are a growing part of the tourism industry. If you want to avoid the crowded roads of the Napa tour and are willing to see the vineyards from a different perspective, you can canoe or kayak on the Russian River north of Santa Rosa, passing nearly one hundred wineries between Guerneville and Cloverdale.

But wineries are not the only attraction of Sonoma-Napa. The coastline from Jenner north to Point Arena is wild and glorious. The ocean pounds furiously against the headlands. Along the coast are fine beaches and Fort Ross, a restored Russian outpost established in 1812.

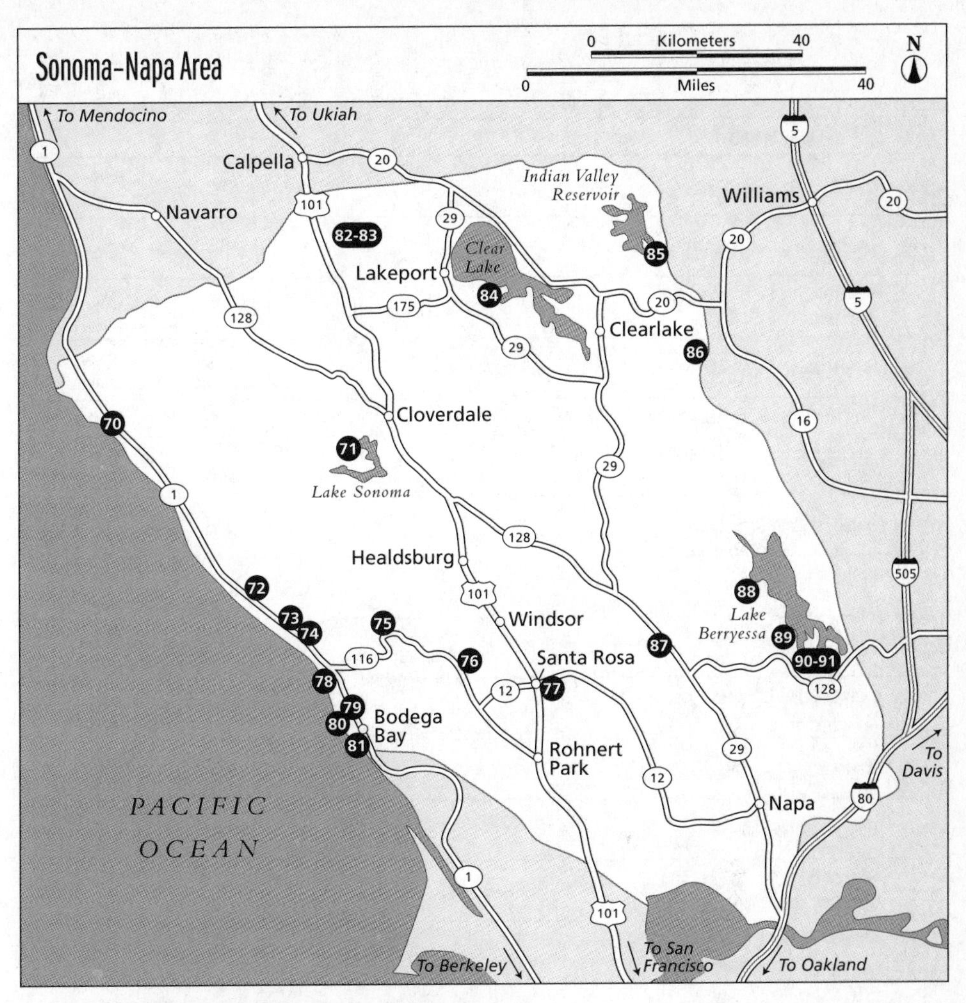


# 70 Gualala Point Regional Park

**Location:** 43 miles north of the community of Bodega Bay

**GPS:** 38.7597103 / -123.5257399

**Sites:** 25 sites for tents and RVs up to 30 feet long

**Facilities:** Tables, fire rings, drinking water, flush toilets, shower, dump station

**Fee per night:** $$$; reservations: (707) 565-2267 or parks.sonomacounty.ca.gov

**Management:** Sonoma County Parks Department, (707) 785-2377

**Activities:** Hiking, fishing, beachcombing, kayaking (river), wading, visitor center

**Finding the campground:** From Bodega Bay, drive north 43 miles on CA 1.

**About the campground:** The campground is situated within a majestic redwood grove along the banks of the Gualala River and close to the coast. Sites are relatively close together. There's access to 2.9 miles of coastal trail along bluffs, through meadows, and overlooking the Gualala River. Steelhead fishing in early winter. There are walk-in sites and a hike & bike site as well. Elevation 52 feet. Stay limit 10 days. Open all year.

| | Name | Group Sites | RV Sites | Max. RV Length | Hookups | Toilets | Showers | Drinking Water | Dump Station | Pets | Wheelchair | Recreation | Fee(s) | Season | Can Reserve |
|---|---|---|---|---|---|---|---|---|---|---|---|---|---|---|---|
| | **SONOMA-NAPA AREA** | | | | | | | | | | | | | | |
| 70 | Gualala Point Regional Park | | * | 30 | | F | * | * | * | * | * | FHB | $$$ | Year-round | * |
| 71 | Liberty Glen (Lake Sonoma) | * | * | | | F | * | * | * | * | * | HR | $$ | Year-round | * |
| 72 | Woodside and Gerstle Cove (Salt Point State Park) | * | * | 27 | | V | | * | * | * | * | HRM | $$$ | Year-round | * |
| 73 | Stillwater Cove Regional Park | | * | 40 | | F | * | * | * | * | * | FHB | $$$ | Year-round | * |
| 74 | Reef (Fort Ross State Historic Park) | | * | 18 | | F | | * | | * | * | HF | $$$ | Apr–Oct | |
| 75 | Bullfrog Pond (Austin Creek State Recreation Area) | | | | | F | | * | | * | | HRF | $$$ | Year-round | * |
| 76 | Sugarloaf Ridge State Park | * | * | 27 | | F | | * | | * | * | HRM | $$$ | Year-round | * |
| 77 | Spring Lake Regional Park | * | * | | | F | * | * | * | * | * | HSFB | $$$ | Year-round | * |
| 78 | Wright's Beach (Sonoma Coast State Beach) | | * | 30 | | F | | * | | * | * | HFR | $$$ | Year-round | * |
| 79 | Bodega Dunes (Sonoma Coast State Beach) | | * | 31 | | F | * | * | * | * | * | HFR | $$$ | Year-round | * |
| 80 | Westside Regional Park | | * | | | F | * | * | * | * | * | FBL | $$$ | Year-round | * |
| 81 | Doran Regional Park | * | * | | | F | * | * | * | * | * | FBHL | $$$ | Year-round | * |
| 82 | Red Mountain (South Cow Mountain Recreation Area) | | * | | | V | | * | | * | | O | None | Year-round | |
| 83 | Mayacmus (North Cow Mountain Recreation Area) | | | | | V | | | | * | | HFR | None | Year-round | |
| 84 | Clear Lake State Park | * | * | 35 | | F | * | * | * | * | * | HSFBL | $$$ | Year-round | * |
| 85 | Blue Oaks (Indian Valley Reservoir) | | * | | | V | | | | | | HSBF | None | Year-round | |
| 86 | Lower Hunting Creek (Knoxville Recreation Area) | | * | | | V | | * | | * | | OM | None | Year-round | |
| 87 | Bothe–Napa Valley State Park | * | * | 31 | | F | * | * | * | * | * | HSR | $$$ | Year-round | * |
| 88 | Putah Canyon (Lake Berryessa) | | * | 38 | | P | | | | * | | FSB | $$$ | Memorial Day–Sept | * |
| 89 | Spanish Flat Recreation Area (Lake Berryessa) | | * | | | V | | * | * | * | * | FSBH | $$$ | Year-round | * |
| 90 | Pleasure Cove (Lake Berryessa) | | * | 40 | EWS | F | * | | * | * | * | FSBHL | $$$$ | Year-round | * |
| 91 | Steele Canyon (Lake Berryessa) | | * | | | P | | | * | * | | FSB | $$$ | Year-round | * |

Toilets: F=flush V=vault P=pit C=Chemical; Fee: $=Under $20 $$=$20-$29 $$$=$30-$39 $$$$ $40 or more; Recreation: H=hiking S=swimming F=fishing B=boating L=boat launch O=Off-highway driving R=horseback riding, M=Mountain biking
Hookups: W=water E=Electric S=Sewer

*The wine country of Sonoma and Napa Counties offers beautiful views of the North Coast Range. Photo by Bubba Seuss*

## 71 Liberty Glen (Lake Sonoma)

**Location:** 13 miles northwest of Healdsburg

**GPS:** 38.7162806 / -123.0577902

**Sites:** 95 sites for tents and RVs; 2 group sites; 1 equestrian group site; 1 cabin

**Facilities:** Tables, fire rings, tent pads, drinking water, flush toilets, showers, playground, dump station

**Fee per night:** $$; reservations: (877) 444-6777 or recreation.gov

**Management:** US Army Corps of Engineers, (707) 431-4533

**Activities:** Hiking, biking, horseback riding

**Finding the campground:** From Healdsburg, drive northwest on Dry Creek Road for 11 miles. Continue over the bridge across Lake Sonoma and drive an additional 2 miles.

**About the campground:** Liberty Glen is situated on a ridge above the Warm Springs Arm of the 9-mile-long Lake Sonoma, offering scenic views. It takes a robust hike of about 1 mile to get to the shoreline. You can also drive 2.5 miles and park for the day. Waterskiing is popular in designated areas of the lake. The marina, located on the western side of the bridge, offers rentals and other services. The fish hatchery next to the visitor center at the park entrance is worth a visit. A dozen wineries lie within a 6-mile radius of the campground, most offering tastings and sales. Also check out the primitive campsites along trails and the boat-in campsites. More than 40 miles of hiking and equestrian trails lead through redwood groves and oak woodlands. Elevation 1,140 feet. Stay limit 14 days. Open all year.

## 72 Woodside and Gerstle Cove (Salt Point State Park)

**Location:** 19 miles north of Jenner
**GPS:** 38.5694926 / -123.3206504
**Sites:** 109 sites for tents and RVs up to 27 feet; 1 group site
**Facilities:** Tables, fire rings, drinking water, vault toilets, dump station
**Fee per night:** $$$; reservations: (800) 444-7275 or reserveamerica.com
**Management:** California Department of Parks and Recreation, (707) 865-2391
**Activities:** Hiking, scuba diving, mountain biking, horseback riding
**Finding the campground:** From Jenner, drive about 19 miles north on CA 1.
**About the campground:** Salt Point Park encompasses almost 6,000 acres and includes 6 miles of rocky shoreline; hard sand beach coves; an underwater preserve; a redwood grove; a pygmy forest; several scenic trails for hikers, equestrians, and mountain bikers; and a small visitor center. There is a primitive boat launch for scuba divers, but the coast is too rough to launch pleasure boats. The waters offshore are a protected marine reserve; no fishing or collecting is permitted. The 2-mile Stump Beach Trail leads along the bluff to a beautiful cove beach lined with driftwood. Adjacent to the park is the Kruse Rhododendron State Reserve, which comes alive with color in April and May. Woodside Campground is located on the east side of the highway in a mixed, mostly pine forest. Gerstle Cove (previously known as Moonrock Campground) is on the ocean side of the highway. Elevation 337 feet. Stay limit 10 days. Open all year.

## 73 Stillwater Cove Regional Park

**Location:** 15 miles north of Jenner
**GPS:** 38.5480288 / -123.2945913
**Sites:** 23 sites for tents and RVs up to 40 feet long; 1 hike & bike site
**Facilities:** Tables, fire rings, drinking water, flush toilets, showers, dump station
**Fee per night:** $$$; reservations: (707) 565-2267 or parks.sonomacounty.ca.gov; walk-ups also available
**Management:** Sonoma County Regional Parks, (707) 847-3245
**Activities:** Fishing, hiking, birding, beach play, kayaking/canoeing, scuba diving
**Finding the campground:** From Bodega Bay, drive north 25 miles on CA 1.
**About the campground:** An attractive campground shaded by tall trees, Stillwater Cove bears the name of the dramatic cove that lies across the highway and is not visible from the campsites. The mile-long Stockoff Creek Loop Trail begins at the campground and travels through a mixed

redwood/Douglas fir forest to a cove used by abalone divers. A 0.5-mile trail leads to the historic one-room Fort Ross Schoolhouse. Elevation 124 feet. Stay limit 14 days. Open all year.

## 74 Reef (Fort Ross State Historic Park)

**Location:** 10 miles north of Jenner
**GPS:** 38.5083994 / -123.2290711
**Sites:** 21 sites for tents and RVs up to18 feet long
**Facilities:** Tables, fire rings, drinking water, flush toilets
**Fee per night:** $$$
**Management:** California Department of Parks and Recreation, (707) 847-3708
**Activities:** Hiking, scuba diving, fishing, historical landmark
**Finding the campground:** From Jenner, drive 10 miles on CA 1. Watch for the campground sign. It is on the west, toward the ocean.
**About the campground:** Fort Ross is the site of a Russian fort built in 1812 to protect the Russian fur trade in California. The Russians withdrew from the area in 1841 due to the decline of the sea otter population. The reconstructed fort consists of several buildings surrounded by a log stockade, including the commandant's house, officers' quarters, and a church. The park includes more than 3,000 upland acres containing some of the world's oldest second-growth redwoods. Although there are no formal trails, hikers are welcome to use the old Russian logging roads that lead through the area. Reef Campground, in a coastal canyon, is 3 miles south of the fort on the west side of the highway on a separate entry road. A trail leads from the campground to Fort Ross Cove, a small beach with an underwater park offshore. It is popular for abalone diving and angling

*A Russian fort, built in 1812 to protect the Russian fur trade in California, is the centerpiece of Fort Ross State Historic Park.*

for rockfish. The trail continues uphill to the fort. Elevation 196 feet. Stay limit 14 days. The fort and park are open all year; the campground and day-use area are open April through October.

## 75 Bullfrog Pond (Austin Creek State Recreation Area)

**Location:** 22 miles northwest of Santa Rosa
**GPS:** 38.5661168 / -123.0112051
**Sites:** 24 sites for tents; 3 tent-only hike-in sites; no trailers
**Facilities:** Tables, fire rings, drinking water, flush toilets
**Fee per night:** $$$; reservations: some sites reservable through hipcamp.com; walk-up registration at Armstrong kiosk
**Management:** California Department of Parks and Recreation, (707) 869-2015
**Activities:** Hiking, horseback riding, fishing, road biking
**Finding the campground:** From the intersection of US 101 and Guerneville Road in Santa Rosa, take the Guerneville Road exit and drive west 8 miles to where the road turns north and becomes CA 116. Continue 9 miles to Guerneville, then drive straight north 2.2 miles on Armstrong Woods Road to Armstrong Redwoods State Reserve. Continue through the reserve for another 2.5 miles. Trailers and RVs over 20 feet long are not permitted on the steep, winding, narrow road to the campground.
**About the campground:** Austin Creek State Recreation Area and Armstrong Redwoods State Reserve are adjoining parks. The campground (Bullfrog Pond) is located in Austin Creek, while most of the redwoods are found in Armstrong. A mile-long loop tours the heart of the Armstrong Reserve, visiting its most famous trees; a strenuous 9-mile loop for hikers and equestrians begins at the campground. A riding concession operates adjacent to the camp, offering rides and pack trips. Half a dozen wineries are located within a 10-mile radius of the campground, most offering tastings and sales. Fishing is not permitted in the streams, just the pond. Elevation 1,260 feet. Stay limit 15 days. Open all year (subject to seasonal closures).

## 76 Sugarloaf Ridge State Park

**Location:** 14 miles east of Santa Rosa
**GPS:** 38.437137 / -122.5159385
**Sites:** 47 sites for tents and RVs up to 27 feet long; 1 group site
**Facilities:** Tables, fire rings, drinking water, flush toilets
**Fee per night:** $$$; reservations: (800) 444-7275 or reserveamerica.com
**Management:** California Department of Parks and Recreation, (707) 833-5712
**Activities:** Hiking, mountain biking, horseback riding
**Finding the campground:** From the intersection of US 101 and CA 12 in Santa Rosa, drive east 11 miles on CA 12. Turn north onto Adobe Canyon Road and drive 3.3 miles.
**About the campground:** Situated in the rugged coastal mountains, on the edge of a meadow shaded by oak trees. Sugarloaf features miles of well-marked trails and service roads. Hikers, bikers, and equestrians can weave through its 4,900 acres on 25 miles of trails, including a 0.75-mile nature trail, a 1.6-mile loop that visits a 25-foot waterfall, and a hike up Bald Mountain. A map is available at the visitor center. Coastal redwoods and large Douglas fir trees can be found in some of the drainages. Elevation 1,200 feet. Stay limit 7 days. Open all year.

# 77 Spring Lake Regional Park

**Location:** In Santa Rosa
**GPS:** 38.4491321 / -122.6504351
**Sites:** 31 sites for tents and RVs; 1 group camp
**Facilities:** Tables, fire rings, drinking water, flush toilets, showers, dump station, boat ramp and rentals
**Fee per night:** $$$; reservations: (707) 565-2267 or sonomacountycamping.org
**Management:** Sonoma County Regional Parks, (707) 539-8092
**Activities:** Hiking, biking, swimming, fishing, boating
**Finding the campground:** From the intersection of US 101 and CA 12 in Santa Rosa, drive east on CA 12 about 5 miles. Turn south onto Newanga Avenue and drive about 1.5 miles to its end at the park.
**About the campground:** Enjoy trails in 320 acres on bike, horse, or foot. Take a refreshing swim in the 3-acre lagoon and fish for largemouth bass, sunfish, and catfish in the 72-acre lake. No motors are permitted on the lake, but kayaking and canoeing are popular and rentals are available. A short trail from the campground leads south to the dam. Elevation 324 feet. Stay limit 10 days. Open May through September; weekends only for the rest of the year. Group campground is open year-round.

*It's an easygoing family camping experience at Spring Lake Campground. Photo by Bubba Seuss*

## 78 Wright's Beach (Sonoma Coast State Beach)

**Location:** 6 miles north of the community of Bodega Bay
**GPS:** 38.400691 / -123.0957076
**Sites:** 27 sites for tents and RVs up to 30 feet long
**Facilities:** Tables, fire rings, drinking water, flush toilets
**Fee per night:** $$$; reservations: (800) 444-7275 or reserveamerica.com
**Management:** California State Parks, (707) 875-3483
**Activities:** Hiking, fishing, tidepools, scuba diving, whale watching, horseback riding
**Finding the campground:** From Bodega Bay, drive north 6 miles on CA 1.
**About the campground:** Situated directly on the beach, the campground doesn't have the wind protection of Bodega Dunes Campground, but it has a wider vista and some trees for shade. Elevation 30 feet. Open all year. See Bodega Dunes (79) for more information.

## 79 Bodega Dunes (Sonoma Coast State Beach)

**Location:** 1 mile north of the community of Bodega Bay
**GPS:** 38.3412258 / -123.0540823
**Sites:** 99 sites for tents and RVs up to 31 feet long
**Facilities:** Tables, fire rings, drinking water, flush toilets, showers, dump station
**Fee per night:** $$$; reservations: (800) 444-7275 or reserveamerica.com (site assigned upon arrival)
**Management:** California State Parks, (707) 875-3483
**Activities:** Hiking, fishing, tidepools, scuba diving, whale watching, horseback riding
**Finding the campground:** From Bodega Bay, drive north 1 mile on CA 1.
**About the campground:** This park of 5,000 acres runs more than 16 miles along the dramatic Sonoma coastline from Bodega Bay to just north of Jenner. At least 13 separate, isolated beaches lie within its borders, most of them reachable by trails from the highway. A visitor center is located in Jenner. The campground is situated in an attractive pine grove behind high dunes that hide the beach. A boardwalk crosses the dunes, leading to 3-mile-long South Salmon Creek Beach. The Bodega Head Trail is a good place to watch for whales December through April. Elevation 88 feet. Stay limit 10 days June through September; 30 days October through May. Open all year.

## 80 Westside Regional Park

**Location:** 2 miles northwest of the community of Bodega Bay
**GPS:** 38.322417 / -123.0556879
**Sites:** 47 sites for tents and RVs
**Facilities:** Tables, fire rings, drinking water, flush toilets, showers, dump station, fish-cleaning station, boat ramp
**Fee per night:** $$$; reservations: (707) 565-2267 or sonomacountycamping.org
**Management:** Sonoma County Regional Parks, (707) 875-3540
**Activities:** Fishing, boating, birding
**Finding the campground:** From Bodega Bay, drive north a short distance on CA 1; turn onto Big Flat Road and continue onto West Shore Road for 2 miles.

**About the campground:** Situated on the west shore of Bodega Bay. Noted for good salmon fishing in early summer and rockfish year-round; lingcod, flounder, and perch are also taken. Elevation 9 feet. Stay limit 10 days. Open all year.

## 81 Doran Regional Park

**Location:** On Bodega Bay
**GPS:** 38.3135881 / -123.0470196
**Sites:** 128 sites for tents or RVs; 10 tent-only; 1 group site, tent-only; 1 hike & bike
**Facilities:** Tables, grills, drinking water, flush toilets, showers, dump station, fish-cleaning station, boat ramp; facilities wheelchair accessible
**Fee per night:** $$$; reservations: (707) 565-2267 or sonomacountycamping.org
**Management:** Sonoma County Regional Parks, (707) 875-3540
**Activities:** Fishing, boating, hiking, beachcombing
**Finding the campground:** From the community of Bodega Bay, drive 1 mile south on CA 1; turn at the campground sign.
**About the campground:** Located on an attractive spit of land dividing Bodega Bay and Bodega Harbor, the campground has water on both sides and is adorned with coastal shrub and ice plant but little shade. Hang out on 2 miles of sandy beach, or launch a sea kayak or fishing boat. Rockfish and lingcod may be caught year-round, perch and flounder from shore, crabbing in winter. Elevation 3 feet. Stay limit 10 days. Open all year.

## 82 Red Mountain (South Cow Mountain Recreation Area)

**Location:** 11 miles southeast of Ukiah
**GPS:** 39.0798135 / -123.0914419
**Sites:** 10 sites for tents; 3 for RVs
**Facilities:** Tables, fire rings, vault toilets; no drinking water
**Fee per night:** None
**Management:** Bureau of Land Management, (707) 468-4000
**Activities:** OHV driving
**Finding the campground:** From the intersection of US 101 and Talmadge Road in Ukiah, drive east 1.5 miles on Talmadge. Turn south onto Old River Road and drive 0.3 mile. Turn east onto Mill Creek Road (which becomes Mendo-Lake Road and Scott Creek Road) and drive 9 miles. Turn northwest onto Red Mountain Camp Road. ***Note:*** Roads to this area are steep and windy. Obtain a free map from the BLM office in Ukiah.
**About the campground:** This south section of the recreation area contains 23,000 acres of rugged terrain set aside primarily for OHV use. There are twenty-five trails and roads (125 miles) graded by difficulty and type of vehicles (motorcycles, ATVs, four-by-four short base, four-by-four long base). The campground is pine-shaded. Best time to visit is spring, fall, and dry winter days. Also in the area is Buckhorn Campground, with 4 sites. Elevation 3,070 feet. Stay limit 14 days. Open all year.

## 83 Mayacmus (North Cow Mountain Recreation Area)

**Location:** 12 miles southeast of Ukiah
**GPS:** 39.0796867 / -123.0911798

**Sites:** 9 sites for tents
**Facilities:** Tables, fire rings, vault toilets; no drinking water
**Fee per night:** None
**Management:** Bureau of Land Management, (707) 468-4000
**Activities:** Hiking, fishing, horseback riding, hunting
**Finding the campground:** From the intersection of US 101 and Talmadge Road in Ukiah, drive east 1.5 miles on Talmadge. Turn south onto Old River Road and drive 0.3 mile. Turn east onto Mill Creek Road and drive 3.5 miles, then turn northwest onto Mendo Rock Road and continue 7 miles.
**About the campground:** This north section of the recreation area contains 27,000 acres of rugged terrain, hot in summer and rainy in winter. Rainbow trout can be found in the colder streams, and some of the small reservoirs have been stocked with sunfish. Nonmotorized trails and roads from the campground are open to hikers and equestrians. There is a rifle range located off Mendo Rock Road, coming into the area. See Red Mountain Campground (82) for OHV use. Nearby Goat Rock campground has 2 sites. Elevation 3,063 feet. Stay limit 14 days. Open all year.

## 84 Clear Lake State Park

**Location:** 11 miles southeast of Lakeport
**GPS:** 39.0105679 / -122.8137362
**Sites:** 146 sites for tents and RVs up to 35 feet long; 2 hike & bike sites; 2 group sites; 8 cabins
**Facilities:** Tables, fire rings, drinking water, flush toilets, showers, dump station, boat ramp, swimming beach
**Fee per night:** $$$; reservations: (800) 444-7275 or reserveamerica.com
**Management:** California Department of Parks and Recreation, (707) 279-4293
**Activities:** Hiking, swimming, fishing, boating, waterskiing, birding, visitor center

*This view of the lake is taken from a nature trail that originates at the Clear Lake State Park campgrounds. Photo by Bubba Seuss*

**Finding the campground:** From Lakeport, drive south 3 miles on CA 29. Turn east onto Soda Bay Road and drive 8 miles; turn north into the state park entrance.

**About the campground:** There are four campgrounds in the park: Cole Creek, Kelsey Creek, Lower Bayview, and Upper Bayview. Clear Lake is the largest natural freshwater lake within the borders of California. It is 19 miles long, covers 40,000 acres, and has 100 miles of shoreline. Fishing is good for largemouth bass, black crappie, channel catfish, bluegill, and Sacramento perch. The water warms up sufficiently in summer for comfortable swimming and waterskiing. Cole Creek Campground is shaded, winding along the creek. Kelsey Creek offers the only lakeside campsites in partial shade. The partially shaded sites in Lower Bayview are up the hill far enough to offer a pleasing view of the lake but close enough to make it a short walk to the beach. Upper Bayview, also partially shaded, offers access to the Dorn Nature Trail. Elevation 2,000 feet. Stay limit 15 days June through September; 30 days October through May. Open all year.

## 85 Blue Oaks (Indian Valley Reservoir)

**Location:** 28 miles west of Williams

**GPS:** 39.0695498 / -122.509175

**Sites:** 6 sites for tents and RVs

**Facilities:** Tables, fire rings, vault toilets; no drinking water

**Fee per night:** None

**Management:** Bureau of Land Management, (707) 468-4000

**Activities:** Swimming, fishing, boating (all at nearby Indian Valley Reservoir), hiking, hunting

**Finding the campground:** From the intersection of I-5 and CA 20 in Williams, drive southwest 21 miles. Turn north onto Walker Ridge Road (gravel) and continue 5.4 miles to the T. Turn west onto Indian Valley Reservoir Road and drive 2.4 miles.

**About the campground:** The primary attraction of this campground is its location, 1.6 miles from the south end of Indian Valley Reservoir. While the lake is not much to look at, it offers excellent bass fishing mid-March through the first week in June. Other times of year offer kokanee salmon, crappie, rainbow trout, bluegill and catfish. A boat ramp is located at the south end of the lake. The 2.5-mile Kowalski trail, starting across the dam, follows the reservoir's west edge. Kayaking the lake is quite pleasant, except in high wind. Elevation 1,807 feet. Stay limit 14 days. Open all year.

## 86 Lower Hunting Creek (Knoxville Recreation Area)

**Location:** 20 miles southeast of Clearlake

**GPS:** 38.8087664 / -122.374165

**Sites:** 5 sites for tents and RVs; 3 overflow sites

**Facilities:** Tables, fire rings, drinking water, vault toilets, ramadas

**Fee per night:** None

**Management:** Bureau of Land Management, (707) 468-4000

**Activities:** Mountain biking, OHV driving

**Finding the campground:** From the intersection of Olympic Drive and CA 29 in Clearlake, drive south 3 miles to Lower Lake. Turn east onto Morgan Valley Road and drive 15 miles. Turn south onto a dirt road and drive 2 miles.

**About the campground:** Located on Hunting Creek. There are 25 miles of trails for OHV driving, plus miles of existing dirt roads for mountain bikes. Elevation 1,115 feet. Stay limit 14 days. Open all year.

# 87 Bothe–Napa Valley State Park

**Location:** 5 miles northwest of St. Helena
**GPS:** 38.5510378 / -122.5216869
**Sites:** 24 sites for tents and RVs up to 31 feet long; 18 tent-only; 10 yurts; 1 group site
**Facilities:** Tables, fire rings, drinking water, flush toilets, showers, dump station, pool (summer only)
**Fee per night:** $$$; reservations: (800) 444-7275 or reserveamerica.com
**Management:** California Department of Parks and Recreation, (707) 942-4575
**Activities:** Hiking, swimming, horseback riding
**Finding the campground:** From St. Helena, drive northwest 5 miles on CA 29.
**About the campground:** Located in the heart of Napa Valley, with two dozen of the nation's most famous wineries within a radius of 18 miles, this 1,900-acre park offers a surprisingly rugged and varied terrain ranging from creek-lined redwoods to dry, chaparral-covered hillsides. A feature of the park is a 1.2-mile trail to Bale Grist Mill, a restored and functioning grinding mill that docents in period dress operate on weekends. The ground flour and products made from it are available for sale. Another excursion, the Redwood Trail–Coyote Peak Loop, offers a 4.7-mile tour of the park, including a view from atop Coyote Peak (1,170 feet). Calistoga, 5 miles west of the campground, is noted for its hot springs and mud baths and for Old Faithful geyser, which spouts 60 feet in the air every 40 minutes. Elevation 432 feet. Stay limit 15 days. Open all year.

# 88 Putah Canyon (Lake Berryessa)

**Location:** 33 miles north of Napa
**GPS:** 38.6252916 / -122.2903077

## LAKE BERRYESSA

East of the Napa Valley, the 30,000-acre Lake Berryessa Recreation Area is a favorite for year-round water sports, both motorized and nonmotorized. Water temperatures can rise to a pleasant 75°F in summer (on often 90-degree days). Anglers fish for mostly native bass and catfish. The lake is stocked annually with rainbow and Eagle Lake trout, Kokanee and Chinook salmon. Campers also enjoy the many miles of beach (about 165 miles of shoreline) and several hiking trails. Lake Berryessa was formed when the Bureau of Reclamation built Monticello Dam on Putah Creek in 1957. Prior to that, the area that is now a body of water was a fertile valley surrounding the bustling town of Monticello. The name Berryessa comes from the Berrelleza brothers (Anglicized to Berryessa) from the Basque region, thought to be the first European settlers in the valley. They owned a large rancho in and around Monticello starting in 1843. The lake is in the shallows between Blue Ridge Natural Area and Cedar Roughs Wilderness, mostly BLM land, with dispersed camping allowed. Concessionaires manage the various campgrounds, day-use areas, and boat launch ramp.

**Sites:** 98 sites for tents and RVs up to 38 feet long
**Facilities:** Table, fire ring, barbecue, pit toilets; no drinking water
**Fee per night:** $$$; reservations: (707) 966-9051
**Management:** Royal Elk Park Management (for Bureau of Reclamation), (707) 966-9051
**Activities:** Fishing, swimming, boating
**Finding the campground:** From Napa, take CA 121 North to CA 128 West. Turn northeast onto Berryessa Knoxville Road to 7600 Knoxville Rd., at the north end of the lake near the bridge.
**About the campground:** Northern most recreation area on Knoxville Road (and on the west shore of Lake Berryessa). Elevation 460 feet. Stay limit 14 days. Open Memorial Day weekend through mid-September.

## 89 Spanish Flat Recreation Area (Lake Berryessa)

**Location:** 26 miles north of Napa
**GPS:** 38.5515031 / -122.230663
**Sites:** 46 sites for tents and RVs; 8 tent-only
**Facilities:** Picnic tables, barbecue, fire rings, drinking water, vault toilets, dump station
**Fee per night:** $$$; reservations: (707) 966-0200
**Management:** Bureau of Reclamation, (707) 966-2111
**Activities:** Fishing, swimming, boating, hiking
**Finding the campground:** From Napa, take CA 121 North to CA 128 West. Turn northeast onto Berryessa Knoxville Road to 4920 Knoxville Rd., at the southwest end of the lake.
**About the campground:** The Bureau of Reclamation installed new amenities at Spanish Flat in 2015, including potable water, an RV dump station, and concrete vault restrooms. Other new amenities include picnic tables and fire rings. One mile north of the campground you will find Spanish Flat Village Center, with the Spanish Flat Country Store & Deli, Berryessa Valley Museum, and Handmade Store & More. Elevation 480 feet. Stay limit 14 days. Open all year.

## 90 Pleasure Cove (Lake Berryessa)

**Location:** 22 miles north of Napa
**GPS:** 38.492347 / -122.1625054
**Sites:** 140 sites for tents and RVs up to 40 feet long (14 full hookups, 13 partial hookups); 24 cabins (no pets in cabins)
**Facilities:** Tables, fire pits, barbecue, flush toilets, showers, boat ramp, boat rentals, dump station; no drinking water
**Fee per night:** $$$$; reservations: (877) 386-4383 or goberryessa.com
**Management:** Forever Resorts (for Bureau of Reclamation), (707) 966-9600
**Activities:** Boating, fishing, swimming, hiking
**Finding the campground:** From Napa, take CA 121 North to CA 128 West, heading north on CA 128 West for 4 miles. Turn west onto Wragg Canyon Road for about 3 miles.
**About the campground:** Pleasure Cove is a busy marina on the southern Wragg Canyon leg of the lake, offering rentals of houseboats, ski boats, pontoons, kayaks, and canoes. It also has cabin rentals. The campground is well situated, but it can be noisy and crowded on summer weekends. There is a limited day-use area for swimming. Elevation 2 feet. Stay limit 14 days. Open all year.

## 91 Steele Canyon (Lake Berryessa)

**Location:** 22 miles north of Napa

**GPS:** 38.5090999 / -122.1954984

**Sites:** 64 sites for tents and RVs; 6 RV-only; 15 tent-only

**Facilities:** Tables, fire pits, barbecue, pit toilets, hand-washing stations, boat ramp, dump station; no drinking water

**Fee per night:** $$$; reservations: (800) 255-5561 or goberryessa.com

**Management:** Forever Resorts (for Bureau of Reclamation), (707) 966-9179

**Activities:** Boating, fishing, swimming

**Finding the campground:** From Napa, take CA 121 North to CA 128 West and then immediately east onto Steele Canyon Road. Continue north for 7 miles. ***Note:*** Check gate times.

**About the campground:** This family campground offers mostly full-sun sites, some shaded, most with excellent views looking north over the lake. At the time of writing, there are plans to add a small marina. There is plenty of lake access. There is only one water spigot, so it's a good idea to bring water; you can refill containers there. Elevation 580 feet. Stay limit 14 days. Open all year.

# San Francisco Bay Area

Ocean access, marvelous views, temperate weather—these define the San Francisco Bay Area. Add the human contributions—the Golden Gate Bridge, Chinatown, cable cars, Fisherman's Wharf, the Embarcadero, and much more—and you have what makes San Francisco such a special city. But the Bay Area is far more than the "city on the hill." Its borders extend from Point Reyes National Seashore in the north to Santa Cruz in the south, and they encompass a variety of natural settings for outdoor recreation.

The 74,000-acre Golden Gate Recreation Area spans several counties and is the world's largest urban park. Point Reyes, only an hour's drive from the city, offers many miles of isolated beaches, hiking and riding trails, and walk-in campsites. Muir Woods, a beautiful redwood grove, is even closer. To the south, 18,000-acre Big Basin State Park preserves more of these giant, ancient trees and offers 80 miles of trails from which to view them. A long string of beaches reaches from Daly City to south of Santa Cruz, while to the east, wooded parks such as Mount Diablo and Henry Coe offer sylvan settings close to the urban sprawl.

The temperature of the San Francisco Bay Area is moderate year-round and varies little from spring through fall. Rainfall is light, averaging from 4.2 inches in January to virtually 0 inch in June, July, and August. Morning fog is common in the coastal areas during the summer months. The average percentage of sunny days is a steady 70 percent spring through fall, dropping to 57 percent in winter.

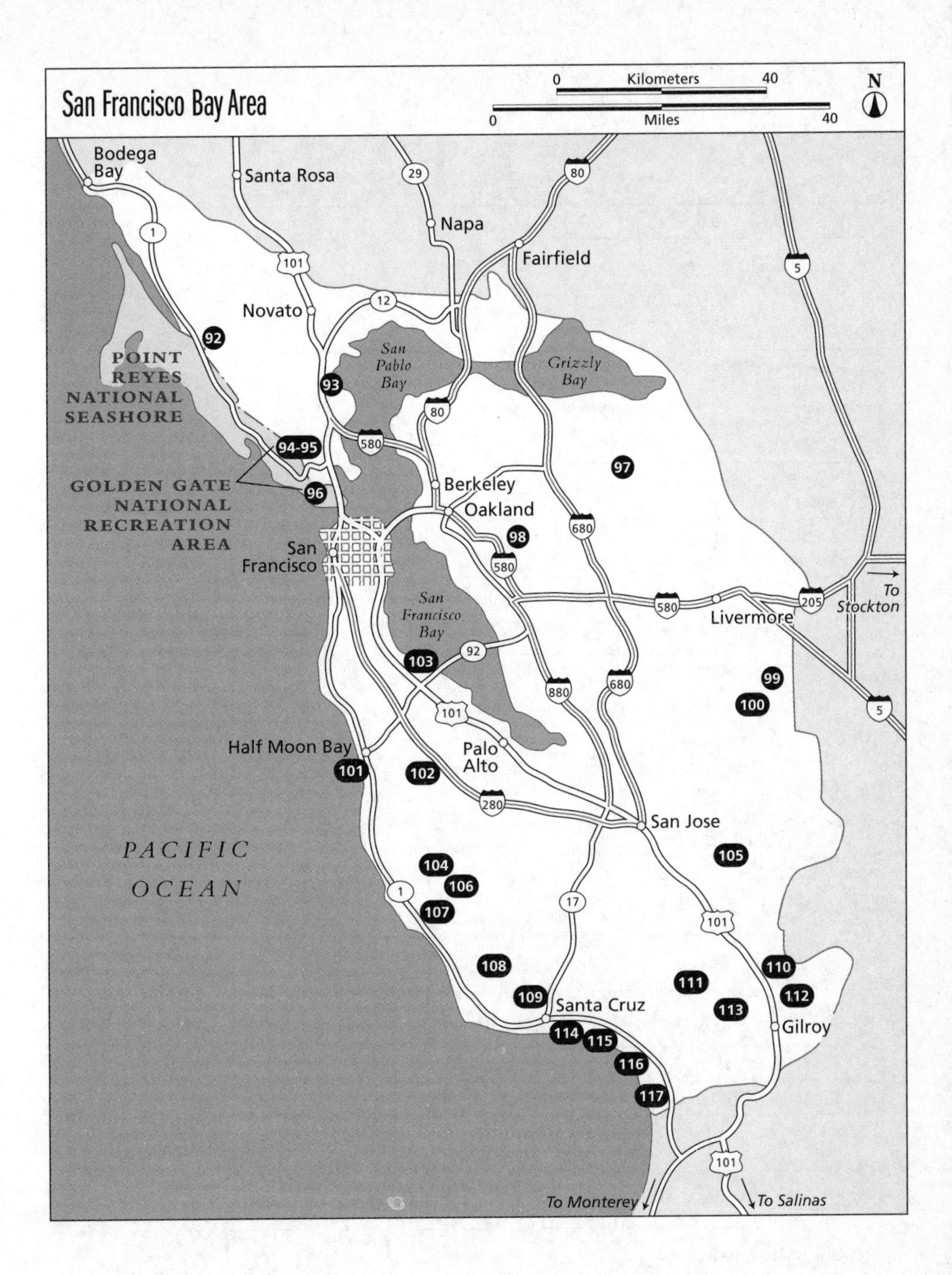
San Francisco Bay Area
0 Kilometers 40
0 Miles 40
N
Bodega Bay
Santa Rosa
Napa
Fairfield
Novato
POINT REYES NATIONAL SEASHORE
San Pablo Bay
Grizzly Bay
GOLDEN GATE NATIONAL RECREATION AREA
Berkeley
Oakland
San Francisco
San Francisco Bay
Livermore
To Stockton
Half Moon Bay
Palo Alto
San Jose
PACIFIC OCEAN
Santa Cruz
Gilroy
To Monterey
To Salinas
1
101
29
80
12
5
580
680
880
205
92
280
17
92
93
94-95
96
97
98
99
100
101
102
103
104
105
106
107
108
109
110
111
112
113
114
115
116
117

| | Name | Group Sites | RV Sites | Max. RV Length | Hookups | Toilets | Showers | Drinking Water | Dump Station | Pets | Wheelchair | Recreation | Fee(s) | Season | Can Reserve |
|---|---|---|---|---|---|---|---|---|---|---|---|---|---|---|---|
| | **SAN FRANCISCO BAY AREA** | | | | | | | | | | | | | | |
| 92 | Samuel P. Taylor State Park | * | * | 18 | | F | * | * | | * | * | HRM | $$$ | Year-round | * |
| 93 | China Camp State Park | * | | | | V | | * | | * | * | HSFBRM | $$$ | Year-round | * |
| 94 | Bootjack (Mount Tamalpais State Park) | | | | | F | | * | | * | * | HRM | $$ | Year-round | |
| 95 | *Pantoll (Mount Tamalpais State Park)* | | | | | F | | * | | * | * | HRM | $$ | Year-round | |
| 96 | Steep Ravine (Mount Tamalpais State Park) | | | | | F | | * | | | * | HFRM | $$-$$$$ | Year-round | * |
| 97 | Juniper and Live Oak Campgrounds (Mount Diablo State Park) | * | * | 25 | | F | | * | | * | * | HRM | $$$ | Year-round | * |
| 98 | Anthony Chabot Regional Park | * | * | 40 | EWS | F | * | * | * | * | * | HF | $$-$$$ | Year-round | * |
| 99 | Carnegie State Vehicular Recreation Area | | * | | | F | * | * | | * | * | O | $ | Year-round | |
| 100 | Del Valle County Park | | * | 40 | EW | F | * | * | * | * | * | HSFB | $$-$$$$ | Year-round | * |
| 101 | Half Moon Bay State Beach | * | * | 40 | | F | * | * | * | * | * | HRF | $$$ | Year-round | * |
| 102 | Toyon Family and Group Camp (Huddart Park) | * | | | | F | | * | | | * | H | $$$ | Year-round | * |
| 103 | Coyote Point Recreation Area | | * | | | F | | | | | * | SBHF | $$$ | Year-round | * |
| 104 | Memorial County Park | * | * | 35 | | F | * | * | * | | * | HR | $$$ | Year-round | * |
| 105 | Joseph D. Grant County Park | * | * | 40 | | F | * | * | * | * | * | HRFM | $$ | Year-round | * |
| 106 | Portola Redwoods State Park | * | * | 24 | | F | * | * | | * | * | HM | $$$ | Apr–Nov | * |
| 107 | Butano State Park | | * | 24 | | V | | * | | * | * | HM | $$$ | Apr–Nov | * |
| 108 | Big Basin Redwoods State Park | * | * | 30 | | FV | * | * | * | * | * | HRM | $$$ | Year-round | * |
| 109 | Henry Cowell Redwoods State Park | | * | 33 | | F | * | * | * | * | * | HF | $$$ | Year-round | * |
| 110 | Henry W. Coe State Park | * | * | 25 | | P | | * | | * | * | HFR | $$$ | Year-round | * |
| 111 | Uvas Canyon County Park | | * | 28 | | F | | * | | * | * | H | $$ | Year-round | * |
| 112 | Coyote Lake Harvey Bear Ranch Park | | * | | | F | | * | | * | * | HRFBL | $$ | Year-round | * |

|  | Name | Group Sites | RV Sites | Max. RV Length | Hookups | Toilets | Showers | Drinking Water | Dump Station | Pets | Wheelchair | Recreation | Fee(s) | Season | Can Reserve |
|---|---|---|---|---|---|---|---|---|---|---|---|---|---|---|---|
| 113 | Mount Madonna County Park |  | * |  | EW | F |  | * | * | * | * | HR | $$-$$$$ | Year-round | * |
| 114 | New Brighton State Beach | * | * | 36 |  | F | * | * | * | * | * | HSF | $$$ | Year-round | * |
| 115 | Seacliff State Beach |  | * | 40 | EWS | F | * | * |  | * | * | SF | $$$$ | Year-round | * |
| 116 | Manresa Uplands (Manresa State Beach) |  |  |  |  | F | * | * |  | * | * | SF | $$$ | Year-round | * |
| 117 | Sunset State Beach | * | * | 31 |  | F | * | * |  | * | * | SF | $$$ | Year-round | * |

Toilets: F=flush V=vault P=pit C=chemical; Fee: $=Under $20 $$=$20-$29 $$$=$30-$39 $$$$ $40 or more; Recreation: H=hiking S=swimming F=fishing B=boating L=boat launch O=off-highway driving R=horseback riding, M=mountain biking
Hookups: W=water E=electric S=sewer

## 92 Samuel P. Taylor State Park

**Location:** 6 miles east of Olema
**GPS:** 38.0193405 / -122.7305033
**Sites:** 29 sites for tents and RVs up to 18 feet long; 22 tent-only; 2 group camps; 1 horse group camp
**Facilities:** Tables, fire rings, drinking water, flush toilets, showers
**Fee per night:** $$$; reservations: (800) 444-7275 or reserveamerica.com
**Management:** California Department of Parks and Recreation, (415) 488-9897
**Activities:** Hiking, cycling, mountain biking, horseback riding
**Finding the campground:** From the intersection of CA 1 and Sir Francis Drake Boulevard in Olema, drive east 6 miles on Drake Highway.
**About the campground:** The sites at the family camp are within a large redwood grove and deeply shaded. The Pioneer Tree Trail makes a 2.5-mile loop through both ancient and second-growth redwoods, and a 9-mile loop trail beginning from the group camp ascends Barnabe Peak. The Cross Marin Bike Trail passes through the park, and fire roads provide challenging ups and downs for mountain bikers. Elevation 230 feet. Stay limit 7 days. Open all year.

## 93 China Camp State Park

**Location:** 6 miles northeast of San Rafael
**GPS:** 38.0060257 / -122.4947624
**Sites:** 31 sites for tents (short walk in); 1 group site; self-contained RVs may overnight in the parking lot
**Facilities:** Tables, grills, drinking water, vault toilets

**Fee per night:** $$$; reservations: (800) 444-7275 or reserveamerica.com
**Management:** California Department of Parks and Recreation, (415) 456-0766
**Activities:** Hiking, swimming, fishing, boating and windsurfing, mountain biking, horseback riding
**Finding the campground:** From San Rafael, drive northeast on North San Pedro Road for 6 miles.
**About the campground:** A historic Chinese fishing village is the centerpiece of the park, which is situated along the southwestern shore of San Pablo Bay. Abandoned in the late nineteenth century as a result of anti-Chinese legislation, the site now contains wooden structures that served as dwellings, a small museum, a Chinese fishing boat, and artifacts and exhibits. A trail leads to the shoreline, and another climbs the ridge behind the park for scenic views over the water. The 15 miles of trails in the park are popular for mountain biking as well as hiking and horseback riding (no dogs allowed on trails). The campground is located in a wooded area, with a meadow and a marsh between it and the bay. Elevation 70 feet. Stay limit 15 days. Open all year.

## 94 Bootjack (Mount Tamalpais State Park)

**Location:** 10 miles northwest of Sausalito
**GPS:** 37.9085578 / -122.6018955
**Sites:** 15 sites for tents
**Facilities:** Tables, fire rings/grills, drinking water, flush toilets
**Fee per night:** $$ (cash only)
**Management:** California Department of Parks and Recreation, (415) 388-2070
**Activities:** Hiking, mountain biking, horseback riding
**Finding the campground:** From the intersection of US 101 and CA 1 northwest of Sausalito, drive 3.5 miles west on CA 1 toward Stinson Beach. Turn right onto Panoramic Highway and drive 5 miles. The road is winding and steep and not recommended for trailers or RVs over 25 feet long.
**About the campground:** You can explore miles of trails on Mount Tamalpais, take in a play in the Mountain Theatre in spring, and enjoy the views from East Peak. If camping with a group and horses, check out Frank Valley Horse Camp (reservation only). For a group site, you want the Alice Eastwood Group Camp. Elevation 1,430 feet. Stay limit 15 days. Open all year. See Pantoll (95) for more information.

## 95 Pantoll (Mount Tamalpais State Park)

**Location:** 10 miles northwest of Sausalito
**GPS:** 37.9036767 / -122.6036786
**Sites:** 16 sites for tents (100 feet from parking area); en-route lot for up to 4 self-contained RVs (first come, first served)
**Facilities:** Tables, fire rings/grills, drinking water, flush toilets
**Fee per night:** $$ (cash only)
**Management:** California Department of Parks and Recreation, (415) 388-2070
**Activities:** Hiking, mountain biking, horseback riding
**Finding the campground:** From the intersection of US 101 and CA 1 northwest of Sausalito, drive 3.5 miles west on CA 1 toward Stinson Beach. Turn right onto Panoramic Highway and drive 5 miles. The road is winding and steep and not recommended for trailers or RVs over 25 feet long.
**About the campground:** Mount Tamalpais is noted for its scenic vistas of San Francisco Bay and the Pacific coast. The Verna Dunshee Trail circles East Peak (2,571 feet), providing views of such

landmarks as the Golden Gate Bridge, Alcatraz, and Mount Diablo. The Steep Ravine Trail (4 miles round-trip) leads into a beautiful gorge with tall redwoods and a rushing stream. The Stapleveldt-Alpine Trail Loop, a forested 4.4-mile hike through impressive redwoods, begins at the Pantoll Ranger Station, near the campground. The Matt Davis Trail also begins at the ranger station and traverses the park's coastal slopes for a little over 4 miles. Elevation 1,560 feet. Stay limit 15 days. Open all year.

## 96 Steep Ravine (Mount Tamalpais State Park)

**Location:** 11 miles northwest of Sausalito
**GPS:** 37.8935907 / -122.6157132
**Sites:** Environmental camp with 7 walk-in sites and 10 primitive cabins
**Facilities:** Tables, fire rings/grills, drinking water, flush toilets
**Fee per night:** Tent sites: $$, cabins: $$$$; reservations: (800) 444-7275 or reserveamerica.com
**Management:** California Department of Parks and Recreation, (415) 388-2070
**Activities:** Hiking, fishing, mountain biking, horseback riding
**Finding the campground:** From the intersection of US 101 and CA 1 northwest of Sausalito, drive 11 miles north on CA 1. One mile South of Stinson Beach, look for a locked entrance gate on the west side of the highway.
**About the campground:** In order to reserve a place at Steep Ravine, you have to phone the moment slots become available. Steep Ravine provides a unique and private camping experience overlooking the Pacific Ocean, with a short walk to a small beach at low tide. Visit Stinson Beach on your way out, or cross the highway to access Mount Tamalpais trails. Elevation 990 feet. Stay limit 15 days. Open all year.

## 97 Juniper and Live Oak Campgrounds (Mount Diablo State Park)

**Location:** 6 miles northeast of Danville
**GPS:** 37.8510998 / -121.9371203
**Sites:** 51 sites for tents and RVs up to 25 feet long; 5 group tent sites
**Facilities:** Tables, fire rings, drinking water, flush toilets
**Fee per night:** $$$; reservations: (800) 444-7275 or reserveamerica.com
**Management:** California Department of Parks and Recreation, (925) 837-2525
**Activities:** Hiking, mountain biking, horseback riding
**Finding the campground:** From I-680 in Danville, take the Diablo Road exit and drive northeast for 6 miles on Diablo Road. The park is also accessible from Walnut Creek via North Gate Road.
**About the campground:** Although only 3,849 feet high, Mount Diablo affords one of the most sweeping views found anywhere in the United States. On clear days the vista extends from Mount Lassen to the Sierra Nevada to the Farallon Islands. An observation tower on the summit provides a 360-degree view and contains a small museum and interpretive center. A 0.7-mile-long trail circles the peak, and a series of trails combine to make the Grand Loop—a 6-mile trip around the mountain for hikers, horses, and mountain bikes. A trail starting near site 20 in Live Oak Campground takes you to Rock City, with its sandstone formations to admire and climb. Juniper offers trails and access to the summit and visitor center atop the mountain. Views are amazing at both camps. Elevation for Live Oak 1,540 feet; 2,880 feet for Juniper. There are also many group camps to choose from. Stay limit 30 days. Open all year.

*Take a tour and scramble up some of the limestone in Rock City, close to Live Oak Campground, and then settle in to camp, enjoying wooded sites or ones with spectacular views of the Las Trampas foothills and San Ramon Valley below.*

## 98 Anthony Chabot Regional Park

**Location:** 17 miles southeast of downtown Oakland
**GPS:** 37.7352446 / -122.0960446
**Sites:** 75 sites for tents and RVs up to 40 feet long (10 with full hookups); 7 group sites
**Facilities:** Tables, fire rings, drinking water, flush toilets, showers, dump station
**Fee per night:** $$–$$$; reservations: (888) 327-2757 or reserveamerica.com
**Management:** East Bay Regional Parks District, (888) 327-2757, option 2
**Activities:** Hiking, fishing, biking
**Finding the campground:** From I-580 in Oakland, exit east on 35th Avenue (which becomes Redwood Road) and drive 7.5 miles.
**About the campground:** The campground is in a eucalyptus grove on a hilltop. Fishing and boating are available at Lake Chabot, about 0.5 mile away, and a trail leads to the lake from the campground. Private boats are not permitted on the lake, but boat rentals are available. Fishing from shore is allowed. The lake is stocked annually with trout and catfish and is also a source of largemouth bass, bluegill, and crappie. A paved path circles most of the lake. Elevation 660 feet. Stay limit 15 days. Open all year.

*The boat docks on Lake Chabot.*

## 99 Carnegie State Vehicular Recreation Area

**Location:** 13 miles southwest of Tracy
**GPS:** 37.6335202 / -121.543855
**Sites:** 23 sites for tents and RVs
**Facilities:** Some tables, fire rings, drinking water, flush toilets, showers, ramadas
**Fee per night:** $
**Management:** California State Parks, OHV Department, (925) 447-0426
**Activities:** OHV driving, bird and nature watching
**Finding the campground:** From the East Bay Area, take I-580 East to exit 57 toward North Greenville Road / Altamont Pass Road. Turn east (slight left) onto Southfront Road and then south onto Greenville Road. Turn east onto Tesla Road and drive for about 10 miles. Continue onto Corral Hollow Road to the park entrance. From Tracy, head west on East 11th Street / 11th Street toward North Central Avenue. Turn south onto Corral Hollow Road and go about 11 miles to the park entrance.
**About the campground:** Carnegie has 1,300 acres of rocky washes, hills, and steep canyons for motocross and ATV riders of all skill levels. At the same time, it is home to a surprisingly wide range of plant and animal life, most especially raptors, which have ample prey in the native bunchgrass. In 1855 clay was found in the coal mines in this canyon, and by 1910 as many as 110,000 bricks each day were being manufactured here and shipped all over the state. The campground is mostly open, with some partial shade. Stay out of bushy areas to avoid rattlesnakes and poison oak. Elevation 650 feet. Open all year.

## 100 Del Valle County Park

**Location:** 10 miles southeast of Livermore
**GPS:** 37.584919 / -121.6964957
**Sites:** 150 sites for tents and RVs up to 40 feet long, 21 with water and electric hookups
**Facilities:** Tables, grills, drinking water, showers, flush toilets, dump station
**Fee per night:** $$–$$$$; reservations: (888) 327-2757, option 2 or reserveamerica.com
**Management:** East Bay Regional Park District, (510) 373-0332
**Activities:** Hiking, swimming, fishing, boating
**Finding the campground:** From the intersection of I-580 and South Vasco Road in Livermore, drive south on South Vasco for 3 miles. Turn right onto Tesla Road and drive 1 mile. Turn left onto Mines Road and drive 3 miles; then bear right onto Del Valle Road and drive 3 miles.
**About the campground:** The campsites are located in open grassland on the shore of Del Valle Reservoir, which provides good fishing, swimming, boating, and windsurfing. Among the trails accessible from the campground is a steep climb to 100-foot Murietta Falls. There are 4,395 acres of rolling hills for hiking and horseback riding. It is also the eastern gateway to the Ohlone Wilderness, where you can explore 28 miles of scenic backcountry trails. During your stay, you can day-trip for tastings at Livermore wineries. Elevation 720 feet. Stay limit 15 days. Open all year.

## 101 Half Moon Bay State Beach

**Location:** In the community of Half Moon Bay
**GPS:** 37.4662863 / -122.4455565
**Sites:** 46 sites for tents and RVs up to 40 feet long; 6 tent only; 1 group tent
**Facilities:** Tables, fire rings, drinking water, flush toilets, showers, dump station
**Fee per night:** $$$; reservations: (800) 444-2757 or reserveamerica.com
**Management:** California Department of Parks and Recreation, (650) 726-8819
**Activities:** Beach play, fishing, surfing, hiking, biking, horseback riding
**Finding the campground:** From the intersection of CA 92 and CA 1 in the community of Half Moon Bay, drive south 0.3 mile on CA 1; turn west onto Kelly Road to the entrance.
**About the campground:** Four beaches compose the Half Moon Bay State Beach complex. The campground is located in an attractive grassy area directly behind the fine sandy stretch known as Francis Beach. Some of the sites are directly on the beach, but most RV sites are standard back-in pads 50 to 100 feet behind the beach. Shoreline fishing for perch can be very good right after the beginning of an incoming tide, and striped bass runs occur occasionally during summer. A 2.3-mile trail for hikers and cyclists runs north from Francis Beach to Dunes Beach. Dogs are not allowed on the beaches. Elevation 22 feet. Stay limit 15 days. Open all year.

## 102 Toyon Family and Group Camp (Huddart Park)

**Location:** 5 miles southwest of Redwood City
**GPS:** 37.4360117 / -122.2992378
**Sites:** Family and group tent sites
**Facilities:** Tables, barbecue grills, drinking water, flush toilets
**Fee per night:** $$$; reservations: (650) 363-4021 or SMCoParks.org

**Management:** San Mateo County Parks and Recreation, Huddart Park, (650) 851-1210
**Activities:** Hiking
**Finding the campground:** From the intersection of I-280 and CA 84 in Redwood City, drive west on CA 84 for 1.8 miles. Turn right onto Kings Mountain Road and drive 3.5 miles.
**About the campground:** In 2015 the group sites were opened to family camping. This well-maintained park is well suited for those who want to get away and enjoy outdoor activities while remaining close to Palo Alto and Redwood City. Elevation 1,280 feet. Stay limit 14 days. Open all year.

## 103 Coyote Point Recreation Area

**Location:** 3 miles northeast of San Mateo
**GPS:** 37.5679606 / -122.2717534
**Sites:** 3 RV-only sites
**Facilities:** Flush toilets, picnic area
**Fee per night:** $$$; reservations: (650) 363-4021 or SMCoParks.org
**Management:** San Mateo County Parks, (650) 363-4020
**Activities:** Swimming, boating, hiking, biking, golf, rifle range, playgrounds, fishing, birding
**Finding the campground:** From US 101 take the Poplar Avenue / Peninsula Avenue exit. Go west on Peninsula Avenue and continue as it becomes Coyote Point Drive. Continue to 1701 Coyote Point Dr.
**About the campground:** This highly developed park features three playgrounds; trails for walking, running, and biking; fishing spots; a gravel beach; a golf course (Poplar Creek); and opportunities for water play galore. Windsurfing, kayaking, and paddleboarding are popular. The Beach Center rents board sport equipment. Eucalyptus and Monterey cypress trees add character to the bluffs above the breakwater. You can also enjoy CuriOdyssey, a museum for family-friendly science. Elevation 0 feet. Stay limit 14 days. Open year-round.

## 104 Memorial County Park

**Location:** 14 miles southwest of Redwood City
**GPS:** 37.2763815 / -122.2965778
**Sites:** 158 sites for tents and RVs up to 35 feet long
**Facilities:** Tables, barbecue pits, drinking water, showers (seasonal), flush toilets, dump station (seasonal)
**Fee per night:** $$$; reservations: (650) 363-4021 or SMCoParks.org
**Management:** San Mateo County Parks and Recreation, (650) 879-0238
**Activities:** Hiking, horseback riding
**Finding the campground:** From the intersection of I-280 and CA 84 in Redwood City, drive west and then south on CA 84 for 11 miles. Turn south onto Pescadero Road and continue about 3 miles to the campground entrance.
**About the campground:** Located in an attractive redwood grove, the campground has hiking and riding trails leading to nearby Portola State Park. Elevation 314 feet. Stay limit 14 days. Open all year on a reduced basis. No showers or dump station November to May, and family camping is reduced to 30 sites during that period. No pets are allowed. For group camping, check out Wurr Flat. For equestrian group camping, there is Jack Brook Horse Camp in nearby Sam McDonald County Park.

## 105 Joseph D. Grant County Park

**Location:** 12 miles east of San Jose
**GPS:** 37.3425697 / -121.7157542
**Sites:** 40 sites for tents and RVs up to 30 feet long; 8 horse camps
**Facilities:** Tables, grills, drinking water, showers, flush toilets, dump station
**Fee per night:** $$; reservations: (408) 355-2201 or gooutsideandplay.org
**Management:** Santa Clara County Parks, (408) 274-6121
**Activities:** Hiking, mountain biking, horseback riding, fishing
**Finding the campground:** From the intersection of US 101 and I-680 in San Jose, drive 2 miles northeast on I-680 to the Alum Rock Avenue exit. Drive east on Alum Rock Avenue for 2.4 miles; turn northeast onto Mount Hamilton Road (CA 130) and drive 8 miles.
**About the campground:** Shaded by oak trees, the campground provides access to 40 miles of hiking and horse trails and 20 miles of dirt roads for mountain biking. The park is a former ranch, and Hall's Valley Loop (5.5 miles) offers a good hiking introduction to its landscape. A lake and several smaller ponds provide warm-water fishing. Elevation 1,590 feet. Stay limit 14 days. Open all year.

## 106 Portola Redwoods State Park

**Location:** 17 miles south of Palo Alto
**GPS:** 37.2529808 / -122.2125159
**Sites:** 5 sites for tents and RVs up to 24 feet long; 1 RV-only; 47 tent-only; 4 group tent sites
**Facilities:** Tables, barbecue grills, drinking water, showers, flush toilets, visitor center
**Fee per night:** $$$; reservations: (800) 444-7275 or reserveamerica.com
**Management:** California Department of Parks and Recreation, (650) 948-9098
**Activities:** Hiking, mountain biking
**Finding the campground:** From I-280, about 3 miles south of Palo Alto, take the Page Mill Road exit and drive south about 7 miles to CA 35 (Skyline Boulevard). Page Mill Road now becomes increasingly narrow and winding. Cross CA 35, where the route becomes known as Alpine Road, and drive about 4 miles. Turn slight left (south) onto Portola Road and drive about 3 miles.
**About the campground:** The narrow, winding access results in fewer visitors than at less-isolated redwood parks. The campground is located in a grove of tall, second-growth redwoods. The 0.7-mile Sequoia Nature Trail reveals seashell deposits from when the area was all under ocean. There are 18 miles of trails to enjoy in the park. There are also 6 hike-in sites 3 miles away on the Slate Creek Trail. Elevation 740 feet. Stay limit 7 days. Open April through November.

## 107 Butano State Park

**Location:** 20 miles south of the community of Half Moon Bay
**GPS:** 37.2020524 / -122.3389378
**Sites:** 18 sites for tents and RVs up to 24 feet long; 17 walk-in sites
**Facilities:** Tables, fire rings, drinking water, vault toilets, nature center
**Fee per night:** $$$; reservations: (800) 444-7275 or reserveamerica.com
**Management:** California Department of Parks and Recreation, (650) 948-9098
**Activities:** Hiking, mountain biking

*The walk-to sites in Butano are worth the effort. They're located in a protected basin of redwoods with much to explore around you.*

**Finding the campground:** From the intersection of CA 92 and CA 1 in the community of Half Moon Bay, drive south 14.5 miles on CA 1; turn east onto Pescadero Road and drive 2.5 miles. Turn southeast onto Cloverdale Road and drive 3 miles.
**About the campground:** This gem of a park encompasses a 3,200-acre rain forest of old-and-new-growth redwoods and large Douglas firs. A stand of tall, mature redwoods gives the campground a dark, cathedral-like aura. Excellent hiking opportunities in the park include Ano Nuevo Lookout (2.7 miles round-trip), the 1.6-mile Little Butano Creek Loop, and the 1.9-mile Jackson Flats/Six Bridges Trail Loop. Longer hikes include Mill Ox Loop (5 miles) and Butano Rim Loop (11 miles). Elevation 255 feet. Stay limit 7 days. Open April through November.

## 108 Big Basin Redwoods State Park

**Location:** 20 miles northwest of Santa Cruz
**GPS:** 37.1729598 / -122.2223731
**Sites:** 35 sites for tents and RVs up to 30 feet long; 67 tent-only; 36 tent walk-ins; 4 group sites
**Facilities:** Tables, fire rings, drinking water, flush and vault toilets, showers, visitor center, snack bar, dump station
**Fee per night:** $$$; reservations: (800) 444-7275 or reserveamerica.com
**Management:** California Department of Parks and Recreation, (831) 338-8860
**Activities:** Hiking, horseback riding, mountain biking
**Finding the campground:** From the intersection of CA 1 and CA 9 in Santa Cruz, take CA 9 north for 11 miles to Boulder Creek. Turn west onto CA 236 and drive 9 miles.

**About the campground:** Big Basin is California's oldest state park, and its 18,000 acres also make it one of the largest. *Sunset* magazine lists the campground as one of the best in the West. A highlight of the park is the Skyline-to-the-Sea Trail—a 37.5-mile equestrian and hiking trail that runs through the park, connecting Castle Rock State Park, high in the Santa Cruz Mountains, and Waddell Beach on the coast. From the visitor center the Redwood Nature Trail makes a 0.6-mile loop through a grove of ancient redwoods, including Mother of the Forest, at 329 feet the tallest tree in the park. Another short trail (1.2 miles) goes to small but pretty Sempervirens Falls. The 10.5-mile hike that takes you to Berry Creek Falls Trail and back is a one-of-a-kind trek featuring four waterfalls. Elevation 1,100 feet. Stay limit 7 days. Open all year.

## 109 Henry Cowell Redwoods State Park

**Location:** 4 miles north of Santa Cruz
**GPS:** 37.0388098 / -122.0573343
**Sites:** 103 sites for tents and RVs up to 33 feet long; 7 tent-only
**Facilities:** Tables, fire rings, drinking water, flush toilets, showers, dump station
**Fee per night:** $$$; reservations: (800) 444-7275 or reserveamerica.com
**Management:** California Department of Parks and Recreation, (408) 335-4598
**Activities:** Hiking, winter fishing, nature center
**Finding the campground:** From the intersection of CA 1 and Graham Hill Road in Santa Cruz, drive north on Graham Hill Road for 4 miles to the campground entrance.
**About the campground:** The park consists of 1,800 acres of diverse forest, including ancient redwoods, pine, and oak. Chaparral covers the ridges, and sycamore, cottonwood, and willow line the banks of the San Lorenzo River, which flows through the park. The campground is located in a well-shaded grove of medium and large trees. While the site doesn't include redwoods, they're not far away. The Eagle Creek Trail (1.8 miles) leads from the campground to Redwood Loop, park headquarters, and a nature center. The Pine Trail (0.6-mile round-trip) leads from the campground to an observation deck. The park provides access to the San Lorenzo River for steelhead fishing in the winter months. Elevation 567 feet. Stay limit 7 days. Open all year (subject to winter closures).

## 110 Henry W. Coe State Park

**Location:** 13 miles northeast of the community of Morgan Hill
**GPS:** 37.1707193 / -121.4201953
**Sites:** 9 sites for tents and RVs up to 25 feet long; 8 tent-only; 11 hike-in group sites; 2 equestrian group sites
**Facilities:** Tables, grills, drinking water, pit toilets, visitor center
**Fee per night:** $$$; reservations (family camping): (800) 444-7275 or reserveamerica.com
**Management:** California Department of Parks and Recreation, (408) 779-2728
**Activities:** Hiking, fishing, horseback riding
**Finding the campground:** From US 101 in Morgan Hill, take the East Dunne Avenue exit and drive northeast for 13 miles on East Dunne. The road becomes narrow and winding shortly after leaving town.
**About the campground:** The park, covering 87,000 acres of rugged grassland and forest, is the largest in California. Flora includes oak, pine, chaparral, and terrific wildflowers in spring. The

campground is located on an open rise with a fine view of the surrounding countryside. The original Coe homestead ranch buildings stand adjacent to the visitor center, which houses a small museum devoted to Coe family memorabilia. Hiking trails range from the 1.6-mile Monument Trail to the 9.3-mile China Hole Loop. Equestrians will find many trails of varying difficulty. Mountain bikers can use the open terrain of the park, as well as former ranch roads. Swimming holes require a hike of 5 to 10 miles to reach. The park contains more than one hundred lakes and ponds, about two dozen offering good fishing. The best fishing is in backcountry lakes, such as Mississippi, Coit, and Paradise, which you must backpack to reach. Elevation 2,600 feet. Stay limit 14 days. Open all year.

## 111 Uvas Canyon County Park

**Location:** 18 miles southwest of the community of Morgan Hill
**GPS:** 37.0845994 / -121.7928103
**Sites:** 30 sites for tents and RVs up to 28 feet long
**Facilities:** Tables, grills, drinking water, flush toilets; boat ramp nearby
**Fee per night:** $$; reservations: (408) 355-2201 or gooutsideandplay.org
**Management:** Santa Clara County Parks, (408) 779-9232
**Activities:** Hiking; fishing and boating 5 miles away
**Finding the campground:** From the intersection of US 101 and East Main Street in Morgan Hill, drive about 1 mile west on East/West Dunne; turn northwest onto Hale Avenue and drive 2.9 miles. Turn southwest onto Willow Springs Road and drive 2.6 miles. Turn west onto Oak Glen Avenue (1.7 miles), south onto CR G8/Uvas Road (1.7 miles), then southwest onto Croy Road and drive 4.4 miles.
**About the campground:** Enjoy 6 miles of hiking trails, including the 1-mile Waterfall Loop, which features several waterfalls. A pamphlet is available online and in the ranger's office for a self-guided nature hike through the lush woods. Elevation 1,090 feet. Stay limit 14 days. Open all year.

## 112 Coyote Lake Harvey Bear Ranch Park

**Location:** 6 miles northeast of Gilroy
**GPS:** 37.0806054 / -121.5307971
**Sites:** 74 sites for tents or RVs
**Facilities:** Tables, fire rings, drinking water, flush toilets, boat ramp
**Fee per night:** $$; reservations: (408) 355-2201 or gooutsideandplay.org
**Management:** Santa Clara County Parks, (408) 842-7800
**Activities:** Hiking, biking, horseback riding, fishing, boating
**Finding the campground:** From the intersection of US 101 and Leavesley Road in Gilroy, drive east on Leavesley for 3 miles; turn north onto New Avenue and drive 0.7 mile. Turn east onto Roop Road (which becomes Gilroy Hot Springs Road) and drive 4 miles. Turn west onto Coyote Reservoir Road and drive about 1 mile.
**About the campground:** The 4,595-acre park in the hills provides many opportunities to view wildlife, including bald eagles. Hikers, bikers, and equestrians have 35 miles of trails to enjoy. You can find a 2-mile paved loop trail at the Bear Ranch Trailhead. Motorized boats are allowed on the 635-acre Coyote Reservoir, which touts "world-class" black bass fishing. Swimming is not allowed. Lake is closed to all boats mid-October to mid-April. Elevation 800 feet. Stay limit 14 days. Open all year.

# 113 Mount Madonna County Park

**Location:** 10 miles west of Gilroy
**GPS:** 37.0031549 / -121.7091719
**Sites:** 11 sites for tents and RVs; 17 RV sites with water and electric hookups; 5 yurts
**Facilities:** Tables, grills, drinking water, flush toilets, dump station
**Fee per night:** $$, yurts: $$$$; reservations: (408) 355-2201 or gooutsideandplay.org
**Management:** Santa Clara County Parks, (408) 842-2341
**Activities:** Hiking, horseback riding
**Finding the campground:** From the east, take US 101 to the CA 152 West exit. From the west, take CA 1 to the CA 152 East exit. The entrance to the park is located at the summit of CA 152 at Pole Line Road. Once it begins climbing Mount Madonna, the road becomes narrow and winding.
**About the campground:** Mount Madonna is a park of considerable beauty, and it provides sweeping views of Monterey and the Santa Clara Valley. More than 18 miles of trails, many of them short and interconnecting, wind through the park. A good introduction is the 2.5-mile Bay View Loop, a combination of short trails beginning at the park entrance station, where a free trail map can be obtained. Horse rentals are available. Several wineries are located within a mile of one another on Hecker Pass Highway, about midway between the campground and Gilroy. They offer tastings, tours, sales, and picnicking. Elevation 1,400 feet. Stay limit 14 days. Open all year.

# 114 New Brighton State Beach

**Location:** 5 miles east of Santa Cruz
**GPS:** 36.9814768 / -121.9352537
**Sites:** 97 sites for tents and RVs up to 36 feet long; 9 tent-only; 3 group sites
**Facilities:** Tables, fire rings, drinking water, showers, flush toilets, dump station
**Fee per night:** $$$; reservations: (800) 444-7275 or reserveamerica.com
**Management:** California Department of Parks and Recreation, (831) 464-6329
**Activities:** Biking, hiking, swimming, fishing, surfing
**Finding the campground:** From Santa Cruz, drive about 4 miles east on CA 1 to the Capitola/Brighton Beach exit. Take the exit road and drive 1 mile south toward the beach.
**About the campground:** Situated on a low bluff overlooking the beach, the campground is shaded by pine and cypress trees. A 0.2-mile path leads to the beach, which is sheltered from the brisk winds that blow along the Santa Cruz coastline. Wineries with tastings are located in Soquet, less than 3 miles from the campground. Elevation 124 feet. Stay limit 7 days. Open all year.

# 115 Seacliff State Beach

**Location:** 5 miles east of Santa Cruz
**GPS:** 36.9726015 / -121.9124056
**Sites:** 26 sites for RVs/trailers only up to 40 feet long; full hookups available
**Facilities:** Tables, grills, drinking water, showers, flush toilets
**Fee per night:** $$$$; reservations: (800) 444-7275 or reserveamerica.com
**Management:** California Department of Parks and Recreation, (831) 685-6442
**Activities:** Swimming, fishing, surfing

**Finding the campground:** From Santa Cruz, drive about 5 miles east on CA 1 to the Seacliff Beach/Aptos exit and then drive south for 0.4 mile.
**About the campground:** Seacliff is classified as a "premium beachfront" campground, hence the higher than usual fees. Its mile-long beach adjoins New Brighton Beach to the west. At the end of the park's pier is the *Palo Alto*, a decomposing World War I supply ship that had a brief reincarnation as a shoreline dining and dancing facility until it broke up in a storm. Fishing from the pier is better than from almost any other shore location on Monterey Bay. The catch is usually perch and kingfish, but striped bass and even halibut are taken occasionally in summer, while winter high tides can bring in mackerel. Elevation 78 feet. Stay limit 7 days. Open all year.

## 116 Manresa Uplands (Manresa State Beach)

**Location:** 6 miles southeast of Aptos
**GPS:** 36.9203029 / -121.8506672
**Sites:** 60 sites for tents
**Facilities:** Tables, fire rings, drinking water, showers, flush toilets
**Fee per night:** $$$; reservations: (800) 444-7275 or reserveamerica.com
**Management:** California Department of Parks and Recreation, (831) 761-1795
**Activities:** Swimming, fishing, surfing
**Finding the campground:** From Aptos, drive southeast 2.5 miles on CA 1; turn north onto San Andreas Road and drive 3 miles. Manresa is the first beach access upon reaching the coast.
**About the campground:** For those willing to lug their camping gear a short distance from the 20-minute loading zone, Manresa offers a relatively isolated retreat without cars driving by the campsites. It is recommended that you bring a wagon to haul your gear. The campground sits on a bluff overlooking the beach, with limited shade from young trees and a small, well-established pine grove. Beach access is via a 170-step staircase. Fishing is fair for surfperch. Clamming is popular in season. Elevation 130 feet. Stay limit 7 days. Open all year.

## 117 Sunset State Beach

**Location:** 8 miles southeast of Aptos
**GPS:** 36.8871619 / -121.830651
**Sites:** 94 sites for tents and RVs up to 31 feet long; 1 group site
**Facilities:** Tables, grills, drinking water, showers, flush toilets
**Fee per night:** $$$; reservations: (800) 444-7275 or reserveamerica.com
**Management:** California Department of Parks and Recreation, (831) 763-7063
**Activities:** Swimming, fishing, surfing
**Finding the campground:** From Aptos, drive southeast 2.5 miles on CA 1; turn south onto San Andreas Road and drive 5 miles. Turn west onto Sunset Beach Road and drive 0.5 mile.
**About the campground:** The campground is located on a bluff back from the beach, shaded by pines and connected to the shore by steep trails. The beach itself is one of the most scenic in the state, but swimming can be dangerous due to surf conditions. Elevation 173 feet. Stay limit 7 days. Open all year.

# Shasta Cascade

Crossing from Oregon to California on I-5, you enter a vast, spectacular outdoor domain. Shasta Cascade boasts within its borders five national forests, a national park, a national monument, a national recreation area, and more than two dozen state and county parks. There is something here for everyone. Soaring mountains, large lakes, rushing streams, deep forests, lava fields, and scenic drives all combine to provide a perfect outdoor experience.

Near the center of this superb scenic region stands awesome Mount Shasta, second highest of the Cascade Range volcanoes after Rainier. Farther south, Shasta Lake provides almost 30,000 acres of paradise for water sports. Other large lakes, such as Eagle, Trinity, and Almanor, offer similar pleasures, while dozens of smaller lakes appeal to those seeking a quieter, more-isolated experience. The Trinity Alps provide a dramatic backdrop for hikers, equestrians, and anglers. Lassen Volcanic National Park and Lava Beds National Monument offer a chance to explore both dormant and active volcanic terrain. Feather Falls, near Lake Oroville, is the sixth-highest waterfall in the United States.

Temperatures in the Shasta Cascade region vary considerably between the mountains and the lowlands of the Sacramento River valley. Precipitation is heaviest in the winter months, and rain lasting several days is not uncommon. Average winter temperatures range from 44°F to 26°F, spring from 60°F to 35°F, summer from 82°F to 48°F, and fall from 65°F to 38°F. The average percentage of sunny days increases from a low of 50 percent in winter to 62 percent in spring and 88 percent in summer. It then declines to 72 percent in the fall.

This guidebook divides Shasta Cascade into five areas: Klamath–Mount Shasta, Shasta-Trinity, Modoc, Lassen, and Plumas.

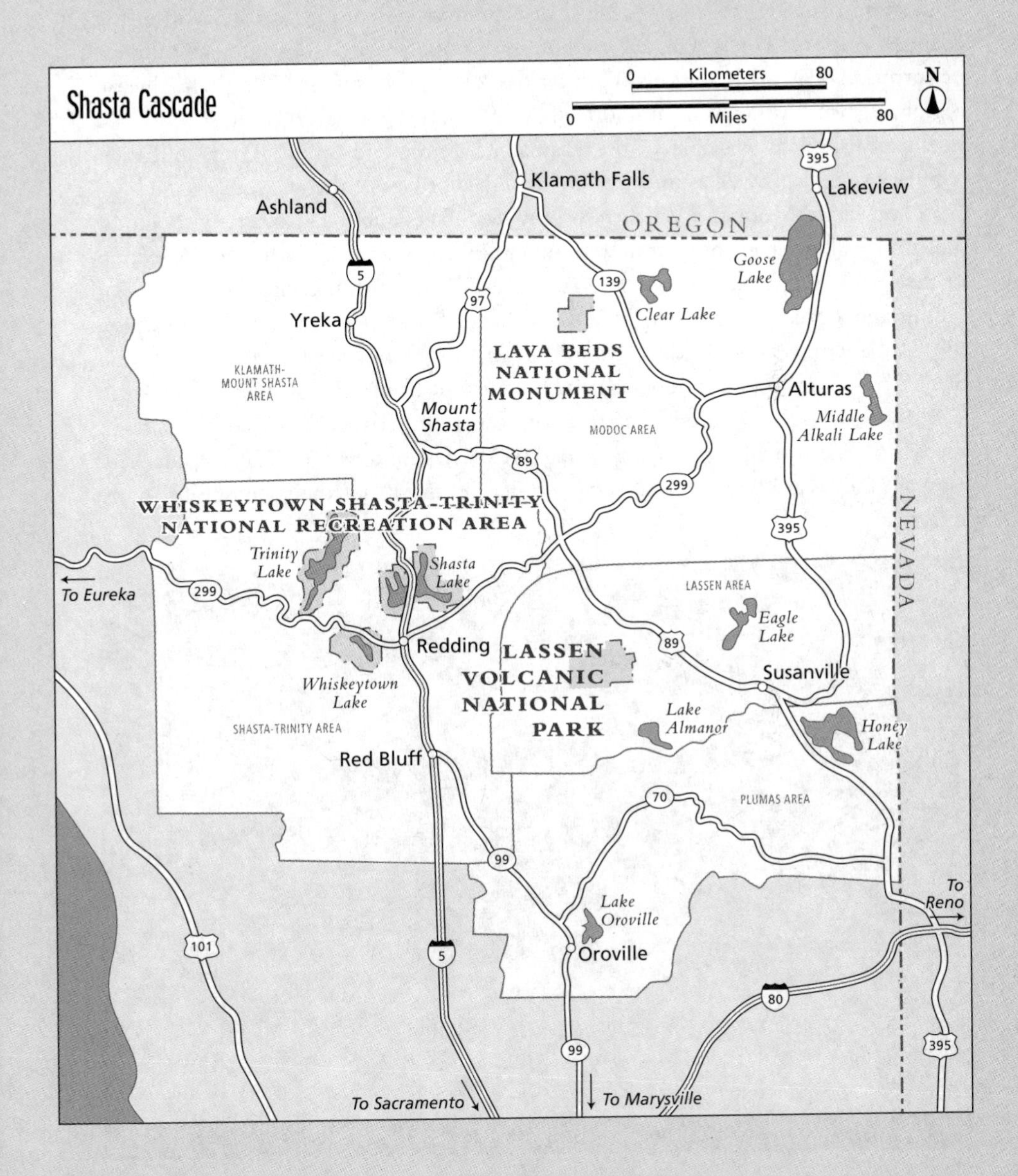
Shasta Cascade
0 Kilometers 80
0 Miles 80
N
Klamath Falls
Ashland
Lakeview
OREGON
Goose Lake
Clear Lake
Yreka
KLAMATH-MOUNT SHASTA AREA
LAVA BEDS NATIONAL MONUMENT
Alturas
Middle Alkali Lake
Mount Shasta
MODOC AREA
WHISKEYTOWN SHASTA-TRINITY NATIONAL RECREATION AREA
NEVADA
Trinity Lake
Shasta Lake
To Eureka
LASSEN AREA
Eagle Lake
Redding
LASSEN VOLCANIC NATIONAL PARK
Susanville
Whiskeytown Lake
Lake Almanor
Honey Lake
SHASTA-TRINITY AREA
Red Bluff
PLUMAS AREA
To Reno
Lake Oroville
Oroville
To Sacramento
To Marysville
5
97
139
395
89
299
70
99
101
80

# Klamath–Mount Shasta Area

The centerpiece of the Klamath–Mount Shasta area is the snow-covered cone of Mount Shasta itself. It rises to an elevation of 14,179 feet and is visible on clear days from more than 100 miles away. Most of the remainder of the area lies within the Klamath National Forest. This 1.7-million-acre woodland provides a host of outdoor opportunities. Klamath National Forest is one of America's most biologically diverse regions. Elevations range from 450 to 8,900 feet above sea level. Trout, salmon, and steelhead fishing is available in the Klamath, Salmon, and Smith Rivers and their tributary streams, as well as in the many small lakes that dot the area.

The Marble Mountain Wilderness provides hikers and backpackers with almost a quarter-million acres of pristine terrain and 89 lakes stocked with trout. A section of the Pacific Crest National Scenic Trail (PCT) passes through the wilderness. For rafting and kayaking enthusiasts, the forest has 200 miles of whitewater, mostly on the Klamath and Salmon Rivers. If you prefer to tour by car, the State of Jefferson Scenic Byway follows the upper Klamath westward from I-5 just north of Yreka to CA 199. Besides the featured campgrounds, you can find many dispersed campsites in the Klamath National Forest, Castle Crags Wilderness, and Mount Shasta Wilderness. Contact the local USDA Forest Service office or check out their website for more information.

*A view from the junction of the Pacific Crest National Scenic Trail and the connector trail down to Toad Lake, where you'll find one of the many dispersed campgrounds in the Mount Shasta Wilderness. The campground is set back from the lake in the trees, center. Photo by Bubba Seuss*

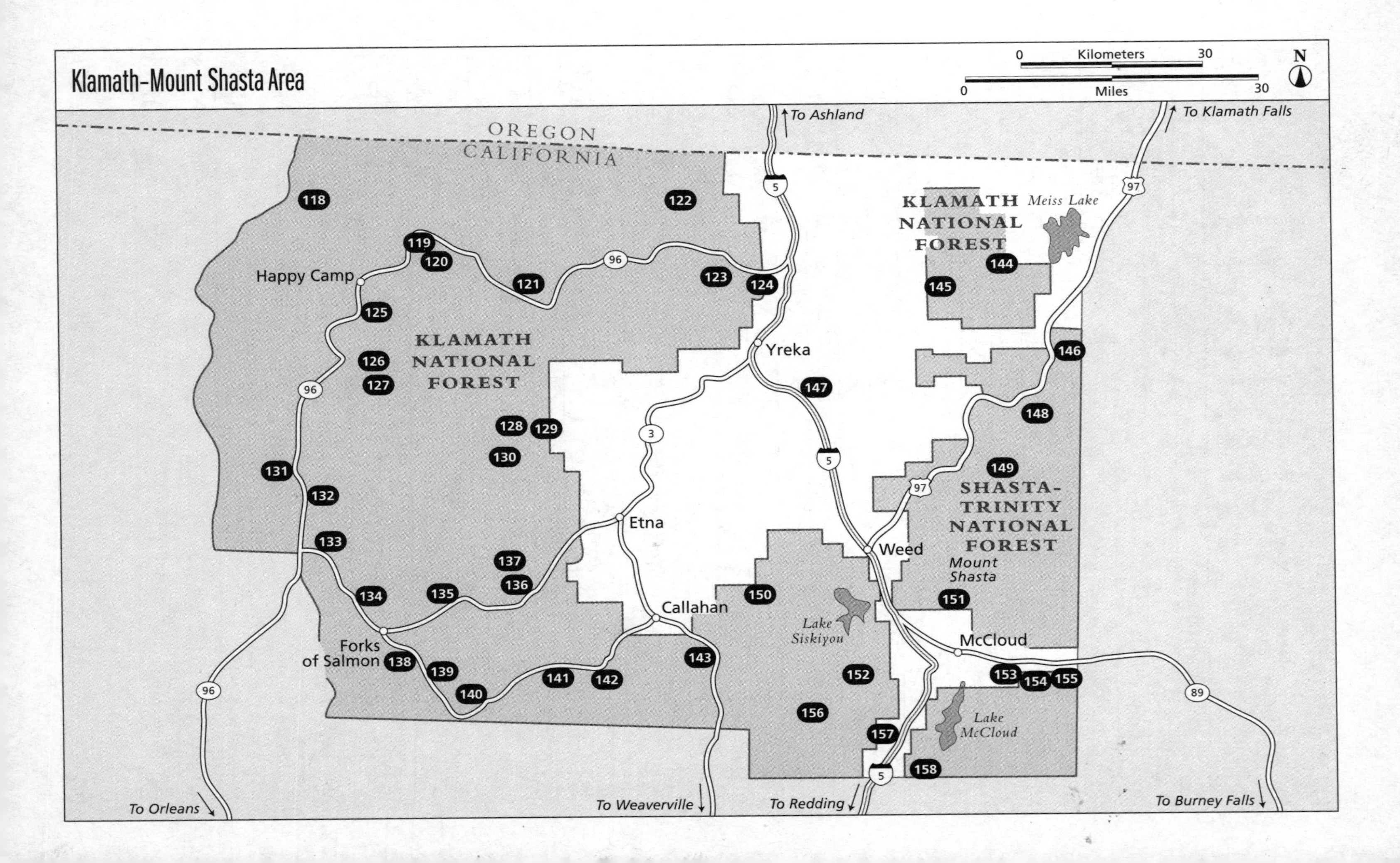
Klamath–Mount Shasta Area
Kilometers
Miles
N
To Ashland
To Klamath Falls
OREGON
CALIFORNIA
KLAMATH NATIONAL FOREST
Meiss Lake
Happy Camp
Yreka
Etna
Callahan
Forks of Salmon
Weed
SHASTA-TRINITY NATIONAL FOREST
Mount Shasta
Lake Siskiyou
McCloud
Lake McCloud
To Orleans
To Weaverville
To Redding
To Burney Falls

| | Name | Group Sites | RV Sites | Max. RV Length | Hookups | Toilets | Showers | Drinking Water | Dump Station | Pets | Wheelchair | Recreation | Fee(s) | Season | Can Reserve |
|---|---|---|---|---|---|---|---|---|---|---|---|---|---|---|---|
| | **KLAMATH–MOUNT SHASTA AREA** | | | | | | | | | | | | | | |
| 118 | West Branch | | * | | | V | | * | | * | | SF | None | May–Oct | |
| 119 | Fort Goff | | | | | V | | | | * | | HBF | None | May–Oct | |
| 120 | Grider Creek | | * | 28 | | V | | | | * | | HFSR | None | May–Oct | |
| 121 | Sarah Totten | | * | 45 | | V | | | | * | * | FBS | $-$$$$ | May–Nov | |
| 122 | Beaver Creek | | * | 28 | | V | | | | * | | FB | None | May–Oct | |
| 123 | Skeahan Bar River Access | | * | | | | | | | * | | FBS | None | May–Oct | |
| 124 | Tree of Heaven | | * | 40 | | V | | * | | * | * | HFB | $ | May–Oct | * |
| 125 | Curly Jack | * | * | | | V | | * | | * | * | FSBH | $-$$$ | Apr–Oct | * |
| 126 | Sulphur Springs | | | | | V | | | | * | | HS | None | May–Oct | |
| 127 | Norcross | | * | | | V | | | | * | * | HFR | None | May–Oct | |
| 128 | Bridge Flat | | * | 30 | | V | | | | | | HFBS | None | May–Oct | |
| 129 | Indian Scotty | * | * | 30 | | V | | * | | * | * | FSH | $-$$$$ | May–Oct | |
| 130 | Lovers Camp | | | | | V | | | | * | | HR | None | May–Oct | |
| 131 | Dillon Creek | | * | 34 | | V | | * | | * | * | HSFB | $ | May–Oct | * |
| 132 | Ti Bar Flat | | * | | | V | | | | * | | FSBL | None | May–Oct | |
| 133 | Oak Bottom | | * | | | V | | * | | * | * | HFS | $ | May–Oct | * |
| 134 | Nordheimer Flat | * | * | | | V | | * | | * | * | FBH | $-$$$$ | May–Oct | * |
| 135 | Red Bank | | * | | | V | | | | | | FS | None | May–Oct | |
| 136 | Idlewild | | * | 24 | | V | | * | | * | | HFSR | $ | May–Oct | |
| 137 | Mule Bridge | | * | | | V | | | | * | | HFSRM | None | May–Oct | |
| 138 | Hotelling | | * | 16 | | V | | | | * | | HFSM | None | May–Oct | |
| 139 | Matthews Creek | | * | 24 | | V | | * | | * | * | FSHB | $ | May–Oct | |
| 140 | East Fork | | * | 16 | | V | | | | * | | HFS | None | May–Oct | |
| 141 | Trail Creek | | * | 20 | | V | | * | | * | | HF | $ | May–Oct | |
| 142 | Hidden Horse | | | | | V | | * | | * | | R | $ | June–Oct | * |
| 143 | Scott Mountain | | * | 15 | | V | | | | * | | HR | None | May–Oct | |
| 144 | Juanita Lake | * | * | 34 | | V | | * | | * | * | HFBM | $-$$$$ | May–Oct | |
| 145 | Martin's Dairy | * | * | | | V | | * | | * | | HFSM | $ | Year-round | |
| 146 | Shafter | | * | 40 | | V | | * | | * | | HF | $ | Year-round | |
| 147 | McBride Springs | | * | 16 | | V | | * | | * | | H | $ | May–Oct | |
| 148 | Orr Lake | | * | 30 | | V | | | | * | | HFSB | None | May–Oct | |
| 149 | Deer Mountain/Chuck Best Snowmobile Park | | * | 30 | | V | | | | * | | HM | None | Year-round | |

| | Name | Group Sites | RV Sites | Max. RV Length | Hookups | Toilets | Showers | Drinking Water | Dump Station | Pets | Wheelchair | Recreation | Fee(s) | Season | Can Reserve |
|---|---|---|---|---|---|---|---|---|---|---|---|---|---|---|---|
| 150 | Kangaroo Lake | | | | | V | | * | | * | * | HFSB | $ | June-Oct | |
| 151 | Panther Meadows | | | | | V | | | | * | | H | None | May-Oct | |
| 152 | Castle Lake | | * | 16 | | V | | | | * | | HFS | None | June-Oct | |
| 153 | Fowlers Camp | | * | 30 | | V | | * | | * | * | HSF | $ | Apr-Oct | |
| 154 | Cattle Camp | | * | 32 | | V | | * | | * | | FSH | $ | May-Oct | |
| 155 | Algoma | | * | 24 | | V | | | | * | | F | None | Apr-Nov | |
| 156 | Gumboot Lake | | * | 10 | | V | | | | * | | FH | None | June-Oct | |
| 157 | Castle Crags State Park | | * | 27 | | F | * | * | | * | * | HFS | $$$ | Year-round | * |
| 158 | Ah-Di-Na | | | | | F | | * | | * | | FH | $ | Apr-Nov | |

Toilets: F=flush V=vault P=pit C=chemical; Fee: $=Under $20 $$=$20-$29 $$$=$30-$39 $$$$ $40 or more; Recreation: H=hiking S=swimming F=fishing B=boating L=boat launch O=off-highway driving R=horseback riding, M=mountain biking Hookups: W=water E=electric S=sewer

# 118 West Branch

**Location:** 12 miles northwest of the community of Happy Camp
**GPS:** 41.9315081 / -123.4750598
**Sites:** 10 sites for tents and RVs
**Facilities:** Tables, fire rings, vault toilets, drinking water (bring extra water)
**Fee per night:** None
**Management:** Klamath National Forest, (530) 842-6131
**Activities:** Swimming, fishing, gold panning, wildlife viewing, scenic drive
**Finding the campground:** From Happy Camp (65 miles west of Yreka on CA 96), drive 12 miles north on Indian Creek Road.
**About the campground:** A quiet and secluded campground in a canyon near Indian Creek. You can enjoy water play off the gravel bar in the West Branch of the creek. It is the last campground on the State of Jefferson Scenic Byway. Elevation 2,200 feet. Stay limit 14 days. Open May through October.

# 119 Fort Goff

**Location:** 53 miles northwest of Yreka
**GPS:** 41.8651259 / -123.2575524
**Sites:** 5 sites for tents
**Facilities:** Tables, fire rings, vault toilet; no drinking water
**Fee per night:** None
**Management:** Klamath National Forest, (530) 842-6131

**Activities:** Hiking, fishing, rafting, kayaking

**Finding the campground:** From Yreka, drive north 8 miles on CA 263; turn west onto CA 96 and drive 45 miles.

**About the campground:** The sites are walk-ins, with parking visible 15 to 35 yards from the campsites. The campground is situated on the banks of the Klamath River, with trout and salmon fishing in late summer and steelhead fishing in winter. A trail runs northwest from the campground along Fort Goff Creek to the Boundary National Recreation Trail. There is a historic cemetery across the road. The town of Seiad Valley is 3 miles away. Elevation 1,300 feet. Stay limit 14 days. Open May through October.

## 120 Grider Creek

**Location:** 52 miles northwest of Yreka

**GPS:** 41.806667 / -123.217222

**Sites:** 10 sites for tents and RVs up to 28 feet long

**Facilities:** Tables, fire rings, vault toilets, corrals; no drinking water

**Fee per night:** None

**Management:** Klamath National Forest, (530) 842-6131

**Activities:** Hiking, fishing, swimming/wading, horseback riding

**Finding the campground:** From Yreka, drive north 8 miles on CA 263; turn west onto CA 96 and drive 42 miles. Turn south onto FR 46N66 and drive 2.2 miles.

**About the campground:** The Pacific Crest National Scenic Trail passes the campground, which is on the banks of Grider Creek. Elevation 1,400 feet. Stay limit 14 days. Open May through October.

## 121 Sarah Totten

**Location:** 39 miles northwest of Yreka

**GPS:** 41.7873537 / -123.0528182

**Sites:** 9 sites for tents and RVs up to 45 feet long; 2 group sites

**Facilities:** Tables, fire rings, vault toilets, gravel boat launch; no drinking water

**Fee per night:** $, group camps: $$$$; reservations: (877) 444-6777 or recreation.gov

**Management:** Klamath National Forest, (530) 842-6131

**Activities:** Fishing, rafting, tubing, swimming, nonmotorized boating

**Finding the campground:** From Yreka, drive north 8 miles on CA 263; turn west onto CA 96 and drive 31 miles.

**About the campground:** Situated on the bank of the Klamath River, with excellent river access. Look for crumpled structures and rock foundations—all that is left of the town of Hamburg, a booming town in the late 1800s. Elevation 1,400 feet. Stay limit 14 days. Open May through November.

## 122 Beaver Creek

**Location:** 26 miles northwest of Yreka

**GPS:** 41.9270781 / -122.8311456

**Sites:** 8 sites for tents and RVs up to 28 feet long

**Facilities:** Tables, fire rings, vault toilets; no drinking water

**Fee per night:** None

**Management:** Klamath National Forest, (530) 842-6131
**Activities:** Fishing, rafting, wading, hunting
**Finding the campground:** From Yreka, drive north 8 miles on CA 263; turn west onto CA 96 and drive 14 miles. Turn north onto Beaver Creek Road (FR 11) and drive 4 miles.
**About the campground:** Beaver Creek offers trout fishing and tube rafting and is a base for fall hunting. Elevation 2,400 feet. Stay limit 14 days. Open May through October.

## 123 Skeahan Bar River Access

**Location:** 17 miles northwest of Yreka
**GPS:** 41.8587736 / -122.7038775
**Sites:** Dispersed
**Facilities:** Picnic tables; no toilets or drinking water. Use of rock fire rings, a barbecue, or a camp stove requires a current California Campfire Permit.
**Fee per night:** None
**Management:** Klamath National Forest, (530) 842-6131
**Activities:** Fishing, kayaking, swimming, riparian wildlife viewing, rockhounding, gold panning (with permit)
**Finding the campground:** From I-5 West, take CA 96 approximately 10 miles to the river access.
**About the campground:** This wooded campsite and Ti-bar Flat are two of more than a dozen dispersed campsites along the Klamath River. Originally named Virginia Bar, Skeahan Bar was a mining claim worked by gold seekers John Skeahan and Joe Davidson in the late 1800s. It is a popular river access point. There is a gravel road to the water's edge. Elevation, 1,900 feet. Stay limit 14 days. Open May through October.

## 124 Tree of Heaven

**Location:** 13 miles north of Yreka
**GPS:** 41.8304659 / -122.6585549
**Sites:** 20 sites for tents and RVs up to 40 feet long
**Facilities:** Tables, fire rings, drinking water, vault toilets
**Fee per night:** $; reservations: (877) 444-6777 or recreation.gov
**Management:** Klamath National Forest, (530) 842-6131
**Activities:** Hiking, fishing, birding, rafting, kayaking
**Finding the campground:** From Yreka, drive north 8 miles on CA 263; turn west onto CA 96 and drive 5 miles.
**About the campground:** On the banks of the Klamath River, with excellent river access. Steelhead and salmon fishing can be good in the winter months. A trail from the campground follows the river. A large day-use area offers horseshoe pits, volleyball, and an open-pit barbecue. Elevation 2,100 feet. Stay limit 14 days. Open May through October.

## 125 Curly Jack

**Location:** In Happy Camp, on Curly Jack Road
**GPS:** 41.7851628 / -123.3916469
**Sites:** 12 sites for tents and RVs; 4 group sites

**Facilities:** Tables, fire rings, drinking water, vault toilets
**Fee per night:** $, group sites: $$$; reservations: (877) 444-6777 or recreation.gov
**Management:** Klamath National Forest, (530) 493-2243
**Activities:** Fishing, swimming, rafting, kayaking, hiking
**Finding the campground:** From Happy Camp (65 miles west of Yreka on CA 96), drive 1 mile southwest on Curly Jack Road.
**About the campground:** On the banks of the Klamath, the campground provides excellent access to the river. The swimming location is among the best on the river. Fishing is good for trout in late spring and early summer, for steelhead in late fall and early winter. Salmon catches are possible in late fall. The campground is also near Elk, Doolittle, Ikes, and Deer Lick Creeks. Elevation 1,075 feet. Stay limit 14 days. Open April through October.

## 126 Sulphur Springs

**Location:** 15 miles south of Happy Camp
**GPS:** 41.6590165 / -123.3203308
**Sites:** 6 sites for tents
**Facilities:** Tables, fire rings, vault toilets; no drinking water
**Fee per night:** None
**Management:** Klamath National Forest, (530) 842-6131
**Activities:** Hiking, swimming
**Finding the campground:** From Happy Camp (65 miles west of Yreka on CA 96), drive 15 miles south on Elk Creek Road.
**About the campground:** Situated on the banks of Elk Creek, the campground is a 50-yard walk from parking. It is the starting point for the Elk Creek Trail, a main route into the beautiful Marble Mountain Wilderness. One of the main attractions of Sulphur Springs Campground is warm springs located along Elk Creek. The temperature of the springs is approximately 75°F, and it can accommodate five or six people at one time. Elevation 3,100 feet. Stay limit 14 days. Open May through October.

## 127 Norcross

**Location:** 17 miles south of the community of Happy Camp
**GPS:** 41.64585355 / -123.3091109
**Sites:** 4 sites for tents and RVs
**Facilities:** Tables, fire rings, vault toilets; no drinking water; water for livestock available
**Fee per night:** None
**Management:** Klamath National Forest, (530) 842-6131
**Activities:** Hiking, fishing, horseback riding
**Finding the campground:** From Happy Camp, drive 16.5 miles south on Elk Creek Road.
**About the campground:** This campground serves as a staging area for various trails that provide access into the Marble Mountain Wilderness. Elevation 2,400 feet. Stay limit 14 days. Open May through October.

# 128 Bridge Flat

**Location:** 34 miles southwest of Yrek
**GPS:** 41.6501325 / -123.1130982
**Sites:** 4 sites for tents and RVs up to 30 feet long
**Facilities:** Tables, fire rings, vault toilets; no drinking water
**Fee per night:** None
**Management:** Klamath National Forest, (530) 842-6131
**Activities:** Fishing, hiking, rafting, swimming, kayaking
**Finding the campground:** From Yreka, drive southwest 17 miles on CA 3 to Fort Jones. Turn northwest onto Scott River Road and drive 17 miles.
**About the campground:** Situated on the bank of the Scott River, Bridge Flat offers easy access to kayaking and whitewater rafting on the river in spring and a waterhole for swimming. Fishing is available throughout the season. The Kelsey National Recreation Trail begins across the road from the campground. This historic route offers excellent scenic day hikes or backpack trips into the Marble Mountain Wilderness. It connects with the Pacific Crest National Scenic Trail approximately 8 miles from the campground at Paradise Lake. Elevation 2,000 feet. Stay limit 14 days. Open May through October.

# 129 Indian Scotty

**Location:** 31 miles southwest of Yreka
**GPS:** 41.6343854 / -123.079158
**Sites:** 28 sites for tents and RVs up to 30 feet long; 1 group site
**Facilities:** Tables, fire rings, drinking water, vault toilets
**Fee per night:** $, group site: $$$$; reservations (required for group site only): (877) 444-6777 or recreation.gov
**Management:** Klamath National Forest, (530) 842-6131
**Activities:** Fishing, swimming, hiking, gold panning (with permit)
**Finding the campground:** From Yreka, drive southwest 17 miles on CA 3 to Fort Jones. Turn northwest onto Scott River Road and drive 14 miles.
**About the campground:** Indian Scotty is situated on the bank of the Scott River, with river access for fishing and swimming. Elevation 2,400 feet. Stay limit 14 days. Open May through October.

# 130 Lovers Camp

**Location:** 39 miles west of Yreka
**GPS:** 41.58874 / -123.14699
**Sites:** 8 sites for tents
**Facilities:** Tables, fire rings, vault toilets, watering and unloading ramp for horses, corrals; no drinking water
**Fee per night:** None
**Management:** Klamath National Forest, (530) 842-6131
**Activities:** Hiking, horseback riding

**Finding the campground:** From Yreka, drive southwest 17 miles on CA 3 to Fort Jones. Turn northwest onto Scott River Road and drive 14 miles. Turn south onto FR 44N45 and drive 8 miles.
**About the campground:** Lovers Camp is shaded and has a good view of the Marble Mountains. It serves as a staging area for backpacking and equestrian trips into the Marble Mountain Wilderness and is the starting point for day hikes to the Sky High Lakes, Deep Lake, and Marble Valley. The campground is very busy during holiday weekends. Elevation 4,300 feet. Stay limit 14 days. Open May through October.

## 131 Dillon Creek

**Location:** 24 miles north of Orleans
**GPS:** 41.5747039 / -123.5402309
**Sites:** 21 sites for tents and RVs up to 34 feet long
**Facilities:** Tables, fire rings, drinking water, vault toilets
**Fee per night:** $; reservations: (877) 444-6777 or recreation.gov
**Management:** Klamath National Forest, (530) 627-3291
**Activities:** Hiking, swimming, fishing, rafting
**Finding the campground:** From Orleans, drive 24 miles north on CA 96.
**About the campground:** Situated on the Klamath River at the site of a spring cascading down Dillon Creek, this campground occupies a scenic setting. The campsites, carved into the mountain slopes, are sheltered and shaded and offer privacy. A path leads to one of the most-scenic natural swimming holes in Northern California. River access is adjacent to the camp, across the highway, with good seasonal fishing for trout, steelhead, and occasional salmon. Excellent rafting and kayaking opportunities exist from the campground south to several takeouts before Somes Bar. The trailhead for Dillon Creek Trail is across the bridge and will take you on a small footpath 100 feet above the creek (not recommended for children). Stay limit 14 days. Open May through October.

## 132 Ti Bar Flat

**Location:** 19 miles north of Orleans
**GPS:** 41.5295069 / -123.528077
**Sites:** Dispersed for tents and RVs
**Facilities:** Tables, fire rings, vault toilets, boat launch; potable water available at Ti-bar Fire Station, just east of the campground
**Fee per night:** None
**Management:** Klamath National Forest, (530) 627-3291
**Activities:** Fishing, swimming, rafting, gold panning (with permit)
**Finding the campground:** From Orleans, drive 19 miles north on CA 96.
**About the campground:** Situated on a large flat on the banks of the Klamath River, the campground has several sites with trees to provide shade from the summer sun. Tents and RVs can disperse over a wide area. There is a boat launch for drift boats and rafts. A campfire permit is required; inquire at the ranger station. Elevation 900 feet. Stay limit 14 days. Open May through October.

## 133 Oak Bottom

**Location:** 9 miles northeast of Orleans
**GPS:** 40.6487597 / -122.5925161
**Sites:** 26 sites for tents and RVs
**Facilities:** Tables, fire rings, drinking water, vault toilets
**Fee per night:** $; reservations: (877) 444-6777 or recreation.gov
**Management:** Six Rivers National Forest, (530) 627-3291
**Activities:** Hiking, fishing, swimming
**Finding the campground:** From Orleans, drive north on CA 96 for 6 miles. Turn east onto Salmon River Road and drive 3 miles.
**About the campground:** Situated across the road from the Salmon River, which offers a few swimming holes and steelhead fishing in the fall. The Oak Bottom River Access, located directly across from the campground, provides access to the Salmon River, which is renowned for its Class III–V whitewater (upriver from the campground). The lower portion of the Salmon offers excellent swimming and tubing opportunities. Elevation 1,290 feet. Stay limit 14 days. Open May through October.

## 134 Nordheimer Flat

**Location:** 4 miles northwest of the community of Forks of Salmon
**Sites:** 12 sites for tents and RVs; 4 group sites
**Facilities:** Tables, fire rings, drinking water, vault toilets
**Fee per night:** $, group sites: $$$$; reservations (group sites only): (877) 444-6777 or recreation.gov
**Management:** Six Rivers National Forest, (530) 627-3291
**Activities:** Fishing, rafting, kayaking, hiking, biking
**Finding the campground:** From Forks of Salmon, drive northwest 4 miles on the Salmon River Road.
**About the campground:** Beautiful and secluded, Nordheimer Flat is located in the center of the Salmon River whitewater area. Rafting activities begin in spring and continue until the water levels drop in early summer. River access is adjacent to the campground. Remnants from historic mining operations can still be seen in this remote but beautiful camping area. A few fruit trees remain from past homesteading activities. The Orleans Trail for hiking and mountain biking begins nearby. A campfire permit is required; inquire at the ranger station. Elevation 900 feet. Stay limit 14 days. Open May through October.

## 135 Red Bank

**Location:** 32 miles southwest of Etna
**GPS:** 41.29791 / -123.23032
**Sites:** 5 sites for tents and RVs
**Facilities:** Tables, fire rings, vault toilets; no drinking water
**Fee per night:** None
**Management:** Klamath National Forest, (530) 842-6131
**Activities:** Fishing, swimming, gold panning (with permit)

**Finding the campground:** From Etna (on CA 3), drive southwest 32 miles on Sawyers Bar Road.

**About the campground:** A shady location next to the North Fork of the Salmon River, with adjacent river access. Elevation 1,760 feet. Stay limit 14 days. Open May through October.

## 136 Idlewild

**Location:** 20 miles southwest of Etna

**GPS:** 41.33153 / -123.06004

**Sites:** 11 sites for tents and RVs up to 24 feet long

**Facilities:** Tables, fire rings, drinking water, vault toilets

**Fee per night:** $

**Management:** Klamath National Forest, (530) 842-6131

**Activities:** Hiking, fishing, swimming, horseback riding, gold panning (with permit)

**Finding the campground:** From Etna (on CA 3), drive southwest 20 miles on Sawyers Bar Road.

**About the campground:** Situated in an open conifer-and-oak grove on the North Fork of the Salmon River, which offers steelhead fishing and swimming. Trailheads to both the Marble Mountain Wilderness (2 miles north) and Russian Wilderness (3 miles east) are within a short drive. Elevation 2,600 feet. Stay limit 14 days. Open May through October.

## 137 Mule Bridge

**Location:** 22 miles southwest of Etna

**GPS:** 41.3583 / -123.0752

**Sites:** 4 sites for tents and RVs

**Facilities:** Tables, fire rings, vault toilets, corrals; no drinking water; water for stock only

**Fee per night:** None

**Management:** Klamath National Forest, (530) 842-6131

**Activities:** Hiking, fishing, swimming, horseback riding, mountain biking

**Finding the campground:** From Etna (on CA 3), drive southwest 20 miles on Sawyers Bar Road. Turn north onto FR 41N37 and drive 2 miles.

**About the campground:** Mule Bridge is the trailhead for the North Fork Trail into the Marble Mountain Wilderness. It roughly parallels the Pacific Crest National Scenic Trail. A campfire permit is required; inquire at the ranger station. Elevation 2,800 feet. Stay limit 14 days. Open May through October.

## 138 Hotelling

**Location:** 3 miles southeast of the community of Forks of Salmon

**GPS:** 41.2396 / -123.2753

**Sites:** 5 sites for tents and RVs up to 16 feet long

**Facilities:** Tables, fire rings, vault toilets; no drinking water

**Fee per night:** None

**Management:** Klamath National Forest, (530) 842-6131

**Activities:** Fishing, swimming, hiking, mountain biking, gold panning (with permit)

**Finding the campground:** From Forks of Salmon, drive 3 miles southeast on the Cecilville Road (FR 93).

**About the campground:** Situated between the highway and the banks of the South Fork of the Salmon River, which offers seasonal steelhead and salmon fishing. Popular with locals in summer. Elevation 1,500 feet. Stay limit 14 days. Open May through October.

## 139 Matthews Creek

**Location:** 8 miles southeast of the community of Forks of Salmon
**GPS:** 41.18680 / -123.21393
**Sites:** 10 sites for tents and RVs up to 24 feet long
**Facilities:** Tables, fire rings, drinking water, vault toilets
**Fee per night:** $
**Management:** Klamath National Forest, (530) 842-6131
**Activities:** Fishing, swimming, hiking, nonmotorized boating
**Finding the campground:** From Forks of Salmon, drive 8 miles southeast on the Cecilville Road (FR 93).
**About the campground:** Dramatically situated in a canyon-like setting along the South Fork of the Salmon River, the campground has a good swimming hole. Fishing here for steelhead and salmon requires skill. A 4-mile trail from the campground leads to the abandoned King Solomon Mine. Elevation 1,760 feet. Stay limit 14 days. Open May through October.

## 140 East Fork

**Location:** 24 miles southwest of Callahan
**GPS:** 41.15403 / -123.10865
**Sites:** 6 sites for tents and RVs up to 16 feet long
**Facilities:** Tables, fire rings, vault toilets; no drinking water
**Fee per night:** None
**Management:** Klamath National Forest, (530) 842-6131
**Activities:** Hiking, fishing, swimming
**Finding the campground:** From Callahan, drive southwest 24 miles on the Callahan-Cecilville Road.
**About the campground:** Situated on the banks of the Salmon River, which offers seasonal steelhead and salmon fishing and has some deep, cold swimming holes. Hiking from the campground provides access to the lakes in the Caribou Basin, Rush Creek, and Little South Fork drainages. Elevation 2,600 feet. Stay limit 14 days. Open May through October.

## 141 Trail Creek

**Location:** 15 miles southwest of Callahan
**GPS:** 41.22903 / -122.97337
**Sites:** 12 sites for tents and RVs up to 20 feet
**Facilities:** Tables, fire rings, drinking water, vault toilets
**Fee per night:** $
**Management:** Klamath National Forest, (530) 842-6131
**Activities:** Hiking, fishing
**Finding the campground:** From Callahan, drive 15 miles southwest on the Callahan-Cecilville Road.

**About the campground:** Situated near the banks of Trail Creek, the campground offers day hikes to Fish and Long Gulch Lakes in the Trinity Alps Wilderness. Access to the Pacific Crest National Scenic Trail is nearby. Elevation 4,700 feet. Stay limit 14 days. Open May through October.

## 142 Hidden Horse

**Location:** 11 miles southwest of Callahan
**GPS:** 41.2188103 / -122.912094
**Sites:** 6 sites for tents
**Facilities:** Tables, fire rings, drinking water, vault toilets
**Fee per night:** $; reservations (site 6 only): (877) 444-6777 or recreation.gov
**Management:** Klamath National Forest, (530) 468-5351
**Activities:** Horseback riding
**Finding the campground:** From Callahan, take the Callahan-Cecilville Road and drive southwest for 11 miles.
**About the campground:** Each campsite is designed for a small group and has a pull-through driveway, four 12 × 12-foot corral stalls, drinking water, and a tent site. There are no stock watering troughs or feed bunks. You must bring your own buckets and hay nets or feed on the ground. A network of interconnecting trails lead to Long Gulch, Trail Gulch, and the Pacific Crest National Scenic Trail, wilderness lakes, and miles of trail beyond. The latter leads into the Trinity Alps Wilderness. Adjacent is the Carter Meadows Group Horse Camp that can accommodate over 25 horses. Elevation 5,800 feet. Stay limit 14 days. Open June through October.

## 143 Scott Mountain

**Location:** 8 miles southeast of Callahan
**GPS:** 41.2761846 / -122.6999149
**Sites:** 7 sites for tents and RVs (up to 15-foot trailers)
**Facilities:** Tables, fire rings, vault toilets; no drinking water
**Fee per night:** None
**Management:** Klamath National Forest, (530) 623-2121
**Activities:** Hiking, horseback riding
**Finding the campground:** From Callahan, drive east and south on CA 3 for 8 miles.
**About the campground:** The Pacific Crest National Scenic Trail passes the campground. Elevation 5,300 feet. Stay limit 14 days. Open May through October.

## 144 Juanita Lake

**Location:** 45 miles northeast of Weed
**GPS:** 41.81663 / -122.1227855
**Sites:** 24 sites for tents and RVs up to 34 feet long; 1 group site for up to 50 people
**Facilities:** Tables, fire rings, drinking water, vault toilets
**Fee per night:** $, group camp: $$$$; reservations (required for group camp): (877) 444-6777 or recreation.gov
**Management:** Klamath National Forest, (530) 842-6131
**Activities:** Hiking, fishing, boating, mountain biking, birding

**Finding the campground:** From the intersection of I-5 and US 97 in Weed, drive northeast 38 miles on US 97. Turn left onto Ball Mountain Road and drive 3 miles. Bear right onto FR 46N04 and drive 3.5 miles.
**About the campground:** Situated on the shoreline of 55-acre Juanita Lake, which is regularly stocked with modest numbers of rainbow and brown trout and has a bass and catfish population. No motorized boats are allowed on the lake. Two fishing jetties provide easy, barrier-free access. A 1.5-mile paved, barrier-free trail circles the lake, and a 6-mile trail climbs 2,700 feet to Ball Mountain Lookout. Elevation 5,100 feet. Stay limit 14 days. Open May through October.

## 145 Martin's Dairy

**Location:** 42 miles northeast of Weed
**GPS:** 41.7956002 / -122.2049175
**Sites:** 6 sites for tents and RVs; 4-unit horse camp
**Facilities:** Tables, fire rings, drinking water, vault toilets, corrals
**Fee per night:** $
**Management:** Klamath National Forest, (530) 842-6131
**Activities:** Hiking, fishing, mountain biking, swimming/wading, birding, hunting (seasonal)
**Finding the campground:** From the intersection of I-5 and US 97 in Weed, drive northeast 30 miles on US 97. Turn west onto West Ball Mountain–Little Shasta Road (FR 70) and drive 10 miles. Turn west onto FR 46N10 and drive 6.1 miles.
**About the campground:** Martin's Dairy is adjacent to a pretty mountain meadow and the Little Shasta River. You can see Mount Shasta in the distance. The river is regularly stocked with rainbow and brown trout. Periwinkles are abundant in the stream and make good trout bait. There are numerous gated logging roads in the area that can be used as trails for hikers, mountain bikers, and equestrians. Elevation 6,000 feet. Stay limit 14 days. Open all year.

## 146 Shafter

**Location:** 46 miles northeast of Weed
**GPS:** 41.7103289 / -121.9805011
**Sites:** 10 sites for tents and RVs up to 40 feet long
**Facilities:** Tables, fire rings, drinking water, vault toilets
**Fee per night:** $
**Management:** Klamath National Forest, (530) 842-6131
**Activities:** Hiking, fishing
**Finding the campground:** From I-5 in Weed, travel northwest on US 97 about 28 miles to Tennant Road. Turn east onto Tennant Road approximately 5 miles to Old State Highway. Turn onto Old State Highway and continue past the town of Bray for a total of 8 miles to the campground.
**About the campground:** Situated on the banks of Butte Creek, which is regularly stocked with rainbow and brown trout and offers good fishing for small trout early in the season. Shafter is a tranquil campground next to meadows that bloom with wildflowers in early spring. The Southern Pacific Railroad tracks go right past the campground, with the occasional train chugging past. During the fall hunting season, the campground fills up quickly. Orr Mountain Lookout, 6 miles south of the campground (last 2 miles by foot or four-wheel-drive vehicle) has fine views of Mount Shasta. Elevation 4,300 feet. Stay limit 14 days. Open all year.

## 147 McBride Springs

**Location:** 5 miles northeast of the community of Mount Shasta
**GPS:** 41.3526525 / -122.2844553
**Sites:** 12 sites for tents and RVs up to 16 feet long
**Facilities:** Tables, fire rings, drinking water, vault toilets
**Fee per night:** $
**Management:** Shasta-Trinity National Forest, Mount Shasta Ranger Station, (530) 926-4511
**Activities:** Hiking
**Finding the campground:** From I-5 in Mount Shasta, take the Central Mount Shasta exit. Turn east onto Lake Street, which becomes Everett Memorial Highway (CR A10/North Washington Drive), and drive about 5 miles.
**About the campground:** Situated on the southwest slope of Mount Shasta at an elevation of 4,900 feet, the campground serves as a base for hiking on and around the mountain. A small, seasonal spring-fed creek runs through the campground. A hand-operated pump provides well water. Elevation 4,860 feet. Stay limit 7 days. Open May 15 through October 31.

## 148 Orr Lake

**Location:** 34 miles northeast of Weed
**GPS:** 41.6671617 / -121.9919224
**Sites:** 4 single sites (east side of lake); 4 double sites (north side) for tents and RVs up to 30 feet long
**Facilities:** Fire rings, picnic tables, vault toilets; no drinking water
**Fee per night:** None.
**Management:** Klamath National Forest, (530) 842-6131
**Activities:** Lake and pond fishing, swimming, boating, riparian wildlife viewing, hiking
**Finding the campground:** From I-5 in Weed, travel northwest on US 97 approximately 28 miles to Tennant Road. Turn east onto Tennant Road and continue approximately 5 miles to Old State Highway. Turn onto Old State Highway and drive to the town of Bray. At Bray turn north onto FR 44N30X; cross the railroad tracks and continue for 2 miles to the campground.
**About the campground:** Orr Lake is popular for fishing trout, bass, and catfish. It boasts a beautiful view of Mount Shasta. A scenic trail along the east edge of the lake provides access to several fishing jetties and follows the lakeshore. A boat ramp on the east shore and a hand-launch boat ramp on the north end provide easy access to the lake. Elevation 5,200 feet. Stay limit 14 days. Open May through October.

## 149 Deer Mountain / Chuck Best Snowmobile Park

**Location:** 21 miles northeast of Weed
**GPS:** 41.5685 / -122.1353
**Sites:** 8 sites for tents and RVs up to 30 feet long
**Facilities:** Fire rings, some picnic tables, vault toilet; no drinking water
**Fee per night:** None
**Management:** Klamath National Forest, (530) 842-6131

**Activities:** Wildlife viewing, hiking, mountain biking; snowmobiling, mushing, and snowshoeing in winter

**Finding the campground:** From I-5 in Weed, travel northwest on US 97 about 17 miles to FR 42N12/ Deer Mountain Road/ FR 19. Turn east about 4 miles to the Deer Mountain Snowpark.

**About the campground:** In winter the campground provides access to a system of 250 groomed snowmobile trails and several warming huts. A popular summer campground, these trails are great for hiking or biking as well. Elevation 5,500 feet. Stay Limit 14 days. Open all year.

## 150 Kangaroo Lake

**Location:** 39 miles southwest of Weed

**GPS:** 41.3345693 / -122.6422301

**Sites:** 18 sites for tents

**Facilities:** Tables, fire rings, drinking water, vault toilets, fishing pier

**Fee per night:** $

**Management:** Klamath National Forest, (530) 842-6131

**Activities:** Hiking, fishing, swimming, boating

**Finding the campground:** From Weed, drive 11 miles north on I-5 to the Edgewood/Gazelle exit; turn southwest and drive 6 miles to Gazelle. From Gazelle, continue southwest on the

*A view of Kangaroo Lake from the Kangaroo Fen Trail. The campground is in the lower left, mostly out of view. Photo by Bubba Seuss*

Gazelle-Callahan Road for about 15 miles to the Kangaroo Lake turnoff. There, turn south onto FR 41N08 and follow the signs for about 7 miles to the campground.

**About the campground:** The lake is within a 5-minute walk of the campsites, and a paved trail leads to the accessible fishing pier. Covering 25 acres, and 110 feet deep, the lake is regularly stocked with catchable rainbow and brown trout. Motorized boats are not allowed. A self-guided interpretive trail connects to the Pacific Crest National Scenic Trail at the top of the ridge. Elevation 6,500 feet. Stay limit 14 days. Open June through October.

## 151 Panther Meadows

**Location:** 25 miles northwest of McCloud

**GPS:** 41.35501402 / -122.2018076

**Sites:** 10 tent-only (short walk from parking lot)

**Facilities:** Tables, fire rings, vault toilet; no drinking water

**Fee per night:** None

**Management:** Mount Shasta Ranger Station, (530) 926-4511

**Activities:** Hiking, wildlife viewing

**Finding the campground:** From I-5 in Mount Shasta, take the Central Mount Shasta exit. Turn east onto Lake Street, which becomes Everett Memorial Highway (CR A10/ North Washington Drive); continue 13.7 miles to the campground entrance.

**About the campground:** This walk-in campground located near timberline is the highest campground on Mount Shasta. It features open vistas and two small, fragile subalpine heather meadows a short distance away. (Please treat meadows with care.) Elevation 7,450 feet. Stay limit 3 days. Open May through October.

## 152 Castle Lake

**Location:** 8 miles southwest of the community of Mount Shasta

**GPS:** 41.2345707 / -122.3773725

**Sites:** 6 sites for tents and RVs up to 16 feet long

**Facilities:** Tables, fire rings, vault toilets; no drinking water

**Fee per night:** None

**Management:** Shasta-Trinity National Forest, (530) 926-4511

**Activities:** Hiking, fishing, swimming

**Finding the campground:** From I-5 in Mount Shasta, take the Central Mount Shasta exit. Turn left at a stop sign, cross back over the highway, and drive 0.4 mile. Turn south at a stop sign onto W A Barr Road (CR 2M020) and drive 7.5 miles.

**About the campground:** Located at the end of the road, the campground sits about 200 feet from the lakeshore. Tents pitch off the road; RVs must camp off the road on the shoulder. A lookout about 0.5 mile back down the road from the campground offers a marvelous view of Mount Shasta. Anglers will find gold shiners and brook and rainbow trout in Castle Lake. Only the west shore of the lake is public; the east is private property. Elevation 5,280 feet. Stay limit 3 days. Open June through October.

*The pristine vista from the end of the road, just a short walk from Castle Lake Campground.*
*Photo by Bubba Seuss*

## 153 Fowlers Camp

**Location:** 6 miles east of McCloud
**GPS:** 41.2454572 / -122.0232698
**Sites:** 39 sites for tents and RVs up to 30 feet long
**Facilities:** Tables, fire rings, drinking water, vault toilets
**Fee per night:** $
**Management:** Shasta-Trinity National Forest, (530) 964-2184
**Activities:** Hiking, swimming, fishing
**Finding the campground:** From McCloud, drive 5 miles east on CA 89. Turn south onto FR 40N44 and drive about 1 mile.
**About the campground:** A popular campground located on the banks of scenic McCloud River. Mediocre fishing for native trout, but the river offers good swimming holes in summer. Three fine waterfalls are accessible on a riverside trail. A 3-mile round-trip will take you to all three. Elevation 2,400 feet. Stay limit 14 days. Open April 15 through October 31.

*Middle McCloud Falls as seen a little ways down the trail from Fowlers Camp Campground. Photo by Bubba Seuss*

# 154 Cattle Camp

**Location:** 10 miles east of McCloud
**GPS:** 41.2597678 / -121.9418552
**Sites:** 27 sites for tents and RVs up to 32 feet long; double sites available
**Facilities:** Tables, fire rings, drinking water, vault toilets
**Fee per night:** $
**Management:** Shasta-Trinity National Forest, (530) 964-2184
**Activities:** Fishing, swimming, hiking
**Finding the campground:** From McCloud, drive 10 miles east on CA 89.
**About the campground:** Situated near the McCloud River. There is a good swimming hole nearby and 12 miles of riverside trail to explore. Elevation 3,700 feet. Stay limit 14 days. Open May through October.

# 155 Algoma

**Location:** 14 miles east of McCloud
**GPS:** 41.25635808 / -121.8830887
**Sites:** 8 sites for tents and RVs up to 24 feet long
**Facilities:** Tables, fire rings, vault toilets; no drinking water
**Fee per night:** None
**Management:** Shasta-Trinity National Forest, (530) 964-2184

**Activities:** Fishing, wading, riparian wildlife viewing
**Finding the campground:** From McCloud, drive east 13 miles on CA 89. Turn south onto FR 39N06 and drive about 1 mile.
**About the campground:** Situated on the McCloud River in an area of fair trout fishing, Algoma offers fairly quiet riverside camping. Elevation 3,800 feet. Stay limit 14 days. Open April through November.

## 156 Gumboot Lake

**Location:** 16 miles southwest of the community of Mount Shasta
**GPS:** 41.21333545 / -122.5094142
**Sites:** 4 sites for tents and RVs up to 10 feet long
**Facilities:** Tables, fire rings, vault toilets; no drinking water
**Fee per night:** None
**Management:** Shasta-Trinity National Forest, (530) 926-4511
**Activities:** Fishing, hiking
**Finding the campground:** From I-5 in Mount Shasta, take exit 738; turn west onto West Lake Street and cross the freeway. Continue onto Hatchery Lane; turn south onto South Old Stage Road. Veer slightly right onto W A Barr Road and drive 9.6 miles. Continue onto FR 40N26 for 4.9 miles.
**About the campground:** Gumboot is a small but very pretty mountain lake with decent fishing for small to midsize rainbow trout. No motorized boats are permitted. A smaller lake lies a short distance to the west. Hikers can drive 2 miles to the Gumboot Trailhead to access the Pacific Crest National Scenic Trail. Enjoy views of Mount Shasta and the Trinity Alps. It is an easy 2.5 miles (one way) south on the Pacific Coast Trail to view and explore the Seven Lakes Basin. Elevation 6,080 feet. Stay limit 14 days. Open June through October.

## 157 Castle Crags State Park

**Location:** 12 miles south of the community of Mount Shasta
**GPS:** 41.1482012 / -122.3210658
**Sites:** 76 sites for tents and RVs up to 27 feet long; 6 environmental sites
**Facilities:** Tables, fire rings, drinking water, showers, flush toilets
**Fee per night:** $$$; reservations (peak season) (800) 444-7275 or reserveamerica.com
**Management:** California Department of Parks and Recreation, (530) 235-2684
**Activities:** Hiking, fishing, swimming
**Finding the campground:** From Mount Shasta, drive south 12 miles on I-5 and take the Castle Crags exit.
**About the campground:** Castle Crags features dramatic granite spires that can be seen from I-5. Campsites are divided between two campgrounds. If you are interested in hiking the trails to the crags, you should use the main campground. If you are interested in swimming, fishing, and hiking along the Sacramento River, use the river campground. A trail connects the two.

There are nearly 30 miles of trails to access in Castle Crag. The Pacific Coast Trail passes through the park as well. A short trail from the end of the access road leads to a great viewpoint with fine views of the crags and Mount Shasta. A 6-mile round-trip trail to the base of the crags also begins here. Trailers and large RVs should not continue on the access road past the campground; it becomes steep, curving, and only one lane wide.

The Indian Creek Interpretive Trail begins at the ranger station and makes a 1-mile loop. From the river campground, a 1.5-mile trail leads upstream along the river, passing fishing spots and swimming holes. Fishing in this section of the river is catch-and-release only. Elevation 2,070 feet. Stay limit 30 days. Open all year.

## 158 Ah-Di-Na

**Location:** 15 miles south of McCloud
**GPS:** 41.1098073 / -122.0988669
**Sites:** 16 sites for tents
**Facilities:** Tables, fire rings, drinking water, flush toilets
**Fee per night:** $
**Management:** Shasta-Trinity National Forest, (530) 964-2184
**Activities:** Fishing, hiking
**Finding the campground:** From McCloud, drive south 11 miles on Squaw Valley Road (FR 11), following the west shore of Lake McCloud. Turn west onto FR 38N53 and drive 4 miles.
**About the campground:** Situated on the scenic banks of the McCloud River. Check fishing regulations, as catch-and-release rules are in effect downstream of the campground. A nature trail follows the river in a nearby Nature Conservancy preserve. Elevation 2,300 feet. Stay limit 14 days. Open April 15 through November 15.

# Shasta-Trinity Area

The core of this area is the Whiskeytown-Shasta-Trinity National Recreation Area—a huge, water-oriented outdoor resource that encompasses three large lakes: Shasta, Trinity, and Whiskeytown. More than three dozen public campgrounds are located throughout the area, most of them on the water. You can enjoy water sports of almost every description, including fishing, waterskiing, and sailing. Boats, canoes, kayaks, sailboards, and personal watercraft are available for rent. Each of the three units composing the recreation area is described separately in the pages that follow.

Much of the northern and western portions of the Shasta-Trinity Area encompass the Shasta-Trinity National Forest—3,453 square miles of public land, the largest national forest in California. It boasts over 6,278 miles of streams and rivers and 365 miles of shoreline. Included is the 525,000-acre Trinity Alps Wilderness, with its granite peaks, fifty-five lakes and streams, and many miles of trails. Camping in the Trinity Alps is dispersed, but you can find established, primitive campsites around most lakeshores.

The Pacific Crest National Scenic Trail traverses the forest in a north–south direction. From it you can get fine views of Mount Shasta, Castle Crags, and the Trinity Alps. The South Fork National Recreation Trail begins at Forest Glen and climbs gradually along the South Fork of the Trinity River to Smokey Creek; the Sisson-Callahan National Recreation Trail traces a historic route from the town of Sisson to the old mining town of Callahan.

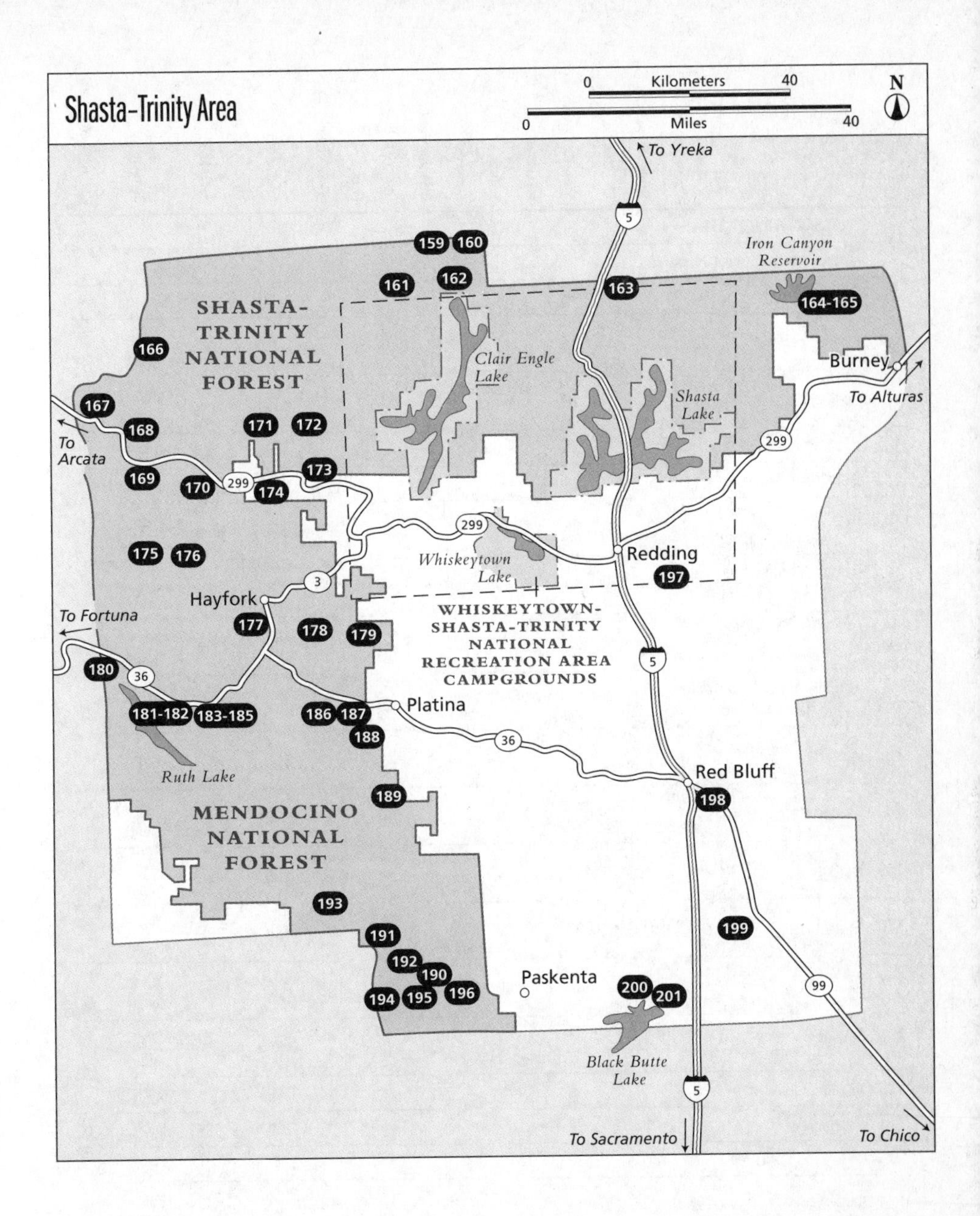


More than 105 miles of Wild and Scenic River have been designated in the forest, many of them along the Trinity. The Trinity Scenic Byway follows the course of the Trinity along CA 299 from the town of Shasta west to Blue Lake. The Trinity Heritage Scenic Byway follows CA 3 along the west bank of Trinity Lake from Weaverville to the town of Mount Shasta, passing through historic towns and mountain landscapes.

| | Name | Group Sites | RV Sites | Max. RV Length | Hookups | Toilets | Showers | Drinking Water | Dump Station | Pets | Wheelchair | Recreation | Fee(s) | Season | Can Reserve |
|---|---|---|---|---|---|---|---|---|---|---|---|---|---|---|---|
| | **SHASTA-TRINITY AREA** | | | | | | | | | | | | | | |
| | **Shasta-Trinity National Forest** | | | | | | | | | | | | | | |
| 159 | Horse Flat | | * | 16 | | V | | | | * | | HR | None | May–Oct | |
| 160 | Eagle Creek | | * | 35 | | V | | * | | * | | F | $ | Year-round | |
| 161 | Goldfield | | * | 16 | | V | | | | * | | H | None | Year-round | |
| 162 | Trinity River | | * | 35 | | V | | * | | * | | F | $ | May–Oct | |
| 163 | Sims Flat | | * | 24 | | FV | | * | | * | * | HFSB | $ | Apr–Nov | |
| 164 | Deadlun (Iron Canyon Reservoir) | | * | 25 | | V | | | | * | | FSB | None | Year-round | |
| 165 | Hawkins Landing (Iron Canyon Reservoir) | | * | 19 | | V | | * | | * | * | FSBL | $ | Apr–Sept | |
| 166 | Denny | | * | 22 | | V | | | | * | | HF | None | Year-round | |
| | **Big Bar Area, Shasta-Trinity National Forest** | | | | | | | | | | | | | | |
| 167 | Burnt Ranch | | * | 25 | | V | | * | | * | * | FSB | $ | Year-round | |
| 168 | Hayden Flat | * | * | 25 | | V | | * | | * | * | FSB | $ | Year-round | |
| 169 | Big Bar | | | | | V | | * | | * | | FSB | None | Year-round | |
| 170 | Big Flat | | * | 22 | | V | | * | | * | | FSB | $ | Year-round | |
| 171 | Hobo Gulch | | | | | V | | | | * | | H | None | Year-round | |
| 172 | Ripstein | | | | | V | | | | * | | H | None | Year-round | |
| 173 | Junction City | | * | 40 | | V | | * | | * | | FSB | $ | May–Nov | |
| 174 | Pigeon Point | * | * | 22 | | V | | | | * | * | FSB | $–$$$$ | May–Oct | |
| | **Hayfork Area** | | | | | | | | | | | | | | |
| 175 | Slide Creek | | | | | V | | | | * | | F | None | Year-round | |
| 176 | Big Slide | | | | | V | | | | * | | FSH | None | Year-round | |
| 177 | Philpot | | * | | | V | | | | * | | H | None | Year-round | |

| | Name | Group Sites | RV Sites | Max. RV Length | Hookups | Toilets | Showers | Drinking Water | Dump Station | Pets | Wheelchair | Recreation | Fee(s) | Season | Can Reserve |
|---|---|---|---|---|---|---|---|---|---|---|---|---|---|---|---|
| 178 | Shiell Gulch | | | | | V | | | | * | | H | None | Year-round | |
| 179 | Deer Lick Springs (Yolla Bolla Area) | | | | | V | | | | * | | HFS | None | Year-round | |
| | **Mad River/Ruth Lake Area** | | | | | | | | | | | | | | |
| 180 | Mad River | | * | 22 | | V | | * | | * | * | F | $ | May-Sept | * |
| 181 | Fir Cove (at Ruth Lake) | | * | 22 | | V | | * | | * | * | FSBHO | $ | Memorial Day-Sept | * |
| 182 | Bailey Canyon (at Ruth Lake) | | * | 22 | | V | | * | | * | * | FSB | $ | Memorial Day-Sept | |
| 183 | Hells Gate | | * | 16 | | V | | * | | * | | FSBH | $ | Year-round | |
| 184 | Scotts Flat | | * | 20 | | V | | | | * | | FSBH | None | Year-round | |
| 185 | Forest Glen | | * | 15 | | V | | * | | * | | FH | $ | Year-round | |
| | **Yolla Bolla Area** | | | | | | | | | | | | | | |
| 186 | White Rock | | | | | | | | | * | | | None | Year-round | |
| 187 | Basin Gulch | | * | 20 | | V | | | | * | | | None | Year-round | |
| 188 | Beegum Gorge | | | | | V | | | | * | | H | None | Year-round | |
| 189 | Tomhead Saddle | | | | | V | | | | * | | HR | None | Year-round | |
| 190 | Sugarfoot Glade | | * | 16 | | V | | | | * | | H | None | Jun-Nov | |
| 191 | Green Springs (Yolla Bolly-Eel River Wilderness) | | * | | | V | | | | * | | HR | None | Jun-Nov | |
| 192 | Three Prong | | * | 16 | | V | | | | * | | H | None | Jun-Nov | |
| 193 | Rock Cabin Trailhead (Yolla Bolly-Eel River Wilderness) | | * | | | | | | | * | | H | None | Year-round | |
| 194 | Wells Cabin | | | | | V | | | | * | | H | None | Jun-Nov | |
| 195 | Kingsley Glade | | * | | | V | | | | * | | HR | None | May-Nov | |
| 196 | Whitlock | | * | 16 | | V | | | | * | | H | None | May-Nov | |
| 197 | Reading Island, Sacramento River Area | * | | | | V | | * | | * | * | FB | $$$$ | Year-round | * |

| | Name | Group Sites | RV Sites | Max. RV Length | Hookups | Toilets | Showers | Drinking Water | Dump Station | Pets | Wheelchair | Recreation | Fee(s) | Season | Can Reserve |
|---|---|---|---|---|---|---|---|---|---|---|---|---|---|---|---|
| | **Mendocino National Forest / Red Bluff Area** | | | | | | | | | | | | | | |
| 198 | Sycamore Cove (Lake Red Bluff) | * | * | 40 | E | FV | * | * | | * | * | FSB | $-$$$ | Mar-Nov | * |
| 199 | Woodson Bridge State Recreation Area | | * | 31 | | F | * | * | * | * | * | FSBH | $$$ | Year-round | * |
| 200 | Buckhorn (Black Butte Lake) | * | * | 45 | | F | * | * | * | * | * | FSBH | $$-$$$$ | Year-round | * |
| 201 | Orland Buttes (Black Butte Lake) | * | * | 45 | | F | * | * | * | * | * | FSBHRL | $-$$$$ | Apr-Sept | * |

Toilets: F=flush V=vault P=pit C=chemical; Fee: $=Under $20 $$=$20-$29 $$$=$30-$39 $$$$ $40 or more; Recreation: H=hiking S=swimming F=fishing B=boating L=boat launch O=off-highway driving R=horseback riding, M=mountain biking
Hookups: W=water E=electric S=sewer

# Shasta-Trinity National Forest

## 159 Horse Flat

**Location:** 47 miles northeast of Weaverville
**GPS:** 41.16651618 / -122.6910963
**Sites:** 10 sites for tents and RVs up to 16 feet long
**Facilities:** Tables, fire rings, vault toilets, hitching rails; no drinking water
**Fee per night:** None
**Management:** Shasta-Trinity National Forest, (530) 623-2121
**Activities:** Hiking, horseback riding
**Finding the campground:** From Weaverville (about 40 miles west of Redding on CA 299), drive 45 miles northeast on CA 3. Turn northwest onto Eagle Creek Loop (FR 36N27) and drive 2 miles.
**About the campground:** The Eagle Creek Trail begins at the campground, providing access to the northern part of the Trinity Alps Wilderness for day hikers, backpackers, and equestrians. Elevation 3,200 feet. Stay limit 14 days. Open mid-May through October.

## 160 Eagle Creek

**Location:** 45 miles northeast of Weaverville
**GPS:** 41.15290955 / -122.6684578
**Sites:** 17 sites for tents and RVs up to 35 feet long
**Facilities:** Tables, fire rings, drinking water, vault toilets
**Fee per night:** $
**Management:** Shasta Recreation Company, (530) 623-2121
**Activities:** Fishing

**Finding the campground:** From Weaverville (about 40 miles west of Redding on CA 299), drive 45 miles northeast on CA 3.

**About the campground:** Situated at the confluence of Eagle Creek and the upper Trinity River, with fair fishing for small trout. Elevation 2,800 feet. Stay limit 14 days. Open all year.

## 161 Goldfield

**Location:** 44 miles northeast of Weaverville
**GPS:** 41.10000775 / -122.7786336
**Sites:** 6 sites for tents and RVs up to 16 feet long
**Facilities:** Tables, fire rings, vault toilets; no drinking water
**Fee per night:** None
**Management:** Shasta-Trinity National Forest, (530) 623-2121
**Activities:** Hiking
**Finding the campground:** From Weaverville, take CA 3 north for 36.6 miles. Turn west onto Coffee Creek Road and drive 4.7 miles. Turn southwest onto the bridge over Coffee Creek (SRV 37N19Y) to the campground.
**About the campground:** The Boulder Creek Trail begins a short distance west of the campground and leads to a series of small lakes in the Trinity Alps Wilderness. Elevation 3,000 feet. Stay limit 14 days. Open all year.

## 162 Trinity River

**Location:** 40 miles northeast of Weaverville
**GPS:** 41.10877789 / -122.7046158
**Sites:** 7 sites for tents and RVs up to 35 feet long
**Facilities:** Tables, fire rings, drinking water, vault toilets
**Fee per night:** $
**Management:** Shasta Recreation Company, (530) 623-2121
**Activities:** Fishing
**Finding the campground:** From Weaverville (about 40 miles west of Redding on CA 299), drive 40 miles northeast on CA 3.
**About the campground:** Situated on the upper Trinity River, this popular campground offers fair fishing for small trout. Elevation 2,500 feet. Stay limit 14 days. Open mid-May through October.

## 163 Sims Flat

**Location:** 21 miles south of the community of Mount Shasta
**GPS:** 41.0609842 / -122.3597335
**Sites:** 19 sites for tents and RVs up to 24 feet long
**Facilities:** Tables, fire rings, drinking water, flush and vault toilets
**Fee per night:** $
**Management:** Shasta-Trinity National Forest, (530) 926-4511
**Activities:** Hiking, fishing, swimming, kayaking, canoeing
**Finding the campground:** From the community of Mount Shasta, drive south 20 miles on I-5. Take the Sims Road exit and drive east about 1 mile on an unmarked road.

**About the campground:** Situated on the banks of the Sacramento River, with good access to it. The river is stocked annually with rainbow trout, including some trophy-size fish. A trail leads east from the campground to the summit of Tombstone Mountain (5,613 feet). It was a Civilian Conservation Corps camp in the 1930s. Union Pacific freight trains make their way through the canyon nearby. Elevation 3,600 feet. Stay limit 14 days. Open April 15 through November 15.

## 164 Deadlun (Iron Canyon Reservoir)

**Location:** 57 miles northeast of Redding
**GPS:** 41.044877 / -121.9843957
**Sites:** 25 sites for tents and RVs up to 24 feet long
**Facilities:** Tables, fire rings, vault toilets; no drinking water
**Fee per night:** None
**Management:** Shasta-Trinity National Forest, (530) 275-1587
**Activities:** Fishing, swimming, boating
**Finding the campground:** From I-5, take CA 299 East 35 miles to Big Bend Road (CR 7M01). On Big Bend Road, drive 17 miles to the town of Big Bend then 5.5 miles to Iron Canyon Reservoir.
**About the campground:** Iron Canyon Reservoir is a lovely 500-acre lake, popular with anglers, hunters and four-wheel-drive enthusiasts. A road around the forested shoreline makes it highly accessible. A boat ramp is located 1 mile south at Hawkins Landing. Elevation 2,750 feet. Stay limit 14 days. Open all year.

## 165 Hawkins Landing (Iron Canyon Reservoir)

**Location:** 56 miles northeast of Redding
**GPS:** 41.051824 / -121.9727761
**Sites:** 10 sites for tents and RVs up to 19 feet long
**Facilities:** Tables, fire rings, drinking water, vault toilets, boat ramp
**Fee per night:** $
**Management:** PG&E, (530) 686-5164
**Activities:** Fishing, swimming, boating
**Finding the campground:** From I-5, take CA 299 East 35 miles to Big Bend Road (CR 7M01). On Big Bend Road, drive 17 miles to the town of Big Bend then 5.5 miles to Iron Canyon Reservoir. At the spillway, turn north onto Iron Canyon Road (lake to the west) for 1.1 miles. Turn south onto a dirt road.
**About the campground:** Powerboats, rowboats, canoes, sailboats, and inflatable boats are allowed on the water. The lake is stocked with rainbow and brook trout. The town of Big Bend is 6 miles southeast. Elevation 2,700 feet. Stay limit 14 days. Open mid-April through mid-September.

## 166 Denny

**Location:** 52 miles northwest of Weaverville
**GPS:** 40.93310237 / -123.3932757
**Sites:** 5 sites for tents and RVs up to 22 feet long
**Facilities:** Tables, fire rings, vault toilets; no drinking water
**Fee per night:** None

**Management:** Shasta-Trinity National Forest, (530) 623-2121
**Activities:** Hiking, fishing
**Finding the campground:** From Weaverville, drive west on CA 299 for 39 miles. Turn north onto CR 402 and drive 13 miles.
**About the campground:** Denny is situated on the New River, a designated Wild and Scenic River like the Trinity, which it flows into. Fishing is fair for small trout. The New River Trail, which leads into the Trinity Alps Wilderness, begins 6 miles north of the campground. Elevation 1,400 feet. Stay limit 14 days. Open all year.

# Big Bar Area, Shasta-Trinity National Forest

## 167 Burnt Ranch

**Location:** 38 miles west of Weaverville
**GPS:** 40.8425381 / -123.4870056
**Sites:** 16 sites for tents and RVs up to 25 feet long
**Facilities:** Tables, fire rings, drinking water, vault toilets
**Fee per night:** $
**Management:** Shasta-Trinity National Forest, (530) 623-2121
**Activities:** Fishing, swimming, paddling
**Finding the campground:** From Weaverville, drive west on CA 299 for 38 miles.
**About the campground:** Burnt Ranch is situated on a bluff above the Wild and Scenic Trinity River. Experienced rafters and kayakers will enjoy this stretch of the river; fishing is good for salmon in summer and steelhead in late fall. Elevation 1,000 feet. Stay limit 14 days. Open all year.

## 168 Hayden Flat

**Location:** 29 miles west of Weaverville
**GPS:** 40.82799522 / -123.4823004
**Sites:** 35 sites for tents and RVs up to 25 feet long
**Facilities:** Tables, fire rings, drinking water, vault toilets
**Fee per night:** $
**Management:** Shasta-Trinity National Forest, (530) 623-6106
**Activities:** Fishing, swimming, paddling
**Finding the campground:** From Weaverville, drive west on CA 299 for 29 miles.
**About the campground:** Hayden Flat is divided in two sections, with some sites along the Trinity River and some across CA 299 in a small grove of trees. The Trinity is a Wild and Scenic River, and experienced rafters and kayakers will enjoy this stretch. Fishing is good for salmon in summer and steelhead in late fall. Campers here have easy access to the river, including a swimming beach. Elevation 1,200 feet. Stay limit 14 days. Open all year.

## 169 Big Bar

**Location:** 22 miles west of Weaverville
**GPS:** 40.737 / -123.253

**Sites:** 3 sites for tents
**Facilities:** Tables, fire rings, drinking water, vault toilets
**Fee per night:** None
**Management:** Shasta-Trinity National Forest, (530) 226-2500
**Activities:** Fishing, swimming, paddling
**Finding the campground:** From Weaverville, drive west on CA 299 for 22 miles.
**About the campground:** Big Bar offers easy access to the Trinity River, a designated Wild and Scenic River. Experienced rafters and kayakers will enjoy this stretch, and fishing is good for salmon in summer and steelhead in late fall. For group camping on the Trinity, try Skunk Point Group Camp. Elevation 1,200 feet. Stay limit 14 days. Open all year.

## 170 Big Flat

**Location:** 19 miles west of Weaverville
**GPS:** 40.7392 / -123.2046
**Sites:** 10 sites for tents and RVs up to 22 feet long
**Facilities:** Tables, fire rings, drinking water, vault toilets
**Fee per night:** $
**Management:** Shasta-Trinity National Forest, (530) 623-2121
**Activities:** Fishing, swimming, paddling.
**Finding the campground:** From Weaverville, drive west on CA 299 for 19 miles.
**About the campground:** Big Flat is on the Trinity River. Elevation 1,300 feet. Stay limit 14 days. Open all year.

## 171 Hobo Gulch

**Location:** 29 miles northwest of Weaverville
**GPS:** 40.92895966 / -123.1533285
**Sites:** 10 sites for tents
**Facilities:** Tables, fire rings, vault toilets; no drinking water
**Fee per night:** None
**Management:** Shasta-Trinity National Forest, (530) 623-2121
**Activities:** Hiking
**Finding the campground:** From Weaverville, drive west on CA 299 for 14 miles. Turn north at Helena onto CR 421 and drive 15 miles.
**About the campground:** Surrounded on three sides by the Trinity Alps Wilderness, the campground serves primarily as a base for hiking and backpacking trips. Trails lead north from the campground toward the Salmon Mountains. Elevation 3,000 feet. Stay limit 14 days. Open all year.

## 172 Ripstein

**Location:** 21 miles northwest of Weaverville
**Sites:** 10 sites for tents.
**GPS:** 40.87615103 / -123.0281703
**Facilities:** Tables, fire rings, vault toilets; no drinking water
**Fee per night:** None

*The view a couple miles down the Canyon Creek Trail from Ripstein campground. Deeper into the canyon you'll find big granite expanses and waterfalls. Photo by Bubba Seuss*

**Management:** Shasta-Trinity National Forest, (530) 623-2121
**Activities:** Hiking
**Finding the campground:** From Weaverville, drive west on CA 299 for 8 miles. At Junction City turn north onto CR 401 (Canyon Creek Road) and drive 13 miles.
**About the campground:** Used primarily as a base for day hikes and backpack trips into the Trinity Alps Wilderness, this campground is 0.5 mile south of the Canyon Creek Trailhead. Trails lead to Little Granite Peak, Sawtooth Mountain, and the Canyon Creek Lakes. Elevation 2,600 feet. Stay limit 14 days. Open all year.

## 173 Junction City

**Location:** 10 miles west of Weaverville
**GPS:** 40.7462665 / -123.0639016
**Sites:** 22 sites for tents and RVs up to 40 feet
**Facilities:** Tables, fire rings, drinking water, vault toilets
**Fee per night:** $
**Management:** Bureau of Land Management, (530) 224-2100
**Activities:** Fishing, swimming, paddling
**Finding the campground:** From Weaverville, drive west on CA 299 for 10 miles.
**About the campground:** Situated on the banks of the Trinity River amid ponderosa pine and madrone. On a good stretch for fishing and challenging whitewater rafting. Elevation 1,500 feet. Stay limit 14 days. Open May through November.

## 174 Pigeon Point

**Location:** 14 miles west of Weaverville
**GPS:** 40.76705358 / -123.1302704
**Sites:** 7 sites for tents and RVs up to 22 feet long; 1 group site
**Facilities:** Tables, fire rings, vault toilets, beach; no drinking water; wheelchair accessible
**Fee per night:** $, group site: $$$$
**Management:** Shasta-Trinity National Forest, (530) 623-2121
**Activities:** Fishing, swimming, paddling
**Finding the campground:** From Weaverville, drive west on CA 299 for 14 miles.
**About the campground:** Pigeon Point is on the Trinity River, and there is a nice beach; however, the campground itself is across the highway from the river. Elevation 1,100 feet. Stay limit 14 days. Open May through October.

# Hayfork Area

## 175 Slide Creek

**Location:** 25 miles northwest of Hayfork
**GPS:** 40.6686 / -123.5035
**Sites:** 5 sites for tents
**Facilities:** Tables, fire rings, vault toilets; no drinking water
**Fee per night:** None
**Management:** Shasta-Trinity National Forest, (530) 628-5227
**Activities:** Fishing
**Finding the campground:** From the intersection of CA 3 and CR 301 in Hayfork (70 miles west of Redding on CA 3), drive about 19 miles northwest on CR 301 to Hyampom. Turn onto CR 311 and drive 5.5 miles.
**About the campground:** Situated on the South Fork of the Trinity River. Elevation 1,250 feet. Stay limit 14 days. Open all year.

## 176 Big Slide

**Location:** 24 miles northwest of Hayfork
**GPS:** 40.66458438 / -123.4974892
**Sites:** 8 sites for tents
**Facilities:** Tables, fire rings, vault toilets; no drinking water
**Fee per night:** None
**Management:** Shasta-Trinity National Forest, (530) 628-5227
**Activities:** Fishing, swimming, hiking
**Finding the campground:** From the intersection of CA 3 and CR 301 in Hayfork (70 miles west of Redding on CA 3), drive about 19 miles northwest on CR 301 to Hyampom. Turn right onto CR 311 and drive 5 miles.

**About the campground:** Situated on the South Fork of the Trinity River; campsites are on the beach. Elevation 1,250 feet. Stay limit 14 days. Open all year.

## 177 Philpot

**Location:** 8 miles south of Hayfork
**GPS:** 40.46596576 / -123.190829
**Sites:** 6 sites for tents and RVs
**Facilities:** Tables, fire rings, vault toilets; no drinking water
**Fee per night:** None
**Management:** Shasta-Trinity National Forest, (530) 628-5227
**Activities:** Hiking
**Finding the campground:** From the intersection of CA 3 and CR 301 in Hayfork (70 miles west of Redding on CA 3), drive 6 miles south on CA 3. Turn west onto the road to Plummer Peak Lookout (initially CR 353) and drive 1.5 miles.
**About the campground:** Situated near a small stream; the road is unpaved to the campsites. You can access the 1.5-mile Philpot Interpretive Trail and have a chance to see some wildlife. Elevation 2,600 feet. Stay limit 14 days. Open all year.

## 178 Shiell Gulch

**Location:** 12 miles southeast of Hayfork
**GPS:** 40.47047737 / -123.0596271
**Sites:** 5 sites for tents
**Facilities:** Tables, fire rings, vault toilets; no drinking water
**Fee per night:** None
**Management:** Shasta-Trinity National Forest, (530) 628-5227
**Activities:** Hiking, wading
**Finding the campground:** From the intersection of CA 3 and CR 301 in Hayfork (70 miles west of Redding on CA 3), drive 5 miles east on CA 3. Turn right (south) onto CR 302 and drive about 7 miles.
**About the campground:** Situated on the banks of Hayfork Creek, the campground offers access to the rugged terrain of the Chanchelulla Wilderness. Elevation 2,600 feet. Stay limit 14 days. Open all year.

## 179 Deer Lick Springs (Yolla Bolla Area)

**Location:** 37 miles southeast of Hayfork
**GPS:** 40.47026159 / -122.9255841
**Sites:** 13 sites for tents
**Facilities:** Tables, fire rings, vault toilets; no drinking water
**Fee per night:** None
**Management:** Shasta-Trinity National Forest, Yolla Bolla Ranger Station, (530) 352-4211
**Activities:** Hiking, fishing, swimming, mineral baths (fee)

**Finding the campground:** From the intersection of CA 3 and CR 301 in Hayfork (70 miles west of Redding on CA 3), drive south 11 miles on CA 3. Turn east onto CA 36 and continue about 16 miles. Turn north onto Harrison Gulch Road and drive about 10 miles.
**About the campground:** Situated on Browns Creek adjacent to Deerlick Springs Resort. Guests flocked here by the hundreds in the 1890s for the cure-all mineral baths. Under renovation during this writing, it will reopen in spring 2016. Trails lead in several directions from the campground, including to Sugarloaf Peak (3 miles). Elevation 3,100 feet. Stay limit 14 days. Open all year.

# Mad River/Ruth Lake Area

## 180 Mad River

**Location:** 39 miles southwest of Hayfork
**GPS:** 40.401649 / -123.465815
**Sites:** 40 sites for tents and RVs up to 22 feet long
**Facilities:** Tables, fire rings, drinking water, vault toilets
**Fee per night:** $; reservations: (877) 444-6777 or recreation.gov
**Management:** Six Rivers National Forest, (707) 442-1721
**Activities:** Fishing
**Finding the campground:** From the intersection of CA 3 and CR 301 in Hayfork (70 miles west of Redding on CA 3), drive south 11 miles on CA 3. Turn west onto CA 36 and drive 23 miles. Turn southwest onto Lower Mad River Road and drive 5 miles.
**About the campground:** Situated on a bluff overlooking the Mad River, which hosts a variety of trout for anglers. Ruth Lake, 3 miles south, also provides fishing as well as boating and swimming. Elevation 2,600 feet. Stay limit 14 days. Open mid-May to mid-September.

## 181 Fir Cove (at Ruth Lake)

**Location:** 45 miles southwest of Hayfork
**GPS:** 40.34417 / -123.40306
**Sites:** 19 sites for tents and RVs up to 22 feet long
**Facilities:** Tables, fire rings, drinking water, vault toilets
**Fee per night:** $; reservations: (877) 444-6777 or recreation.gov
**Management:** Six Rivers National Forest, (707) 574-6233
**Activities:** Fishing, swimming, boating, waterskiing, hiking, hunting, OHV driving
**Finding the campground:** From the intersection of CA Highway 3 and CR 301 in Hayfork (70 miles west of Redding on CA 3), drive south 11 miles on CA 3. Turn west onto CA 36 and drive 23 miles. Turn southwest onto Lower Mad River Road and drive 11 miles.
**About the campground:** Fir Cove is on the eastern shore of 13,800-acre Ruth Lake, situated in a thick forest on a seasonal creek. Many sites overlook the lake, which is a short walk away. It contains small- and largemouth bass, catfish, rainbow trout, kokanee salmon, bluegill, and crappie. Elevation 2,800 feet. Stay limit 14 days. Open Memorial Day through September.

## 182 Bailey Canyon (at Ruth Lake)

**Location:** 45 miles southwest of Hayfork
**GPS:** 40.3404231 / -123.3997506
**Sites:** 25 sites for tents and RVs up to 22 feet long
**Facilities:** Tables, fire rings, drinking water, vault toilets
**Fee per night:** $
**Management:** Six Rivers National Forest, (707) 574-6233
**Activities:** Fishing, swimming, boating, waterskiing
**Finding the campground:** From the intersection of CA 3 and CR 301 in Hayfork (70 miles west of Redding on CA 3), drive south 11 miles on CA 3. Turn west onto CA 36 and drive 23 miles. Turn southwest onto Lower Mad River Road and drive a little over 11 miles.
**About the campground:** The campground is just east of Fir Cove Campground on Ruth Lake; no reservation is required. Elevation 2,780 feet. Stay limit 14 days. Open Memorial Day through Mid-September.

## 183 Hells Gate

**Location:** 19 miles southwest of Hayfork
**GPS:** 40.3706906 / -123.313568
**Sites:** 17 sites for tents and RVs up to 16 feet long
**Facilities:** Tables, fire rings, drinking water, vault toilets
**Fee per night:** $
**Management:** Shasta-Trinity National Forest, (530) 628-5227
**Activities:** Fishing, swimming, hiking, paddling, birding
**Finding the campground:** From the intersection of CA 3 and CR 301 in Hayfork (70 miles west of Redding on CA 3), drive south 11 miles on CA 3. Turn west onto CA 36 and drive 8 miles.
**About the campground:** Situated in an attractive location on the South Fork of the Trinity River, Hells Gate offers a beach and easy river access. The South Fork National Recreation Trail begins at the campground. Elevation 2,300 feet. Stay limit 14 days. Open all year.

## 184 Scotts Flat

**Location:** 20 miles southwest of Hayfork
**GPS:** 40.36607156 / -123.3091884
**Sites:** 10 sites for tents and RVs up to 20 feet long
**Facilities:** Tables, fire rings, vault toilets; no drinking water
**Fee per night:** None
**Management:** Shasta-Trinity National Forest, (530) 628-5227
**Activities:** Fishing, swimming, hiking, paddling
**Finding the campground:** From the intersection of CA 3 and CR 301 in Hayfork (70 miles west of Redding on CA 3), drive south 11 miles on CA 3. Turn west onto CA 36 and drive 8.5 miles.
**About the campground:** On the South Fork of the Trinity River, with some good swimming holes, fishing, and hiking. Elevation 2,450 feet. Stay limit 14 days. Open all year.

## 185 Forest Glen

**Location:** 20 miles southwest of Hayfork
**GPS:** 40.3762564 / -123.3275276
**Sites:** 15 sites for tents and RVs up to 15 feet long
**Facilities:** Tables, fire rings, drinking water, vault toilets; wheelchair accessible
**Fee per night:** $
**Management:** Shasta-Trinity National Forest, (530) 628-5227
**Activities:** Fishing, hiking
**Finding the campground:** From the intersection of CA 3 and CR 301 in Hayfork (70 miles west of Redding on CA 3), drive south 11 miles on CA 3. Turn west onto CA 36 and drive 9 miles.
**About the campground:** Situated near the emerald waters of the South Fork of the Trinity River, with swimming holes, whitewater rafting, and fishing for trout and salmon. Elevation 2,300 feet. Stay limit 14 days. Open all year.

# Yolla Bolla Area

## 186 White Rock

**Location:** 33 miles south of Hayfork
**GPS:** 40.25318848 / -123.0228627
**Sites:** 3 sites for tents
**Facilities:** Tables, fire rings; no toilets; no drinking water
**Fee per night:** None.
**Management:** Shasta-Trinity National Forest, (530) 352-4211
**Activities:** None
**Finding the campground:** From the intersection of CA 3 and CR 301 in Hayfork (70 miles west of Redding on CA 3), drive south 11 miles on CA 3. Turn east onto CA 36 and continue about 7 miles. Turn south onto FR 30 (Wild Mad Road) and drive 8.8 miles. Turn east onto Little Black Rock Road, continuing straight on Little Black Rock Road for about 5 miles. Turn south at Junction Road (FR 28N19); turn north to stay on FR 28N19 approximately 0.1 mile.
**About the campground:** It's a long, winding drive to this primitive and isolated site. Elevation 4,800 feet. Stay limit 14 days. Open all year.

## 187 Basin Gulch

**Location:** 29 miles southeast of Hayfork
**GPS:** 40.35207599 / -122.958743
**Sites:** 13 sites for tents and RVs up to 20 feet long
**Facilities:** Tables, fire rings, vault toilets; no drinking water
**Fee per night:** None
**Management:** Shasta-Trinity National Forest, (530) 352-4211
**Activities:** None

**Finding the campground:** From the intersection of CA 3 and CR 301 in Hayfork (70 miles west of Redding on CA 3), drive south 11 miles on CA 3. Turn east onto CA 36 and proceed about 17 miles to Yolla Bolla Ranger Station. Turn right onto FR 28N10 and drive 1 mile.
**About the campground:** Situated near a small creek with sparse vegetation, this rarely used campground may appeal to those seeking solitude. Elevation 2,700 feet. Stay limit 14 days. Open all year.

## 188 Beegum Gorge

**Location:** 37 miles southeast of Hayfork
**GPS:** 40.31378305 / -122.9333562
**Sites:** 2 sites for tents
**Facilities:** Tables, fire rings, vault toilets; no drinking water
**Fee per night:** None
**Management:** Shasta-Trinity National Forest, (530) 352-4211
**Activities:** Hiking
**Finding the campground:** From the intersection of CA 3 and CR 301 in Hayfork (70 miles west of Redding on CA 3), drive south 11 miles on CA 3. Turn east onto CA 36 and continue about 21 miles to Platina. Turn right onto FR 29N06 and drive 5 miles. The road is not recommended for trailers.
**About the campground:** Situated in dry country with sparse vegetation, Beegum Gorge has little to make the long trip there worthwhile. A trail leads west from the campground along Beegum Creek. Elevation 2,200 feet. Stay limit 14 days. Open all year.

## 189 Tomhead Saddle

**Location:** 36 miles west of Red Bluff
**GPS:** 40.14053414 / -122.8291488
**Sites:** 5 sites for tents
**Facilities:** Tables, fire rings, vault toilets, corral; no drinking water
**Fee per night:** None
**Management:** Shasta-Trinity National Forest, (530) 352-4211
**Activities:** Hiking, horseback riding
**Finding the campground:** From the intersection of I-5 and CA 36 in Red Bluff, drive west 13 miles on CA 36. Turn left onto Cannon Road and go approximately 23.5 miles on this gravel road (the name will change to Pettijohn Road); stay on this road to the National Forest Boundary sign. Continue another 1.6 miles to FR 27N06; turn left and travel about 1 mile to the campground.
**About the campground:** This campground will mainly interest equestrians and hikers. Trails extend west from the campground into the Yolla Bolly–Middle Eel Wilderness; several loop back to camp. The area is dry and sparsely vegetated and better suited to horses than hikers. Elevation 5,600 feet. Stay limit 14 days. Open all year.

## 190 Sugarfoot Glade

**Location:** Located 50 miles east of Covelo
**GPS:** 39.885038 / -122.777093
**Sites:** 6 sites for tents and RVs up to 16 feet long
**Facilities:** Picnic tables, vault toilet; no drinking water

**Fee per night:** None
**Management:** Mendocino National Forest, (530) 934-3316
**Activities:** Hiking, seasonal creek walks
**Finding the campground:** From Red Bluff, take I-5 south to Corning; go west on Corning Road. Continue on Paskenta Road past Flournoy to Paskenta; past Paskenta, continue on Toomes Camp Road. Continue south onto FR M2 (FR 23N01). Continue south onto FR 24N0. The entrance is on the north side of the road.
**About the campground:** A small creek flows through camp early in the season (dry in late season). The camp is situated amid oaks and ponderosa pines. Elevation 4,200 feet. Stay limit 14 days. Open June through November.

## 191 Green Springs (Yolla Bolly–Eel River Wilderness)

**Location:** 40 miles northeast of Covelo
**GPS:** 39.972375 / -122.9338967
**Sites:** 4 sites for tents and RVs
**Facilities:** Fire rings, corrals, vault toilet; no drinking water
**Fee per night:** None
**Management:** Mendocino National Forest, (530) 934-3316
**Activities:** Hiking, horseback riding
**Finding the campground:** From Covelo, take CA 162 East; it will become Mendocino Pass Road. Turn northeast onto CR M1 (Indian Dick Road). It will become FR 1N02 for about 2 miles, then FR 24N06 for 7 miles. Turn north onto FR 24N02 (Pacific Crest Road), then make a sharp left onto FR M2 to the campground.
**About the campground:** The campground provides trailhead access to the Yolla Bolly–Eel River Wilderness for hikers and equestrians. Elevation 6,000 feet. Stay limit 14 days. Open June through November.

## 192 Three Prong

**Location:** 25 miles west of Paskenta
**GPS:** 39.920478 / -122.792384
**Sites:** 6 sites for tents and RVs up to 16 feet long
**Facilities:** Tables, fire rings, vault toilet; no drinking water
**Fee per night:** None
**Management:** Mendocino National Forest, (530) 824-5196
**Activities:** Hiking
**Finding the campground:** From Paskenta, drive west on FR 23N01 (also signed FR M2); turn left onto FR 24N13 and continue to the campground. The route is well marked.
**About the campground:** Situated in a grove of fir and pine trees along the edge of a large meadow. Elevation 5,800 feet. Stay limit 14 days. Open June through November.

## 193 Rock Cabin Trailhead (Yolla Bolly–Eel River Wilderness)

**Location:** 27 miles northwest of Paskenta
**GPS:** 40.008005 / -123.085134

**Sites:** 3 sites for tents and RVs
**Facilities:** Tables, fire rings, grills; no drinking water
**Fee per night:** None
**Management:** Mendocino National Forest, (530) 934-3316
**Activities:** Hiking
**Finding the campground:** From Paskenta, drive west for 27 miles on FR M2. A campground sign will be on the right.
**About the campground:** A long, winding dirt road leads to the isolated campground. Access to the Rocky Cabin Trail and remote wilderness of the Eel River. Elevation 5,000 feet. Stay limit 14 days. Open all year.

## 194 Wells Cabin

**Location:** 33 miles west of Paskenta
**GPS:** 39.836520 / -122.949034
**Sites:** 25 sites for tents
**Facilities:** Tables, fire rings, stoves, vault toilets; no drinking water
**Fee per night:** None
**Management:** Mendocino National Forest, (530) 934-3316
**Activities:** Hiking
**Finding the campground:** From Paskenta, drive west for about 30 miles on FR 23N02. Turn north onto FR 23N69 and drive about 3 miles.
**About the campground:** Situated in a red fir forest, with beautiful high-elevation scenery. Nearby Anthony Peak Lookout provides excellent views all the way to the Pacific Ocean on a clear day. Elevation 6,300 feet. Stay limit 14 days. Open June to November.

## 195 Kingsley Glade

**Location:** 22 miles west of Paskenta
**GPS:** 39.903396 / -122.767371
**Sites:** 6 sites for tents and RVs
**Facilities:** Tables, fire rings, vault toilets; no drinking water
**Fee per night:** None
**Management:** Mendocino National Forest, (530) 934-3316
**Activities:** Hiking, horseback riding
**Finding the campground:** From Paskenta, drive west on FR 23N01 (also signed FR M2). Turn left onto FR 24N01 and continue to the campground. The route is well marked.
**About the campground:** Situated in forest at the edge of a meadow, with riding and hiking trails leading from camp. Thomes Creek, located about 5 road miles from the camp, is a popular fishing and swimming spot. Elevation 4,500 feet. Stay limit 14 days. Open May to November.

## 196 Whitlock

**Location:** 55 miles southwest of Red Bluff
**GPS:** 39.919896 / -122.686533
**Sites:** 3 sites for tents and RVs up to 16 feet long

**Facilities:** Tables, fire rings, grill, vault toilet; no drinking water
**Fee per night:** None
**Management:** Mendocino National Forest, (530) 934-3316
**Activities:** Hiking
**Finding the campground:** From the intersection of CA Highway 36 and I-5 in Red Bluff, drive 18 miles south on I-5. Take the Corning exit and drive west on Corning Road for 21 miles to Paskenta. Drive west on FR 23N01 (also signed FR M2) for about 15 miles; turn right onto FR 24N41 and drive about 1 mile.
**About the campground:** A small, quiet campground in a grove of large oaks and ponderosa pines. Elevation 4,300 feet. Stay limit 14 days. Open May to November.

## 197 Reading Island, Sacramento River Area

**Location:** 21 miles south of Reading
**GPS:** 40.3907418 / -122.194851
**Sites:** 1 group site for up to 20 people
**Facilities:** Tables, fire rings, drinking water, vault toilets; boat ramp nearby
**Fee per night:** $$$$; reservations: (530) 224-2100
**Management:** Bureau of Land Management, (530) 224-2100
**Activities:** Fishing, boating, birding
**Finding the campground:** From the intersection of CA 44 and I-5 in Redding, drive south 16 miles on I-5. Turn east onto Balls Ferry Road and drive 5 miles.
**About the campground:** Though a group site and not a family site, this campground has its own entry because there are little other opportunities to camp in this area except for boat-in campgrounds. Situated on the banks of the Sacramento River, with fishing for trout, salmon, steelhead, and bass. This Class I and II section is popular for rafts, kayaks, and canoes. Swimming is not recommended. Elevation 360 feet. Stay limit 14 days. Open all year.

# Mendocino National Forest / Red Bluff Area

## 198 Sycamore Cove (Lake Red Bluff)

**Location:** 3 miles southeast of Red Bluff
**GPS:** 40.155136 / -122.201132
**Sites:** 30 sites for tents and RVs up to 40 feet long (10 with electric hookups)
**Facilities:** Tables, fire rings, drinking water (except in winter), showers, flush and vault toilets, boat ramps, bathhouse
**Fee per night:** $, double site: $$$, hookup sites: $$, group (16 people): $$$; reservations: (877) 444-6777 or recreation.gov
**Management:** Mendocino National Forest, (530) 527-1196 or (530) 527-2813
**Activities:** Fishing, swimming, boating, waterskiing, birding
**Finding the campground:** From the intersection of I-5 and CA Highway 36 in Red Bluff, drive about 100 yards east on CA 36 to the first turnoff, which is Sale Lane. Turn south and travel about 0.5 mile to the end of the road.

**About the campground:** You can find all camping conveniences here. This part of the Sacramento River offers riparian forest, flowering grasslands, wetlands, and oak woodlands. Trout and a variety of fish inhabit this stretch of the river year-round, and 125 species of birds have been identified here. The Sacramento River Discovery Center offers wonderful outdoor education. Elevation 265 feet. Stay limit 14 days. Open March to November. For larger groups, take a look at the nearby Camp Discovery Group Campground.

## 199 Woodson Bridge State Recreation Area

**Location:** 26 miles south of Red Bluff
**GPS:** 39.9178588 / -122.0926012
**Sites:** 37 sites, for tents and RVs up to 31 feet long; 1 group site
**Facilities:** Tables, fire rings, drinking water, showers, flush toilets, dump station, playground; boat ramp nearby
**Fee per night:** $$$; reservations (high season only): (800) 444-7275 or reserveamerica.com.
**Management:** American Land and Leisure for California State Parks, (530) 839-2112
**Activities:** Fishing, boating, swimming, hiking
**Finding the campground:** From the intersection of I-5 and CA 99 in Red Bluff, take CA 99 south for 24 miles. Turn west onto South Avenue (CR A9) and drive 2 miles.
**About the campground:** Situated in an attractive oak grove on the banks of the Sacramento River, this campground is just a short walk away from a gravel swimming beach. Shad, catfish, striped and largemouth bass, steelhead, and bluegill are all possible catches in the river. A short nature loop trail begins at the campground. Stay limit 15 days peak summer; 30 days off-peak. Open all year.

## 200 Buckhorn (Black Butte Lake)

**Location:** 40 miles southwest of Red Bluff
**GPS:** 39.8124618 / -122.3574319
**Sites:** 87 sites for tents and RVs up to 45 feet long; 5 walk-in sites; 1 group site
**Facilities:** Tables, fire rings, drinking water, flush toilets, showers, dump station, boat ramp, fish-cleaning station, playgrounds, beach
**Fee per night:** $$, walk-in: $, group: $$$$; reservations: (800) 444-7275 or reserveamerica.com
**Management:** US Army Corps of Engineers, (530) 865-4781
**Activities:** Fishing, swimming, boating, hiking
**Finding the campground:** From the intersection of CA 36 and I-5 in Red Bluff, drive south on I-5 for 27 miles. Take the Black Butte Lake exit and drive northwest 12 miles on Newville Road. Turn left onto Buckhorn Road and drive 1 mile.
**About the campground:** Buckhorn is situated on the north shore of Black Butte Lake, which is 7 miles long, covers a surface area of almost 4,500 acres, and has 40 miles of shoreline. Fishing is best in spring; catches include crappie, bass, catfish, and bluegill. The lake is subject to heavy water drawdowns in summer and fall. Summers are usually hot. Three self-guided nature trails are located at different parts of the lake. Elevation 450 feet. Stay limit 14 days. Open all year.

## 201 Orland Buttes (Black Butte Lake)

**Location:** 40 miles southwest of Red Bluff
**GPS:** 39.7852931 / -122.3407807

**Sites:** 35 sites for tents and RVs up to 45 feet long; 1 group site
**Facilities:** Tables, fire rings, drinking water, flush toilets, showers, dump station, boat ramp, fish-cleaning station
**Fee per night:** $, group site: $$$$; reservations: (800) 444-7275 or reserveamerica.com
**Management:** US Army Corps of Engineers, (530) 865-4781
**Activities:** Fishing, swimming, boating, hiking, horseback riding
**Finding the campground:** From I-5, take the Black Butte Lake exit at Orland. Travel west on CR 200 (Newville Road) for 6 miles. Turn left onto CR 206 and drive 4 miles to the campground.
**About the campground:** This family-friendly camp is on the shores of Black Buttes Lake. There is a boat ramp and an eighteen-hole disc golf course, as well as spring wildflowers and volcanic buttes. Elevation 675 feet. Stay limit 14 days. Open April through September.

# Trinity Unit

## 202 Big Flat

**Location:** 60 miles north of Weaverville
**GPS:** 41.0673 / -122.9352
**Sites:** 5 sites for tents and RVs up to 16 feet long
**Facilities:** Tables, fire rings, vault toilets; no drinking water
**Fee per night:** None
**Management:** Shasta-Trinity/Klamath National Forest, (530) 623-2121
**Activities:** Hiking
**Finding the campground:** From Weaverville (about 40 miles west of Redding on CA 299), drive 38 miles northeast on CA 3. Turn west at the Coffee Creek Ranger Station onto CR 104 and drive 22 miles.
**About the campground:** Deep within the Trinity Alps Wilderness, the campground offers an ideal base for day hikes and backpacking trips. Trails lead north, west, and south to lovely small lakes and abandoned gold mines. Elevation 5,000 feet. Stay limit 14 days. Open all year.

## 203 Preacher Meadow

**Location:** 29 miles northeast of Weaverville
**GPS:** 40.96313183 / -122.7304608
**Sites:** 45 sites for tents and RVs up to 40 feet long
**Facilities:** Tables, fire rings, Klamath ovens, drinking water, vault toilets
**Fee per night:** $
**Management:** Shasta-Trinity National Forest, (530) 623-2121
**Activities:** Hiking
**Finding the campground:** From Weaverville, take CA 3 north for 27 miles. Turn left at the campground sign; the campground is 0.5 mile from the turnoff.
**About the campground:** Serene, private sites under mature cedar and ponderosa pine. Access to Swift Creek Trail. Elevation 2,900 feet. Stay limit 14 days. Open mid-May through mid-October.

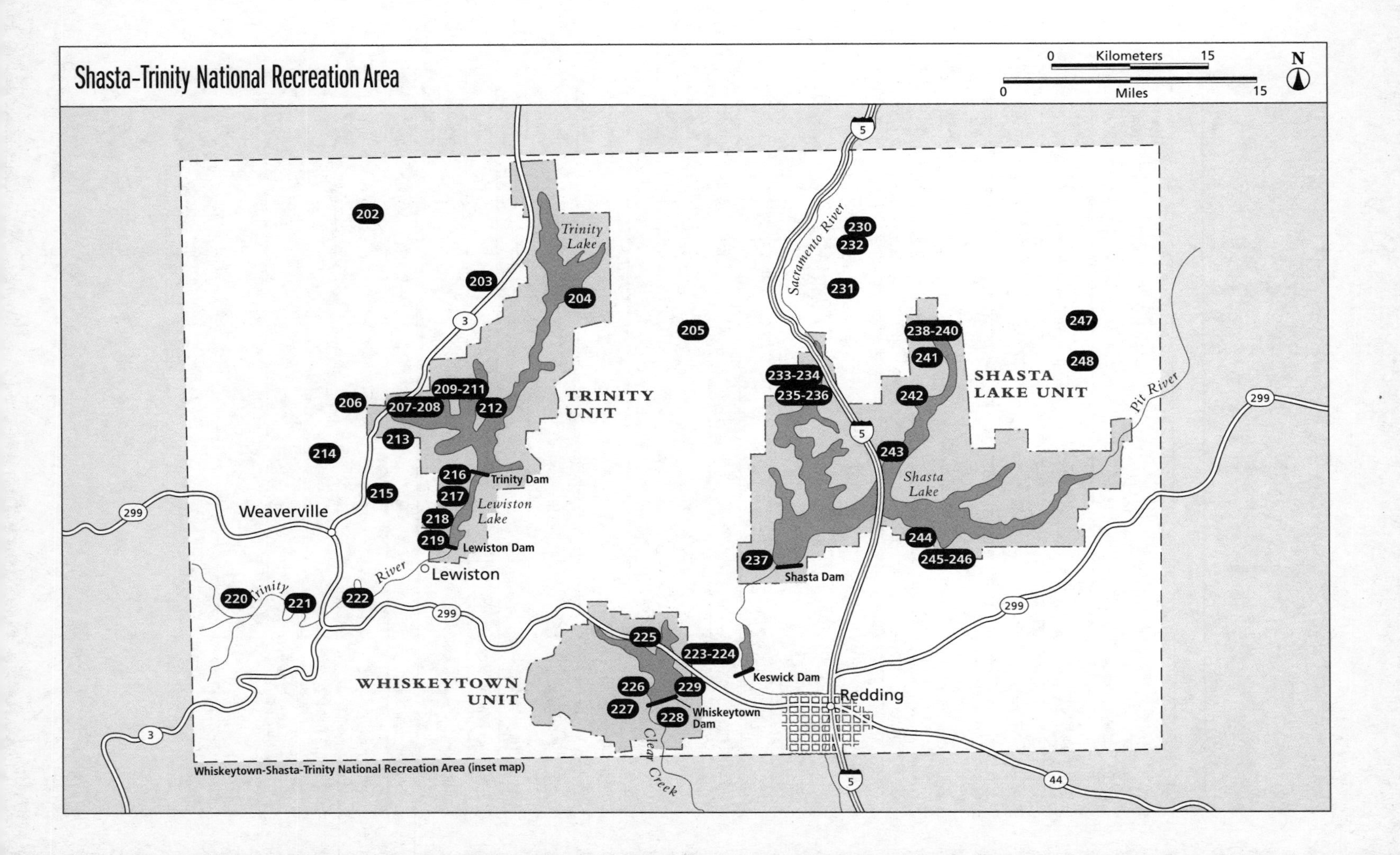
Shasta-Trinity National Recreation Area
0 Kilometers 15
0 Miles 15
N
Trinity Lake
TRINITY UNIT
Lewiston Lake
Trinity Dam
Lewiston Dam
Weaverville
Lewiston
Trinity River
Sacramento River
SHASTA LAKE UNIT
Shasta Lake
Pit River
Shasta Dam
Keswick Dam
Redding
WHISKEYTOWN UNIT
Whiskeytown Dam
Clear Creek
Whiskeytown-Shasta-Trinity National Recreation Area (inset map)
202
203
204
205
206
207-208
209-211
212
213
214
215
216
217
218
219
220
221
222
223-224
225
226
227
228
229
230
231
232
233-234
235-236
237
238-240
241
242
243
244
245-246
247
248
299
3
5
44

| | Name | Group Sites | RV Sites | Max. RV Length | Hookups | Toilets | Showers | Drinking Water | Dump Station | Pets | Wheelchair | Recreation | Fee(s) | Season | Can Reserve |
|---|---|---|---|---|---|---|---|---|---|---|---|---|---|---|---|
| | **Trinity Unit** | | | | | | | | | | | | | | |
| 202 | Big Flat | | * | 16 | | V | | | | * | | H | None | Year-round | |
| 203 | Preacher Meadow | | * | 40 | | V | | * | | * | | H | $ | May–Oct | |
| 204 | Jackass Springs | | * | 32 | | V | | | | * | | FS | None | Year-round | |
| 205 | Clear Creek | | * | 22 | | V | | | | * | | | None | Year-round | |
| 206 | Bridge Camp | | * | 20 | | V | | * | | * | | HR | $ | Year-round | |
| 207 | Stoney Point | * | | | | F | | * | | * | | BFS | $ | May–Oct | |
| 208 | Bushytail | * | * | 40 | E | F | * | * | | * | * | BFSL | $-$$$$ | May–Oct | * |
| 209 | Minersville | | * | 36 | E | FV | | * | | * | * | BFSL | $-$$ | Year-round | * |
| 210 | Clark Springs | | * | 25 | | F | | * | | * | | FBSH | $ | Apr–Sept | |
| 211 | Hayward Flat | | * | 40 | | F | | * | | * | | BFS | $–$$ | May–Sept | * |
| 212 | Alpine View | | * | 32 | | F | | * | | * | | BFS | $-$$ | May–Sept | |
| 213 | Tannery Gulch | | * | 40 | | F | | * | | * | | FBSH | $-$$ | May–Oct | * |
| 214 | East Weaver | | * | 25 | | V | | * | | * | | FH | $ | Year-round | |
| 215 | Rush Creek | | * | 20 | | V | | | | * | | F | $ | May–Sept | |
| 216 | Ackerman | | * | 40 | | F | | * | * | * | | FB | $ | Year-round | * |
| 217 | Tunnel Rock | | * | 15 | | V | | * | | * | | FB | $ | Year-round | |
| 218 | Cooper Gulch | | * | 16 | | V | | * | | * | * | FBH | $ | Apr–Oct | |
| 219 | Mary Smith | | | | | FV | | * | | * | | FB | $ | May–Oct | * |
| 220 | Steiner Flat | | | | | V | | | | * | | FB | None | Year-round | |
| 221 | Douglas City | | * | 28 | | FV | | * | | * | | FSB | $ | May–Oct | |
| 222 | Steel Bridge | | * | 20 | | V | | | | * | | FSB | $ | Year-round | |
| | **Whiskeytown National Recreation Area (Whiskeytown Unit)** | | | | | | | | | | | | | | |
| 223 | Crystal Creek | | | | | V | | | | * | | H | $$ | Year-round | |
| 224 | Coggins Park | | * | 25 | | V | | | | * | | H | $$ | Year-round | |

| | Name | Group Sites | RV Sites | Max. RV Length | Hookups | Toilets | Showers | Drinking Water | Dump Station | Pets | Wheelchair | Recreation | Fee(s) | Season | Can Reserve |
|---|---|---|---|---|---|---|---|---|---|---|---|---|---|---|---|
| 225 | Oak Bottom | | * | | | F | * | * | * | * | * | SFBHM | $$ | Year-round | * |
| 226 | Brandy Creek RV | | * | 35 | | | | | * | * | | SFBH | $ | Year-round | |
| 227 | Sheep Camp | | | | | V | | | | * | | H | $$ | Year-round | |
| 228 | Peltier Bridge | | | | | V | | | | * | | H | $$ | Year-round | |
| 229 | Horse Camp | | * | 25 | | V | | | | * | | HR | $$ | Year-round | |
| | **Shasta Lake Unit** | | | | | | | | | | | | | | |
| 230 | Antlers | | * | 30 | | FV | | * | | * | | SFB | $$–$$$ | Mar–Oct | * |
| 231 | Gregory Beach | | * | 30 | | V | | | | * | | SF | None | May–Labor Day | |
| 232 | Gregory Creek | | * | 16 | | V | | * | | * | | SF | $ | Year-round | |
| 233 | Lakeshore East | | * | 30 | | F | | * | | * | * | SFB | $$–$$$$ | Apr–Oct | * |
| 234 | Beehive Point Shoreline | | * | 31 | | C | | | | * | | SFB | $ | Year-round | |
| 235 | Nelson Point | * | * | 16 | | V | | | | * | | SFB | $–$$$$ | June–Sept | |
| 236 | Lower Salt Creek | | * | 30 | | C | | | | * | | SFB | $ | Year-round | |
| 237 | Shasta Campground (Chappie-Shasta OHV Area) | | * | 30 | | V | | * | | * | | FHO | $ | Year-round | |
| 238 | Ellery Creek | | * | 30 | | V | | * | | * | * | SFB | $$ | Apr–Labor Day | * |
| 239 | Pine Point | * | * | 24 | | V | | * | | * | | SFB | $–$$$$ | June–Sept | |
| 240 | McCloud Bridge | | * | 16 | | FV | | * | | * | * | FS | $$ | Apr–Oct | |
| 241 | Moore Creek | * | * | 16 | | V | | * | | * | * | SFB | $$ | May–Sept | * |
| 242 | Hirz Bay | * | * | 30 | | F | | * | | * | * | SFBL | $$–$$$$ | Year-round | * |
| 243 | Bailey Cove | | * | 30 | | F | | * | | * | * | SFBHLM | $–$$ | Year-round | * |
| 244 | Mariners Point Shoreline | | * | 16 | | | | | | * | | SFB | None | May–Sept | |
| 245 | Upper and Lower Jones Valley | | * | 16 | | V | | * | | * | | FB | $ | Year-round | |
| 246 | Jones Valley Inlet Shoreline | | * | 30 | | C | | * | | * | | SFBH | $ | Mar–Oct | |

| | Name | Group Sites | RV Sites | Max. RV Length | Hookups | Toilets | Showers | Drinking Water | Dump Station | Pets | Wheelchair | Recreation | Fee(s) | Season | Can Reserve |
|---|---|---|---|---|---|---|---|---|---|---|---|---|---|---|---|
| 247 | Madrone | | * | 16 | | V | | | | * | | FH | None | Year-round | |
| 248 | Chirpchatter | | * | 24 | | V | | | | * | | H | None | Year-round | |

Toilets: F=flush V=vault P=pit C=chemical; Fee: $=Under $20 $$=$20-$29 $$$=$30-$39 $$$$ $40 or more; Recreation: H=hiking S=swimming F=fishing B=boating L=boat launch O=off-highway driving R=horseback riding, M=mountain biking Hookups: W=water E=electric S=sewer

## 204 Jackass Springs

**Location:** 34 miles north of Weaverville
**GPS:** 40.96183574 / -122.6609193
**Sites:** 10 sites for tents and RVs up to 32 feet long
**Facilities:** Tables, fire rings, vault toilets; no drinking water
**Fee per night:** None
**Management:** Shasta-Trinity National Forest, (530) 623-2121
**Activities:** Fishing, swimming
**Finding the campground:** From Weaverville, take CA 3 north for 34.2 miles. Turn right onto CR 106, crossing over Carrville Bridge. Stay on CR 106 for 12.4 miles to the Jackass Springs Road junction. Turn right and continue 5 miles to the campground.
**About the campground:** This is the only campground on the isolated eastern shore of the lake. It is situated in an attractive cove, and there is an island offshore. The setting is affected by water drawdowns in the fall. Elevation 2,600 feet. Stay limit 14 days. Open all year.

## 205 Clear Creek

**Location:** 44 miles northwest of Redding
**GPS:** 40.93079995 / -122.5859239
**Sites:** 6 sites for tents and RVs up to 22 feet long
**Facilities:** Tables, fire rings, vault toilets; no drinking water
**Fee per night:** None
**Management:** Shasta-Trinity National Forest, (530) 623-2121
**Activities:** Hunting
**Finding the campground:** From the intersection of I-5 and CA 299 at Redding, take CA 299 west for 17 miles. Turn right (north) onto Trinity Lake Road and continue 14 miles. Turn right (north) onto East Side Road (CR 106) and drive 11 miles, then turn right onto Dog Creek Road and drive 2 miles.
**About the campground:** An isolated campground off the beaten path or a seasonal hunting base camp. Elevation 3,400 feet. Stay limit 14 days. Open all year.

## 206 Bridge Camp

**Location:** 18 miles north of Weaverville
**GPS:** 40.87287582 / -122.9153598
**Sites:** 10 sites for tents and RVs up to 20 feet long
**Facilities:** Tables, fire rings, drinking water (May–Oct only), vault toilets, corrals
**Fee per night:** $ (free off-season)
**Management:** Shasta-Trinity National Forest, (530) 623-2121
**Activities:** Hiking, horseback riding
**Finding the campground:** From Weaverville (about 40 miles west of Redding on CA 299), drive 14 miles north on CA 3. Turn left onto Trinity Alps Road (CR 112) and drive past the resort. The last 2 miles are dirt road.
**About the campground:** Bridge Camp is one of the major starting points for hikes into the Trinity Alps Wilderness. The Stuarts Fork Trail (for hikers and equestrians) begins 0.5 mile northwest of the campground and leads to Alpine Lake (7 miles) and Emerald and Sapphire Lakes (11 and 13 miles, respectively). The campground is 3 miles from the shore of Trinity Lake. Elevation 2,700 feet. Stay limit 14 days. Open all year.

## 207 Stoney Point

**Location:** 13 miles northeast of Weaverville
**GPS:** 40.84842468 / -122.8584044
**Sites:** 22 sites for tents
**Facilities:** Tables, fire rings, drinking water, flush toilets; boat ramp 0.5 mile northwest at Stuart Fork
**Fee per night:** $
**Management:** Shasta-Trinity National Forest, (530) 623-2121
**Activities:** Boating, fishing, swimming, waterskiing
**Finding the campground:** From Weaverville, drive 13.3 miles northeast on CA 3.
**About the campground:** Situated on the southwest shore of Trinity Lake, with a swimming beach nearby. Private sites, but highway traffic can be heard. Elevation 2,400 feet. Stay limit 14 days. Open May through October. For groups of from 9 to 50 people, check out nearby Stoney Creek Group Camp; Fawn Group Camp can accommodate up to 300 people. Reservations are required for group camps; call (800) 280-CAMP.

## 208 Bushytail

**Location:** 18 miles northeast of Weaverville
**GPS:** 40.85445579 / -122.8167159
**Sites:** 11 sites for tents and RVs up to 40 feet long and for groups
**Facilities:** Tables, fire rings, grills, drinking water, flush toilets, showers, bear lockers, electric hookups; boat ramp 0.7 mile away
**Fee per night:** $–$$$$; reservations: (877) 444-6777 or recreation.gov
**Management:** Shasta Recreation Company, (530) 623-2121
**Activities:** Boating, fishing, swimming, waterskiing

**Finding the campground:** From Weaverville, drive 16.5 miles northeast on CA 3.

**About the campground:** Situated about 0.5 mile from the shore of Trinity Lake, with a swimming beach nearby. Bushytail offers single, double, triple, and quad sites, all nestled in a grove of tall Douglas firs and ponderosa pines. Sites lack privacy. Lots of wildlife in the area. Elevation 2,500 feet. Stay limit 14 days. Open May through October.

## 209 Minersville

**Location:** 19 miles northeast of Weaverville

**GPS:** 40.85182609 / -122.8116255

**Sites:** 14 sites for tents and RVs up to 36 feet long (some doubles); 1 electric hookup; 6 hike-in sites

**Facilities:** Tables, fire rings, drinking water (Apr–Oct only), flush and vault toilets, boat ramp

**Fee per night:** $$ peak season, $ winter; reservations: (800) 444-7275 or reserveamerica.com

**Management:** Shasta-Trinity National Forest, (530) 623-2121

**Activities:** Boating, fishing, swimming, waterskiing

**Finding the campground:** From Weaverville, drive 15 miles northeast on CA 3. Turn right onto Granite Peak/Minersville Road for 1 mile.

**About the campground:** Situated close to the shore of Trinity Lake, with a swimming beach and excellent waterskiing nearby. A popular, well-developed campground with good views. The hike-ins are shoreside. Elevation 2,400 feet. Stay limit 14 days. Open all year.

## 210 Clark Springs

**Location:** 17 miles northeast of Weaverville

**GPS:** 40.8571 / -122.8135

**Sites:** 21 sites for tents (including 4 walk-in) and RVs up to 25 feet long

**Facilities:** Tables, fire rings, drinking water, flush toilets; boat ramp nearby

**Fee per night:** $

**Management:** Shasta Recreation Company, (530) 623-2121

**Activities:** Boating, fishing, swimming, waterskiing, hiking

**Finding the campground:** From Weaverville, drive 16 miles northeast on CA 3. Turn right onto Clarks Springs Road for 0.5 mile.

**About the campground:** Situated on the shore of Trinity Lake, with a swimming beach nearby. Rugged campground includes four secluded walk-in tent sites next to a brook. Adjacent to the Clark Springs picnic area, swim beach, and boat ramp. Hikers can access the 4-mile Trinity Lakeshore Trail. Elevation 2,400 feet. Stay limit 14 days. Open April through mid-September.

## 211 Hayward Flat

**Location:** 20 miles northeast of Weaverville

**GPS:** 40.87422669 / -122.7675828

**Sites:** 98 sites for tents and RVs up to 40 feet long

**Facilities:** Tables, fire rings, drinking water, flush toilets, swimming beach, interpretive programs

**Fee per night:** $–$$ (double); reservations: (877) 444-6777 or recreation.gov

**Management:** Shasta Recreation Company, (530) 623-2121

**Activities:** Boating, fishing, swimming, waterskiing
**Finding the campground:** From Weaverville, drive 17.5 miles northeast on CA 3. Turn east onto FR 35N26Y (at Hayward sign) and drive 2 miles.
**About the campground:** A popular campground, favored by the water sports crowd; situated in an attractive spot on the shore of Trinity Lake (boat ramp is about 3 miles away). It has its own private swimming beach and plenty of shade. Elevation 2,400 feet. Stay limit 14 days. Open mid-May through mid-September.

## 212 Alpine View

**Location:** 27 miles northeast of Weaverville
**GPS:** 40.88706482 / -122.7658164
**Sites:** 53 sites for tents and RVs up to 32 feet long, including 4 double sites
**Facilities:** Tables, fire rings, drinking water, flush toilets; boat ramp 0.5 mile north
**Fee per night:** $, double: $$
**Management:** Shasta-Trinity National Forest, (530) 623-2121
**Activities:** Boating, fishing, swimming, waterskiing
**Finding the campground:** From Weaverville, drive 25 miles northeast on CA 3. Turn right (east) onto CR 160 and drive 2 miles.
**About the campground:** As the name implies, this shoreline campground has great views across the water toward the Trinity Alps. Great choice for children and the elderly. Popular with boaters, since Bowerman boat ramp is just 0.25 mile down the road. Elevation 2,400 feet. Stay limit 14 days. Open mid-May through mid-September.

## 213 Tannery Gulch

**Location:** 12 miles northeast of Weaverville
**GPS:** 40.83548477 / -122.8451525
**Sites:** 82 family sites; 4 double sites for tents and RVs up to 40 feet long
**Facilities:** Tables, fire rings, drinking water, flush toilets, boat ramp, amphitheater
**Fee per night:** $, double: $$; reservations: (877) 444-6777 or recreation.gov
**Management:** Shasta-Trinity National Forest, (530) 623-2121
**Activities:** Boating, fishing, swimming, waterskiing, hiking, nature trail
**Finding the campground:** From Weaverville, drive 10.5 miles north on CA 3. Take the Tannery Gulch exit; the campground is located 1 mile from the exit.
**About the campground:** Situated on the southwest shore of Trinity Lake among tall pines, firs, and oaks, with a good swimming beach nearby. Campsites in every loop except loop A have a view of lake. Although there are patches of middle-story, most campsites are close to one another, making privacy minimal. A hiking trail follows the shoreline east from the campground. Elevation 2,400 feet. Stay limit 14 days. Open May through October.

## 214 East Weaver

**Location:** 4 miles north of Weaverville
**GPS:** 40.77300079 / -122.9209875
**Sites:** 10 sites for tents and RVs up to 25 feet long

**Facilities:** Tables, fire rings, drinking water, vault toilets
**Fee per night:** $
**Management:** Shasta Recreation Company, (530) 623-2121
**Activities:** Fishing, hiking
**Finding the campground:** From Weaverville, drive 2 miles north on CA 3. Turn left onto CR 228 and drive 1.5 miles.
**About the campground:** Situated on the East Branch of Weaver Creek. A trail leads northwest from the campground into the Monument Peak area of the Trinity Alps Wilderness. Town is only 1.5 miles away. Elevation 2,500 feet. Stay limit 14 days. Open all year (full services April through October).

## 215 Rush Creek

**Location:** 8 miles northeast of Weaverville
**GPS:** 40.81875082 / -122.8972609
**Sites:** 10 sites for tents and RVs up to 20 feet long
**Facilities:** Tables, fire rings, vault toilets; no drinking water

### WHISKEYTOWN-SHASTA-TRINITY NATIONAL RECREATION AREA: TRINITY UNIT

Trinity Lake, also known briefly as Clair Engle Lake, is the westernmost and second-largest of the three major lakes that make up the Whiskeytown-Shasta-Trinity National Recreation Area. The Trinity Unit contains twenty-four public campgrounds, most of them either on the lake or a tributary stream. In addition, there are several private camping resorts and three full-service marinas. Boat rentals are available, including houseboats.

Man-made Trinity Lake occupies 17,000 acres of surface area at an elevation of 2,400 feet and is surrounded by scenic mountains. Fishing is varied, but the lake is noted particularly for smallmouth bass. Trout fishing is also good; each year the lake is stocked with rainbow trout and Chinook salmon. Other catches include largemouth bass, bullhead, kokanee, and catfish. The Trinity Heritage National Scenic Byway begins at Weaverville and follows CA 3 along the western shore of the lake. Area campgrounds provide an excellent base from which to explore the beautiful Trinity Alps Wilderness, which lies to the west.

For car and RV campers who have boats and want to get away from the road-bound crowd for a day or so, Trinity Lake features four boat-in campgrounds. Three are on the southwestern arm of the lake, and one is farther northeast. They all have picnic tables, fire rings, and vault toilets. They have no drinking water, and no fee is charged. The campgrounds are Ridgeville, 21 sites; Ridgeville Island, 3 sites; Mariners Roost, 7 sites; and Captains Point, 3 sites. From the first three, you have great views of the Trinity Alps.

**Fee per night:** $
**Management:** Shasta Recreation Company, (530) 623-2121
**Activities:** Fishing
**Finding the campground:** From Weaverville, drive 8 miles north on CA 3. Turn left at the Rush Creek Campground sign and drive 0.5 mile.
**About the campground:** Situated on Rush Creek; most campsites are well separated, providing good privacy. Fishing is good for brook trout. Road is unpaved. Elevation 2,400 feet. Stay limit 14 days. Open mid-May through mid-September.

## 216 Ackerman

**Location:** 8 miles north of Lewiston
**GPS:** 40.78621842 / -122.770651
**Sites:** 51 sites for tents and RVs up to 40 feet long
**Facilities:** Tables, fire rings, drinking water (Apr–Oct only), flush toilets, dump station; boat ramp 2 miles south
**Fee per night:** $; reservations: (877) 444-6777 or recreation.gov
**Management:** Shasta Recreation Company, (530) 623-2121
**Activities:** Fishing, canoeing, kayaking, birding
**Finding the campground:** From Lewiston (27 miles west of Redding via CA 299 and CR 105), drive 8 miles north on CR 105.
**About the campground:** On the shores of Lewiston Lake. There is a 10-mile-per-hour speed limit on the lake, which is stocked annually with catchable-size rainbow trout. Lewiston is a magnet for water birds and other birds and is a designated wildlife viewing area. Elevation 2,400 feet. Stay limit 14 days. Open all year.

## 217 Tunnel Rock

**Location:** 7 miles north of Lewiston
**GPS:** 40.77239619 / -122.7784136
**Sites:** 6 sites for tents and RVs up to 15 feet long
**Facilities:** Tables, fire rings, vault toilets, drinking water; boat ramp 1 mile south
**Fee per night:** $
**Management:** Shasta-Trinity National Forest, (530) 623-2121
**Activities:** Fishing, canoeing, kayaking, birding
**Finding the campground:** From Lewiston (27 miles west of Redding via CA 299 and CR 105), drive 7 miles north on CR 105.
**About the campground:** The campground has shaded sites and is across the road from Lewiston Lake near a popular fishing spot. Elevation 2,400 feet. Stay limit 14 days. Open all year.

## 218 Cooper Gulch

**Location:** 4 miles north of Lewiston
**GPS:** 40.74592569 / -122.8042848
**Sites:** 5 sites for tents and RVs up to 16 feet long
**Facilities:** Tables, fire rings, drinking water, vault toilets; boat ramp 2 miles north

**Fee per night:** $
**Management:** Shasta Recreation Company, (530) 623-2121
**Activities:** Fishing, hiking, nonmotorized boating, birding
**Finding the campground:** From Lewiston (27 miles west of Redding via CA 299 and CR 105), drive 4 miles north on CR 105.
**About the campground:** On the water's edge, a favorite of kayakers and anglers. Accesses Baker Gulch Trail. Elevation 2,400 feet. Stay limit 14 days. Open April through October.

## 219 Mary Smith

**Location:** 2 miles north of Lewiston
**GPS:** 40.73179586 / -122.8072276
**Sites:** 17 sites for tents
**Facilities:** Tables, fire rings, drinking water, flush and vault toilets; boat ramp 3 miles north
**Fee per night:** $; reservations: (877) 444-6777 or recreation.gov
**Management:** Shasta Recreation Company, (530) 623-2121
**Activities:** Fishing, canoeing, kayaking, birding
**Finding the campground:** From Lewiston (27 miles west of Redding via CA 299 and CR 105), drive 2 miles north on CR 105.
**About the campground:** Situated on Lewiston Lake, this campground is small but in a beautiful setting south of Trinity Dam. Car-top boats may be launched from the campground, and a boat ramp is located 3 miles north. The campsites, each with a view of the lake or Trinity Alps, offer varying degrees of privacy. Elevation 2,000 feet. Stay limit 14 days. Open May through October.

## 220 Steiner Flat

**Location:** 9 miles south of Weaverville
**GPS:** 40.6571027 / -122.9665326
**Sites:** 8 sites for tents or small trailers
**Facilities:** Fire rings, vault toilet, primitive boat ramp; no drinking water
**Fees per night:** None
**Management:** Bureau of Land Management, (530) 224-2100
**Activities:** Fishing, canoeing, kayaking
**Finding the campground:** From Weaverville, take CA 299 East/CA 3 South for 6.3 miles. Turn southwest onto Riverview Road and west onto Steiner Flat Road for about 2.2 miles.
**About the campground:** Primitive tent camping on the Trinity River. The Trinity is a designated Wild and Scenic River, and experienced rafters and kayakers will enjoy this stretch. Elevation 1,500 feet. Stay limit 14 days. Open all year.

## 221 Douglas City

**Location:** 7 miles south of Weaverville
**GPS:** 40.6468821 / -122.9531054
**Sites:** 20 sites for tents and RVs up to 28 feet long
**Facilities:** Tables, fire rings, drinking water, flush and vault toilets, beach
**Fee per night:** $

**Management:** Bureau of Land Management, (530) 224-2100
**Activities:** Fishing, swimming, paddling
**Finding the campground:** From Weaverville, drive south on CA 299 East/CA 3 South for 6 miles. Turn right onto Riverview Road/Steiner Flat Road and drive 0.5 mile.
**About the campground:** Situated on the bank of the Trinity amid ponderosa pine, Douglas fir, and oak trees, with good access to the river. Fishing is good for salmon in summer and steelhead in late fall. Elevation 1,600 feet. Stay limit 14 days. Open May through October.

## 222 Steel Bridge

**Location:** 9 miles south of Weaverville
**GPS:** 40.6743698 / -122.910433
**Sites:** 12 sites for tents and RVs up to 20 feet long
**Facilities:** Tables, fire rings, vault toilets; no drinking water
**Fee per night:** $
**Management:** Bureau of Land Management, (530) 224-2100
**Activities:** Fishing, swimming, paddling
**Finding the campground:** From Weaverville, drive south on CA 299/CA 3 South for 7 miles. Turn left onto Steel Bridge Road and drive 2 miles.
**About the campground:** Shaded and partially shaded sites on the Trinity River. Elevation 1,700 feet. Stay limit 14 days. Open all year.

# Whiskeytown National Recreation Area

## 223 Crystal Creek

**Location:** 8 plus miles northwest of Redding
**GPS:** 40.6148336 / -122.5197165
**Sites:** 2 sites for tents or small pop-up tent trailer.
**Facilities:** Tables, fire pits, food lockers, lantern poles, vault toilet; no drinking water
**Fee per night:** $$ (permit and daily fee)
**Management:** Whiskeytown National Recreation Area, (530) 246-1225
**Activities:** Hiking, riparian wildlife viewing
**Finding the campground:** Take CA 299 West about 7 miles to the Whiskeytown National Recreation Area Visitor Center on J. F. Kennedy Memorial Road. Purchase a permit and get directions to the campground from here.
**About the campground:** Primitive campground in a forest setting on the creek. Near to Crystal Creek Falls, one of four waterfalls you can hike to in Whiskeytown. Elevation 1,390 feet. Stay limit 14 days. Open all year (may be closed in winter).

## 224 Coggins Park

**Location:** 8 plus miles northwest of Redding
**GPS:** 40.6148336 / -122.5197165
**Sites:** 1 site for tent or small pop-up tent trailer

**Facilities:** Tables, fire pits, food lockers, lantern poles, vault toilet; no drinking water
**Fee per night:** $$ (permit and daily fee)
**Management:** Whiskeytown National Recreation Area, (530) 246-1225
**Activities:** Hiking
**Finding the campground:** Take CA 299 West about 7 miles to the Whiskeytown National Recreation Area Visitor Center on J. F. Kennedy Memorial Road. Purchase a permit and get directions to the campground from here.
**About the campground:** Primitive campground in a forest setting inside Whiskeytown parkland. Four-wheel drive recommended. Elevation 1,390 feet. Stay limit 14 days. Open all year (may be closed in winter).

## 225 Oak Bottom

**Location:** 14 miles west of Redding
**GPS:** 40.6487597 / -122.5925161
**Sites:** 94 sites for tents and 22 spaces for RVs in a large parking area
**Facilities:** Tables, fire rings, drinking water, showers, flush toilets, dump station, store, boat ramp and rentals
**Fee per night:** $$ ($ in winter); reservations (mid-Apr to mid-Oct): (530) 359-2269
**Management:** Whiskeytown National Recreation Area, (530) 359-2269
**Activities:** Swimming, fishing, boating, waterskiing, hiking, mountain biking, nature programs
**Finding the campground:** From Redding, drive west 14 miles on CA 299.
**About the campground:** The best sites go to the tents in this large campground on the northern shore of the lake, but the location is excellent for both lake access and hiking and mountain biking trails. Elevation 1,230 feet. Stay limit 14 days May 15 to October 15; 30 days remainder of year. Open all year.

### WHISKEYTOWN-SHASTA-TRINITY NATIONAL RECREATION AREA: WHISKEYTOWN UNIT

Whiskeytown Lake, with a 3,200-acre surface area and 36 miles of shoreline, is the central attraction of this smallest of the three units in the national recreation area. In addition to most water sports (including scuba diving), you can hike 45 miles of trails, including ones through old-growth forests; take the waterfall challenge (hikes to four waterfalls); explore historical gold rush sites; and pan for gold (with permit fee; check at the visitor center for permit and best panning locations). OHV enthusiasts can drive a four-wheel-drive vehicle to the summit of Shasta Bally. The lake is stocked annually with rainbow and brook trout and Chinook salmon. There is also a resident population of largemouth, smallmouth, and spotted bass, as well as kokanee salmon. A visit to the Camden House Historic District is worthwhile for gold rush–era enthusiasts.

# 226 Brandy Creek RV

**Location:** 14 miles west of Redding
**GPS:** 40.6157046 / -122.5750152
**Sites:** 32 sites for self-contained RVs up to 35 feet long
**Facilities:** Dump station; drinking water (shut off in winter) and boat ramp are nearby; no toilets
**Fee per night:** $
**Management:** Whiskeytown-Shasta-Trinity National Recreation Area, (530) 242-3412
**Activities:** Swimming, fishing, boating, waterskiing, hiking
**Finding the campground:** From Redding, drive west 10 miles on CA 299. Turn left at the Whiskeytown Unit Visitor Center and drive 4 miles.
**About the campground:** For self-contained vehicles only; no tents allowed. Situated on Brandy Creek less than 0.25 mile from the lakeshore, this looks more like a parking lot than a campground. A marina and boat ramp are located within 0.25 mile. Elevation 1,315 feet. Stay limit 14 days mid-May through mid-September; 30 days October through April. Open all year. Not to be confused with Brandy Creek primitive camp with 2 tent sites over a mile from the lake.

# 227 Sheep Camp

**Location:** 8 plus miles northwest of Redding
**GPS:** 40.5997425 / -122.5943876
**Sites:** 4 sites for tents or small pop-up tent trailer
**Facilities:** Tables, fire pits, food lockers, lantern poles, vault toilet; no drinking water
**Fee per night:** $$ (permit and daily fee)
**Management:** Whiskeytown National Park, (530) 246-1225
**Activities:** Hiking
**Finding the campground:** Take CA 299 West about 7 miles to the Whiskeytown National Recreation Area Visitor Center on J. F. Kennedy Memorial Road. Purchase a permit and get directions to the campground from here.
**About the campground:** Primitive campground in a forest setting inside Whiskeytown parkland. Elevation 1,840 feet. Stay limit 14 days. Open all year (subject to closure in winter).

# 228 Peltier Bridge

**Location:** 11 miles west of Redding
**GPS:** 40.58525 / -122.5522
**Sites:** 7 sites for tents or small pop-up tent trailer
**Facilities:** Tables, fire pits, food lockers, lantern poles, vault toilet; no drinking water
**Fee per night:** $$ (permit and daily fee)
**Management:** Whiskeytown National Park, (530) 246-1225
**Activities:** Hiking
**Finding the campground:** Take CA 299 West about 7 miles to the Whiskeytown National Recreation Area Visitor Center on J. F. Kennedy Memorial Road. Purchase a permit. Continuing on J. F. Kennedy Memorial Road, go straight on to Paige Bar Road just before you cross the dam, about 1.2 miles, and then turn right toward Peltier Bridge. Cross the bridge to the campgrounds.

**About the campground:** Primitive campground. Up the dirt road 2.7 miles is the Peltier Trail, a 3-mile loop. This trail connects to the Kanaka Peak Loop and Salt Gulch Trails. Decent catch and release fishing. Elevation 1,070 feet. Stay limit 14 days. Open all year (subject to closure in winter).

## 229 Horse Camp

**Location:** 8 plus miles northwest of Redding
**GPS:** 40.6148336 / -122.5197165
**Sites:** 2 sites for tents and small trailers
**Facilities:** Tables, fire pits, food lockers, lantern poles, vault toilet; no drinking water
**Fee per night:** $$ (permit and daily fee)
**Management:** Whiskeytown National Recreation Area, (530) 246-1225
**Activities:** Hiking, horseback riding
**Finding the campground:** Take CA 299 West about 7 miles to the Whiskeytown National Recreation Area Visitor Center on J. F. Kennedy Memorial Road. Purchase a permit and get directions to the campground from here.
**About the campground:** Primitive campground in a forest setting inside Whiskeytown parkland. Equestrians can reserve Horse Camp as a group camp (call 530-242-3412). Elevation 1,380 feet. Stay limit 14 days. Open all year (may be closed in winter).

# Shasta Lake Unit

## 230 Antlers

**Location:** 25 miles north of Redding
**GPS:** 40.8946237 / -122.3743501
**Sites:** 41 single and 18 double sites for tents and RVs up to 30 feet long
**Facilities:** Tables, fire rings, bear boxes, drinking water, flush and vault toilets; boat ramp 0.5 mile south.
**Fee per night:** $$–$$$; reservations: (877) 444-6777 or recreation.gov
**Management:** Shasta-Trinity National Forest, (530) 275-1589
**Activities:** Swimming, fishing, boating, waterskiing
**Finding the campground:** From the intersection of CA 44 and I-5 in Redding, drive north 24 miles on I-5. Take exit 702 for Lakeshore Drive toward Antlers Road and take Antlers Road 1.5 miles.
**About the campground:** Situated in forest on the upper Sacramento River Arm of Shasta Lake. Elevation 1,100 feet. Stay limit 14 days. Open March through October.

## 231 Gregory Beach

**Location:** 25 miles north of Redding
**GPS:** 40.88490158 / -122.3705088
**Sites:** Dispersed sites for tents and trailers to 30 feet long
**Facilities:** Vault toilet; no drinking water
**Fee per night:** None
**Management:** Shasta-Trinity National Forest, (530) 275-1589

**Activities:** Swimming, fishing
**Finding the campground:** From the intersection of CA 44 and I-5 in Redding, drive north 20 miles on I-5. Take the Salt Creek exit and drive 4 miles north on Gregory Creek Road (Salt Creek Road).
**About the campground:** Situated on the eastern shore of the Sacramento River Arm of the lake, above the lakeshore, this is a pack-in, pack-out campground. Some years the vault toilet may not be provided. Elevation 1,100 feet. Stay limit 14 days. Open mid-May through Labor Day.

## 232 Gregory Creek

**Location:** 24 miles north of Redding
**GPS:** 40.8893677 / -122.3697541
**Sites:** 18 tents and trailers up to 16 feet long

### WHISKEYTOWN-SHASTA-TRINITY NATIONAL RECREATION AREA: SHASTA UNIT

Shasta Lake, with its 29,500-acre surface area and 370 miles of shoreline, gets large numbers of visitors, especially during the summer months. Yet its numerous arms, inlets, and coves can provide privacy for those willing to seek it. Much of the shoreline is accessible only by boat, providing opportunities for exploration. I-5, which runs north–south, bisects the lake neatly, facilitating access to many campgrounds, resorts, and marinas. Shasta Dam is the tallest dam in the United States and the second largest in volume. It is open for tours.

The lake supports twenty-one varieties of fish and is stocked annually with a large mix of rainbow and brown trout and Chinook salmon. There are seven public boat ramps on the lake. They all charge a fee. You can rent a boat at eleven commercial marinas around the lake. There are no developed shoreline swimming areas, but many people swim at their campgrounds and from boats.

The USDA Forest Service maintains four boat-in campgrounds on Shasta Lake. They all have vault toilets, no drinking water, and no fee and are open all year. Arbuckle Flat (Pit River Arm) has eleven sites; Ski Island (Pit River Arm) has twenty-three sites; Greens Creek (McCloud River Arm) has nine sites; and Gooseneck Cove (Sacramento River Arm) offers eight sites.

Hiking trails at Packers Bay, Bailey Cove, Hirz Bay, and Jones Valley offer moderate hiking and good shoreline fishing access. Mountain biking is permitted on most of the trails. The Chappie-Shasta Off Highway Vehicle Area provides trails and roads for adventurous off-road driving, as well as a nearby campground. Shasta Caverns (commercially operated) and Samwel Cave (no charge) are open to visitors year-round.

Two visitor centers provide brochures, maps, exhibits, campfire permits, and general information:

1. Shasta Lake Visitor Information Center; Mountain Gate/Wonderland Boulevard exit from I-5; (530) 275-1589
2. Shasta Dam Visitor Information Center; Shasta Dam Boulevard exit from I-5; (530) 275-4463

**Facilities:** Tables, fire rings, drinking water, vault toilets
**Fee per night:** $
**Management:** Shasta-Trinity National Forest, (530) 275-1587
**Activities:** Swimming, fishing
**Finding the campground:** From the intersection of CA 44 and I-5 in Redding, drive north 20 miles on I-5. Take the Salt Creek exit and drive 4.5 miles north on Gregory Creek Road (Salt Creek Road).
**About the campground:** Pine-shaded campground situated on the upper eastern shore of the Sacramento River Arm of the lake. As the lake level drops, the drop-off to the water gets steeper, especially nearest Gregory Beach. Nearest boat ramp is at Antlers. Elevation 1,100 feet. Stay limit 14 days. Open all year (subject to closure to protect bald eagles).

## 233 Lakeshore East

**Location:** 26 miles north of Redding
**GPS:** 40.87223567 / -122.3875378
**Sites:** 17 single and 6 double sites for tents and RVs up to 30 feet long; 3 yurts
**Facilities:** Tables, fire rings, drinking water, flush toilets; boat ramp 1 mile south
**Fee per night:** $$, doubles: $$$, yurts: $$$$; reservations: (877) 444-6777 or recreation.gov
**Management:** Shasta-Trinity National Forest, (530) 275-1589
**Activities:** Swimming, fishing, boating
**Finding the campground:** From the intersection of CA 44 and I-5 in Redding, drive north 24 miles on I-5. Take the Antlers Road exit and turn west at the stop sign. Go under the freeway, turn south onto Lakeshore Drive, and go 2 miles.
**About the campground:** Situated on the west shore of the Sacramento River Arm of the lake, close to both the Antlers and Sugarloaf boat ramps. Not much scenery and subject to noise from passing trains. Elevation 1,060 feet. Stay limit 14 days. Open April through October.

## 234 Beehive Point Shoreline

**Location:** 28 miles north of Redding
**GPS:** 40.8467142 / -122.4129987
**Sites:** Open shoreline camping for tents and RVs up to 30 feet long
**Facilities:** Portable restrooms (May–Sept only); no drinking water; boat ramp 1 mile north
**Fee per night:** $ (free off-season)
**Management:** Shasta-Trinity National Forest, (530) 275-8113
**Activities:** Swimming, fishing, boating
**Finding the campground:** From the intersection of CA 44 and I-5 in Redding, drive north 24 miles on I-5. Take the Antlers Road exit and turn west at the stop sign. Go under the freeway, turn south onto Lakeshore Drive, and go 4 miles.
**About the campground:** Situated on the upper Sacramento River Arm of the lake, campsites are undesignated in a semi-wooded shoreline area. Elevation 1,070 feet. Stay limit 14 days. Open all year.

## 235 Nelson Point

**Location:** 21 miles north of Redding
**GPS:** 40.8482559 / -122.3446712

**Sites:** 8 sites for tents and RVs up to 16 feet long; may be reserved as a group camp (up to 60 people)
**Facilities:** Tables, fire rings, tent pads, vault toilets; no drinking water
**Fee per night:** $, group: $$$$; reservations (group only): (877) 444-6777 or recreation.gov
**Management:** Shasta-Trinity National Forest, (530) 275-1589
**Activities:** Swimming, fishing, boating, waterskiing
**Finding the campground:** From the intersection of CA 44 and I-5 in Redding, drive north 20 miles on I-5. Take the Salt Creek/Gilman Road exit, turning southwest onto Gilman. Turn northwest onto Salt Creek Road for 3 miles, then west onto Conflict Point Road for about 2 miles.
**About the campground:** Situated on the shore of Salt Creek Inlet. Elevation 1,130 feet. Stay limit 14 days. Open June to September.

## 236 Lower Salt Creek

**Location:** 25 miles north of Redding
**GPS:** 40.84289039 / -122.3542097
**Sites:** Dispersed sites for tents or RVs up to 30 feet long
**Facilities:** Portable restrooms (May–Sept only); no drinking water
**Fee per night:** $ (free off-season)
**Management:** Shasta Recreation Company, (530) 275-8113
**Activities:** Swimming, fishing, boating
**Finding the campground:** From the intersection of CA 44 and I-5 in Redding, drive north 20 miles on I-5. Take the Salt Creek/Gilman Road exit, turning southwest onto Gilman. Turn northwest onto Salt Creek Road and then southwest onto Salt Creek Lodge Road for about 1 mile.
**About the campground:** There are no permanent facilities at the Lower Salt Creek area. During the off-season, please pack it in, pack it out. Elevation 1,100 feet. Stay limit 14 days. Open all year.

## 237 Shasta Campground (Chappie-Shasta OHV Area)

**Location:** 13 miles north of Redding.
**GPS:** 40.71310085 / -122.4357897
**Sites:** 27 sites for tents and RVs up to 30 feet long
**Facilities:** Tables, fire rings, drinking water, vault toilets; boat ramp 1.5 miles east
**Fee per night:** $
**Management:** Redding Bureau of Land Management, (530) 224-2100
**Activities:** OHV driving, fishing, hiking
**Finding the campground:** From Redding, take I-5 north about 10 miles to the Shasta Dam exit. Follow Shasta Dam Boulevard 2 miles; turn north onto Lake Boulevard (CR A18) to Shasta Dam. To cross Shasta Dam you must present a valid driver's license and vehicle registration; your vehicle and trailer may be subject to inspection. After crossing Shasta Dam, turn left and travel 2 miles to the facilities.
**About the campground:** Situated on the Sacramento River adjacent to the Chappie-Shasta Off Highway Vehicle Area, this campground is of primary interest to OHV enthusiasts. A boat ramp at Centimudi, 1.5 miles to the east, provides access to Shasta Lake. The 4.5-mile Dry Fork Creek Trail begins at the western end of Shasta Dam, providing shoreline fishing access, swimming opportunities, and great views of Mount Shasta. Elevation 620 feet. Stay limit 14 days. Open all year.

## 238 Ellery Creek

**Location:** 34 miles north of Redding
**GPS:** 40.91584323 / -122.2416307
**Sites:** 19 sites for tents and RVs up to 30 feet long
**Facilities:** Tables, fire rings, tent pads, bear boxes, drinking water, vault toilets
**Fee per night:** $$; reservations: (877) 444-6777 or recreation.gov
**Management:** Shasta-Trinity National Forest, (530) 275-1589
**Activities:** Swimming, fishing, boating, waterskiing
**Finding the campground:** From the intersection of CA 44 and I-5 in Redding, drive north 20 miles on I-5. Take the Salt Creek/Gilman exit and drive 13.5 miles northeast on Gilman Road (CR 7H009).
**About the campground:** Situated on the McCloud River Arm of the lake, this is a popular forested site. When the lake is at its highest, boats can be moored on the shore. Water levels can drop rapidly in summer. Elevation 1,070 feet. Stay limit 14 days. Open April through Labor Day.

## 239 Pine Point

**Location:** 35 miles north of Redding
**GPS:** 40.92747159 / -122.2469047
**Sites:** 14 sites for tents and RVs up to 24 feet long or group (up to 100 people)
**Facilities:** Tables, fire rings, drinking water, vault toilets
**Fee per night:** $, group: $$$$; reservations (group only): (877) 444-6777 or recreation.gov
**Management:** Shasta-Trinity National Forest, (530) 275-1589
**Activities:** Swimming, fishing, boating
**Finding the campground:** From the intersection of CA 44 and I-5 in Redding, drive north 20 miles on I-5. Take the Salt Creek/Gilman exit and drive 14 miles northeast on Gilman Road (CR 7H009).
**About the campground:** Situated on the McCloud River Arm of the lake. Elevation 1,100 feet. Stay limit 14 days. Open June through September.

## 240 McCloud Bridge

**Location:** 36 miles north of Redding
**GPS:** 40.938333 / -122.245
**Sites:** 11 single sites and 3 doubles for tents and RVs up to 16 feet long
**Facilities:** Tables, fire rings, tent pads, bear boxes, drinking water, flush and vault toilets
**Fee per night:** $$
**Management:** Shasta-Trinity National Forest, (530) 275-1589
**Activities:** Fishing, swimming
**Finding the campground:** From the intersection of CA 44 and I-5 in Redding, drive north 20 miles on I-5. Take the Salt Creek/Gilman exit and drive 14 miles northeast on Gilman Road (CR 7H009).
**About the campground:** This popular campground is located on an old ranch site on the McCloud River Arm of the lake. Adjacent to the McCloud Bridge Day Use Area, allowing easy lake access. Elevation 1,100 feet. Stay limit 14 days. Open April through October.

## 241 Moore Creek

**Location:** 31 miles north of Redding
**GPS:** 40.88860608 / -122.2239995
**Sites:** 12 sites for tents and RVs up to 16 feet long; may be reserved as a group camp (maximum 90 people)
**Facilities:** Tables, fire rings, tent pads, bear boxes, drinking water, vault toilets
**Fee per night:** $$; reservations: (877) 444-6777 or recreation.gov
**Management:** Shasta-Trinity National Forest, (530) 275-1589
**Activities:** Swimming, fishing, boating, waterskiing
**Finding the campground:** From the intersection of CA 44 and I-5 in Redding, drive north 20 miles on I-5. Take the Salt Creek/Gilman exit and drive about 20 miles northeast on Gilman Road (CR 7H009).
**About the campground:** Though primarily a group campground, it is also provides overflow for single-site family campers. Situated on the McCloud River Arm of the lake. Elevation 1,100 feet. Stay Limit 14 days. Open May through September.

## 242 Hirz Bay

**Location:** 29 miles north of Redding
**GPS:** 40.86644193 / -122.249355
**Sites:** 37 single sites, 11 double sites, 2 group sites for tents and RVs up to 30 feet long
**Facilities:** Tables, fire rings, drinking water, flush toilets; boat ramp 0.5 mile south
**Fee per night:** $$, doubles: $$$, group: $$$$; reservations (peak season): (877) 444-6777 or recreation.gov
**Management:** Shasta-Trinity National Forest, (530) 275-1589
**Activities:** Swimming, fishing, boating, waterskiing
**Finding the campground:** From the intersection of CA 44 and I-5 in Redding, drive north 20 miles on I-5. Take the Salt Creek/Gilman exit and drive 9 miles northeast on Gilman Road (CR 7H009).
**About the campground:** Situated on the McCloud River Arm of Shasta Lake. The scenic Hirz Bay Trail begins at the campground and follows the shoreline to the Dekkas Rock Day Use Area. Elevation 1,150 feet. Stay limit 14 days. Open all year.

## 243 Bailey Cove

**Location:** 18 miles north of Redding
**GPS:** 40.80030183 / -122.3191469
**Sites:** 5 single and 2 double sites for tents and RVs up to 30 feet long
**Facilities:** Tables, fire rings, drinking water, flush toilets, boat ramp
**Fee per night:** $, doubles: $$; reservations: (877) 444-6777 or recreation.gov
**Management:** Shasta-Trinity National Forest, (530) 275-1589
**Activities:** Swimming, fishing, boating, waterskiing, hiking, mountain biking, birding
**Finding the campground:** From the intersection of CA 44 and I-5 in Redding, drive north 17 miles on I-5. Take the Lake Shasta Caverns exit and drive 1 mile east.

**About the campground:** Popular, pretty, wooded campground situated on the lower McCloud River Arm of the lake. Well-used boat ramp and day-use area are nearby. Provides access to the 3-mile Bailey Cove Trail. The Lake Shasta Caverns are also on the McCloud Arm, with tours available for a fee. Elevation 1,130 feet. Stay limit 14 days. Open all year.

## 244 Mariners Point Shoreline

**Location:** 14 miles northeast of Redding
**GPS:** 40.75248409 / -122.2536076
**Sites:** Open camping for tents and RVs up to 16 feet long
**Facilities:** 7 tables, 7 fire pits; no toilets; no drinking water
**Fee per night:** None
**Management:** Shasta-Trinity National Forest, (530) 275-1589
**Activities:** Swimming, fishing, boating, waterskiing
**Finding the campground:** Take exit 680 off of I-5 for CA 299/Lake Boulevard. Follow signs for Burney/Alturas/CA 299 East and merge onto CA 299 East/Lake Boulevard East for about 6.7 miles. Turn left and follow Bear Mountain Road 9 miles to Dry Creek Road. Turn north onto Dry Creek Road for 5.5 miles and continue straight as it becomes Bear Mountain Road and then Silverthorn Road (CR 5J050). From there it is approximately 4 miles to the campground.
**About the campground:** Situated on the shoreline of the Pit River Arm of the lake, this is a pack-in, pack-out site with no services. Elevation 1,085 feet. Stay limit 14 days. Open May through September.

## 245 Upper and Lower Jones Valley

**Location:** 13 miles northeast of Redding
**GPS:** 40.73007774 / -122.230025 (continue 0.1 mile to Lower Jones Valley)
**Sites:** 8 in Upper Jones, 11 in Lower Jones for tents and RVs up to 16 feet long
**Facilities:** Tables, fire rings, drinking water, vault toilets
**Fee per night:** $
**Management:** Shasta Recreation Company, (530) 275-1589
**Activities:** Fishing, boating
**Finding the campground:** From the intersection of I-5 and CA 299 in Redding, drive east 5 miles on CA 299. Turn north onto Dry Creek Road (CR 4J02) and drive 6.5 miles. Bear right (northeast) at the Y intersection and drive 1 mile.
**About the campground:** Two adjacent campgrounds near an attractive cove in the Pit River Arm of the lake. A boat ramp is located about 1 mile north. This campground is located in a small canyon adjacent to the lake. The Jones Valley boat ramp and the Clikapudi Trail are located nearby. Spurs are unpaved in Upper Jones, paved in Lower Jones. Elevation 1,125 feet. Stay limit 14 days. Open all year.

## 246 Jones Valley Inlet Shoreline

**Location:** 13 miles northeast of Redding
**GPS:** 40.733056 / -122.231944

**Sites:** Open camping for tents and RVs up to 30 feet long
**Facilities:** Drinking water, portable toilets
**Fee per night:** $
**Management:** Shasta-Trinity National Forest, (530) 275-1589
**Activities:** Swimming, fishing, boating, waterskiing, hiking
**Finding the campground:** From the intersection of I-5 and CA 299 in Redding, drive east 5 miles on CA 299. Turn left (north) onto Dry Creek Road (CR 4J02) and drive 6.5 miles. Bear right (northeast) at the Y intersection and drive 1.5 miles.
**About the campground:** Situated on the shoreline of the Pit River arm of the lake. The Clikapudi Trail—a pretty, 4-mile loop—samples the forest and shoreline coves in the area and is open to hikers, mountain bikers, and equestrians. Elevation 1,150 feet. Stay limit 14 days. Open March through October.

## 247 Madrone

**Location:** 44 miles northeast of Redding
**GPS:** 40.9243209 / -122.0952793
**Sites:** 10 sites for tents and RVs up to 16 feet long
**Facilities:** Tables, fire rings, vault toilets; no drinking water
**Fee per night:** None
**Management:** Shasta-Trinity National Forest, (530) 275-1589
**Activities:** Fishing, hiking, hunting
**Finding the campground:** From the intersection of I-5 and CA 299, drive 29 miles northeast on CA 299. Turn north onto Fenders Ferry Road (FR 27) and drive 15 miles.
**About the campground:** An isolated campground on the bank of Squaw Creek. A trail leads north from the campground along Beartrap Creek. Elevation 1,500 feet. Stay limit 14 days. Open all year.

## 248 Chirpchatter

**Location:** 51 miles north of Redding
**GPS:** 40.8687326 / -122.1197489
**Sites:** Dispersed sites for tents and RVs up to 24 feet long
**Facilities:** Picnic tables, vault toilets; no drinking water
**Fee per night:** None
**Management:** Shasta Lake Ranger Station, (530) 275-1587
**Activities:** Hiking, hunting (seasonal)
**Finding the campground:** From I-5 North, take exit 698 to Gilman Road toward Salt Creek Road. Continue on Gilman Road about 15 miles until it becomes Fenders Ferry Road over the bridge. After 13 miles it becomes CR N8G01. Continue east 0.5 mile; cross a bridge and turn south onto CR N7K02 for 0.5 mile.
**About the campground:** This is a remote, wooded campground located east of Shasta Lake but with no lake access. Popular in the fall during hunting season. You have to cross the country road to access Squaw Creek. Elevation 1,285 feet. Stay limit 14 days. Open all year.

# Modoc Area

Most of this area lies within the borders of the Modoc National Forest, 1.6 million acres of varied terrain that includes meadows, wetlands, forests, and lava fields. The national forest shelters more than 300 species of wildlife, including pronghorn, wild horses and burros, and bald eagles.

The Medicine Lake Shield Volcano, about 10 miles south of Lava Beds National Monument, is one of North America's most unusual geological features. At about 20 miles in diameter, it is the largest volcano in California. Its gently sloping profile hides the fact that, in mass, it is larger than nearby Mount Shasta.

This sprawling area northeast of CA 89 contains extensive lava flows, cinder cones, pumice deposits, and lava tubes. Scenic attractions include Lava Beds National Monument, Giant Crater, Tilted Rocks, and Burnt Lava Flows.

## 249 Lava Beds National Monument: Indian Well

**Location:** 48 miles northwest of Canby

**GPS:** 41.716627 / -121.5045619

**Sites:** 43 sites for tents and RVs up to 30 feet long; 1 group site for up to 40 people

**Facilities:** Tables, fire rings, grills, drinking water, flush toilets

**Fee per night:** $, group: $$$$; reservations (group site): (530) 667-8113

**Management:** Lava Beds National Monument, (530) 667-8113

**Activities:** Hiking, cave exploring

**Finding the campground:** From Canby, drive northwest on CA 139 for 30 miles. Turn southwest onto FR 97 (FR 44N01) and drive about 2.6 miles. Turn northwest onto Lava Beds National Monument Road for 13.5 miles, continuing straight as it becomes Hill Road (FR 48N04) and FS Road 10. Head north on Lava Beds Campground Road for 0.4 mile.

**About the campground:** Indian Well offers a unique opportunity to explore more than thirty caves and lava tubes and to hike over ancient lava beds and fields. While ranger-led tours of the caves are offered, visitors are encouraged to explore the tubes on their own. You may check out a flashlight free of charge at the visitor center, which also provides maps and information about the caves and hiking trails. Some of the more popular caves are Mushpot, the only illuminated cave, located at the visitor center; Skull Cave, a deep hole with a staircase leading down to a narrow tube; and Sentinel, more than 0.67 mile long, with entrances at each end. A trail leads to the top of Schonchin Butte, a 30,000-year-old cinder cone with an excellent view of Mount Shasta. The area was also the stronghold for the last stand of the Modoc Indians against the US Army in the 1870s, and several interesting historical sites are located throughout the monument. Elevation 4,650 feet. Stay limit 14 days. Open all year. Backcountry camping is permitted in Lava Beds.

## 250 Hemlock (Medicine Lake)

**Location:** 60 miles northeast of the community of Mount Shasta

**GPS:** 41.58611111 / -121.5886111

**Sites:** 19 sites for tents and RVs up to 22 feet long

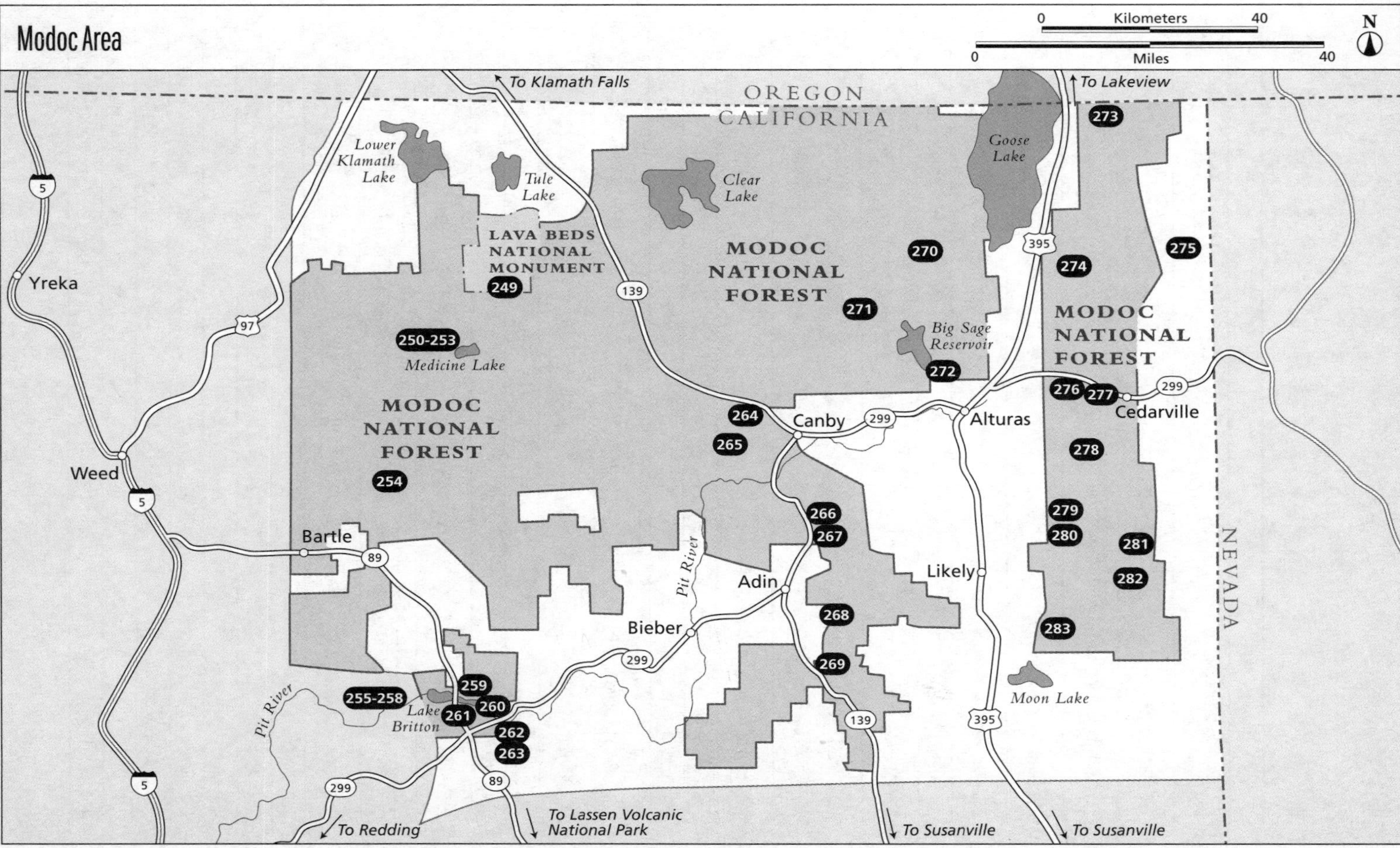
Modoc Area
0
Kilometers
40
0
Miles
40
N
To Klamath Falls
To Lakeview
OREGON
CALIFORNIA
NEVADA
Lower Klamath Lake
Tule Lake
Clear Lake
Goose Lake
Big Sage Reservoir
Medicine Lake
Moon Lake
Lake Britton
Pit River
LAVA BEDS NATIONAL MONUMENT
MODOC NATIONAL FOREST
MODOC NATIONAL FOREST
MODOC NATIONAL FOREST
Yreka
Weed
Bartle
Bieber
Adin
Canby
Alturas
Likely
Cedarville
249
250-253
254
255-258
259
260
261
262
263
264
265
266
267
268
269
270
271
272
273
274
275
276
277
278
279
280
281
282
283
5
97
139
89
299
395
To Redding
To Lassen Volcanic National Park
To Susanville
To Susanville

| | Name | Group Sites | RV Sites | Max. RV Length | Hookups | Toilets | Showers | Drinking Water | Dump Station | Pets | Wheelchair | Recreation | Fee(s) | Season | Can Reserve |
|---|---|---|---|---|---|---|---|---|---|---|---|---|---|---|---|
| | **MODOC AREA** | | | | | | | | | | | | | | |
| 249 | Lava Beds National Monument: Indian Well | * | * | 30 | | F | | * | | * | * | H | $-$$$$ | Year-round | |
| 250 | Hemlock (Medicine Lake ) | | * | 22 | | V | | * | * | * | * | HSFBL | $ | Late May-Oct | |
| 251 | A. H. Hogue (Medicine Lake) | | * | 30 | | V | | * | | * | * | HSFBL | $ | Late May-Oct | |
| 252 | Medicine (Medicine Lake) | | * | 22 | | V | | * | | * | * | HSFBL | $ | Late May-Oct | |
| 253 | Headquarters (Medicine Lake) | | * | 18 | | V | | * | | * | * | HSFBL | $ | Late May-Oct | |
| 254 | Harris Spring | | * | 32 | | V | | * | | * | | H | None | June-Oct | |
| 255 | Madesi River Access | | * | 40 | | V | | | | * | | FSB | None | Year-round | |
| 256 | Ruling Creek | * | * | 40 | | V | | | | * | * | FB | $ | Apr-Oct | |
| 257 | Gravel Bar River | | | | | | | | | * | | F | None | Year-round | |
| 258 | Pit 5 Dam River Access | | | | | | | | | * | | F | None | Year-round | |
| 259 | Northshore (Lake Britton) | | * | 16 | | V | | * | | * | | HSFB | $$ | Apr-Sept | |
| 260 | Dusty (Lake Britton) | * | * | 20 | | V | | | | * | | HSFB | $ | Apr-Nov | * |
| 261 | McArthur-Burney Falls Memorial State Park | | * | 32 | | F | * | * | * | * | * | HSFBL | $$$ | Year-round | * |
| 262 | Pit River | * | * | | | V | | | | * | | F | $ | Year-round | |
| 263 | Cassel | | * | 20 | | V | | * | | | | F | $ | Apr-Nov | * |
| 264 | Howard's Gulch | | * | 22 | | V | | * | | * | * | H | $ | May-Oct | |
| 265 | Cottonwood Flat | | * | 22 | | V | | | | * | | | None | Year-round | |
| 266 | Upper Rush Creek | | * | 22 | | V | | | | * | | F | None | Year-round | |
| 267 | Lower Rush Creek | | * | 22 | | V | | | | * | | F | None | Year-round | |
| 268 | Ash Creek | | * | 22 | | V | | | | * | | FHRM | None | May-Oct | |
| 269 | Willow Creek | | * | 32 | | V | | * | | * | * | F | $ | May-Oct | |
| 270 | Jane's Reservoir | | * | 22 | | V | | | | * | | FB | None | May-Oct | |
| 271 | Reservoir C | | * | 22 | | V | | | | * | | FB | None | May-Oct | |
| 272 | Big Sage Reservoir | | * | 22 | | V | | | | * | | FB | None | May-Oct | |
| 273 | Cave Lake | | * | 16 | | V | | * | | * | | FBS | None | July-Oct | |
| 274 | Plum Valley | | * | 16 | | V | | | | * | | F | None | June-Oct | |

| | Name | Group Sites | RV Sites | Max. RV Length | Hookups | Toilets | Showers | Drinking Water | Dump Station | Pets | Wheelchair | Recreation | Fee(s) | Season | Can Reserve |
|---|---|---|---|---|---|---|---|---|---|---|---|---|---|---|---|
| 275 | Fee Reservoir | | * | 24 | | V | | | | * | | BFH | None | May-Oct | |
| 276 | Cedar Pass | | * | 16 | | V | | | | * | | | None | May-Oct | |
| 277 | Stough Reservoir | | * | 22 | | V | | * | | * | | FB | None | May-Oct | |
| 278 | Pepperdine | | * | 15 | | V | | * | | * | | H | None | July-Oct | |
| 279 | Soup Spring | | * | 22 | | V | | * | | * | | HR | None | June-Oct | |
| 280 | Mill Creek Falls | | * | 22 | | V | | * | | * | | HF | $ | June-Oct | |
| 281 | Emerson | | * | 16 | | V | | | | * | | HF | None | July-Oct | |
| 282 | Patterson | | * | 16 | | V | | * | | * | | H | None | July-Oct | |
| 283 | Blue Lake | | * | 32 | | V | | * | | * | * | SBFHL | $ | May-Oct | |

Toilets: F=flush V=vault P=pit C=chemical; Fee: $=Under $20 $$=$20-$29 $$$=$30-$39 $$$$ $40 or more; Recreation: H=hiking S=swimming F=fishing B=boating L=boat launch O=off-highway driving R=horseback riding, M=mountain biking
Hookups: W=water E=electric S=sewer

**Facilities:** Tables, fire rings, drinking water, vault toilets, dump station; boat ramp located on the east shore of the lake
**Fee per night:** $
**Management:** Modoc National Forest, (530) 677-2246
**Activities:** Hiking, swimming, fishing, boating, waterskiing
**Finding the campground:** From the intersection of I-5 and CA 89 in Mount Shasta, drive east on CA 89 for 29 miles to Bartle. Just past town, turn left onto FR 49 (Medicine Lake Road) and drive north about 31 miles. Turn left (east) at the campground sign.
**About the campground:** Medicine Lake, 1.5 miles long by about 1 mile wide, is the crater of a former volcano. It receives much attention from anglers. Fishing is good from a trolling boat and the shore, especially in the morning and the evening. Waterskiing is restricted to the hours between 10 a.m. and 5 p.m. All sites offer views of the lake and vary from partially shaded by pines to forest settings. There are many hiking trails nearby. Elevation 6,700 feet. Stay limit 14 days. Open from snowmelt (late May to July) through October.

## 251 **A. H. Hogue (Medicine Lake)**

**Location:** 60 miles northeast of the community of Mount Shasta
**GPS:** 41.58661389 / -121.5916667
**Sites:** 24 sites for tents and RVs up to 30 feet long
**Facilities:** Tables, fire rings, drinking water, vault toilets; boat ramp located on the east shore of the lake
**Fee per night:** $
**Management:** Modoc National Forest, (530) 677-2246
**Activities:** Hiking, swimming, fishing, boating, waterskiing

**Finding the campground:** From the intersection of I-5 and CA 89 in Mount Shasta, drive east on CA 89 for 29 miles to Bartle. Just past town, turn left onto FR 49 (Medicine Lake Road) and drive north about 31 miles. Turn left (east) at the campground sign and continue west a short distance past Hemlock Campground (250).

**About the campground:** Hogue is the largest and most spacious of the four campgrounds on Medicine Lake located on the north shore. Beach access is on the eastern shore. Elevation 6,700 feet. Stay limit 14 days. Open from snowmelt (late May to July) through October.

## 252 Medicine (Medicine Lake)

**Location:** 60 miles northeast of the community of Mount Shasta
**GPS:** 41.5875 / -121.5947222
**Sites:** 22 sites for tents and RVs up to 22 feet long
**Facilities:** Tables, fire rings, drinking water, vault toilets; boat ramp and beach located on the east shore of the lake
**Fee per night:** $
**Management:** Modoc National Forest, (530) 677-2246
**Activities:** Hiking, swimming, fishing, boating, waterskiing
**Finding the campground:** From the intersection of I-5 and CA 89 in Mount Shasta, drive east on CA 89 for 29 miles to Bartle. Just past town, turn left onto FR 49 (Medicine Lake Road) and drive north about 31 miles. Turn left (east) at the campground sign and continue west a short distance past A. H. Hogue Campground (251).
**About the campground:** The campground offers views of surrounding peaks. Besides recreation around the lake, you can take off for a scenic drive along the Modoc Backcountry Discovery Trail—a 200-mile segment of the statewide system that runs past the Medicine Lake area. Elevation 6,700 feet. Stay limit 14 days. Open from snowmelt (late May to July) through October.

## 253 Headquarters (Medicine Lake)

**Location:** 60 miles northeast of the community of Mount Shasta
**GPS:** 41.585 / -121.6147222
**Sites:** 16 sites for tents and RVs up to 18 feet long
**Facilities:** Tables, fire rings, drinking water, vault toilets
**Fee per night:** $
**Management:** Modoc National Forest, (530) 677-2246
**Activities:** Hiking, swimming, fishing, boating, waterskiing
**Finding the campground:** From the intersection of I-5 and CA 89 in Mount Shasta, drive east on CA 89 for 29 miles to Bartle. Just past town, turn left onto FR 49 (Medicine Lake Road) and drive north about 31 miles. Turn east at the campground sign and continue west 1.5 miles beyond Medicine Campground (252).
**About the campground:** Located on the west side of the lake, away from the other campgrounds. Elevation 6,700 feet. Stay limit 14 days. Open from snowmelt (late May to July) through October.

## 254 Harris Spring

**Location:** 32 miles northeast of McCloud
**GPS:** 41.45656342 / -121.7847204
**Sites:** 15 sites for tents and RVs up to 32 feet long
**Facilities:** Tables, fire rings, drinking water, vault toilets
**Fee per night:** None
**Management:** Shasta-Trinity National Forest, (530) 964-2184
**Activities:** Sightseeing, hiking, hunting
**Finding the campground:** From McCloud, drive 16 miles east on CA 89. Turn north at Bartle onto FR 15 (Volcanic National Scenic Byway) and drive 16 miles.
**About the campground:** Harris Spring is best used as an overnight stop or as a base camp for exploring the lava flows, cinder cones, and craters of the surrounding Medicine Lake Highlands Volcanic Area. Popular with hunters in fall. Elevation 4,800 feet. Stay limit 14 days. Open June through October.

## 255 Madesi River Access

**Location:** 3.5 miles southeast of Big Bend
**GPS:** 40.9958922 / -121.8725807
**Sites:** 5 sites for tents and RVs up to 40 feet
**Facilities:** Fire rings, picnic area, vault toilet, fishing pier; no drinking water
**Fee per night:** None

*Camping at the Madesi River Access overlooking the Pit River. Photo by Scott Waters*

**Management:** PG&E, (530) 335-2199
**Activities:** Fishing, swimming, river rafting
**Finding the campground:** From CA 299 East, turn onto Big Bend Road for 13.5 miles. Turn right onto Ready Camp Road; take the first left to stay on Ready Camp Road. Continue straight onto Hagen Flat Road for 1.5 miles and turn left onto a dirt road.
**About the campground:** Secluded site on the Pit River, which is popular for fly fishing. Easy river access. Elevation 1,700 feet. Stay limit 14 days. Open all year.

## 256 Ruling Creek

**Location:** 12 miles southeast of Big Bend
**GPS:** 40.9816483 / -121.7789086
**Sites:** 8 sites for tents and RVs up to 40 feet long; 1 group site
**Facilities:** Tables, fire rings, vault toilet; no drinking water
**Fee per night:** $
**Management:** PG&E, (530) 335-2199
**Activities:** Fishing, fly fishing, rafting
**Finding the campground:** From CA 89, 9.7 miles north of the junction with CA 299, turn west onto Clark Creek Road. Drive 4.4 miles; merge onto Pit River Road and go 8 miles.
**About the campground:** Built on the edge of the Pit River, Ruling Creek offers great access to the water. Available for group camping as well. Elevation 2,450 feet. Stay limit 14 days. Open mid-April to mid-October.

## 257 Gravel Bar River

**Location:** 11 miles southeast of Big Bend
**GPS:** 40.9716179 / -121.7809209
**Sites:** 3 sites for tents
**Facilities:** Fire rings; no drinking water or toilets.
**Fee per night:** None
**Management:** PG&E, (530) 335-2199
**Activities:** Fishing, riparian wildlife watching
**Finding the campground:** From CA 89, turn onto FR 37N05 and drive 5 miles.
**About the campground:** Remote campground on the Pit River in a forested area. It would be difficult to pull a trailer or RV into this location. Elevation 2,370 feet. Stay limit 14 days. Open all year.

## 258 Pit 5 Dam River Access

**Location:** 3.5 miles southeast of Big Bend
**GPS:** 40.9916484 / -121.8681946
**Sites:** 3 walk-in tent sites
**Facilities:** Fire rings; no toilets; no drinking water
**Fee per night:** None
**Management:** PG&E, (530) 335-2199
**Activities:** Fishing

**Finding the campground:** From the town of Big Bend, head south on Big Bend Road toward Hot Springs Road. Take the second left onto Hagen Flat Road for 1.2 miles. Turn left to stay on Hagen Flat Road for 1.7 miles.

**About the campground:** With no restrooms or other facilities, this is a true back-to-nature experience on the Pit River, but with a lovely view of the water. Recommended for 4x4 vehicles only. Elevation 2,100 feet. Stay limit 14 days. Open all year.

## 259 Northshore (Lake Britton)

**Location:** 15 miles north of Burney
**GPS:** 41.0337717 / -121.6508208
**Sites:** 30 sites for tents or RVs up to 16 feet long
**Facilities:** Tables, grills, drinking water, vault toilets, boat ramp
**Fee per night:** $$
**Management:** PG&E, (916) 386-5164
**Activities:** Hiking, swimming, fishing, boating
**Finding the campground:** From Burney, drive 5 miles northeast on CA 299. Turn left onto CA 89 and drive 9 miles. Turn left onto Clark Creek Road and drive 1 mile.
**About the campground:** Northshore is attractively located on Lake Britton, and many campsites have direct access to the lake and views over the water. See McArthur-Burney Falls Memorial State Park Campground (261) for area information. Elevation 2,800 feet. Stay limit 14 days. Open mid-April to mid-September.

## 260 Dusty (Lake Britton)

**Location:** 13 miles northeast of Burney, near Lake Britton
**GPS:** 41.0157153 / -121.6113779
**Sites:** 9 sites for tents and RVs up to 20 feet long; 2 group sites (maximum 25 people)
**Facilities:** Tables, fire rings, vault toilets; no drinking water
**Fee per night:** $; reservations: (530) 335-2199 or http://recreation.pge.com
**Management:** PG&E, (916) 386-5164
**Activities:** Hiking, swimming, fishing, boating
**Finding the campground:** From Burney, drive 5 miles northeast on CA 299. Turn left onto CA 89 and drive 8 miles.
**About the campground:** Located in a wooded setting on the north bank of the Pit River, just before its juncture with Lake Britton. See McArthur-Burney Falls Memorial State Park Campground (261) for area information. Elevation 2,800 feet. Stay limit 14 days. Open mid-April to November.

## 261 McArthur-Burney Falls Memorial State Park

**Location:** 11 miles northeast of Burney
**GPS:** 41.0151448 / -121.6480134
**Sites:** 102 sites for tents and RVs up to 32 feet long; hike & bike and primitive walk-ins available; 24 cabins
**Facilities:** Tables, grills, drinking water, flush toilets, showers, dump station, store, snack bar, boat launch and rentals

*Burney Falls in all its glory. Photo by Scott Waters*

**Fee per night:** $$$; reservations (May–Sept only): (800) 444-7275 or reserveamerica.com
**Management:** California Department of Parks and Recreation, (916) 335-2777
**Activities:** Hiking, swimming, fishing, boating
**Finding the campground:** From Burney, drive 5 miles northeast on CA 299. Turn left onto CA 89 and drive 6 miles.
**About the campground:** On the shores of Lake Britton and encompassing a beautiful waterfall and several hiking trails, this 875-acre forested park provides a full range of outdoor recreation. Campsites are well spaced in an attractive forest of tall pines, with some scattered oaks. Most campsites are only a short walk from 129-foot Burney Falls, a lovely double waterfall. One hundred million gallons of water spill over the falls daily, year-round.

Access to Lake Britton is at the end of the campground access road, where there is a boat launch, marina, and swimming beach. The lake contains bass, bluegill, trout, and crappie, although catches of the last two are not particularly good. The Falls Trail leads from the store parking lot to the bottom of the falls, crosses the creek, and ascends on the other side of the falls. Two trails, Headwaters Trail and the Fall Creek Loop Trail, explore different aspects of the falls and Burney Creek. Elevation 3,000 feet. Stay limit 15 days June through September; 30 days October through May. Open all year.

## 262 Pit River

**Location:** 12 miles northeast of Burney
**GPS:** 40.9918064 / -121.5072441
**Sites:** 7 sites for tents or RVs; 1 group site
**Facilities:** Tables, fire rings, vault toilets; no drinking water

**Fee per night:** $
**Management:** Bureau of Land Management, (916) 257-5381
**Activities:** Fishing, riparian wildlife watching
**Finding the campground:** From Burney, drive about 12 miles northeast on CA 299. After Burney, continue 12 miles east until you see the sign "Pit #1 Power House." Turn onto the road and follow the signs downhill to the campground.
**About the campground:** The Pit River is the largest river in Northeastern California. Trout fishing along the Pit River is good if you are willing to fight the brush along its banks and do a lot of wading. The south fork is stocked in summer with rainbows. Elevation 2,860 feet. Stay limit 14 days. Open all year.

## 263 Cassel

**Location:** 11 miles northeast of Burney
**GPS:** 40.9215113 / -121.5517309
**Sites:** 27 sites for tents and RVs up to 20 feet long
**Facilities:** Tables, grills, drinking water, vault toilets
**Fee per night:** $; reservations: (530) 335-2199 or http://recreation.pge.com
**Management:** PG&E, (530) 335-2199
**Activities:** Fishing, fly fishing
**Finding the campground:** From Burney, drive 7.5 miles northeast on CA 299. Turn right onto Cassel Road and drive 3.5 miles.
**About the campground:** Cassel is on the banks of Lower Hat Creek, a stream famous for fly fishing for large trout. Check for catch-and-release regulations. Elevation 3,190 feet. Stay limit 15 days. Open April to November.

## 264 Howard's Gulch

**Location:** 6 miles northwest of Canby
**GPS:** 41.48583333 / -120.9688889
**Sites:** 6 sites for tents and RVs up to 22 feet long
**Facilities:** Tables, fire rings, drinking water, vault toilets
**Fee per night:** $
**Management:** Modoc National Forest, (530) 279-6116
**Activities:** Hiking
**Finding the campground:** From Canby, drive 6 miles northwest on CA 139.
**About the campground:** This campground sits in an attractive setting–a mixed forest of pines with some aspens along the fringe of a meadow. It is especially nice in the fall, when the aspen leaves turn golden. Elevation 4,700 feet. Stay limit 14 days. Open mid-May through October.

## 265 Cottonwood Flat

**Location:** 12 miles west of Canby
**GPS:** 41.4298883 / -121.0635841
**Sites:** Sites for tents and RVs up to 22 feet long
**Facilities:** Tables, fire rings, vault toilet; no drinking water
**Fee per night:** None

**Management:** Modoc National Forest, (530) 233-5811
**Activities:** None
**Finding the campground:** From Canby, drive southwest 4 miles on CA 139/ CA 299. Turn right onto FR 84 and drive west 7.6 miles.
**About the campground:** A remote, primitive camp, situated on lava flats strewn with junipers. Elevation 4,770 feet. Stay limit 14 days. Open all year (inaccessible during inclement weather).

# 266 Upper Rush Creek

**Location:** 10 miles northeast of Adin
**GPS:** 41.298538 / -120.8522306
**Sites:** 13 sites for tents and RVs up to 22 feet long
**Facilities:** Tables, fire rings, vault toilet; no drinking water
**Fee per night:** None
**Management:** Modoc National Forest, (530) 233-5811
**Activities:** Fishing
**Finding the campground:** From the intersection of CA 139 and CA 299 in Adin, drive 10 miles northeast on CA 299.
**About the campground:** Situated along the banks of Upper Rush Creek, this primitive campground offers fair fishing for small trout. Elevation 5,200 feet. Stay limit 14 days. Open all year (inaccessible during inclement weather).

# 267 Lower Rush Creek

**Location:** 9 miles northeast of Adin
**GPS:** 41.29333333 / -120.8780556
**Sites:** 10 sites for tents and RVs up to 22 feet long
**Facilities:** Tables, fire rings, vault toilets; no drinking water
**Fee per night:** None
**Management:** Modoc National Forest, (530) 299-3215
**Activities:** Fishing
**Finding the campground:** From the intersection of CA 139 and CA 299 in Adin, drive 8 miles northeast on CA 299. Turn right at the campground sign and drive 0.5 mile.
**About the campground:** Situated on the banks of a small stream, with fair fishing for small native trout. The campground is on the Adin, Canby, Lookout Auto Tour Loop. You can pick up a copy of this auto loop at any office of the Modoc National Forest. Elevation 4,400 feet. Stay limit 14 days. Open all year (inaccessible during inclement weather).

# 268 Ash Creek

**Location:** 9 miles southeast of Adin
**GPS:** 41.16138889 / -120.8280556
**Sites:** 7 sites for tents and RVs up to 22 feet long
**Facilities:** Tables, fire rings, vault toilet; no drinking water
**Fee per night:** None
**Management:** Modoc National Forest, (530) 299-3215

**Activities:** Fishing, fly fishing, hiking, mountain biking, horseback riding
**Finding the campground:** From Adin, drive southeast on Ash Valley Road (CR 527) for 8 miles. Turn left at a sign for the campground and drive 1 mile.
**About the campground:** Within walking distance of the campground are several good fly-fishing spots. Stocked annually, Ash Creek is fairly reliable for anglers. Just past Ash Creek Campground is the south trailhead for 22-mile Red Tail Rim Trail, open to equestrians, mountain bikers, and hikers. Elevation 4,800 feet. Stay limit 14 days. Open May through October.

## 269 Willow Creek

**Location:** 14 miles southeast of Adin
**GPS:** 41.01305556 / -120.8280556
**Sites:** 8 sites for tents and RVs up to 32 feet long
**Facilities:** Tables, fire rings, drinking water, vault toilets
**Fee per night:** $
**Management:** Modoc National Forest, (530) 299-3215
**Activities:** Fishing
**Finding the campground:** From the intersection of CA 299 and CA 139 in Adin, drive southeast 14 miles on CA 139.
**About the campground:** Features shaded sites and a day-use area. Fishing in Willow Creek is possible directly from the campground. The catch is small rainbow trout, which are lightly stocked annually. Elevation 5,200 feet. Stay limit 14 days. Open mid-May through October.

## 270 Jane's Reservoir

**Location:** 30 miles north of Alturas
**GPS:** 41.87981111 / -120.764
**Sites:** 8 sites for tents and RVs up to 22 feet long
**Facilities:** Fire pits, vault toilets; no drinking water
**Fee per night:** None
**Management:** Modoc National Forest, (530) 233-5811
**Activities:** Nonmotorized boating, fishing
**Finding the campground:** From Alturas travel west on CA 299 for 3 miles. Turn north onto Crowder Flat Road (CR 73) and travel approximately 29 miles to the Jane's Reservoir turnoff, on the left.
**About the campground:** Located in the Devil's Garden area of Modoc on the Modoc Plateau—a 25 million-year-old, mile-high area of lava flows featuring cinder cones, juniper flats, pine forests, and seasonal lakes. The campground circles the southeastern section of the lake, with a dirt boat ramp north of the entrance. Elevation 5,000 feet. Stay limit 14 days. Open mid-May through October (as weather permits). For a similar camping experience nearby, check out Reservoir F.

## 271 Reservoir C

**Location:** 19 miles northwest of Alturas
**GPS:** 41.66027778 / -120.7738889
**Sites:** Sites for tents and RVs up to 22 feet long
**Facilities:** Tables, vault toilets; no drinking water

**Fee per night:** None
**Management:** Modoc National Forest, (530) 233-5811
**Activities:** Fishing, nonmotorized boating, birding
**Finding the campground:** From the intersection of CA 299 and US 395 in Alturas, drive west on CA 299 for 3.6 miles. Turn right onto FR 73 (Crowder Flat Road) and drive 9.2 miles. Turn left onto FR 43N18 (Triangle Ranch Road) and drive 5.6 miles. Then turn right onto FR 44N32 and drive 0.7 mile.
**About the campground:** This small lake, which hosts migratory birds, is stocked annually with trout. Fishing is best in early summer, before water drawdowns take place. With virtually no light pollution, this is a great spot for stargazing. Elevation 4,900 feet. Stay limit 14 days. Open mid-May through October.

## 272 Big Sage Reservoir

**Location:** 13 miles northwest of Alturas
**GPS:** 41.57888889 / -120.6280556
**Sites:** 11 sites for tents and RVs up to 22 feet long
**Facilities:** Tables, vault toilets, boat ramp; no drinking water
**Fee per night:** None
**Management:** Modoc National Forest, (530) 233-5811
**Activities:** Fishing, boating
**Finding the campground:** From the intersection of CA 299 and US 395 in Alturas, drive west on CA 299 for 3.6 miles. Turn right onto FR 73 (Crowder Flat Road) and drive 5.6 miles. Turn right onto CR 180 and drive 3.3 miles.
**About the campground:** You can catch largemouth bass and catfish at Big Sage Reservoir, stocked annually. The reservoir encompasses several thousand acres. Elevation 5,100 feet. Stay limit 14 days. Open May through October.

## 273 Cave Lake

**Location:** 44 miles northeast of Alturas
**GPS:** 41.97861111 / -120.2044444
**Sites:** 6 sites for tents and RVs up to 16 feet long
**Facilities:** Tables, fire rings, drinking water, vault toilets
**Fee per night:** None
**Management:** Modoc National Forest, (530) 279-6116
**Activities:** Fishing, nonmotorized boating, swimming
**Finding the campground:** From the intersection of CA 299 and US 395 in Alturas, drive north on US 395 for 38 miles. Turn right onto FR 2 and drive 6 miles.
**About the campground:** The campground provides access to two nearby lakes: Cave and Lily. Trout fishing in both lakes is fair to good, but it's usually better in Lily Lake. Both lakes are stocked annually. FR 2 is a steep dirt road, not recommended for trailers or large RVs. The Modoc Back-country Discovery Trail for scenic driving runs past the Cave Lake Campground. Elevation 6,600 feet. Stay limit 14 days. Open July through October.

## 274 Plum Valley

**Location:** 22 miles northeast of Alturas
**GPS:** 41.712272 / -120.3268579
**Sites:** 7 sites for tents and RVs up to 16 feet long
**Facilities:** Tables, fire rings, vault toilet; no drinking water
**Fee per night:** None
**Management:** Modoc National Forest, (530) 279-6116
**Activities:** Fishing
**Finding the campground:** From the intersection of CA 299 and US 395 in Alturas, drive north on US 395 for 19 miles. Turn right onto CR 11 and drive 2 miles. Bear right onto FR 45N35 and drive 1 mile.
**About the campground:** Plum Valley features a small creek and wooded solitude. Elevation 5,600 feet. Stay limit 14 days. Open June through October.

## 275 Fee Reservoir

**Location:** 34 miles north of Cedarville
**GPS:** 41.8300271 / -120.0290843
**Sites:** 7 sites for tents and RVs up to 24 feet
**Facilities:** Tables, fire rings, vault toilets; no drinking water
**Fee per night:** None
**Management:** Bureau of Land Management, Applegate Field Office, (530) 233-4666
**Activities:** Boating, fishing, hiking, biking, wildlife viewing
**Finding the campground:** From the Intersection of CA 299 and CR 1, travel north on CR 1 for 26 miles to Fort Bidwell. Turn right (east) at the T intersection onto CR 6 (Barrel Springs Road). Travel east on Barrel Springs Road approximately 4.5 miles to a fork. Take the right fork and continue approximately 3 miles to Fee Reservoir.
**About the campground:** Ample opportunity for recreation and solitude. Contact BLM for dispersed camping in this region. Elevation 5,300 feet. Stay limit 14 days. Open about May through October.

## 276 Cedar Pass

**Location:** 15 miles northeast of Alturas
**GPS:** 41.5593776 / -120.2939023
**Sites:** 17 sites for tents and RVs up to 16 feet long
**Facilities:** Tables, fire rings, vault toilets; no drinking water
**Fee per night:** None
**Management:** Modoc National Forest, (530) 279-6116
**Activities:** Riparian wildlife viewing
**Finding the campground:** From the intersection of CA 299 and US 395 in Alturas, drive north on combined US 395/CA 299 for 5.6 miles. Turn right onto CA 299 and drive east 9.2 miles.
**About the campground:** Best used as an overnight stop. Nonpotable water is available from two small streams adjacent to the campground. Elevation 5,900 feet. Stay limit 14 days. Open May through October.

## 277 Stough Reservoir (sometimes called Stowe)

**Location:** 17 miles northeast of Alturas
**GPS:** 41.5626711 / -120.2552258
**Sites:** 8 sites for tents and RVs up to 22 feet long
**Facilities:** Tables, fire rings, drinking water, vault toilets
**Fee per night:** None
**Management:** Modoc National Forest, (530) 279-6116
**Activities:** Fishing, nonmotorized boating, birding
**Finding the campground:** From the intersection of CA 299 and US 395 in Alturas, drive north on combined US 395/CA 299 for 5.6 miles. Turn right onto CA 299 and drive east 11.2 miles.
**About the campground:** The campground is under tall trees with views of the reservoir. Though small, the reservoir is regularly stocked for good fishing. Creek fishing is available nearby. Stough Reservoir is Number 4 on the Basin & Range Birding Trail, so bring your binoculars. Elevation 6,200 feet. Stay limit 14 days. Open May through October.

## 278 Pepperdine

**Location:** 19 miles east of Alturas
**GPS:** 41.45027778 / -120.2408333
**Sites:** 7 sites for tents and RVs up to 15 feet long
**Facilities:** Tables, fire rings, drinking water, vault toilets
**Fee per night:** None

*The view of the mountains and valley below from a couple miles down the Warner Summit Trail. The trail departs from the Pepperdine Campground. Photo by Bubba Seuss*

**Management:** Modoc National Forest, (530) 279-6116
**Activities:** Hiking
**Finding the campground:** From the intersection of CA 299 and US 395 in Alturas, drive south on US 395 for 1.2 miles. Turn left onto CR 56 and drive east for 13 miles to a fork in the road. Bear left at the fork onto FR 31 (Parker Creek Road) and drive 5 miles to the campground access sign.
**About the campground:** A trail leads from the campground to the summit of Squaw Peak (8,646 feet; 4 miles round-trip). The Summit Trail leads to Patterson Lake in the South Warner Wilderness (12 miles round-trip). For equestrian camping in the vicinity, see Pepperdine Equestrian Campground. Elevation 6,680 feet. Stay limit 14 days. Open July through October.

## 279 Soup Spring

**Location:** 39 miles southeast of Alturas
**GPS:** 41.30916667 / -120.2772222
**Sites:** 8 sites for tents and RVs up to 22 feet long
**Facilities:** Tables, fire rings, drinking water, vault toilets; corrals nearby
**Fee per night:** None
**Management:** Modoc National Forest, (530) 279-6116
**Activities:** Hiking, horseback riding
**Finding the campground:** From the intersection of CA 299 and US 395 in Alturas, drive south on US 395 for 19 miles to the town of Likely. Turn left onto CR 64 (Jess Valley Road) and drive 9 miles. Turn left onto FR 5 (also still CR 64) and drive 4.5 miles. Turn right onto FR 40N24 and drive 6 miles.
**About the campground:** A spur trail leads from the campground to the Mill Creek Trail and the Summit Trail in the South Warner Wilderness. The corrals are located at the equestrian trailhead; horses are not allowed in the campground. Elevation 6,800 feet. Stay limit 14 days. Open June through October.

## 280 Mill Creek Falls

**Location:** 33 miles southeast of Alturas
**GPS:** 41.27666667 / -120.2880556
**Sites:** 8 sites for tents and RVs up to 22 feet long; additional tent sites
**Facilities:** Tables, fire rings, drinking water, vault toilets
**Fee per night:** $
**Management:** Modoc National Forest, (530) 279-6116
**Activities:** Hiking, fishing
**Finding the campground:** From the intersection of CA 299 and US 395 in Alturas, drive south on US 395 for 19 miles to the town of Likely. Turn left (east) onto CR 64 (Jess Valley Road) and drive for 12 miles, bearing left when FR 5 joins CR 64 from the south. Turn left onto FR 40N46 and drive 1.5 miles.
**About the campground:** Located on the banks of Mill Creek. A trail leads from the campground to Mill Creek Falls; the Poison Flat Trail connects the campground to Mill Creek, Summit, and East Creek Trails in the South Warner Wilderness. Less than a mile hike uphill is Clear Lake. It is not stocked. Elevation 5,700 feet. Stay limit 14 days. Open June through October.

## 281 Emerson

**Location:** 20 miles south of Cedarville
**GPS:** 41.26388889 / -120.1377778
**Sites:** 4 sites for tents and RVs up to 16 feet long
**Facilities:** Tables, fire rings, vault toilets; no drinking water
**Fee per night:** None
**Management:** Modoc National Forest, (530) 279-6116
**Activities:** Hiking, fishing
**Finding the campground:** From the intersection of CA 299 and CR 1 in Cedarville, drive south 17 miles on CR 1. Turn right onto CR 40 and drive 3 miles.
**About the campground:** The steep, dirt access road contributes to the seclusion here. There is stream fishing in Emerson Creek. The Emerson Trail leads from the campground into the South Warner Wilderness, connecting to the Summit Trail. Elevation 6,000 feet. Stay limit 14 days. Open July through October.

## 282 Patterson

**Location:** 44 miles southeast of Alturas
**GPS:** 41.19805556 / -120.1861111
**Sites:** 6 sites for tents and RVs up to 16 feet long
**Facilities:** Tables, fire rings, drinking water, vault toilets
**Fee per night:** None
**Management:** Modoc National Forest, (530) 279-6116
**Activities:** Hiking
**Finding the campground:** From the intersection of CA 299 and US 395 in Alturas, drive south on US 395 for 19 miles to the town of Likely. Turn left onto CR 64 (Jess Valley Road) and drive 9 miles. Turn right onto FR 64 and drive 16 miles.
**About the campground:** The Summit and East Creek Trails lead north from the campground into the South Warner Wilderness. Elevation 7,200 feet. Stay limit 14 days. Open July through October.

## 283 Blue Lake

**Location:** 36 miles southeast of Alturas
**GPS:** 41.14277778 / -120.28
**Sites:** 48 sites for tents and RVs up to 32 feet long
**Facilities:** Tables, fire rings, drinking water, vault toilets, boat ramp, fishing pier
**Fee per night:** $
**Management:** Modoc National Forest, (530) 279-6116
**Activities:** Swimming, boating, fishing, hiking
**Finding the campground:** From the intersection of CA 299 and US 395 in Alturas, drive south on US 395 for 19 miles to the town of Likely. Turn left onto CR 64 (Jess Valley Road) and drive 9 miles. Turn right onto FR 64 and drive 6 miles. Then turn right onto FR 38N60 and drive 2 miles.
**About the campground:** Campsites are situated to provide views of Blue Lake and the surrounding mountains. White fir and ponderosa pine surround the lake, which is noted for large brown

trout. The lake is also stocked annually with rainbow trout. A 5 mph speed limit is in effect on the lake, which is circled by a 3-mile trail. Elevation 4,900 feet. Stay limit 14 days. Open mid-May through October.

## Lassen Area

Welcome to "The Crossroads," where the lava of the Modoc Plateau, the granite of the Sierra Nevada, and the sagebrush of the Great Basin meet and blend. This is one of the most fascinating and geologically diverse areas of California. The centerpiece is Lassen Volcanic National Park, but other attractions also lure outdoor enthusiasts. Lassen National Forest offers miles of wooded trails, streams, and the Thousand Lakes Wilderness. Eagle Lake is the second-largest natural lake in the state, and Lake Almanor is one of the most beautiful of the man-made ones. Hat Creek offers challenging trout fishing, and Subway Cave features a self-guided tour through the largest lava tube in California. Lassen National Scenic Byway makes a 170-mile loop through four major geophysical regions, providing an excellent tour of The Crossroads.

*It's an easy walk from the Butte Lake Campground in the Lassen area to see the colorful Painted Dunes. Photo by Bubba Seuss*

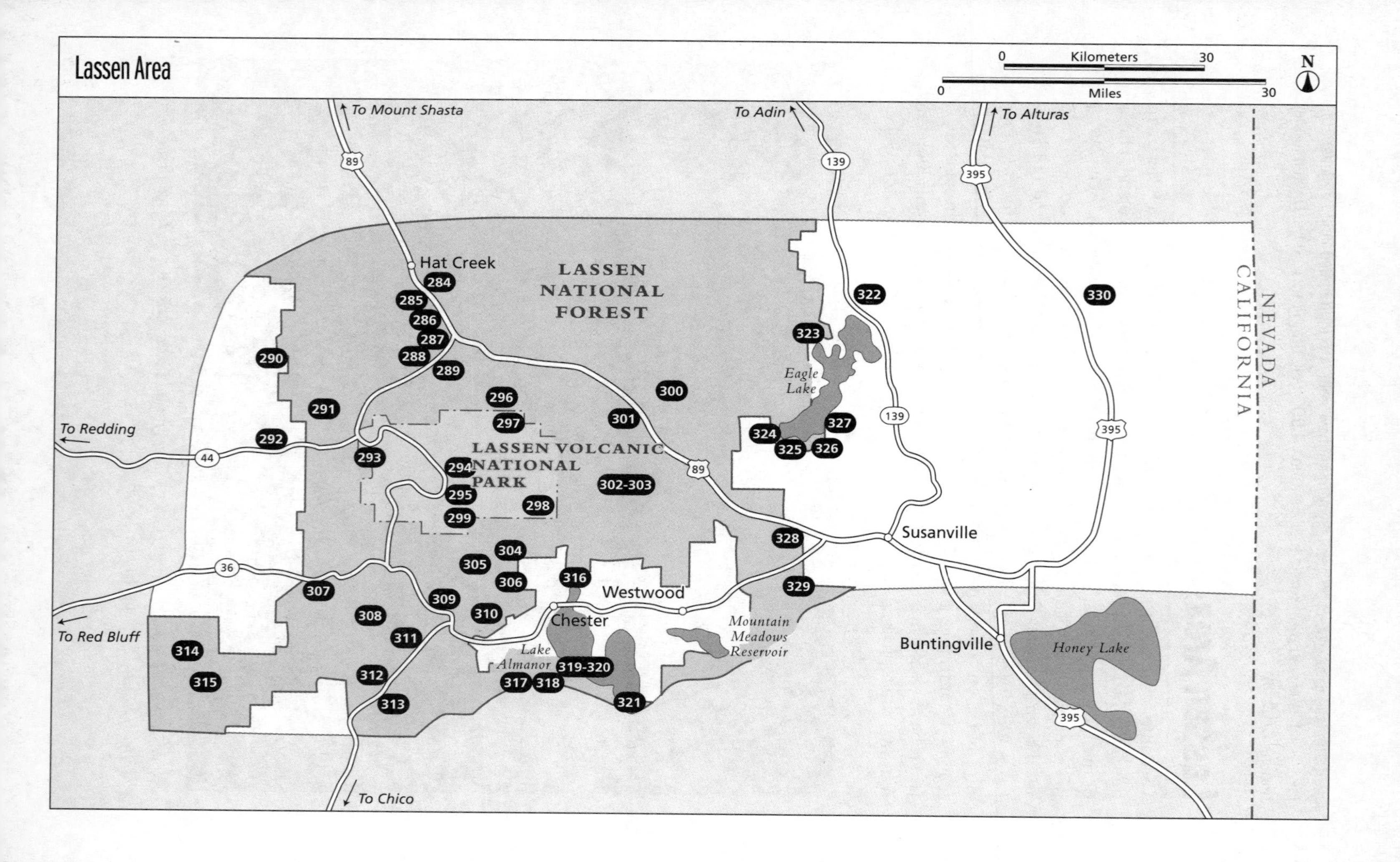

Lassen Area
Kilometers
0
30
Miles
0
30
N
To Mount Shasta
To Adin
To Alturas
To Redding
To Red Bluff
To Chico
NEVADA
CALIFORNIA
LASSEN NATIONAL FOREST
LASSEN VOLCANIC NATIONAL PARK
Hat Creek
Susanville
Westwood
Chester
Buntingville
Eagle Lake
Lake Almanor
Mountain Meadows Reservoir
Honey Lake
89
139
395
44
36
284
285
286
287
288
289
290
291
292
293
294
295
296
297
298
299
300
301
302-303
304
305
306
307
308
309
310
311
312
313
314
315
316
317
318
319-320
321
322
323
324
325
326
327
328
329
330

| | Name | Group Sites | RV Sites | Max. RV Length | Hookups | Toilets | Showers | Drinking Water | Dump Station | Pets | Wheelchair | Recreation | Fee(s) | Season | Can Reserve |
|---|---|---|---|---|---|---|---|---|---|---|---|---|---|---|---|
| | **LASSEN AREA** | | | | | | | | | | | | | | |
| 284 | Honn | | | | | V | | | | * | | F | $ | Apr–Oct | |
| 285 | Bridge | | * | 22 | | V | | | | * | | HF | $ | Apr–Oct | |
| 286 | Rocky | | | | | V | | | | * | | HF | $ | Apr–Oct | |
| 287 | Cave | | * | 22 | | V | | * | | * | * | HF | $ | Year-round | |
| 288 | Hat Creek | | * | 23 | | FV | | * | | * | | HF | $ | Apr–Oct | |
| 289 | Big Pine | | * | 22 | | V | | * | | * | | F | $ | May–Oct | |
| 290 | Latour Demonstration State Forest | | * | | | VP | | | | * | | HFM | None | June–Nov | |
| 291 | North Battle Creek Reservoir | | * | | | V | | * | | * | | FBSL | $ | Year-round | * |
| 292 | Macumber Reservoir | | * | | | V | | * | | * | | SFBL | $ | Year-round | * |
| 293 | Manzanita Lake (Lassen Volcanic National Park) | | * | 35 | | F | * | * | * | * | * | HFBSL | $$ | May–Oct | * |
| 294 | Summit Lake North (Lassen Volcanic National Park) | | * | 35 | | F | | * | | * | * | HFSB | $$ | June–Oct | * |
| 295 | Summit Lake South (Lassen Volcanic National Park) | | * | 35 | | V | | * | | * | * | HFSB | $$ | June–Oct | * |
| 296 | Butte Creek | | * | 22 | | P | | | | * | | FH | None | May–Oct | |
| 297 | Butte Lake (Lassen Volcanic National Park) | * | * | 35 | | F | | * | | * | * | HSFBL | $$ | June–Oct | * |
| 298 | Juniper Lake (Lassen Volcanic National Park) | * | | | | V | | | | * | | HSB | $ | June–Oct | |
| 299 | Warner Valley (Lassen Volcanic National Park) | | | | | V | | * | | * | * | H | $ | May–Oct | |
| 300 | Crater Lake | | * | 22 | | V | | * | | * | | FBSH | $ | May–Oct | |
| 301 | Bogard | | * | 25 | | V | | * | | * | | FH | None | May–Oct | |
| 302 | Rocky Knoll (Silver Lake) | | * | | | V | | * | | * | | FSHBL | $ | May–Oct | |
| 303 | Silver Bowl (Silver Lake) | | * | | | V | | * | | * | | FSHBL | $ | May–Oct | |
| 304 | Warner Creek | | | | | V | | | | * | | F | $ | May–Oct | |
| 305 | Domingo Springs | | | | | V | | * | | * | | HF | $ | May–Oct | |
| 306 | High Bridge | | | | | V | | * | | * | | HF | $ | May–Oct | |
| 307 | Battle Creek | | * | | | FV | | * | | * | | HF | $ | Apr–Oct | |
| 308 | Hole in the Ground | | * | | | V | | * | | * | | HF | $ | Apr–Oct | |
| 309 | Gurnsey Creek | | * | | | V | | * | | * | | HF | $ | May–Oct | |
| 310 | Willow Springs | | | | | V | | | | * | | F | None | May–Oct | |
| 311 | Elam | | * | | | V | | * | | * | | F | $ | Apr–Oct | |

| | Name | Group Sites | RV Sites | Max. RV Length | Hookups | Toilets | Showers | Drinking Water | Dump Station | Pets | Wheelchair | Recreation | Fee(s) | Season | Can Reserve |
|---|---|---|---|---|---|---|---|---|---|---|---|---|---|---|---|
| 312 | Alder Creek | | * | | | V | | | | * | | HF | $ | Apr-Oct | |
| 313 | Potato Patch | | * | | | V | | * | | * | * | HF | $ | May-Oct | |
| 314 | South Antelope | | | | | V | | | | * | | HF | None | Year-round | |
| 315 | Black Rock | | | | | V | | | | * | | HF | None | Year-round | |
| 316 | Last Chance Creek | * | * | 37 | | V | | * | | * | * | FHR | $$ | May-Oct | * |
| 317 | Soldier Meadow | | * | | | V | | | | * | | FH | $ | May-Oct | |
| 318 | Legacy | | * | | | V | | * | * | * | | HSBF | $$$ | May-Oct | |
| 319 | Almanor South (Lake Almanor) | * | * | 40 | | V | | * | | * | * | HSBFM | $-$$$$ | May-Oct | * |
| 320 | Almanor North (Lake Almanor) | | * | 40 | | V | | * | | | | HSBFLM | $ | May-Oct | * |
| 321 | Rocky Point (Lake Almanor) | * | * | 45 | | V | | * | | * | * | HSBF | $$ | May-Oct | * |
| 322 | North Eagle Lake (Eagle Lake) | | * | 35 | | V | | * | * | * | | HSBFL | $ | May-Nov | |
| 323 | Rocky Point East (Eagle Lake) | | * | 40 | | V | | | | * | | HSBF | None | May-Nov | |
| 324 | Christie (Eagle Lake) | * | * | 40 | | F | | * | | * | * | HSBF | $$-$$$ | May-Sept | * |
| 325 | Merrill (Eagle Lake) | * | * | 40 | EWS | F | | * | * | * | * | HSBF | $$-$$$ | May-Nov | * |
| 326 | Eagle (Eagle Lake) | * | * | 40 | E | F | | * | | * | * | HSBF | $$-$$$ | May-Nov | * |
| 327 | Aspen (Eagle Lake) | | | | | F | | * | | * | | HSBF | $$ | May-Oct | * |
| 328 | Goumaz | | * | 30 | | V | | * | | * | | HFRM | None | May-Oct | |
| 329 | Roxie Peconom | | | | | V | | * | | * | | HF | None | May-Oct | |
| 330 | Ramhorn Springs | | * | 27 | | V | | | | * | | HR | None | Year-round | |

Toilets: F=flush V=vault P=pit C=chemical; Fee: $=Under $20 $$=$20-$29 $$$=$30-$39 $$$$ $40 or more; Recreation: H=hiking S=swimming F=fishing B=boating L=boat launch O=off-highway driving R=horseback riding, M=mountain biking Hookups: W=water E=electric S=sewer

## 284 **Honn**

**Location:** 17 miles southeast of Burney
**GPS:** 40.77925 / -121.503
**Sites:** 6 sites for tents
**Facilities:** Tables, grills, vault toilets; no drinking water
**Fee per night:** $
**Management:** Lassen National Forest, (530) 336-5521
**Activities:** Fishing

**Finding the campground:** From Burney, drive 5.5 miles northeast on CA 299. Turn right onto CA 89 and drive southeast for 12 miles.

**About the campground:** In the shadow of Lassen Peak, Honn is one of six campgrounds located along Hat Creek, providing opportunities for trophy trout fishing, hiking, camping, and wildlife observation. Lava tubes, dormant and extinct volcanoes, lava flows, and fault lines all attest to a turbulent volcanic past. The campgrounds are used almost exclusively by anglers during the fishing season, and Upper Hat Creek is stocked annually with abundant trout. Honn is not recommended for trailers due to limited turnaround space. Elevation 3,500 feet. Stay limit 14 days. Open April through mid-October.

## 285 Bridge

**Location:** 23 miles southeast of Burney
**GPS:** 40.7309894 / -121.4394483
**Sites:** 25 sites for tents and RVs up to 22 feet long
**Facilities:** Tables, grills, vault toilets; no drinking water
**Fee per night:** $
**Management:** Lassen National Forest, (530) 336-5521
**Activities:** Fishing, hiking
**Finding the campground:** From Burney, drive 5.5 miles northeast on CA 299. Turn right onto CA 89 and drive southeast for 17 miles.
**About the campground:** There is access to the Fisherman's Access Trail, 4.25 miles along picturesque Hat Creek between Bridge and Cave Campgrounds. Elevation 4,000 feet. Stay limit 14 days. Open April through mid-October.

## 286 Rocky

**Location:** 24 miles southeast of Burney
**GPS:** 40.7259049 / -121.4285588
**Sites:** 8 sites for tents; no RVs
**Facilities:** Tables, grills, vault toilets; no drinking water
**Fee per night:** $
**Management:** Lassen National Forest, (530) 336-5521
**Activities:** Fishing, hiking
**Finding the campground:** From Burney, drive 5.5 miles northeast on CA 299. Turn right onto CA 89 and drive southeast for 18 miles.
**About the campground:** Fishing and hiking are available along Hat Creek. Not recommended for trailers because of tight turnaround. Elevation 4,000 feet. Stay limit 14 days. Open April through October.

## 287 Cave

**Location:** 27 miles southeast of Burney
**GPS:** 40.6841814 / -121.4238632
**Sites:** 46 sites for tents and RVs up to 22 feet long
**Facilities:** Tables, grills, drinking water (none in winter), vault toilets
**Fee per night:** $

**Management:** Lassen National Forest, (530) 336-5521
**Activities:** Fishing, hiking, cave touring
**Finding the campground:** From Burney, drive 5.5 miles northeast on CA 299. Turn right onto CA 89 and drive southeast for 21 miles.
**About the campground:** Located on the banks of Hat Creek at a point where the stream is stocked with rainbow trout every two weeks during fishing season. A trail runs along the creek; part of it is wheelchair accessible. Directly across the highway from the campground is Subway Cave, a large lava tube 0.7 mile long, with interpretive displays along its length. The cave is not illuminated, so bring a flashlight. For more day hikes and interpretive information, visit the Old Station Visitor Center 1 mile south. The campground is 15 miles northeast of the entrance to Lassen Volcanic National Park. Elevation 4,400 feet. Stay limit 14 days. Sites 1–16 are open all year.

## 288 Hat Creek

**Location:** 29 miles southeast of Burney
**GPS:** 40.6691618 / -121.4439978
**Sites:** 73 sites for tents and RVs up to 22 feet long
**Facilities:** Tables, grills, drinking water, flush and vault toilets
**Fee per night:** $
**Management:** Lassen National Forest, (530) 336-5521
**Activities:** Fishing, hiking
**Finding the campground:** From Burney, drive 5.5 miles northeast on CA 299. Turn right onto CA 89 and drive southeast for 23 miles.
**About the campground:** Just across the street is the Spatter Cones Trail—a 1.5-mile self-guided interpretive loop showing the origins of the Hat Creek Lava Flow. The campground is about 12 miles northeast of the entrance to Lassen Volcanic National Park. Elevation 4,390 feet. Stay limit 14 days. Open April through October.

## 289 Big Pine

**Location:** 32 miles southeast of Burney
**GPS:** 40.6328829 / -121.4671842
**Sites:** 19 sites for tents and RVs up to 22 feet long
**Facilities:** Tables, grills, hand-pumped drinking water, vault toilets
**Fee per night:** $
**Management:** Lassen National Forest, (530) 336-5521
**Activities:** Fishing
**Finding the campground:** From Burney, drive 5.5 miles northeast on CA 299. Turn right onto CA 89 and drive south for 26 miles.
**About the campground:** For an area description, see Honn Campground (number 284). Elevation 4,700 feet. Stay limit 14 days. Open May through October.

## 290 Latour Demonstration State Forest

**Location:** 19 miles south of Burney
**GPS:** 40.688212 / -121.744435 (Old Cow Creek)

**Sites:** Total of 7 sites for tents and RVs in 4 primitive campgrounds within 2 miles of one another: Old Cow Creek (2 sites), South Cow Creek Meadows (2 sites), Butcher's Gulch (1 site), and Old Headquarters (2 sites)
**Facilities:** Tables, grills, drinking water, vault or pit toilets
**Fee per night:** None
**Management:** Latour Demonstration State Forest, (530) 225-2438
**Activities:** Hiking, mountain biking, fishing, hunting
**Finding the campground:** From Burney, drive about 3 miles west on CA 299. Turn south onto Tamarack Road and continue 16 miles to Old Cow Creek. A series of crisscrossing dirt roads can be confusing here; call for a brochure before visiting the forest.
**About the campground:** The purpose of this remote 9,000-acre state forest is to teach and demonstrate conservation logging practices. It also protects a unique stand of old-growth sugar pines, many of which are 40 to 60 inches in diameter. Elevation 5,500–5,900 feet. Stay limit 15 days. Open June to November.

## 291 North Battle Creek Reservoir

**Location:** 45 miles south of Burney
**GPS:** 40.5944536 / -121.6521626
**Sites:** 10 sites for tents and RVs; 5 walk-in sites
**Facilities:** Tables, grills, drinking water, vault toilets, boat ramp
**Fee per night:** $; reservations: http://recreation.pge.com
**Management:** PG&E, (530) 335-2199
**Activities:** Fishing, nonmotorized boating, swimming
**Finding the campground:** From Burney, drive 5.5 miles northeast on CA 299. Turn southeast onto CA 89 and drive south for 34 miles. Turn west onto FR 32N31 and drive 5 miles.
**About the campground:** Fishing can be good at this little-known lake. No gas engines are allowed on the lake. Lassen Volcanic National Park is 8 miles to the southeast. Elevation 5,600 feet. Stay limit 14 days. Open all year.

## 292 Macumber Reservoir

**Location:** 37 miles east of Redding
**GPS:** 40.5385729 / -121.7304467
**Sites:** 8 sites for tents and RVs; 5 walk-ins
**Facilities:** Tables, grills, drinking water, vault toilets, boat ramp
**Fee per night:** $; reservations (all but walk-ins): http://recreation.pge.com
**Management:** PG&E, (530) 335-2199
**Activities:** Swimming, fishing, nonmotorized boating
**Finding the campground:** From Redding, go east on CA 44 toward Viola/Lassen National Park to Lake Macumber Road (which becomes Deer Flat Road). Drive 2 miles to the reservoir and campground.
**About the campground:** This small, often-overlooked lake is usually stocked annually with rainbow trout. No gas engines are allowed on the lake. Elevation 3,500 feet. Stay limit 14 days. Open all year.

## 293 Manzanita Lake (Lassen Volcanic National Park)

**Location:** 46 miles east of Redding
**GPS:** 40.5312504 / -121.5620932
**Sites:** 179 sites for tents and RVs up to 35 feet long
**Facilities:** Tables, grills, drinking water, showers, flush toilets, dump station, laundry, store, boat launch
**Fee per night:** $$; reservations: (877) 444-6777 or recreation.gov
**Management:** Lassen Volcanic National Park, (530) 595-4480
**Activities:** Hiking, fishing, nonmotorized boating, swimming
**Finding the campground:** From Redding, drive about 45 miles east on CA 44. Turn south onto CA 89 and drive less than 1 mile to the park entrance station. Continue a short distance and make a right (southeast) turn onto the campground entrance road.
**About the campground:** Small but beautiful Manzanita Lake is one of the main attractions of the park. It offers great reflections of Mount Lassen and Chaos Crags, and the campground gets heavy use. To accommodate the crowds, the sites are closer together than at other park campgrounds. The park visitor center is also here, on CA 89 just past the campground entrance road. The Nobles Emigrant Trail leads northeast to Chaos Crags and beyond. Trout fishing can be good, but catch-and-release rules are in effect. None of the lakes in Lassen Volcanic National Park are stocked. Elevation 5,900 feet. Stay limit 15 days. Open May through October. If you are camping with a group, check out Lost Creek Group Camp, about 6 miles east of the Manzanita Visitor Center.

*Lassen Peak and Chaos Crags are seen from the loop trail around Manzanita Lake. Photo by Bubba Seuss*

## 294 Summit Lake North (Lassen Volcanic National Park)

**Location:** 12 miles east of the Manzanita Visitor Center
**GPS:** 40.4944437 / -121.4235308
**Sites:** 46 sites for tents and RVs up to 35 feet long
**Facilities:** Tables, grills, drinking water, flush toilets
**Fee per night:** $$; reservations: (877) 444-6777 or recreation.gov
**Management:** Lassen Volcanic National Park, (530) 595-4480
**Activities:** Hiking, fishing, swimming, boating
**Finding the campground:** From the Manzanita Visitor Center, drive 12 miles north and then southeast on CA 89.
**About the campground:** Summit is a small but beautiful lake. Deer often graze in a nearby meadow. Campsites are not on the shoreline but are close to it. They are also close together, as at Manzanita. The Summit Lake Trail (8 miles round-trip) begins at the north end of the lake and leads to Echo Lake and Upper and Lower Twin Lakes. Elevation 6,700 feet. Stay limit 15 days. Open June through October.

## 295 Summit Lake South (Lassen Volcanic National Park)

**Location:** 13 miles east of the Manzanita Visitor Center
**GPS:** 40.490509 / -121.4267327
**Sites:** 48 sites for tents and RVs up to 35 feet long
**Facilities:** Tables, grills, drinking water, vault toilets
**Fee per night:** $$; reservations: (877) 444-6777 or recreation.gov
**Management:** Lassen Volcanic National Park, (530) 595-4480
**Activities:** Hiking, fishing, swimming, boating
**Finding the campground:** From the Manzanita Visitor Center, drive 12.5 miles north and then southeast on CA 89.
**About the campground:** See Summit Lake North Campground (294) for lake and area information.

## 296 Butte Creek

**Location:** 40 miles southeast of Burney
**GPS:** 40.6109964 / -121.2960831
**Sites:** 10 sites for tents and RVs up to 22 feet long
**Facilities:** Tables, fire rings, pit toilets; no drinking water
**Fee per night:** None
**Management:** Lassen National Forest, (530) 258-2141
**Activities:** Fishing, hiking
**Finding the campground:** From Burney, drive 5.5 miles northeast on CA 299. Turn right onto CA 89 and drive southeast for 21 miles. Turn left onto CA 44 and drive 11 miles; then turn right onto FR 32N21 and drive 3 miles.
**About the campground:** This is a fairly primitive campground. Fishing is generally only fair in this stream and best in spring. Butte Lake Campground in Lassen Volcanic National Park lies 4 miles to the south on the same road. Elevation 5,600 feet. Stay limit 14 days. Open May through October.

## 297 Butte Lake (Lassen Volcanic National Park)

**Location:** 89 miles east of Redding
**GPS:** 40.5649205 / -121.3025868
**Sites:** 101 sites for tents and RVs up to 35 feet long; 6 group sites
**Facilities:** Tables, grills, food lockers, drinking water, flush toilets, boat ramp (mid-September to closing, vault toilets and no drinking water)
**Fee per night:** $$; reservations (Loop B sites and group sites): (877) 444-6777 or recreation.gov
**Management:** Lassen Volcanic National Park, (530) 595-4480
**Activities:** Hiking, swimming, fishing, nonmotorized boating
**Finding the campground:** From Redding, drive east 82 miles on CA 44. Turn south onto FR 32N21 and drive about 7 miles.
**About the campground:** A 4-mile round-trip hike leads from the campground to the top of Cinder Cone (6,907 feet), from which there are excellent views of the surrounding wilderness. Good place to enjoy the night sky. Elevation 6,100 feet. Stay limit 15 days. Open June through October.

## 298 Juniper Lake (Lassen Volcanic National Park)

**Location:** 12 miles north of Chester
**GPS:** 40.4498812 / -121.2943766
**Sites:** 18 sites for tents (RVs not recommended); 2 group sites for up to 15 people each
**Facilities:** Fire rings, vault toilets, boat ramp; no drinking water
**Fee per night:** $
**Management:** Lassen Volcanic National Park, (530) 595-4480
**Activities:** Hiking, swimming, nonmotorized boating
**Finding the campground:** From Chester, on the north end of Lake Almanor, take Warner Valley Road north for 1 mile. Bear left onto Juniper Lake Road and drive 11 miles. The dirt road is rough and not suitable for RVs.
**About the campground:** The campground is on the east side of the lake. The last 6 miles of road is rough dirt not suitable for buses, motor homes, or trailers. Fishing is only fair, as the lake is not stocked. On the north end of the lake, a 0.5-mile climb of Inspiration Point affords wide views of the park. Elevation 6,800 feet. Stay limit 14 days. Open June through October.

## 299 Warner Valley (Lassen Volcanic National Park)

**Location:** 16 miles north of Chester
**GPS:** 40.421375 / -121.3687539
**Sites:** 17 sites for tents (RVs and trailers not recommended)
**Facilities:** Tables, fire rings, drinking water, vault toilets
**Fee per night:** $
**Management:** Lassen Volcanic National Park, (530) 595-4480
**Activities:** Hiking
**Finding the campground:** From Chester, drive north on Warner Valley Road for 16 miles. The dirt road, often rutted, is not recommended for large RVs.

**About the campground:** The Drake Lake Trail begins 0.5 mile north of the campground and ascends steeply in just over 2 miles to emerald-green Drake Lake. Other nearby trailheads include Terminal Geyser, Boiling Springs Lake, and Devil's Kitchen. Nearby Drakesbad Guest Ranch offers dining, horseback riding, massage, and thermal pool swimming (reservations required). Elevation 5,650 feet. Stay limit 15 days. Open May through October.

## 300 Crater Lake

**Location:** 57 miles southeast of Burney
**GPS:** 40.6268342 / -121.0427415
**Sites:** 17 sites for tents and RVs up to 22 feet long
**Facilities:** Tables, fire rings, drinking water (hand-pumped), vault toilets
**Fee per night:** $
**Management:** Lassen National Forest, (530) 257-4188
**Activities:** Fishing, nonmotorized boating, swimming, hiking
**Finding the campground:** From Burney, drive 5.5 miles northeast on CA 299. Turn right onto CA 89 and drive southeast for 21 miles. Turn left onto CA 44 and drive east 23 miles to Bogard Work Center. Turn left onto FR 32N08 and drive 7 miles.
**About the campground:** The pretty lake is stocked annually with Eagle Lake trout. Elevation 6,800 feet. Stay limit 14 days. Open mid-May through October.

## 301 Bogard

**Location:** 54 miles southeast of Burney
**GPS:** 40.5759998 / -121.0994097
**Sites:** 11 sites for tents and RVs up to 25 feet long
**Facilities:** Tables, fire rings, drinking water (hand-pumped), vault toilets
**Fee per night:** None
**Management:** Lassen National Forest, (530) 257-4188
**Activities:** Hiking, fishing
**Finding the campground:** From Burney, drive 5.5 miles northeast on CA 299. Turn right onto CA 89 and drive southeast for 21 miles. Turn left onto CA 44 and drive east 23 miles to Bogard Work Center. Continue on CA 44 for 2 miles; turn right onto FR 31N26 and drive 1.6 miles. Turn right onto FR 31N21 and drive almost 0.5 mile.
**About the campground:** Elevation 5,600 feet. Stay limit 14 days. Open May through October.

## 302 Rocky Knoll (Silver Lake)

**Location:** 20 miles northwest of Westwood
**GPS:** 40.4990541 / -121.1563557
**Sites:** 18 sites for tents and RVs
**Facilities:** Tables, fire rings, drinking water (hand-pumped), vault toilets, boat ramp
**Fee per night:** $
**Management:** Lassen National Forest, (530) 258-2141
**Activities:** Hiking, swimming, fishing, boating

**Finding the campground:** From Westwood (20 miles west of Susanville on CA 36), drive north on CR A21 for 12 miles. Turn left onto CR 110 (Silver Lake Road) and drive 8 miles to Silver Lake. Turn left at the lake.

**About the campground:** Silver Lake is a small but beautiful lake adjacent to the Caribou Wilderness. It is stocked with brown and Eagle Lake trout. Only car-top boats are allowed. There are two campgrounds on the lakeshore less than 0.5 mile apart (see Silver Bowl Campground, number 303). Trails lead into the wilderness and to other nearby lakes. Elevation 6,400 feet. Stay limit 14 days. Open May through October.

## 303 Silver Bowl (Silver Lake)

**Location:** 20 miles northwest of Westwood
**GPS:** 40.4993317 / -121.1641338
**Sites:** 18 sites for tents and RVs
**Facilities:** Tables, fire rings, drinking water, vault toilets, boat ramp
**Fee per night:** $
**Management:** Lassen National Forest, (530) 258-2141
**Activities:** Hiking, swimming, fishing, boating
**Finding the campground:** From Westwood (20 miles west of Susanville on CA 36), drive north on CR A21 for 12 miles. Turn left onto CR 110 (Silver Lake Road) and drive 8 miles to Silver Lake. Turn right at the lake.
**About the campground:** A nature trail encircles the lake, with access to two picnic areas. See Rocky Knoll Campground (302) for more information.

## 304 Warner Creek

**Location:** 7 miles northwest of Chester
**GPS:** 40.362530 / -121.308042
**Sites:** 13 sites for tents (RVs with trailers not recommended)
**Facilities:** Tables, fire rings, vault toilets; no drinking water
**Fee per night:** $
**Management:** Lassen National Forest, (530) 258-2141
**Activities:** Fishing
**Finding the campground:** From the intersection of CA 36 and CR 312 (Warner Valley Road) in Chester, drive northwest on CR 312 for 7 miles.
**About the campground:** See High Bridge Campground (number 306) for area information.

## 305 Domingo Springs

**Location:** 8 miles northwest of Chester
**GPS:** 40.3601613 / -121.3449711
**Sites:** 18 sites for tents (RVs with trailers not recommended)
**Facilities:** Tables, fire rings, drinking water, vault toilets
**Fee per night:** $
**Management:** Lassen National Forest, (530) 258-2141
**Activities:** Hiking, fishing

**Finding the campground:** From the intersection of CA 36 and CR 312 (Warner Valley Road) in Chester, drive northwest on CR 312 for 6 miles. Bear left onto CR 311 and drive 2.2 miles.
**About the campground:** The Pacific Crest National Scenic Trail passes 0.5 mile west of the campground on its way north to Lassen Volcanic National Park (4 miles). The dirt road to the campground is not suitable for large vehicles. The local Maidu Indians referred to this spot as the "center of the universe." Elevation 5,060 feet. Stay limit 14 days. Open May through October.

## 306 High Bridge

**Location:** 5 miles northwest of Chester
**GPS:** 40.33772 / -121.30763
**Sites:** 12 sites for tents (RVs with trailers not recommended)
**Facilities:** Tables, fire rings, drinking water, vault toilets
**Fee per night:** $
**Management:** Lassen National Forest, (530) 258-2141
**Activities:** Hiking, fishing
**Finding the campground:** From the intersection of CA 36 and CR 312 (Warner Valley Road) in Chester, drive northwest on CR 312 for 5 miles.
**About the campground:** Trout fishing can be good in the usually overlooked stream that flows beside the campground. The Warner Valley entrance to Lassen Volcanic National Park is 9 miles to the north. CR 312 is a dirt road, often rough, and is not suited for large vehicles. Elevation 5,200 feet. Stay limit 14 days. Open May through October.

## 307 Battle Creek

**Location:** 41 miles east of Red Bluff
**GPS:** 40.348144 / -121.627731
**Sites:** 50 sites for tents and RVs
**Facilities:** Tables, fire rings, drinking water, vault and flush toilets
**Fee per night:** $
**Management:** Lassen National Forest, (530) 258-2141
**Activities:** Fishing, hiking
**Finding the campground:** From Red Bluff, drive east 41 miles on CA 36.
**About the campground:** Located on the banks of Battle Creek, the campground provides access to good trout fishing. The stream is well stocked annually with trout, mostly rainbows. The campground is 10 miles southwest of the southwest entrance to Lassen Volcanic National Park. Elevation 4,800 feet. Stay limit 14 days. Open April through October.

## 308 Hole in the Ground

**Location:** 50 miles east of Red Bluff
**GPS:** 40.309813 / -121.560859
**Sites:** 13 sites for tents and RVs
**Facilities:** Tables, fire rings, drinking water (hand-pumped), vault toilets
**Fee per night:** $
**Management:** Lassen National Forest, (530) 258-2141

**Activities:** Fishing, hiking
**Finding the campground:** From Red Bluff, drive east 43 miles on CA 36 to Mineral. Turn right onto CR 172 and drive 5 miles. Turn right almost 180 degrees onto FR 28N05 and drive 2 miles.
**About the campground:** This tree-shaded campground is located on the banks of Mill Creek, which is stocked annually with rainbow trout. An 18-mile trail, following the creek most of the way, leads to Black Rock, where a primitive campground is also located. Elevation 4,300 feet. Stay limit 14 days. Open April through October.

## 309 Gurnsey Creek

**Location:** 54 miles east of Red Bluff
**GPS:** 40.309512 / -121.427937
**Sites:** 52 sites for tents and RVs
**Facilities:** Tables, grills, drinking water, vault toilets
**Fee per night:** $
**Management:** Lassen National Forest, (530) 258-2141
**Activities:** Fishing, hiking
**Finding the campground:** From Red Bluff, drive east 54 miles on CA 36 to the campground sign.
**About the campground:** Fishing is fair in spring, when the water level of the creek is highest. The stream is stocked annually with a small number of rainbow trout. Elevation 4,700 feet. Stay limit 14 days. Open May through October.

## 310 Willow Springs

**Location:** 57 miles east of Red Bluff
**GPS:** 40.3045663 / -121.3727145
**Sites:** 8 sites for tents (RVs with trailers not recommended)
**Facilities:** Tables, fire rings, vault toilet; no drinking water
**Fee per night:** None
**Management:** Lassen National Forest, (530) 258-2141
**Activities:** Fishing
**Finding the campground:** From Red Bluff, drive east 51 miles on CA 36. Turn left onto CR 769 and drive 1.3 miles. Turn right onto FR 29N19 and drive 5 miles.
**About the campground:** Dispersed camping on the banks of Lost Creek. Elevation 5,200 feet. Stay limit 14 days. Open May through October.

## 311 Elam

**Location:** 59 miles east of Red Bluff
**GPS:** 40.249116 / -121.448599
**Sites:** 15 sites for tents and RVs
**Facilities:** Tables, fire rings, drinking water, vault toilets
**Fee per night:** $
**Management:** Lassen National Forest, (530) 258-2141
**Activities:** Fishing

**Finding the campground:** From Red Bluff, drive east 56 miles on CA 36. Turn right onto CA 32 and drive 3 miles.

**About the campground:** Located on the banks of Deer Creek, which is one of the better trout streams in the area. The creek is known as one of the last streams in the northern Sierra that still supports threatened spring run Chinook salmon and winter steelhead. Elevation 4,400 feet. Stay limit 14 days. Open April through October.

## 312 Alder Creek

**Location:** 63 miles east of Red Bluff
**GPS:** 40.209283 / -121.496702
**Sites:** 6 sites for tents only (RVs with trailers not recommended)
**Facilities:** Tables, fire rings, vault toilet; no drinking water
**Fee per night:** $
**Management:** Lassen National Forest, (530) 258-2141
**Activities:** Hiking, fishing
**Finding the campground:** From Red Bluff, drive east 56 miles on CA 36. Turn right onto CA 32 and drive 7 miles.
**About the campground:** A lovely site on Deer Creek; see Elam Campground (number 311) for fishing information. Elevation 3,900 feet. Stay limit 14 days. Open April through October.

## 313 Potato Patch

**Location:** 66 miles east of Red Bluff
**GPS:** 40.188347 / -121.532717
**Sites:** 32 sites for tents and RVs
**Facilities:** Tables, fire rings, drinking water, vault toilets
**Fee per night:** $
**Management:** Lassen National Forest, (530) 258-2141
**Activities:** Fishing, hiking
**Finding the campground:** From Red Bluff, drive east 56 miles on CA 36. Turn right onto CA 32 and drive 9.6 miles.
**About the campground:** This popular campground is shaded by pines and firs. See Elam Campground (311) for fishing information. Elevation 3,400 feet. Stay limit 14 days. Open May through October.

## 314 South Antelope

**Location:** 41 miles east of Red Bluff
**GPS:** 40.2545442 / -121.7585997
**Sites:** 4 sites for tents
**Facilities:** Tables, fire rings, vault toilet; no drinking water
**Fee per night:** None
**Management:** Lassen National Forest, (530) 258-3844
**Activities:** Hiking, fishing

**Finding the campground:** From Red Bluff, drive east on CA 36 for about 24 miles. Turn right (south) onto Plum Creek Road and drive 8 miles. Turn right (south) onto Ponderosa Way and drive 9 miles.

**About the campground:** Catches of small native trout are possible in the South Fork of Antelope Creek, and hikers can use its course for off-trail hiking. Better hiking options are available at Black Rock Campground (315), which is a gateway to the Ishi Wilderness. Elevation 2,700 feet. Stay limit 14 days. Open all year.

## 315 Black Rock

**Location:** 50 miles east of Red Bluff
**GPS:** 40.1847836 / -121.7104695
**Sites:** 6 sites for tents
**Facilities:** Tables, fire rings, vault toilet; no drinking water
**Fee per night:** None
**Management:** Lassen National Forest, (530) 258-2141
**Activities:** Hiking, fishing
**Finding the campground:** From Red Bluff, drive east on CA 36 for about 24 miles. Turn right (south) onto Plum Creek Road and drive 8 miles. Turn right (south) onto Ponderosa Way and drive 18 miles.
**About the campground:** Located on the banks of Mill Creek and at the base of Black Rock, one of the oldest geological features of the area. A trail leads west from the campground into the Ishi Wilderness. Elevation 2,100 feet. Stay limit 14 days. Open all year.

## 316 Last Chance Creek

**Location:** 6 miles north of Chester
**GPS:** 40.3537741 / -121.2241328
**Sites:** 12 sites for tents and RVs up to 37 feet long; 13 group sites
**Facilities:** Tables, fire grills, drinking water, vault toilets
**Fee per night:** $$; reservations: http://recreation.pge.com
**Management:** PG&E, (530) 284-1785
**Activities:** Fishing, hiking, horseback riding
**Finding the campground:** From the Chester fire station, drive east 2.3 miles on CA 36 (crossing the causeway); turn left (north) and drive 3.2 miles.
**About the campground:** Situated where Last Chance Creek flows into the north end of Lake Almanor. Includes horseshoe pits, a sand volleyball court, and an area for horses. Elevation 4,500 feet. Stay limit 14 days. Open May through October.

## 317 Soldier Meadow

**Location:** 7 miles west of Almanor
**GPS:** 40.2132172 / -121.2746879
**Sites:** 15 sites for tents/RVs
**Facilities:** Tables, fire rings with grills, vault toilets; no drinking water
**Fee per night:** $

**Management:** Lassen National Forest, (530) 258-2141
**Activities:** Fishing, hiking, riparian wildlife watching
**Finding the campground:** From Almanor, take CA 89 west about 1 mile. Turn southwest onto Humbug Humboldt Cross Road. In about 0.5 mile turn west onto Humboldt Road and follow it 4.4 miles to the campground.
**About the campground:** Located in a meadow near Soldier Creek in a pine-and-fir forest. Close enough to Lake Almanor for day trips. Elevation 4,890 feet. Stay limit 14 days. Open May to October.

## 318 Legacy

**Location:** 2 miles west of Prattville
**GPS:** 40.216420 / -121.191175
**Sites:** 14 tent and RV sites; double sites available
**Facilities:** Tables, fire rings with grills, drinking water, vault toilets, dump station, water hookups
**Fee per night:** $$$
**Management:** Lassen National Forest, Almanor Ranger District, (530) 258-2141
**Activities:** Hiking, swimming, boating, fishing
**Finding the campground:** From CA 89 in Prattville, turn west at the "Almanor Campground" sign.
**About the campground:** Wooded large, level, paved sites. It is a 1-mile walk to Lake Almanor on a bike and walking path. Elevation 4,585 feet. Stay limit 14 days. Open May to October.

## 319 Almanor South (Lake Almanor)

**Location:** 9 miles southeast of Chester
**GPS:** 40.217182 / -121.176337
**Sites:** 53 sites for tents and RVs up to 40 feet long; 1 group site
**Facilities:** Tables, fire rings, drinking water, vault toilets
**Fee per night:** $, group site: $$$$; reservations: (877) 444-6777 or recreation.gov; walk-ins available
**Management:** Lassen National Forest, (530) 258-2141
**Activities:** Swimming, fishing, boating, waterskiing, hiking, mountain biking
**Finding the campground:** From Chester, take CA 36 West to CA 89 South. Turn left onto CA 89 and continue about 6 miles to Almanor Drive West (not to be confused with the Almanor West development and Almanor West Drive). Turn left onto Almanor Drive West (directly across from the Almanor Group Camp and rest area) and continue approximately 1 mile to Almanor South Campground.
**About the campground:** Lake Almanor, 27 miles west of Susanville, is one of the largest man-made lakes in California. Its sapphire-blue waters reflect Mount Lassen from almost any angle, providing great photos for camera buffs. Virtually all water sports may be enjoyed on the lake, and Almanor offers good fishing for trout, salmon, and smallmouth bass. The lake is stocked annually. Fishing is best in early spring and fall. Boat ramps, docks, and marinas are located along the shores of the lake.

The family campground is less than a 0.25-mile walk to the lake. You can access the 9-mile Lake Almanor Recreation Trail within the campground. Elevation 4,500 feet. Stay limit 14 days. Open May through October.

*Lake Almanor Campground sprawls along almost 2 miles of shoreline, with plenty of beach space for swimming and sunbathing. Photo by John Protopappas*

## 320 Almanor North (Lake Almanor)

**Location:** 9 miles southeast of Chester
**GPS:** 40.218612 / -121.176337
**Sites:** 50 sites for tents and RVs up to 40 feet long
**Facilities:** Tables, fire rings, drinking water, vault toilets, boat ramp
**Fee per night:** $; reservations: (877) 444-6777 or recreation.gov; walk-ins available
**Management:** Lassen National Forest, (530) 258-2141
**Activities:** Swimming, fishing, boating, waterskiing, hiking, mountain biking
**Finding the campground:** From Chester, take CA 36 West to CA 89 South. Turn left onto CA 89 and continue about 6 miles to Almanor Drive West (not to be confused with the Almanor West development and Almanor West Drive). Turn left onto Almanor Drive West (directly across from the Almanor Group Camp and rest area) and continue approximately 1 mile to Almanor North Campground, on the left.
**About the campground:** Next to the Almanor boat launch and Lake Almanor. See Almanor South (319) for more information.

## 321 Rocky Point (Lake Almanor)

**Location:** 13 miles south of Chester
**GPS:** 40.1907205 / -121.1052388
**Sites:** 109 sites for tents and RVs up to 45 feet long; 2 group camps
**Facilities:** Tables, fire rings, vault toilets, drinking water
**Fee per night:** $$; reservations: http://recreation.pge.com; walk-ins available
**Management:** PG&E (530) 284-1785
**Activities:** Boating, fishing, swimming, waterskiing, hiking
**Finding the campground:** From CA 70 North, turn left onto CA 89 North; continue 24 miles to Lake Almanor. Turn left at the campground.

**About the campground:** Among ponderosa pines with views of the lake and Mount Lassen. Some sites are on the shoreline. Access to the paved Lake Almanor Recreation Trail. Elevation: 4,500 feet. Stay limit 14 days. Open May through October.

## 322 North Eagle Lake (Eagle Lake)

**Location:** 41 miles north of Susanville
**GPS:** 40.7329664 / -120.723926
**Sites:** 20 sites for tents and RVs up to 35 feet long
**Facilities:** Tables, fire rings, drinking water, vault toilets; dump station and boat ramp nearby (fee charged)
**Fee per night:** $
**Management:** Bureau of Land Management, (530) 257-0456
**Activities:** Fishing, swimming, boating, waterskiing, hiking
**Finding the campground:** From Susanville, drive north on CA 139 for 40 miles. Turn east onto CR A1 (Eagle Lake Road) and drive 0.5 mile.
**About the campground:** Eagle Lake is the second-largest natural lake in California. Six campgrounds are located on its pine-lined shores—this one at the north end of the lake and five on the south shore. All water activities can be enjoyed here, and the lake is known for its trophy-size trout, which average 3 to 5 pounds. Eagle Lake is stocked annually. This campground offers direct access to the water. Elevation 5,100 feet. Stay limit 14 days. Open mid-May to November.

## 323 Rocky Point East (Eagle Lake)

**Location:** 23 miles north of Susanville
**GPS:** 40.6912803 / -120.7462249
**Sites:** Dispersed sites for tents and RVs up to 35 feet long
**Facilities:** Vault toilet; no drinking water
**Fee per night:** None (donation requested)
**Management:** Bureau of Land Management, (530) 257-0456
**Activities:** Fishing, swimming, boating, waterskiing, hiking
**Finding the campground:** From Susanville, travel north on CA 139 for 30 miles. Turn west (left) onto CR A-1 and travel approximately 5 miles. Turn south (left) onto Lakeside drive in the Bucks Bay subdivision. Travel south to the Rocky Point access road; watch for signs to Rocky Point. Follow the unimproved dirt road south along the shoreline until you reach the campground area.
**About the campground:** This small, undeveloped campground is best suited for self-contained camping. You can launch small boats along the shoreline in the campground area. Elevation 5,100 feet. Stay limit 14 days. Open mid-May to November. An alternative is the smaller Rocky Point West, on the other side of the lake (call BLM or check out their website: blm.gov/ca/st/en/fo/eaglelake/eaglelakecamping.html).

## 324 Christie (Eagle Lake)

**Location:** 19 miles northwest of Susanville
**GPS:** 40.5663889 / -120.8387833
**Sites:** 69 sites for tents and RVs up to 40 feet long, including some pull-throughs; 9 group sites

**Facilities:** Tables, grills, drinking water, flush toilets
**Fee per night:** $$, group: $$$; reservations: (877) 444-6777 or recreation.gov
**Management:** Lassen College Foundation, (530) 825-3212
**Activities:** Fishing, swimming, boating, waterskiing, hiking, biking
**Finding the campground:** From the junction of CA 139 and CA 36 in Susanville, drive west on CA 36 for 3 miles. Turn right (northeast) onto CR A1 and drive 16 miles.
**About the campground:** Spacious, wooded sites; next to Christie day-use area, at the end of the Eagle Lake Recreation Area paved hiking and biking trail. Because it is 5 miles from the marina and other amenities (hot showers, groceries, dump station), it is the most private of the Lassen College campgrounds. Elevation 5,100 feet. Stay limit 14 days. Open mid-May through mid-September.

## 325 Merrill (Eagle Lake)

**Location:** 17 miles northwest of Susanville
**GPS:** 40.5496152 / -120.8119014
**Sites:** 173 sites for tents and RVs up to 40 feet long; 2 group hookup sites (up to 16 people)
**Facilities:** Tables, grills, drinking water, flush toilets, hookups, dump station (for fee)
**Fee per night:** $$, group: $$$; reservations: (877) 444-6777 or recreation.gov
**Management:** Lassen College Foundation, (530) 825-3212
**Activities:** Fishing, swimming, boating, waterskiing, hiking, biking
**Finding the campground:** From the junction of CA 139 and CA 36 in Susanville, drive west on CA 36 for 3 miles. Turn right (northeast) onto CR A1 and drive 14 miles.
**About the campground:** Situated on the south shore of the lake in a pine grove. Easy access to the store, pay showers, and full-service marina via the paved hiking and biking trail. Guests can moor boats along the shoreline and hand-launch kayaks and canoes for no fee. The 5-mile South Shore Trail is ideal for cycling or hiking. Renovated in 2005, some sites will accommodate the largest RV. Elevation 5,100 feet. Stay limit 14 days. Open May through November.

## 326 Eagle (Eagle Lake)

**Location:** 17 miles northwest of Susanville
**GPS:** 40.5489785 / -120.7797207
**Sites:** 50 sites for tents and RVs up to 40 feet long; 2 group sites
**Facilities:** Tables, grills, drinking water, flush toilets
**Fee per night:** $$–$$$ (partial and full hookups); reservations: (877) 444-6777 or recreation.gov; walk-ins available
**Management:** Lassen College Foundation, (530) 825-3212
**Activities:** Fishing, swimming, boating, waterskiing, hiking, biking
**Finding the campground:** From the junction of CA 139 and CA 36 in Susanville, drive west on CA 36 for 3 miles. Turn right (northeast) onto CR A1 and drive 13 miles. Turn right (east) onto CR 231 and drive a little over 1 mile.
**About the campground:** Located 0.5 mile from the marina and waterfront and featuring 10 tent-only sites, this campground is popular with families and anglers. Elevation 5,100 feet. Stay limit 14 days. Open mid-May through November. (Self-contained campers are welcome to stay until December 31, weather permitting.)

## 327 Aspen (Eagle Lake)

**Location:** 18 miles northwest of Susanville
**GPS:** 40.5550194 / -120.7744139
**Sites:** 28 sites for tents
**Facilities:** Tables, grills, drinking water, flush toilets
**Fee per night:** $$; reservations: (877) 444-6777 or recreation.gov; walk-ins available
**Management:** Lassen College Foundation, (530) 825-3212
**Activities:** Fishing, swimming, boating, waterskiing, hiking, biking
**Finding the campground:** From the junction of CA 139 and CA 36 in Susanville, drive west on CA 36 for 3 miles. Turn right (northeast) onto CR A1 and drive 13 miles. Turn right (east) onto CR 231 and drive 2.2 miles.
**About the campground:** With no generators allowed and wheelbarrows on hand to move in your gear from the parking lot, you get a quiet, natural experience in Aspen (sometimes called Aspen Grove). Easy walk to marina, store, and showers. Elevation 5,100 feet. Stay limit 14 days. Open mid-May to October.

## 328 Goumaz

**Location:** 16 miles west of Susanville
**GPS:** 40.398 / -120.836
**Sites:** 5 sites for tents and RVs up to 30 feet long
**Facilities:** Tables, fire rings, drinking water, vault toilets
**Fee per night:** None
**Management:** Lassen National Forest, (530) 257-4118
**Activities:** Hiking, fishing, mountain biking, horseback riding
**Finding the campground:** Take CA 44 approximately 10 miles northwest of Susanville. Turn south on FR 30N03 and follow this dirt road 3 miles to the campground. The road is not suitable for passenger cars.
**About the campground:** Located on the banks of the Susan River, the camp is not far from the Bizz Johnson Trail, a 26-mile former railway right-of-way that offers fine views of the river as it passes through rugged, primitive Susan River Canyon. It is used by hikers, mountain bikers, and equestrians, as well as snowmobilers and cross-country skiers in winter. Elevation 5,200 feet. Stay limit 14 days. Open May through October.

## 329 Roxie Peconom

**Location:** 11 miles southwest of Susanville
**GPS:** 40.365 / -120.804
**Sites:** 10 sites for tents
**Facilities:** Tables, fire rings, drinking water, vault toilets
**Fee per night:** None
**Management:** Lassen National Forest, (530) 257-4188
**Activities:** Hiking, fishing

**Finding the campground:** From the intersection of CA 139 and CA 36 in Susanville, drive west 9 miles on CA 36. Turn left (south) onto FR 29N03 and drive 2 miles.
**About the campground:** Quiet sites in Douglas fir forest. Elevation 4,800 feet. Stay limit 14 days. Open May through October.

## 330 Ramhorn Springs

**Location:** 52 miles northeast of Susanville
**GPS:** 40.7071998718107 / -120.252973354492
**Sites:** 10 sites for tents and RVs up to 27 feet long
**Facilities:** Tables, grills, vault toilets, corrals; no drinking water
**Fee per night:** None (donation requested)
**Management:** Bureau of Land Management, (530) 257-5381
**Activities:** Hiking, horseback riding, hunting (seasonal)
**Finding the campground:** From Susanville, drive east and then north 50 miles on US 395. Turn right (east) onto Post Camp Road and drive 2 miles.
**About the campground:** High-desert camping without much shade, this campground is better in cooler months. Hiking and horseback riding on undeveloped trails, not far from Shinn Peak (7,562 feet). Elevation 5,100 feet. Stay limit 14 days. Open all year.

# Plumas Area

Plumas National Forest covers most of this region, providing more than 1.1 million acres of opportunity for nature lovers. The forest contains more than 1,000 miles of rivers and streams and over 100 lakes. Lake Oroville, which lies outside the national forest, is one of California's larger lakes. It offers good fishing for trout and salmon on more than 15,000 surface acres.

The Feather River National Scenic Byway, which begins about 10 miles north of Oroville on CA 70, travels along the rugged canyon of the North Fork of the Feather River, climbing over the Sierra crest at Beckwourth Pass and passing huge rock formations, waterfalls, and forested slopes en route. Feather Falls, a spectacular 410-foot drop, can be reached either by boat from Lake Oroville or via the Feather Falls National Recreation Trail, a strenuous 9-mile round-trip with a 2,500-foot elevation gain. Frazier Falls (248-foot cascade), near Gold Lake, can be reached by an easy 0.25-mile hike.

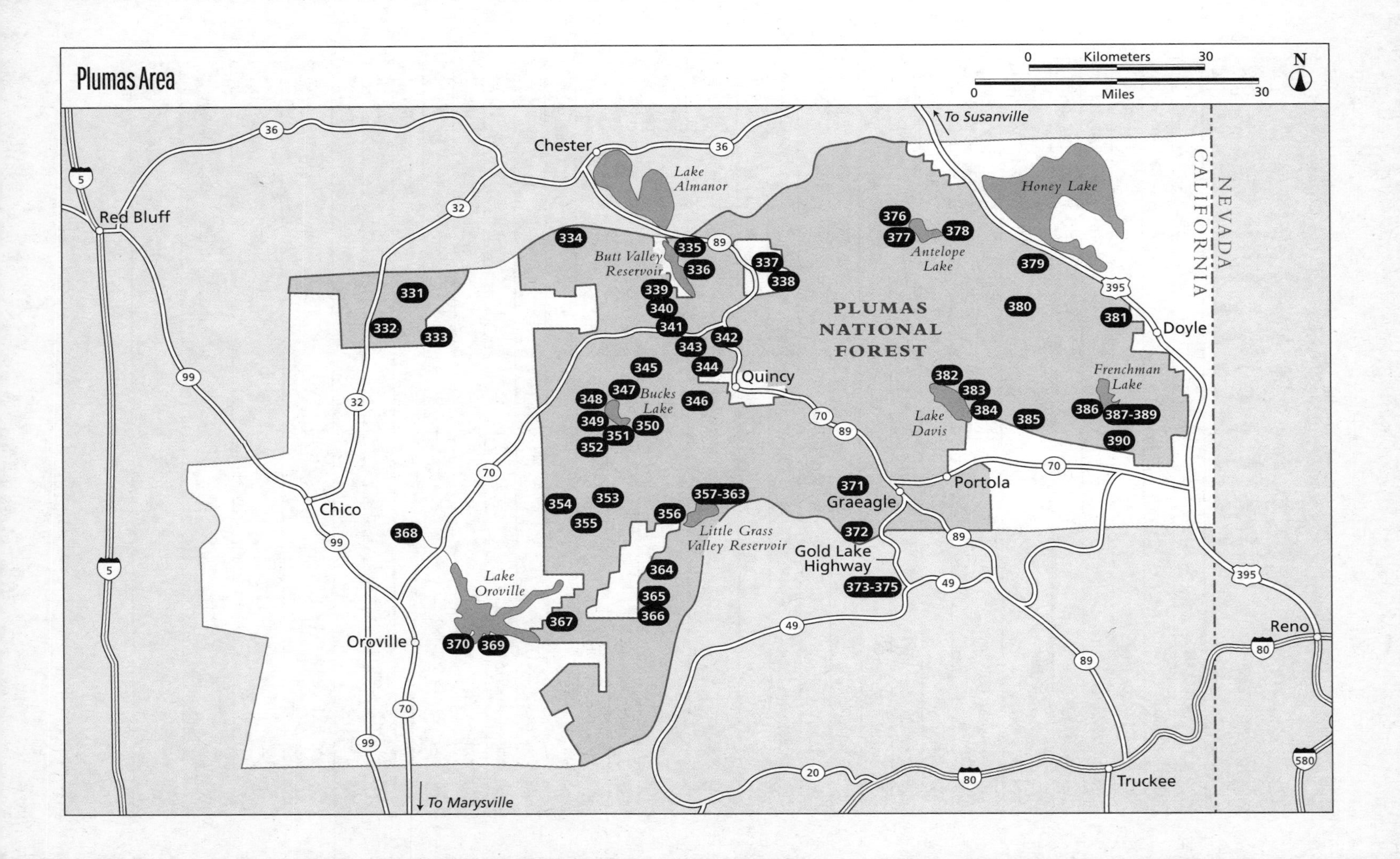
Plumas Area
Kilometers
0
30
Miles
0
30
N
To Susanville
Chester
Red Bluff
Lake Almanor
Honey Lake
Butt Valley Reservoir
Antelope Lake
PLUMAS NATIONAL FOREST
NEVADA
CALIFORNIA
Doyle
Quincy
Bucks Lake
Frenchman Lake
Lake Davis
Portola
Graeagle
Chico
Little Grass Valley Reservoir
Gold Lake Highway
Lake Oroville
Oroville
Reno
Truckee
To Marysville
331
332
333
334
335
336
337
338
339
340
341
342
343
344
345
346
347
348
349
350
351
352
353
354
355
356
357-363
364
365
366
367
368
369
370
371
372
373-375
376
377
378
379
380
381
382
383
384
385
386
387-389
390

| | Name | Group Sites | RV Sites | Max. RV Length | Hookups | Toilets | Showers | Drinking Water | Dump Station | Pets | Wheelchair | Recreation | Fee(s) | Season | Can Reserve |
|---|---|---|---|---|---|---|---|---|---|---|---|---|---|---|---|
| | **PLUMAS AREA** | | | | | | | | | | | | | | |
| 331 | Cherry Hill | | * | | | V | | * | | * | | F | $ | Apr–Nov | |
| 332 | Butte Meadows | | * | | | V | | * | | * | | F | $ | Apr–Oct | |
| 333 | Philbrook Lake | | * | | | V | | * | | * | * | SFB | $$ | May–Oct | * |
| 334 | Yellow Creek | | | | | V | | * | | * | | F | $ | May–Oct | |
| 335 | Ponderosa Flat (Butt Valley Reservoir) | | | | | V | | * | | * | * | SFBL | $$ | May–Sept | * |
| 336 | Cool Springs (Butt Valley Reservoir) | | * | | | V | | * | | * | * | SFB | $$ | May–Sept | * |
| 337 | Greenville | | * | | | V | | * | * | * | | H | $$ | May–Sept | |
| 338 | Taylorsville County Park | | * | | | FV | * | * | * | * | * | HR | $ | Apr–Oct | |
| 339 | Queen Lily | | * | 17 | | F | | * | | * | | HSF | $$ | May–Oct | |
| 340 | North Fork | | * | 32 | | F | | * | * | * | * | HSF | $$-$$$ | May–Oct | |
| 341 | Gansner Bar | | * | 31 | | F | | * | | * | * | HF | $$ | Apr–Oct | |
| 342 | Spanish Creek | | * | 40 | | V | | * | | * | * | HFS | $$ | May–Sept | * |
| 343 | Hallsted | | * | 23 | E | F | | * | | * | * | SF | $$-$$$ | May–Sept | * |
| 344 | Snake Lake | | * | | | V | | * | | * | | FBHRO | None | Year-round | |
| 345 | Silver Lake | | | | | V | | | | * | | FBHOM | None | Year-round | |
| 346 | Deanes Valley | | * | | | V | | | | * | | FO | None | Apr–Oct | |
| 347 | Mill Creek (Bucks Lake) | | * | | | V | | * | | * | | HSFB | $$ | Apr–Nov | |
| 348 | Sundew (Bucks Lake) | | * | 22 | | V | | * | | * | | HSFBM | $$ | Apr–Nov | |
| 349 | Lower Bucks (Bucks Lake) | | * | | | V | | * | | * | | HSFBO | $$ | Apr–Nov | |
| 350 | Whitehorse (Bucks Lake) | | * | | | V | | * | | * | | HR | $$ | May–Sept | |
| 351 | Haskins Valley (Bucks Lake) | | * | 40 | | V | | * | * | * | | SFBHL | $$ | Apr–Nov | * |
| 352 | Grizzly Creek (Bucks Lake) | | * | | | V | | | | * | | FH | $$ | Apr–Nov | |
| 353 | Little North Fork | | * | small | | V | | * | | * | * | HFSM | None | Apr–Nov | |
| 354 | Rogers Cow Camp | | * | | | V | | * | | * | * | O | None | Apr–Nov | |
| 355 | Milsap Bar | | | | | V | | | | * | | FB | None | Apr–Sept | |
| 356 | Black Rock (Little Grass Valley Reservoir) | | * | | | V | | | | * | * | HFSBL | $$ | May–Oct | |
| 357 | Peninsula (Little Grass Valley Reservoir) | | | | | F | | * | | * | * | HFSBL | $$ | May–Oct | |
| 358 | Tooms (Little Grass Valley Reservoir) | | * | | | V | | * | * | * | * | HFSBL | $$ | May–Oct | * |
| 359 | Wyandotte (Little Grass Valley Reservoir) | | * | | | F | | * | * | * | * | HFSBL | $$-$$$ | May–Oct | * |

| | Name | Group Sites | RV Sites | Max. RV Length | Hookups | Toilets | Showers | Drinking Water | Dump Station | Pets | Wheelchair | Recreation | Fee(s) | Season | Can Reserve |
|---|---|---|---|---|---|---|---|---|---|---|---|---|---|---|---|
| 360 | Little Beaver (Little Grass Valley Reservoir) | | * | | | F | | * | * | * | * | HFSBL | $$ | May–Oct | * |
| 361 | Red Feather (Little Grass Valley Reservoir) | | * | | | F | | * | * | * | * | HFSBL | $$ | May–Oct | * |
| 362 | Running Deer (Little Grass Valley Reservoir) | | * | | | F | | * | * | * | * | HFSBL | $$ | Apr–Oct | * |
| 363 | Horse Camp (Little Grass Valley Reservoir) | | * | | | V | | * | * | * | * | HFSBRL | $$ | Year-round | * |
| 364 | Golden Trout | | * | | | V | | * | | * | | BFS | None | Year-round | |
| 365 | Sly Creek (Sly Creek Reservoir) | | * | | | V | | * | | * | * | FBSOL | $$ | May–Oct | |
| 366 | Strawberry (Sly Creek Reservoir) | | * | | | V | | * | | * | * | FBSL | $$ | May–Oct | |
| 367 | Feather Falls Trailhead | | | | | V | | * | | * | | H | None | Year-round | |
| 368 | Lime Saddle (Lake Oroville State Recreation Area) | * | * | 40 | EWS | F | | * | * | * | * | FBSHRL | $$-$$$ | Year-round | * |
| 369 | Bidwell Canyon (Lake Oroville State Recreation Area) | * | * | 40 | EWS | F | * | * | * | * | * | FBSHRL | $$-$$$ | Year-round | * |
| 370 | Loafer Creek (Lake Oroville State Recreation Area) | * | * | 40 | | F | * | * | * | * | * | FBSHRL | $$-$$$$ | Year-round | * |
| 371 | Upper Jamison (Plumas-Eureka State Park) | * | * | 24 | | F | * | * | * | * | * | HF | $$$ | May–Oct | * |
| 372 | Lakes Basin | | * | 26 | | V | | * | | * | | HSFM | $$ | Year-round | |
| 373 | Gold Lake | | | | | CV | | | | * | * | FBRHSM | $ | Year-round | |
| 374 | Goose Lake | | | | | V | | | | * | | FBRHSM | $ | Year-round | |
| 375 | Haven Lake | | | | | V | | | | * | | FBRHSM | $ | Year-round | |
| 376 | Lone Rock (Antelope Lake) | | * | 45 | | V | | * | * | * | * | SFBH | $$ | May–Sept | * |
| 377 | Boulder Creek (Antelope Lake) | | * | 30 | | V | | * | * | * | * | SFBH | $$ | May–Sept | * |
| 378 | Long Point (Antelope Lake) | * | * | 45 | | V | | * | | * | * | SFBH | $$ | May–Sept | * |
| 379 | Laufman | | * | | | V | | | | * | | | None | Year-round | |
| 380 | Conklin Park | | * | | | V | | | | * | | FO | None | Year-round | |
| 381 | Meadow View | | * | | | V | | * | | * | | R | None | Year-round | |
| 382 | Lightning Tree (Lake Davis) | | * | 45 | | V | | * | | * | * | SFBLM | $$ | May–Oct | * |

| | Name | Group Sites | RV Sites | Max. RV Length | Hookups | Toilets | Showers | Drinking Water | Dump Station | Pets | Wheelchair | Recreation | Fee(s) | Season | Can Reserve |
|---|---|---|---|---|---|---|---|---|---|---|---|---|---|---|---|
| 383 | Grasshopper Flat (Lake Davis) | * | * | 35 | | F | | * | * | * | * | SFBLM | $$ | May–Oct | * |
| 384 | Grizzly (Lake Davis) | | * | 45 | | F | | * | * | * | * | SFBL | $$ | May–Oct | * |
| 385 | Crocker | | * | | | V | | | | * | | F | None | May–Nov | |
| 386 | Cottonwood Springs (Frenchman Lake Recreation Area) | * | * | 45 | | V | | * | * | * | * | SFBH | $$ | Apr–Sept | * |
| 387 | Frenchman (Frenchman Lake Recreation Area) | | * | 45 | | V | | * | | * | * | SFBL | $$ | Apr–Oct | * |
| 388 | Spring Creek (Frenchman Lake Recreation Area) | | * | 45 | | V | | * | | * | * | SFB | $$ | Apr–Oct | * |
| 389 | Big Cove (Frenchman Lake Recreation Area) | | * | 45 | | F | * | * | | * | * | SFBH | $$ | Apr–Oct | * |
| 390 | Chilcoot | | * | 40 | | F | | * | | * | * | HF | $$ | Apr–Oct | * |

Toilets: F=flush V=vault P=pit C=chemical; Fee: $=Under $20 $$=$20–$29 $$$=$30–$39 $$$$ $40 or more; Recreation: H=hiking S=swimming F=fishing B=boating L=boat launch O=off-highway driving R=horseback riding, M=mountain biking
Hookups: W=water E=electric S=sewer

*Breathtaking Feather Falls lie on the Fall River, a tributary of the Middle Fork Feather River.*

## 331 Cherry Hill

**Location:** 36 miles northeast of Chico
**GPS:** 40.102799 / -121.497186
**Sites:** 26 sites for tents and RVs
**Facilities:** Tables, fire rings, drinking water, vault toilets
**Fee per night:** $
**Management:** Lassen National Forest, (530) 258-2141
**Activities:** Fishing
**Finding the campground:** From the intersection of CA 99 and CA 32 in Chico, drive northeast about 27 miles on CA 32. Turn right (northeast) onto Humboldt Road and drive 8.6 miles.
**About the campground:** Situated on the banks of Butte Creek, with some walk-in sites across the creek, home to native Chinook salmon and steelhead trout. Elevation 4,700 feet. Stay limit 14 days. Open April to November.

## 332 Butte Meadows

**Location:** 32 miles northeast of Chico
**GPS:** 40.078517 / -121.558811
**Sites:** 13 sites for tents and RVs
**Facilities:** Tables, fire rings, drinking water, vault toilets
**Fee per night:** $
**Management:** Lassen National Forest, (530) 258-2141
**Activities:** Fishing
**Finding the campground:** From the intersection of CA 99 and CA 32 in Chico, drive northeast about 27 miles on CA 32. Turn right (northeast) onto Humboldt Road and drive 5 miles.
**About the campground:** Located on the banks of Butte Creek, which serves as an important watershed for the area and is shaded by Douglas fir and oak trees. Elevation 4,300 feet. Stay limit 14 days. Open April through October.

## 333 Philbrook Lake

**Location:** 42 miles northeast of Chico
**GPS:** 40.0269127 / -121.4668395
**Sites:** 20 sites for tents and RVs
**Facilities:** Tables, grills, drinking water, vault toilets
**Fee per night:** $$; reservations: http://recreation.pge.com
**Management:** PG&E, (530) 413-8143
**Activities:** Swimming, fishing, boating
**Finding the campground:** From the intersection of CA 99 and CA 32 in Chico, drive northeast about 27 miles on CA 32. Turn right (northeast) onto Humboldt Road and drive 5 miles. Drive southeast 4.5 miles on Skyway Road; turn left onto Humbug Summit Road and drive 1.5 miles. Turn right onto West Branch Road (which becomes Philbrook Road) and drive 3.5 miles.
**About the campground:** The campground is near the shoreline of Philbrook Reservoir, a pretty lake that hosts some trout and non-native catfish that feed river otters, raptors, and other wildlife. Elevation 5,600 feet. Stay limit 14 days. Open May through October.

## 334 Yellow Creek

**Location:** 15 miles south of Chester
**GPS:** 40.1259934 / -121.3860728
**Sites:** 11 sites for tents
**Facilities:** Tables, grills, drinking water, vault toilets
**Fee per night:** $
**Management:** PG&E, (530) 284-1785
**Activities:** Fishing
**Finding the campground:** From Chester, drive 2 miles south on CA 36. Turn left onto CA 89 and drive 5 miles. Turn right onto Humbug Road (CR 308/309) and drive 0.7 mile. Bear left onto CR 309 and drive 1.3 miles. Turn right onto CR 307 and drive 4.5 miles; turn left at a Y intersection and drive 1.2 miles.
**About the campground:** Located in the Humbug Valley, the campground boasts spring wildflowers. Sites shaded by ponderosa pines. No paved access for RVs. Elevation 4,400 feet. Stay limit 14 days. Open May through October.

## 335 Ponderosa Flat (Butt Valley Reservoir)

**Location:** 12 miles south of Chester
**GPS:** 40.1662788 / -121.1874295
**Sites:** 63 sites for tents
**Facilities:** Tables, grills, drinking water, vault toilets, boat ramp
**Fee per night:** $$; reservations: http://recreation.pge.com
**Management:** PG&E, (530) 284-1785
**Activities:** Swimming, fishing, boating
**Finding the campground:** From Chester, drive 2 miles south on CA 36. Turn left onto CA 89 and drive 7 miles. Turn right onto Butt Valley Road (CR 305) and drive 3 miles.
**About the campground:** Located on the north end of Butt Valley Reservoir, which is subject to heavy drawdowns of water. It contains small amounts of trophy-size brown, brook, and rainbow trout. Elevation 4,150 feet. Stay limit 14 days. Open mid-May to mid-September.

## 336 Cool Springs (Butt Valley Reservoir)

**Location:** 14 miles south of Chester
**GPS:** 40.1451684 / -121.16854
**Sites:** 25 sites for tents and RVs; 5 walk-ins
**Facilities:** Tables, grills, drinking water, vault toilets
**Fee per night:** $$; reservations: http://recreation.pge.com
**Management:** PG&E, (530) 284-1785
**Activities:** Swimming, fishing, boating
**Finding the campground:** From Chester, drive 2 miles south on CA 36. Turn left onto CA 89 and drive 7 miles. Turn right onto Butt Valley Road (CR 305) and drive 5 miles.
**About the campground:** On the eastern shore, enjoying the calm waters of Butt Valley Reservoir. Elevation 4,150 feet. Stay limit 14 days. Open mid-May to mid-September.

## 337 Greenville

**Location:** miles north of Greenville
**GPS:** 40.157 / -120.954
**Sites:** 19 sites for tents and RVs
**Facilities:** Tables, fire rings, grills, drinking water, vault toilets, dump station
**Fee per night:** $$
**Management:** Royal Elk Park Management, (707) 799-4453
**Activities:** Hiking, biking
**Finding the campground:** From Greenville, drive north on CA 89 for 1.5 miles.
**About the campground:** A partially wooded location close to town, with a stream nearby and horseshoe pits. Nine miles from Lake Almanor and 3.5 miles from Round Valley Reservoir. Elevation 3,670 feet. Stay limit 14 days. Open May to September.

## 338 Taylorsville County Park

**Location:** At the east end of Taylorsville
**GPS:** 40.075 / -120.829
**Sites:** 60+ sites for tents and RVs, divided into a lower and an upper level
**Facilities:** Tables, drinking water, showers, flush and vault toilets, dump station, group kitchen area (fee), tennis court, horseshoe pits
**Fee per night:** $
**Management:** Plumas County Facilities, (530) 283-6299
**Activities:** Biking, hiking, horseback riding
**Finding the campground:** From Taylorsville, drive east on CR 207 to the park, at the end of town.
**About the campground:** A wooded site close to town beside Indian Creek and across from the Indian Valley Riding and Roping Club (rodeo grounds). Most campsites have makeshift fire rings, and campfires are permitted. Beach access for swimming and fishing. Elevation 3,540 feet. Stay limit 14 days. Open mid-April through mid-October.

## 339 Queen Lily

**Location:** 53 miles northeast of Oroville
**GPS:** 40.045 / -121.217
**Sites:** 12 sites for tents and RVs up to 17 feet long
**Facilities:** Tables, fire rings, drinking water, flush toilets
**Fee per night:** $$
**Management:** Royal Elk Park Management, (707) 799-4453
**Activities:** Hiking, swimming, fishing
**Finding the campground:** From Oroville, drive northeast 50 miles on CA 70 to Gansner Ranch Ranger Station, at the intersection with Caribou Road. Turn left (north) onto Caribou and drive 3 miles.
**About the campground:** On the banks of the North Fork of the Feather River. Rock climbing at nearby Grizzly Dome. Elevation 2,600 feet. Stay limit 14 days. Open May through October.

## 340 North Fork

**Location:** 52 miles northeast of Oroville
**GPS:** 40.040 / -121.219
**Sites:** 21 sites for tents and RVs up to 32 feet long
**Facilities:** Tables, grills, bear boxes, drinking water, flush toilets, dump station
**Fee per night:** $$, with electric: $$$
**Management:** Royal Elk Park Management, (707) 799-4453
**Activities:** Hiking, biking, swimming, fishing
**Finding the campground:** From Oroville, drive northeast 50 miles on CA 70 to Gansner Ranch Ranger Station, at the intersection with Caribou Road. Turn left (north) onto Caribou and drive 2 miles.
**About the campground:** On the banks of the North Fork of the Feather River, which is stocked annually with rainbow trout. Facilities were upgraded in 2014. There is nearby fishing and berry picking in late summer. Elevation 2,600 feet. Stay limit 14 days. Open May through October.

## 341 Gansner Bar

**Location:** 51 miles northeast of Oroville
**GPS:** 40.019 / -121.221
**Sites:** 14 sites for tents and RVs up to 31 feet long
**Facilities:** Tables, fire rings, drinking water, flush toilets
**Fee per night:** $$
**Management:** Royal Elk Park Management, (707) 799-4453
**Activities:** Hiking, fishing, wading
**Finding the campground:** From Oroville, drive northeast 50 miles on CA 70 to Gansner Ranch Ranger Station, at the intersection with Caribou Road. Turn left (north) onto Caribou and drive 0.5 mile.
**About the campground:** Shady and quiet, with some streamside sites, on the North Fork of the Feather River. Elevation 2,300 feet. Stay limit 14 days. Open April through October.

## 342 Spanish Creek

**Location:** 8 miles west of Quincy
**GPS:** 40.0383804 / -120.9834995
**Sites:** 21 sites for tents/RVs up to 40 feet long
**Facilities:** Tables, fire rings, bear boxes, lantern posts, drinking water, vault toilets
**Fee per night:** $$; reservations: (877) 444-6777 or recreation.gov
**Management:** Plumas National Forest, (530) 283-0555
**Activities:** Fishing, hiking, swimming
**Finding the campground:** Located off CA 70, just 8 miles west of Quincy.
**About the campground:** New Interpretive panels are located at the entrance to the campground, which is on Spanish Creek and near Clear Creek. Elevation 2945 feet. Stay limit 14 days. Open May through September.

# 343 Hallsted

**Location:** 60 miles northeast of Oroville
**GPS:** 40.0175908 / -121.0743078
**Sites:** 20 sites for tents and RVs up to 23 feet long
**Facilities:** Tables, fire rings, drinking water, flush toilets, electric hookups
**Fee per night:** $$, hookups: $$$; reservations: (877) 444-6777 or recreation.gov
**Management:** Royal Elk Park Management, (707) 799-4453
**Activities:** Swimming, fishing
**Finding the campground:** From Oroville, drive northeast on CA 70 for 60 miles.
**About the campground:** Located on the banks of the East Branch of the North Fork of the Feather River. In 2015, the campground was renovated, including new restroom facilities. A walking path through the forest leads to the river. Elevation 2,800 feet. Stay limit 14 days. Open May through September.

# 344 Snake Lake

**Location:** 7 miles northwest of Quincy
**GPS:** 39.97 / -121.01
**Sites:** 17 sites for tents/RVs
**Facilities:** Tables, fire rings, vault toilets, drinking water, corrals
**Fee per night:** None
**Management:** Plumas National Forest, (530) 283-0555
**Activities:** Fishing, boating, hiking, biking, horseback riding, OHV driving
**Finding the campground:** From Quincy, drive 5 miles west on Bucks Lake Road (FR 119). Turn right onto CR 422 and drive 1.6 miles. Turn right onto Snake Lake Access Road and drive 0.5 mile.
**About the campground:** Shady lakeside campsites for tents, RVs, OHVs, and horses. Snake Lake is relatively shallow, allowing catfish, bass, and bluegill to thrive. Elevation 4,200 feet. Stay limit 14 days. Open all year (no water or restrooms in winter).

# 345 Silver Lake

**Location:** 15 miles west of Quincy
**GPS:** 39.959 / -121.134
**Sites:** 7 sites for tents
**Facilities:** Tables, fire rings, vault toilets; no drinking water
**Fee per night:** None
**Management:** Plumas National Forest, (530) 283-0555
**Activities:** Fishing, boating, hiking, mountain biking, OHV driving, hunting (seasonal)
**Finding the campground:** From Quincy, drive 8 miles west on Bucks Lake Road (FR 119). Turn north onto Silver Lake Road (FR 24N29X) and drive 5 miles.
**About the campground:** No powerboats or swimming are allowed on this beautiful, secluded lake. Fishing is limited to small trout. There are trailheads for both Gold Lake and Granite Gap Trails. Elevation 5,800 feet. Stay limit 14 days. Open all year.

## 346 Deanes Valley

**Location:** 13 miles southwest of Quincy
**GPS:** 39.88 / -121.022
**Sites:** 7 sites for tents and RVs
**Facilities:** Tables, fire rings, vault toilets; no drinking water
**Fee per night:** None
**Management:** Plumas National Forest, (530) 283-0555
**Activities:** Fishing, OHV driving, hunting (seasonal)
**Finding the campground:** From Quincy, drive west 3.5 miles on Bucks Lake Road (FR 119). Turn left onto FR 24N28 and drive 5 miles.
**About the campground:** Located on the South Fork of Rock Creek, with some creekside sites. Fishing is limited to small trout. Elevation 4,400 feet. Stay limit 14 days. Open April through October.

## 347 Mill Creek (Bucks Lake)

**Location:** 21 miles west of Quincy
**GPS:** 39.913 / -121.186
**Sites:** 10 sites for tents and RVs
**Facilities:** Tables, fire rings, bear boxes, drinking water, vault toilets
**Fee per night:** $$
**Management:** Royal Elk Park Management, (707) 799-4453
**Activities:** Hiking, swimming, fishing, boating, waterskiing
**Finding the campground:** From Quincy, drive west 16 miles on Bucks Lake Road (FR 119). Turn right onto Bucks Lake Dam Road (FR 33) and drive 5 miles.
**About the campground:** Noted for good trout fishing, Bucks Lake is stocked annually with rainbow, brook, and brown trout. Two boat ramps are located on the south shore of the lake, and there's one on the north shore. If camping with a group of 10 to 25 people, you might consider nearby Hutchins Group Camp on Bucks Lake. Supplies and boat rentals are available at resorts on the lake. Elevation 5,200 feet. Stay limit 14 days. Open April to November.

## 348 Sundew (Bucks Lake)

**Location:** 19 miles west of Quincy
**GPS:** 39.90 / -121.20
**Sites:** 22 sites for tents and RVs up to 22 feet long
**Facilities:** Tables, fire rings, drinking water, vault toilets
**Fee per night:** $$
**Management:** Royal Elk Park Management, (707) 799-4453
**Activities:** Swimming, fishing, boating, waterskiing, hiking, mountain biking
**Finding the campground:** From Quincy, drive west 16 miles on Bucks Lake Road (FR 119). Turn right onto Bucks Lake Dam Road (FR 33) and drive 3.3 miles.
**About the campground:** On the banks of Bucks Lake. Elevation 5,200 feet. Stay limit 14 days. Open April to November.

## 349 Lower Bucks (Bucks Lake)

**Location:** 24 miles west of Quincy
**GPS:** 39.901 / -121.213
**Sites:** 7 sites for tents and RVs
**Facilities:** Tables, fire rings, bear boxes, vault toilets, drinking water
**Fee per night:** $$
**Management:** Royal Elk Park Management, (707) 799-4453
**Activities:** Swimming, fishing, boating, waterskiing, hiking, biking, OHV driving
**Finding the campground:** From Quincy, drive west 16 miles on Bucks Lake Road (FR 119). Turn right onto Bucks Lake Dam Road (FR 33) and drive 3 miles.
**About the campground:** Shady and lakeside sites. Elevation 5,200 feet. Stay limit 14 days. Open April to November.

## 350 Whitehorse (Bucks Lake)

**Location:** 15 miles west of Quincy
**GPS:** 39.888 / -121.141
**Sites:** 20 sites for tents and RVs (includes 3 equestrian sites)
**Facilities:** Tables, fire rings, drinking water, vault toilets
**Fee per night:** $$
**Management:** Royal Elk Park Management, (707) 799-4453
**Activities:** Hiking, biking, horseback riding
**Finding the campground:** From Quincy, drive west 15 miles on Bucks Lake Road (FR 119).
**About the campground:** Whitehorse is on the banks of Bucks Creek, about 0.5 mile east of Bucks Lake. Adjoins Bucks Lake Loop Trail for mountain bikes. Elevation 5,200 feet. Stay limit 14 days. Open May to September.

## 351 Haskins Valley (Bucks Lake)

**Location:** 17 miles west of Quincy
**GPS:** 39.871713 / -121.1751612
**Sites:** 65 sites for tents and RVs up to 40 feet
**Facilities:** Tables, grills, drinking water, vault toilets, dump station, dock, boat ramp, Internet
**Fee per night:** $$; reservations: (530) 335-2199 or http://recreation.pge.com
**Management:** PG&E, (530) 283-0256
**Activities:** Swimming, fishing, boating, waterskiing, hiking, biking
**Finding the campground:** From Quincy, drive west 17 miles on Bucks Lake Road (FR 119).
**About the campground:** Sites are under pine trees in a cove at the south end of Bucks Lake. Elevation 5,200 feet. Stay limit 14 days. Open April to November.

## 352 Grizzly Creek (Bucks Lake)

**Location:** 21 miles west of Quincy
**GPS:** 39.867 / -121.206

**Sites:** 11 sites for tents and RVs
**Facilities:** Tables, fire rings, vault toilets; no drinking water
**Fee per night:** $$
**Management:** Royal Elk Park Management, (707) 799-4453
**Activities:** Fishing, hiking, road cycling, hunting (seasonal)
**Finding the campground:** From Quincy, drive west about 18 miles on Bucks Lake Road (FR 119). Continue straight onto Big Creek Road about 10 miles. Continue onto Bucks Lake Road/Oroville-Quincy Road and continue about 2 miles.
**About the campground:** This creekside campground is approximately 2 miles from the Buck's Lake Marina. Elevation 5,400 feet. Stay limit 14 days. Open April to November.

## 353 Little North Fork

**Location:** 37 miles northeast of Oroville
**GPS:** 39.782 / -121.259
**Sites:** 6 sites for tents and small RVs (trailers not recommended)
**Facilities:** Tables, fire rings, drinking water, vault toilets
**Fee per night:** None
**Management:** Plumas National Forest, (530) 534-6500
**Activities:** Hiking, mountain biking, fishing, swimming
**Finding the campground:** From the intersection of CA 70 and CA 162 in Oroville, drive east and then north on CA 162 (Olive Highway) for about 30 miles, passing the Brush Creek Work Center. Turn west onto FR 60 and drive about 7 miles on a narrow, winding dirt road not suitable for trailers or large RVs.
**About the campground:** This is an out-of-the-way site on the Middle Fork Feather River. Facilities were updated in 2015. Elevation 4,000 feet. Stay limit 14 days. Open April to November.

## 354 Rogers Cow Camp

**Location:** 32 miles northeast of Oroville
**GPS:** 39.768 / -121.310
**Sites:** 6 sites for tents and RVs
**Facilities:** Tables, fire rings, drinking water (hand-pump from well), vault toilets
**Fee per night:** None
**Management:** Plumas National Forest, (530) 534-6500
**Activities:** Biking, OHV driving
**Finding the campground:** From the intersection of CA 70 and CA 162 in Oroville, drive east and then north on CA 162 (Olive Highway) for 32 miles, passing the Brush Creek Work Center. Watch for the campground sign on the left side of the road.
**About the campground:** The campground is near a singletrack trail popular for mountain bikes and OHV motorbikes. Elevation 4,100 feet. Stay limit 14 days. Open April to November.

## 355 Milsap Bar

**Location:** 33 miles northeast of Oroville
**GPS:** 39.706 / -121.268

**Sites:** 20 sites for tents
**Facilities:** Tables, fire rings, vault toilets; no drinking water
**Fee per night:** None
**Management:** Plumas National Forest, (530) 534-6500
**Activities:** Fishing, kayaking, rafting
**Finding the campground:** From the intersection of CA 70 and CA 162 in Oroville, drive east and then north on CA 162 (Olive Highway) for 24 miles to the Brush Creek Work Center. Turn south onto FR 62 (Milsap Bar Road) and drive about 9 miles. FR 62 is a narrow, winding dirt road not suitable for trailers or large RVs.
**About the campground:** Milsap Bar provides access to Middle Fork Feather River, a designated National Wild and Scenic River. The portion of the river fronting the campground is called the Milsap Bar Scenic River Zone. It is 3.6 miles long and suitable for experienced kayakers. However, since it is bordered on both the north and south by wild-river zones (precipitous cliffs, waterfalls, and huge boulders), local knowledge of the area is essential. Elevation 1,600 feet. Stay limit 14 days. Open April to September.

## 356 Black Rock (Little Grass Valley Reservoir)

**Location:** 53 miles northeast of Oroville
**GPS:** 39.7293363 / -121.0105105
**Sites:** 20 walk-in sites for tents; RV parking in the parking lot
**Facilities:** Tables, fire rings, drinking water, vault toilets, boat ramp
**Fee per night:** $$
**Management:** Plumas National Forest, (530) 534-6500
**Activities:** Hiking, fishing, swimming, boating, waterskiing
**Finding the campground:** From the intersection of CA 70 and CA 162 in Oroville, drive east 8 miles on CA 162 (Olive Highway). Turn right onto Forbestown Road (signed to Challenge/La Porte) and drive about 40 miles, passing through Forbestown, Challenge, Strawberry Valley, and La Porte. Turn left onto Little Grass Valley Road (CR 514) and drive about 5 miles.
**About the campground:** Sites are on the shoreline. The reservoir is a popular water sports location, and eight campgrounds line its shores. Black Rock is the only one on the western shore. The lake is stocked annually with rainbow trout and kokanee. Elevation 5,060 feet. Stay limit 14 days. Open May through October.

## 357 Peninsula (Little Grass Valley Reservoir)

**Location:** 50 miles northeast of Oroville
**GPS:** 39.720 / -120.979
**Sites:** 25 sites for tents
**Facilities:** Tables, fire rings, drinking water, flush toilets, boat ramp
**Fee per night:** $$
**Management:** Plumas National Forest, (530) 534-6500
**Activities:** Hiking, fishing, horseback riding, swimming, boating, waterskiing
**Finding the campground:** From the intersection of CA 70 and CA 162 in Oroville, drive east 8 miles on CA 162 (Olive Highway). Turn right onto Forbestown Road (signed to Challenge/La Porte) and drive about 40 miles, passing through Forbestown, Challenge, Strawberry Valley, and La Porte.

Turn left onto Little Grass Valley Road (CR 514) and drive about 2 miles to the campground road on the right.
**About the campground:** The campground is adjacent to Pancake Beach Day Use Area. Elevation 5,060 feet. Stay limit 14 days. Open May through October.

## 358 Tooms (Little Grass Valley Reservoir)

**Location:** 50 miles northeast of Oroville
**GPS:** 39.749 / -120.99
**Sites:** 20 sites for RVs only; no tents
**Facilities:** Drinking water, vault toilets, boat ramp, fish-washing and RV dump stations
**Fee per night:** $$
**Management:** Plumas National Forest, (530) 534-6500
**Activities:** Hiking, fishing, swimming, boating, waterskiing
**Finding the campground:** From the intersection of CA 70 and CA 162 in Oroville, drive east 8 miles on CA 162 (Olive Highway). Turn right onto Forbestown Road (signed to Challenge/La Porte) and drive about 40 miles, passing through Forbestown, Challenge, Strawberry Valley, and La Porte. Turn left onto Little Grass Valley Road (CR 514) and drive about 2 miles to the campground road on the right. Tooms is adjacent to Peninsula Campground (357).
**About the campground:** The "campground" is actually the upper parking lot of the Tooms boat ramp. Elevation 5,060 feet. Stay limit 14 days. Open May through October.

## 359 Wyandotte (Little Grass Valley Reservoir)

**Location:** 50 miles northeast of Oroville
**GPS:** 39.7450041 / -120.989694
**Sites:** 28 individual sites and 2 double sites for tents and RVs
**Facilities:** Tables, fire rings, drinking water, flush toilets, dump station, boat ramp
**Fee per night:** $$, double: $$$; reservations: (877) 444-6777 or recreation.gov; some walk-ins
**Management:** Plumas National Forest, (530) 534-6500
**Activities:** Hiking, fishing, swimming, boating, waterskiing
**Finding the campground:** Take the La Porte–Quincy Road from Brownsville or CA 70 to the town of La Porte. Travel 3 miles northeast of town to Little Grass Valley Road. Drive about 0.25 mile beyond Peninsula Campground (357).
**About the campground:** Little Grass Valley reservoir is a 1600 acre, clear mountain lake with plenty of wildlife, including bald eagles. Elevation 5,060 feet. Stay limit 14 days. Open from May through October.

## 360 Little Beaver (Little Grass Valley Reservoir)

**Location:** 51 miles northeast of Oroville
**GPS:** 39.720 / -120.953
**Sites:** 120 sites for tents and RVs
**Facilities:** Tables, fire rings, drinking water, flush toilets, dump station, boat ramp
**Fee per night:** $$; reservations: (877) 444-6777 or recreation.gov; some walk-ins

**Management:** Plumas National Forest, (530) 534-6500
**Activities:** Hiking, fishing, swimming, boating, waterskiing
**Finding the campground:** From the intersection of CA 70 and CA 162 in Oroville, drive east 8 miles on CA 162 (Olive Highway). Turn right onto Forbestown Road (signed to Challenge/La Porte) and drive about 40 miles, passing through Forbestown, Challenge, Strawberry Valley, and La Porte. Turn left onto Little Grass Valley Road (CR 514) and drive 1 mile. Make a sharp right turn onto FR 22N68 and drive 2 miles.
**About the campground:** The campground is adjacent to Maidu Boat Ramp and Blue Water Beach Day Use Area. Elevation 5,060 feet. Stay limit 14 days. Open May through October.

## 361 Red Feather (Little Grass Valley Reservoir)

**Location:** 52 miles northeast of Oroville
**GPS:** 39.735 / -120.95
**Sites:** 60 sites for tents and RVs
**Facilities:** Tables, fire rings, drinking water, flush toilets, dump station, boat ramp
**Fee per night:** $$; reservations: (877) 444-6777 or recreation.gov; some walk-in
**Management:** Plumas National Forest, (530) 534-6500
**Activities:** Hiking, fishing, swimming, boating, waterskiing
**Finding the campground:** From the intersection of CA 70 and CA 162 in Oroville, drive east 8 miles on CA 162 (Olive Highway). Turn right onto Forbestown Road (signed to Challenge/La Porte) and drive about 40 miles, passing through Forbestown, Challenge, Strawberry Valley, and La Porte. Turn left onto Little Grass Valley Road (CR 514) and drive 1 mile. Make a sharp right turn onto FR 22N68 and drive almost 2.5 miles.
**About the campground:** Located on the eastern shore of the Little Grass Valley Reservoir, 12 units are on the lake. Elevation 5,060 feet. Stay limit 14 days. Open May through October.

## 362 Running Deer (Little Grass Valley Reservoir)

**Location:** 52 miles northeast of Oroville
**GPS:** 39.735 / -120.95
**Sites:** 40 sites for tents and RVs
**Facilities:** Tables, fire rings, drinking water, flush toilets, dump station, boat ramp
**Fee per night:** $$; reservations: (877) 444-6777 or recreation.gov
**Management:** Plumas National Forest, (530) 534-6500
**Activities:** Hiking, fishing, swimming, boating, waterskiing
**Finding the campground:** From the intersection of CA 70 and CA 162 in Oroville, drive east 8 miles on CA 162 (Olive Highway). Turn right onto Forbestown Road (signed to Challenge/La Porte) and drive about 40 miles, passing through Forbestown, Challenge, Strawberry Valley, and La Porte. Turn left onto Little Grass Valley Road (CR 514) and drive 1 mile. Make a sharp right turn onto FR 22N68 and drive about 3 miles.
**About the campground:** The campground is located on the eastern shore of the Little Grass Valley Reservoir. Elevation 5,060 feet. Stay limit 14 days. Open April through October.

## 363 Horse Camp (Little Grass Valley Reservoir)

**Location:** 53 miles northeast of Oroville
**GPS:** 39.73528 / -120.95306
**Sites:** 10 sites for tents and RVs
**Facilities:** Tables, fire rings, drinking water, vault toilets, 10 hitching posts, boat launch
**Fee per night:** $$; reservations: (877) 444-6777 or recreation.gov
**Management:** Plumas National Forest, (530) 534-6500
**Activities:** Hiking, fishing, swimming, boating, waterskiing, horseback riding
**Finding the campground:** From the intersection of CA 70 and CA 162 in Oroville, drive east 8 miles on CA 162 (Olive Highway). Turn right onto Forbestown Road (signed to Challenge/La Porte) and drive about 40 miles, passing through Forbestown, Challenge, Strawberry Valley, and La Porte. Turn left onto Little Grass Valley Road (CR 514) and drive 1 mile. Make a sharp right turn onto FR 22N68 and drive about 3.5 miles. The camp is near the point at which the South Fork Feather River enters the lake.
**About the campground:** Adjacent to the campground is the Bald Rock Trailhead, which ties to the Pacific Crest National Scenic Trail. Around the lake, you can ride horses only on the northern portion of the Lakeside Trail. In winter there is no fee, and you need to pack out trash. Elevation 5,000 feet. Stay limit 14 days. Open all year.

## 364 Golden Trout

**Location:** 7 miles north of Strawberry Valley
**GPS:** 39.605 / -121.139
**Sites:** 10 sites for tents and RVs
**Facilities:** Tables, fire rings with grills, drinking water (hand-pump), vault toilets
**Fee per night:** None
**Management:** Plumas National Forest, (530) 283-2050
**Activities:** Boating, swimming, fishing
**Finding the campground:** From La Porte Road, go southwest and turn northwest onto Lost Creek Dam Road for about 0.8 mile. Go north on Moreville Ridge Road for about 4 miles.
**About the campground:** The campground is located on FR 22N24, which spans the South Fork Feather River. The Feather offers excellent fly fishing, being one of the largest steelhead runs in California's Central Valley. The facilities were updated in 2015. Elevation 4,000 feet. Stay limit 14 days. Open all year.

## 365 Sly Creek (Sly Creek Reservoir)

**Location:** 40 miles northeast of Oroville
**GPS:** 39.576 / -121.120
**Sites:** 23 sites for tents and RVs
**Facilities:** Tables, fire rings, drinking water, vault toilets, boat ramp
**Fee per night:** $$
**Management:** South Feather Water & Power, (530) 534-1221, ext. 215
**Activities:** Fishing, swimming, boating, OHV driving

**Finding the campground:** From the intersection of CA 70 and CA 162 in Oroville, drive east 8 miles on CA 162 (Olive Highway). Turn right onto Forbestown Road (signed to Challenge/La Porte) and drive about 15 miles to Challenge. From there, drive 12 miles northeast on La Porte Road. Turn left at the campground turnoff and drive 4.5 miles.
**About the campground:** The campground is on the southwest shore of the lake, which offers reasonably good trout fishing. The lake is great for paddling. Elevation 3,530 feet. Stay limit 14 days. Open May through October.

## 366 Strawberry (Sly Creek Reservoir)

**Location:** 41 miles northeast of Oroville
**GPS:** 39.588 / -121.08
**Sites:** 17 sites for tents and RVs
**Facilities:** Tables, fire rings, drinking water, vault toilets, boat ramp
**Fee per night:** $$
**Management:** South Feather Water & Power, (530) 534-1221, ext. 215
**Activities:** Fishing, swimming, boating
**Finding the campground:** From the intersection of CA 70 and CA 162 in Oroville, drive east 8 miles on CA 162 (Olive Highway). Turn right onto Forbestown Road (signed to Challenge/La Porte) and drive about 15 miles to Challenge. From there, drive 16 miles northeast on La Porte Road. Turn left at the campground turnoff and drive 2 miles.
**About the campground:** The campground is situated on the eastern shore of the lake. See Sly Creek Campground (365) for more information.

## 367 Feather Falls Trailhead

**Location:** 27 miles northeast of Oroville
**GPS:** 39.6141861 / -121.2662372
**Sites:** 5 sites for tents
**Facilities:** Tables, fire rings, drinking water, vault toilet
**Fee per night:** None
**Management:** Plumas National Forest, (530) 534-6500
**Activities:** Hiking
**Finding the campground:** From the intersection of CA 70 and CA 162 in Oroville, drive east 8 miles on CA 162 (Olive Highway). Turn east onto Forbestown Road and drive 7 miles. Turn north onto Lumpkin Road and drive 10 miles to the trailhead turnoff. Turn north and drive 1.5 miles.
**About the campground:** Feather Falls National Recreation Trail, which leads to the falls, is actually two loop trails. Choose an 8-mile round-trip with a 2,500-foot elevation gain that passes over Frey Creek and its falls—famous in winter as a stopping point for migrating ladybugs—or a 9.5-mile round-trip that provides an easier climb. Elevation 2,500 feet. Stay limit 14 days. Open all year.

## 368 Lime Saddle (Lake Oroville State Recreation Area)

**Location:** Lake Oroville
**GPS:** 39.6824892 / -121.559894
**Sites:** 30 sites for tent and 15 RVs up to 40 feet long; 1 group site

## LAKE OROVILLE STATE RECREATION AREA

Created by the tallest earth-filled dam in the United States in 1969, Lake Oroville is one of California's larger lakes—more than 15,800 acres of surface area and 167 miles of mostly undeveloped shoreline. It is primarily a boater's lake, in that much of the shoreline is accessible only by boat. Recreation areas, including boat-in campgrounds, are located at various places around the lake. Boaters may land at any point to explore the shoreline and surrounding country, which is state-owned from 300 feet to as much as 1 mile from the high-water line.

Lake Oroville is known for its bass fishing and is stocked annually with coho salmon from the Feather River Fish Hatchery. The lake also has a sizable population of other fish, including rainbow trout, bluegill, crappie, and catfish. Feather Falls, with its spectacular 410-foot drop, is a highlight of the recreation area. You can reach it by boat or trail. When the lake is at high water, boats can get to within 0.25 mile of the falls. Hikers must drive about 16 miles to reach the Feather Falls National Recreation Trail, an 8-mile round-trip to the falls with a 2,500-foot elevation gain.

The recreation area is divided into two parts: Lake Oroville itself and the much smaller North and South Forebays, about 5 miles to the north.

**Facilities:** Tables, fire pits, flush toilets, drinking water, boat launch, dump station, concessions
**Fee per night:** $$, full hookups: $$$; (800) 444-7275 or reserveamerica.com
**Management:** California Department of Parks and Recreation, (530) 876-8516
**Activities:** Fishing, boating, waterskiing, swimming, hiking, biking, horseback riding
**Finding the campground:** Head north of Sacramento on CA 70 to Pentz Road. Go north on Pentz Road, then northeast on Lime Saddle Road. Turn right (south) at the campground entrance sign and proceed to the kiosk.
**About the campground:** The campground is located on the lake's northern end, close to the Lake Oroville Marina. Elevation 1,070 feet. Stay limit 30 days. Open all year.

## 369 Bidwell Canyon (Lake Oroville State Recreation Area)

**Location:** 9 miles east of Oroville
**GPS:** 39.5332198 / -121.4585785
**Sites:** 75 sites with full hookups; primarily for RVs up to 40 feet long, but tents allowed
**Facilities:** Tables, grills, drinking water, showers, flush toilets, dump station, boat ramp, boat rentals, marina, store
**Fee per night:** $$, full hookups: $$$; reservations: (800) 444-7275 or reserveamerica.com
**Management:** California Department of Parks and Recreation, (530) 538-2218
**Activities:** Fishing, boating, waterskiing, swimming, hiking, biking, horseback riding

**Finding the campground:** From the intersection of CA 70 and CA 162 in Oroville, drive east on CA 162 (Olive Highway) for 6.5 miles. Turn north onto Kelly Ridge Road and drive 2.5 miles.
**About the campground:** The campground is not on the shore of the lake but on a small hill just above the marina; it is the most central of the lake's campgrounds. The nearby visitor center features an open-air lookout tower with views over the lake. Elevation 934 feet. Stay limit 30 days. Open all year.

## 370 Loafer Creek (Lake Oroville State Recreation Area)

**Location:** 8 miles east of Oroville
**GPS:** 39.5247466 / -121.4474866
**Sites:** 137 sites for tents and RVs up to 40 feet long; 6 group sites; horse camp
**Facilities:** Tables, grills, drinking water, showers, flush toilets, dump station, boat ramp, swimming beach
**Fee per night:** $$–$$$$; reservations: (800) 444-7275 or reserveamerica.com
**Management:** California Department of Parks and Recreation, (530) 538-2217
**Activities:** Fishing, boating, waterskiing, swimming, hiking, biking, horseback riding
**Finding the campground:** From the intersection of CA 70 and CA 162 in Oroville, drive east on CA 162 (Olive Highway) for 8 miles to the campground entrance on the left.
**About the campground:** More rustic and spacious than Bidwell Canyon (369), Loafer Creek is located in a mixed deciduous forest. It has a swimming beach and a 4.6-mile forested loop trail. Elevation 1,030. Stay limit 30 days. Open all year. For horse camping, check out Loafer Creek Horse Camp. Groups might enjoy Loafer Creek Group Camp.

## 371 Upper Jamison (Plumas-Eureka State Park)

**Location:** 15 miles west of Portola
**GPS:** 39.7407228 / -120.7059636
**Sites:** 60 sites for tents and RVs up to 24 feet long; 1 group tent-only site
**Facilities:** Tables, grills, showers, flush toilets, laundry, dump station
**Fee per night:** $$$; reservations: (800) 444-7275 or reserveamerica.com
**Management:** California Department of Parks and Recreation, (530) 836-2380
**Activities:** Hiking, fishing
**Finding the campground:** From Portola, drive west on CA 70 for about 10 miles. Go southwest onto Mohawk Highway Road for 0.5 mile and then west onto Johnsville Road for 4 miles. Turn west onto Johnsville McCrea Road and continue 1.3 miles.
**About the campground:** The park blends the history of California's hard-rock gold-mining period with the beauty of the northern Sierra Nevada peaks, lakes, and meadows. A mining museum and a restored stamp mill are located at the park headquarters, and the historic mining town of Johnsville is nearby. Two small lakes, Eureka and Madora, lie within the park. A 1.5-mile loop trail circles Madora. Another loop trail, 3 miles long, climbs 1,300 feet to the summit of Eureka Peak (7,447 feet).

The campground is located under tall pine trees, with trails leading to the museum/mining complex, Jamison Mine, and Grass and Smith Lakes (outside the park boundary). Elevation 4,700 feet. Stay limit 15 days. Open May 1 through October 15.

## 372 Lakes Basin

**Location:** 9 miles southwest of Graeagle
**GPS:** 39.700 / -120.660
**Sites:** 23 individual sites for tents and RVs up to 26 feet long; 1 double site
**Facilities:** Tables, fire rings, drinking water, vault toilets
**Fee per night:** $$
**Management:** Thousand Trails Management (Plumas National Forest), (530) 836-2575
**Activities:** Hiking, mountain biking, swimming, fishing
**Finding the campground:** Just out of Graeagle, take CR 519 off CA 89. Proceed north approximately 9 miles to the campground turnoff.
**About the campground:** A scenic alpine landscape, 25 lakes and ponds connected by a well-maintained trail system, and unusual geological features make this campground an ideal base for exploration. A 0.5-mile-long trail leads from the campground to 175-foot-high Frazier Falls, best visited in spring, when the water level is highest and wildflowers are in bloom. Elevation 6,400 feet. Stay limit 14 days. Open all year (no services or fees September to Memorial Day).

## 373 Gold Lake

**Location:** 9 miles southwest of Graeagle
**GPS:** 39.668 / -120.661
**Sites:** 37 sites for tents and trailers
**Facilities:** Tables, fire pits, food lockers, vault and portable toilets, boat ramp; no drinking water
**Fee per night:** $
**Management:** Plumas National Forest, (530) 836-2575
**Activities:** Fishing, boating, hunting (seasonal), mountain biking, horseback riding, hiking, swimming, windsurfing
**Finding the campground:** Take CA 89 southeast from Graegle for 2 miles. Turn south onto Gold Lake Highway and proceed 10 miles to Gold Lake.
**About the campground:** The campground is set on the shores of Gold Lake, with lovely scenery and special geological features, as well as access (by hiking trails) to more than 20 small lakes nearby. In winter, visitors come to snowmobile, cross-country ski, and snowshoe. Elevation 6400 feet. Stay limit 14 days. Open all year (no services or fees September to Memorial Day).

## 374 Goose Lake

**Location:** 9 miles southwest of Graeagle
**GPS:** 39.6755301 / -120.6364793
**Sites:** 13 sites for tents and small trailers
**Facilities:** Fire rings, vault toilets, tables at most sites, food lockers; no drinking water
**Fee per night:** $
**Management:** Plumas National Forest, (530) 836-2575
**Activities:** Fishing, boating, hunting (seasonal), mountain biking, horseback riding, hiking, swimming, windsurfing

**Finding the campground:** Take CA 89 southeast from Graeagle for 2 miles. Turn south onto Gold Lake Highway and proceed 12 miles to Goose Lake.
**About the campground:** Located in the Lakes Basin Recreation Area. See Gold Lake (373) and Lakes Basin (372) for details. Elevation 6,700 feet. Stay limit 14 days. Open all year (no services or fees September to Memorial Day).

## 375 Haven Lake

**Location:** 11 miles south of Graeagle
**GPS:** 39.6724406 / -120.6306844
**Sites:** 4 sites for tents and small trailers
**Facilities:** Fire rings, tables, vault toilet; no drinking water
**Fee per night:** $ (none October to mid-May)
**Management:** Plumas National Forest, (530) 836-2575
**Activities:** Fishing, boating, mountain biking, horseback riding, hiking, swimming
**Finding the campground:** Take CA 89 southeast for 2 miles. Turn south onto Gold Lake Highway and proceed 12 miles to Haven Lake.
**About the campground:** See Gold Lake (373) and Lakes Basin (372) for details. Elevation 6,700 feet. Stay limit 14 days. Open all year (no services or fees September to Memorial Day).

## 376 Lone Rock (Antelope Lake)

**Location:** 33 miles southeast of Susanville
**GPS:** 40.191 / -120.611
**Sites:** 87 sites for tents and RVs up to 45 feet long
**Facilities:** Tables, fire rings, grills, drinking water, vault toilets, dump station, boat ramp
**Fee per night:** $$; reservations: (877) 444-6777 or recreation.gov
**Management:** Royal Elk Park Management, (530) 283-0555
**Activities:** Swimming, fishing, boating, waterskiing, hiking
**Finding the campground:** From Susanville, drive southeast for 10 miles on US 395. Turn south onto Janesville Grade for 5 miles. Go east on FR 28N01 for 9 miles, and then turn right onto FS 28N03 for 2 miles.
**About the campground:** Located on quiet Antelope Lake, some lakefront sites are shady with pines and firs. Anglers may enjoy well-stocked trout, bass, and catfish populations. Elevation 5,000 feet. Stay limit 14 days. Open May through September.

## 377 Boulder Creek (Antelope Lake)

**Location:** 31 miles southeast of Susanville
**GPS:** 40.195 / -120.617
**Sites:** 44 sites for tents and RVs up to 30 feet long
**Facilities:** Tables, fire rings, grills, drinking water, vault toilets, dump station
**Fee per night:** $$; reservations: (877) 444-6777 or recreation.gov
**Management:** Royal Elk Park Management, (530) 283-0555
**Activities:** Swimming, fishing, boating, waterskiing, hiking, biking

**Finding the campground:** From Susanville, drive southeast for 10 miles on US 395. Turn right just past Janesville onto CR 208 (which becomes FR 28N01) and drive 15 miles. Turn right onto FR 28N03 and drive 6 miles.

**About the campground:** One of the more-remote lakes in the Plumas National Forest, Antelope Lake is a good wildlife viewing area. The lake is well stocked annually with rainbow and brook trout, as well as Eagle Lake trout fingerlings. The campground is on the shoreline in an attractive pine forest. The dump station is located at Boulder Creek Work Center, about 0.5 mile northeast of the campground. The boat ramp is at Lost Cove, on the north shore of the lake, about 2 miles east of the campground. Elevation 5,000 feet. Stay limit 14 days. Open May through September.

## 378 Long Point (Antelope Lake)

**Location:** 29 miles southeast of Susanville
**GPS:** 40.178 / -120.578
**Sites:** 24 sites for tents and RVs up to 45 feet long; 4 group sites
**Facilities:** Tables, fire rings, grills, drinking water, vault toilets
**Fee per night:** $$; reservations: (877) 444-6777 or recreation.gov
**Management:** Royal Elk Park Management, (530) 283-0555
**Activities:** Swimming, fishing, boating, waterskiing, hiking
**Finding the campground:** From Susanville, drive southeast for 10 miles on US 395. Turn right onto CR 208 and drive 15 miles. Turn right onto FR 28N03 and drive 2 miles. Then turn right onto FR 27N41 and drive 1.5 miles.

**About the campground:** The campground has a wheelchair-accessible nature trail and fishing dock. Bass and trouth fishing are popular with anglers. It's a lovely lake for sailboats and paddlers. See Boulder Creek Campground (377) for more information.

## 379 Laufman

**Location:** 23 miles southeast of Susanville
**GPS:** 40.135 / -120.347
**Sites:** 6 sites for tents and RVs
**Facilities:** Tables, fire rings, vault toilet; no drinking water
**Fee per night:** None
**Management:** Plumas National Forest, (530) 836-2575
**Activities:** None
**Finding the campground:** From Susanville, drive southeast 20 miles on US 395. Turn right onto CR 336 and drive 3 miles.

**About the campground:** There's not much at Laufman, but it is a free place to stop for a night. Elevation 5,100 feet. Stay limit 14 days. Open all year.

## 380 Conklin Park

**Location:** 31 miles southeast of Susanville
**GPS:** 40.047 / -120.366
**Sites:** 9 sites for tents and RVs
**Facilities:** Tables, fire rings, vault toilets; no drinking water

**Fee per night:** None
**Management:** Plumas National Forest, (530) 836-2575
**Activities:** Fishing, OHV driving, hunting (seasonal)
**Finding the campground:** From Susanville, drive southeast 20 miles on US 395. Turn right onto CR 336 and drive 11 miles. CR 336 becomes FR 70 when the pavement begins.
**About the campground:** Situated in a quiet location on the banks of Willow Creek, which has a population of small, native trout. Eight miles northwest of Frenchman Lake. Elevation 5,900 feet. Stay limit 14 days. Open all year.

## 381 Meadow View

**Location:** 6 miles west of Doyle
**GPS:** 40.035 / -120.212
**Sites:** 6 sites for tents and RVs
**Facilities:** Tables, fire rings, drinking water (hand-pumped), vault toilets
**Fee per night:** None
**Management:** Plumas National Forest, (530) 836-2575
**Activities:** Horseback riding
**Finding the campground:** From the intersection of US 395 and CR 331 in Doyle, drive west 6 miles on CR 331. Proceed west 1 mile to the campground.
**About the campground:** This is a family and equestrian campground, and there is a horse corral across the road with a table and fire ring. Elevation 6,100 feet. Stay limit 14 days. Open all year.

## 382 Lightning Tree (Lake Davis)

**Location:** 12 miles north of Portola
**GPS:** 39.9313657 / -120.5014801
**Sites:** 19 family sites; 21 double sites for tents and RVs up to 45 feet long
**Facilities:** Tables, fire rings, drinking water, vault toilets, boat ramp
**Fee per night:** $$; reservations: (877) 444-6777 or recreation.gov
**Management:** Thousand Trails Management, (530) 836-2575
**Activities:** Swimming, fishing, boating, mountain biking, hunting (seasonally)
**Finding the campground:** From Portola, drive east 3 miles on CA 70. Turn left onto CR 112 (Grizzly Road) and drive 9 miles.
**About the campground:** The campground is on the northeast shore of the lake. Davis is a beautiful mountain lake destination, but it is prone to frequent strong winds. Waterskiing and personal watercraft are not permitted. Stocked with Eagle Lake trout and hosting bass, anglers can enjoy fishing year-round. Elevation 5,900 feet. Stay limit 14 days. Open May through October.

## 383 Grasshopper Flat (Lake Davis)

**Location:** 9 miles north of Portola
**GPS:** 39.890 / -120.477
**Sites:** 70 sites for tents and RVs up to 35 feet long; group sites
**Facilities:** Tables, fire rings, grills, drinking water, flush toilets, dump station, boat ramp

**Fee per night:** $$; reservations: (877) 444-6777 or recreation.gov
**Management:** Plumas National Forest, (530) 832-1076
**Activities:** Swimming, fishing, boating, mountain biking, hunting (seasonally)
**Finding the campground:** From Portola, drive east 3 miles on CA 70. Turn left onto CR 112 (Grizzly Road) and drive 6 miles. The campground is on the shoreline of the lake, a short distance beyond Grizzly Campground (384).
**About the campground:** Coin operated showers are available at Honker Cove boat ramp, adjacent to Grasshopper. The RV dump station is across from the campground. See Lightning Tree Campground (382) for more information.

## 384 Grizzly (Lake Davis)

**Location:** 9 miles north of Portola
**GPS:** 39.867 / -121.206
**Sites:** 57 sites for tents and RVs up to 45 feet long
**Facilities:** Tables, fire rings, grills, drinking water, flush toilets, dump station, boat ramp
**Fee per night:** $$; reservations: (877) 444-6777 or recreation.gov
**Management:** Thousand Trails management, (530) 832-1076
**Activities:** Swimming, fishing, boating
**Finding the campground:** From Portola, drive east 3 miles on CA 70. Turn left onto CR 112 (Grizzly Road) and drive 6 miles.
**About the campground:** Located on the eastern shore, just a few non-motorized campsites have lake views. Davis is a beautiful mountain lake destination for those seeking a water sports vacation. Lake Davis, created in 1967, covers 4,000 acres and has 32 miles of shoreline. Smith Peak State Game Refuge borders the lake to the east and south, hosting an abundance of birds and other wildlife. Elevation 5,900 feet. Stay limit 14 days. Open May through October.

## 385 Crocker

**Location:** 11 miles northeast of Portola
**GPS:** 39.891 / -120.422
**Sites:** 10 sites for tents and RVs
**Facilities:** Tables, fire rings, vault toilets; no drinking water
**Fee per night:** None
**Management:** Plumas National Forest, (530) 836-2575
**Activities:** Fishing, hunting (seasonal)
**Finding the campground:** From Portola, drive 5 miles east on CA 70. Turn left onto CR 111 at Beckwourth and drive north 6 miles.
**About the campground:** Situated on the banks of intermittent Crocker Creek, where a few wild trout may be available. Elevation 5,600 feet. Stay limit 14 days. Open May through November.

## 386 Cottonwood Springs (Frenchman Lake Recreation Area)

**Location:** 26 miles northeast of Portola
**GPS:** 39.8909 / -120.208

**Sites:** 20 sites for tents and RVs up to 45 feet long; 2 group sites
**Facilities:** Tables, grills, drinking water, vault toilets; dump station across the road
**Fee per night:** $$; reservations: (800) 444-7275 or reserveamerica.com
**Management:** Thousand Trails, (530) 258-7606
**Activities:** Swimming, fishing, boating, waterskiing, hiking, biking
**Finding the campground:** From Portola, drive 18 miles east on CA 70. Turn left in Chilcoot onto FR 176 and drive 9 miles. At the lake, take the left fork and drive 1.5 miles.
**About the campground:** Frenchman Lake Recreation Area contains four campgrounds, three along the lakeshore (Frenchman, Spring Creek, and Big Cove) and one on a stream 1.5 miles west of the lake (Cottonwood Springs). The lake provides a good place for a complete water sport vacation. A shoreline 21 miles long ends at the 129-foot-tall earthen dam, which rises to an elevation of 5,607 feet. Reno, Nevada, is 38 miles away. Elevation 5,700 feet. Stay limit 14 days. Open April through September.

## 387 Frenchman (Frenchman Lake Recreation Area)

**Location:** 29 miles northeast of Portola
**GPS:** 39.89 / -120.186
**Sites:** 38 sites for tents and RVs up to 45 feet long
**Facilities:** Tables, grills, drinking water, vault toilets, boat ramp.
**Fee per night:** $$; reservations: (877) 444-6777 or recreation.gov
**Management:** Thousand Trails Management, (530) 258-7606
**Activities:** Swimming, fishing, boating, waterskiing
**Finding the campground:** From Portola, drive 18 miles east on CA 70. Turn left in Chilcoot onto FR 176 and drive 9 miles. At the lake, take the right fork and drive 1.5 miles.
**About the campground:** Located at the southeastern peninsula of the lake, with widely spaced and rather private sites. The terrain is rather steep and rugged in places. Elevation 5,700 feet. Stay limit 14 days. Open April through October.

## 388 Spring Creek (Frenchman Lake Recreation Area)

**Location:** 28 miles northeast of Portola
**GPS:** 39.89 / -120.176
**Sites:** 35 sites for tents and RVs up to 45 feet long
**Facilities:** Tables, grills, drinking water, vault toilets
**Fee per night:** $$; reservations: (800) 444-7275 or reserveamerica.com
**Management:** Thousand Trails Management, (530) 258-7606
**Activities:** Swimming, fishing, boating, waterskiing
**Finding the campground:** From Portola, drive 18 miles east on CA 70. Turn left in Chilcoot onto FR 176 and drive 9 miles. At the lake, take the right fork and drive 1.7 miles.
**About the campground:** Spring Creek is the only campground on the lake that has some sites directly on the water, making swimming and small boat inputs possible right from the campsite. Larger boats may launch at the ramp at Frenchman or the beach at Spring Creek. Elevation 5,800 feet. Stay limit 14 days. Open April through October.

## 389 Big Cove (Frenchman Lake Recreation Area)

**Location:** 29 miles northeast of Portola
**GPS:** 39.902 / -120.172
**Sites:** 42 sites for tents and RVs up to 45 feet long
**Facilities:** Tables, grills, drinking water, flush toilets, showers
**Fee per night:** $$; reservations: (800) 444-7275 or reserveamerica.com
**Management:** Thousand Trails Management, (530) 258-7606
**Activities:** Swimming, fishing, boating, waterskiing, hiking
**Finding the campground:** From Portola, drive 18 miles east on CA 70. Turn left in Chilcoot onto FR 176 and drive 9 miles. At the lake, take the right fork and drive 2.5 miles.
**About the campground:** For a description of Frenchman Lake Recreation Area, see Frenchman Campground (387). Big Cove has an overflow area across the road from the main campground. Elevation 5,800 feet. Stay limit 14 days. Open April through October.

## 390 Chilcoot

**Location:** 23 miles northeast of Portola
**GPS:** 39.865 / -120.166
**Sites:** 40 sites for tents and RVs up to 40 feet long
**Facilities:** Tables, fire rings, drinking water, flush toilets
**Fee per night:** $$; reservations: (800) 444-7275 or reserveamerica.com
**Management:** Thousand Trails Management, (530) 258-7606
**Activities:** Hiking, fishing
**Finding the campground:** From Portola, drive 18 miles east on CA 70. Turn left in Chilcoot onto FR 176 and drive 5 miles.
**About the campground:** Situated on Little Last Chance Creek, about 4 miles south of Frenchman Lake. See Cottonwood Springs Campground (number 386) for lake activities. Elevation 5,100 feet. Stay limit 14 days. Open April to October.

# Central Valley

California's Central Valley is one of the most productive farming areas in the world. A drive along I-5 through the Sacramento Valley reveals an astoundingly diverse agricultural bounty rarely seen anywhere. Miles and miles of orchards, vineyards, rice, and vegetable crops seem to stretch to an endless horizon. To a traveler accustomed to the smaller farms of the eastern United States, California agriculture boggles the mind.

But not all the Central Valley is farmland. The eastern foothills of the Sierra Nevada offer a variety of outdoor adventures. Large lakes provide opportunities for a full range of water sports, and the foothills offer miles of hiking, equestrian, and mountain biking trails, as well as picnicking and wildlife-watching opportunities.

Cool winters and warm summers produce a long growing season, which contributes significantly to the Central Valley's agricultural bounty. In summer the average low temperature is 65°F; the average high is 98°F. In winter the low averages 38°F and the high 57°F. Spring sees readings of between 76°F and 49°F. Fall temperatures are somewhat warmer, with an average high of 80°F and low of 44°F. The percentage of average days of sunshine is 91 percent in summer, 71 percent in fall, 44 percent in winter, and 61 percent in the spring, with a lot more in drought years.

Although the Central Valley Tour Region (as defined by the California Division of Tourism) extends into Southern California, this book features only the campgrounds in its northern half. For the southern campgrounds, please see the companion FalconGuide *Camping Southern California* by Richard McMahon.

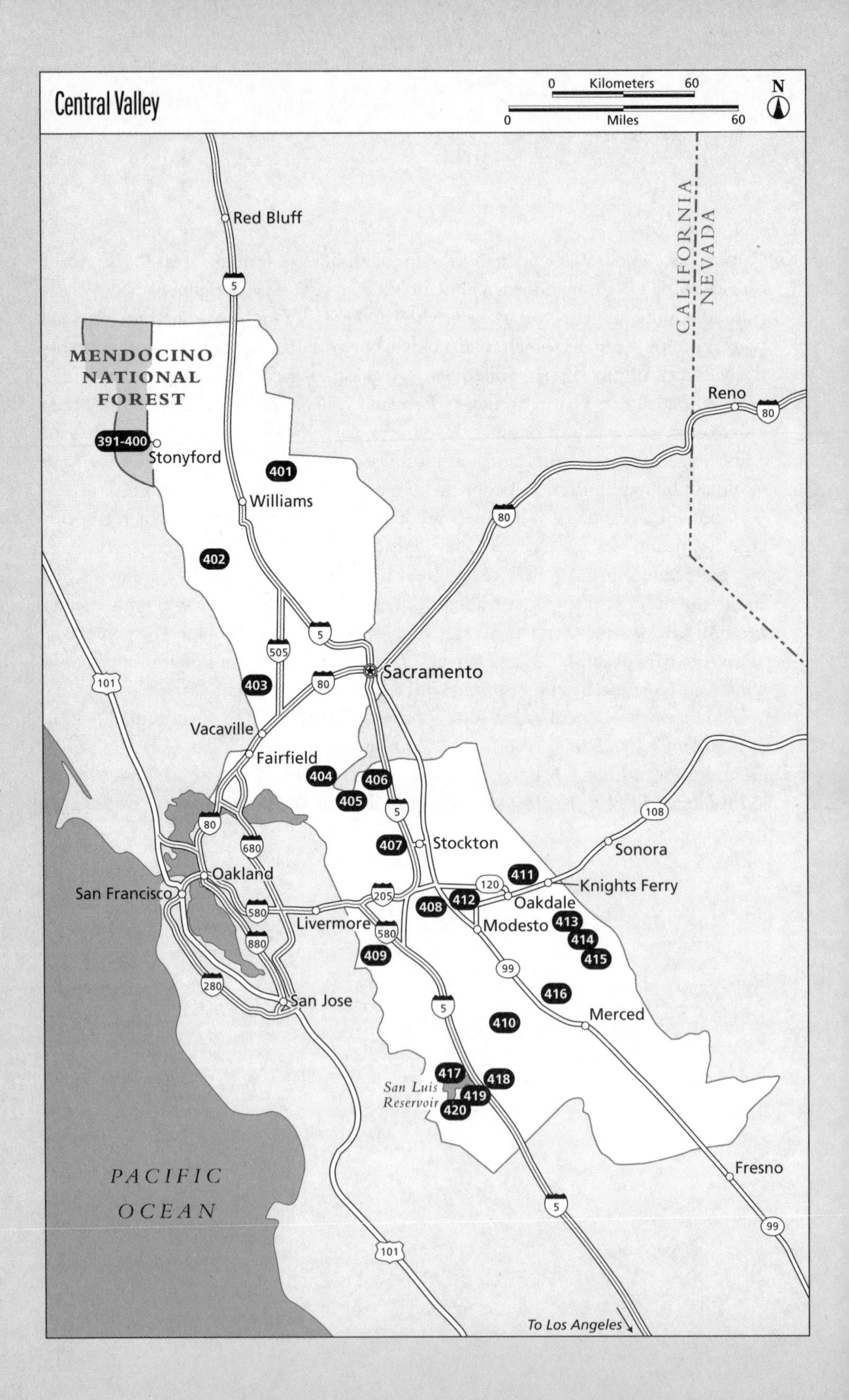

Central Valley
0
Kilometers
60
0
Miles
60
N
MENDOCINO
NATIONAL
FOREST
CALIFORNIA
NEVADA
Red Bluff
Stonyford
Williams
Reno
Sacramento
Vacaville
Fairfield
Stockton
Sonora
Knights Ferry
Oakland
San Francisco
Oakdale
Livermore
Modesto
San Jose
Merced
San Luis
Reservoir
Fresno
PACIFIC
OCEAN
To Los Angeles
391-400
401
402
403
404
405
406
407
408
409
410
411
412
413
414
415
416
417
418
419
420
5
80
101
505
680
580
880
280
205
120
108
99

|  | Name | Group Sites | RV Sites | Max. RV Length | Hookups | Toilets | Showers | Drinking Water | Dump Station | Pets | Wheelchair | Recreation | Fee(s) | Season | Can Reserve |
|---|---|---|---|---|---|---|---|---|---|---|---|---|---|---|---|
|  | **CENTRAL VALLEY** |  |  |  |  |  |  |  |  |  |  |  |  |  |  |
| 391 | Mill Creek |  |  |  |  | V |  |  |  | * |  | FO | $ | Year-round |  |
| 392 | Fouts |  | * | 16 |  | V |  |  |  | * | * | FO | $ | Year-round |  |
| 393 | Davis Flat |  | * |  |  | V |  |  |  | * |  | 0 | $ | Year-round |  |
| 394 | South Fork & North Fork |  | * |  |  | V |  |  |  | * |  | FO | $ | South: Year-round; North: May–Nov |  |
| 395 | Old Mill |  | * |  |  | V |  |  |  | * |  | HO | None | May–Nov |  |
| 396 | Cedar Camp |  | * | 16 |  | V |  |  |  | * |  | HO | None | May–Nov |  |
| 397 | Little Stony |  | * | small |  | V |  |  |  | * |  | FO | $ | Year-round |  |
| 398 | Dixie Glade |  | * |  |  | V |  |  |  | * |  | HR | $ | Apr–Nov |  |
| 399 | Mill Valley |  | * |  |  | V |  |  |  | * |  | HO | $ | May–Oct |  |
| 400 | Letts Lake Complex |  | * | 24 |  | V |  | * |  | * | * | FSBH | $ | May–Oct |  |
| 401 | Colusa-Sacramento River State Recreation Area |  | * | 37 | E | F | * | * | * | * | * | FBHL | $$–$$$$ | Year-round | * |
| 402 | Cache Creek Canyon Regional Park | * | * |  |  | F | * | * | * | * | * | FSBHL | $$–$$$$ | Year-round | * |
| 403 | Lake Solano County Park |  | * | 40 | EW | F | * | * | * | * | * | FSBHL | $$$–$$$$ | Year-round | * |
| 404 | Sandy Beach County Park |  | * | 45 | EW | F | * | * | * | * | * | FBL | $$$ | Year-round | * |
| 405 | Brannan Island State Recreation Area | * | * | 36 | EW | F |  | * | * | * | * | FSBHL | $$$–$$$$ | Year-round | * |
| 406 | Westgate Landing County Park |  | * |  |  | F |  | * |  | * | * | FSB | $$ | Year-round | * |
| 407 | Dos Reis County Park |  | * |  |  | F | * | * |  | * | * | FBL | $$ | Year-round | * |
| 408 | Caswell Memorial State Park | * | * | 24 |  | F | * | * |  | * | * | FSH | $$$ | Year-round | * |
| 409 | Frank Raines–Deer Creek OHV Park |  | * |  | EWS | F | * | * |  | * | * | 0 | $ | Year-round |  |
| 410 | George J. Hatfield State Recreation Area | * | * | 30 |  | F |  | * |  | * | * | FSB | $$–$$$$ | Year-round | * |
| 411 | Woodward Reservoir County Park | * | * |  | EWS | F | * | * | * | * | * | FSBL | $$–$$$$ | Year-round | * |

| | Name | Group Sites | RV Sites | Max. RV Length | Hookups | Toilets | Showers | Drinking Water | Dump Station | Pets | Wheelchair | Recreation | Fee(s) | Season | Can Reserve |
|---|---|---|---|---|---|---|---|---|---|---|---|---|---|---|---|
| 412 | McHenry Recreation Area | * | | | | F | | * | | * | * | BFSH | $ | Year-round | * (permit only) |
| 413 | Modesto Reservoir Regional Park | | * | | EWS | F | * | * | * | | * | SFBL | $$ | Year-round | |
| 414 | Turlock Lake State Recreation Area | | * | 27 | | F | * | * | | * | * | FSBL | $$$ | Year-round | * |
| 415 | LaGrange OHV Park | | * | | | F | | * | | * | | O | $ | Year-round | |
| 416 | McConnell State Recreation Area | * | * | 30 | | F | * | * | | * | * | FS | $$$-$$$$ | Mar-Sept | * |
| 417 | San Luis Creek (San Luis Reservoir State Recreation Area) | * | * | 30 | EW | C | | * | * | * | * | FSBL | $$$$ | Year-round | * |
| 418 | Los Banos Creek Reservoir (San Luis Reservoir State Recreation Area) | | | | | V | | * | * | * | * | FSBL | $$ | Year-round | |
| 419 | Medeiros (San Luis Reservoir State Recreation Area) | | * | | | C | | * | | * | * | FSB | $$ | Year-round | |
| 420 | Basalt (San Luis Reservoir State Recreation Area) | | * | 30 | | F | * | * | * | * | * | FBSHL | $$$ | Year-round | * |

Toilets: F=flush V=vault P=pit C=chemical; Fee: $=Under $20 $$=$20-$29 $$$=$30-$39 $$$$ $40 or more; Recreation: H=hiking S=swimming F=fishing B=boating L=boat launch O=off-highway driving R=horseback riding, M=mountain biking Hookups: W=water E=electric S=sewer

# 391 Mill Creek

**Location:** 8 miles west of Stonyford
**GPS:** 39.355780 / -122.654079
**Sites:** 6 sites for tents
**Facilities:** Tables, fire rings, grills, vault toilet; no drinking water
**Fee per night:** $
**Management:** Mendocino National Forest, (530) 934-3316
**Activities:** Fishing, OHV driving
**Finding the campground:** From Stonyford, drive west on Fouts Spring Road (FR M10), staying on it as it becomes FR 18N01/Fouts Springs Road for a total of about 8 miles.

**About the campground:** Situated on Mill Creek, in an area where vegetation is pretty much limited to brush and digger pine trees. The campground receives high OHV use October through June. Stream flow is best in winter and early spring. Elevation 1,700 feet. Stay limit 14 days. Open all year.

## 392 Fouts

**Location:** 9 miles west of Stonyford
**GPS:** 39.3582812 / -122.6542004
**Sites:** 11 sites for tents and RVs up to 16 feet long
**Facilities:** Tables, fire rings, grills, vault toilets; no drinking water
**Fee per night:** $
**Management:** Mendocino National Forest, (530) 934-3316
**Activities:** Fishing, OHV driving
**Finding the campground:** From Stonyford, drive west on Fouts Spring Road (FR M10), staying on it as it becomes FR 18N01/Fouts Springs Road for a total of about 8.3 miles to Fouts Springs OHV Staging Area. Turn north at the sign and drive about 0.2 mile to the campground, on right.
**About the campground:** Situated on a bluff overlooking Mill Creek, campsites are mainly sunlit due to fires some years ago. OHV access is the best reason to stay here. Elevation 1,700 feet. Stay limit 14 days. Open all year.

## 393 Davis Flat

**Location:** 9 miles west of Stonyford
**GPS:** 39.3619628 / -122.655009
**Sites:** 20 dispersed sites for tents and RVs
**Facilities:** Tables, fire rings, vault toilets; no drinking water
**Fee per night:** $
**Management:** Mendocino National Forest, (530) 934-3316
**Activities:** OHV driving
**Finding the campground:** From Stonyford, drive west on Fouts Spring Road (FR M10), staying on it as it becomes FR 18N01/Fouts Springs Road for a total of about 8.3 miles to Fouts Springs OHV Staging Area. Turn north at the sign and drive about 1 mile.
**About the campground:** Situated in the Davis Flat OHV Driving Area, the campground is used mainly for this purpose, especially October through June. There are only tables and fire rings for the 20 campsites, plus more open-space camping. Elevation 1,700 feet. Stay limit 14 days. Open all year.

## 394 South Fork & North Fork

**Location:** 10 miles west of Stonyford
**GPS:** North Fork: 39.379100 / -122.648233; South Fork: 39.361507 / -122.653590
**Sites:** 10 sites for tents and RVs at North Fork; open-space camping at South Fork
**Facilities:** Tables, fire rings, vault toilet; no drinking water
**Fee per night:** $
**Management:** Mendocino National Forest, (530) 934-3316
**Activities:** OHV driving, fishing

**Finding the campground:** From Stonyford, drive west on Fouts Spring Road (FR M10), staying on it as it becomes FR 18N01/Fouts Springs Road for a total of about 8.3 miles to Fouts Springs OHV Staging Area. Turn north at the sign and drive about 1.5 miles.
**About the campground:** Situated on the South Fork of Stony Creek, this campground is in an area of high OHV use, especially October through June. North Fork is adjacent to a year-long stream in an open grove of oak trees. Elevation 1,500 feet. Stay limit 14 days. South Fork is open all year; North Fork is open May through November.

## 395 Old Mill

**Location:** 10 miles southwest of Stonyford
**GPS:** 39.308528 / -122.645133
**Sites:** 10 sites for tents and RVs up to 16 feet long
**Facilities:** Tables, fire rings, vault toilets; no drinking water
**Fee per night:** None
**Management:** Mendocino National Forest, (530) 934-3316
**Activities:** Hiking, OHV driving
**Finding the campground:** From Stonyford, drive west 6 miles on Fouts Spring Road (FR M10). Turn south onto Trough Springs Road (FR M5), and drive about 5 miles. FR M5 is a narrow dirt road, not recommended for large vehicles or trailers.
**About the campground:** Located in a mature stand of mixed pine and fir. Best suited for OHV riders. Elevation 3,700 feet. Stay limit 14 days. Open May through November.

## 396 Cedar Camp

**Location:** 19 miles southwest of Stonyford
**GPS:** 39.264322 / -122.698635
**Sites:** 5 sites for tents and small RVs
**Facilities:** Tables, fire rings, vault toilets; no drinking water
**Fee per night:** None
**Management:** Mendocino National Forest, (530) 934-3316
**Activities:** Hiking, OHV driving
**Finding the campground:** From Stonyford, drive west about 5 miles on Fouts Spring Road (FR M10). Turn south onto Trough Springs Road (FR M5) and drive about 11 miles. FR M5 is a narrow dirt road, not recommended for large vehicles or trailers.
**About the campground:** Situated in an area of mature fir and pine near the base of Goat Mountain (6,121 feet), this campground is best used for OHV trail access. Elevation 4,300 feet. Stay limit 14 days. Open May through November.

## 397 Little Stony

**Location:** 9 miles southwest of Stonyford
**GPS:** 39.286417 / -122.576463
**Sites:** 8 sites for tents and small RVs
**Facilities:** Tables, fire rings, vault toilets; no drinking water
**Fee per night:** $

**Management:** Mendocino National Forest, (530) 934-3316
**Activities:** OHV driving, fishing
**Finding the campground:** From Stonyford, drive south 5 miles on Lodoga-Stonyford Road. Turn southwest onto Goat Mountain Road and drive about 4 miles. The access road is not suited to trailers.
**About the campground:** With Little Stony OHV Staging Area nearby, the area receives high OHV use October 1 to June 1. Most popular in winter, when Stony Creek is in full flow. Elevation 1,500 feet. Stay limit 14 days. Open all year.

## 398 Dixie Glade

**Location:** 12 miles west of Stonyford
**GPS:** 39.336276 / -122.703479
**Sites:** 7 sites for tents and RVs
**Facilities:** Tables, fire rings, vault toilets, hitching posts and corrals; no drinking water
**Fee per night:** $
**Management:** Mendocino National Forest, (530) 963-3128
**Activities:** Hiking, horseback riding
**Finding the campground:** From Stonyford, drive west 12 miles on Fouts Spring Road (FR M10).
**About the campground:** Situated in a small, quiet location amid ponderosa pine, Douglas fir, and oak, the campground is suitable for horse camping. The Bathhouse Trail (0.8 mile) leads to Deafy Glade Trail, providing access to the Snow Mountain Wilderness. Elevation 3,700 feet. Stay limit 14 days. Open April through November.

## 399 Mill Valley

**Location:** 16 miles west of Stonyford
**GPS:** 39.3174871 / -122.7111552
**Sites:** 15 sites for tents and RVs
**Facilities:** Tables, fire rings, drinking water, vault toilets
**Fee per night:** $
**Management:** Mendocino National Forest, (530) 963-3128
**Activities:** OHV driving, hiking
**Finding the campground:** From Stonyford, drive west about 14.5 miles on Fouts Spring Road (FR M10). Turn east onto FR 17N02 and drive 1.5 miles.
**About the campground:** Situated beside pretty Lily Pond (a meadow in drier months). Hiking is on forest/OHV roads. Trout fishing and nonmotorized boating are available 1.5 miles south at Upper Letts Lake. Elevation 4,200 feet. Stay limit 14 days. Open May through October.

## 400 Letts Lake Complex

**Location:** 17 miles west of Stonyford
**GPS:** 39.302844 / -122.707693
**Sites:** 42 campsites for tents and RVs up to 24 feet long
**Facilities:** Tables, fire rings, drinking water, vault toilets, fishing pier
**Fee per night:** $.

**Management:** Mendocino National Forest, (530) 934-3316
**Activities:** Fishing, swimming, nonmotorized boating, hiking
**Finding the campground:** From Stonyford, drive west about 14 miles on Fouts Spring Road (FR M10). Turn east onto FR 17N02 and drive 3 miles.
**About the campground:** Campsites are distributed throughout a mixed pine forest with access to 35-acre Letts Lake. The lake features an accessible fishing pier, from which you can try your hand at catching rainbow trout, black bass, and catfish. A scenic 1-mile trail follows the shoreline. Elevation 4,500 feet. Stay limit 14 days. Open May through October.

## 401 Colusa-Sacramento River State Recreation Area

**Location:** In Colusa
**GPS:** 39.217246 / -122.014836
**Sites:** 14 sites for tents and RVs up to 37 feet long
**Facilities:** Tables, fire rings, drinking water, flush toilets, hookups, showers, laundry, dump station, boat ramp
**Fee per night:** $$, primitive: $, electric hookups: $$$–$$$$; reservations: (800) 444-7275 or reserveamerica.com
**Management:** California Department of Parks and Recreation, (530) 458-4740, ext. 104
**Activities:** Fishing, boating, hiking, birding
**Finding the campground:** From the junction of I-5 and CA 20 near Williams, drive east on CA 20 for 9 miles to Colusa. Turn left (north) onto 10th Street and drive 1 mile.
**About the campground:** Situated on the Sacramento River, with a variety of fishing options: striped bass in spring, shad in summer, salmon in late summer–early fall, and sturgeon in winter. Other catches include catfish, bluegill, and carp. The boat ramp is for small boats only. You can walk by the river or into downtown Colusa. On the Pacific Flyway, the area is home to an abundant number of birds. Elevation 70 feet. Stay limit 15 days June through September; 30 days October through May. Open all year.

## 402 Cache Creek Canyon Regional Park

**Location:** 44 miles northwest of Woodland
**GPS:** 38.9170155 / -122.3133016
**Sites:** 49 sites for tents and RVs, including 4 group sites
**Facilities:** Tables, fire rings, drinking water, flush toilets, showers, dump station, store, playground
**Fee per night:** $$, group sites: $$$$; reservations: (530) 406-4880 or apm.activecommunities .com/yolocountyparks
**Management:** Yolo County Parks and Recreation, (530) 406-4880
**Activities:** Fishing, swimming, hiking, kayaking, rafting
**Finding the campground:** From the intersection of I-505 and CA 16 (10 miles west of Woodland), drive about 34 miles northwest on CA 16.
**About the campground:** Cache Creek is the closest whitewater rafting to the San Francisco Bay area. The stretch near the campground can be good fishing grounds for catfish and sometimes for bass. Note that it can be over 100°F by day in summer (50°F at night). Elevation 790 feet. Stay limit 14 days. Open all year.

## 403 Lake Solano County Park

**Location:** 18 miles north of Vacaville
**GPS:** 38.4917018 / -122.0290617
**Sites:** 58 sites for tents and RVs up to 40 feet long
**Facilities:** Tables, fire rings, drinking water, flush toilets, showers, dump station, boat ramp and rentals, water and electric hookups, nature center
**Fee per night:** $$$, hookups: $$$$; reservations: (530) 795-2990 or parkreservations.solano county.com
**Management:** Solano County Parks Department, (530) 795-2990
**Activities:** Fishing, fly fishing, nonmotorized boating, swimming, hiking
**Finding the campground:** From the intersection of I-80 and I-505 at Vacaville, drive north 11 miles on I-505. Turn west onto CA 128 and drive 7 miles. Turn south onto Pleasants Valley Road and drive about 300 yards.
**About the campground:** This small lake is actually a dammed section of Putah Creek, and its size varies. It is stocked with rainbow trout, and you can also catch catfish and sunfish. It has a popular beach and day-use picnic area. Elevation 165 feet. Stay limit 14 days. Open all year.

## 404 Sandy Beach County Park

**Location:** 25 miles west of Stockton
**GPS:** 38.1401068 / -121.6960312
**Sites:** 42 sites for tents and RVs up to 45 feet long
**Facilities:** Tables, fire rings, drinking water, flush toilets, showers, electric and water hookups, dump station, playground, boat ramp, sand volleyball, horseshoes
**Fee per night:** $$$; reservations: (707) 374-2097 or parkreservations.solanocounty.com
**Management:** Sacramento County Parks Department, (707) 374-2097
**Activities:** Fishing, boating
**Finding the campground:** From Stockton, drive north 7 miles on I-5, turn left (west) onto CA 12 and drive 17 miles. After crossing the Sacramento River and entering Rio Vista, turn left onto Main Street and then right onto Second Street and proceed to Beach Avenue. Follow Beach Avenue to the campground.
**About the campground:** The site is on the Sacramento River at a popular fishing location. For fishing information see Colusa–Sacramento River Campground (401). There is a beach, but no swimming is permitted due to strong currents. Elevation 20 feet. Stay limit 14 days. Open all year.

## 405 Brannan Island State Recreation Area

**Location:** 26 miles west of Stockton
**GPS:** 38.11456 / -121.6933284
**Sites:** 140 sites for tents and RVs up to 36 feet long; cabins; group sites
**Facilities:** Tables, fire rings, drinking water, flush toilets, dump station, boat ramp, swimming area, water and electric hookups
**Fee per night:** $$$; hookups, cabins, group sites: $$$$; reservations: (800) 444-7275 or reserveamerica.com

*Spring, when the grass is green, is a great time for camping at Brannan Island, whether the fish are biting or not.*

**Management:** California Department of Parks and Recreation, (530) 777-6671
**Activities:** Swimming, fishing, boating, waterskiing, hiking, biking, birding
**Finding the campground:** From Stockton, drive north 7 miles on I-5. Turn west onto CA 12 and drive 16 miles. Turn south onto CA 160 and drive 3 miles.
**About the campground:** Situated on the Sacramento River, the campground provides an excellent base for fishing and exploring the many miles of waterway in the Sacramento–San Joaquin Delta. There are multiple fishing piers and a large picnic area. A paved bike and walking path circles the island and includes a nature trail. For fishing information see Colusa–Sacramento River Campground (401). Nearby Frank's Tract is ideal for waterskiing. Elevation 30 feet. Stay limit 15 days. Open all year.

## 406 Westgate Landing County Park

**Location:** 13 miles northwest of Stockton
**GPS:** 38.123957 / -121.492904
**Sites:** 14 sites for tents and RVs
**Facilities:** Tables, grills, drinking water, flush toilets, boat slips
**Fee per night:** $$; reservations: (209) 953-8800 or (209) 331-7400
**Management:** San Joaquin County Parks Department, (209) 953-8800 or (209) 331-7400
**Activities:** Swimming, fishing, boating, waterskiing
**Finding the campground:** From Stockton, drive north 7 miles on I-5. Turn west onto CA 12 and drive 5 miles. Turn north onto Glasscock Road and drive 1 mile.

**About the campground:** Situated on the South Mokelumne River, the campground provides access to the waterways of the Sacramento–San Joaquin Delta. For fishing information, see Colusa–Sacramento River Campground (401). Elevation 2 feet. Stay limit 14 days. Open all year.

## 407 Dos Reis County Park

**Location:** In Stockton
**GPS:** 37.8313168 / -121.3106683
**Sites:** 26 sites for RVs with full hookups; tents accepted
**Facilities:** Tables, grills, drinking water, flush toilets, showers, boat ramp
**Fee per night:** $$; reservations: (209) 953-8800
**Management:** San Joaquin County Parks Department, (209) 953-8800
**Activities:** Fishing, boating
**Finding the campground:** From I-5 in Stockton, take the Lathrop exit west to an immediate right onto Manthey Road. Drive about 1 mile; turn left onto Dos Reis Road and drive a short distance.
**About the campground:** Situated on the San Joaquin River, where fishing for striped bass is sometimes good. Elevation 16 feet. Stay limit 14 days. Open all year.

## 408 Caswell Memorial State Park

**Location:** 6 miles south of Manteca
**GPS:** 37.6926358 / -121.1847167
**Sites:** 65 sites for tents and RVs up to 24 feet long; hike & bike sites; 1 group site
**Facilities:** Tables, fire rings, drinking water, flush toilets, showers, visitor center
**Fee per night:** $$$; reservations: (800) 444-7275 or reserveamerica.com
**Management:** California Department of Parks and Recreation, (209) 599-3810
**Activities:** Fishing, hiking, biking, swimming
**Finding the campground:** From the intersection of CA 120 and CA 99 at Manteca, drive southeast 1 mile on CA 99. Turn right onto Austin Road and drive 4.5 miles.
**About the campground:** Situated on the Stanislaus River in one of the last remaining oak-riparian woodlands, which once flourished throughout the valley. Although parts of the river are fairly well stocked with rainbow trout, this section of sluggish green water more often yields catfish. There are many wonderful nature trails. ***Note:*** It can get to over 100°F in summer. Come prepared for mosquitoes too. Elevation 60 feet. Stay limit 15 days. Open all year.

## 409 Frank Raines–Deer Creek OHV Park

**Location:** 23 miles west of Patterson
**GPS:** 37.4218623 / -121.3775344
**Sites:** 34 sites for tents and RVs
**Facilities:** Tables, grills, drinking water, flush toilets, showers, electric and sewer hookups, playground
**Fee per night:** $
**Management:** Stanislaus County Department of Parks and Recreation, (408) 897-3127
**Activities:** OHV driving

**Finding the campground:** From I-5 at Patterson, take the Patterson exit. Turn west onto Del Puerto Canyon Road and drive 23 miles.
**About the campground:** This park encompasses 860 acres of steep terrain for OHV use (all-terrain vehicles, dune buggies, motorcycles, four-wheel-drive vehicles). Elevation 1,150 feet. Stay limit 14 days. Open all year.

## 410 George J. Hatfield State Recreation Area

**Location:** 42 miles west of Merced
**GPS:** 37.356222 / -120.9593082
**Sites:** 21 sites for tents and RVs up to 30 feet long; 1 group site
**Facilities:** Tables, grills, drinking water, flush toilets
**Fee per night:** $$, group site: $$$$; reservations (group site only): (800) 444-7275 or reserveamerica.com
**Management:** California Department of Parks and Recreation, (203) 632-1852
**Activities:** Fishing, swimming, paddling, birding, riparian wildlife viewing
**Finding the campground:** From the intersection of CA 99 and CA 140 in Merced, drive west on CA 140 for 33 miles. Turn right (north) onto CA 33 and drive 3.7 miles to Newman. Turn right onto Merced Street (which becomes Hills Ferry Road, then Kelley Road) and drive about 5 miles.
**About the campground:** Situated on the Merced River near its confluence with the San Joaquin, with a lot of riverside waterfront to wander. Catfish are the main catch. Elevation 75 feet. Stay limit 15 days. Open all year.

## 411 Woodward Reservoir County Park

**Location:** 5 miles north of Oakdale
**GPS:** 37.8471234 / -120.8770056
**Sites:** 155 sites for tents and RVs; 1 group site
**Facilities:** Tables, grills, drinking water, flush toilets, showers, dump station, store, boat ramp and rentals, full hookups, go-kart track, radio-controlled airplane field
**Fee per night:** $$, group site: $$$$; reservations (group site only): (209) 847-3304
**Management:** Stanislaus County Department of Parks and Recreation, (408) 897-3127
**Activities:** Swimming, fishing, boating, waterskiing, duck hunting (seasonal)
**Finding the campground:** From the intersection of CA 120 and CR J14 in Oakdale, drive north on CR J14 (26 Mile Road) for 5 miles.
**About the campground:** Woodward Reservoir covers almost 3,000 acres and has more than 20 miles of shoreline. Boating rules separate the lake into fishing and waterskiing areas. The lake is stocked annually with rainbow trout; redear sunfish, largemouth bass, channel catfish, and bluegill can also be taken. Many park facilities were renovated in 2016. Elevation 210 feet. Stay limit 14 days. Open all year.

## 412 McHenry Recreation Area

**Location:** 11 miles west of Oakdale
**GPS:** 37.7537835 / -121.0114824
**Sites:** 10 sites for tents only; group camp

**Facilities:** Tables, fire pits, flush toilets, drinking water
**Fee per night:** $; by permit only: (209) 881-3517
**Management:** US Army Corp of Engineers, (209) 881-3517
**Activities:** Boating, fishing, swimming, hiking
**Finding the campground:** From Oakdale, go southwest on CA 108 West about 6 miles. Go north on 1st Street/Santa Fe Road for 1.8 miles, then west on East River Road for 3.5 miles.
**About the campground:** On the Stanislaus River, this is a popular place for float tubing on summer weekends. Access is by boat, foot, or bicycle only. You will need to park and walk in. Trout, smallmouth bass, striped bass, carp, channel and white catfish, and black crappie tempt anglers here. This is part of a larger system of Stanislaus River Parks. Elevation 95 feet. Stay limit 14 days. Open all year. Also consider Valley Oak Recreation Area, a walk-in, tent-only site on the river about a 0.25 mile away.

## 413 Modesto Reservoir Regional Park

**Location:** 21 miles east of Modesto
**GPS:** 37.6598589 / -120.6532201
**Sites:** 150 sites for tents and RVs
**Facilities:** Tables, barbecues, drinking water, showers, flush toilets, dump station, boat ramp, full hookups
**Fee per night:** $$
**Management:** Stanislaus County Parks Department, (209) 874-9540
**Activities:** Swimming, fishing, boating, waterskiing, birding, archery, radio-controlled airplane flying
**Finding the campground:** From the intersection of CA 99 and CA 132 in Modesto, drive east on CA 132 about 19 miles. Turn north onto Reservoir Road and drive 2 miles.
**About the campground:** Modesto Reservoir is a medium-size lake covering about 2,800 acres. It has 30 miles of shoreline. Small to medium-size bass and trout are the main catches. A portion of the southern part of the lake has a 5 mph speed limit, which prevents waterskiing and benefits anglers. Elevation 210 feet. Stay limit 15 days. Open all year. No pets allowed.

## 414 Turlock Lake State Recreation Area

**Location:** 26 miles east of Modesto
**GPS:** 37.6258628 / -120.5894457
**Sites:** 54 sites for tents and RVs up to 27 feet long
**Facilities:** Tables, fire rings, drinking water, showers, flush toilets, boat ramp, fishing pier
**Fee per night:** $$$; reservations: (800) 444-7275 or reserveamerica.com
**Management:** California State Parks, (209) 874-2056
**Activities:** Fishing, swimming, boating, waterskiing
**Finding the campground:** From the intersection of CA 99 and CA 132 in Modesto, drive east on CA 132 for about 23 miles. Turn south onto Roberts Ferry Road and drive 1 mile. Turn east onto Lakeside Road and drive 2 miles.
**About the campground:** Turlock Lake has 26 miles of shoreline and covers 3,500 acres. However, this surface area can be cut in half during summer due to heavy drawdowns. The lake can provide good trout fishing in spring and fair bass fishing in summer. It is stocked annually with rainbow trout. Other catches include bluegill, crappie, and catfish. Elevation 270 feet. Stay limit 15 days. Open all year.

## 415 LaGrange OHV Park

**Location:** 21 miles east of Waterford
**GPS:** 37.6317112 / -120.4640472
**Sites:** Dispersed camping for tents and RVs
**Facilities:** Tables, fire pits, barbecue grills, drinking water, flush toilets
**Fee per night:** $
**Management:** Stanislaus County Department of Parks and Recreation, (209) 525-6750
**Activities:** OHV driving
**Finding the campground:** Take CA 132 east for 17.5 miles. Turn south onto La Grange Road for about 2.5 miles.
**About the campground:** What used to be an active gold dredge is now an OHV park with open play areas, hills, trails, a mud bog, and motocross tracks, sometimes used for race events. There is limited shade. Elevation 435 feet. Stay limit 15 days. Open all year.

## 416 McConnell State Recreation Area

**Location:** 13 miles southeast of Turlock
**GPS:** 37.4161907 / -120.710805
**Sites:** 21 sites for tents and RVs up to 30 feet long; group sites
**Facilities:** Tables, grills, drinking water, showers, flush toilets, swimming beach, campfire center
**Fee per night:** $$$, group sites: $$$$; reservations: (800) 444-7275 or reserveamerica.com
**Management:** California Department of Parks and Recreation, (203) 394-7755
**Activities:** Fishing, swimming
**Finding the campground:** From the intersection of CR J-17 and CA 99 in Turlock, drive southeast on CA 99 for 5.7 miles. Take the El Capitan Way exit and drive east 4.5 miles. Turn south onto Pepper Street and drive 2.7 miles.
**About the campground:** This 74-acre park enjoys an attractive location on the banks of the Merced River. Large sycamores and evergreens shade spacious lawns in the campsite area. Fishing is primarily for catfish, bass, and perch. Elevation 125 feet. Stay limit 15 days. Open March through September.

## 417 San Luis Creek (San Luis Reservoir State Recreation Area)

**Location:** 15 miles west of Los Banos
**GPS:** 37.0944909 / -121.0629491
**Sites:** 53 sites for tents and RVs up to 30 feet long; 2 group sites (with showers)
**Facilities:** Tables with shade ramadas, fire rings, drinking water, tent pads, chemical toilets, water and electric hookups, dump station, boat ramp
**Fee per night:** $$$$; reservations: (800) 444-7275 or reserveamerica.com
**Management:** California Department of Parks and Recreation, (209) 826-1197
**Activities:** Fishing, swimming, boating, waterskiing, sailboarding, cycling
**Finding the campground:** From the intersection of CA 165 and CA 152 in Los Banos, drive 13 miles west on CA 152. Turn north at the campground entry sign and drive about 2 miles.

**About the campground:** Situated on the northwest shore of O'Neill Forebay, with fishing for striped bass, crappie, bluegill, and catfish. Access to the California Aqueduct Bikeway is 0.2 mile north of the campground. Elevation 245 feet. Stay limit 15 days June through September; 30 days October through May. Open all year.

## 418 Los Banos Creek Reservoir (San Luis Reservoir State Recreation Area)

**Location:** 11 miles south of Los Banos
**GPS:** 36.9865112 / -120.9392583
**Sites:** 20 sites for tents only
**Facilities:** Tables with shade ramada, fire rings, vault toilets, boat ramp; no drinking water
**Fee per night:** $$
**Management:** California Department of Parks and Recreation, (209) 826-1197
**Activities:** Fishing, swimming, boating, sailboarding, hiking
**Finding the campground:** From the intersection of CA 165 and CA 152 in Los Banos, drive 5 miles west on CA 152. Turn south onto Volta Road and drive 1 mile. Turn east onto Pioneer Road and drive 1 mile, then south onto Canyon Road and drive about 4 miles.
**About the campground:** Situated on the eastern shore of Los Banos Creek Reservoir, which is stocked annually in fall and winter with rainbow trout. You can also catch bluegill, black bass, crappie, and catfish. Elevation 350 feet. Stay limit 15 days June through September; 30 days October through May. Open all year.

## 419 Medeiros (San Luis Reservoir State Recreation Area)

**Location:** 11 miles west of Los Banos
**GPS:** 37.0650949 / -121.0291893
**Sites:** Primitive sites for tents and RVs
**Facilities:** Tables, fire rings, ramadas, drinking water, chemical toilets, boat ramp
**Fee per night:** $$
**Management:** California Department of Parks and Recreation, (203) 826-1197
**Activities:** Fishing, swimming, boating, waterskiing, sailboarding
**Finding the campground:** From the intersection of CA 165 and CA 152 in Los Banos, drive 10 miles west on CA 152. Turn right (north) onto CA 33 and drive about 1 mile.
**About the campground:** Situated on the southeast shore of O'Neill Forebay, with fishing for striped bass, crappie, bluegill, and catfish. Elevation 235 feet. Stay limit 15 days June through September; 30 days October through May. Open all year.

## 420 Basalt (San Luis Reservoir State Recreation Area)

**Location:** 14 miles west of Los Banos
**GPS:** 37.03169 / -121.0658524
**Sites:** 79 sites for tents and RVs up to 30 feet long
**Facilities:** Tables, fire rings, drinking water, flush toilets, showers, dump station, boat ramp
**Fee per night:** $$$; reservations: (800) 444-7275 or reserveamerica.com

## SAN LUIS RESERVOIR STATE RECREATION AREA

This recreation area encompasses more than 26,000 acres of low, grassy hills in the eastern Diablo Mountains. It features three man-made lakes: San Luis Reservoir, O'Neill Forebay, and Los Banos Creek Reservoir. San Luis Reservoir is the largest, covering 14,000 acres, with 65 miles of virtually treeless shoreline. Its water can be drawn down significantly during summer and fall. O'Neill Forebay, below the San Luis Dam, covers about 2,000 acres and has 14 miles of mostly treeless shoreline. Its water level is more constant than that of San Luis Reservoir. Los Banos Creek Reservoir, the most scenic of the three, has a 12-mile shoreline and occupies 400 acres in a narrow, steep-sided canyon. High winds can blow up quickly on San Luis Reservoir and O'Neill Forebay in spring and early summer. The recreation area contains four campgrounds—two on O'Neill Forebay and one on each of the other lakes.

**Management:** California Department of Parks and Recreation, (209) 826-1197
**Activities:** Fishing, swimming, boating, waterskiing, sailboarding, cycling, hiking
**Finding the campground:** From the intersection of CA 165 and CA 152 in Los Banos, drive 12 miles west on CA 152. Turn south at the campground entry sign and drive about 2 miles.
**About the campground:** Situated on the eastern shore of San Luis Reservoir in a shaded valley protected from the wind. Striped bass, crappie, bluegill, and catfish are the main catches. A 1.5-mile loop trail leads from the campground to a hilltop viewpoint. Access to the California Aqueduct Bikeway is 0.2 mile north of San Luis Creek Campground (417). Elevation 615 feet. Stay limit 15 days June through September; 30 days October through May. Open all year.

# Gold Country

The glitter of gold once lured more than 300,000 fortune hunters to this region from all over the world. Boomtowns were created almost overnight, and then, when the gold panned out, the towns disappeared almost as quickly. Fortunes were indeed made, but mostly by wily merchants and saloon owners, who knew where the real gold was. Today the Gold Country still attracts visitors seeking different kinds of riches: history, natural beauty, and outdoor recreation.

CA 49, which runs from Mariposa in the south part of the region to Downieville in the north, forges a pathway through the center of Gold Country. It passes through towns and districts whose very names evoke the days of the gold rush: Coulterville, Sonora, Angel's Camp, Placerville, and Nevada City. Lining the route are old mines and mining towns—some preserved, some restored, and some slowly fading away.

Sacramento, the capital of the Golden State, is a sophisticated city with a gold rush past. Its Old Sacramento district, on the riverfront, encompasses 26 acres of restaurants and shops in buildings dating from 1849 to 1870. It also includes the California State Railroad Museum. To the northeast, a large portion of Tahoe National Forest provides forested lakes, streams, and rivers in the high country.

Temperatures in Gold Country vary considerably from summer to winter and from the high forest in the northeast to the lowlands of the Sacramento River valley, but the area is said to have a Mediterranean climate. Indeed, there are more than one hundred wineries in the Gold Country. Average precipitation is about 30 inches. Summers can be hot and dry, with heat waves peaking into the low 100s. In winter the range is high 20s to the mid-50s.

This guidebook divides Gold Country into two areas: the High Forest and Mother Lode Territory.

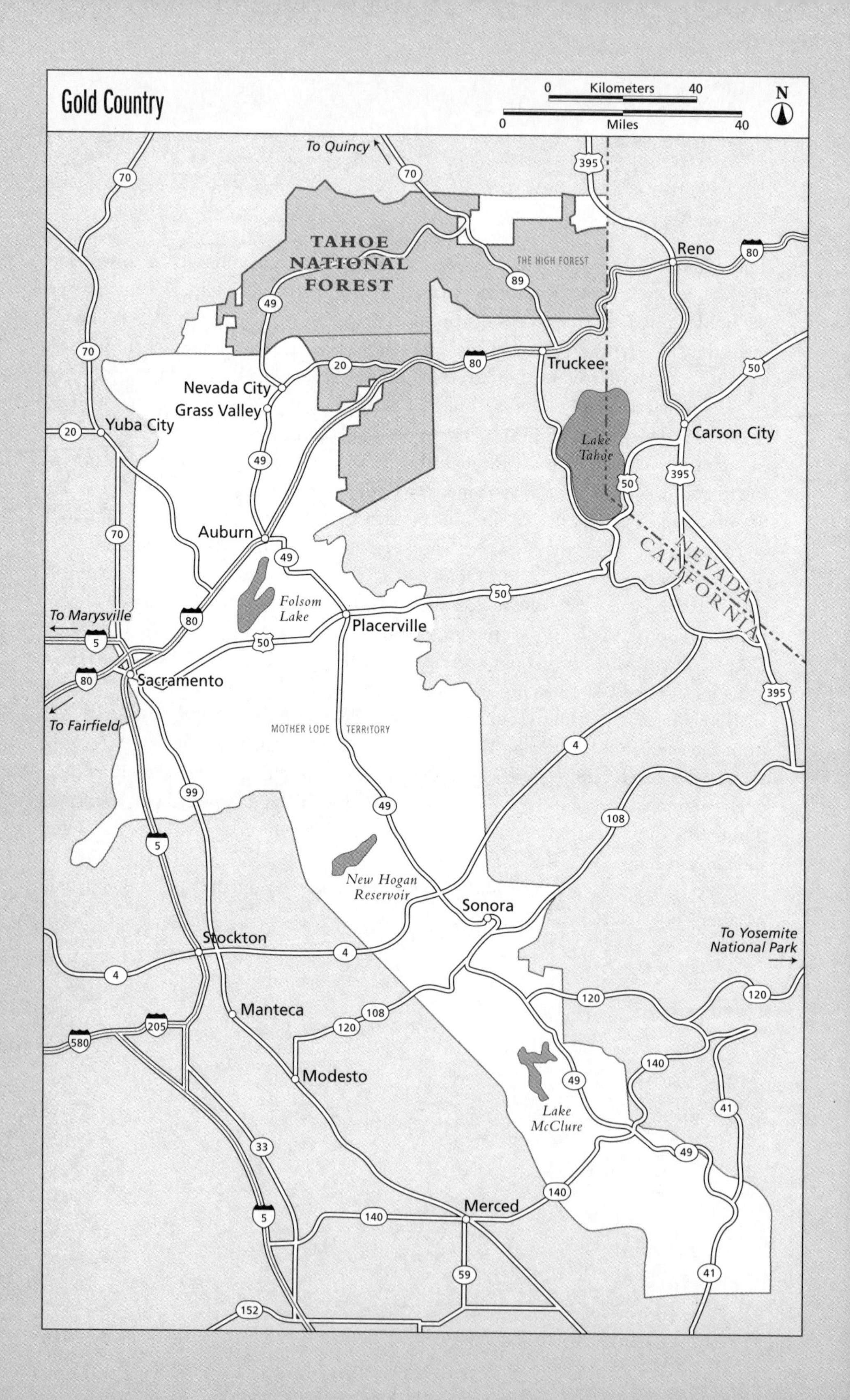

Gold Country
0 Kilometers 40
0 Miles 40
N
To Quincy
TAHOE NATIONAL FOREST
THE HIGH FOREST
Reno
Truckee
Nevada City
Grass Valley
Yuba City
Lake Tahoe
Carson City
Auburn
NEVADA
CALIFORNIA
Folsom Lake
To Marysville
Placerville
Sacramento
To Fairfield
MOTHER LODE TERRITORY
New Hogan Reservoir
Sonora
Stockton
To Yosemite National Park
Manteca
Modesto
Lake McClure
Merced
70
395
80
89
49
20
50
5
99
4
108
120
580
205
140
41
33
59
152

# The High Forest

A large portion of Tahoe National Forest covers most of the High Forest, providing woodlands, lakes, rivers, and streams for outdoor enjoyment. Five large man-made lakes offer a variety of water sports. The era of the gold rush is brought to life along the Yuba Donner National Scenic Byway, which travels to both slopes of the Sierra Nevada as it follows the North Yuba River from Truckee to Nevada City. Of particular interest is the portion of the byway between Bassetts and Oregon Creek, known as "49 Miles on Highway 49," with its quaint gold rush towns along the river.

## 421 Dark Day (New Bullards Bar Reservoir)

**Location:** 22 miles northwest of Nevada City
**GPS:** 39.428614 / -121.109886
**Sites:** 10 sites for tents; double and triple sites available
**Facilities:** Tables, fire rings, drinking water, vault toilets, boat ramp
**Fee per night:** $$; reservations: (877) 692-3201 or bullardsbar.com/dark-day-campground
**Management:** Emerald Cove Marina, (530) 692-3200
**Activities:** Hiking, swimming, fishing, boating
**Finding the campground:** From the intersection of CA 20 and CA 49 in Nevada City, drive 18 miles northwest on CA 49 to North Yuba Ranger Station in Log Cabin. Turn west onto FR 8 (Marysville Road) and drive 3.5 miles.

*New Bullards Bar Dam is a 635-foot wall of concrete on the North Yuba River. When completed in 1970, it formed New Bullards Bar Reservoir. Photo by Richard Easterling (hotspringsfinder.com)*

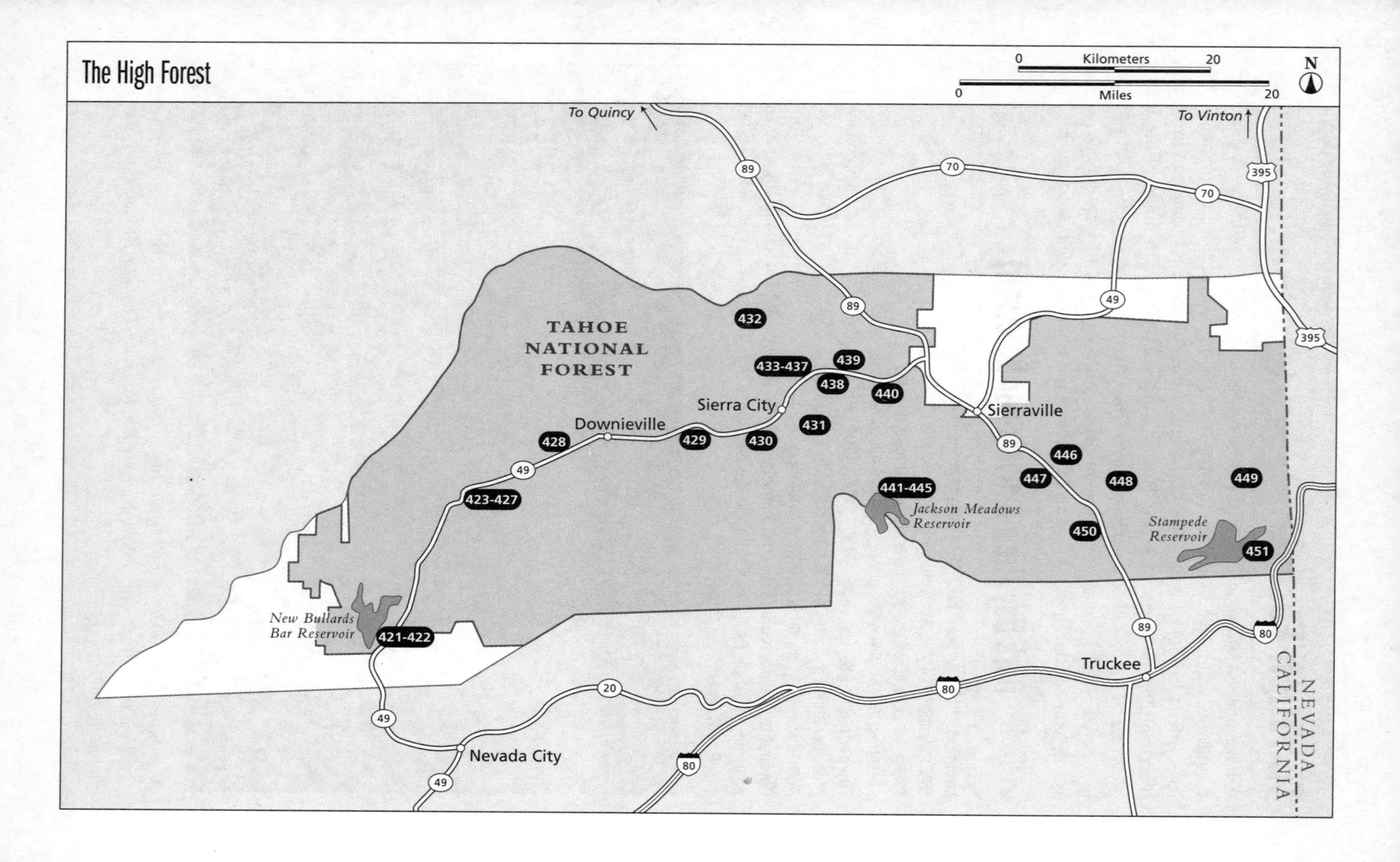

The High Forest
0
Kilometers
20
0
Miles
20
N
To Quincy
To Vinton
TAHOE
NATIONAL
FOREST
Downieville
Sierra City
Sierraville
Truckee
Nevada City
Jackson Meadows
Reservoir
Stampede
Reservoir
New Bullards
Bar Reservoir
NEVADA
CALIFORNIA
421-422
423-427
428
429
430
431
432
433-437
438
439
440
441-445
446
447
448
449
450
451
89
70
395
49
20
80

| # | Name | Group Sites | RV Sites | Max. RV Length | Hookups | Toilets | Showers | Drinking Water | Dump Station | Pets | Wheelchair | Recreation | Fee(s) | Season | Can Reserve |
|---|---|---|---|---|---|---|---|---|---|---|---|---|---|---|---|
| | **THE HIGH FOREST** | | | | | | | | | | | | | | |
| 421 | Dark Day (New Bullards Bar Reservoir) | | | | | V | | * | * | * | * | HSFB | $$ | May–Oct | * |
| 422 | Schoolhouse (New Bullards Bar Reservoir) | * | * | 45 | | F | | * | | * | * | HSFB | $$ | May–Oct | * |
| 423 | Rocky Rest | | * | 30 | | V | | * | | * | | HFSBR | $$ | Apr–Oct | * |
| 424 | Indian Valley | | * | 40 | | V | | * | | * | | HSFBM | $$ | Apr–Oct | * |
| 425 | Fiddle Creek | | | | | V | | * | | * | * | HSFB | $$ | Apr–Oct | * |
| 426 | Cal-Ida | | * | 40 | | V | | * | | * | | HSFB | $$ | May–Sept | * |
| 427 | Carlton Flat | | * | 15 | | V | | * | | * | | HSFB | $$ | May–Sept | * |
| 428 | Ramshorn | | * | 25 | | V | | * | | * | | HSFB | $$ | May–Sept | * |
| 429 | Union Flat | | * | 23 | | V | | * | | * | * | HSFB | $$ | May–Sept | * |
| 430 | Loganville | | * | 30 | | V | | * | | * | | HSF | $$ | May–Oct | * |
| 431 | Wild Plum | | * | 25 | | V | | * | | * | | HF | $$ | May–Oct | * |
| 432 | Snag Lake | | * | 19 | | V | | | | * | | FSB | None | June–Oct | |
| 433 | Salmon Creek | | * | 25 | | V | | * | | * | | HF | $$ | May–Oct | * |
| 434 | Sardine | | * | 25 | | V | | * | | * | | HSFB | $$ | May–Oct | * |
| 435 | Diablo | | * | 45 | | V | | | | * | | HF | $$ | May–Oct | * |
| 436 | Berger | | * | 45 | | V | | | | * | | HF | $$ | May–Oct | * |
| 437 | Packsaddle | | * | 45 | | V | | | | * | | HFRM | $$ | May–Oct | * |
| 438 | Sierra | | * | 45 | | V | | | | * | | FS | $$ | June–Oct | * |
| 439 | Chapman Creek | | * | 35 | | V | | * | | * | | FSH | $$ | June–Oct | * |
| 440 | Yuba Pass | | * | 45 | | V | | * | | * | * | HM | $$ | June–Oct | * |
| 441 | Pass Creek (Jackson Meadows Reservoir) | * | * | 23 | | F | | * | * | * | * | HFSBLM | $$ | June–Oct | * |
| 442 | East Meadow (Jackson Meadows Reservoir) | | * | 45 | | F | | * | | * | | HSFB | $$ | June–Oct | * |
| 443 | Firtop (Jackson Meadows Reservoir) | | * | 43 | | F | | * | | * | * | HSFB | $$ | June–Oct | * |
| 444 | Findley (Jackson Meadows Reservoir) | | * | 45 | | F | | * | | * | * | HSFB | $$ | June–Oct | * |
| 445 | Woodcamp (Jackson Meadows Reservoir) | | * | 42 | | F | | * | | * | * | HSFB | $$ | June–Oct | * |
| 446 | Cottonwood Creek | | * | 40 | | V | | * | | * | | H | $$ | May–Oct | * |
| 447 | Cold Creek | | * | 30 | | V | | * | | * | | H | $ | May–Oct | * |
| 448 | Bear Valley | | * | | | V | | * | | * | | MO | None | June–Oct | |
| 449 | Lookout | | * | 45 | | V | | | | * | | HF | $ | June–Sept | * |
| 450 | Upper Little Truckee and Lower Little Truckee | | * | 45 | | V | | * | | * | * | HFM | $$ | May–Oct | * |
| 451 | Logger (Stampede Reservoir) | * | * | 40 | | V | | * | * | * | * | HSFBM | $$–$$$$ | May–Oct | * |

Toilets: F=flush V=vault P=pit C=chemical; Fee: $=Under $20 $$=$20–$29 $$$=$30–$39 $$$$ $40 or more; Recreation: H=hiking S=swimming F=fishing B=boating L=boat launch O=off-highway driving R=horseback riding, M=mountain biking
Hookups: W=water E=electric S=sewer

**About the campground:** Although listed as a walk-in campground, Dark Day is only a short distance from the parking lot. The campsites are almost close enough to the lakeshore to be considered on the water. Bullards Bar is an attractive lake with 55 miles of shoreline. Fishing can be excellent, as the lake is heavily stocked. Two boat-in campgrounds are located on the north shore of the lake. Elevation 2,200 feet. Stay limit 14 days. Open May through October.

## 422 Schoolhouse (New Bullards Bar Reservoir)

**Location:** 22 miles northwest of Nevada City
**GPS:** 39.415878 / -121.121903
**Sites:** 56 sites for tents and RVs up to 45 feet long; double sites available
**Facilities:** Tables, fire rings, drinking water, flush toilets; boat ramp 0.5 mile away at Dark Day Campground
**Fee per night:** $$; reservations: (877) 692-3201 or bullardsbar.com/dark-day-campground
**Management:** Emerald Cove Marina, (530) 692-3200
**Activities:** Hiking, swimming, fishing, boating
**Finding the campground:** From the intersection of CA 20 and CA 49 in Nevada City, drive 18 miles northwest on CA 49 to North Yuba Ranger Station in Log Cabin. Turn west onto FR 8 (Marysville Road) and drive about 4 miles.
**About the campground:** See Dark Day Campground (421). Large groups can be accommodated at the Hornswoggle Group Camp, just across the road. Elevation 2,000 feet. Stay limit 14 days. Open May through October.

## 423 Rocky Rest

**Location:** 9 miles west of Downieville
**GPS:** 39.513481 / -120.977741
**Sites:** 10 sites for tents and RVs up to 30 feet long
**Facilities:** Tables, fire rings, drinking water, vault toilets
**Fee per night:** $$; reservations: (800) 444-7275 or reserveamerica.com
**Management:** Tahoe National Forest, (530) 994-3231
**Activities:** Hiking, fishing, swimming, boating, horseback riding, gold panning, hunting (seasonal)
**Finding the campground:** From Downieville, drive 9 miles west on CA 49.
**About the campground:** Situated on the banks of the North Yuba River, one of the prettiest rivers in the region. Although this is a stocked trout stream, it is impacted by gold-mining operations. You can access the 7.5-mile North Yuba Trail in the campground, as well as a rocky beach and swimming hole. Also features good river access and a footbridge across the North Yuba River. Elevation 2,300 feet. Stay limit 14 days. Open April through October.

## 424 Indian Valley

**Location:** 10 miles west of Downieville
**GPS:** 39.513669 / -120.979713
**Sites:** 19 sites for tents and RVs up to 40 feet long
**Facilities:** Tables, fire rings, drinking water, vault toilets
**Fee per night:** $$; reservations: (800) 444-7275 or reserveamerica.com

**Management:** Tahoe National Forest, (530) 994-3231
**Activities:** Hiking, fishing, swimming, boating, mountain biking, gold panning
**Finding the campground:** From Downieville, drive 9.5 miles west on CA 49.
**About the campground:** Tumbled rock piles from early gold dredging activity are scattered around the campground. Sites are shaded. See Rocky Rest Campground (423) for more information. Elevation 2,300 feet. Stay limit 14 days. Open April through October.

## 425 Fiddle Creek

**Location:** 11 miles west of Downieville
**GPS:** 39.518253 / -120.992564
**Sites:** 15 sites for tents
**Facilities:** Tables, fire rings, drinking water, vault toilets
**Fee per night:** $$; reservations: (877) 444-6777 or recreation.gov
**Management:** Tahoe National Forest, (530) 994-3231
**Activities:** Hiking, fishing, boating, swimming, gold panning
**Finding the campground:** From Downieville, drive 11 miles west on CA 49.
**About the campground:** Tubing and rafting are popular on the river. See Rocky Rest Campground (423) for more information. Elevation 2,200 feet. Stay limit 14 days. Open April through October.

## 426 Cal-Ida

**Location:** 11 miles west of Downieville
**GPS:** 39.520888 / -120.997019
**Sites:** 19 sites for tents and RVs up to 40 feet long
**Facilities:** Tables, fire rings, drinking water, vault toilets
**Fee per night:** $$; reservations: (877) 444-6777 or recreation.gov
**Management:** Tahoe National Forest, (530) 994-3231
**Activities:** Hiking, fishing, swimming, boating, gold panning
**Finding the campground:** From Downieville, drive 11.3 miles west on CA 49. Turn right onto Eurka Diggins Road. The campground is immediately on the left.
**About the campground:** Across the highway from the North Yuba River with shaded sites. See Rocky Rest Campground (423) for more information. Elevation 2,350 feet. Stay limit 14 days. Open May through September.

## 427 Carlton Flat

**Location:** 11 miles west of Downieville
**GPS:** 39.519430 / -120.999794
**Sites:** 17 sites for tents and RVs up to 15 feet long
**Facilities:** Tables, fire rings, drinking water, vault toilets
**Fee per night:** $$; reservations: (877) 444-6777 or recreation.gov
**Management:** Tahoe National Forest, (530) 994-3231
**Activities:** Hiking, fishing, swimming, boating, gold panning
**Finding the campground:** From Downieville, drive 11.3 miles west on CA 49.

**About the campground:** Surrounded by pines and oak trees. See Rocky Rest Campground (423) for more information. Elevation 2,200 feet. Stay limit 14 days. Open May through September.

## 428 Ramshorn

**Location:** 5 miles west of Downieville
**GPS:** 39.538850 / -120.912299
**Sites:** 16 sites for tents and RVs up to 25 feet long
**Facilities:** Tables, fire rings, drinking water, vault toilets
**Fee per night:** $$; reservations: (800) 444-7275 or reserveamerica.com
**Management:** Tahoe National Forest, (530) 994-3231
**Activities:** Fishing, swimming, boating, hiking, gold panning, berry picking (seasonal)
**Finding the campground:** From Downieville, drive west 5 miles on CA 49.
**About the campground:** Recreational gold panning is featured at the campground, but be careful not to infringe on commercial claims in the vicinity. Blackberry bushes are abundant around the camp and the berries can be picked in the fall. A network of trails crisscrosses the surrounding area, including the 5.8-mile Halls Ranch Trail. See Rocky Rest Campground (423) for more information. Elevation 2,600 feet. Stay limit 14 days. Open May through September.

## 429 Union Flat

**Location:** 5 miles east of Downieville
**GPS:** 39.568224 / -120.744873
**Sites:** 11 sites for tents and RVs up to 23 feet long
**Facilities:** Tables, fire rings, drinking water, vault toilets
**Fee per night:** $$; reservations: (877) 444-6777 or recreation.gov
**Management:** Tahoe National Forest, (530) 994-3231
**Activities:** Hiking, fishing, swimming, boating, gold panning
**Finding the campground:** From Downieville, drive 5 miles east on CA 49.
**About the campground:** Surrounded by oak and maple trees. An area downstream is available for recreational mining. See Rocky Rest Campground (423) for more information. Elevation 3,400 feet. Stay limit 14 days. Open May through September.

## 430 Loganville

**Location:** 2 miles west of Sierra City
**GPS:** 39.565880 / -120.662141
**Sites:** 19 sites for tents and RVs up to 30 feet long
**Facilities:** Tables, fire rings, drinking water, vault toilets
**Fee per night:** $$; reservations: (800) 444-7275 or reserveamerica.com
**Management:** Tahoe National Forest, (530) 994-3231
**Activities:** Hiking, fishing, swimming, hunting (seasonal)
**Finding the campground:** From Sierra City, drive 2 miles west on CA 49.
**About the campground:** Situated on the North Yuba River, a stocked trout stream impacted by area gold-mining operations. Gold panning is prohibited here. Kentucky Mine and Sierra County Historic Park are fun nearby sties. Elevation 4,000 feet. Stay limit 14 days. Open May through October.

*The Sierra Butts above Sierra City, visible from many of the campgrounds in the area. Photo by Richard Easterling (Hotspringsfinder.com)*

## 431 Wild Plum

**Location:** 2 miles east of Sierra City
**GPS:** 39.5663886 / -120.6012877
**Sites:** 47 sites for tents and RVs up to 25 feet long
**Facilities:** Tables, fire rings, drinking water, vault toilets
**Fee per night:** $$; reservations: (800) 444-7275 or reserveamerica.com
**Management:** Tahoe National Forest, (530) 994-3231
**Activities:** Hiking, fishing
**Finding the campground:** From Sierra City, drive 2 miles east on Wild Plum Road.
**About the campground:** Located on the banks of a small creek, with several attractive waterfalls in the vicinity. The Haypress Creek Trail (6 miles round-trip) passes by the campground, rises steeply along the creek, and goes through a canyon into an old-growth forest and past a scenic waterfall. Elevation 4,400 feet. Stay limit 14 days. Open May through October.

## 432 Snag Lake

**Location:** 8 miles north of Sierra City
**GPS:** 39.670908 / -120.626453
**Sites:** 12 sites for tents and RVs up to 19 feet long

**Facilities:** Tables, fire rings, vault toilets; no drinking water
**Fee per night:** None
**Management:** Tahoe National Forest, (530) 994-3231
**Activities:** Fishing, swimming, canoeing, kayaking
**Finding the campground:** From Sierra City, drive 3 miles northeast on CA 49. Turn left (west) at Bassetts onto Gold Lake Road and drive 5 miles.
**About the campground:** Only hand-launched boats are permitted on this small, peaceful lake, which is stocked annually with a modest number of rainbow trout. The campground is only 2 miles from Gold Lake and scenic Lakes Basin (in the Plumas Area). Here, an alpine landscape, 25 lakes and ponds connected by a well-maintained trail system, unusual geological features, and 175-foot-high Frazier Falls provide a memorable outdoor experience. Elevation 6,600 feet. Stay limit 14 days. Open June through October.

## 433 Salmon Creek

**Location:** 5 miles north of Sierra City
**GPS:** 39.623440 / -120.612011
**Sites:** sites for tents and RVs up to 25 feet long
**Facilities:** Tables, fire rings, drinking water, vault toilets
**Fee per night:** $$; reservations: (800) 444-7275 or reserveamerica.com
**Management:** Tahoe National Forest, (530) 994-3231
**Activities:** Hiking, fishing
**Finding the campground:** From Sierra City, drive 3 miles northeast on CA 49. Turn left (west) at Bassetts onto Gold Lake Road and drive 2 miles.
**About the campground:** Situated at the junction of Salmon and Packer Creeks. Elevation 5,800 feet. Stay limit 14 days. Open May through October.

## 434 Sardine

**Location:** 5 miles north of Sierra City
**GPS:** 39.621668 / -120.615222
**Sites:** 23 for tents and RVs up to 25 feet long
**Facilities:** Tables, fire rings, drinking water, vault toilets
**Fee per night:** $$; reservations: (800) 444-7275 or reserveamerica.com
**Management:** Tahoe National Forest, (530) 994-3231
**Activities:** Hiking, fishing, swimming, boating
**Finding the campground:** From Sierra City, drive 3 miles northeast on CA 49. Turn left (west) at Bassetts onto Gold Lake Road and drive 1.5 miles. Turn left onto Packer Lake Road and drive less than 0.25 mile, bearing left at the fork.
**About the campground:** Situated 1 mile east of Lower Sardine Lake—along with Upper Sardine Lake, the prettiest pair of lakes in the northern Sierra Nevada. The lower lake is well stocked annually with brook and rainbow trout; the upper lake is not stocked. Elevation 5,800 feet. Stay limit 14 days. Open May through October.

# 435 Diablo

**Location:** 6 miles north of Sierra City
**GPS:** 39.629859 / -120.639347
**Sites:** 19 sites for tents and RVs up to 45 feet long
**Facilities:** Tables, fire rings, vault toilets; no drinking water
**Fee per night:** $$; reservations: (800) 444-7275 or reserveamerica.com
**Management:** Tahoe National Forest, (530) 994-3231
**Activities:** Fishing, hiking
**Finding the campground:** From Sierra City, drive 3 miles northeast on CA 49. Turn left (west) at Bassetts onto Gold Lake Road and drive 1.5 miles. Turn left onto Packer Lake Road and drive about 1 mile, bearing right at the fork.
**About the campground:** Located on the banks of Packer Creek. Several hiking trails are nearby, and lakes are scattered around the area. Elevation 5,800 feet. Stay limit 14 days. Open May through October.

# 436 Berger

**Location:** 7 miles north of Sierra City
**GPS:** 39.628385 / -120.644612
**Sites:** 8 sites for tents and RVs up to 45 feet long
**Facilities:** Tables, fire rings, vault toilets; no drinking water
**Fee per night:** $$; reservations: (800) 444-7275 or reserveamerica.com
**Management:** Tahoe National Forest, (530) 994-3231
**Activities:** Fishing, hiking
**Finding the campground:** From Sierra City, drive 3 miles northeast on CA 49. Turn left (west) at Bassetts onto Gold Lake Road and drive 1.5 miles. Turn left onto Packer Lake Road and drive about 2 miles, bearing right at the fork.
**About the campground:** Berger is mainly used as an overflow campground if others in the Lakes Basin area are full. Elevation 5,900 feet. Stay limit 14 days. Open May through October.

# 437 Packsaddle

**Location:** 7 miles north of Sierra City
**GPS:** 39.624645 / -120.649854
**Sites:** 14 sites for tents and RVs up to 45 feet long
**Facilities:** Tables, fire rings, vault toilets, hitching posts; no drinking water
**Fee per night:** $$; reservations: (877) 444-6777 or recreation.gov
**Management:** Tahoe National Forest, (530) 994-3231
**Activities:** Hiking, fishing, horseback riding, mountain biking
**Finding the campground:** From Sierra City, drive 3 miles northeast on CA 49. Turn left (west) at Bassetts onto Gold Lake Road and drive 1.5 miles. Turn left onto Packer Lake Road and drive about 2.5 miles, bearing right at the fork.
**About the campground:** There are a number of trails to choose from in the area that access lakes and the Pacific Crest National Scenic Trail. The Sierra Buttes Trail climbs 2,500 feet to one of the

finest lookouts in the state, located at 8,587 feet. En route it passes the Tamarack Lakes, a lovely and easier destination. There is no extra charge for horses at the campground, and equestrians may hitch their horses at the campsite. Elevation 6,000 feet. Stay limit 14 days. Open May through October.

## 438 Sierra

**Location:** 7 miles northeast of Sierra City
**GPS:** 39.631608 / -120.557749
**Sites:** 16 sites for tents and RVs up to 45 feet long
**Facilities:** Tables, fire rings, vault toilets; no drinking water
**Fee per night:** $$; reservations: (800) 444-7275 or reserveamerica.com
**Management:** Tahoe National Forest, (530) 994-3231
**Activities:** Fishing, swimming
**Finding the campground:** From Sierra City, drive northeast 7 miles on CA 49.
**About the campground:** Situated on the banks of the North Fork Yuba River, which is stocked with rainbow trout annually. Elevation 5,700 feet. Stay limit 14 days. Open June through October.

## 439 Chapman Creek

**Location:** 8 miles northeast of Sierra City
**GPS:** 39.629529 / -120.544789
**Sites:** 27 sites for tents and RVs up to 35 feet long
**Facilities:** Tables, fire rings, vault toilets, drinking water
**Fee per night:** $$; reservations: (877) 444-6777 or recreation.gov
**Management:** Tahoe National Forest, (530) 994-3231
**Activities:** Fishing, swimming, hiking
**Finding the campground:** From Sierra City, drive northeast 8 miles on CA 49.
**About the campground:** Situated on the banks of Chapman Creek at its junction with the North Fork Yuba River. For fishing information, see Sierra Campground (438). The Chapman Creek Trail begins at the campground and follows the creek through a thick forest, gaining a modest 500 feet in elevation in 1.5 miles. Elevation 6,000 feet. Stay limit 14 days. Open June through October.

## 440 Yuba Pass

**Location:** 11 miles northeast of Sierra City
**GPS:** 39.615878 / -120.490072
**Sites:** 19 sites for tents and RVs up to 45 feet long
**Facilities:** Tables, fire rings, drinking water, vault toilets
**Fee per night:** $$; reservations: (877) 444-6777 or recreation.gov
**Management:** Tahoe National Forest, (530) 994-3231
**Activities:** Hiking, mountain biking, birding
**Finding the campground:** From Sierra City, drive northeast 11 miles on CA 49. At the top of the pass, turn left onto Yuba Pass–Webber Lake Road. The campground is immediately on the right.

**About the campground:** Situated at the top of the pass in cool mountain forest. The Lakes Basin Recreation area lies a short drive to the west. Elevation 6,700 feet. Stay limit 14 days. Open June through October.

## 441 Pass Creek (Jackson Meadows Reservoir)

**Location:** 30 miles northwest of Truckee
**GPS:** 39.505686 / -120.532998
**Sites:** 30 sites for tents and RVs up to 23 feet long
**Facilities:** Tables, fire rings, drinking water, flush toilets, dump station, boat ramp
**Fee per night:** $$; reservations: (877) 444-6777 or recreation.gov
**Management:** Tahoe National Forest, (530) 994-3401
**Activities:** Hiking, fishing, boating, swimming, mountain biking, waterskiing
**Finding the campground:** From the intersection of I-80 and CA 89 in Truckee, drive north 14 miles on CA 89. Turn west onto FR 07 (Henness Pass Road) and drive 16 miles.
**About the campground:** Jackson Meadows is a high-mountain reservoir with beautiful views of the surrounding mountains. It offers cool weather in summer and provides good fishing. Nearly 35,000 rainbow and brown trout, 10 to 12 inches long, are stocked annually, as are 50,000 fingerlings, mostly rainbows. Pass Creek Campground is on the northeastern shoreline of the lake. A swimming beach is nearby at Aspen Creek Picnic Area. The Pacific Crest National Scenic Trail passes 0.5 mile east of the campground. Elevation 6,100 feet. Stay limit 14 days. Open June through October. Camping with horses? Call about nearby Little Laiser Meadow Horse Camp (6 sites with corrals). For group camping, Aspen Group Camp and Silver Tip Group Camp are both nearby.

## 442 East Meadow (Jackson Meadows Reservoir)

**Location:** 30 miles northwest of Truckee
**GPS:** 39.501158 / -120.532890
**Sites:** 46 sites for tents and RVs up to 45 feet long
**Facilities:** Tables, fire rings, drinking water, flush toilets; dump station and boat ramp at Pass Creek Campground (441), 2 miles north
**Fee per night:** $$; reservations: (877) 444-6777 or recreation.gov
**Management:** Tahoe National Forest, (530) 994-3401
**Activities:** Hiking, fishing, boating, swimming
**Finding the campground:** From the intersection of I-80 and CA 89 in Truckee, drive north 14 miles on CA 89. Turn west onto FR 07 (Henness Pass Road) and drive 15 miles. Turn south onto the campground entrance road and drive 1 mile.
**About the campground:** Situated near the shoreline in a wooded cove on the eastern shore of the lake. See Pass Creek Campground (441) for lake and area description. Elevation 6,100 feet. Stay limit 14 days. Open June through October.

## 443 Firtop (Jackson Meadows Reservoir)

**Location:** 34 miles northwest of Truckee
**GPS:** 39.486172 / -120.551590
**Sites:** 12 sites for tents and RVs up to 43 feet long
**Facilities:** Tables, fire rings, drinking water, flush toilets; boat ramp nearby; dump station and swimming beach available at Pass Creek Campground (441), 3 miles to the north
**Fee per night:** $$; reservations: (877) 444-6777 or recreation.gov
**Management:** Tahoe National Forest, (530) 994-3401
**Activities:** Hiking, fishing, boating, swimming
**Finding the campground:** From the intersection of I-80 and CA 89 in Truckee, drive north 14 miles on CA 89. Turn left (west) onto FR 07 (Henness Pass Road) and drive 16.5 miles to the dam. (FR 07 becomes FR 956 en route.) Cross over the dam and continue along the west shore of the lake for about 2 miles. Turn left and proceed into the campground.
**About the campground:** The campground lies on the western shore in a forest of pine and fir trees. See Pass Creek Campground (441) for lake and area description. Elevation 6,200 feet. Stay limit 14 days. Open June through October.

## 444 Findley (Jackson Meadows Reservoir)

**Location:** 34 miles northwest of Truckee
**GPS:** 39.484428 / -120.553673
**Sites:** 11 sites for tents and RVs up to 45 feet long
**Facilities:** Tables, fire rings, drinking water, flush toilets; boat ramp nearby; dump station and swimming beach available at Pass Creek Campground (441), 3.5 miles to the north
**Fee per night:** $$; reservations: (800) 444-7275 or reserveamerica.com
**Management:** Tahoe National Forest, (530) 994-3231
**Activities:** Hiking, fishing, boating, swimming
**Finding the campground:** From the intersection of I-80 and CA 89 in Truckee, drive north 14 miles on CA 89. Turn left (west) onto FR 07 (Henness Pass Road) and drive 16.5 miles to the dam. (FR 07 becomes FR 956 en route.) Cross over the dam and continue along the west shore of the lake for about 2 miles. Turn left and proceed into the campground.
**About the campground:** On the western shore of the lake. See Pass Creek Campground (441) for lake and area description. Elevation 6,200 feet. Stay limit 14 days. Open June through October.

## 445 Woodcamp (Jackson Meadows Reservoir)

**Location:** 34 miles northwest of Truckee
**GPS:** 39.485207 / -120.548811
**Sites:** 16 sites for tents and RVs up to 42 feet long
**Facilities:** Tables, fire rings, drinking water, flush toilets; boat ramp nearby; dump station and swimming beach available at Pass Creek Campground (441), 4 miles to the north
**Fee per night:** $$; reservations: (877) 444-6777 or recreation.gov
**Management:** Tahoe National Forest, (530) 994-3401
**Activities:** Hiking, fishing, boating, swimming

**Finding the campground:** From the intersection of I-80 and CA 89 in Truckee, drive north 14 miles on CA 89. Turn left (west) onto FR 07 (Henness Pass Road) and drive 16.5 miles to the dam. (FR 07 becomes FR 956 en route.) Cross over the dam and continue along the west shore of the lake for about 2 miles. Turn left and proceed into the campground.
**About the campground:** A half-mile interpretive nature trail meanders Woodcamp. See Pass Creek Campground (441) for lake and area description. Elevation 6,100 feet. Stay limit 14 days. Open June through October.

## 446 Cottonwood Creek

**Location:** 5 miles southeast of Sierraville
**GPS:** 39.3196283 / -120.2326987
**Sites:** 48 sites for tents and RVs up to 40 feet long
**Facilities:** Tables, fire rings, drinking water, vault toilets
**Fee per night:** $$; reservations: (800) 444-7275 or reserveamerica.com
**Management:** Tahoe National Forest, (530) 994-3401
**Activities:** Hiking
**Finding the campground:** From Sierraville, drive southeast on CA 89 for 4.5 miles.
**About the campground:** A short interpretive trail makes a loop from the campground. Elevation 5,960 feet. Stay limit 14 days. Open May through October.

## 447 Cold Creek

**Location:** 5 miles southeast of Sierraville
**GPS:** 39.544387 / -120.315806
**Sites:** 13 sites for tents and RVs up to 30 feet long
**Facilities:** Tables, fire rings, drinking water, vault toilets
**Fee per night:** $; reservations: (800) 444-7275 or reserveamerica.com
**Management:** Tahoe National Forest, (530) 994-3401
**Activities:** Hiking
**Finding the campground:** From Sierraville, drive southeast on CA 89 for 5 miles.
**About the campground:** On the banks of Cold Creek, the campground is a relaxing spot with a few short scenic trails a couple minutes away. The Lake District lies 30 minutes to the west. Elevation 5,700 feet. Stay limit 14 days. Open May through October.

## 448 Bear Valley

**Location:** 12 miles southeast of Sierraville
**GPS:** 39.557194 / -120.237005
**Sites:** 10 sites for tents and RVs
**Facilities:** Tables, fire rings, drinking water, vault toilets
**Fee per night:** None
**Management:** Tahoe National Forest, (530) 994-3401
**Activities:** OHV driving, mountain biking
**Finding the campground:** From Sierraville, drive southeast on CA 89 for 8 miles. Turn left (north) onto FR 451 and drive 4 miles.

**About the campground:** The region surrounding the camp was burned extensively by a forest fire in 1994, but time has long since begun to heal the scars. Routes suitable for OHV driving radiate in almost every direction from the campground, and mountain bikers can use many of them. One route leads to Sardine Peak (8,134 feet), which overlooks the burn area. Elevation 6,625 feet. Stay limit 14 days. Open June through October.

## 449 Lookout

**Location:** 30 miles northeast of Truckee
**GPS:** 39.590066 / -120.074110
**Sites:** 17 sites for tents and RVs up to 45 feet long
**Facilities:** Tables, fire rings, vault toilets, tent pads; no drinking water
**Fee per night:** $; reservations: (877) 444-6777 or recreation.gov
**Management:** Toiyabe National Forest, (775) 882-2766
**Activities:** Hiking, fishing
**Finding the campground:** From the intersection of I-80 and CA 89 in Truckee, drive northeast on I-80 for 20 miles (into Nevada). Take the Verdi exit and drive north on Dog Valley Road for 10 miles.
**About the campground:** A former quartz crystal mine is located a short distance from the campground on a well-maintained trail. Limit one bucket of crystals per week. Elevation 6,800 feet. Stay limit 14 days. Open June through September.

## 450 Upper Little Truckee and Lower Little Truckee

**Location:** 11 miles north of Truckee
**GPS:** Upper: 39.491462 / -120.244708; Lower: 39.486037 / -120.236684
**Sites:** Upper: 26 sites for tents and RVs up to 45 feet long; Lower: 14 sites for tents and RVs up to 40 feet long
**Facilities:** Tables, fire rings, drinking water, vault toilets
**Fee per night:** $$; reservations: (800) 444-7275 or reserveamerica.com
**Management:** Tahoe National Forest, (530) 994-3401
**Activities:** Hiking, fishing, mountain biking, hunting (seasonal)
**Finding the campground:** From the intersection of I-80 and CA 89 in Truckee, drive north 11 miles to Lower Little Truckee; 0.3 mile more on CA 89 for Upper Little Truckee.
**About the campground:** Both are situated on the banks of the Little Truckee River, an attractive and fairly productive trout stream. Elevation 6,200 feet. Stay limit 14 days. Open May through October.

## 451 Logger (Stampede Reservoir)

**Location:** 16 miles northeast of Truckee
**GPS:** 39.464821 / -120.121558
**Sites:** 201 sites for tents and RVs up to 40 feet long
**Facilities:** Tables, fire rings, drinking water, vault toilets, dump station; boat ramp 1 mile north

**Fee per night:** $$, double and triple sites: $$$$; reservations: (800) 444-7275 or reserve america.com
**Management:** Tahoe National Forest, (530) 587-3558
**Activities:** Hiking, Fishing, swimming, boating, mountain biking
**Finding the campground:** From the intersection of I-80 and CA 89 in Truckee, drive northeast on I-80 for 6 miles. Take the Boca-Hirschdale exit and drive north on CR 894/270 for about 8 miles. Turn left (west) onto CR 261 and drive 2 miles.
**About the campground:** Beautiful Stampede Reservoir encompasses almost 3,500 acres of surface area. Annual fish stockings include 20,000 rainbow trout and a quarter-million kokanee fingerlings. Because the reservoir is heavily drawndown in summer and fall, fishing is best in spring. The Commemorative Overland Emigrant Trail passes the campground, running east to Dutch Flat and west to Nevada City. A scenic trail follows the lake's high-water mark. A boat ramp is located just northwest of the campground. Elevation 6,000 feet. Stay limit 14 days. Open May through October. For group camping, check out Emigrant Group Camp.

# Mother Lode Territory

Tourists traveling to Mother Lode Territory from the north via the Golden Chain Highway (CA 49) are welcomed to the region by the gold rush towns of Nevada City and Grass Valley. Once rivaling San Francisco and Sacramento in population, Nevada City has reinvented itself, turning from gold fields to grape fields as it hosts a flourishing wine industry, most around Murphys. North of the town lies Malakoff Diggins, the world's largest hydraulic mining site; to the south, Empire Mine State Historic Park preserves what was once California's largest and richest hard-rock mine.

Farther south, at Coloma, a replica of Sutter's Mill stands on the original site of the 1848 gold discovery that started the worldwide rush to California. Placerville—once called "Hangtown" because of its speedy law enforcement—has the distinction of owning its own gold mine, which is open for tours. Columbia State Historic Park, near Sonora, provides the opportunity to tour an actual gold rush–era town, with its original buildings, covered boardwalks, and storefronts. Coulterville, listed on the National Register of Historic Places, once had fifty saloons.

But all that glitters in Mother Lode Territory is not gold. Twelve large lakes offer their shining surfaces to water sports enthusiasts. This represents a very favorable lake-to-population ratio, enhanced by the fact that the lakes are spread out almost evenly from north to south through the region. The Indian Grinding Rock State Historic Park, about 9 miles east of Jackson, features a museum and a large, flat rock outcropping pitted by more than 1,000 mortar holes used by early peoples for grinding acorns into flour.

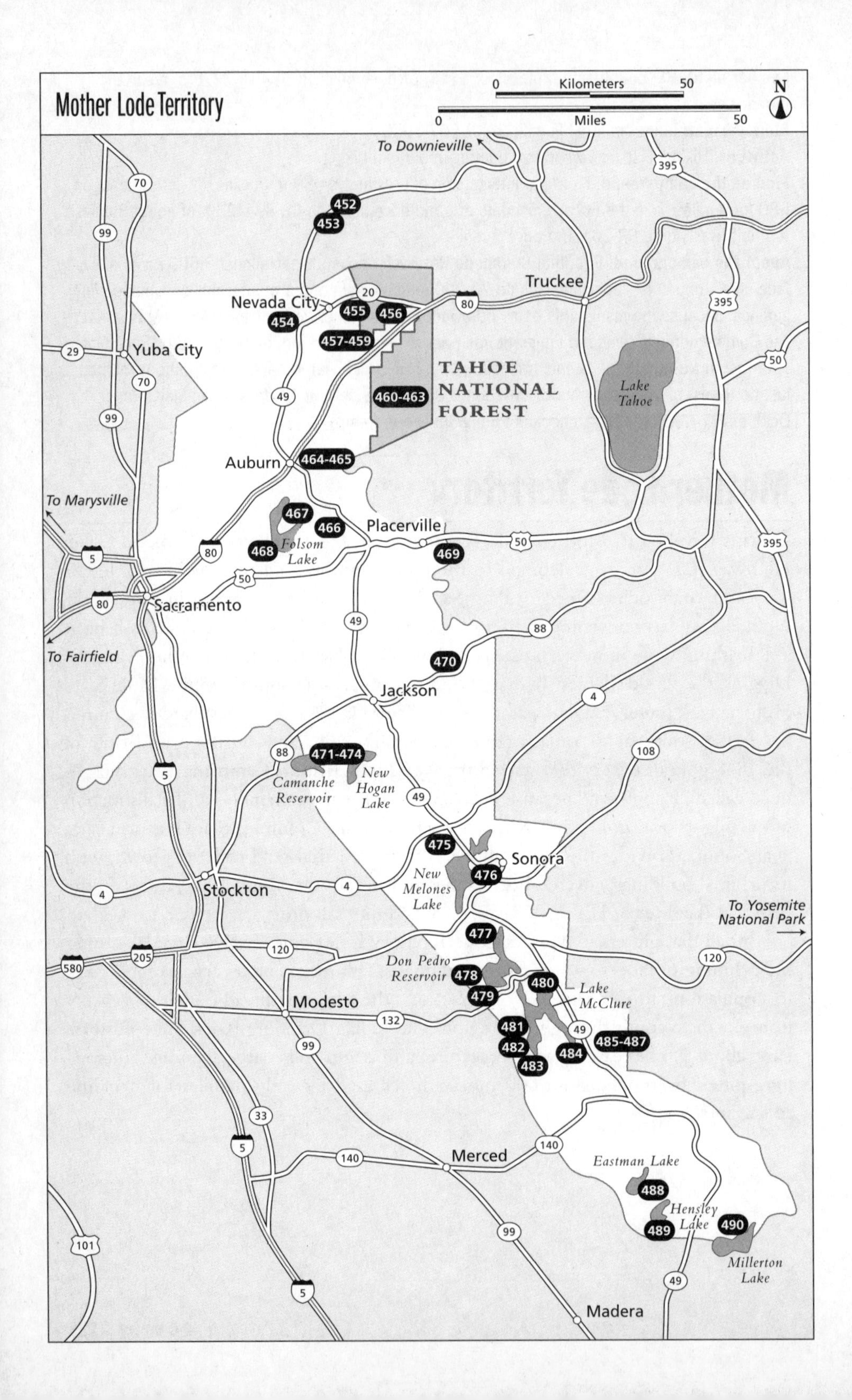
Mother Lode Territory
0 Kilometers 50
0 Miles 50
N
To Downieville
395
70
452
453
99
Truckee
Nevada City
20
455
456
80
454
395
457-459
29
Yuba City
TAHOE
NATIONAL
FOREST
50
Lake Tahoe
70
460-463
49
99
Auburn
464-465
To Marysville
467
466
Placerville
468
Folsom Lake
50
469
395
5
80
50
80
Sacramento
49
To Fairfield
88
470
Jackson
4
108
88
471-474
5
Camanche Reservoir
New Hogan Lake
49
475
Sonora
476
New Melones Lake
Stockton
4
4
To Yosemite National Park
477
580
205
120
Don Pedro Reservoir
478
480
120
479
Lake McClure
Modesto
132
481
49
485-487
482
484
99
483
33
5
140
140
Merced
Eastman Lake
488
Hensley Lake
489
490
99
Millerton Lake
101
49
5
Madera

| | Name | Group Sites | RV Sites | Max. RV Length | Hookups | Toilets | Showers | Drinking Water | Dump Station | Pets | Wheelchair | Recreation | Fee(s) | Season | Can Reserve |
|---|---|---|---|---|---|---|---|---|---|---|---|---|---|---|---|
| | **MOTHER LODE TERRITORY** | | | | | | | | | | | | | | |
| 452 | Chute Hill (Malakoff Diggins State Historic Park) | * | * | 24 | | F | | * | | * | | HSF | $$$-$$$$ | Year-round | * |
| 453 | South Yuba | | * | 27 | | P | | * | | * | | HRMSB | $ | Mar–Oct | |
| 454 | Nevada County Fairgrounds | | * | 45 | | F | | * | * | * | * | | $$-$$$$ | Year-round | * |
| 455 | Scotts Flat Lake Recreation Area | * | * | 45 | | F | * | * | * | * | * | SFB | $$-$$$ | Year-round | * |
| 456 | White Cloud | * | * | 35 | | F | | * | | * | | HRM | $$ | May–Oct | * |
| 457 | Orchard Springs (Rollins Reservoir) | | * | 45 | | F | * | * | | * | * | SFBL | $$$-$$$$ | Year-round | * |
| 458 | Peninsula (Rollins Reservoir) | * | * | 40 | | F | * | * | | * | * | SFBL | $$$-$$$$ | Year-round | * |
| 459 | Long Ravine (Rollins Reservoir) | * | * | 40 | EWS | F | * | * | * | * | * | SFBL | $$-$$$$ | Year-round | * |
| 460 | Parker Flat OHV Staging Area | | * | small | | V | | * | | * | | 0 | None | May–Oct | |
| 461 | Giant Gap (Sugar Pine Reservoir) | * | * | 40 | | V | | * | | * | * | HSFBO | $$-$$$$ | May–Oct | * |
| 462 | Shirttail Creek (Sugar Pine Reservoir) | | * | 45 | | V | | * | | * | * | HSFBO | $$-$$$$ | May–Oct | * |
| 463 | Big Reservoir & Morning Star (Big Reservoir) | | * | 27 | | V | | * | | * | * | SFBO | $$-$$$$ | May–Oct | * |
| 464 | Mineral Bar (Auburn State Recreation Area) | | * | | | P | | | | * | | HSFBRM | $$ | Year-round | |
| 465 | Ruck-a-Chucky (Auburn State Recreation Area) | | | | | V | | | | * | | HBF | $$ | May–Oct | |
| 466 | Marshall Gold Discovery State Historic Park | | * | 45 | EWS | F | * | * | * | * | * | HB | $$-$$$ | Year-round | * |
| 467 | Peninsula (Folsom Lake State Recreation Area) | | * | 38 | | F | | * | * | * | * | FBHMRL | $$-$$$ | Apr–Sept | * |
| 468 | Beal's Point (Folsom Lake State Recreation Area) | | * | 31 | EWS | F | * | * | * | * | * | FBHMRL | $-$$$$ | Year-round | * |
| 469 | Sly Park (Jenkinson Lake) | * | * | | | V | | * | | * | | SFBRL | $-$$$$ | Year-round | * |
| 470 | Chaw'se (Indian Grinding Rock State Historic Park) | | * | 27 | | F | * | * | | * | * | | $$$ | Year-round | |
| 471 | North Shore (Camanche Reservoir) | * | * | 45 | | FC | * | * | * | * | * | BFHL | $-$$$$ | Year-round | * |
| 472 | South Shore (Camanche Reservoir) | * | * | 45 | EWS | FC | * | * | * | * | * | BFHL | $-$$$$ | Year-round | * |
| 473 | Acorn East & West (New Hogan Lake) | | * | 45 | | F | * | * | * | * | * | SFB | $$ | Year-round | * |

| # | Name | Group Sites | RV Sites | Max. RV Length | Hookups | Toilets | Showers | Drinking Water | Dump Station | Pets | Wheelchair | Recreation | Fee(s) | Season | Can Reserve |
|---|---|---|---|---|---|---|---|---|---|---|---|---|---|---|---|
| 474 | Oak Knoll (New Hogan Lake) | * | * | 45 | | V | | * | | * | | SFB | $ | Apr–Oct | * |
| 475 | Glory Hole (New Melones Lake) | | * | 40 | | F | * | * | * | * | * | SFBM | $-$$ | Year-round | * |
| 476 | Tuttletown Recreation Area (New Melones Lake) | * | * | 45 | | F | * | * | * | * | * | SFBM | $-$$$$ | Year-round | * |
| 477 | Moccasin Point (Don Pedro Reservoir) | | * | | EWS | F | * | * | * | | * | SFBH | $$-$$$$ | Year-round | * |
| 478 | Fleming Meadows (Don Pedro Reservoir) | | * | | | F | * | * | * | | * | SFBH | $-$$ | Year-round | * |
| 479 | Blue Oaks (Don Pedro Reservoir) | | * | | | F | * | * | * | | * | SFBH | $$-$$$$ | Year-round | * |
| 480 | Horseshoe Bend Recreation Area (Lake McClure) | | * | | EW | F | * | * | * | * | * | SFB | $-$$$ | Year-round | * |
| 481 | Barrett Cove Recreation Area (Lake McClure) | | * | | EW | F | * | * | * | * | * | SFBM | $-$$$ | Year-round | * |
| 482 | McClure Point Recreation Area (Lake McClure) | | * | | EW | F | * | * | | * | * | SFBL | $-$$$ | Year-round | * |
| 483 | Lake McSwain Recreation Area | | * | | EW | F | * | * | * | * | * | SFBL | $-$$$ | Year-round | * |
| 484 | Bagby Recreation Area (Lake McClure) | | * | | | F | * | * | | * | * | SFB | $-$$$ | Year-round | * |
| 485 | McCabe Flat (Merced River Recreation Area) | | * | | | V | | | | * | * | HSFBR | $ | Year-round | |
| 486 | Willow Placer (Merced River Recreation Area) | | * | | | V | | | | * | | HSFBRM | $ | Year-round | |
| 487 | Railroad Flat (Merced River Recreation Area) | | * | | | V | | | | * | | HSFBR | $ | Year-round | |
| 488 | Codorniz Recreation Area (Eastman Lake) | | * | | EWS | F | * | * | * | * | | FBSR | $$-$$$ | Year-round | * |
| 489 | Hidden View (Hensley Lake) | * | * | 45 | | F | * | * | * | * | * | FBS | $$-$$$ | Year-round | * |
| 490 | Millerton Lake State Recreation Area | * | * | 36 | | F | * | * | * | * | * | HSFBRL | $$$-$$$$ | Year-round | * |

Toilets: F=flush V=vault P=pit C=chemical; Fee: $=Under $20 $$=$20–$29 $$$=$30–$39 $$$$ $40 or more; Recreation: H=hiking S=swimming F=fishing B=boating L=boat launch O=off-highway driving R=horseback riding, M=mountain biking Hookups: W=water E=electric S=sewer

## 452 Chute Hill (Malakoff Diggins State Historic Park)

**Location:** 25 miles northeast of Nevada City
**GPS:** 39.376825 / -120.900555
**Sites:** 29 sites for tents and RVs up to 24 feet long; 3 rustic cabins; 1 group site
**Facilities:** Tables, grills, drinking water, flush toilets
**Fee per night:** $$$, cabins and group site: $$$$; reservations: (800) 444-7275 or reserveamerica.com
**Management:** Malakoff Diggins State Historic Park, (530) 265-2740
**Activities:** Hiking, swimming, fishing, gold panning
**Finding the campground:** From the intersection of CA 20 and CA 49 in Nevada City, drive west and then north on CA 49 for 10.5 miles. Turn east onto Tyler Foote Crossing Road (which becomes Backbone Road) and drive about 14 miles. The last 2 miles of the road are unpaved and steep.
**About the campground:** Malakoff Diggins was once the world's largest hydraulic mining site, and North Bloomfield was a thriving community. Today visitors can explore the "diggins" and walk the town's now-deserted streets, which are lined with restored original buildings. The park also features a museum, picnic sites, gold panning, and a small lake for swimming and shoreline fishing (bass, bluegill, and catfish). Diggins Trail, a 3-mile loop, tours the mining pit, its rim, and the surrounding facilities, including a tunnel used to bring water to the site (flashlight required). Elevation 3,400 feet. Stay limit 30 days. Open all year.

## 453 South Yuba

**Location:** 23 miles northeast of Nevada City
**GPS:** 39.342241 / -120.973029
**Sites:** 16 sites for tents and RVs up to 27 feet long
**Facilities:** Tables, fire rings, drinking water, pit toilets
**Fee per night:** $
**Management:** Bureau of Land Management, (916) 941-3101
**Activities:** Hiking, mountain biking, horseback riding; swimming, fishing, kayaking, gold panning, 1 mile north
**Finding the campground:** From the intersection of CA 20 and CA 49 in Nevada City, drive west and then north on CA 49 for 10.5 miles. Turn east onto Tyler Foote Crossing Road and drive about 9 miles. Turn south onto Grizzly Hills Road and drive 3 miles. Turn east onto North Bloomfield Road and drive about 0.25 mile.
**About the campground:** Situated about 1 mile north of the South Yuba River in a thick pine forest, the campground is a good base from which to explore the Mother Lode Territory. Malakoff Diggins and the Empire Mine are close by (see above). The South Yuba provides trout fishing and white-water kayaking and rafting. The campground is also one of the trailheads for the South Yuba River Trail, a wheelchair-accessible trail running east–west 15 miles through the scenic Yuba River Canyon. This historic trail features flumes, waterworks, and the remains of equipment used in hydraulic mining. Another access to the trail is on CA 49, 8 miles northwest of Nevada City. Elevation 2,600 feet. Stay limit 14 days. Open March through October.

*On the South Yuba Trail. Photo by Richard Easterling (hotspringsfinder.com)*

## 454 Nevada County Fairgrounds

**Location:** 4 miles southwest of Nevada City
**GPS:** 39.203848 / -121.080339
**Sites:** 145 sites for RVs (only up to 45 feet long); no tents
**Facilities:** Drinking water, flush toilets, electric and full hookups, dump station
**Fee per night:** $$, full hookups: $$$$; reservations: (530) 273-6217, ext. 221
**Management:** Nevada County Fairgrounds, (530) 273-6217
**Activities:** None, unless a fair or festival is in progress
**Finding the campground:** From the junction of CA 20 and CA 49 in Nevada City, drive southwest on CA 20/49 for about 4 miles. Take the McCourtney Street exit (large "Fairgrounds" sign) and follow the signs to the fairgrounds.
**About the campground:** The fairgrounds became home to the Strawberry Musical Festival in 2015 and hosts many other exciting events. At other times, this campground is best used as an overnight stop or as a base from which to explore the surrounding Mother Lode Territory. The North Star Mining Museum and Empire Mine State Historic Park are nearby, and Malakoff Diggins State Historic Park (Chute Hill, 452) is about 30 miles to the north. The Empire Mine was formerly one of the largest and richest hard-rock gold mines in the state. Elevation 2,300 feet. Stay limit 14 days. Open all year.

## 455 Scotts Flat Lake Recreation Area

**Location:** 8 miles east of Nevada City
**GPS:** 39.278218 / -120.9392749
**Sites:** 169 sites for tents and RVs up to 45 feet long; yurts; group sites
**Facilities:** Tables, fire rings, grills, drinking water, flush toilets, showers, laundry, dump station, playground, store; boat ramp less than 0.5 mile away
**Fee per night:** $$–$$$; reservations: (530) 265-5302 or orchardspringscampground.com
**Management:** Nevada Irrigation District, (530) 265-5302
**Activities:** Swimming, fishing, boating, waterskiing, horseshoes, volleyball
**Finding the campground:** From the intersection of CA 20 and CA 49 in Nevada City, drive northeast 4 miles on CA 20. Turn right (south) onto Scotts Flat Road and drive 4 miles.
**About the campground:** This very attractive lake is stocked annually with rainbow and brown trout but hosts a wide variety of fish. There are two separate gates to the campground. Elevation 3,000 feet. Stay limit 15 days. Open all year.

## 456 White Cloud

**Location:** 10 miles northeast of Nevada City
**GPS:** 39.320164 / -120.846173
**Sites:** 45 sites for tents and RVs up to 35 feet long
**Facilities:** Tables, fire rings, drinking water, flush toilets
**Fee per night:** $$; reservations: (800) 444-7275 or reserveamerica.com
**Management:** Tahoe National Forest, (530) 288-3231
**Activities:** Hiking, mountain biking, horseback riding
**Finding the campground:** From the intersection of CA 20 and CA 49 in Nevada City, drive northeast on CA 20 for 10 miles.
**About the campground:** The Pioneer Trail, the first wagon route used by gold seekers in 1850, runs by the campground. It has become a popular mountain biking route, especially in the downhill direction (east to west). Elevation 4,300 feet. Stay limit 14 days. Open May through October. If camping with horses, try Skillman Horse Campground, 4 more miles east along CA 20 (available for groups or individuals, with or without horses).

## 457 Orchard Springs (Rollins Reservoir)

**Location:** 12 miles southeast of Nevada City
**GPS:** 39.141156 / -120.956346
**Sites:** 91 sites for tents and RVs up to 45 feet long
**Facilities:** Tables, grill, drinking water, flush toilets, showers, boat ramp, store, restaurant, volleyball
**Fee per night:** $$$–$$$$; reservations: (530) 346-0073 or orchardspringscampground.com
**Management:** Orchard Springs Resort, (530) 346-0073
**Activities:** Swimming, fishing, boating, waterskiing
**Finding the campground:** From the intersection of CA 20 and CA 49 in Nevada City, drive 2 miles south on CA 49. Turn southeast onto CA 174 and drive 9 miles. Turn left (east) onto Orchard Springs Road and drive 1 mile.

**About the campground:** Rollins has 13 miles of shoreline and 300 acres to explore. The lake hosts a wide variety of trout, bass, and catfish. Saturday nights, you can generally watch a movie in the meadow. Elevation 2,200 feet. Stay limit 14 days. Open all year.

## 458 Peninsula (Rollins Reservoir)

**Location:** 14 miles southeast of Nevada City
**GPS:** 39.155665 / -120.946583
**Sites:** 70 sites for tents and RVs up to 40 feet; group sites and cabins
**Facilities:** Tables, grill, drinking water, showers, flush toilets, boat ramp, volleyball, horseshoes, store, boat rental
**Fee per night:** $$$–$$$$; reservations: (530) 477-9413 or orchardspringscampground.com
**Management:** Family Camping Resort, (530) 477-9413
**Activities:** Swimming, fishing, boating, waterskiing, hiking
**Finding the campground:** From the intersection of CA 20 and CA 49 in Nevada City, drive 2 miles south on CA 49. Turn southeast onto CA 174 and drive 5 miles. Turn left (east) onto You Bet Road and drive 7 miles.
**About the campground:** See Orchard Springs Campground (457) for information.

## 459 Long Ravine (Rollins Reservoir)

**Location:** 15 miles southeast of Nevada City
**GPS:** 39.139487 / -120.938332
**Sites:** 18 sites for RVs; 40 sites for tents; group sites
**Facilities:** Tables, grills, drinking water, flush toilets, boat ramp, dump station, electric and full hookups, store and restaurant
**Fee per night:** $$–$$$$; reservations: (530) 265-8861 or orchardspringscampground.com
**Management:** Long Ravine Resort, (530) 265-8861
**Activities:** Swimming, fishing, boating, waterskiing
**Finding the campground:** From the intersection of CA 20 and CA 49 in Nevada City, drive 2 miles south on CA 49. Turn southeast onto CA 174 and drive about 11 miles to Shady Glen. Make a hard left and drive about 2 miles northeast to the access road, on the left.
**About the campground:** See Orchard Springs Campground (457) for information.

## 460 Parker Flat OHV Staging Area

**Location:** 27 miles northeast of Auburn
**GPS:** 39.127410 / -120.761446
**Sites:** 6 sites for tents or small RVs
**Facilities:** Tables, fire rings, drinking water, vault toilets
**Fee per night:** None
**Management:** Tahoe National Forest, (530) 367-2224
**Activities:** OHV driving

**Finding the campground:** From I-80 at the north end of Auburn, take the Foresthill Road exit and drive about 24 miles northeast on Foresthill Road. Turn left (west) onto Sugar Pine Road (FR 10) and drive 3 miles.

**About the campground:** The campground is a staging area for off-highway drivers and their vehicles. It could possibly be used as an overflow spot if the campgrounds at Sugar Pine Lake are full. A series of trails for motorcycles and ATVs extends in several directions from the campground. Elevation 3,700 feet. Stay limit 14 days. Open May through October. Just north is Sugar Pine OHV Staging Area, with undesignated sites for RVs only.

## 461 Giant Gap (Sugar Pine Reservoir)

**Location:** 32 miles northeast of Auburn

**GPS:** 39.139720 / -120.791546

**Sites:** 25 sites for tents and RVs up to 40 feet long; group sites at Forbes Creek

**Facilities:** Tables, fire rings, drinking water, vault toilets, swimming beach; dump station 2 miles southeast; boat ramp 2.5 miles southeast

**Fee per night:** $$–$$$$; reservations: (800) 444-7275 or reserveamerica.com

**Management:** Tahoe National Forest, (530) 367-2224

**Activities:** Hiking, swimming, fishing, boating, OHV driving

**Finding the campground:** From I-80 at the north end of Auburn, take the Foresthill Road exit and drive about 24 miles northeast. Turn west onto Sugar Pine Road (FR 10) and drive just under 3 miles to a fork. Bear left and continue 4.5 miles around the lake.

**About the campground:** Sugar Pine Reservoir is 2 miles long and 1 mile wide at its widest point. It is stocked with rainbow and brown trout annually. There is a 10 mph speed limit for boats on the lake. A paved trail circles the lakeshore, and a series of OHV trails run north and east of the campground. You'll find a swimming beach near the Manzanita Picnic Area. Elevation 3,725 feet. Stay limit 14 days. Open May through October. For groups up to 50 people, try nearby Forbes Creek Group Camp.

## 462 Shirttail Creek (Sugar Pine Reservoir)

**Location:** 32 miles northeast of Auburn

**GPS:** 39.141916 / -120.786442

**Sites:** 29 sites for tents and RVs up to 45 feet long

**Facilities:** Tables, fire rings, drinking water, vault toilets; dump station 2.5 miles southeast; boat ramp 3 miles southeast

**Fee per night:** $$–$$$$: reservations: (800) 444-7275 or reserveamerica.com

**Management:** Tahoe National Forest, (530) 367-2224

**Activities:** Hiking, swimming, fishing, boating, mountain biking, OHV driving

**Finding the campground:** From I-80 at the north end of Auburn, take the Foresthill Road exit and drive about 24 miles northeast. Turn left (west) onto Sugar Pine Road (FR 10) and drive just under 3 miles to a fork. Bear left and continue 4.5 miles around the lake, past Giant Gap Campground.

**About the campground:** The campground is adjacent to the Manzanita Picnic Area, on the north shore of Sugar Pine Reservoir. A paved, nonmotorized trail circles the campground. The North Fork of the American River is nearby, offering additional fishing and swimming and miles of hiking, biking, and OHV trails. Elevation 3,600 feet. Stay limit 14 days. Open May through October.

## 463 Big Reservoir & Morning Star (Big Reservoir)

**Location:** 29 miles northeast of Auburn
**GPS:** 39.141762 / -120.752741
**Sites:** 100 sites for tents and RVs up to 27 feet long
**Facilities:** Tables, fire rings, drinking water, vault toilets
**Fee per night:** $$–$$$$, group sites: $$$$; reservations: (530) 367-2129
**Management:** Tahoe National Forest, (530) 367-2224
**Activities:** Swimming, fishing, boating, OHV driving
**Finding the campground:** From I-80 at the north end of Auburn, take the Foresthill Road exit and drive about 24 miles northeast. Turn left (west) onto Sugar Pine Road (FR 10) and drive just under 3 miles. Turn right onto FR 24 and drive about 2 miles.
**About the campground:** This attractive 70-acre lake does not permit boats with motors, making it a good place for canoeing and kayaking. Fishing is poor but may improve, since private stocking of the lake with trout began a few years ago. Elevation 4,000 feet. Stay limit 14 days. Open May through October.

## 464 Mineral Bar (Auburn State Recreation Area)

**Location:** 18 miles northeast of Auburn
**GPS:** 39.100493 / -120.923883
**Sites:** 18 sites for tents and small RVs
**Facilities:** Tables, fire rings, pit toilets; no drinking water
**Fee per night:** $$
**Management:** California Department of Parks and Recreation, (530) 885-4527
**Activities:** Hiking, swimming, fishing, boating, waterskiing, kayaking, rafting, horseback riding, mountain biking, gold panning
**Finding the campground:** From Auburn, drive east on I-80 for 13 miles to Colfax. Take the Canyon Way exit and turn left onto Canyon Way. Continue for 1 mile and turn right onto Iowa Hill Road. Follow it for 0.6 mile before turning right to stay on Iowa Hill Road. In another 0.4 mile turn left to stay on Iowa Hill Road. Stay on it for 2 more miles. Cross over the American River to reach the campground.
**About the campground:** The 42,000 acres of this historic placer-mining area encompass 30 miles of the North and Middle Forks of the American River. Over 50 miles of hiking, biking, and equestrian trails (including an 11-mile segment of the Western States Pioneer Express Trail, which runs from Sacramento to Carson City, Nevada) run through the park along the Middle Fork of the American River, past inviting pools for swimming. A 3-mile round-trip to Ruck-a-Chucky Falls begins at the campground and leads to an attractive waterfall and deep pool. Both the North and the Middle Forks of the river provide challenging runs for rafters and kayakers; nearby Lake Clementine offers water sports. Elevation 1,175 feet. Stay limit 14 days. Open all year.

## 465 Ruck-a-Chucky (Auburn State Recreation Area)

**Location:** 8 miles northeast of Auburn
**GPS:** 38.963140 / -120.932384
**Sites:** 5 sited for tents; no RVs permitted on the access road

**Facilities:** Fire rings, tables, vault toilets; no drinking water
**Fee per night:** $$
**Management:** Auburn State Recreation Area, (530) 885-4527
**Activities:** Hiking, boating, fishing
**Finding the campground:** Exit I-80 at Foresthill Road. Going toward Foresthill, turn right onto Drivers Flat Road, a 2.5-mile dirt road down to the site and river.
**About the campground:** Primitive campsites located on the Placer County side of the Middle Fork of the American River accessed by a gravel/dirt road. There are boat launches for rafters. The historic Western States Trail, a gold rush–era thoroughfare, continues along the banks of the river upstream from the campground. Elevation 740 feet. Stay limit 14 days. Open May through October.

## 466 Marshall Gold Discovery State Historic Park

**Location:** 18 miles southeast of Auburn, in Coloma
**GPS:** 38.802255 / -120.889480
**Sites:** 80 sites for tents and RVs up to 45 feet long; tent cabins
**Facilities:** Tables, grills, drinking water, showers, flush toilets, full hookups available, dump station, kayak/raft put-in and takeout, store
**Fee per night:** $$; tent cabins: $$$; reservations: (800) 238-2298
**Management:** Coloma Resort, (530) 621-2267
**Activities:** Hiking, rafting, gold panning, sightseeing
**Finding the campground:** From the intersection of I-80 and CA 49 in Auburn, drive south about 18 miles on CA 49 to Coloma. Turn left onto Bridge Street and cross the single-lane bridge over the American River. The campground entrance is on the right, immediately after clearing the bridge.
**About the campground:** We are including this privately owned campground (an exception to the parameters of this book) because the site is unique. The campground is surrounded by the Marshall Gold Discovery State Historic Park, the site of Sutter's Mill, where gold was first discovered in California in 1848 and the town that grew up around it. The mill has been reconstructed, and some of its original timbers are housed at the site. The town contains a visitor center and museum and some of the original buildings, survivors of the gold rush days. The campground is along the American River, and most of its campsites are directly on the riverbank. Elevation 770 feet. No stay limit. Open all year.

## 467 Peninsula (Folsom Lake State Recreation Area)

**Location:** 20 miles south of Auburn
**GPS:** 38.755798 / -121.107681
**Sites:** 75 sites for tents and RVs up to 38 feet long
**Facilities:** Tables, grills, drinking water, flush toilets, dump station, boat launch
**Fee per night:** $$–$$$; reservations: (800) 444-7275 or reserveamerica.com
**Management:** Folsom Lake State Recreation Area, (916) 988-0205
**Activities:** Hiking, swimming, fishing, boating, waterskiing, sailboarding, cycling, mountain biking, horseback riding
**Finding the campground:** From the intersection of I-80 and CA 49 in Auburn, drive south about 10 miles on CA 49. Turn right (west) onto Rattlesnake Bar Road and drive another 10 miles.

**About the campground:** See Beal's Point Campground (468) for area information. The Darrington Trail, open to hikers and mountain bikers, follows the South Fork American River for almost 8 miles. Elevation 550 feet. Stay limit 7 days. Open April through September. Group sites are available at Negro Bar.

## 468 Beal's Point (Folsom Lake State Recreation Area)

**Location:** 13 miles southwest of Auburn
**GPS:** 38.720661 / -121.172722
**Sites:** 69 sites for tents and RVs up to 31 feet long
**Facilities:** Tables, grills, drinking water, showers, flush toilets, dump station, boat launch and rentals, swimming beach, full hookups
**Fee per night:** $$, hookups: $$$$; reservations: (800) 444-7275 or reserveamerica.com
**Management:** Folsom Lake State Recreation Area, (916) 988-0205
**Activities:** Hiking, swimming, fishing, boating, waterskiing, sailboarding, cycling, mountain biking, horseback riding
**Finding the campground:** From the intersection of I-80 and Auburn-Folsom Road in Auburn, drive southwest 13 miles on Auburn-Folsom Road.
**About the campground:** This 18,000-acre lake with 75 miles of shoreline is a complete water sports destination serving the heavily populated area between Auburn and Sacramento. Campground reservations are a good idea, especially in summer. Folsom is stocked annually and contains rainbow trout, kokanee, and bass. In addition, the lake has a decent catfish population, and even sturgeon have been caught in the deeper waters. Landlubbers too will find lots to do. The American River Bikeway runs from Beal's Point to Discovery Park in Old Town Sacramento, providing 32 paved miles of excellent cycling along the shores of Folsom and Natoma Lakes and the American River. Equestrians and hikers will enjoy the section of the Western States Pioneer Express Trail that passes near the campground. Elevation 550 feet. Stay limit 7 days June through September; 30 days October through April. Open all year.

## 469 Sly Park (Jenkinson Lake)

**Location:** 17 miles east of Placerville
**GPS:** 38.724856 / -120.569568
**Sites:** 191 sites for tents and RVs; 5 group sites; equestrian camp
**Facilities:** Tables, fire rings, drinking water, vault toilets, boat ramp
**Fee per night:** $, group sites: $$$$; reservations: (530) 295-6810
**Management:** El Dorado Irrigation District, (530) 644-2545
**Activities:** Swimming, fishing, boating, waterskiing, horseback riding
**Finding the campground:** From Placerville, drive east on US 50 for 12 miles. Take the Sly Park Road exit and drive south 4 miles. Turn left onto the campground access road and drive 0.5 mile.
**About the campground:** The campground is on the north shore of Jenkinson Lake, a good fishing location for trout in spring and bass in summer. There is a 5 mph speed limit on the upper end of the lake. Nine miles of horse trails circle the lake, and there are several hiking trails in the area. Elevation 3,500 feet. Stay limit 14 days. Open all year.

## 470 Chaw'se (Indian Grinding Rock State Historic Park)

**Location:** 11 miles northeast of Jackson
**GPS:** 38.422371 / -120.642388
**Sites:** 22 sites for tents and RVs up to 27 feet long; environmental group camp
**Facilities:** Tables, fire rings, drinking water, showers, flush toilets, food lockers
**Fee per night:** $$$
**Management:** Indian Grinding Rock State Historic Park, (209) 296-7488
**Activities:** Sightseeing
**Finding the campground:** From the intersection of CA 49 and CA 88 in Jackson, drive 8.5 miles northeast on CA 88. Turn left onto Pine Grove Volcano Road and continue 1.5 miles to the park.
**About the campground:** *Chaw'se* is the Miwok Indian word for a grinding rock used to grind acorns and other seeds into meal. The main rock in the park contains more than 1,100 circular depressions created by this grinding, the largest grouping of such bedrock mortars in North America. The site also includes a museum, a reconstructed Miwok village and ceremonial roundhouse, and a 0.5-mile-long nature trail. The family campground sits on a wooded hill above the field of grinding rocks. The environmental group camp consists of seven bark houses in a secluded part of the park where all supplies, including water, must be hauled in on foot. Elevation 2,400 feet. Stay limit 15 days. Open all year.

## 471 North Shore (Camanche Reservoir)

**Location:** 15 miles northwest of Lodi
**GPS:** 38.239214 / -120.955521
**Sites:** 181 sites for tents and RVs up to 45 feet long; yurts; cottages; primitive and group sites available
**Facilities:** Tables, fire rings, flush and chemical toilets, drinking water, showers, dump station, playground, basketball court, boat ramp
**Fee per night:** $–$$$$; reservations: (866) 763-5121 or lakecamancheresort.com
**Management:** California Parks Company, (209) 763-5915
**Activities:** Boating, fishing, swimming, biking, hiking, waterskiing, boat rentals
**Finding the campground:** From Victor Road and CA 99 in Lodi, drive east on Victor Road for 5 miles. Turn left onto CA 88 and continue 7 miles before veering left to stay on CA 88. Proceed 3 miles and turn left onto Liberty Road; drive another 3 miles. The road becomes Camanche Parkway; stay on it for another 4.5 miles.
**About the campground:** Located in the Sierra Foothills, you'll find 12 square miles of lake and 53 miles of shoreline. Personal watercraft and windsurfing are popular on the lake. Visitors can also play tennis and basketball. Boaters may rent open or covered slips year-round at both shores, and patio and fishing boats also are available for rent. Both north and south shore resorts offer a variety of campgrounds and camping experiences, as well as rental cottages with kitchens. The facilities vary at the different areas. Elevation 290 feet. Stay limit 14 days. Open all year.

## 472 South Shore (Camanche Reservoir)

**Location:** 15 miles northwest of Lodi
**GPS:** 38.218302 / -120.928205

**Sites:** 517 sites for tents and RVs up to 45 feet long; group and equestrian sites and cottages available
**Facilities:** Tables; fire rings; drinking water; flush and chemical toilets; showers; full hookups; laundry; boat ramp; store; basketball, volleyball, and tennis courts; amphitheater
**Fee per night:** $–$$$$; reservations: (866) 763-5121 or lakecamancheresort.com
**Management:** California Parks Company, (209) 763-5915
**Activities:** Boating, fishing, swimming, biking, hiking, waterskiing, boating, boat rentals, store
**Finding the campground:** From Victor Road and CA 99 in Lodi drive east on Victor Road for 5 miles. Turn left onto CA 88 and continue 7 miles before staying straight and proceeding on CA 12 for 5 miles. Turn left onto Camanche Parkway South and follow signs to the South Shore area.
**About the campground:** Ten different campgrounds at South Shore provide a variety of experiences, from alcohol-free family areas to full hookup RV-only areas. The facilities vary at the different areas. Turkey Hill offers equestrian camping. See North Shore (471) for more information. Elevation 260 feet. Stay limit 14 days. Recreational vehicles can hook up for 1 night or up to 6 months. Open all year.

## 473 Acorn East & West (New Hogan Lake)

**Location:** 10 miles west of San Andreas
**GPS:** 38.176292 / -120.799741
**Sites:** 132 sites for tents and RVs up to 45 feet long
**Facilities:** Tables, fire rings, drinking water, showers, flush toilets, dump station; East only: fish-cleaning station, boat ramp
**Fee per night:** $$; reservations: (877) 444-6777 or recreation.gov
**Management:** US Army Corps of Engineers, (209) 772-1343

*Created with an earth-filled dam, New Hogan Lake in the Sierra Nevada foothills came into being in 1965. It provides hydroelectric power, water for drinking and irrigation, and every kind of water recreation for those who camp near its shores.*

**Activities:** Swimming, fishing, boating, waterskiing

**Finding the campground:** From San Andreas, drive northwest on CA 49 for 1 mile. Turn left (west) onto CA 12 and drive 6 miles. Turn left onto Lime Creek Road and drive 0.5 mile; turn left onto South Petersburg Road and drive 2.5 miles.

**About the campground:** New Hogan Lake has a surface area of 4,400 acres and 50 miles of shoreline. You can catch bass, bluegill, crappie, and catfish here. A good portion of the campsites are on the lakeshore, and boats can be anchored or beached at the sites. Some sites were renovated in 2016. Elevation 760 feet. Stay limit 14 days. Open all year.

## 474 Oak Knoll (New Hogan Lake)

**Location:** 10 miles west of San Andreas

**GPS:** 38.182630 / -120.793655

**Sites:** 50 sites for tents and RVs up to 45 feet long

**Facilities:** Tables, fire rings, drinking water, vault toilets

**Fee per night:** $; reservations: (800) 444-7275 or reserveamerica.com

**Management:** US Army Corps of Engineers, (209) 772-1343

**Activities:** Swimming, fishing, boating, waterskiing

**Finding the campground:** From San Andreas, drive northwest on CA 49 for 1 mile. Turn left (west) onto CA 12 and drive 6 miles. Turn left onto Lime Creek Road and drive 0.5 mile; turn left onto South Petersburg Road and drive 2.5 miles.

**About the campground:** See Acorn East Campground (473) for lake information. A boat ramp and dump station are available at Acorn East. Elevation 750 feet. Stay limit 14 days. Open April through October as needed for overflow. For group camping, check out Coyote Point Group Camp.

## 475 Glory Hole (New Melones Lake)

**Location:** 19 miles northwest of Sonora

**GPS:** 38.008133 / -120.538406

**Sites:** 140 sites for tents and RVs up to 40 feet long

**Facilities:** Tables, grills, drinking water, showers, flush toilets, dump station, playground, marina; boat ramp 0.7 mile south

**Fee per night:** $–$$; reservations: (877) 444-6777 or recreation.gov

**Management:** US Bureau of Reclamation, (209) 536-9094

**Activities:** Swimming, fishing, boating, waterskiing, biking, mountain biking

**Finding the campground:** From Sonora, drive about 15 miles northwest on CA 49; turn left (west) onto Glory Hole Road and drive 4 miles.

**About the campground:** See Tuttletown Recreation Area (476) for area information. Open all year.

## 476 Tuttletown Recreation Area (New Melones Lake)

**Location:** 10 miles west of Sonora

**GPS:** 37.985629 / -120.505993

**Sites:** 164 sites for tents and RVs up to 45 feet long; group sites

**Facilities:** Tables, grills, drinking water, showers, flush toilets, dump station, playground, boat ramp

**Fee per night:** $–$$, group sites: $$$$; reservations: (877) 444-6777 or recreation.gov

**Management:** US Bureau of Reclamation, (209) 536-9094
**Activities:** Swimming, fishing, boating, waterskiing, biking, mountain biking
**Finding the campground:** From Sonora, drive about 8 miles northwest on CA 49 to Tuttletown. Turn left (west) onto Reynolds Ferry Road and drive 2 miles.
**About the campground:** This large reservoir, the fifth-largest lake in California, has a surface area of more than 12,000 acres and almost 100 miles of shoreline. Rainbow trout, bass, bluegill, and catfish are the catches here, and the lake is heavily stocked annually with rainbow trout. Nearby is Natural Bridges, accessible from Parrott's Ferry Road, with a hiking trail and a creek that flows through a marble cave. The Table Mountain Trail climbs to the top of an extensive lava flow that occurred over 9 million years ago. Elevation 1,100 feet. Stay limit 14 days. Open all year.

## 477 Moccasin Point (Don Pedro Reservoir)

**Location:** 15 miles south of Sonora
**GPS:** 37.828514 / -120.336981
**Sites:** 96 sites for tents and RVs, including 18 with full hookups
**Facilities:** Tables, grills, fire rings, drinking water, showers, flush toilets, dump station, boat ramp and rentals, store, snack bar
**Fee per night:** $$–$$$$; reservations: (209) 852-2396, ext. 3, or donpedrolake.com/reservations
**Management:** Don Pedro Recreation Agency, Turlock Irrigation District, (209) 852-2396
**Activities:** Swimming, fishing, boating, waterskiing, hiking, biking
**Finding the campground:** From the intersection of CA 108 and CA 49 just south of Sonora, drive south 14 miles on CA 49.
**About the campground:** A large lake with 160 miles of shoreline and covering more than 12,000 acres, Don Pedro provides good trout and bass fishing, with the added possibility of catching kokanee and bluegill. The lake is heavily stocked annually with mature rainbow trout and bass fingerlings. Elevation 900 feet. Stay limit 14 days. Open all year.

## 478 Fleming Meadows (Don Pedro Reservoir)

**Location:** 40 miles east of Modesto
**GPS:** 37.697969 / -120.403402
**Sites:** 238 sites for tents and RVs, including 89 with full hookups
**Facilities:** Tables, grills, fire rings, drinking water, showers, flush toilets, dump station; boat ramp nearby
**Fee per night:** $–$$; reservations: (209) 852-2396, ext. 3, or donpedrolake.com/reservations
**Management:** Don Pedro Recreation Agency, Turlock Irrigation District, (209) 852-2396
**Activities:** Swimming, fishing, boating, waterskiing, hiking, biking
**Finding the campground:** From the intersection of CA 99 and CA 132 in Modesto, drive east on CA 132 about 33 miles. Turn left (north) onto CR J59 (La Grange Road) and drive 5 miles. Turn right (east) onto Bonds Flat Road and drive about 2 miles.
**About the campground:** A large lake with 160 miles of shoreline and covering more than 12,000 acres, Don Pedro provides good trout and bass fishing, with the added possibility of catching kokanee and bluegill. The lake is heavily stocked annually with mature rainbow trout and bass fingerlings. Elevation 860 feet. Stay limit 14 days. Open all year. No pets allowed.

## 479 Blue Oaks (Don Pedro Reservoir)

**Location:** 39 miles east of Modesto
**GPS:** 37.704718 / -120.432966
**Sites:** 161 sites for tents and 34 for RVs with partial hookups, including water and electric hookups
**Facilities:** Tables, grills, fire rings, drinking water, showers, flush toilets, dump station; boat ramp nearby
**Fee per night:** $$–$$$$; reservations: (209) 852-2396, ext. 3, or donpedrolake.com/reservations
**Management:** Don Pedro Recreation Agency, Turlock Irrigation District, (209) 852-2396
**Activities:** Swimming, fishing, boating, waterskiing, hiking, biking
**Finding the campground:** From the intersection of CA 99 and CA 132 in Modesto, drive east on CA 132 about 33 miles. Turn left (north) onto CR J59 (La Grange Road) and drive 5 miles. Turn right (east) onto Bonds Flat Road and drive about 1 mile.
**About the campground:** A large lake with 160 miles of shoreline and covering more than 12,000 acres, Don Pedro provides good trout and bass fishing, with the added possibility of catching kokanee and bluegill. The lake is heavily stocked annually with mature rainbow trout and bass fingerlings. Elevation 885 feet. Stay limit 14 days. Open all year. No pets allowed.

## 480 Horseshoe Bend Recreation Area (Lake McClure)

**Location:** 3 miles west of Coulterville
**GPS:** 37.701967 / -120.244219
**Sites:** 97 sites for tents and RVs, including 35 with water and electric hookups
**Facilities:** Tables, drinking water, showers, flush toilets, dump station, two-lane boat ramp, swimming lagoon, fish-cleaning station, store, laundry
**Fee per night:** $–$$$; reservations: (855) 800-2267 or reservations.lakemcclure.com
**Management:** Merced Irrigation District, (209) 378-2521
**Activities:** Swimming, fishing, boating, waterskiing
**Finding the campground:** From the intersection of CA 49 and CA 132 in Coulterville, drive west on CA 132 about 3 miles.
**About the campground:** Shaped like a huge letter H, Lake McClure has more than 80 miles of shoreline and is noted for its waterskiing and houseboats. The lake has populations of salmon, bluegill, crappie, shad, and catfish spread generally throughout the lake. Trout can best be caught in the eastern leg of the H, and bass seem to favor the western leg. The lake is heavily stocked annually with rainbow trout. Elevation 950 feet. Stay limit 14 days. Open all year.

## 481 Barrett Cove Recreation Area (Lake McClure)

**Location:** 44 miles east of Modesto
**GPS:** 37.644374 / -120.294307
**Sites:** 249 sites for tents and RVs, including 89 with water and electric hookups
**Facilities:** Tables, drinking water, showers, flush toilets, dump station, playground, swimming area, five-lane boat ramp, marina and boat rentals (including houseboats), store, fish-cleaning station, laundry, gas station

**Fee per night:** $-$$$; reservations: (855) 800-2267 or reservations.lakemcclure.com
**Management:** Merced Irrigation District, (209) 378-2521
**Activities:** Swimming, fishing, boating, waterskiing, mountain biking
**Finding the campground:** From the intersection of CA 99 and CA 132 in Modesto, drive east about 38 miles on CA 132. Turn right (south) onto Merced Falls Road and drive 3.5 miles. Turn left (east) onto Barrett Cove Road and drive 2 miles.
**About the campground:** See Horseshoe Bend Recreation Area (480) for area information. A trail leads from the campground to the Exchequer Bike Park, offering exciting trails for mountain bikers.

## 482 McClure Point Recreation Area (Lake McClure)

**Location:** 41 miles east of Modesto
**GPS:** 37.607871 / -120.281567
**Sites:** 100 sites for tents and RVs, including 52 with water and electric hookups
**Facilities:** Tables, drinking water, showers, flush toilets, three-lane boat ramp, marina and boat rentals, swimming lagoon, fish-cleaning station, store, laundry, gas station
**Fee per night:** $-$$$; reservations: (855) 800-2267 or reservations.lakemcclure.com
**Management:** Merced Irrigation District, (209) 378-2521
**Activities:** Swimming, fishing, boating, waterskiing
**Finding the campground:** From the intersection of CA 99 and CR J16 just southeast of Modesto, drive east on CR J16 about 33 miles to Merced Falls. Turn right onto Lake McClure Road and drive about 8 miles.
**About the campground:** See Horseshoe Bend Recreation Area (480) for area information.

## 483 Lake McSwain Recreation Area

**Location:** 34 miles east of Modesto
**GPS:** 37.523304 / -120.303756
**Sites:** 111 sites for tents and RVs, including 65 with water and electric hookups
**Facilities:** Tables, drinking water, showers, flush toilets, dump station, playground, two-lane boat ramp, marina and boat rentals, swimming lagoon, store, laundry, gas station
**Fee per night:** $-$$$; reservations: (855) 800-2267 or reservations.lakemcclure.com
**Management:** Merced Irrigation District, (209) 378-2521
**Activities:** Swimming, fishing, boating, kayaking
**Finding the campground:** From the intersection of CA 99 and CR J16 just southeast of Modesto, drive east on CR J16 about 33 miles to Merced Falls. Turn right onto Lake McClure Road and drive about 1 mile.
**About the campground:** Lake McSwain is small compared to its neighboring reservoirs—roughly 2 miles long by 0.5 mile wide. It is stocked annually with more than 35,000 catchable-size trout, which makes for good fishing until summer's hot weather. Elevation 430 feet. Stay limit 14 days. Open all year.

## 484 Bagby Recreation Area (Lake McClure)

**Location:** 10 miles south of Coulterville
**GPS:** 37.6101853 / -120.1308051

**Sites:** 31+ sites for tents and RVs, including 10 with water and electric hookups and 10 primitive sites along the river
**Facilities:** Tables, drinking water, flush toilets, showers, fish-cleaning station, boat ramp
**Fee per night:** $–$$$; reservations: (855) 800-2267 or reservations.lakemcclure.com
**Management:** Merced Irrigation District, (209) 378-2521
**Activities:** Swimming, fishing, boating, waterskiing
**Finding the campground:** From the intersection of CA 49 and CA 132 in Coulterville, drive south about 10 miles on CA 49.
**About the campground:** Located just below the Wild & Scenic Merced River at the inlet of Lake McClure. See Horseshoe Bend Recreation Area (480) for area information.

*Originating in the high country of Yosemite National Park, the Merced River rushes headlong through glacially carved valleys and rugged mountains before spilling into the San Joaquin River.*

## 485 McCabe Flat (Merced River Recreation Area)

**Location:** 18 miles north of Mariposa
**GPS:** 37.597433 / -120.003020
**Sites:** 11 walk-in sites for tents; 3 sites for RVs
**Facilities:** Tables, fire rings, vault toilets; no drinking water
**Fee per night:** $
**Management:** Bureau of Land Management, (209) 966-3192
**Activities:** Hiking, fishing, swimming, rafting, horseback riding, gold panning, mountain biking
**Finding the campground:** From Mariposa, drive 15 miles north on CA 140. Turn left at Briceburg BLM Visitor Center and cross the Merced River Bridge (not recommended for large RVs and trailers over 18 feet long). Turn left and drive downriver 2.5 miles.
**About the campground:** Situated in a great setting on the scenic Merced River, the campground is also adjacent to the old Yosemite Railroad Grade, which is now a trail for hikers, mountain bikers, and equestrians. Rafting access is also available to the Class III–Class V rapids of the Merced. Swimming is usually excellent, if cold. The river is stocked in summer with rainbow trout. Recreational gold panning is permitted along this section of the Merced. As if all this is not enough, the main entrance to Yosemite National Park (Arch Rock) is only 18 miles to the east. Elevation 1,080 feet. Stay limit 14 days. Open all year.

## 486 Willow Placer (Merced River Recreation Area)

**Location:** 19 miles north of Mariposa
**GPS:** 37.609210 / -120.007713
**Sites:** 9 walk-in sites for tents; 1 RV site
**Facilities:** Tables, fire rings, vault toilets; no drinking water
**Fee per night:** $
**Management:** Bureau of Land Management, (209) 966-3192
**Activities:** Hiking, fishing, swimming, rafting, horseback riding, gold panning, mountain biking
**Finding the campground:** From Mariposa, drive 15 miles north on CA 140. Turn left at Briceburg BLM Visitor Center and cross the Merced River Bridge (not recommended for large RVs and trailers over 18 feet long). Turn left and drive downriver 3.8 miles.
**About the campground:** Pine and oak trees provide shade. See McCabe Flat Campground (485) for area information.

## 487 Railroad Flat (Merced River Recreation Area)

**Location:** 21 miles north of Mariposa
**GPS:** 37.617124 / -120.019972
**Sites:** 3 walk-in sites for tents; 6 RV sites
**Facilities:** Tables, fire rings, vault toilets; no drinking water
**Fee per night:** $
**Management:** Bureau of Land Management, (209) 966-3192
**Activities:** Hiking, fishing, swimming, rafting, horseback riding, gold panning

**Finding the campground:** From Mariposa, drive 15 miles north on CA 140. Turn left at Briceburg BLM Visitor Center and cross the Merced River Bridge (not recommended for large RVs and trailers over 18 feet long). Turn left and drive downriver 5.8 miles.
**About the campground:** Nice shaded sites on the river and not far from the entrance to Yosemite. See McCabe Flat Campground (485) for area information.

## 488 Codorniz Recreation Area (Eastman Lake)

**Location:** 24 miles northeast of Chowchilla
**GPS:** 37.207134 / -119.966408
**Sites:** 65 sites for tents and RVs, including 6 with full hookups and 4 with water and electric; 3 group sites; equestrian site with corrals
**Facilities:** Tables, fire rings/grills, lantern holders, drinking water, flush toilets, showers, dump station, boat ramp, fish-cleaning stations, playground
**Fee per night:** $$–$$$; reservations: (877) 444-6777 or recreation.gov
**Management:** US Army Corps of Engineers, (559) 689-3255
**Activities:** Fishing, boating, swimming, waterskiing, horseback riding
**Finding the campground:** From CA 99 in Chowchilla, take the Avenue 26 exit and drive east 16 miles. Turn left onto CR 29 and drive about 8 miles.
**About the campground:** A first-class campground. Campsites are above the lakes, some with water views. Trails lead down to small coves for swimming or shore fishing. Largemouth bass, rainbow trout, crappie, bluegill, sunfish, and catfish can be taken here. Elevation 715 feet. Stay limit 14 days. Open all year.

## 489 Hidden View (Hensley Lake)

**Location:** 16 miles northeast of Madera
**GPS:** 37.124676 / -119.897568
**Sites:** 55 sites for tents and RVs up to 45 feet long; 2 group sites
**Facilities:** Tables, barbecue grills, fire rings, lantern holders, drinking water, flush toilets, showers, dump station, boat ramp, swimming beach, fish-cleaning stations
**Fee per night:** $$–$$$, group site: $$$$; reservations: (877) 444-6777 or recreation.gov
**Management:** US Army Corps of Engineers, (559) 673-5151
**Activities:** Fishing, boating, swimming, waterskiing
**Finding the campground:** From the intersection of CA 99 and CA 145 in Madera, go east on CA 145 for 7.2 miles. Turn north onto CR 33 for about one mile. Bear left (northeast) on River Road (CR 400) and drive about 7 miles. Turn left (northwest) onto Daulton Road CR 603 for one mile then right (north) onto CR 407 for 2 miles.
**About the campground:** Located in dry, rolling hill country, where the grass only greens up in spring, Hensley and nearby Eastman Lake ( Codorniz Recreation Area, 488) provide the only standing water for miles. The sites are well situated to take advantage of waterfront locations and views over the lake. Ramadas and trees provide shade. The lake is a good place to fish for largemouth bass; it is also stocked with rainbow trout annually. Bluegill, crappie, and catfish are also caught. Shore fishing is good from the lake's many coves, including those at the campground. Elevation 540 feet. Stay limit 14 days. Open all year.

## 490 Millerton Lake State Recreation Area

**Location:** 26 miles east of Madera
**GPS:** 37.021104 / -119.685634
**Sites:** 135 sites for tents and RVs up to 36 feet long; 2 equestrian sites; 2 group sites
**Facilities:** Tables, fire rings, grills, drinking water, showers, flush toilets, dump station, boat ramp
**Fee per night:** $$$–$$$$, group sites: $$$$; reservations: (800) 444-7275 or reserveamerica.com
**Management:** Millerton Lake State Recreation Area, (559) 822-2332
**Activities:** Hiking, swimming, fishing, boating, sailboarding, waterskiing, horseback riding
**Finding the campground:** From the intersection of CA 99 and CA 145 in Madera, drive east about 20 miles on CA145. Turn right (north) onto Oneal Road and drive 1.7 miles. Turn left (east) onto Millerton Road and drive about 4 miles.
**About the campground:** This 15-mile-long lake provides excellent sailing and sailboarding, as well as access to the scenic San Joaquin River Gorge. Its main fish catch is small- to medium-size bass. A multipurpose trail circles the landward side of the campground, and a 1.2-mile round-trip hiking trail climbs to Buzzard's Roost, a fine overlook of the lake and the surrounding area. Campsites are spread out along several attractive coves on the north shore of the lake. Scattered trees supply some shade. Campsite 59 sits alone on a small peninsula at least 300 yards from its nearest neighbor. It is completely private, with its own small cove and beach. Elevation 640 feet. Stay limit 15 days June through September; 30 days October through May. Open all year.

# The Sierra Nevada

Some of the most majestic scenery in all of California is found in the high country that separates the fertile Sacramento Valley in the west from the arid Nevada desert to the east. The Sierra Nevada, the highest mountain range in the contiguous forty-eight states, is the centerpiece of this tour region. Extending like a giant spine from north to south, its rugged peaks and granite-walled valleys deny access to its interior to all but hikers and backpackers. The region is a year-round paradise for outdoor enthusiasts, and virtually every type of outdoor activity takes place within its borders.

Yosemite, the crown jewel of the National Park Service, lies within this region, as do six national forests encompassing more than 5 million acres and containing hundreds of miles of roads, trails, and breathtaking scenery. Hundreds of lakes, large and small, dot the landscape. Many of them are in wild, remote places—havens of solitude where nothing but an angler's line disturbs their placid surfaces. Others, such as Lake Tahoe, North America's largest alpine lake, are more easily accessible by car and RV and welcome powerboats and water-skiers. Stands of giant sequoia, the largest trees on earth, are found along the western slopes of the Sierra Nevada. Wild and Scenic Rivers beckon kayakers and whitewater rafters, while special trails attract equestrians, mountain bikers, and off-highway drivers. Ski areas cater to both downhill and cross-country skiers.

Although most campgrounds in the Sierra Nevada are closed in winter, national forests permit camping anywhere within their borders as long as certain rules are followed (see "How to Use This Guide"). This allows the self-contained RVer and the hardy all-seasons camper the opportunity to enjoy these special places in their wonderful winter settings.

The climate of the Sierra Nevada is typical of mountainous areas: warm summers, cool springs and falls, and cold winters—although the winters here are relatively moderate for a mountain environment. High temperatures in summer can reach well into the 80s. The low in winter is about 15°F. Of course altitude affects the climate; the higher elevations have colder averages, while the lowest elevations tend to be warmer. The percentage of average days of sunshine is fairly consistent year-round: 80 percent in summer, 79 percent in the fall, 74 percent in winter, and 77 percent in spring.

Although the High Sierra region, as defined by the California Division of Tourism, extends into Southern California, this book features campgrounds only in its northern half. For the southern campgrounds, please see the FalconGuide *Camping Southern California* by Richard McMahon.

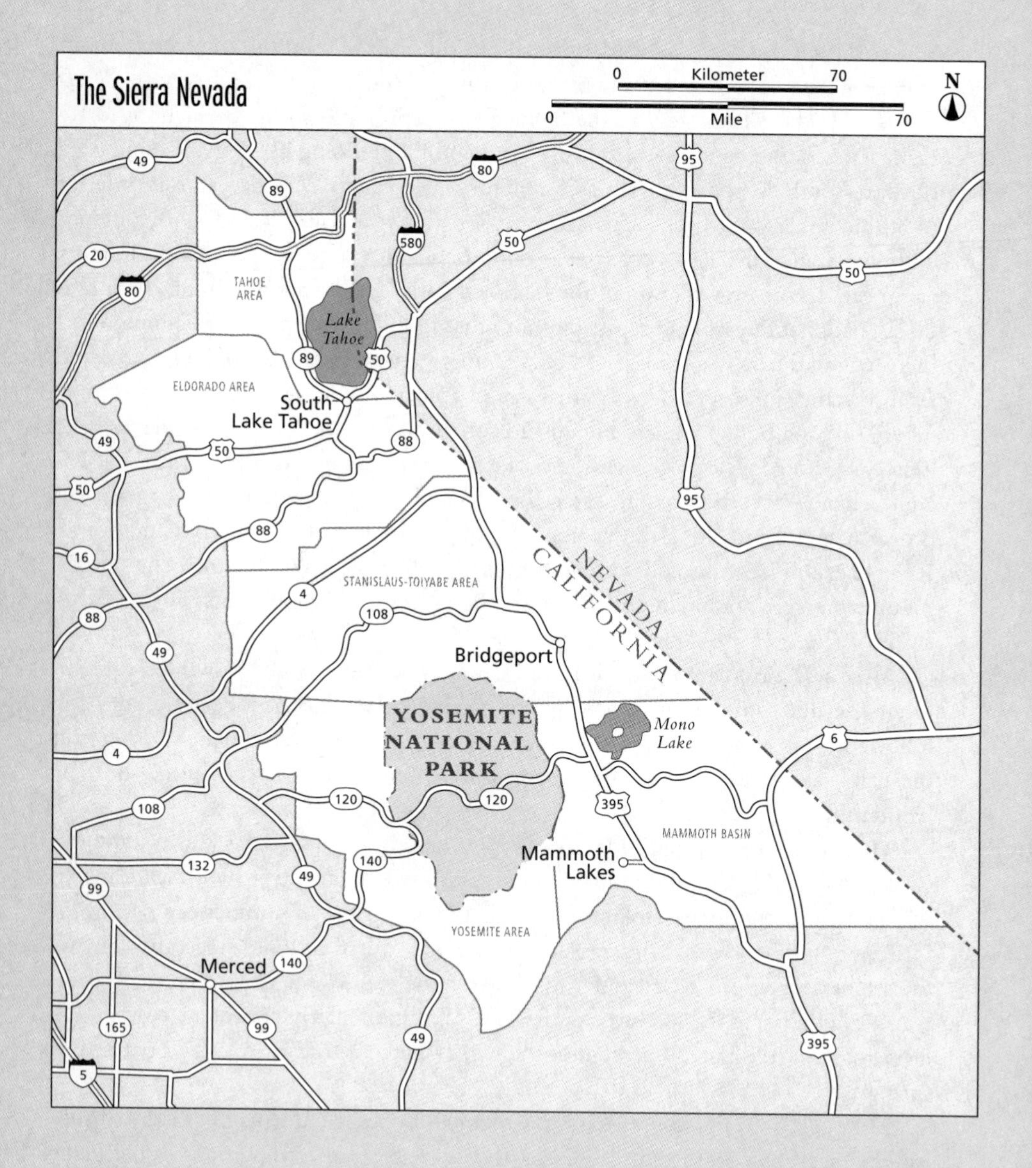

The Sierra Nevada
0
Kilometer
70
0
Mile
70
N
TAHOE AREA
Lake Tahoe
ELDORADO AREA
South Lake Tahoe
STANISLAUS-TOIYABE AREA
NEVADA
CALIFORNIA
Bridgeport
YOSEMITE NATIONAL PARK
Mono Lake
MAMMOTH BASIN
Mammoth Lakes
YOSEMITE AREA
Merced
49
89
80
580
95
50
20
88
16
4
108
120
395
6
132
140
99
165
5

This book divides the Sierra Nevada into four areas: Tahoe, Eldorado, Stanislaus-Toiyabe, and Yosemite. Each contains a variety of campgrounds that will satisfy virtually all lovers of the outdoors, whatever their preferred activities may be.

## Tahoe Area

The centerpiece of this area is magnificent Lake Tahoe. Ringed by snowcapped mountains and lying at an elevation of 6,225 feet, it is the largest and deepest alpine lake in North America. Smaller, less-crowded lakes are located in the surrounding Tahoe National Forest, which also features half a million acres of woodland, rivers, and streams and hundreds of miles of hiking, equestrian, OHV, and mountain biking trails. Also located within the forest is Big Trees Grove, the northernmost stand of giant sequoia in the Sierra Nevada.

*Lake Tahoe at sunset. Photo by Nicole Uhlig*

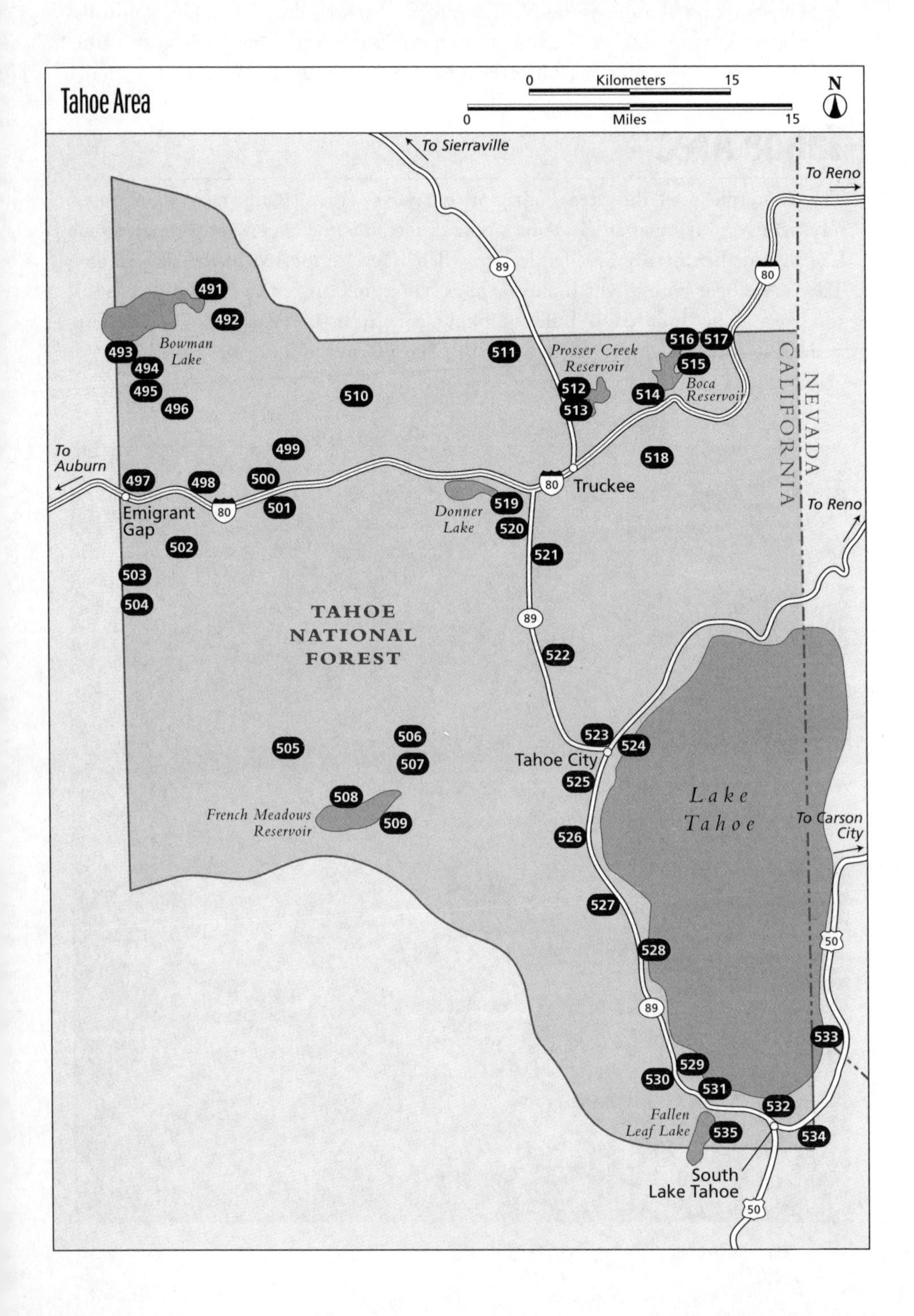
Tahoe Area
0 Kilometers 15
0 Miles 15
N
To Sierraville
To Reno
89
80
491
492
Bowman Lake
493
494
495
496
510
511
Prosser Creek Reservoir
512
513
516
517
515
514
Boca Reservoir
NEVADA
CALIFORNIA
To Auburn
497
498
499
500
501
80
Emigrant Gap
518
80
Truckee
Donner Lake
519
520
521
To Reno
502
503
504
TAHOE NATIONAL FOREST
89
522
523
524
Tahoe City
505
506
507
508
509
French Meadows Reservoir
525
526
Lake Tahoe
To Carson City
527
528
50
89
533
529
530
531
532
Fallen Leaf Lake
535
534
South Lake Tahoe
50

| | Name | Group Sites | RV Sites | Max. RV Length | Hookups | Toilets | Showers | Drinking Water | Dump Station | Pets | Wheelchair | Recreation | Fee(s) | Season | Can Reserve |
|---|---|---|---|---|---|---|---|---|---|---|---|---|---|---|---|
| | **TAHOE AREA** | | | | | | | | | | | | | | |
| 491 | Jackson Creek | | | | | V | | * | | * | | FHM | None | Jun-Oct | |
| 492 | Canyon Creek | | | | | V | | | | * | | FHM | None | Jun-Oct | |
| 493 | Bowman Lake | | | | | V | | | | * | | SFBHM | None | Jun-Oct | |
| 494 | Lindsey Lake | | | | | V | | | | * | | SFBHM | $ | Jun-Oct | |
| 495 | Carr Lake | | | | | V | | | | * | | SFBHM | $ | Jun-Oct | |
| 496 | Grouse Ridge | | * | 17 | | V | | | | * | | SFBHM | None | Jun-Oct | |
| 497 | Lake Spaulding | | * | | | F | | * | | * | * | SFBL | $$ | May-Oct | |
| 498 | Indian Springs | | * | 27 | | V | | * | | * | | SFO | $$ | May-Oct | * |
| 499 | Sterling Lake | | | | | V | | | | * | | HFO | $ | Jun-Oct | |
| 500 | Woodchuck | | * | 17 | | V | | | | * | | HO | $ | May-Oct | |
| 501 | Hampshire Rocks | | * | 23 | | V | | * | | * | | HF | $$ | May-Oct | * |
| 502 | Lodgepole (Lake Valley Reservoir) | | * | 23 | | V | | * | | * | | SFB | $$ | May-Oct | |
| 503 | North Fork | | * | 17 | | V | | * | | * | | HFM | $$ | May-Oct | * |
| 504 | Mumford Bar | | * | | | V | | | | * | | HR | None | May-Oct | |
| 505 | Robinson Flat | | | | | V | | * | | * | | H | None | May-Oct | |
| 506 | Talbot | | | | | V | | | | * | | FHR | None | Jun-Oct | |
| 507 | Ahart (French Meadows Reservoir) | | * | 23 | | V | | | | * | | HSF | $$ | May-Nov | * |
| 508 | Lewis (French Meadows Reservoir) | | * | 23 | | V | | | | * | * | HFSB | $$ | Jun-Oct | * |
| 509 | French Meadows (French Meadows Reservoir) | * | * | 23 | | F | | * | | * | * | HFSB | $$ | Jun-Oct | * |
| 510 | Meadow Lake | | | | | V | | | | * | | HFSBO | $ | Jun-Oct | |
| 511 | Sagehen Creek | | * | 17 | | V | | | | * | | HROM | None | May-Oct | |
| 512 | Lakeside (Prosser Reservoir) | | * | 40 | | V | | * | | * | | FBSMO | $$ | May-Oct | * |
| 513 | Prosser Family (Prosser Reservoir) | | * | 41 | | V | | * | | * | | FBSMR | $$ | May-Oct | * |
| 514 | Boca (Boca Reservoir) | | * | 27 | | V | | | | * | | FBSHMOL | $$ | May-Oct | * |
| 515 | Boca Rest (Boca Reservoir) | | * | 40 | | V | | * | | * | | FBSHM | $$ | May-Oct | * |
| 516 | Boca Spring (Boca Reservoir) | | * | 19 | | V | | * | | * | | HRMO | $$ | May-Oct | * |
| 517 | Boyington Mill | | * | 32 | | V | | | | * | | FOM | $$ | May-Oct | * |
| 518 | Martis Creek Lake | | * | 30 | | V | | * | | * | * | FB | $$ | May-Oct | |
| 519 | Donner Memorial State Park | | * | 28 | | F | * | * | | * | * | HFSB | $$$ | Memorial Day-Sept | * |
| 520 | Granite Flat | | * | | | V | | * | | * | * | HFBS | $$ | May-Oct | * |
| 521 | Goose Meadow | | * | 31 | | V | | * | | * | * | HFBS | $$ | May-Oct | * |
| 522 | Silver Creek | | * | | | V | | * | | * | * | HFB | $$ | May-Oct | * |

| | Name | Group Sites | RV Sites | Max. RV Length | Hookups | Toilets | Showers | Drinking Water | Dump Station | Pets | Wheelchair | Recreation | Fee(s) | Season | Can Reserve |
|---|---|---|---|---|---|---|---|---|---|---|---|---|---|---|---|
| | **LAKE TAHOE** | | | | | | | | | | | | | | |
| 523 | Tahoe State Recreation Area | | * | 30 | | F | * | * | | * | | SFH | $$$ | May-Sept | * |
| 524 | Lake Forest | | * | 25 | | F | | * | | * | * | SFBL | $$ | Apr-Oct | |
| 525 | William Kent | | * | 24 | | F | | * | | * | * | SF | $$ | May-Oct | * |
| 526 | Kaspian | | * | | | F | | * | | * | * | SHFM | $$ | May-Oct | * |
| 527 | General Creek (Ed Z'berg Sugar Pine Point State Park) | * | * | 32 | | F | * | * | * | * | * | SFH | $$$ | Year-round | * |
| 528 | Meeks Bay | | * | 20 | | F | | * | | * | | SBF | $$ | May-Oct | * |
| 529 | D. L. Bliss State Park | | * | 18 | | F | * | * | | * | | HSFB | $$$-$$$$ | June-Oct | * |
| 530 | Bayview | | * | 20 | | V | | | | * | * | HR | $ | June-Oct | |
| 531 | Eagle Point (Emerald Bay State Park) | | * | 21 | | F | * | * | | * | | SFHB | $$$ | June-Sept | * |
| 532 | Camp Richardson Resort | * | * | | | F | * | * | * | * | * | SHFBRL | $$ | Apr-Oct | * |
| 533 | Nevada Beach | * | * | 40 | | F | | * | | * | | SFB | $$$ | May-Oct | * |
| 534 | Campground by the Lake | | * | | E | F | * | * | * | * | * | SF | $$$$ | Apr-Oct | * |
| 535 | Fallen Leaf | | * | 40 | | F | | * | | * | * | SFB | $$$ | May-Oct | * |

Toilets: F=flush V=vault P=pit C=chemical; Fee: $=Under $20 $$=$20-$29 $$$=$30-$39 $$$$ $40 or more; Recreation: H=hiking S=swimming F=fishing B=boating L=boat launch O=off-highway driving R=horseback riding, M=mountain biking Hookups: W=water E=electric S=sewer

# 491 Jackson Creek

**Location:** 39 miles northeast of Nevada City
**GPS:** 39.457177 / -120.601095
**Sites:** 14 sites for tents
**Facilities:** Tables, fire rings, vault toilets; no drinking water
**Fee per night:** None
**Management:** Tahoe National Forest, (530) 288-3231
**Activities:** Fishing, hiking, mountain biking
**Finding the campground:** From the intersection of CA 49 and CA 20 in Nevada City, drive east 22 miles on CA 20. Turn left (north) onto Bowman Road (FR 18) and drive about 17 miles to the campground. When FR 18 reaches Bowman Lake, it intersects Meadow Lake Road (CR 843). This section of the road may be difficult for conventional vehicles in wet weather.
**About the campground:** Situated on the banks of Jackson Creek, about 0.5 mile east of its confluence with Bowman Lake. A trailhead 1 mile south of the campground leads to an area of small, pretty lakes. See Grouse Ridge Campground (496). Elevation 5,600 feet. Stay limit 14 days. Open June through October.

# 492 Canyon Creek

**Location:** 41 miles northeast of Nevada City
**GPS:** 39.437595 / -120.579748
**Sites:** 16 sites for tents
**Facilities:** Tables, fire rings, vault toilets; no drinking water
**Fee per night:** None
**Management:** Tahoe National Forest, (530) 288-3231
**Activities:** Fishing, hiking, mountain biking
**Finding the campground:** From the intersection of CA 49 and CA 20 in Nevada City, drive east 22 miles on CA 20. Turn left (north) onto Bowman Road (FR 18) and drive about 17 miles to Jackson Creek Campground (491). When FR 18 reaches Bowman Lake, it intersects Meadow Lake Road (CR 843). From Jackson Creek Campground, take the road that intersects Meadow Lake Road near the entrance to the campground and drive south about 2 miles. The last 7 miles to the campground is rough gravel road that may not be suitable for large RVs or trailers.
**About the campground:** Sawmill Lake is 1 mile north of the campground; Faucherie Lake is 1 mile south. Faucherie receives a good annual stock of rainbow and brown trout fingerlings. The trailhead at the north end of Sawmill Lake leads to a series of small, attractive lakes. See Grouse Ridge Campground (496). Elevation 6,000 feet. Stay limit 14 days. Open June through October.

# 493 Bowman Lake

**Location:** 35 miles northeast of Nevada City
**GPS:** 39.460601 / -120.611254
**Sites:** 7 sites for tents
**Facilities:** Tables, fire rings, vault toilets; no drinking water
**Fee per night:** None
**Management:** Tahoe National Forest, (530) 288-3231
**Activities:** Swimming, fishing, boating, hiking, mountain biking
**Finding the campground:** From the intersection of CA 49 and CA 20 in Nevada City, drive east 22 miles on CA 20. Turn left (north) onto Bowman Road (FR 18) and drive about 13 miles. The last 3-mile stretch of the gravel road is rough and may not be suitable for large RVs.
**About the campground:** Bowman, a scenic 3-mile-long lake, is heavily stocked annually with rainbow trout fingerlings. It is also a good place to fish for brown trout. Elevation 5,670 feet. Stay limit 14 days. Open June through October.

# 494 Lindsey Lake

**Location:** 33 miles northeast of Nevada City
**GPS:** 39.412843 / -120.644360
**Sites:** 7 sites for tents
**Facilities:** Tables, fire rings, vault toilets; no drinking water
**Fee per night:** $
**Management:** PG&E, (530) 389-2236
**Activities:** Swimming, fishing, boating, hiking, mountain biking

**Finding the campground:** From the intersection of CA 49 and CA 20 in Nevada City, drive east 22 miles on CA 20. Turn left (north) onto Bowman Road (FR 18) and drive about 10 miles. Turn right (east) onto a gravel road signed "Lindsey Lake" and drive 1 mile.
**About the campground:** An 8-mile loop trail leads northeast from the campground, passing half a dozen small, pretty lakes. Elevation 5,900 feet. Stay limit 14 days. Open June through October.

## 495 Carr Lake

**Location:** 33 miles northeast of Nevada City
**GPS:** 39.402115 / -120.643082
**Sites:** 11 sites for tents
**Facilities:** Tables, fire rings, vault toilets; no drinking water
**Fee per night:** $
**Management:** PG&E, (530) 389-2236
**Activities:** Swimming, fishing, boating, hiking, mountain biking
**Finding the campground:** From the intersection of CA 49 and CA 20 in Nevada City, drive east 22 miles on CA 20. Turn left (north) onto Bowman Road (FR 18) and drive 8.5 miles. Turn right (east) onto FR 17 and drive 2.5 miles. Park and make the short hike in.
**About the campground:** Situated on the shore of a small lake, the campground provides hiking access to many small, beautiful lakes in rocky terrain nearby. Elevation 6,700 feet. Stay limit 14 days. Open June through October.

## 496 Grouse Ridge

**Location:** 33 miles northeast of Nevada City
**GPS:** 39.387459 / -120.609958
**Sites:** 9 sites for tents and RVs up to 17 feet long
**Facilities:** Tables, fire rings, vault toilets; no drinking water
**Fee per night:** None.
**Management:** Tahoe National Forest, (530) 288-3231
**Activities:** Swimming, fishing, boating, hiking, mountain biking
**Finding the campground:** From I-80, take the CA 20 cutoff and head west for approximately 5 miles. Turn right onto Bowman Lake Road (FR 18). Continue for 5 miles and turn right onto Grouse Ridge Road (FR 14). This road is unimproved dirt for 6 miles until it reaches the campground.
**About the campground:** Situated near the shore of tiny Sanford Lake, the campground serves as the trailhead for hikes to a dozen small lakes within a 3-mile radius north and west of the camp, as well as to Five Lakes Basin, 3 miles to the east. A 0.5-mile hike up to Grouse Ridge Lookout (7,707 feet) provides a fine view of the many small lakes in the area. Grouse Ridge Road is rough gravel, and its condition sometimes makes driving difficult for large vehicles. Elevation 7,400 feet. Stay limit 14 days. Open June through October.

## 497 Lake Spaulding

**Location:** 7 miles east of Emigrant Gap
**GPS:** 39.320832 / -120.635180
**Sites:** 25 sites for tents and RVs

**Facilities:** Tables, grills, drinking water, flush toilets, boat ramp
**Fee per night:** $$; reservations (for a week or more): http://recreation.pge.com
**Management:** PG&E, (530) 389-2236
**Activities:** Swimming, fishing, boating, waterskiing
**Finding the campground:** From Emigrant Gap, drive east 4.5 miles on I-80. Exit at CA 20 and drive west 1.5 miles. Turn right (north) onto Lake Spaulding Road and drive 0.5 mile.
**About the campground:** Situated in a granite bowl, Lake Spaulding's cold water provides good trout fishing for rainbows and browns as well as kokanee. A mix of trout fingerlings is stocked annually. Elevation 5,000 feet. Stay limit 14 days. Open May through October.

## 498 Indian Springs

**Location:** 8 miles east of Emigrant Gap
**GPS:** 39.329499 / -120.569301
**Sites:** 35 sites for tents and RVs up to 27 feet long
**Facilities:** Tables, fire rings, drinking water, vault toilets
**Fee per night:** $$; reservations: (800) 444-7275 or reserveamerica.com
**Management:** Tahoe National Forest, (530) 288-3231
**Activities:** Swimming, fishing, OHV driving
**Finding the campground:** From Emigrant Gap, drive east on I-80 for 7 miles. Take the Eagle Lakes exit and drive north 1 mile on Eagle Lakes Road.
**About the campground:** Situated on the banks of the South Fork of the Yuba River at one of its most scenic points, this campground offers sparkling water tumbling over large boulders and deep pools for swimming, but only fair trout fishing. An OHV trail begins about 1 mile northwest of the campground. Elevation 5,600 feet. Stay limit 14 days. Open May through October.

## 499 Sterling Lake

**Location:** 15 miles northeast of Emigrant Gap
**GPS:** 39.352960 / -120.493844
**Sites:** 8 sites for tents
**Facilities:** Tables, fire rings, vault toilets; no drinking water
**Fee per night:** $
**Management:** Tahoe National Forest, (530) 288-3231
**Activities:** Hiking, fishing, OHV driving
**Finding the campground:** From Emigrant Gap, drive east on I-80 for about 8 miles. Take the Cisco Grove exit north and turn left onto the frontage road. Drive less than 0.5 mile to Fordyce Lake Road (FR 85); turn right (northeast) onto Fordyce and drive 5 miles. Then turn left onto Sterling Lake Road and drive 2 miles. The road is steep and winding and not suitable for trailers or large RVs.
**About the campground:** Situated on the western shore of a secluded, scenic lake, with fair trout fishing. The 5-mile Mossy Pond loop trail circles a series of attractive mountain ponds north of the camp. An OHV trail just west of the campground leads from Fordyce Lake to Meadow Lake and beyond. Elevation 7,000 feet. Stay limit 14 days. Open June through October.

## 500 Woodchuck

**Location:** 11 miles northeast of Emigrant Gap
**GPS:** 39.333249 / -120.519383
**Sites:** 8 sites for tents and RVs up to 17 feet long
**Facilities:** Tables, fire rings, vault toilets; no drinking water
**Fee per night:** $
**Management:** Tahoe National Forest, (530) 288-3231
**Activities:** Fishing, OHV driving
**Finding the campground:** From Emigrant Gap, drive east on I-80 for about 8 miles. Take the Cisco Grove exit north and turn left onto the frontage road. Drive less than 0.5 mile to Fordyce Lake Road (FR 85); turn right (northeast) onto Fordyce and drive 3 miles. The road is steep and winding and not suitable for trailers or large RVs.
**About the campground:** Situated on the banks of Rattlesnake Creek. Elevation 6,300 feet. Stay limit 14 days. Open May through October.

## 501 Hampshire Rocks

**Location:** 11 miles east of Emigrant Gap
**GPS:** 39.310722 / -120.499983
**Sites:** 30 sites for tents and RVs up to 23 feet long
**Facilities:** Tables, fire rings, drinking water, vault toilets
**Fee per night:** $$; reservations: (877) 444-6777 or recreation.gov
**Management:** Tahoe National Forest, (530) 367-2224
**Activities:** Hiking, fishing
**Finding the campground:** From Emigrant Gap, drive east on I-80 for about 9 miles. Take the Big Bend exit south; turn left onto the frontage road and drive east 1.5 miles.
**About the campground:** Though close to I-80, the campground is situated on the South Fork Yuba River, which offers fair trout fishing and several swimming holes. For group camping in this area, check out Big Bend Group Campground, about 2 miles to the west. A trail begins south of Big Bend and leads to the Loch Leven Lakes (2 miles) and beyond. Elevation 5,800 feet. Stay limit 14 days. Open May through October.

## 502 Lodgepole (Lake Valley Reservoir)

**Location:** 6 miles east of Emigrant Gap
**GPS:** 39.2971239 / -120.5946537
**Sites:** 18 sites for tents and RVs up to 23 feet long
**Facilities:** Tables, grills, drinking water, vault toilets; boat ramp nearby
**Fee per night:** $$; reservations (a week or more): http://recreation.pge.com
**Management:** PG&E, (530) 386-5164
**Activities:** Swimming, fishing, boating
**Finding the campground:** From Emigrant Gap, drive east almost 4 miles on I-80. Take the Yuba Gap exit and drive south 0.25 mile. Turn right onto Lake Valley Road and drive about 2 miles, bearing right at the fork.

**About the campground:** Situated on the North Fork of the American River, just below the Lake Valley Reservoir, a scenic high-country lake. Trout fishing in the lake for rainbows is fair to good. A mix of catchable-size trout and fingerlings is stocked annually. Elevation 6,380 feet. Stay limit 14 days. Open May through October.

## 503 North Fork

**Location:** 6 miles south of Emigrant Gap
**GPS:** 39.271489 / -120.658139
**Sites:** 17 sites for tents and RVs up to 17 feet long
**Facilities:** Tables, fire rings, drinking water, vault toilets
**Fee per night:** $$; reservations: (877) 444-6777 or recreation.gov
**Management:** Tahoe National Forest, (530) 367-2224
**Activities:** Hiking, fishing, mountain biking
**Finding the campground:** From I-80, take the exit at Emigrant Gap and drive south about 0.25 mile. Turn right (west) onto Texas Hill Road (FR 19) and drive 5.5 miles.
**About the campground:** An attractive location on the banks of one of the forks of the American River. Elevation 4,400 feet. Stay limit 14 days. Open May through October.

## 504 Mumford Bar

**Location:** 17 miles northeast of Foresthill
**GPS:** 39.178278 / -120.640988
**Sites:** 4 sites for tent, RVs, or equestrians
**Facilities:** Hitching posts, vault toilet; no drinking water
**Fee per night:** None
**Management:** Tahoe National Forest, (530) 367-2224
**Activities:** Hiking, horseback riding
**Finding the campground:** From I-80 take the Foresthill Road exit in Auburn. Travel 18 miles to the town of Foresthill. Continue past Foresthill for 17 miles; Mumford Bar will be on your left-hand side.
**About the campground:** On Foresthill Divide Road. This small campground is located at the roadside, near the Mumford Bar Trailhead. Mumford Bar Trail offers hiking, mountain biking, or equestrian access to the North Fork of the American River. Elevation 5200 feet. Stay limit 14 days. Open May through October.

## 505 Robinson Flat

**Location:** 40 miles northeast of Auburn
**GPS:** 39.156320 / -120.502824
**Sites:** 7 sites for tents; an additional 7 sites for equestrians
**Facilities:** Tables, fire rings, well water, vault toilets
**Fee per night:** None
**Management:** Tahoe National Forest, (530) 367-2224
**Activities:** Hiking
**Finding the campground:** From I-80 at the north end of Auburn, take the Foresthill Road exit and drive about 40 miles northeast. The latter part of the road is gravel, narrow, and winding.

**About the campground:** The historic Western States Trail passes the campground, leading down to French Meadows Reservoir (6 miles). The historic trail crossed the Sierra Nevada and connected the Great Basin to the Central Valley. It was an important highway during the gold rush. The Little Bald Mountain Trail departs from the campground and climbs to excellent views. Elevation 6,800 feet. Stay limit 14 days. Open May through October.

## 506 Talbot

**Location:** 58 miles northeast of Auburn
**GPS:** 39.188128 / -120.373292
**Sites:** 5 sites for tents
**Facilities:** Tables, fire rings, vault toilets; no drinking water
**Fee per night:** None
**Management:** Tahoe National Forest, (530) 367-2224
**Activities:** Hiking, fishing, horseback riding
**Finding the campground:** From I-80 at the north end of Auburn, take the Foresthill Road exit and drive 15 miles to the Foresthill Work Center. Turn right onto Mosquito Ridge Road (FR 96) and drive about 33 miles to Anderson Dam. Continue around the south side of the lake for 5 miles to a fork in the road at the east end of the lake. Bear right at the fork onto FR 96 and drive 5 more miles.
**About the campground:** Situated on the banks of the Middle Fork of the American River, about 4 miles north of French Meadows Reservoir. The Western States Trail passes near the campground. The camp serves as a trailhead for hikers and equestrians and has 10 stalls for horses. Elevation 5,600 feet. Stay limit 14 days. Open June through October.

## 507 Ahart (French Meadows Reservoir)

**Location:** 55 miles northeast of Auburn
**GPS:** 39.145923 / -120.408195
**Sites:** 12 sites for tents and RVs up to 23 feet long
**Facilities:** Tables, fire rings, vault toilets; no drinking water; boat ramp 3 miles southwest
**Fee per night:** $$; reservations: (877) 444-6777 or recreation.gov
**Management:** Tahoe National Forest, (530) 367-2224
**Activities:** Hiking, fishing, swimming
**Finding the campground:** From I-80 at the north end of Auburn, take the Foresthill Road exit and drive 15 miles to the Foresthill Work Center. Turn right onto Mosquito Ridge Road (FR 96) and drive about 33 miles to Anderson Dam. Continue around the south side of the lake for 6.5 miles, bearing right at the fork at the east end of the lake.
**About the campground:** Situated on the bank of the Middle Fork of the American River near French Meadows Reservoir and in proximity to Granite Chief Wilderness. Elevation 5,300 feet. Stay limit 14 days. Open May to November.

## 508 Lewis (French Meadows Reservoir)

**Location:** 55 miles northeast of Auburn
**GPS:** 39.131975 / -120.416393
**Sites:** 40 sites for tents and RVs up to 23 feet long

**Facilities:** Tables, fire rings, drinking water, vault toilets; boat ramp 1 mile southwest
**Fee per night:** $$; reservations: (800) 444-7275 or reserveamerica.com
**Management:** Tahoe National Forest, (530) 367-2224
**Activities:** Hiking, fishing, swimming, boating
**Finding the campground:** From I-80 at the north end of Auburn, take the Foresthill Road exit and drive 15 miles to the Foresthill Work Center. Turn right onto Mosquito Ridge Road (FR 96) and drive about 33 miles to Anderson Dam. Continue around the south side of the lake for 6.5 miles, bearing left at the fork at the east end of the lake.
**About the campground:** The Western States Trail passes Lewis Campground. See French Meadows Campground (509).

## 509 French Meadows (French Meadows Reservoir)

**Location:** 52 miles northeast of Auburn
**GPS:** 39.113705 / -120.421291
**Sites:** 75 sites for tents and RVs up to 23 feet long
**Facilities:** Tables, fire rings, drinking water, flush toilets; boat ramp 0.5 mile west
**Fee per night:** $$; reservations: (800) 444-7275 or reserveamerica.com
**Management:** Tahoe National Forest, (530) 367-2224
**Activities:** Hiking, fishing, swimming, boating
**Finding the campground:** From I-80 at the north end of Auburn, take the Foresthill Road exit and drive 15 miles to the Foresthill Work Center. Turn right onto Mosquito Ridge Road (FR 96) and drive about 33 miles to Anderson Dam. Continue around the south side of the lake for 4 miles.
**About the campground:** Situated on the southeast shore of the reservoir, which is 4 miles long and 1 mile wide and which covers about 2,000 acres when full. French Meadows is one of the better trout fishing lakes in the region and is well stocked annually with rainbows. Elevation 5,300 feet. Stay limit 14 days. Open June through October. For group camping, you have the choice of 4 sites at Coyote Group Camp or 3 sites at Gates Group Camp.

## 510 Meadow Lake

**Location:** 18 miles northeast of Truckee
**GPS:** 39.408132 / -120.502684
**Sites:** 10 sites for tents and small trailers
**Facilities:** Tables, fire pits and grills, vault toilets, informal boat launch; no drinking water
**Fee per night:** $
**Management:** PG&E, (530) 994-3401
**Activities:** Hiking, fishing, swimming, boating, OHV driving
**Finding the campground:** From Truckee, travel north on CA 89 for 17 miles to FR 7. Turn left and travel west to the Meadow Lake turnoff. Turn left onto FR 86, which becomes Nevada CR 843, traveling south for approximately 10 miles. Most of the route is paved, but the last few miles are unpaved and become very rough.
**About the campground:** Access to the Fordyce Jeep Trail is nearby. There are an additional 10 campsites at the Meadow Lake Shoreline Campground. For group camping, PG&E's Meadow Knolls is right next door. Lots of lakes within a short distance make excellent day hikes. Elevation 7,315 feet. Stay limit 14 days. Open June through October.

## 511 Sagehen Creek

**Location:** 10 miles north of Truckee
**GPS:** 39.43350 / -120.255438
**Sites:** 10 sites for tents and RVs up to 17 feet long
**Facilities:** Tables, fire rings, vault toilets; no drinking water
**Fee per night:** None
**Management:** Tahoe National Forest, (530) 587-3558
**Activities:** Hiking, fishing, mountain biking, OHV driving
**Finding the campground:** From the intersection of I-80 and CA 89 in Truckee, drive north 8 miles on CA 89. Turn left (west) onto Sagehen Summit Road and drive 2 miles.
**About the campground:** Shaded by lodgepole pines and adjacent to a picturesque meadow. Elevation 6,500 feet. Stay limit 14 days. Open May through October.

## 512 Lakeside (Prosser Reservoir)

**Location:** 5 miles north of Truckee
**GPS:** 39.380638 / -120.168938
**Sites:** 30 sites for tents and RVs up to 40 feet long
**Facilities:** Tables, fire rings, drinking water, vault toilets; boat ramp about 1 mile east at Prosser Ranch Group Camp (513)
**Fee per night:** $$; reservations: (800) 444-7275 or reserveamerica.com
**Management:** Tahoe National Forest, (530) 587-3558
**Activities:** Fishing, boating, swimming, mountain biking, OHV driving
**Finding the campground:** From the intersection of I-80 and CA 89 in Truckee, drive north 4 miles on CA 89. Turn right (east) onto the campground entrance road and drive about 1 mile.
**About the campground:** Prosser is the most attractive of three large lakes just north of Truckee, and the campground is situated in a pretty cove on its northwestern shore. The lake is stocked annually with rainbow trout. There is a 5 mph speed limit for all boats operating on the lake. This campground is popular for OHVs when the lake's level drops. Elevation 5,800 feet. Stay limit 14 days. Open May through October.

## 513 Prosser Family (Prosser Reservoir)

**Location:** 5 miles north of Truckee
**GPS:** 39.377216 / -120.162032
**Sites:** 29 sites for tents and RVs up to 45 feet long
**Facilities:** Tables, fire rings, drinking water, vault toilets
**Fee per night:** $$; reservations: (800) 444-7275 or reserveamerica.com
**Management:** Tahoe National Forest, (530) 587-3558
**Activities:** Fishing, boating, swimming, mountain biking, horseback riding
**Finding the campground:** From the intersection of I-80 and CA 89 in Truckee, drive north 4 miles on CA 89. Turn right (east) onto the campground entrance road and drive about 1.2 miles.
**About the campground:** Situated on a wooded rise overlooking the lake. See Lakeside Campground (512) for a description of the lake. A boat ramp is located less than 0.5 mile east at

Prosser Ranch Group Camp, which has 1 site that will accommodate 50 people. Elevation 5,800 feet. Stay limit 14 days. Open May through October.

## 514 Boca (Boca Reservoir)

**Location:** 7 miles northeast of Truckee
**GPS:** 39.391598 / -120.106106
**Sites:** 20 sites for tents and RVs up to 27 feet long
**Facilities:** Tables, fire rings, vault toilets; no drinking water; boat ramp 0.5 mile east
**Fee per night:** $$; reservations: (800) 444-7275 or reserveamerica.com
**Management:** Tahoe National Forest, (530) 587-3558
**Activities:** Fishing, boating, swimming, waterskiing, hiking, mountain biking, OHV driving
**Finding the campground:** From the intersection of I-80 and CA 89 in Truckee, drive northeast on I-80 for 6 miles. Turn northwest (left) at the Boca-Hirschdale exit (Exit 194) onto Hirschdale. In 0.3 mile, continue on Stampede Meadows Rd. for 0.8 mile. Turn west (left) on Boca Dam Reservoir Rd and continue onto Boca Rd. about 1 mile.
**About the campground:** On a peninsula of the western shore of attractive Boca Reservoir, which is stocked annually with cutthroat trout and Kokanee fingerlings. Sites are shaded by mature Jeffrey pine and fir trees. Elevation 5,680 feet. Stay limit 14 days. Open May through October.

## 515 Boca Rest (Boca Reservoir)

**Location:** 9 miles northeast of Truckee
**GPS:** 39.419282 / -120.086332
**Sites:** 29 sites for tents and RVs up to 40 feet long
**Facilities:** Tables, fire rings, drinking water, vault toilets
**Fee per night:** $$; reservations: (800) 444-7275 or reserveamerica.com
**Management:** Tahoe National Forest, (530) 587-3558
**Activities:** Fishing, boating, swimming, waterskiing, hiking, mountain biking
**Finding the campground:** From the intersection of I-80 and CA 89 in Truckee, drive northeast on I-80 for 6 miles. Turn north at the Boca-Hirschdale exit and drive north on CR 894/270 for 3.5 miles.
**About the campground:** Located on the northeastern shore, some sites are along the waterfront. There is little shade, but good space between sites. See Boca Campground (514) for more information.

## 516 Boca Spring (Boca Reservoir)

**Location:** 10 miles northeast of Truckee
**GPS:** 39.428167 / -120.075062
**Sites:** 17 sites for tents and RVs up to 19 feet long
**Facilities:** Tables, fire rings, drinking water, vault toilets
**Fee per night:** $$; reservations: (800) 444-7275 or reserveamerica.com
**Management:** Tahoe National Forest, (530) 587-3558
**Activities:** Hiking, horseback riding, mountain biking, OHV driving

**Finding the campground:** From the intersection of I-80 and CA 89 in Truckee, drive northeast on I-80 for 6 miles. Turn north at the Boca-Hirschdale exit and drive north on CR 894/270 for 2.8 miles. Veer right onto FR 72 and proceed 1 mile to the campground.
**About the campground:** Located near a spring and lush meadow about 1 mile east of the water activities at Boca Reservoir. See Boca Campground (514) for a lake description. The campground permits horses at no additional charge. Elevation 5,950 feet. Stay limit 14 days. Open May through October.

## 517 Boyington Mill

**Location:** 11 miles northeast of Truckee
**GPS:** 39.438430 / -120.088791
**Sites:** 13 sites for tents and RVs up to 32 feet long
**Facilities:** Tables, fire rings, vault toilets; no drinking water
**Fee per night:** $$; reservations: (800) 444-7275 or reserveamerica.com
**Management:** Tahoe National Forest, (530) 587-3558
**Activities:** Fishing, OHV driving, mountain biking
**Finding the campground:** From the intersection of I-80 and CA 89 in Truckee, drive northeast on I-80 for 6 miles. Turn north at the Boca-Hirschdale exit and drive north on CR 894/270 for 4.5 miles.
**About the campground:** Located on the banks of the Little Truckee River, 2 miles north of the water activities of Boca Reservoir. There are abundant hiking, moutain biking, and off-road opportunities nearby. See Boca Campground (514) for a lake description. Fly-fishermen ply the river from trails in nearby meadows. Elevation 5,700 feet. Stay limit 14 days. Open May through October.

## 518 Martis Creek Lake

**Location:** 5 miles east of Truckee
**GPS:** 39.320014 / -120.122677
**Sites:** 25 sites for tents and RVs up to 30 feet long
**Facilities:** Tables, grills, drinking water, vault toilets
**Fee per night:** $$
**Management:** US Army Corps of Engineers, (530) 587-8113
**Activities:** Fishing, boating
**Finding the campground:** From Truckee, drive southeast 2.6 miles on CA 267. Turn left onto a dirt road; drive east and then north for 2.2 miles.
**About the campground:** The lake and campground are rather stark, especially when the water level is low. There are few big trees, and other vegetation is sparse. Fishing is catch-and-release, with only artificial lures and single barbless hooks permitted. No motorized boats are allowed on the lake. Elevation 5,800 feet. Stay limit 14 days. Open May through October.

## 519 Donner Memorial State Park

**Location:** 3 miles west of Truckee
**GPS:** 39.323616 / -120.234621
**Sites:** 152 sites for tents and RVs up to 28 feet long

**Facilities:** Tables, grills, drinking water, showers, flush toilets
**Fee per night:** $$$; reservations: (800) 444-7275 or reserveamerica.com
**Management:** Donner Memorial State Park, (530) 582-7892
**Activities:** Hiking, fishing, swimming, boating
**Finding the campground:** From I-80 at Truckee, take the CA 89 South exit (1.5 miles west of town) and drive a short distance north. Turn left (west) onto Donner Pass Road and drive 1.5 miles.
**About the campground:** Donner is a beautiful lake in a mountain setting, but its proximity to the highway detracts somewhat from its ambience. Although the lake receives an annual stocking of rainbow trout and kokanee fingerlings, fishing is only fair. The park commemorates the Donner Party, pioneers marooned near this spot by a snowstorm in 1846 and forced to resort to cannibalism before the survivors were finally rescued. The park includes a museum, two interpretive trails, and a swimming beach. A public boat ramp is located at the northwestern end of the lake. The campground is on the southeastern shore. Elevation 5,900 feet. Stay limit 15 days. Open Memorial Day through mid-September.

## 520 Granite Flat

**Location:** 3 miles southwest of Truckee
**GPS:** 39.302651 / -120.205334
**Sites:** 7 sites for tents and RVs, including walk-in sites
**Facilities:** Tables, fire rings, drinking water, vault toilets
**Fee per night:** $$; reservations: (800) 444-7275 or reserveamerica.com
**Management:** Tahoe National Forest, (530) 587-3558
**Activities:** Hiking, fishing, rafting, swimming
**Finding the campground:** From I-80 at Truckee, take the CA 89 South exit (1.5 miles west of town) and drive south on CA 89 for 1.5 miles.
**About the campground:** Situated on the bank of the Truckee River, which is a good trout stream and populated by rafters and tubers in summer. It is just 3 miles from Truckee. Elevation 5,900 feet. Stay limit 14 days. Open May through October.

## 521 Goose Meadow

**Location:** 6 miles southwest of Truckee
**GPS:** 39.258438 / -120.211462
**Sites:** 24 sites for tents and RVs up to 31 feet long
**Facilities:** Tables, fire rings, drinking water, vault toilets
**Fee per night:** $$; reservations: (800) 444-7275 or reserveamerica.com
**Management:** Tahoe National Forest, (530) 587-3558
**Activities:** Hiking, fishing, rafting, swimming
**Finding the campground:** From I-80 at Truckee, take the CA 89 South exit (1.5 miles west of town) and drive south on CA 89 for 4.5 miles.
**About the campground:** Situated on the bank of the Truckee River, a good trout stream. Elevation 6,000 feet. Stay limit 14 days. Open May through October.

# 522 Silver Creek

**Location:** 9 miles southwest of Truckee
**GPS:** 39.223235 / -120.202667
**Sites:** 27 sites for tents and RVs
**Facilities:** Tables, fire rings, drinking water, vault toilets
**Fee per night:** $$; reservations: (800) 444-7275 or reserveamerica.com
**Management:** Tahoe National Forest, (530) 587-3558
**Activities:** Hiking, fishing, rafting
**Finding the campground:** From I-80 at Truckee, take the CA 89 South exit (1.5 miles west of town) and drive south on CA 89 for 7.5 miles.
**About the campground:** Situated on the bank of the Truckee River. A paved trail starts just a few miles south of the campground at the entrance to Squaw Valley. Enjoy tubing and swimming on the river as well. The Deer Creek Trail runs from the campground northeast toward Mount Pluto (8,617 feet). Elevation 6,000 feet. Stay limit 14 days. Open May through October.

# Lake Tahoe

# 523 Tahoe State Recreation Area

**Location:** North side of Tahoe City
**GPS:** 39.175501 / -120.135694
**Sites:** 23 spaces for tents and RVs up to 30 feet long
**Facilities:** Tables, grills, fire rings, drinking water, showers, flush toilets, pier
**Fee per night:** $$$; reservations: (800) 444-7275 or reserveamerica.com
**Management:** Tahoe State Recreation Area, (530) 583-3074
**Activities:** Swimming, fishing, hiking
**Finding the campground:** Off CA 28 on the north side of town.
**About the campground:** This site is tucked into a corner of Tahoe City. Lodgepole pine, alder, and willows partially shade this campground directly on the shore of Lake Tahoe. A pier and a 100-foot-long rocky beach provide access to the lake. A 5-mile loop trail runs through adjacent Burton Creek State Park. The *Tahoe Gal* makes daily lake cruises from a pier next to the campground, and a shopping center is within walking distance. Elevation 6,300 feet. Stay limit 15 days. Open May through September.

# 524 Lake Forest

**Location:** 1 mile northeast of Tahoe City
**GPS:** 39.184374 / -120.120354
**Sites:** 20 spaces for tents and RVs up to 25 feet long
**Facilities:** Tables, grills, drinking water, flush toilets; boat ramp 0.5 mile west
**Fee per night:** $$
**Management:** Tahoe City Parks Department, (530) 583-3796
**Activities:** Swimming, fishing, boating

**Finding the campground:** From Tahoe City, drive 1.3 miles northeast on CA 28 and turn right at the sign for Lake Forest Park. Located a few blocks away from Lake Forest Beach.
**About the campground:** Elevation 6,200 feet. Stay limit 14 days. Open April through October.

## 525 William Kent

**Location:** 2 miles south of Tahoe City
**GPS:** 39.139598 / -120.154440
**Sites:** 84 sites for tents and RVs up to 24 feet long
**Facilities:** Tables, grills, drinking water, flush toilets
**Fee per night:** $$; reservations: (877) 444-6777 or recreation.gov
**Management:** California Land Management, (530) 583-3642
**Activities:** Swimming, fishing
**Finding the campground:** From the intersection of CA 28 and CA 89 in Tahoe City, drive south 2 miles on CA 89.
**About the campground:** Set in a stand of lodgepole pines, the campground is across the highway from the lakeshore, but a pebbly beach/picnic area belonging to the campground is on the lake side of the road. Elevation 6,260 feet. Stay limit 14 days. Open May through October.

## 526 Kaspian

**Location:** 4 miles south of Tahoe City
**GPS:** 39.113364 / -120.159161
**Sites:** 9 walk-in sites for tents; parking lot for RVs
**Facilities:** Tables, grills, drinking water, flush toilets
**Fee per night:** $$; reservations: (877) 444-6777 or recreation.gov
**Management:** California Land Management, (530) 544-0426
**Activities:** Swimming, hiking, fishing, biking
**Finding the campground:** From the intersection of CA 28 and CA 89 in Tahoe City, drive south 4 miles on CA 89.
**About the campground:** Directly across the highway from the lake, the campground has a small picnic area and lake access on the lake side of the highway. Great for campers wanting to bike around the lake. All campers must park in the parking lot. Tenters climb a staircase to wooded campsites, while RVs use the parking lot. Kaspian also has access to the trailhead to Barker Peak (8,166 feet), where you can get a magnificent view of Lake Tahoe. Elevation 6,300 feet. Stay limit 14 days. Open May through October.

## 527 General Creek (Ed Z'berg Sugar Pine Point State Park)

**Location:** 9 miles south of Tahoe City
**GPS:** 39.057662 / -120.122493
**Sites:** 106 sites for tents and RVs up to 32 feet long; 10 group sites
**Facilities:** Tables, grills, drinking water, showers, flush toilets, dump station
**Fee per night:** $$$; reservations: (800) 444-7275 or reserveamerica.com
**Management:** Ed Z'berg Sugar Pine Point State Park, (530) 525-7982
**Activities:** Swimming, fishing, hiking, mountain biking

**Finding the campground:** From the intersection of CA 28 and CA 89 in Tahoe City, drive south 9 miles on CA 89.

**About the campground:** This 2,000-acre park contains nearly 2 miles of shoreline. However, the campground is on the opposite side of the highway from the lake, in a tall pine forest. Its sites are well spaced, affording relative privacy. The Dolder Nature Trail makes a 2-mile loop through the lakeside forest; the General Creek Loop (for hikers and mountain bikers) makes a 5-mile circuit from the campground to Lily Pond through meadows and stands of lodgepole pine. Also of interest is the Hellman-Ehrman Mansion, a Queen Anne–style residence that was once the summer home of a frontier banker. Elevation 6,365 feet. Stay limit 15 days June through September; 30 days October through May. Open all year.

## 528 Meeks Bay

**Location:** 11 miles south of Tahoe City
**GPS:** 39.035639 / -120.124995
**Sites:** 35 sites for tents and RVs up to 20 feet long
**Facilities:** Tables, grills, drinking water, flush toilets
**Fee per night:** $$; reservations: (800) 444-7275 or reserveamerica.com
**Management:** California Land Management, (530) 544-0426
**Activities:** Swimming, boating, fishing, cycling
**Finding the campground:** From the intersection of CA 28 and CA 89 in Tahoe City, drive south 11 miles on CA 89.

**About the campground:** The campground is in a stand of pine trees immediately behind a fine, sandy beach. The sites are fairly close together, but access to a beach makes a stay here worthwhile. Elevation 6,250 feet. Stay limit 14 days. Open May through October.

## 529 D. L. Bliss State Park

**Location:** 11 miles northwest of South Lake Tahoe
**GPS:** 38.977846 / -120.102936
**Sites:** 150 sites for tents and RVs up to 18 feet long
**Facilities:** Tables, grills, drinking water, showers, flush toilets
**Fee per night:** $$$–$$$$; reservations: (800) 444-7275 or reserveamerica.com
**Management:** D. L. Bliss State Park, (530) 525-7277
**Activities:** Hiking, swimming, fishing, kayaking
**Finding the campground:** From the intersection of US 50 and CA 89 in South Lake Tahoe, take CA 89 northwest for 11 miles.

**About the campground:** This state park preserves one of the most beautiful locations on the Lake Tahoe shoreline. Its campground has been selected by *Sunset* magazine as one of the 100 best in the western United States. The camp is laid out in three separate loops. The northernmost lies just behind Lester Beach, the finest beach on the Tahoe shore, and Catawee Cove beach, a close second. A 1-mile-long loop trail leads to Balancing Rock, a favorite geological feature of the Tahoe area since the 1800s. The premier hike along the lakeshore is the 4.5-mile Rubicon Trail, which connects D. L. Bliss and Emerald Bay State Parks and ends at Vikingsholm, a replica of an ancient Norse fortress. Elevation 6,830 feet. Stay limit 14 days. Open June through October.

## 530 Bayview

**Location:** 7 miles northwest of South Lake Tahoe
**GPS:** 38.945984 / -120.098339
**Sites:** 13 sites for tents and RVs up to 20 feet long
**Facilities:** Fire rings, vault toilet; no drinking water
**Fee per night:** $
**Management:** Lake Tahoe Basin Management Unit, (530) 543-2600
**Activities:** Hiking, horseback riding
**Finding the campground:** From the intersection of US 50 and CA 89 in South Lake Tahoe, take CA 89 west for 6.5 miles to the campground entrance, on the left, near the Inspiration Point parking lot.
**About the campground:** A trail leading southwest from the campground connects with the Pacific Crest National Scenic Trail. Elevation 7,100 feet. Stay limit 2 days. Open June through October.

## 531 Eagle Point (Emerald Bay State Park)

**Location:** 6 miles west of South Lake Tahoe
**GPS:** 38.959477 / -120.080671
**Sites:** 100 sites for tents and RVs up to 21 feet long
**Facilities:** Tables, grills, drinking water, showers, flush toilets
**Fee per night:** $$$; reservations: (800) 444-7275 or reserveamerica.com
**Management:** Emerald Bay State Park, (530) 525-7273
**Activities:** Swimming, fishing, hiking, kayaking
**Finding the campground:** From the intersection of US 50 and CA 89 in South Lake Tahoe, take CA 89 west for 6 miles.
**About the campground:** The campground is laid out in two sections (Upper and Lower Eagle Point) overlooking beautiful Emerald Bay. The upper campground (sites 35–100) has some sites with great views overlooking the bay, but most are small and not level. The lower campground also has access to a trail leading to a beach on the bay and a 1.5-mile trail to Vikingsholm. Elevation 6,450 feet. Stay limit 15 days. Open June through September.

## 532 Camp Richardson Resort

**Location:** 2.5 miles west of South Lake Tahoe
**GPS:** 38.933572 / -120.038166
**Sites:** 332 sites for tents and RVs, many with full or partial hookups; group sites; cabins
**Facilities:** Tables, fire rings, drinking water, showers, flush toilets, dump station, playground, boat ramp and rental, horse rental, recreation hall, restaurant, store
**Fee per night:** $$; reservations: (800) 544-1801 or camprichardson.com
**Management:** Camp Richardson Inc., (530) 541-1801
**Activities:** Swimming, hiking, fishing, boating, waterskiing, cycling, horseback riding
**Finding the campground:** From the intersection of US 50 and CA 89 in South Lake Tahoe, take CA 89 west for 2.5 miles.
**About the campground:** Situated on both sides of the highway in a pine forest, with sites close to but not on the shoreline, Camp Richardson has all the facilities of an upscale commercial

campground, with the advantages of a woodland and lakeshore setting. The atmosphere can be more resort than nature at times though. The USDA Forest Service Lake Tahoe Visitor Center is 1 mile west of the campground on CA 89. Hiking and equestrian trails lead from the campground; a 3.2-mile bicycle path connects the camp with the visitor center and Baldwin Beach to the west and South Lake Tahoe and Poe Beach to the east. Parasailing, swimming beaches, and cruise boats are available in nearby South Lake Tahoe; gambling casinos are located a few miles past the state line in Nevada. Elevation 6,300 feet. Stay limit 14 days. Open mid-April through mid-October. No pets allowed.

## 533 Nevada Beach

**Location:** In Nevada, 6 miles northeast of South Lake Tahoe
**GPS:** 38.981873 / -119.951408
**Sites:** 49 sites for tent and RVs up to 40 feet long; 2 group sites
**Facilities:** Tables, fire rings, drinking water, flush toilets
**Fee per night:** $$$; reservations: (877) 444-6777 or recreation.gov
**Management:** California Land Management, (775) 588-5562
**Activities:** Swimming, fishing, canoeing, kayaking
**Finding the campground:** From the intersection of US 50 and CA 89 in South Lake Tahoe, take US 50 northeast for 5 miles. Turn left onto the road to Elk Point and drive 1 mile.
**About the campground:** Although in Nevada, this campground is only a short distance across the state line and is a good place to enjoy the attractions of the south shore of the lake if the California campgrounds are full. Elevation 6,200 feet. Stay limit 14 days. Open May through October.

## 534 Campground by the Lake

**Location:** In South Lake Tahoe
**GPS:** 38.943053 / -119.973529
**Sites:** 170 sites for tents and RVs; cabins
**Facilities:** Tables, grills, drinking water, showers, flush toilets, dump station, playground, swimming pool, tennis and volleyball courts, electric hookups
**Fee per night:** $$$$; reservations: (530) 542-6096 or cityofslt.us
**Management:** City of South Lake Tahoe, (530) 542-6096
**Activities:** Swimming, fishing, cycling
**Finding the campground:** From the intersection of US 50 and CA 89 in South Lake Tahoe, take US 50 northeast for 2.8 miles. Turn right onto Rufus Allen Boulevard.
**About the campground:** Although not directly on the lakeshore, the campground is just across the highway from El Dorado Beach and a boat launch. Parasailing, swimming beaches, and cruise boats are available in nearby South Lake Tahoe; gambling casinos are located a few miles past the state line in Nevada. Free shuttles to the casinos stop at the campground entrance. The Tahoe Vista Trail begins at the top of the Heavenly Valley Tram. (From the campground, drive east on US 50 for about 2 miles; turn right onto Ski Run Boulevard and follow the signs to Heavenly Valley Ski Resort.) Traversing a ridge more than 2,000 feet above the lakeshore, this self-guided trail combines natural beauty with panoramic views over the entire Tahoe Basin. Elevation 6,200 feet. Stay limit 14 days. Open April through October. ***Note:*** This campground was formerly called South Lake Tahoe El Dorado Recreation Area.

*Lake Tahoe as seen from the Flume Trail, a 14-mile challenging mountain bike trail on the Nevada side of the lake. Photo by Richard Easterling (hotspringsfinder.com)*

## 535 **Fallen Leaf**

**Location:** 4 miles west of South Lake Tahoe
**GPS:** 38.929140 / -120.048029
**Sites:** 205 sites for tents and RVs up to 40 feet long
**Facilities:** Tables, fire rings, drinking water, flush toilets
**Fee per night:** $$$; reservations: (877) 444-6777 or recreation.gov
**Management:** California Land Management, (530) 544-0426
**Activities:** Swimming, fishing, boating
**Finding the campground:** From the intersection of US 50 and CA 89 in South Lake Tahoe, drive west 3 miles on CA 89. Turn left (south) onto Fallen Leaf Road and drive 1 mile.
**About the campground:** A little more than 1 mile from the south shore of Lake Tahoe, the campground is situated on the north shore of Fallen Leaf Lake, which is 3 miles long, 1 mile wide, and 430 feet deep. The lake is stocked annually. Fishing is for rainbow, cutthroat, Mackinaw and brown trout and Kokanee salmon. A boat ramp is located at the south end of the lake, about 3 miles from camp. There is another ramp at Pope Beach (Lake Tahoe), about 2 miles to the northeast. Elevation 6,300 feet. Stay limit 14 days. Open May through October.

# Eldorado Area

The Eldorado National Forest is the main feature of this area, with its 4 rivers, 170 lakes, and 400 miles of trails for hikers, equestrians, and mountain bikers. The Carson National Scenic Byway (CA 88) winds for 58 miles across the forest, offering fine views of mountains and glacier-carved valleys. Camping, fishing, hiking, and mountain biking locations are available along or not far off the route.

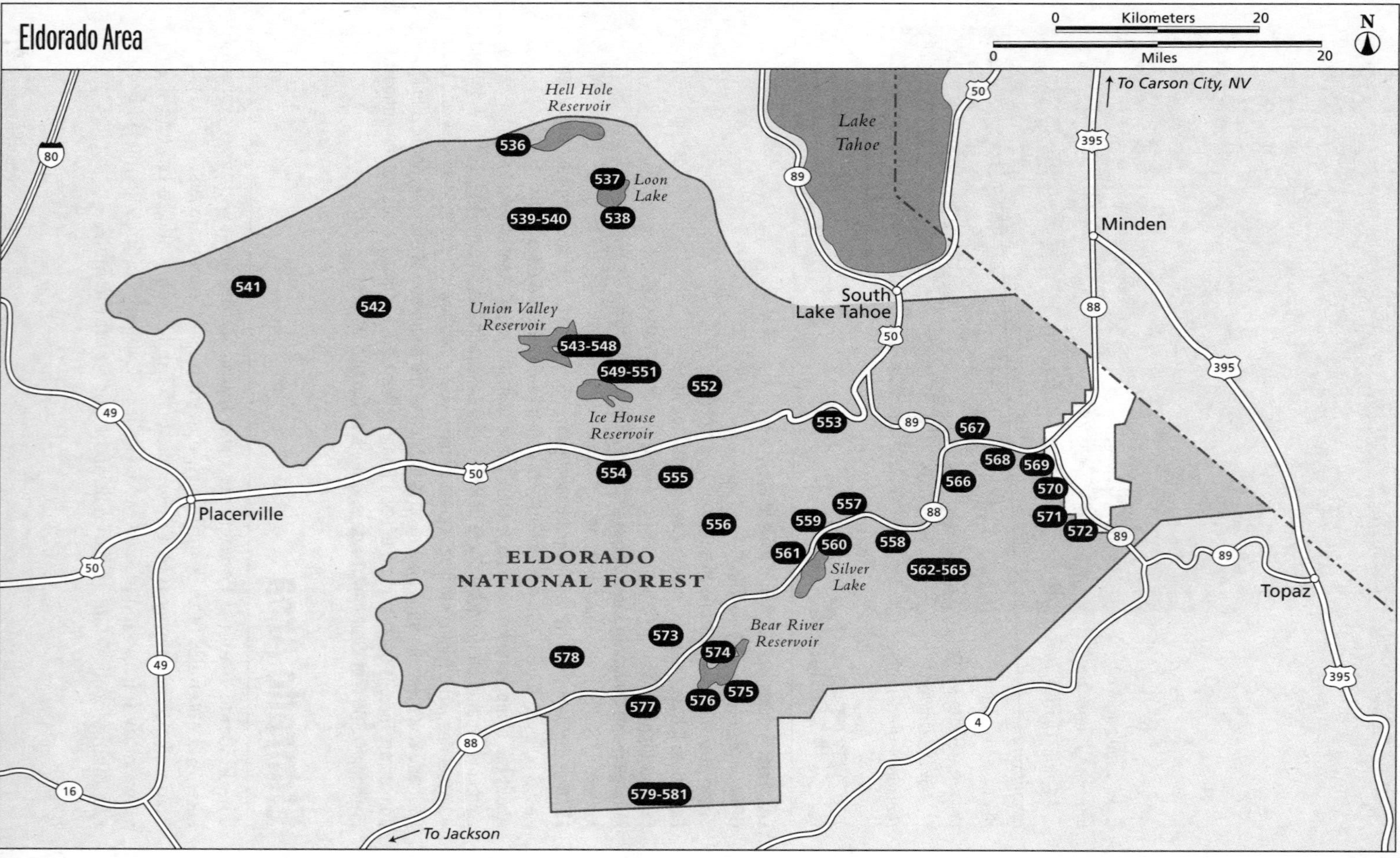
Eldorado Area
0 Kilometers 20
0 Miles 20
N
To Carson City, NV
Hell Hole Reservoir
Loon Lake
Lake Tahoe
Minden
South Lake Tahoe
Union Valley Reservoir
Ice House Reservoir
Placerville
ELDORADO NATIONAL FOREST
Silver Lake
Bear River Reservoir
Topaz
To Jackson
536
537
538
539-540
541
542
543-548
549-551
552
553
554
555
556
557
558
559
560
561
562-565
566
567
568
569
570
571
572
573
574
575
576
577
578
579-581
80
50
89
395
88
49
16
4

| | Name | Group Sites | RV Sites | Max. RV Length | Hookups | Toilets | Showers | Drinking Water | Dump Station | Pets | Wheelchair | Recreation | Fee(s) | Season | Can Reserve |
|---|---|---|---|---|---|---|---|---|---|---|---|---|---|---|---|
| | **ELDORADO AREA** | | | | | | | | | | | | | | |
| 536 | Big Meadows | | * | 27 | | FV | | * | | * | * | HFBL | $-$$ | May–Nov | |
| 537 | Northshore (Loon Lake) | | * | | | V | | | | * | * | HFSB | $ | May–Nov | |
| 538 | Loon Lake | | * | | | V | | * | | * | * | HFSBL | $$-$$$$ | June–Sept | * |
| 539 | Gerle Creek Reservoir | | * | 23 | | V | | * | | * | * | HFSB | $$-$$$$ | June–Oct | * |
| 540 | Airport Flat | | * | 23 | | V | | | | * | * | FH | None | June–Oct | |
| 541 | Dru Barner Equestrian Camp | | * | 23 | | V | | * | | * | | HR | $ | Year-round | |
| 542 | Stumpy Meadows | * | * | | | V | | * | | * | * | HFBL | $$-$$$$ | May–Oct | * |
| 543 | Jones Fork, (Union Valley Reservoir) | | * | 27 | | V | | | | * | | SFBL | $ | May–Oct | * |
| 544 | Fashoda (Union Valley Reservoir) | | | | | V | * | * | * | * | * | SFB | $$ | May–Oct | * |
| 545 | Sunset (Union Valley Reservoir) | | * | | | V | | * | * | * | * | SFBLM | $$-$$$$ | May–Oct | * |
| 546 | Wench Creek (Union Valley Reservoir) | | * | | | FV | | * | | * | | SFB | $$-$$$$ | May–Oct | * |
| 547 | Yellowjacket (Union Valley Reservoir) | | * | 23 | | FV | | * | | * | | SFBL | $$ | May–Oct | * |
| 548 | Wolf Creek (Union Valley Reservoir) | | * | | | V | | * | | * | * | SFB | $$-$$$$ | May–Oct | * |
| 549 | Ice House (Ice House Reservoir) | | * | 25 | | V | | * | | * | * | SFB | $$-$$$ | June–Oct | * |
| 550 | Northwind (Ice House Reservoir) | | * | | | V | | | | * | * | SFBM | $ | May–Oct | |
| 551 | Strawberry Point (Ice House Reservoir) | | * | | | V | | | | * | * | SFB | $ | May–Oct | |
| 552 | Wrights Lake | | * | | | V | | * | | * | * | SFBHR | $$-$$$ | June–Oct | * |
| 553 | Lovers Leap | | | | | V | | * | | * | | HFO | $ | May–Oct | |
| 554 | Sand Flat | | * | | | V | | * | | * | * | FS | $$-$$$$ | Apr–Nov | |
| 555 | China Flat | | * | | | V | | * | | * | * | FSH | $$-$$$$ | Apr–Oct | |
| 556 | Silver Fork | | * | | | V | | * | | * | * | FSHO | $$-$$$$ | May–Oct | |
| 557 | Caples Lake | | * | | | V | | * | | * | | HFSBOL | $$-$$$$ | June–Oct | |
| 558 | Woods Lake | | * | | | V | | * | | * | * | HFSB | $$-$$$$ | June–Oct | |
| 559 | Kirkwood Lake | | | | | V | | * | | * | | HFB | $$-$$$$ | June–Oct | |
| 560 | Silver Lake East | | * | | | V | | * | | * | | HFSBL | $$-$$$ | June–Oct | * |
| 561 | Silver Lake West | | * | 24 | | V | | * | | * | | HFSBL | $$ | May–Oct | |
| 562 | Lower Blue Lake (Blue Lake) | | * | | | V | | * | | * | | HSFBL | $$ | June–Oct | |
| 563 | Middle Creek and Middle Creek Expansion (Blue Lake) | | * | 45 | | V | | * | | * | | HSFBL | $$ | June–Oct | |

| # | Name | Group Sites | RV Sites | Max. RV Length | Hookups | Toilets | Showers | Drinking Water | Dump Station | Pets | Wheelchair | Recreation | Fee(s) | Season | Can Reserve |
|---|---|---|---|---|---|---|---|---|---|---|---|---|---|---|---|
| 564 | Upper Blue Lake Dam (Blue Lake) | | * | | | V | | * | | * | | HSFBL | $$ | Jun-Oct | |
| 565 | Upper Blue Lake (Blue Lake) | | * | | | V | | * | | * | | HSFBL | $$ | Jun-Oct | |
| 566 | Hope Valley | | * | | | V | | * | | * | * | FH | $$-$$$$ | May-Sept | * |
| 567 | Kit Carson | | * | 23 | | V | | * | | * | | F | $ | May-Sept | |
| 568 | Snowshoe Springs | | | | | V | | | | * | | F | $ | May-Sept | |
| 569 | Crystal Springs | | * | 23 | | V | | * | | * | | F | $ | May-Sept | |
| 570 | Turtle Rock | | * | | | V | | * | | * | * | | $ | May-Oct | |
| 571 | Grover Hot Springs State Park | | * | 27 | | F | * | * | | * | * | HFS | $$$ | Year-round | * |
| 572 | Markleeville | | * | 23 | | V | | * | | * | | F | $ | Apr-Sept | |
| 573 | Middle Fork Cosumnes River | | | | | V | | | | * | | FSH | $ | June-Oct | |
| 574 | Sugar Pine Point (Bear River Reservoir) | | * | 25 | | V | | | | * | | FSBO | $$-$$$$ | June-Nov | |
| 575 | Pardoes Point (Bear River Reservoir) | | * | | | V | | | | * | | FSBO | $$-$$$$ | June-Nov | |
| 576 | South Shore (Bear River Reservoir) | | * | 25 | | V | | * | | * | | FSBO | $$-$$$$ | June-Nov | |
| 577 | Lumberyard | | * | | | V | | | | * | | | None | June-Oct | |
| 578 | PiPi | | * | | | V | | * | | * | * | SFH | $$-$$$$ | Apr-Nov | * |
| 579 | Mokelumne River | | * | 45 | | V | | | | * | | FS | None | Year-round | |
| 580 | Moore Creek | | | | | V | | | | * | | FS | None | Year-round | |
| 581 | White Azalea | | | | | V | | | | * | | FSH | None | Year-round | |

Toilets: F=flush V=vault P=pit C=chemical; Fee: $=Under $20 $$=$20-$29 $$$=$30-$39 $$$$ $40 or more; Recreation: H=hiking S=swimming F=fishing B=boating L=boat launch O=off-highway driving R=horseback riding, M=mountain biking Hookups: W=water E=electric S=sewer

## 536 **Big Meadows**

**Location:** 57 miles northeast of Auburn
**GPS:** 39.073092 / -120.429463
**Sites:** 53 sites for tents and RVs up to 27 feet long
**Facilities:** Tables, fire rings, drinking water, flush and vault toilets; boat ramp 1.5 miles south
**Fee per night:** $, double sites: $$
**Management:** Eldorado National Forest, (530) 333-4312

**Activities:** Hiking, fishing, boating
**Finding the campground:** From I-80 at the north end of Auburn, take the Foresthill Road exit; drive 15 miles to the Foresthill Work Center. Turn right onto Mosquito Ridge Road (FR 96) and drive about 33 miles to Anderson Dam. Cross the dam, turn left (east) onto FR 22, and drive 4.5 miles. Turn right onto FR 2 and drive about 4 miles. The access road is long, winding, and narrow; not suitable for larger trailers and RVs.
**About the campground:** This is the only vehicle-accessible campground near Hell Hole Reservoir, 1.5 miles to the southeast. There are walk-in sites as well. Hell Hole is situated in a huge rock-walled gorge and has virtually no shoreline. It is a beautiful setting. Fishing can be good for rainbow trout, which are stocked annually. Elevation 5,300 feet. Stay limit 14 days. Open mid-May through mid-November.

## 537 Northshore (Loon Lake)

**Location:** 54 miles northeast of Placerville
**GPS:** 38.999588 / -120.318761
**Sites:** 15 sites for tents and RVs
**Facilities:** Tables, fire rings, vault toilets; no drinking water
**Fee per night:** $
**Management:** El Dorado National Forest, (530) 647-5415
**Activities:** Hiking, fishing, swimming, boating, sailboarding
**Finding the campground:** From the intersection of CA 49 and US 50 in Placerville, drive east on US 50 for 21 miles. Turn left (north) onto Ice House Road and drive about 30 miles. Turn left onto Loon Lake Road (FR 13N18) and drive 3 miles. Also on this side of the lake is Red Fir Group Camp (maximum 25 people and 6 vehicles).
**About the campground:** Rustic campground on the waterfront in a landscape dominated by tall pines and granite rock. Most amenities are on the other side of the lake. See Loon Lake Campground (538).

## 538 Loon Lake

**Location:** 51 miles northeast of Placerville
**GPS:** 38.979886 / -120.317020
**Sites:** 53 sites for tents and RVs; 15 sites for self-contained RVs at adjacent Loon Lake Boat Ramp
**Facilities:** Tables, fire rings, drinking water, vault toilets, boat ramp, swimming beach
**Fee per night:** $$–$$$$; reservations: (800) 444-7275 or reserveamerica.com
**Management:** American Land and Leisure, (530) 647-5415
**Activities:** Hiking, fishing, swimming, boating, sailboarding, waterskiing
**Finding the campground:** From the intersection of CA 49 and US 50 in Placerville, drive east on US 50 for 21 miles. Turn left (north) onto Ice House Road and drive about 30 miles.
**About the campground:** Situated on the south shore of the lake which is abundant in water activities and covers about 600 acres and is well stocked annually with rainbow trout. Adjacent are Look Lake Equestrian Camp and Loon Lake Group Camp. Elevation 6,475 feet. Stay limit 14 days. Open June through September.

## 539 Gerle Creek Reservoir

**Location:** 50 miles northeast of Placerville
**GPS:** 38.979483 / -120.391564
**Sites:** 50 sites for tents and RVs up to 23 feet long
**Facilities:** Tables, fire rings, drinking water, vault toilets, fishing pier
**Fee per night:** $$–$$$$; reservations: (877) 444-6777 or recreation.gov
**Management:** El Dorado National Forest, (530) 647-5415
**Activities:** Hiking, fishing, swimming, boating
**Finding the campground:** From the intersection of CA 49 and US 50 in Placerville, drive east on US 50 for 21 miles. Turn left (north) onto Ice House Road and drive about 27 miles. Turn left onto FR 33 and drive 1.5 miles; turn left onto the campground access road and drive 0.5 mile.
**About the campground:** Situated on the shore of Gerle Creek Reservoir, a small lake covering a little more than 100 acres. The lake is not stocked, but there are brown, rainbow, and brook trout for the wily angler. There is a wheelchair-accessible fishing platform. No motorized boats are allowed. Elevation 5,300 feet. Stay limit 14 days. Open June through mid-October.

## 540 Airport Flat

**Location:** 50 miles northeast of Placerville
**GPS:** 38.984977 / -120.380698
**Sites:** 16 sites for tents and RVs up to 23 feet long
**Facilities:** Tables, fire rings, vault toilets; no drinking water
**Fee per night:** None
**Management:** Eldorado National Forest, (530) 644-6048
**Activities:** Fishing, hiking
**Finding the campground:** From the intersection of CA 49 and US 50 in Placerville, drive east on US 50 for 21 miles. Turn left (north) onto Ice House Road and drive about 27 miles. Turn left onto FR 33 and drive 2 miles.
**About the campground:** Situated on Gerle Creek. The Summer Harvest Trail begins at the campground, highlighting plants gathered for food by Native Americans. Elevation 5,300 feet. Stay limit 14 days. Open June through October.

## 541 Dru Barner Equestrian Camp

**Location:** 21 miles north of Placerville
**GPS:** 38.942930 / -120.764091
**Sites:** 47 sites for tents and RVs up to 23 feet long
**Facilities:** Tables, fire rings, vault toilets, drinking water
**Fee per night:** $
**Management:** Eldorado National Forest, (530) 647-5415
**Activities:** Hiking, horseback riding
**Finding the campground:** From Placerville, drive north on CA 193 for 13 miles to Georgetown. Turn right (east) onto Wentworth Springs Road and drive 6 miles to Balderson Station. Turn left onto Bypass Road (FR 13N58) and drive 1.5 miles.

**About the campground:** Primarily for use of equestrians, but family camping is also permitted. A riding trail is near the campground. Elevation 3,250 feet. Stay limit 14 days. Open all year.

## 542 Stumpy Meadows

**Location:** 30 miles northeast of Placerville
**GPS:** 38.904649 / -120.590167
**Sites:** 40 sites for tents and RVs, including 2 double sites
**Facilities:** Tables, fire rings, drinking water, vault toilets; boat ramp nearby
**Fee per night:** $$–$$$$; reservations: (877) 444-6777 or recreation.gov
**Management:** Eldorado National Forest, (530) 647-5415
**Activities:** Hiking, fishing, boating
**Finding the campground:** From Placerville, drive north on CA Highway 193 for 13 miles to Georgetown. Turn right (east) onto Wentworth Springs Road and drive 17 miles.
**About the campground:** Situated on the shore of Stumpy Meadows Reservoir, which covers 320 acres and offers good spring trout fishing. The lake is stocked annually with rainbow and brown trout. There is a 5 mph speed limit for boats. Elevation 4,400 feet. Stay limit 14 days. Open mid-May to mid-October. Also on the reservoir is Black Oak Group Camp, with 4 sites (minimum 10 people; maximum up to 75).

## 543 Jones Fork (Union Valley Reservoir)

**Location:** 33 miles northeast of Placerville
**GPS:** 38.858332 / -120.383767
**Sites:** 10 sites for tents and RVs up to 27 feet long
**Facilities:** Tables, fire rings, vault toilets; no drinking water; dump station and boat ramp nearby
**Fee per night:** $
**Management:** Eldorado National Forest, (530) 647-5415
**Activities:** Swimming, fishing, boating
**Finding the campground:** From the intersection of CA 49 and US 50 in Placerville, drive east on US 50 for 21 miles. Turn left (north) onto Ice House Road and drive about 12 miles.
**About the campground:** Situated on the southeastern shore of Union Valley Reservoir, a 3,000-acre lake that is well stocked annually with rainbow and brook trout. Elevation 4,900 feet. Stay limit 14 days. Open May through October.

## 544 Fashoda (Union Valley Reservoir)

**Location:** 35 miles northeast of Placerville
**GPS:** 38.867862 / -120.397603
**Sites:** 30 walk-in sites for tents
**Facilities:** Tables, fire rings, drinking water, shower, vault toilets, picnic area
**Fee per night:** $$; reservations: (800) 444-7275 or reserveamerica.com
**Management:** American Land and Leisure, (530) 647-5415
**Activities:** Swimming, fishing, boating

**Finding the campground:** From the intersection of CA 49 and US 50 in Placerville, drive east on US 50 for 21 miles. Turn left (north) onto Ice House Road and drive about 12.5 miles. Turn left (west) onto FR 12N35 and drive 1.5 miles.
**About the campground:** See Jones Fork Campground (543). Fashoda has walk-in tent only sites. Cars must remain in the parking lot above the campground.

## 545 Sunset (Union Valley Reservoir)

**Location:** 35 miles northeast of Placerville
**GPS:** 38.867245 / -120.401344
**Sites:** 131 sites for tents and RVs, including 8 double sites
**Facilities:** Tables, fire rings, drinking water, vault toilets; dump station, boat ramp, and swimming beach nearby
**Fee per night:** $$–$$$$; reservations: (800) 444-7275 or reserveamerica.com
**Management:** American Land and Leisure, (530) 647-5415
**Activities:** Swimming, fishing, boating
**Finding the campground:** From the intersection of CA 49 and US 50 in Placerville, drive east on US 50 for 21 miles. Turn left (north) onto Ice House Road and drive about 12.5 miles. Turn left (west) onto FR 12N35 and drive 1.5 miles, just past Fashoda Campground.
**About the campground:** See Jones Fork Campground (543) for area information. The campground is situated on a peninsula jutting into the lake. Overflow camping is available for a small fee at the Sunset Boat Ramp.

## 546 Wench Creek (Union Valley Reservoir)

**Location:** 36 miles northeast of Placerville
**GPS:** 38.889271 / -120.370317
**Sites:** 100 sites for tents and RVs; 2 group sites for up to 50 people each
**Facilities:** Tables, fire rings, drinking water, flush and vault toilets; dump station, boat ramp, and swimming beach 2 miles away
**Fee per night:** $$, group: $$$$; reservations: (800) 444-7275 or reserveamerica.com
**Management:** American Land and Leisure, (530) 647-5415
**Activities:** Swimming, fishing, boating, mountain biking
**Finding the campground:** From the intersection of CA 49 and US 50 in Placerville, drive east on US 50 for 21 miles. Turn left (north) onto Ice House Road and drive about 15 miles.
**About the campground:** Located in a Ponderosa forest on the east shore mountain bikers can explore the Union Valley Bike Trail and hikers the Bassi Falls Trail. See Jones Fork Campground (543) for area information.

## 547 Yellowjacket (Union Valley Reservoir)

**Location:** 42 miles northeast of Placerville
**GPS:** 38.8887948 / -120.3863075
**Sites:** 40 sites for tents and RVs up to 23 feet long
**Facilities:** Tables, fire rings, drinking water, flush and vault toilets, boat ramp; dump station nearby
**Fee per night:** $$; reservations: (877) 444-6777 or recreation.gov

**Management:** American Land and Leisure, (530) 647-5415
**Activities:** Swimming, fishing, boating
**Finding the campground:** From the intersection of CA 49 and US 50 in Placerville, drive east on US 50 for 21 miles. Turn left (north) onto Ice House Road and drive about 19 miles. Turn left (west) onto FR 12N78 and drive 0.5 mile; take the left fork and drive another 1.5 miles.
**About the campground:** Surrounded by cedar and pine forest. See Jones Fork Campground (543) for area information.

## 548 Wolf Creek (Union Valley Reservoir)

**Location:** 43 miles northeast of Placerville
**GPS:** 38.885307 / -120.39948
**Sites:** 42 sites for tents and RVs, including 4 double sites
**Facilities:** Tables, fire rings, drinking water, vault toilets; boat ramp and dump station nearby
**Fee per night:** $$–$$$$; reservations: (800) 444-7275 or reserveamerica.com
**Management:** American Land and Leisure, (530) 647-5415
**Activities:** Swimming, fishing, boating
**Finding the campground:** From the intersection of CA 49 and US 50 in Placerville, drive east on US 50 for 21 miles. Turn left (north) onto Ice House Road and drive about 19 miles. Turn left (west) onto FR 12N78 and drive 1.5 miles. Located on the north shore.
**About the campground:** See Jones Fork Campground (543) for area information.

## 549 Ice House (Ice House Reservoir)

**Location:** 32 miles northeast of Placerville
**GPS:** 38.832178 / -120.358847
**Sites:** 83 sites for tents and RVs up to 25 feet long, including 6 double units
**Facilities:** Tables, fire rings, drinking water, vault toilets; dump station and boat ramp nearby
**Fee per night:** $$–$$$; reservations: (800) 444-7275 or reserveamerica.com
**Management:** American Land and Leisure, (530) 647-5415
**Activities:** Swimming, fishing, boating
**Finding the campground:** From the intersection of CA 49 and US 50 in Placerville, drive east on US 50 for 21 miles. Turn left (north) onto Ice House Road and drive 11 miles.

### CRYSTAL BASIN RECREATION AREA

About 35 miles northeast of Placerville, off US 50, the Crystal Basin Recreation Area encompasses an extensive, scenic area of lakes, forested streams, and hiking trails. The area was named for the crystalline effect of snow covering the granite ridges and outcroppings of the Sierra Nevada. Three large lakes—Ice House and Union Valley Reservoirs and Loon Lake—provide the area's major attraction, water sports. They also host most of Crystal Basin's nineteen campgrounds. Big Hill Lookout, south of Union Valley Reservoir, provides a panoramic view over the region.

**About the campground:** Ice House is the first of three major lakes of the Crystal Basin Recreation Area north of US 50. It encompasses 650 acres at high water and provides good trout fishing. A mix of brown, rainbow, and brook trout are stocked annually. Elevation 5,500 feet. Stay limit 14 days. Open June through October.

## 550 Northwind (Ice House Reservoir)

**Location:** 33 miles northeast of Placerville
**GPS:** 38.832255 / -120.351027
**Sites:** 9 sites for self-contained RVs
**Facilities:** Tables, fire rings, vault toilets; no drinking water; dump station and boat ramp 1 mile west
**Fee per night:** $
**Management:** Eldorado National Forest, (530) 647-5415
**Activities:** Swimming, fishing, boating
**Finding the campground:** From the intersection of CA 49 and US 50 in Placerville, drive east on US 50 for 21 miles. Turn left (north) onto Ice House Road and drive 11 miles. From Ice House Campground (549), take the left fork in the road and continue 1 mile east along the north shore of the lake.
**About the campground:** Situated on a rise just above the lake. See Ice House Campground (549). Elevation 5,500 feet. Stay limit 14 days. Open May through October.

## 551 Strawberry Point (Ice House Reservoir)

**Location:** 34 miles northeast of Placerville
**GPS:** 38.829041 / -120.339137
**Sites:** 10 sites for self-contained RVs
**Facilities:** Tables, fire rings, vault toilets; no drinking water; dump station and boat ramp 2 miles west
**Fee per night:** $
**Management:** Eldorado National Forest, (530) 647-5415
**Activities:** Swimming, fishing, boating, mountain biking
**Finding the campground:** From the intersection of CA 49 and US 50 in Placerville, drive east on US 50 for 21 miles. Turn left (north) onto Ice House Road and drive 11 miles. From Ice House Campground (549), take the left fork in the road and continue 2 miles east along the north shore of the lake.
**About the campground:** Ice Bike Trailhead is the entrance road for mountain bikers. See Ice House Campground (549). Elevation 5,500 feet. Stay limit 14 days. Open from May through October.

## 552 Wrights Lake

**Location:** 39 miles northeast of Placerville
**GPS:** 38.844427 / -120.236565
**Sites:** 67 sites for tents and RVs, including 3 double sites and 15 equestrian sites

**Facilities:** Tables, fire rings, drinking water, vault toilets
**Fee per night:** $$–$$$; reservations: (800) 444-7275 or reserveamerica.com
**Management:** Eldorado National Forest, (530) 644-6048
**Activities:** Swimming, fishing, boating, hiking, horseback riding
**Finding the campground:** From the intersection of CA 49 and US 50 in Placerville, drive east on US 50 for 21 miles. Turn left (north) onto Ice House Road and drive 11 miles. Take the left fork in the road and continue 5 miles east on FR 32. Turn left onto Wrights Lake Road (FR 4) and drive 2 miles.
**About the campground:** Situated on the shoreline of a scenic, alpine lake that is stocked annually with brown and rainbow trout. No motorized boats are allowed on the lake. Trails depart from the lake for lake-to-alpine lakes high in the Desolation Wilderness. Elevation 7,000 feet. Stay limit 14 days. Open June through October.

## 553 Lovers Leap

**Location:** 16 miles southwest of South Lake Tahoe
**GPS:** 38.799155 / -120.141680
**Sites:** 21 sites for tents
**Facilities:** Tables, fire rings, drinking water, vault toilets
**Fee per night:** $
**Management:** Eldorado National Forest, (530) 644-2324
**Activities:** Hiking, fishing, rock climbing, OHV driving
**Finding the campground:** From the northern intersection of CA 89 and US 50 in South Lake Tahoe, drive southwest on US 50 for 16 miles.
**About the campground:** Lovers Leap is a massive cliff famous for some of the best rock climbing in the Sierra Nevada, with multiple-pitch routes from novice level to expert. The campground is also used as an overnight starting point for backpackers hiking into the Desolation Wilderness. An OHV trail runs south from the campground. Horsetail Falls, just north of CA 50 at Twin Falls, is a spectacular cascade plunging into Pyramid Canyon. Elevation 5,800 feet. Stay limit 14 days. Open May 15 through October 31.

## 554 Sand Flat

**Location:** 28 miles east of Placerville
**GPS:** 38.763980 / -120.324402
**Sites:** 29 sites for tents and RVs, including 1 double site
**Facilities:** Tables, fire rings, drinking water, vault toilets
**Fee per night:** $$, double: $$$$
**Management:** American Land and Leisure, (530) 647-5415
**Activities:** Fishing, swimming
**Finding the campground:** From the intersection of CA 49 and US 50 in Placerville, drive east on US 50 for 28 miles.
**About the campground:** Situated in an attractive setting on the South Fork of the American River, adjacent to US 50. Trout fishing is mediocre to poor. Elevation 3,900 feet. Stay limit 14 days. Open April through November.

# 555 China Flat

**Location:** 33 miles east of Placerville
**GPS:** 38.753949 / -120.266576
**Sites:** 19 sites for tents and RVs, including 1 double site
**Facilities:** Tables, fire rings, drinking water, vault toilets
**Fee per night:** $$, double: $$$$
**Management:** American Land and Leisure, (530) 647-5415
**Activities:** Fishing, swimming, hiking, gold panning
**Finding the campground:** From the intersection of CA 49 and US 50 in Placerville, drive east on US 50 for 30 miles. Turn right (south) at Kyburz onto Silver Fork Road and drive 2.6 miles.
**About the campground:** Situated on both sides of the Silver Fork of the American River, which offers much better trout fishing than the South Fork. The Silver Fork is stocked annually with rainbow trout. The two halves of the campground are connected by a bridge. Elevation 4,800 feet. Stay limit 14 days. Open April through October.

# 556 Silver Fork

**Location:** 38 miles east of Placerville
**GPS:** 38.733581 / -120.245170
**Sites:** 35 sites for tents and RVs, including 4 double sites
**Facilities:** Tables, fire rings, drinking water, vault toilets
**Fee per night:** $$, double: $$$$
**Management:** American Land and Leisure, (530) 647-5415
**Activities:** Fishing, swimming, hiking, OHV driving
**Finding the campground:** From the intersection of CA 49 and US 50 in Placerville, drive east on US 50 for 30 miles. Turn right (south) at Kyburz onto Silver Fork Road and drive 8 miles.
**About the campground:** Situated on the Silver Fork of the American River, which offers much better trout fishing than the South Fork. The Silver Fork is stocked annually with rainbow trout. Trails for off-highway driving lead eastward from the campground. Elevation 5,600 feet. Stay limit 14 days. Open May through October.

# 557 Caples Lake

**Location:** 27 miles south of South Lake Tahoe
**GPS:** 38.704012 / -120.052809
**Sites:** 34 sites for tents and RVs
**Facilities:** Tables, fire rings, drinking water, vault toilets; boat ramp nearby
**Fee per night:** $$, doubles: $$$$
**Management:** Sierra Recreation Managers, (209) 296-8895
**Activities:** Hiking, fishing, swimming, boating, OHV driving
**Finding the campground:** From the northern intersection of CA 89 and US 50 in South Lake Tahoe, drive south and then east on CA 89 for 15 miles. Turn right (south) onto CA 88 and drive 12 miles. You will pass the entrance to the Kirkwood Ski Area 1 mile before you reach the campground.

**About the campground:** Caples is an attractive lake on CA 88. It covers about 600 acres and offers good trout fishing in late spring and early summer. Each year the lake is stocked with a heavy mix of rainbow, brown, and brook trout. There is a 10 mph speed limit for boats. An 8-mile round-trip trail leads from the campground along the southwest shore of the lake to Emigrant Lake. AN OHV trail runs north from the Kirkwood ski area. Next to the lake is Caples Resort, with cabins and a small store for snacks and bait. Elevation 7,800 feet. Stay limit 14 days. Open June through October.

## 558 Woods Lake

**Location:** 26 miles south of South Lake Tahoe
**GPS:** 38.688050 / -120.009258
**Sites:** 25 sites for tents, including 2 double sites
**Facilities:** Tables, fire rings, drinking water (hand-pumped), vault toilets
**Fee per night:** $$, doubles: $$$$
**Management:** Sierra Recreation Managers, (209) 296-8895
**Activities:** Hiking, fishing, swimming, boating
**Finding the campground:** From the northern intersection of CA 89 and US 50 in South Lake Tahoe, drive south and then east on CA 89 for 15 miles. Turn right (south) onto CA 88 and drive 10 miles. Turn left (south) at Woods Lake turnoff and drive 1 mile.
**About the campground:** A small, scenic lake in a secluded location, Woods is stocked annually with rainbow trout. No motors are permitted on the lake. A spectacular 3.5-mile loop trail to Round Top and Winnemucca Lakes begins at the campground. Elevation 8,200 feet. Stay limit 14 days. Open July through October.

## 559 Kirkwood Lake

**Location:** 30 miles south of South Lake Tahoe
**GPS:** 38.706682 / -120.087538
**Sites:** 12 sites for tents
**Facilities:** Tables, fire rings, drinking water, vault toilets
**Fee per night:** $$, doubles: $$$$
**Management:** Sierra Recreation Managers, (209) 296-8895
**Activities:** Hiking, fishing, boating
**Finding the campground:** From the northern intersection of CA 89 and U.S 50 in South Lake Tahoe, drive south and then east on CA 89 for 15 miles. Turn right (south) onto CA 88 and drive 15 miles.
**About the campground:** A small lake in a beautiful setting, Kirkwood yields only small trout. No motors are allowed on the lake. Elevation 7,600 feet. Stay limit 14 days. Open June through October.

## 560 Silver Lake East

**Location:** 34 miles south of South Lake Tahoe
**GPS:** 38.672226 / -120.120325
**Sites:** 62 sites for tents and RVs

*Thunder Mountain captures the colors of the sunset over beautiful Silver Lake.*

**Facilities:** Tables, fire rings, drinking water, vault toilets; boat ramp and rentals and store nearby
**Fee per night:** $$, doubles: $$$$; reservations: (877) 444-6777 or recreation.gov
**Management:** Sierra Recreation Managers, (209) 295-4251
**Activities:** Hiking, fishing, swimming, boating, waterskiing
**Finding the campground:** From the northern intersection of CA 89 and US 50 in South Lake Tahoe, drive south and then east on CA 89 for 15 miles. Turn right (south) onto CA 88 and drive 19 miles.
**About the campground:** Two miles long and 1 mile wide at its widest point, Silver Lake enjoys a classic Sierra setting at the base of a granite cirque. It offers good fishing, with an annual stock of rainbow, brook, and brown trout. Unlike on smaller lakes in the area, waterskiing is permitted. The campground is on the northeast side, with a short walk to the lake. Day hikes to wildflowers, other lakes, and plateaus are abundant in the area. Elevation 7,300 feet. Stay limit 14 days. Open June through October.

## 561 Silver Lake West

**Location:** 34 miles south of South Lake Tahoe
**GPS:** 38.671923 / -120.121000
**Sites:** 42 sites for tents and RVs up to 24 feet long
**Facilities:** Tables, fire rings, drinking water, vault toilets; boat ramp and rentals nearby
**Fee per night:** $$
**Management:** El Dorado Irrigation District, (530) 295-6824
**Activities:** Hiking, fishing, swimming, boating
**Finding the campground:** From the northern intersection of CA 89 and US 50 in South Lake Tahoe, drive south and then east on CA 89 for 15 miles. Turn right (south) onto CA 88 and drive 19 miles.
**About the campground:** See Silver Lake East Campground (560) for lake and area information. The campground is across the highway from the lake and Silver Lake East Campground. It features a short hike to the Pot Holes, a series of swimming holes carved into the granite by the Silver Fork of the American River. Elevation 7,300 feet. Stay limit 14 days. Open mid-May to mid-October.

# 562 Lower Blue Lakes (Blue Lakes)

**Location:** 30 miles south of South Lake Tahoe
**GPS:** 38.610475 / -119.925044
**Sites:** 17 sites for tents and RVs
**Facilities:** Tables, fire rings and grills, drinking water, vault toilets, boat ramp
**Fee per night:** $$
**Management:** PG&E, (530) 314-8278
**Activities:** Hiking, swimming, fishing, boating
**Finding the campground:** From the northern intersection of CA 89 and US 50 in South Lake Tahoe, drive south and then east on CA 89 for 15 miles. Turn right (south) onto CA 88 and drive 2.5 miles. Turn left (south) onto Blue Lakes Road and drive 12 miles.
**About the campground:** Situated on the south shore of the lake, which has good fishing for trout. Catchable-size rainbow and fingerling brook trout are stocked annually. Elevation 8,100 feet. Stay limit 14 days. Open June through October.

# 563 Middle Creek and Middle Creek Expansion (Blue Lakes)

**Location:** 31 miles south of South Lake Tahoe
**GPS:** 38.626949 / -119.936688
**Sites:** 40 sites for tents and RVs up to 45 feet
**Facilities:** Tables, fire rings and grills, drinking water, vault toilets; boat ramp nearby
**Fee per night:** $$
**Management:** PG&E, (530) 314-8278
**Activities:** Hiking, swimming, fishing, boating
**Finding the campground:** From the northern intersection of CA 89 and US 50 in South Lake Tahoe, drive south and then east on CA 89 for 15 miles. Turn right (south) onto CA 88 and drive 2.5 miles. Turn left (south) onto Blue Lakes Road and drive 12 miles. From Lower Blue Lake Campground (562), drive north along the lake 1.5 miles.
**About the campground:** The majority of sites are in the newer Middle Creek Expansion area across the road from the original Middle Creek campground, offering shaded, roomy sites. See Lower Blue Lake Campground (562) for lake and area information. Elevation 8,100 feet. Stay limit 14 days. Open June through October.

# 564 Upper Blue Lakes Dam (Blue Lakes)

**Location:** 32 miles south of South Lake Tahoe
**GPS:** 38.62986 / -119.939028
**Sites:** 10 sites for tents and RVs
**Facilities:** Tables, fire rings and grills, drinking water, vault toilets; boat ramp nearby
**Fee per night:** $$
**Management:** PG&E, (530) 314-8278
**Activities:** Hiking, swimming, fishing, boating
**Finding the campground:** From the northern intersection of CA 89 and US 50 in South Lake Tahoe, drive south and then east on CA 89 for 15 miles. Turn right (south) onto CA 88 and drive

2.5 miles. Turn left (south) onto Blue Lakes Road and drive 12 miles. From Lower Blue Lake Campground (562), drive north along the lake 2 miles.
**About the campground:** See Lower Blue Lake Campground (562) for lake and area information. Elevation 8,200 feet. Open June through October.

## 565 Upper Blue Lakes (Blue Lakes)

**Location:** 33 miles south of South Lake Tahoe
**GPS:** 38.640799 / -119.954891
**Sites:** 32 sites for tents and RVs
**Facilities:** Tables, fire rings and grills, drinking water, vault toilets; boat ramp nearby
**Fee per night:** $$
**Management:** Pacific Gas and Electric, (530) 314-8278
**Activities:** Hiking, swimming, fishing, boating
**Finding the campground:** From the northern intersection of CA 89 and US 50 in South Lake Tahoe, drive south and then east on CA 89 for 15 miles. Turn right (south) onto CA 88 and drive 2.5 miles. Turn left (south) onto Blue Lakes Road and drive 12 miles. From Lower Blue Lake Campground (562), drive north along the lake 3 miles.
**About the campground:** See Lower Blue Lake Campground (562) for lake and area information. Elevation 8,200 feet. Stay limit 14 days. Open June through October.

## 566 Hope Valley

**Location:** 19 miles southeast of South Lake Tahoe
**GPS:** 38.730959 / -119.930430
**Sites:** 28 sites for tents and RVs
**Facilities:** Tables, fire rings, drinking water, vault toilets
**Fee per night:** $$, doubles: $$$$; reservations: (800) 444-7275 or reserveamerica.com
**Management:** Westrek Services, (530) 694-1002
**Activities:** Fishing, hiking, biking
**Finding the campground:** From the northern intersection of CA 89 and US 50 in South Lake Tahoe, drive south and then east on CA 89 for 15 miles. Turn right onto CA 88 and drive 2.6 miles. Turn left (south) onto Blue Lakes Road and drive 1.5 miles.
**About the campground:** Situated on the bank of the West Fork of the Carson River, at the southern end of a large meadow. The river is well stocked annually with rainbow trout. Fishing is best in late spring and early summer. Elevation 7,300 feet. Stay limit 14 days. Open May through September.

## 567 Kit Carson

**Location:** 16 miles southeast of South Lake Tahoe
**GPS:** 38.776751 / -119.894898
**Sites:** 12 sites for tents and RVs up to 23 feet long
**Facilities:** Tables, fire rings, drinking water, vault toilets
**Fee per night:** $
**Management:** Westrek Services, (530) 694-1002
**Activities:** Fishing

**Finding the campground:** From the northern intersection of CA 89 and US 50 in South Lake Tahoe, drive south and then east on CA 89 for 15 miles. Turn left onto CA 88/89 and drive 1.2 miles.
**About the campground:** Situated on the bank of the West Fork of the Carson River, which is well stocked annually with rainbow trout. Fishing is best in late spring and early summer. Elevation 6,900 feet. Stay limit 14 days. Open May through September.

## 568 Snowshoe Springs

**Location:** 17 miles southeast of South Lake Tahoe
**GPS:** 38.775759 / -119.893998
**Sites:** 13 sites for tents
**Facilities:** Tables, fire rings, vault toilets; no drinking water
**Fee per night:** $
**Management:** Toiyabe National Forest, (702) 882-2766
**Activities:** Fishing
**Finding the campground:** From the northern intersection of CA 89 and US 50 in South Lake Tahoe, drive south and then east on CA 89 for 15 miles. Turn left onto CA 88/89 and drive 1.5 miles.
**About the campground:** Dispersed, primitive camping. For area information, see Kit Carson Campground (567). Elevation 6,600 feet. Stay limit 14 days. Open May through September.

## 569 Crystal Springs

**Location:** 20 miles southeast of South Lake Tahoe
**GPS:** 38.7633885 / -119.8525408
**Sites:** 19 sites for tents and RVs up to 23 feet long
**Facilities:** Tables, fire rings, drinking water, vault toilets
**Fee per night:** $
**Management:** Toiyabe National Forest, (702) 882-2766
**Activities:** Fishing
**Finding the campground:** From the northern intersection of CA 89 and US 50 in South Lake Tahoe, drive south and then east on CA 89 for 15 miles. Turn left onto CA 88/89 and drive 5 miles.
**About the campground:** A small campground in wooded setting. See Kit Carson Campground (567). Elevation 6,000 feet. Stay limit 14 days. Open May through September.

## 570 Turtle Rock

**Location:** 25 miles southeast of South Lake Tahoe
**GPS:** 38.721941 / -119.802028
**Sites:** 38 sites for tents and RVs
**Facilities:** Tables, grills, drinking water, vault toilets
**Fee per night:** $
**Management:** Alpine County Community Development, (530) 694-2140
**Activities:** None
**Finding the campground:** From the northern intersection of CA 89 and US 50 in South Lake Tahoe, drive southeast on CA 89 for 25 miles.

**About the campground:** A wooded campground close to CA 89, best used as an overnight stop or if the campground at Grover Hot Springs (571) is full. There are trails through an adjacent county park (6 miles south; see below). Elevation 5,500 feet. No stay limit. Open May through October.

## 571 Grover Hot Springs State Park

**Location:** 32 miles southeast of South Lake Tahoe
**GPS:** 38.698851 / -119.837195
**Sites:** 76 sites for tents and RVs up to 27 feet
**Facilities:** Tables, fire grills, drinking water, showers, flush toilets, mineral spring pools
**Fee per night:** $$$; reservations: (800) 444-7275 or reserveamerica.com
**Management:** Grover Hot Springs State Park, (530) 694-2248
**Activities:** Hiking, fishing, swimming
**Finding the campground:** From the northern intersection of CA 89 and US 50 in South Lake Tahoe, drive south on CA 89 for 28 miles to Markleeville. Turn right (west) onto Hot Springs Road and drive 3.5 miles.
**About the campground:** This camp features sites well spaced in a tall pine forest. The hot springs—one hot pool and one cold—are 0.3 mile by trail or 0.5 mile by road from the campground. The hot pool is fed by the runoff from six mineral springs; it surfaces at 148°F, but cold water is added to bring it down to 104°F. The mountain setting is impressive, and the pools are open all year, closing only for cleaning and for the Thanksgiving, Christmas, and New Year holidays. The campground is open May to September, but camping is permitted in winter in the day-use area adjacent to the park entrance. A trout creek runs through the park and hiking trails set out. Elevation 6,000 feet. Stay limit 15 days. Open all year.

## 572 Markleeville

**Location:** 28 miles southeast of South Lake Tahoe
**GPS:** 38.697564 / -119.773437
**Sites:** 10 sites for tents and RVs up to 23 feet long
**Facilities:** Tables, fire rings, drinking water, vault toilets
**Fee per night:** $
**Management:** Toiyabe National Forest, (702) 882-2766
**Activities:** Fishing
**Finding the campground:** From the northern intersection of CA 89 and US 50 in South Lake Tahoe, drive south on CA 89 for 28 miles.
**About the campground:** Situated on the banks of Markleeville Creek, which provides fishing for small trout. This campground provides an option if the campground at Grover Hot Springs (571; 3.5 miles west) is full. Elevation 5,500 feet. Stay limit 14 days. Open April through September.

## 573 Middle Fork Cosumnes River

**Location:** 42 miles northeast of Jackson
**GPS:** 38.584286 / -120.300105
**Sites:** 19 sites for tents
**Facilities:** Tables, fire rings, vault toilet; no drinking water

**Fee per night:** $
**Management:** Eldorado National Forest, (209) 295-4251
**Activities:** Fishing, swimming, hiking
**Finding the campground:** From the intersection of CA 49 and CA 88 in Jackson, take CA 88 northeast for 38 miles. Turn left (north) onto FR 8N23 and drive 3.5 miles.
**About the campground:** Situated on the bank of the river, with a swimming hole nearby. Fishing is fair for small native trout. Elevation 6,800 feet. Stay limit 14 days. Open June through October.

## 574 Sugar Pine Point (Bear River Reservoir)

**Location:** 46 miles northeast of Jackson
**GPS:** 38.547483 / -120.240434
**Sites:** 8 sites for tents, plus 2 sites for RVs up to 25 feet long
**Facilities:** Tables, fire rings, vault toilet; no drinking water
**Fee per night:** $$–$$$$
**Management:** Sierra Recreation Managers, (209) 296-8895
**Activities:** Fishing, swimming, boating, waterskiing, OHV driving
**Finding the campground:** From the intersection of CA 49 and CA 88 in Jackson, take CA 88 northeast for 40 miles. Turn right (south) onto Bear River Reservoir Road and drive 2.5 miles to a Y intersection. Turn left onto an unpaved road and drive 3 miles.
**About the campground:** About 3 miles long and up to 0.5 mile wide, the granite-ringed reservoir covers 725 acres. Fishing can be very good, as the lake is well stocked. The campground is on the north shore of the lake. Bear River Lake Resort, a commercial campground 2 miles west of the campground (you pass it on the way here), offers a boat ramp, dump station, showers, laundry, store, restaurant, and hookup sites if the public campground is full. Elevation 6,000 feet. Stay limit 14 days. Open June through November.

## 575 Pardoes Point (Bear River Reservoir)

**Location:** 45 miles northeast of Jackson
**GPS:** 38.534804 / -120.237289
**Sites:** 10 sites for tents
**Facilities:** Tables, fire rings, vault toilets; no drinking water
**Fee per night:** $$–$$$$
**Management:** Sierra Recreation Managers, (209) 296-8895
**Activities:** Fishing, swimming, boating, waterskiing, OHV driving
**Finding the campground:** From the intersection of CA 49 and CA 88 in Jackson, take CA 88 northeast for 40 miles. Turn right (south) onto Bear River Reservoir Road and drive 5 miles.
**About the campground:** See Sugar Pine Point Campground (574). For group camping, contact the Eldorado National Forest about Bear River Group Camp.

## 576 South Shore (Bear River Reservoir)

**Location:** 44 miles northeast of Jackson
**GPS:** 38.535541 / -120.244836
**Sites:** 19 sites for tents and RVs up to 25 feet long, including 4 double sites

**Facilities:** Tables, fire rings, drinking water, vault toilets; boat ramp 2 miles northeast
**Fee per night:** $$–$$$$
**Management:** Sierra Recreation Managers, (209) 296-8895
**Activities:** Fishing, swimming, boating, waterskiing, OHV driving
**Finding the campground:** From the intersection of CA 49 and CA 88 in Jackson, take CA 88 northeast for 40 miles. Turn right (south) onto Bear River Reservoir Road and drive 4 miles.
**About the campground:** See Sugar Pine Point Campground (574) for area information. Large groups can also use the nearby Bear River Group Camp, located 1.25 miles from South Shore, bearing left after 1 mile.

## 577 Lumberyard

**Location:** 37 miles northeast of Jackson
**GPS:** 38.547554 / -120.307027
**Sites:** 5 sites for tents and RVs
**Facilities:** Tables, fire rings, vault toilet; no drinking water
**Fee per night:** None
**Management:** Eldorado National Forest, (209) 295-4251
**Activities:** None
**Finding the campground:** From the intersection of CA 49 and CA 88 in Jackson, take CA 88 northeast for 37 miles.
**About the campground:** This campground is best used as an overnight stop along the Carson Pass National Scenic Byway (CA 88). Elevation 6,517 feet. Stay limit 14 days. Open June to mid-October.

## 578 PiPi

**Location:** 34 miles northeast of Jackson
**GPS:** 38.5672343 / -120.4380146
**Sites:** 51 sites for tents and RVs, including double sites
**Facilities:** Tables, fire rings, drinking water, vault toilets, fishing piers.
**Fee per night:** $$–$$$$; reservations: (800) 444-7275 or reserveamerica.com
**Management:** Sierra Recreation Managers, (209) 296-8895
**Activities:** Swimming, fishing, hiking
**Finding the campground:** From the intersection of CA 49 and CA 88 in Jackson, take CA 88 northeast for 26 miles. Turn left (north) onto Omo Ranch Road and drive 1.5 miles. Turn right (north) onto North South Road (FR 6) and drive 6 miles.
**About the campground:** Situated on the bank of the Middle Fork of the Cosumnes River, with good swimming holes nearby. A barrier-free interpretive trail highlights Native American history and mid-1800s mining activity in the area. The fishing piers are also barrier-free. Elkins Flat, an OHV staging area about 2 miles north of PiPi, permits open camping at no cost. Except for vault toilets, there are no facilities there. Elevation 4,100 feet. Stay limit 14 days. Open mid-April to mid-November.

## 579 Mokelumne River

**Location:** 46 miles northeast of Jackson
**GPS:** 38.478636 / -120.271169
**Sites:** 13 sites for tents and RVs up to 45 feet long
**Facilities:** Tables, fire rings, vault toilet; no drinking water
**Fee per night:** None
**Management:** Eldorado National Forest, (209) 295-4251
**Activities:** Fishing, swimming
**Finding the campground:** From the intersection of CA 49 and CA 88 in Jackson, take CA 88 northeast for 37 miles. Turn right (south) onto Ellis Road (FR 92) and drive about 9 miles.
**About the campground:** Situated in the canyon of the North Fork of the Mokelumne River, which offers several nearby swimming holes and fishing for small trout. Elevation 3,200 feet. Stay limit 14 days. Open all year.

## 580 Moore Creek

**Location:** 46 miles northeast of Jackson
**GPS:** 38.4796388 / -120.2690555
**Sites:** 8 sites for tents
**Facilities:** Tables, fire rings, vault toilet; no drinking water
**Fee per night:** None
**Management:** Eldorado National Forest, (209) 295-4251
**Activities:** Fishing, swimming
**Finding the campground:** From the intersection of CA 49 and CA 88 in Jackson, take CA 88 northeast for 37 miles. Turn right (south) onto Ellis Road (FR 92) and drive about 9 miles on a steep, narrow road to the campground, just beyond Mokelumne River Campground.
**About the campground:** You can camp here to access Salt Springs Reservoir and the trailhead there into the Mokelumne Wilderness. See Mokelumne River Campground (579) for area information.

## 581 White Azalea

**Location:** 47 miles northeast of Jackson
**GPS:** 38.483441 / -120.264458
**Sites:** 6 sites for tents
**Facilities:** Vault toilet; no drinking water
**Fee per night:** None
**Management:** Eldorado National Forest, (209) 295-4251
**Activities:** Fishing, swimming, hiking
**Finding the campground:** From the intersection of CA 49 and CA 88 in Jackson, take CA 88 northeast for 37 miles. Turn right (south) onto Ellis Road (FR 92) and drive about 10 miles.
**About the campground:** See Mokelumne River Campground (579). A trailhead 3 miles east of the campground leads 4 miles along the north shore of Salt Springs Reservoir to Blue Hole and Salt Springs. Elevation 3,500 feet. Stay limit 14 days. Open all year.

# Stanislaus-Toiyabe Area

The Stanislaus National Forest and a portion of the Toiyabe National Forest make up most of this area of the High Sierra region. The Stanislaus covers almost 900,000 acres and contains 800 miles of rivers and streams, of which 29 miles of the Tuolumne and 11 miles of the Merced are designated Wild and Scenic Rivers. Nearly 500 miles of trails and 1,000 miles of abandoned roads are available for use by hikers and equestrians, while 150 miles of trails and 2,000 miles of dirt roads are open to mountain bikers. Inhabiting the forest are 325 species of wildlife and 18 species of fish.

Although Toiyabe is the largest national forest in the contiguous forty-eight states, only a small part of it, northwest of Mono Lake, lies within California; the rest is scattered around Nevada. You can drive and access wilderness in three high passes over the Sierra Nevada in this region, a rare thing: Carson, Ebbetts, and Sonora. The scenery throughout is breathtaking.

## 582 Centerville Flats

**Location:** 34 miles southeast of South Lake Tahoe
**GPS:** 38.631222 / -119.723458
**Sites:** Open camping for tents and RVs
**Facilities:** Tables, fire rings, vault toilets; no drinking water
**Fee per night:** None
**Management:** Toiyabe National Forest, (702) 882-2766
**Activities:** Fishing
**Finding the campground:** From the northern intersection of CA 89 and US 50 in South Lake Tahoe, drive south on CA 89 for 32 miles. Turn right (south) onto CA 4 and drive 2 miles.
**About the campground:** Dispersed, primitive site situated near the East Fork of the Carson River, which is well stocked annually with rainbow trout. Elevation 6,000 feet. Stay limit 16 days. Open all year. For group camping nearby, try Silver Creek group campground.

## 583 Silver Creek

**Location:** 39 miles southeast of South Lake Tahoe
**GPS:** 38.588912 / -119.786993
**Sites:** 27 sites for tents and RVs up to 45 feet long
**Facilities:** Tables, fire rings, drinking water, vault toilets
**Fee per night:** $–$$$; reservations: (877) 444-6777 or recreation.gov
**Management:** Westrek Services, (530) 694-1002
**Activities:** Fishing, hiking
**Finding the campground:** From the northern intersection of CA 89 and US 50 in South Lake Tahoe, drive southeast on CA 89 for 32 miles. Turn right (south) onto CA 4 and drive 7 miles.
**About the campground:** Silver Creek was the site of a mining boom in the 1860s. When the silver quickly ran out, the thriving community became a ghost town. Some of the buildings were moved to Markeerville. Hikes take you to some of the abandoned mines in the area. Situated near Silver

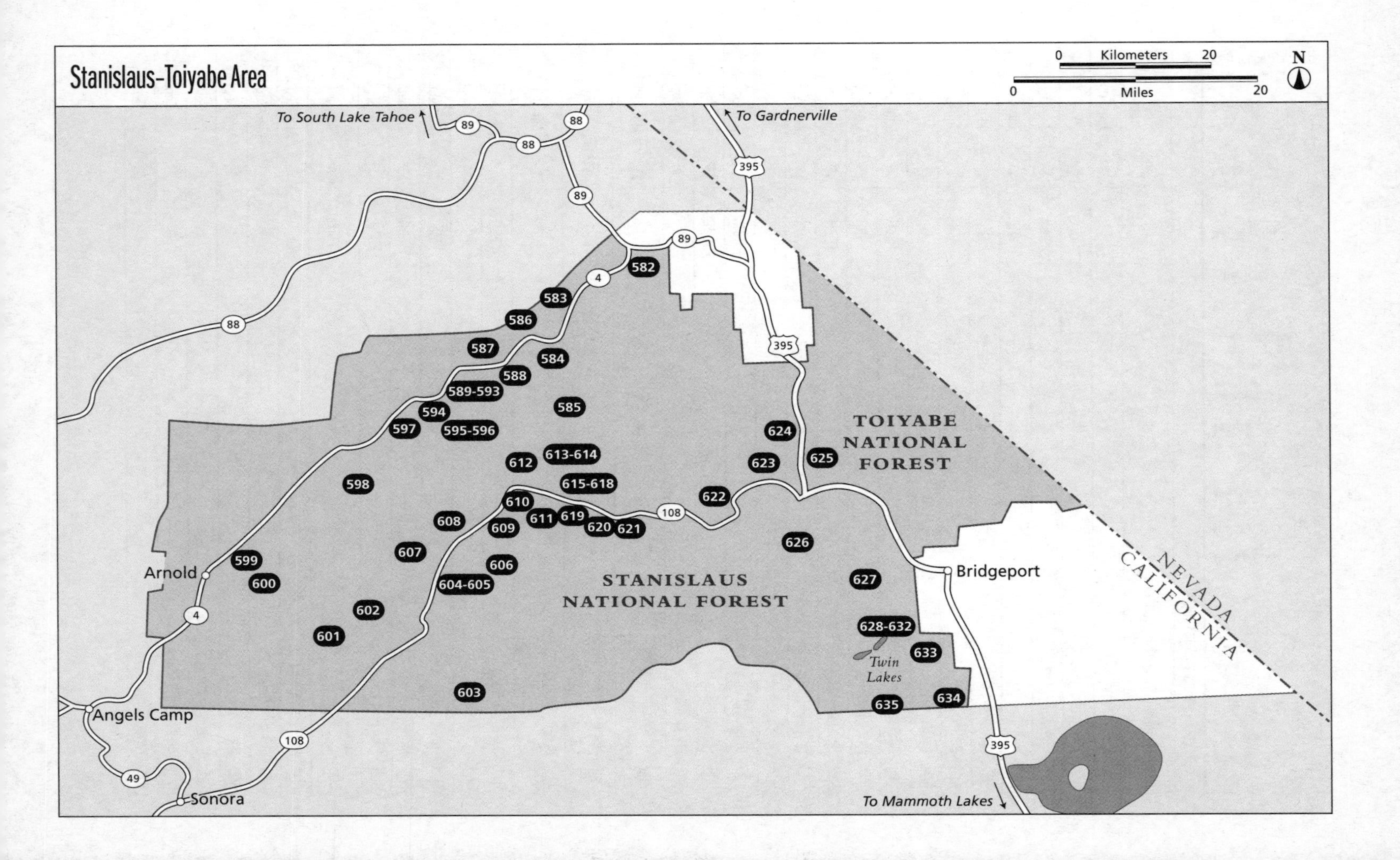
Stanislaus–Toiyabe Area
0 Kilometers 20
0 Miles 20
N
To South Lake Tahoe
To Gardnerville
89
88
88
395
89
89
582
4
583
586
88
587
584
588
589-593
585
594
597
595-596
624
TOIYABE
NATIONAL
FOREST
612
613-614
625
623
598
615-618
622
610
108
608
611
619
609
620
621
626
599
607
606
Arnold
600
604-605
STANISLAUS
NATIONAL FOREST
627
Bridgeport
NEVADA
CALIFORNIA
602
4
601
628-632
633
Twin
Lakes
603
634
635
Angels Camp
108
395
49
Sonora
To Mammoth Lakes

| | Name | Group Sites | RV Sites | Max. RV Length | Hookups | Toilets | Showers | Drinking Water | Dump Station | Pets | Wheelchair | Recreation | Fee(s) | Season | Can Reserve |
|---|---|---|---|---|---|---|---|---|---|---|---|---|---|---|---|
| | **STANISLAUS-TOIYABE AREA** | | | | | | | | | | | | | | |
| 582 | Centerville Flats | * | * | | | V | | | | * | | F | None | Year-round | |
| 583 | Silver Creek | | * | | | V | | * | | * | | F | $-$$ | Jun-Sep | * |
| 584 | Bloomfield | | * | | | V | | * | | * | | F | $ | Jun-Oct | |
| 585 | Highland Lakes | | * | | | V | | * | | * | | FSBHL | $ | Jun-Oct | |
| 586 | Hermit Valley | | * | | | V | | * | | * | | FH | None | Jun-Oct | |
| 587 | Mosquito Lakes | | * | | | V | | | | * | | FH | $ | Jun-Oct | |
| 588 | Pacific Valley | | * | | | V | | * | | * | | FH | $ | Jun-Oct | |
| 589 | Lake Alpine | | * | | | FV | * | * | | * | * | FSBHL | $$ | Jun-Sept | |
| 590 | Backpackers (Lake Alpine) | | | | | F | | * | | * | | FSBH | $$ | May-Oct | |
| 591 | Pine Marten (Lake Alpine) | | * | | | F | | * | | * | | FSBH | $$ | Jun-Sept | |
| 592 | Silver Valley (Lake Alpine) | | * | | | F | | * | | * | * | FSBH | $$ | Jun-Sept | |
| 593 | Silvertip (Lake Alpine) | | * | | | F | | * | | * | | FSBH | $$ | Jun-Sept | |
| 594 | Stanislaus River | | * | | | V | | * | | * | | FS | $ | Jun-Sept | |
| 595 | Utica and Union Reservoirs | | * | | | V | | | | * | | FSBHM | $ | Jun-Oct | |
| 596 | Spicer Reservoir | | * | 28 | | V | | * | | * | * | FSBHRL | $$ | Jun-Sept | |
| 597 | Big Meadow | * | * | | | V | | * | | * | | H | $ | May-Sept | |
| 598 | Wa Ka Luu Hep Yoo (Wild River) | | * | 45 | | FV | * | * | | * | * | F | $$ | May-Oct | |
| 599 | North Grove (Calaveras Big Trees State Park) | * | * | | | F | * | * | * | * | * | HSF | $$$-$$$$ | Year-round | * |
| 600 | Oak Hollow (Calaveras Big Trees State Park) | | * | | | F | * | * | * | * | * | HSF | $$$ | Apr-Oct | |
| 601 | Sand Bar Flat | | * | | | V | | * | | * | * | FS | $-$$ | May-Sept | |
| 602 | Fraser Flat | | * | | | V | | * | | * | * | FS | $-$$$ | May-Sept | |
| 603 | Hull Creek | | * | | | V | | * | | * | | FO | $ | May-Sept | |
| 604 | Meadowview (Pinecrest Lake) | | * | | | F | | * | * | * | | FSBHL | $$ | May-Sept | |
| 605 | Pinecrest (Pinecrest Lake) | | * | | | | | * | * | * | * | FSBH | $$ | May-Sept | * |
| 606 | Herring Creek /(Herring Creek Reservoir) | | * | | | P | | | | * | | FSH | None | May-Oct | |
| 607 | Beardsley Dam | | * | | | V | | * | | * | | FSBHL | $ | May-Sept | |
| 608 | Cascade Creek | | * | | | V | | | | * | | | $ | May-Sept | |
| 609 | Mill Creek | | * | | | V | | | | * | | | $ | May-Sept | |
| 610 | Niagara Creek | | * | | | V | | | | * | | | $ | May-Sept | |
| 611 | Niagara OHV Camp | | * | | | V | | | | * | | FO | $ | May-Sept | |
| 612 | Fence Creek | | * | | | P | | | | * | | F | $ | May-Sept | |

| | Name | Group Sites | RV Sites | Max. RV Length | Hookups | Toilets | Showers | Drinking Water | Dump Station | Pets | Wheelchair | Recreation | Fee(s) | Season | Can Reserve |
|---|---|---|---|---|---|---|---|---|---|---|---|---|---|---|---|
| 613 | Clark Fork | | * | 23 | | FV | | * | * | * | * | HFR | $-$$$$ | May-Sept | |
| 614 | Sand Flat | | * | | | V | | * | * | * | | F | $ | May-Sept | |
| 615 | Boulder Flat | | * | | | V | | * | | * | | F | $-$$$ | May-Sept | |
| 616 | Brightman Flat | | * | | | V | | | | * | | F | $ | May-Sept | |
| 617 | Dardanelles | | * | | | V | | * | | * | | F | $-$$$ | May-Sept | |
| 618 | Pigeon Flat | | | | | V | | | | * | | FH | $ | May-Sept | |
| 619 | Eureka Valley | | * | 23 | | V | | * | | * | | FH | $ | May-Sept | |
| 620 | Baker | | * | 23 | | V | | * | | * | | F | $$-$$$$ | May-Oct | |
| 621 | Deadman | | * | 23 | | V | | * | | * | | FH | $$-$$$$ | May-Sept | |
| 622 | Leavitt Meadows | | * | 23 | | V | | * | | * | | FH | $$ | May-Oct | |
| 623 | Sonora Bridge | | * | 35 | | V | | * | | * | | F | $ | May-Oct | |
| 624 | Bootleg | | * | | | V | | * | | * | | F | $$ | May-Sept | |
| 625 | Chris Flat | | * | | | V | | * | | * | | F | $$ | Apr-Oct | |
| 626 | Obsidian | | * | | | V | | | | * | | HF | $ | May-Oct | |
| 627 | Buckeye | | * | 30 | | F | | | | * | | HFS | $ | Apr-Sep | |
| 628 | Honeymoon Flat | | * | 45 | | V | | * | | * | | F | $-$$$$ | Apr-Oct | * |
| 629 | Robinson Creek, South and North | | * | | | F | | * | | * | | FH | $$-$$$$ | Apr-Oct | * |
| 630 | Paha | | * | 32 | | F | | * | | * | * | FHL | $$-$$$$ | Apr-Oct | * |
| 631 | Crags | | * | | | F | | * | | * | | FHL | $$-$$$$ | Apr-Oct | * |
| 632 | Lower Twin Lakes | | * | 36 | | F | | * | | * | | HFSBL | $$ | Apr-Oct | * |
| 633 | Green Creek | * | * | 35 | | V | | * | | * | | HF | $$ | May-Oct | |
| 634 | Lower Virginia Creek | | * | | | V | | | | * | | H | None | June-Sept | |
| 635 | Trumbull Lake | | * | 45 | | V | | * | | * | | HFB | $$-$$$$ | July-Oct | * |

Toilets: F=flush V=vault P=pit C=chemical; Fee: $=Under $20 $$=$20-$29 $$$=$30-$39 $$$$ $40 or more; Recreation: H=hiking S=swimming F=fishing B=boating L=boat launch O=off-highway driving R=horseback riding, M=mountain biking Hookups: W=water E=electric S=sewerr

Creek, which provides fishing in early summer for small trout. Elevation 6,800 feet. Stay limit 14 days. Open June through September.

## 584 **Bloomfield**

**Location:** 62 miles northeast of Angels Camp
**GPS:** 38.5379685 / -119.8279289
**Sites:** 20 sites for tents and smaller RVs (not recommended for trailers)
**Facilities:** 5 tables and fire rings, drinking water (hand-pumped), vault toilets

**Fee per night:** $
**Management:** Stanislaus National Forest, (209) 795-1381
**Activities:** Fishing
**Finding the campground:** From the intersection of CA 49 and CA 4 in Angels Camp, drive northeast about 60 miles on CA 4 (passing Lake Alpine at milepoint 47). Turn right (southeast) onto Highland Lake Road and drive 1.5 miles.
**About the campground:** Situated on the bank of the North Fork of the Mokelumne River. This campground is good for solitude on the river. A campfire permit is required. Elevation 7,800 feet. Stay limit 14 days. Open June through October.

## 585 Highland Lakes

**Location:** 66 miles northeast of Angels Camp
**GPS:** 38.489390 / -119.806573
**Sites:** 35 sites for tents and smaller RVs (not recommended for trailers)
**Facilities:** Tables, fire rings, drinking water, vault toilets; boat ramp 1 mile northeast
**Fee per night:** $
**Management:** Stanislaus National Forest, (209) 795-1381
**Activities:** Fishing, swimming, boating, hiking
**Finding the campground:** From the intersection of CA 49 and CA 4 in Angels Camp, drive northeast about 60 miles on CA 4 (passing Lake Alpine at milepoint 47). Turn right (southeast) onto Highland Lake Road and drive 5.5 miles.
**About the campground:** Situated on the shoreline of the southernmost of two small, alpine lakes in a beautiful panoramic setting. The lakes provide only mediocre fishing for small brook trout. The boat ramp is on the northernmost of the two lakes. Trails lead from the campground into the Carson-Iceberg Wilderness. A campfire permit is required. Elevation 8,600 feet. Stay limit 14 days. Open June through October.

## 586 Hermit Valley

**Location:** 56 miles northeast of Angels Camp
**GPS:** 38.538376 / -119.897684
**Sites:** 25 sites for tents and RVs
**Facilities:** Tables, fire rings, vault toilets; no drinking water
**Fee per night:** None
**Management:** Stanislaus National Forest, (209) 795-1381
**Activities:** Fishing, hiking
**Finding the campground:** From the intersection of CA 49 and CA 4 in Angels Camp, drive northeast about 56 miles on CA 4.
**About the campground:** Situated near the confluence of Grouse Creek and the North Fork of the Mokelumne River. Trout fishing is fair to poor. A trail leads north from the campground into the Mokelumne Wilderness. Further dispersed camping is available 1 mile east on CA 4 at the Grouse Flat area, a former campground. A campfire permit is required. Elevation 7,500 feet. Stay limit 14 days. Open June through October.

## 587 Mosquito Lakes

**Location:** 53 miles northeast of Angels Camp
**GPS:** 38.515786 / -119.914112
**Sites:** 11 sites for tents and RVs
**Facilities:** Tables, fire rings, vault toilets; no drinking water
**Fee per night:** $
**Management:** Stanislaus National Forest, (209) 795-1381
**Activities:** Fishing, hiking
**Finding the campground:** From the intersection of CA 49 and CA 4 in Angels Camp, drive northeast about 53 miles on CA 4.
**About the campground:** Situated across the highway from a small, pretty lake that offers fair fishing for small trout. Trailheads at the lake and 1 mile to the west of the campground lead into the Carson-Iceberg and Mokelumne Wildernesses, respectively. A campfire permit is required. Elevation 8,060 feet. Stay limit 14 days. Open June through October.

## 588 Pacific Valley

**Location:** 54 miles northeast of Angels Camp
**GPS:** 38.514878 / -119.902027
**Sites:** 15 sites for tents and RVs
**Facilities:** Tables, fire rings, vault toilets, drinking water
**Fee per night:** $
**Management:** Stanislaus National Forest, (209) 795-1381
**Activities:** Fishing, hiking
**Finding the campground:** From the intersection of CA 49 and CA 4 in Angels Camp, drive northeast about 54 miles on CA 4.
**About the campground:** Situated near the bank of Pacific Creek. A trail leads south from the campground into the Carson-Iceberg Wilderness. A campfire permit is required. Elevation 7,600 feet. Stay limit 14 days. Open June through October.

## 589 Lake Alpine

**Location:** 47 miles northeast of Angels Camp
**GPS:** 38.477337 / -120.008006
**Sites:** 26 sites for tents and RVs
**Facilities:** Tables, fire rings, drinking water, showers, flush and vault toilets, boat ramp; store within walking distance
**Fee per night:** $$
**Management:** Stanislaus National Forest, (209) 795-1381
**Activities:** Fishing, swimming, boating, hiking
**Finding the campground:** From the intersection of CA 49 and CA 4 in Angels Camp, drive northeast about 47 miles on CA 4.
**About the campground:** Located on the southwest shore of a beautiful lake that is stocked annually with rainbow trout. A 4-mile loop trail circles the lake, with an optional spur up Inspiration Point. Elevation 7,300 feet. Stay limit 14 days. Open June through September.

## 590 **Backpackers (Lake Alpine)**

**Location:** 48 miles northeast of Angels Camp
**GPS:** 38.4762368 / -120.0084616
**Sites:** 8 sites for tents (RVs prohibited)
**Facilities:** Tables, fire rings, drinking water, flush toilets, and parking located across the road at Chickaree Picnic Area; boat ramp and store 1 mile away
**Fee per night:** $$
**Management:** Stanislaus National Forest, (209) 795-1381
**Activities:** Fishing, swimming, boating, hiking
**Finding the campground:** From the intersection of CA 49 and CA 4 in Angels Camp, drive northeast about 48 miles on CA 4.
**About the campground:** See Lake Alpine Campground (589) for area information. The campground, in a lodgepole pine and fir forest with a lake view, is primarily for the use of backpackers hiking into the Mokelumne and Carson-Iceberg Wildernesses, but it can serve as an overnight stop if other campgrounds are full. Elevation 7,300 feet. Stay limit 1 night. Open May through October.

## 591 **Pine Marten (Lake Alpine)**

**Location:** 48 miles northeast of Angels Camp
**GPS:** 38.480689 / -119.988496
**Sites:** 32 sites for tents and RVs
**Facilities:** Tables, fire rings, drinking water, flush toilets; boat ramp and store 1 mile away
**Fee per night:** $$
**Management:** Stanislaus National Forest, (209) 795-1381
**Activities:** Fishing, swimming, boating, hiking
**Finding the campground:** From the intersection of CA 49 and CA 4 in Angels Camp, drive northeast about 48 miles on CA 4.
**About the campground:** In conifer forest along the shore. See Lake Alpine Campground (589) for area information.

## 592 **Silver Valley (Lake Alpine)**

**Location:** 48 miles northeast of Angels Camp
**GPS:** 38.4759008 / -120.0019384
**Sites:** 21 sites for tents and RVs
**Facilities:** Tables, fire rings, drinking water, flush toilets; boat ramp and store 1 mile away
**Fee per night:** $$
**Management:** Stanislaus National Forest, (209) 795-1381
**Activities:** Fishing, swimming, boating, hiking
**Finding the campground:** From the intersection of CA 49 and CA 4 in Angels Camp, drive northeast about 48 miles on CA 4.
**About the campground:** See Lake Alpine Campground (589) for area information. A trail from the campground leads to connecting trails in the Carson-Iceberg Wilderness, including trips to Inspiration point and meadow-bound Duck Lake.

## 593 Silvertip (Lake Alpine)

**Location:** 46 miles northeast of Angels Camp
**GPS:** 38.4804667 / -120.0179635
**Sites:** 2 sites for tents and RVs
**Facilities:** Tables, fire rings, drinking water, flush toilets; boat ramp and store 1 mile away
**Fee per night:** $$
**Management:** Stanislaus National Forest, (209) 795-1381
**Activities:** Fishing, swimming, boating, hiking (all at Lake Alpine, 1 mile east)
**Finding the campground:** From the intersection of CA 49 and CA 4 in Angels Camp, drive northeast about 46 miles on CA 4.
**About the campground:** See Lake Alpine Campground (589) for area information. Silvertip can be used as an overflow area when lakeside campgrounds are full. An official overflow area, Lodgepole, is 1 mile west of Silvertip on CA 4. A pleasant trail heads south from the camp to the top of Osborne Hill, with great views to the west. Elevation 7,600 feet. Stay limit 14 days. Open mid-June through September.

## 594 Stanislaus River

**Location:** 44 miles northeast of Angels Camp
**GPS:** 38.422953 / -120.046849
**Sites:** 25 sites for tents and RVs
**Facilities:** Tables, fire rings, drinking water (hand-pumped), vault toilets
**Fee per night:** $
**Management:** Stanislaus National Forest, (209) 795-1381
**Activities:** Fishing, swimming
**Finding the campground:** From the intersection of CA 49 and CA 4 in Angels Camp, drive northeast about 41 miles on CA 4. Turn right (east) onto Spicer Reservoir Road (FR 7N01) and drive about 3 miles.
**About the campground:** A wooded location on the banks of the North Fork of the Stanislaus River. Elevation 6,200 feet. Stay limit 14 days. Open June through September.

## 595 Utica and Union Reservoirs

**Location:** 49 miles northeast of Angels Camp
**GPS:** 38.418327 / -120.007520
**Sites:** 23 sites at Utica Reservoir, 29 sites at Union Reservoir; both for tents and small RVs
**Facilities:** Tables, fire rings, vault toilets; no drinking water
**Fee per night:** $
**Management:** Stanislaus National Forest, (209) 795-1381
**Activities:** Fishing, swimming, kayaking, canoeing, hiking, mountain biking
**Finding the campground:** From the intersection of CA 49 and CA 4 in Angels Camp, drive northeast about 41 miles on CA 4. Turn right (east) onto Spicer Reservoir Road (FR 7N01) and drive about 6.5 miles. Turn left onto FR 7ON75; proceed 0.5 mile to a fork. To reach Utica Reservoir, turn left at the fork and drive 1 mile to the first of two small campgrounds. The second lies a few hundred yards farther down the road. To reach Union Reservoir, go right at the fork; go 0.3 mile to

a second fork. Staying left leads to the first of two campgrounds. To the right, the final campground lies 0.8 mile ahead.

**About the campground:** The twin, scenic lakes both boast good kayaking and great off-trail exploration in the Sierra Nevada landscape. Four small campgrounds are found here, two per lake. Some sites are shaded; some are in open, rocky, pretty terrain. Many sites are right on the water. Union Reservoir has a small, rustic boat launch. Utica Reservoir is managed for nonmotorized use. Mountain bikers will enjoy the 7-mile loop from Union Reservoir over Summit Lake Road on trail and gravel road. Elevation 7,000 feet. Stay limit 14 days. Open June through October.

## 596 Spicer Reservoir

**Location:** 49 miles northeast of Angels Camp
**GPS:** 38.406399 / -119.999093
**Sites:** 43 sites for tents and RVs up to 28 feet long
**Facilities:** Tables, fire rings, drinking water, vault toilets, boat ramp
**Fee per night:** $$
**Management:** Sierra Recreation Managers, (209) 296-8895
**Activities:** Fishing, swimming, boating, hiking, horseback riding
**Finding the campground:** From the intersection of CA 49 and CA 4 in Angels Camp, drive northeast about 41 miles on CA 4. Turn right (east) onto Spicer Reservoir Road (FR 7N01) and drive about 8 miles.

**About the campground:** Six miles long and up to 1 mile wide, Spicer Reservoir covers only about 230 acres. Low-speed boating is allowed, except in the northern arm, which opens to the Carson-Iceberg Wilderness. Fishing is fairly good for annually stocked rainbow and brown trout. The campground is timbered and close to the reservoir. The adjacent Spicer Reservoir Group Camp requires a reservation; call (209) 296-8895. Elevation 6,300 feet. Stay limit 14 days. Open June through September.

## 597 Big Meadow

**Location:** 38 miles northeast of Angels Camp
**GPS:** 38.417010 / -120.106533
**Sites:** 68 sites for tents and RVs; 1 group site
**Facilities:** Tables, fire rings, drinking water, vault toilets
**Fee per night:** $
**Management:** Stanislaus National Forest, (209) 795-1381
**Activities:** Hiking, hunting (seasonal)
**Finding the campground:** From the intersection of CA 49 and CA 4 in Angels Camp, drive northeast about 38 miles on CA 4.

**About the campground:** Situated on a bluff high over the North Fork of the Stanislaus River amid cool forest. An adjacent group camp can accept large groups. Elevation 6,500 feet. Stay limit 14 days. Open mid-May to September.

## 598 Wa Ka Luu Hep Yoo (Wild River)

**Location:** 11 miles northeast of Arnold

**GPS:** 38.3222868 / -120.217103
**Sites:** 49 sites for tents and RVs up to 45 feet long
**Facilities:** Picnic tables, flush and vault toilets, showers, drinking water
**Fee per night:** $$
**Management:** Stanislaus National Forest, (209) 795-1381
**Activities:** Interpretive site, fishing (swimming not recommended in untamed river), programs on flint-knapping and basket weaving offered at this campground (seasonal)
**Finding the campground:** Head northeast on CA 4 East to Dorrington. Turn south onto Board's Crossing–Sourgrass Road for about 4.7 miles.
**About the campground:** This beautiful campground is set in mature conifer-and-oak forest on the North Fork Stanislaus River. The campground is located on the site of an ancient Miwuk Indian village, within the Sourgrass Recreation Complex. Significant Native American artifacts such as grinding stones and middens have been preserved. Nearby fishing, a picnic/day-use area, river shore trails, and whitewater boating launch. Day-use area on the other side of the river. Elevation 3,900 feet. Stay limit 14 days. Open May through October.

## 599 North Grove (Calaveras Big Trees State Park)

**Location:** 26 miles northeast of Angels Camp
**GPS:** 38.277313 / -120.308785
**Sites:** 74 sites for tents and RVs; 1 group site
**Facilities:** Tables, fire rings, stone barbecues, drinking water (spigot at each site), flush toilets, showers, dump station, visitor center
**Fee per night:** $$$–$$$$; reservations: (800) 444-7275 or reserveamerica.com
**Management:** California Department of Parks and Recreation, (209) 795-2334
**Activities:** Hiking, swimming, fishing
**Finding the campground:** From the intersection of CA 49 and CA 4 in Angels Camp, drive 26 miles northeast on CA 4.
**About the campground:** Campsites are well spaced along intermittent Big Trees Creek, in a forest composed mainly of pines. A boardwalk through a scenic meadow connects parts of the campground. Elevation 4,800 feet. Stay limit 15 days. Open all year.

### CALAVERAS BIG TREES STATE PARK

This park encompasses more than 6,000 acres and contains more than 1,000 ancient sequoia trees in two separate groves about 5 miles apart. The 1-mile-long North Grove Loop Trail, which passes through the better known of the groves, begins in the North Grove Campground and visits, among other attractions, the Abraham Lincoln Tree. The park's second and larger stand of sequoias, the South Grove, is actually 5 miles northeast of North Grove. You can reach it via the park's Memorial Parkway. The South Grove Trail (5.2 miles round-trip) visits the Agassiz Tree, the largest in the park. Self-guiding brochures to both groves may be purchased at the visitor center.

## 600 **Oak Hollow (Calaveras Big Trees State Park)**

**Location:** 28 miles northeast of Angels Camp
**GPS:** 38.273581 / -120.291400
**Sites:** 54 sites for tents and RVs
**Facilities:** Tables, fire rings, stone barbecues, drinking water, flush toilets, showers, dump station, visitor center
**Fee per night:** $$$; reservations: (800) 444-7275 or reserveamerica.com
**Management:** California Department of Parks and Recreation, (209) 795-2334
**Activities:** Hiking, swimming, fishing
**Finding the campground:** From the intersection of CA 49 and CA 4 in Angels Camp, drive 26 miles northeast on CA 4. From North Grove Campground (599), continue 2 miles past the entrance station on Memorial Parkway (River Road).
**About the campground:** Features spacious sites, mostly walk-ins, under the shade of redwoods and conifers. See North Grove Campground (599) for area information. Stay limit 15 days. Open April through October.

## 601 **Sand Bar Flat**

**Location:** 33 miles northeast of Sonora
**GPS:** 38.184902 / -120.155025
**Sites:** 10 sites for tents and RVs
**Facilities:** Tables, stoves, drinking water, vault toilets
**Fee per night:** $–$$
**Management:** Stanislaus National Forest, (209) 586-3234
**Activities:** Fishing, swimming, hunting (seasonal)
**Finding the campground:** From the intersection of CA 49 and CA 108 in Sonora, drive 23 miles northeast on CA 108. Turn left (north) onto Spring Gap Road (FR 4N01) and drive 10 miles.
**About the campground:** Situated on an attractive part of the South Fork Stanislaus River, which is stocked annually with rainbow trout. Elevation 3,000 feet. Stay limit 14 days. Open May through September.

## 602 **Fraser Flat**

**Location:** 26 miles northeast of Sonora
**GPS:** 38.170532 / -120.071134
**Sites:** 38 sites for tents and RVs
**Facilities:** Tables, stoves, drinking water, vault toilets
**Fee per night:** $–$$$
**Management:** Dodge Ridge Corporation, (209) 965-3474
**Activities:** Fishing, swimming, hunting (seasonal)
**Finding the campground:** From the intersection of CA 49 and CA 108 in Sonora, drive 23 miles northeast on CA 108. Turn left (north) onto Spring Gap Road (FR 4N01) and drive 3 miles.

**About the campground:** Situated on the South Fork Stanislaus River, a pretty stream that is stocked annually with rainbow trout. Elevation 4,800 feet. Stay limit 14 days. Open May through September.

## 603 Hull Creek

**Location:** 28 miles northeast of Sonora
**GPS:** 38.093323 / -120.042710
**Sites:** 18 sites for tents and RVs
**Facilities:** Tables, fire rings, drinking water, vault toilets
**Fee per night:** $
**Management:** Stanislaus National Forest, (209) 586-3234
**Activities:** Fishing, OHV driving
**Finding the campground:** From the intersection of CA 49 and CA 108 in Sonora, drive 17 miles northeast on CA 108 to Long Barn. Turn right onto Hull Meadow Road (FR 31) and drive 11 miles.
**About the campground:** Situated in a secluded spot on the banks of Hull Creek, a stream too small for good fishing. The area is popular with off-road enthusiasts. Elevation 5,600 feet. Stay limit 14 days. Open May through September; winter camping permitted at no cost.

## 604 Meadowview (Pinecrest Lake)

**Location:** 27 miles northeast of Sonora
**GPS:** 38.186481 / -120.003832
**Sites:** 100 sites for tents and RVs
**Facilities:** Tables, stoves, drinking water, flush toilets, dump station; boat ramp 1 mile

*The beaches at Pinecrest Lake fill up on warm summer days, but there is always room for more. The trail around the lake takes you to quieter scenes of granite rock and sparkling lake.*

**Fee per night:** $$
**Management:** Dodge Ridge Corporation, (209) 965-3474
**Activities:** Fishing, swimming, boating, hiking; all at Pinecrest Lake, 1 mile east
**Finding the campground:** From the intersection of CA 49 and CA 108 in Sonora, drive 27 miles northeast on CA 108.
**About the campground:** Located about a mile from the lake with mostly shady sites. See Pinecrest Campground (605) for area information. Elevation 5,600 feet. Stay limit 14 days. Open May to September.

## 605 Pinecrest Campground (Pinecrest Lake)

**Location:** 28 miles northeast of Sonora
**GPS:** 38.190802 / -119.997484
**Sites:** 200 sites for tents and RVs
**Facilities:** Tables, stoves, drinking water, flush toilets, dump station, boat ramp
**Fee per night:** $$; reservations: (800) 444-7275 or reserveamerica.com
**Management:** Dodge Ridge Corporation, (209) 965-3474
**Activities:** Fishing, swimming, boating, hiking, biking
**Finding the campground:** From the intersection of CA 49 and CA 108 in Sonora, drive 27 miles northeast on CA 108.

*Recreation opportunities are abundant at Pinecrest Lake, and bicycles are a great way to get around the area from Pinecrest Campground.*

**About the campground:** Situated on the southwest shore of Pinecrest Lake, which is 1 mile long and 0.5 mile wide and covers about 300 acres. There is a 20 mph speed limit for boats on the lake. Fishing is good for small rainbow trout. A hiking trail circles the lake, and there is a 2-mile round-trip side trip to tiny Catfish Lake. Elevation 5,600 feet. Stay limit 14 days. Open May through September. Winter camping is permitted free of charge, but fewer facilities are available. For group camping there is Pioneer Trail Group Camp on Pinecrest, with 3 sites.

## 606 Herring Creek (Herring Creek Reservoir)

**Location:** 36 miles northeast of Sonora
**GPS:** 38.248678 / -119.936433
**Sites:** 42 sites for tents and RVs at Herring Reservoir; 9 additional sites at Herring Creek
**Facilities:** Fire grills, pit toilets; no drinking water
**Fee per night:** None
**Management:** Stanislaus National Forest, (209) 965-3434
**Activities:** Fishing, swimming, hiking
**Finding the campground:** From the intersection of CA 49 and CA 108 in Sonora, drive 28 miles northeast on CA 108. About 1 mile north of Strawberry, turn right (east) onto FR 4N12 and drive 7.5 miles.
**About the campground:** Situated on the shore of small Herring Creek Reservoir. A trail leads from the campground northeast along Herring Creek and then into the Emigrant Wilderness. Elevation 7,350 feet. Stay limit 14 days. Open May through October.

## 607 Beardsley Dam

**Location:** 40 miles northeast of Sonora
**GPS:** 38.213481 / -120.074756
**Sites:** 16 sites for tents and RVs
**Facilities:** Tables, stoves, drinking water, vault toilets; boat ramp nearby
**Fee per night:** $
**Management:** Stanislaus National Forest, (209) 965-3434
**Activities:** Fishing, swimming, boating, hiking
**Finding the campground:** From the intersection of CA 49 and CA 108 in Sonora, drive 32 miles northeast on CA 108. Turn left (west) on FR 52 and drive 7.5 miles. After crossing the dam, the road follows the lakeshore for about 0.5 mile; the campground is along the road.
**About the campground:** Situated along the west shore of Beardsley Reservoir, which is about 2 miles long and up to 1 mile wide. The lake is heavily stocked with rainbow trout annually, but it is subject to such heavy water drawdowns that the only rewarding time to fish is early spring. Elevation 3,400 feet. Stay limit 14 days. Open May through September.

## 608 Cascade Creek

**Location:** 37 miles northeast of Sonora
**GPS:** 38.2810135 / -119.972476
**Sites:** 14 sites for tents and RVs
**Facilities:** Tables, fire rings, vault toilets; no drinking water

**Fee per night:** $
**Management:** Stanislaus National Forest, (209) 965-3434
**Activities:** None
**Finding the campground:** From the intersection of CA 49 and CA 108 in Sonora, drive 37 miles northeast on CA 108.
**About the campground:** Located on Cascade Creek, the campground, in a mixed conifer forest, is a good overflow option if the sites at Beardsley Dam and Pinecrest Lake happen to fill up. Elevation 6,000 feet. Stay limit 14 days. Open May through September.

## 609 Mill Creek

**Location:** 40 miles northeast of Sonora
**GPS:** 38.301699 / -119.938674
**Sites:** 17 sites for tents and RVs
**Facilities:** Tables, fire rings, vault toilets; no drinking water
**Fee per night:** $
**Management:** Stanislaus National Forest, (209) 965-3434
**Activities:** None
**Finding the campground:** From the intersection of CA 49 and CA 108 in Sonora, drive 40 miles northeast on CA 108.
**About the campground:** This campground tucked away on the bank of Mill Creek. Elevation 6,200 feet. Stay limit 14 days. Open May through September.

## 610 Niagara Creek

**Location:** 43 miles northeast of Sonora
**GPS:** 38.324046 / -119.916538
**Sites:** 10 sites for tents and RVs
**Facilities:** Tables, stoves, vault toilets; no drinking water
**Fee per night:** $
**Management:** Stanislaus National Forest, (209) 965-3434
**Activities:** Fishing
**Finding the campground:** From the intersection of CA 49 and CA 108 in Sonora, drive 42 miles northeast on CA 108. Turn right onto FR 6N24 and drive less than 1 mile.
**About the campground:** Situated on the bank of small Niagara Creek. Elevation 6,600 feet. Stay limit 14 days. Open May through September.

## 611 Niagara OHV Camp

**Location:** 45 miles northeast of Sonora
**GPS:** 38.310715 / -119.890158
**Sites:** 10 sites for tents and RVs
**Facilities:** Tables, fire rings, vault toilets; no drinking water
**Fee per night:** $
**Management:** Stanislaus National Forest, (209) 965-3434
**Activities:** OHV driving, fishing

**Finding the campground:** From the intersection of CA 49 and CA 108 in Sonora, drive 42 miles northeast on CA 108. Turn right onto FR 6N24 and drive less than 0.25 mile. Turn right onto FR 5N01 and drive 2.5 miles.

**About the campground:** Situated on the bank of small Niagara Creek, the campground has four-wheel-drive and off-highway trails and roads leading north and east. Elevation 7,000 feet. Stay limit 14 days. Open May through September.

## 612 Fence Creek

**Location:** 48 miles northeast of Sonora
**GPS:** 38.365724 / -119.873212
**Sites:** 338 sites for tents and RVs
**Facilities:** Tables, fire rings, pit toilets; no drinking water
**Fee per night:** $
**Management:** Stanislaus National Forest, (209) 965-3434
**Activities:** Fishing
**Finding the campground:** From the intersection of CA 49 and CA 108 in Sonora, drive 47 miles northeast on CA 108. Turn left onto Clark Fork Road and drive 1 mile.
**About the campground:** Nestled at the bottom of a canyon on the border of the Carson-Iceberg Wilderness, the campground is only a 0.25-mile walk from both the Clark Fork and Middle Fork of the Stanislaus River. The confluence lies just downstream. Elevation 5,650 feet. Stay limit 14 days. Open May through September.

## 613 Clark Fork

**Location:** 52 miles northeast of Sonora
**GPS:** 38.398509 / -119.801747
**Sites:** 88 sites for tents and RVs up to 23 feet long; double sites available
**Facilities:** Tables, stoves, drinking water, flush and vault toilets, dump station
**Fee per night:** $–$$$$
**Management:** American Land and Leisure, (209) 965-3434
**Activities:** Hiking, fishing, horseback riding
**Finding the campground:** From the intersection of CA 49 and CA 108 in Sonora, drive 47 miles northeast on CA 108. Turn left onto Clark Fork Road and drive 5 miles.
**About the campground:** Trails lead north from the campground into the Carson-Iceberg Wilderness. A mile further along the road is Clark Fork Horse Camp, with 14 sites for tents and RVs up to 23 feet long. Elevation 6,200 feet. Stay limit 14 days. Open May through September.

## 614 Sand Flat

**Location:** 53 miles northeast of Sonora
**GPS:** 38.4038039 / -119.7890385
**Sites:** 53 sites for tents and RVs; 15 walk-in sites for tents
**Facilities:** Tables, stoves, drinking water, vault toilets; dump station nearby
**Fee per night:** $
**Management:** American Land and Leisure, (800) 342-2267

**Activities:** Fishing
**Finding the campground:** From the intersection of CA 49 and CA 108 in Sonora, drive 47 miles northeast on CA 108. Turn left onto Clark Fork Road and drive 6 miles.
**About the campground:** West of the campground, trails lead north into the Carson-Iceberg Wilderness. Elevation 6,200 feet. Stay limit 14 days. Open May through September.

## 615 Boulder Flat

**Location:** 48 miles northeast of Sonora
**GPS:** 38.353867 / -119.861291
**Sites:** 20 sites for tents and RVs, including some double sites
**Facilities:** Tables, stoves, drinking water, vault toilets
**Fee per night:** $–$$$
**Management:** Dodge Ridge Corporation, (209) 965-3474
**Activities:** Fishing
**Finding the campground:** From the intersection of CA 49 and CA 108 in Sonora, drive 48 miles northeast on CA 108.
**About the campground:** Situated on the bank of the Middle Fork of the Stanislaus River, which is stocked annually with rainbow trout, though heavy fishing keeps fish size small. Elevation 5,600 feet. Stay limit 14 days. Open May through September.

## 616 Brightman Flat

**Location:** 49 miles northeast of Sonora
**GPS:** 38.352000 / -119.848548
**Sites:** 32 sites for tents and RVs
**Facilities:** Tables, fire rings, vault toilets; no drinking water
**Fee per night:** $
**Management:** Dodge Ridge Corporation, (209) 965-3474
**Activities:** Fishing
**Finding the campground:** From the intersection of CA 49 and CA 108 in Sonora, drive 49 miles northeast on CA 108.
**About the campground:** Sites are in mixed conifers on the Stanislaus River. See Boulder Flat Campground (615) for area information. Elevation 5,700 feet. Stay limit 14 days. Open May through September.

## 617 Dardanelle

**Location:** 50 miles northeast of Sonora
**GPS:** 38.341239 / -119.833345
**Sites:** 28 sites for tents and RVs, including some double sites
**Facilities:** Tables, stoves, drinking water, vault toilets
**Fee per night:** $–$$$
**Management:** Dodge Ridge Corporation, (209) 965-3474
**Activities:** Fishing

**Finding the campground:** From the intersection of CA 49 and CA 108 in Sonora, drive 50 miles northeast on CA 108.
**About the campground:** See Boulder Flat Campground (615) for area information. Elevation feet. Stay limit 14 days. Open May through September.

## 618 Pigeon Flat

**Location:** 51 miles northeast of Sonora
**GPS:** 38.340178 / -119.805212
**Sites:** 7 sites for tents
**Facilities:** Tables, fire rings, vault toilet; no drinking water
**Fee per night:** $
**Management:** Dodge Ridge Corporation, (209) 965-3474
**Activities:** Fishing, hiking
**Finding the campground:** From the intersection of CA 49 and CA 108 in Sonora, drive 51 miles northeast on CA 108.
**About the campground:** See Boulder Flat Campground (615) for area information. An interpretive trail leads from the campground to the Columns of the Giants, an interesting formation of columnar basalt similar to that at Devils Postpile National Monument. Elevation 5,960 feet. Stay limit 14 days. Open May through September.

## 619 Eureka Valley

**Location:** 51 miles northeast of Sonora
**GPS:** 38.341233 / -119.791847
**Sites:** 28 sites for tents and RVs up to 23 feet long
**Facilities:** Tables, fire rings, drinking water, vault toilets
**Fee per night:** $
**Management:** Dodge Ridge Corporation, (209) 965-3474
**Activities:** Fishing, hiking
**Finding the campground:** From the intersection of CA 49 and CA 108 in Sonora, drive 51 miles northeast on CA 108.
**About the campground:** See Boulder Flat Campground (615) for area information. A trail 0.5 mile east of the campground leads north to the Carson-Iceberg Wilderness. The campground is 1 mile east of the Columns of the Giants, an interesting formation of columnar basalt similar to that at Devils Postpile National Monument. Elevation 6,100 feet. Stay limit 14 days. Open May through September.

## 620 Baker

**Location:** 54 miles northeast of Sonora
**GPS:** 38.324192 / -119.752445
**Sites:** 44 sites for tents and RVs up to 23 feet long; double sites available
**Facilities:** Tables, stoves, drinking water, vault toilets
**Fee per night:** $$–$$$$
**Management:** American Land and Leisure, (800) 342-2267
**Activities:** Fishing

**Finding the campground:** From the intersection of CA 49 and CA 108 in Sonora, drive 54 miles northeast on CA 108.
**About the campground:** In mixed conifers on the Stanislaus River. See Boulder Flat Campground (615) for area information. Elevation 6,200 feet. Stay limit 14 days. Open May through October.

## 621 Deadman

**Location:** 55 miles northeast of Sonora
**GPS:** 38.317999 / -119.748488
**Sites:** 17 sites for tents and RVs up to 23 feet long; double sites available
**Facilities:** Tables, stoves, drinking water, vault toilets
**Fee per night:** $$–$$$$
**Management:** American Land and Leisure, (800) 342-2267
**Activities:** Fishing, hiking
**Finding the campground:** From the intersection of CA 49 and CA 108 in Sonora, drive 55 miles northeast on CA 108.
**About the campground:** See Boulder Flat Campground (615) for area information. A trail from the campground leads south to several destinations in the Emigrant Wilderness, including Relief Reservoir (4 miles) and Kennedy Lake (7 miles). Elevation 6,200 feet. Stay limit 14 days. Open May through September.

## 622 Leavitt Meadows

**Location:** 22 miles northwest of Bridgeport
**GPS:** 38.3329697 / -119.5521135
**Sites:** 10 sites for tents and RVs up to 23 feet long
**Facilities:** Tables, fire rings, drinking water, vault toilets
**Fee per night:** $$
**Management:** Westrek Services, (530) 694-1002
**Activities:** Hiking, fishing
**Finding the campground:** From Bridgeport, drive 16 miles northwest on US 395. Turn left (west) onto CA 108 and drive 6 miles.
**About the campground:** Located on the bank of the West Walker River, a good trout stream. Leavitt Falls is about 1 mile away, and a 2-mile trail leads from the campground to Secret Lake, with Roosevelt Lake and others not far beyond. Elevation 7,160 feet. Stay limit 14 days. Open May through October.

## 623 Sonora Bridge

**Location:** 18 miles northwest of Bridgeport
**GPS:** 38.362449 / -119.474536
**Sites:** 23 sites for tents and RVs up to 35 feet long
**Facilities:** Tables, fire rings, drinking water, vault toilets
**Fee per night:** $
**Management:** Westrek Services, (530) 694-1002
**Activities:** Fishing

**Finding the campground:** From Bridgeport, drive 16 miles northwest on US 395. Turn left (west) onto CA 108 and drive 2 miles.
**About the campground:** Situated about 1 mile from the West Walker River, a popular trout stream with good fishing for rainbows. Elevation 6,800 feet. Stay limit 14 days. Open May through October.

## 624 Bootleg

**Location:** 66 miles southeast of South Lake Tahoe
**GPS:** 38.419670 / -119.450250
**Sites:** 63 sites for tents and RVs
**Facilities:** Tables, fire rings, drinking water, flush toilets
**Fee per night:** $$
**Management:** Westrek Services, (530) 694-1002
**Activities:** Fishing
**Finding the campground:** From the northern intersection of CA 89 and US 50 in South Lake Tahoe, drive southeast on CA 89 for about 48 miles. Turn right (south) onto US 395 and drive 18 miles.
**About the campground:** Situated across the highway from the West Walker River, a popular trout stream with good fishing for rainbows. Elevation 6,600 feet. Stay limit 14 days. Open May through September.

## 625 Chris Flat

**Location:** 68 miles southeast of South Lake Tahoe
**GPS:** 38.394836 / -119.452660
**Sites:** 15 sites for tents and RVs
**Facilities:** Tables, fire rings, drinking water, vault toilets
**Fee per night:** $$
**Management:** Westrek Services, (530) 694-1002
**Activities:** Fishing
**Finding the campground:** From the northern intersection of CA 89 and US 50 in South Lake Tahoe, drive south on CA 89 for about 48 miles. Turn right (south) onto US 395 and drive 20 miles.
**About the campground:** Situated along the bank of the West Walker River, with easy access from the campground to this popular trout stream with good fishing for rainbows. Elevation 6,600 feet. Stay limit 14 days. Open April through October.

## 626 Obsidian

**Location:** 20 miles northwest of Bridgeport
**GPS:** 38.297598 / -119.448521
**Sites:** 12 sites for tents and RVs
**Facilities:** Tables, fire rings, vault toilets; no drinking water
**Fee per night:** $
**Management:** Westrek Services, (530) 694-1002

**Activities:** Hiking, fishing
**Finding the campground:** From Bridgeport, drive northwest on US 395 for about 17 miles. Turn left (south) onto FR 066 (dirt road) and drive 3 miles.
**About the campground:** Situated on the bank of Molybdenite Creek. Two trails lead from the campground south to the Hoover Wilderness, one along the creek and the other through Burt Canyon. The nearby trail to lonely Emma Lake is spectacular. Elevation 7,800 feet. Stay limit 14 days. Open May through October.

## 627 Buckeye

**Location:** 10 miles west of Bridgeport
**GPS:** 38.237749 / -119.342401
**Sites:** 68 sites for tents and RVs up to 30 feet long; 1 group site
**Facilities:** Tables, fire rings, flush toilets; no drinking water
**Fee per night:** $
**Management:** Westrek Services, (530) 694-1002
**Activities:** Hiking, fishing, swimming, hot springs
**Finding the campground:** From the intersection of US 395 and CR 420 (Twin Lakes Road) in Bridgeport, drive southwest on CR 420 about 7 miles. Turn right (north) onto FR 017 (Buckeye Road) and drive 3 miles.
**About the campground:** A natural, undeveloped hot spring is within a 2-mile walk of the campground. Nearby Buckeye Creek can be a good place to find large trout. Several trails lead out from the camp. One follows Buckeye Creek southwest to the Hoover Wilderness and on into Yosemite National Park; another traces Eagle Creek southward. Elevation 7,000 feet. Stay limit 14 days. Open mid-April through September.

## 628 Honeymoon Flat

**Location:** 8 miles southwest of Bridgeport
**GPS:** 38.201232 / -119.320490
**Sites:** 45 sites for tents and RVs up to 45 feet long
**Facilities:** Tables, fire rings, drinking water, vault toilets
**Fee per night:** $, double: $$$$; reservations: (800) 444-7275 or reserveamerica.com
**Management:** Westrek Services, (760) 932-7092
**Activities:** Fishing
**Finding the campground:** From the intersection of US 395 and CR 420 (Twin Lakes Road) in Bridgeport, drive southwest on CR 420 about 8 miles.
**About the campground:** Situated on the bank of Robinson Creek, which is heavily stocked with rainbow trout. The western loop is nicer, with sites on the creek bank. Elevation 7,000 feet. Stay limit 14 days. Open mid-April through October.

## 629 Robinson Creek, South and North

**Location:** 9 miles southwest of Bridgeport
**GPS:** 38.184607 / -119.322784

**Sites:** 54 sites for tents and RVs
**Facilities:** Tables, fire rings, drinking water, flush toilets
**Fee per night:** $$–$$$$; reservations: (877) 444-6777 or recreation.gov
**Management:** Westrek Services, (530) 694-1002
**Activities:** Fishing, hiking
**Finding the campground:** From the intersection of US 395 and CR 420 (Twin Lakes Road) in Bridgeport, drive southwest on CR 420 about 9 miles.
**About the campground:** Situated on the bank of Robinson Creek, which is heavily stocked with rainbow trout. The Twin Lakes area is nearby for additional recreation. Elevation 7,000 feet. Stay limit 14 days. Open mid-April through October.

## 630 Paha

**Location:** 10 miles southwest of Bridgeport
**GPS:** 38.180608 / -119.32510
**Sites:** 20 sites for tents and RVs up to 32 feet long; 1 yurt
**Facilities:** Tables, fire rings, drinking water, flush toilets; boat ramp nearby
**Fee per night:** $$–$$$$; reservations: (800) 444-7275 or reserveamerica.com
**Management:** Westrek Services, (760) 932-7092
**Activities:** Fishing, hiking
**Finding the campground:** From the intersection of US 395 and CR 420 (Twin Lakes Road) in Bridgeport, drive southwest on CR 420 about 9.5 miles.
**About the campground:** Situated about 1.5 miles from the water activities at Lower Twin Lakes (632). Elevation 7,000 feet. Stay limit 14 days. Open mid-April through October.

## 631 Crags

**Location:** 10 miles southwest of Bridgeport
**GPS:** 38.172111 / -119.323010
**Sites:** 27 sites for tents and RVs
**Facilities:** Tables, fire rings, drinking water, flush toilets; boat ramp nearby
**Fee per night:** $$–$$$$; reservations: (877) 444-6777 or recreation.gov
**Management:** Westrek Services, (760) 932-7092
**Activities:** Fishing, hiking
**Finding the campground:** From the intersection of US 395 and CR 420 (Twin Lakes Road) in Bridgeport, drive southwest on CR 420 about 10 miles.
**About the campground:** Situated about 0.25 mile from the water activities at Lower Twin Lakes. The camp has three loops, some of which are fairly close to the lake. The third loop is down the road and separated from the rest of the camp. Robinson Creek is a popular hiking trail in the area. Elevation 7,000 feet. Stay limit 14 days. Open mid-April through October.

## 632 Lower Twin Lakes

**Location:** 11 miles southwest of Bridgeport
**GPS:** 38.171254 / -119.323825

**Sites:** 14 sites for tents and RVs up to 36 feet long
**Facilities:** Tables, fire rings, drinking water, flush toilets; boat ramp nearby
**Fee per night:** $$; reservations: (800) 444-7275 or reserveamerica.com
**Management:** Westrek Services, (760) 932-7092
**Activities:** Hiking, fishing, swimming, boating
**Finding the campground:** From the intersection of US 395 and CR 420 (Twin Lakes Road) in Bridgeport, drive southwest on CR 420 about 10.5 miles.
**About the campground:** The two largest brown trout caught in California—both over 26 pounds—were taken from Lower Twin Lake. In addition to the chance to land a large brown, you can fish for rainbows, with which the lake is heavily stocked each year. Elevation 7,000 feet. Stay limit 14 days. Open mid-April through October.

## 633 Green Creek

**Location:** 11 miles south of Bridgeport
**GPS:** 38.108914 / -119.277716
**Sites:** 14 sites for tents and RVs up to 35 feet long: 1 group camp
**Facilities:** Tables, fire rings, drinking water, vault toilets
**Fee per night:** $$
**Management:** Westrek Services, (530) 694-1002
**Activities:** Hiking, fishing
**Finding the campground:** From Bridgeport, drive south on US 395 for about 4 miles. Turn right (south) onto Green Lakes Road (dirt) and continue about 7 miles.
**About the campground:** Situated on the bank of Green Creek, a fairly good stream for small trout. A trail leads southwest from the campground to a series of small, secluded lakes (2–6 miles) and then continues into Yosemite National Park. Elevation 7,500 feet. Stay limit 14 days. Open mid-May through October.

## 634 Lower Virginia Creek

**Location:** 16 miles south of Bridgeport
**GPS:** 38.0676042 / -119.228294
**Sites:** 22 sites for tents and RVs
**Facilities:** Fire rings, bear boxes, vault toilets; no drinking water
**Fee per night:** None
**Management:** Westrek Services, (760) 932-7070
**Activities:** Hiking, riparian nature study
**Finding the campground:** From Bridgeport, head southeast on US 395. Turn west onto Virginia Lakes Road for about 3 miles.
**About the campground:** Rustic campsites with fire rings in Jeffrey pine forest near Virginia Creek. Close to easy alpine trails in the Hoover Wilderness. Pack out trash. Elevation 8,500 feet. Open June to September (subject to weather conditions). Upper Virginia Creek Campground, with 15 sites, is about 0.8 mile farther along Virginia Lakes Road (RVs up to 25 feet).

## MONO LAKE

Located 24 miles south of Bridgeport on I-395, Mono Lake is worth a visit. An otherworldly sight, it is a large, shallow saline soda lake set in a desert landscape. Jagged tufa formations rise out of the water, and the lake's islands are covered with flapping and resting seagulls and other aquatic birds. Home to thriving brine shrimp and blackflies, the lake is a critical nesting habitat to some 2 million migratory birds. For birding, geology, history, preservation, and a unique view, visit Mono Lake while camping near Bridgeport.

## 635 Trumbull Lake

**Location:** 19 miles south of Bridgeport
**GPS:** 38.049377 / -119.258578
**Sites:** 33 sites for tents and RVs up to 45 feet long
**Facilities:** Tables, fire rings, drinking water, vault toilets
**Fee per night:** $$–$$$$; reservations: (800) 444-7275 or reserveamerica.com
**Management:** Westrek Services, (760) 932-7070
**Activities:** Hiking, fishing, nonmotorized boating
**Finding the campground:** From Bridgeport, drive south on US 395 for about 13 miles. Turn right (west) onto Virginia Lakes Road (dirt) and drive about 6 miles.
**About the campground:** Trumbull Lake and the nearby Virginia Lakes are stocked annually with rainbows and offer fair fishing for small trout. A trail from the campground (4 miles round-trip) visits six tiny lakes. The same trail continues a total of 9 miles to Green Creek Campground (633), passing more than a dozen small lakes en route. It also provides access to Yosemite National Park. Elevation 9,980 feet. Stay limit 14 days. Open July through mid-October.

# Yosemite Area

Magnificent Yosemite National Park is the centerpiece of this area of the Sierra Nevada. But the Sierra and Inyo National Forests also contribute deep woods, sparkling lakes, soaring mountains, and wonderful vistas to the scene. The Sierra is home to 315 different animal species and 31 species of fish and contains hundreds of miles of trails, rivers, and streams. The Sierra Vista National Scenic Byway traverses many of the most dramatic parts of Sierra National Forest, including Fresno Dome and Nelder Grove, home to 106 mature sequoia intermingled with second-growth fir and cedar.

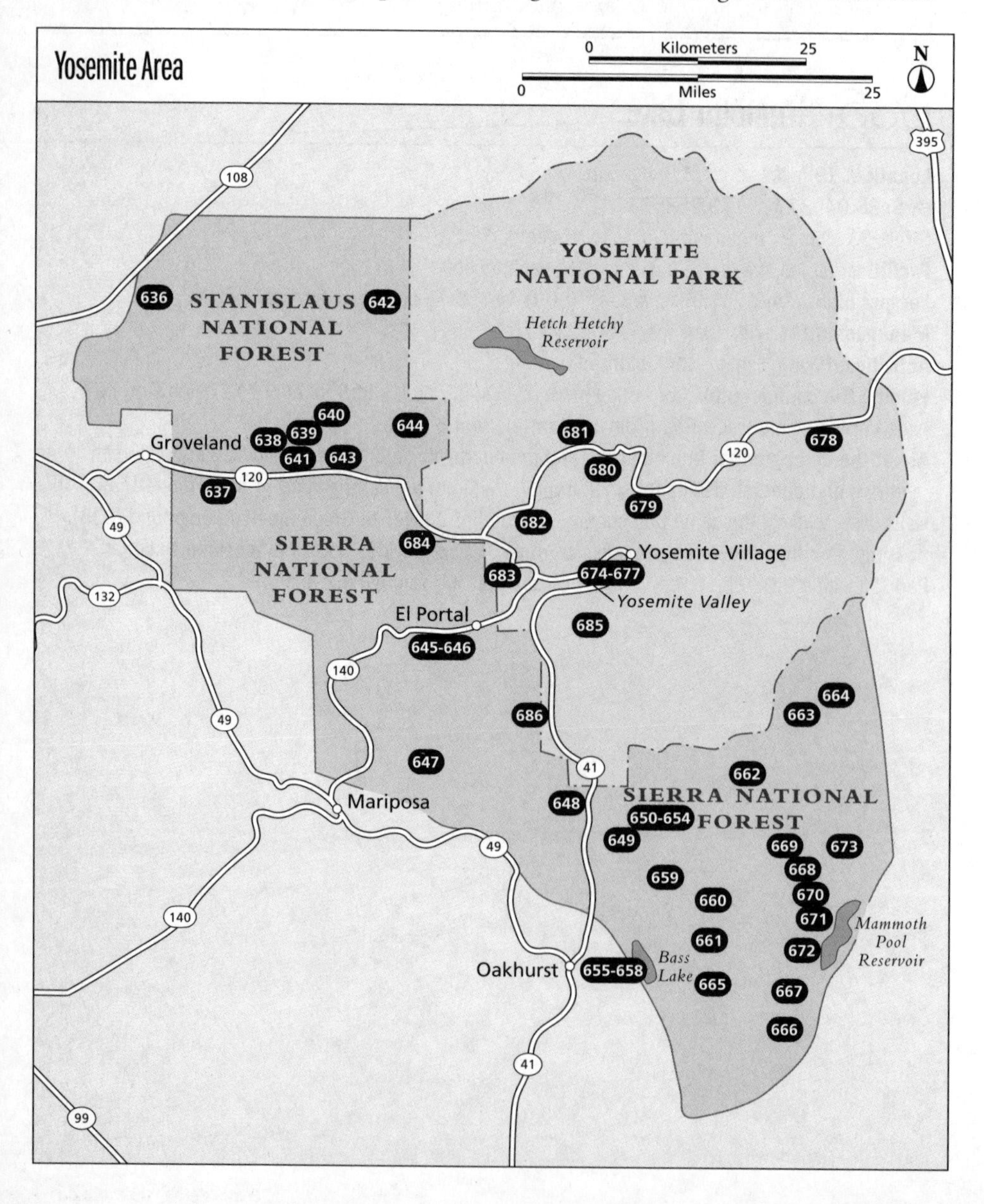

| | Name | Group Sites | RV Sites | Max. RV Length | Hookups | Toilets | Showers | Drinking Water | Dump Station | Pets | Wheelchair | Recreation | Fee(s) | Season | Can Reserve |
|---|---|---|---|---|---|---|---|---|---|---|---|---|---|---|---|
| | **YOSEMITE AREA** | | | | | | | | | | | | | | |
| 636 | River Ranch | | * | | | F | | * | | * | | F | $$ | Mar–Nov | |
| 637 | The Pines | * | * | | | V | | * | | * | | H | $-$$$$ | May–Sept | |
| 638 | Lumsden | | | | | V | | | | * | | FBH | None | Year-round | |
| 639 | South Fork | | | | | V | | | | * | | FB | None | Year-round | |
| 640 | Lumsden Bridge | | | | | V | | | | * | | FB | None | Year-round | |
| 641 | Lost Claim | | * | small | | V | | * | | * | * | F | $ | May–Sept | * |
| 642 | Cherry Valley | | * | 32 | | V | | * | | * | | HFSB | $$-$$$$ | June–Sept | * |
| 643 | Sweetwater | | * | 32 | | V | | * | | * | | F | $$ | Mar–Labor Day | * |
| 644 | Dimond O | | * | | | V | | * | | * | * | F | $$-$$$$ | May–Sept | * |
| 645 | Dirt Flat | | | | | V | | * | | * | * | HSF | $$ | Year-round | * |
| 646 | Dry Gulch | | | | | V | | * | | * | | HSF | $$ | Year-round | * |
| 647 | Jerseydale | | | | | V | | * | | * | | | None | May–Nov | |
| 648 | Summerdale | | * | 30 | | V | | * | | * | | FS | $$ | May–Sept | * |
| 649 | Nelder Grove | | * | | | V | | | | * | | H | None | May–Sept | |
| 650 | Soquel | | * | 23 | | V | | | | * | | F | $$-$$$$ | June–Oct | * |
| 651 | Greys Mountain | | * | 23 | | V | | | | * | | F | $$-$$$$ | May–Oct | |
| 652 | Kelty Meadow | | * | 23 | | V | | | | * | | R | $$-$$$$ | June–Oct | * |
| 653 | Fresno Dome | | * | 23 | | V | | | | * | | HF | $$-$$$$ | May–Oct | |
| 654 | Big Sandy | | * | 20 | | V | | | | * | | F | $$ | June–Nov | |
| 655 | Forks (Bass Lake) | | * | 35 | | F | * | * | | * | * | HSFBL | $$-$$$$ | May–Sept | * |
| 656 | Lupine-Cedar Bluffs (Bass Lake) | | * | 40 | | F | | * | | * | * | HSFBL | $$-$$$$ | May–Sept | * |
| 657 | Spring Cove (Bass Lake) | | * | 31 | | F | | * | | * | * | HSFBL | $$-$$$$ | May–Sept | * |
| 658 | Wishon Point (Bass Lake) | | * | | | F | | * | | * | * | HSFBL | $$-$$$$ | May–Sept | * |
| 659 | Chilkoot | | * | 30 | | V | | | | * | | F | $$-$$$$ | May–Sept | * |
| 660 | Gaggs Camp | | * | 19 | | V | | | | * | | F | $$-$$$$ | June–Oct | |
| 661 | Whiskers | | * | | | V | | | | * | | F | $$-$$$$ | June–Oct | |
| 662 | Upper Chiquito | | * | 23 | | V | | | | * | | H | None | June–Sept | |
| 663 | Clover Meadow | | * | 19 | | V | | * | | * | | H | None | June–Sept | |
| 664 | Granite Creek | | * | | | V | | | | * | | HFS | None | June–Sept | |
| 665 | Whisky Falls | | * | | | V | | | | * | | F | None | May–Sept | |

| | Name | Group Sites | RV Sites | Max. RV Length | Hookups | Toilets | Showers | Drinking Water | Dump Station | Pets | Wheelchair | Recreation | Fee(s) | Season | Can Reserve |
|---|---|---|---|---|---|---|---|---|---|---|---|---|---|---|---|
| 666 | Fish Creek | | * | 20 | | V | | | | * | | HF | $$-$$$$ | Apr-Oct | * |
| 667 | Rock Creek | | * | 32 | | V | | * | | * | | HFS | $$-$$$$ | Apr-Oct | * |
| 668 | Soda Springs | | * | 23 | | V | | | | * | | FS | $$-$$$$ | Apr-Oct | |
| 669 | Lower Chiquito | | * | 25 | | V | | | | * | | FS | $$-$$$$ | May-Sept | |
| 670 | Placer | | | | | V | | | | * | | F | $$-$$$$ | Apr-Sept | |
| 671 | Sweet Water | | * | 17 | | V | | | | * | | FS | $$-$$$$ | May-Oct | * |
| 672 | Mammoth Pool | * | * | | | V | | | | * | | FSBH | $$-$$$$ | Apr-Oct | * |
| 673 | Little Jackass | | * | | | V | | | | * | | F | None | May-Oct | |
| | **YOSEMITE NATIONAL PARK** | | | | | | | | | | | | | | |
| 674 | Lower Pines (Yosemite National Park, Yosemite Valley) | * | * | 40 | | F | | * | | * | * | HFSBR | $$-$$$ | Mar-Oct | * |
| 675 | Upper Pines (Yosemite National Park, Yosemite Valley) | | * | 35 | | F | | * | | * | * | HFSBR | $$ | Mar-Oct | * |
| 676 | North Pines (Yosemite National Park, Yosemite Valley) | | * | 40 | | F | | | | * | * | HFSBR | $$ | Mar-Oct | * |
| 677 | Camp 4 Walk-in (Yosemite National Park, Yosemite Valley) | | | | | F | | * | | | | HSF | $ | Year-round | |
| 678 | Tuolumne Meadows (Yosemite National Park) | * | * | 35 | | F | | * | * | * | * | HSFR | $$-$$$$ | Jun-Sept | * |
| 679 | Porcupine Flat (Yosemite National Park) | | * | 40 | | V | | | | * | * | H | $ | July-Sept | |
| 680 | Yosemite Creek (Yosemite National Park) | | * | small | | P | | | | * | * | HF | $ | July-Sept | |
| 681 | White Wolf (Yosemite National Park) | | * | 27 | | F | | * | | * | | HF | $ | July-Sept | |
| 682 | Tamarack Flat (Yosemite National Park) | | * | small | | P | | | | | * | H | $ | June-Sept | |
| 683 | Crane Flat (Yosemite National Park) | | * | 35 | | F | | * | | * | * | H | $$ | July-Oct | |
| 684 | Hodgdon Meadow (Yosemite National Park) | * | * | 35 | | F | | * | | * | | | $$-$$$$ | Year-round | * |
| 685 | Bridalveil Creek (Yosemite National Park) | * | * | 35 | | F | | * | | * | | HFR | $$-$$$$ | July-Sept | * |
| 686 | Wawona (Yosemite National Park) | * | * | 35 | | F | | * | * | * | * | HSFR | $$ | Year-round | * |

Toilets: F=flush V=vault P=pit C=chemical; Fee: $=Under $20 $$=$20-$29 $$$=$30-$39 $$$$ $40 or more; Recreation: H=hiking S=swimming F=fishing B=boating L=boat launch O=off-highway driving R=horseback riding, M=mountain biking
Hookups: W=water E=electric S=sewer

## 636 River Ranch

**Location:** 13 miles east of Sonora
**GPS:** 37.9933 / -120.1815
**Sites:** 38 sites for tents and RVs
**Facilities:** Tables, grills, drinking water, showers, flush toilets
**Fee per night:** $$
**Management:** Mi Wok RD and River Ranch Campground, (209) 928-3708
**Activities:** Fishing
**Finding the campground:** From the intersection of CA 49 and CA 108 in Sonora, drive 2 miles east on CA 108. Turn right (southeast) onto Tuolumne Road (CR E18) and drive 6.5 miles. Turn right onto Cottonwood Road and drive 4 miles.
**About the campground:** Situated in a meadow at the confluence of Basin Creek and the North Fork Tuolumne River, which is stocked with rainbow trout annually. It is adjacent to the private River Ranch Campground (reservations accepted). Elevation 2,500 feet. Stay limit 14 days. Open March to November.

## 637 The Pines

**Location:** 9 miles east of Groveland
**GPS:** 37.8192362 / -120.095426
**Sites:** 12 sites for tents and small RVs; 1 group site
**Facilities:** Tables, fire rings, drinking water, vault toilets
**Fee per night:** $, group site: $$$$
**Management:** American Land and Leisure, (800) 342-2267
**Activities:** Hiking
**Finding the campground:** From Groveland, drive 9 miles east on CA 120. The campground is adjacent to the Groveland Ranger District Office.
**About the campground:** The Pines is best used as an overnight stop or as a base from which to explore the Tuolumne Wild and Scenic River Area. The campground is adjacent to the Little Golden Forest Trail and is 14 miles west of the Big Oak Flat entrance to Yosemite National Park and 20 miles southwest of the Hetch Hetchy entrance. Yosemite Valley is 28 miles to the southeast, making The Pines a good alternative camping spot if Yosemite campgrounds are full. The adjacent Pines Group Camp is a good option for larger groups. Elevation 3,200 feet. Stay limit 14 days. Open May through September.

## 638 Lumsden

**Location:** 15 miles east of Groveland
**GPS:** 37.838238 / -120.050932
**Sites:** 11 tent sites
**Facilities:** Tables, grills, vault toilets; no drinking water
**Fee per night:** None
**Management:** Stanislaus National Forest, (209) 962-7825
**Activities:** Fishing, rafting, nonmotorized boating, hiking

**Finding the campground:** From Groveland, drive 10 miles east on CA 120. Turn left onto Ferretti Road and drive about 1 mile. Turn right onto Lumsden Road and drive 4 miles. This is a steep, narrow dirt road that is subject to closure in wet weather. It is not suitable for trailers or RVs larger than pickups.
**About the campground:** Situated close to the bank of the Tuolumne, a nationally designated Wild and Scenic River, the campground is an access point for rafting the river. The three forks of the Tuolumne are stocked with rainbow trout. Nearby hiking trails include Tuolumne River Canyon Trail and the Andresen Mine Trail. The area was burned in the 2013 Rim Fire. Elevation 1,500 feet. Stay limit 14 days. Open all year.

## 639 South Fork

**Location:** 16 miles east of Groveland
**GPS:** 37.839808 / -120.045855
**Sites:** 8 tent sites
**Facilities:** Tables, grills, vault toilets; no drinking water
**Fee per night:** None
**Management:** Stanislaus National Forest, (209) 962-7825
**Activities:** Fishing, rafting
**Finding the campground:** From Groveland, drive 10 miles east on CA 120. Turn left onto Ferretti Road and drive about 1 mile. Turn right onto Lumsden Road and drive 4.5 miles. This is a steep, narrow dirt road that is subject to closure in wet weather. It is not suitable for trailers or RVs larger than pickups.
**About the campground:** Situated near the confluence of the South Fork and the Main Fork of the Tuolumne River. See Lumsden Campground (638) for area information.

## 640 Lumsden Bridge

**Location:** 17 miles east of Groveland
**GPS:** 37.847740 / -120.032255
**Sites:** 9 tent sites
**Facilities:** Tables, grills, vault toilets; no drinking water
**Fee per night:** None
**Management:** Stanislaus National Forest, (209) 962-7825
**Activities:** Fishing, rafting
**Finding the campground:** From Groveland, drive 10 miles east on CA 120. Turn left onto Ferretti Road and drive about 1 mile. Turn right onto Lumsden Road and drive 5.5 miles. This is a steep, narrow dirt road that is subject to closure in wet weather. It is not suitable for trailers or RVs larger than pickups.
**About the campground:** In low elevation pine and oak forest beside the Tuolumne RIver. See Lumsden Campground (638) for area information.

## 641 Lost Claim

**Location:** 12 miles east of Groveland
**GPS:** 37.8239 / -120.0049

**Sites:** 10 sites for tents and small RVs
**Facilities:** Tables, grills, well water, vault toilets
**Fee per night:** $; reservations: (800) 444-7275 or reserveamerica.com
**Management:** American Land and Leisure, (800) 342-2267
**Activities:** Fishing, biking
**Finding the campground:** From Groveland, drive 12 miles east on CA 120.
**About the campground:** Situated on a small tributary of the Tuolumne, the campground is also about 0.5 mile from the South Fork of the river. It is 11 miles west of the Big Oak Flat entrance to Yosemite National Park and 17 miles southwest of the Hetch Hetchy entrance. Yosemite Valley is 25 miles to the southeast, making Lost Claim a good alternative camping spot if Yosemite campgrounds are full. The area is rejuvenating from the 2013 Rim Fire. Elevation 3,100 feet. Stay limit 14 days. Open May through mid-September.

## 642 Cherry Valley

**Location:** 35 miles northeast of Groveland
**GPS:** 37.9809 / -119.9214
**Sites:** 46 sites for tents and RVs up to 32 feet long, including some multifamily units
**Facilities:** Tables, grills, drinking water, vault toilets; boat ramp 1.3 miles south
**Fee per night:** $$, multifamily: $$$$; reservations: (877) 444-6777 or recreation.gov
**Management:** American Land and Leisure, (800) 342-2267
**Activities:** Hiking, fishing, swimming, boating
**Finding the campground:** From Groveland, drive east on CA 120 for 15 miles. Turn left (north) onto Cherry Valley Road (FR 1N07) and drive 20 miles.
**About the campground:** Situated at a scenic location on the southwest shore of Cherry Lake, which is stocked annually. Trails from Cherry Lake Dam (1.5 miles south of the campground) lead north into the Emigrant Wilderness and east to Lake Eleanor, Hetch Hetchy, and other points in Yosemite National Park. In an area recovering from the 2013 Rim Fire. Elevation 4,700 feet. Stay limit 14 days. Open June to mid-September.

## 643 Sweetwater

**Location:** 15 miles east of Groveland
**GPS:** 37.8239 / -120.0050
**Sites:** 13 sites for tents and RVs up to 32 feet long
**Facilities:** Tables, grills, drinking water, vault toilets
**Fee per night:** $$; reservations: (877) 444-6777 or recreation.gov
**Management:** American Land and Leisure, (800) 342-2267
**Activities:** Fishing
**Finding the campground:** From Groveland, drive 15 miles east on CA 120.
**About the campground:** Near the South Fork of the Tuolumne River. The campground is 8 miles west of the Big Oak Flat entrance to Yosemite National Park and 14 miles southwest of the Hetch Hetchy entrance. Yosemite Valley is 22 miles to the southeast, making Sweetwater a good alternative camping spot if Yosemite campgrounds are full. The area is recuperating from the 2013 Rim Fire. Elevation 3,000 feet. Stay limit 14 days. Open mid-March to Labor Day.

## 644 **Dimond O**

**Location:** 28 miles east of Groveland
**GPS:** 37.8633 / -119.8693
**Sites:** 38 sites for tents and small RVs
**Facilities:** Tables, grills, drinking water, vault toilets
**Fee per night:** $$–$$$$; reservations: (877) 444-6777 or recreation.gov
**Management:** Stanislaus National Forest, (209) 962-7825
**Activities:** Fishing
**Finding the campground:** From Groveland, drive 24 miles east on CA 120. Turn left (north) onto Evergreen Road and drive about 4 miles.
**About the campground:** Situated near the Middle Fork of the Tuolumne River, which is stocked annually with rainbow trout. It is 3 miles south of the Hetch Hetchy entrance to Yosemite National Park and 5 miles north of the Big Oak Flat entrance. Yosemite Valley is only 18 miles to the southeast, making Dimond O a good alternative camping spot if Yosemite campgrounds are full. Elevation 4,400 feet. Stay limit 14 days. Open May through September.

## 645 **Dirt Flat**

**Location:** 14 miles northeast of Mariposa
**GPS:** 37.671175 / -119.836203
**Sites:** 20 sites for tents
**Facilities:** Tables, grills, drinking water, vault toilets
**Fee per night:** $$; reservations: (877) 444-6777 or recreation.gov
**Management:** Sierra National Forest, (559) 877-2218
**Activities:** Hiking, swimming, fishing
**Finding the campground:** From Mariposa, drive north 26 miles on CA 140. Turn left onto Foresta Road and cross the bridge over the river. Turn left onto Incline Road and proceed 1.3 miles.
**About the campground:** Though small, this campground is located right alongside the mighty Merced River. It is a scenic spot and not far from the entrance to Yosemite National Park. Elevation 1,600. Stay limit 14 days. Open all year.

## 646 **Dry Gulch**

**Location:** 14 miles northeast of Mariposa
**GPS:** 37.668677 / -119.838686
**Sites:** 20 sites for tents
**Facilities:** Tables, grills, drinking water, vault toilets
**Fee per night:** $$; reservations: (877) 444-6777 or recreation.gov
**Management:** Sierra National Forest, (559) 877-2218
**Activities:** Hiking, swimming, fishing
**Finding the campground:** From Mariposa, drive north 26 miles on CA 140. Turn left onto Foresta Road and cross the bridge over the river. Turn left onto Incline Road and proceed 1.5 miles.
**About the campground:** Though small, this campsite is located right alongside the mighty Merced River. It is a scenic spot and not far from the entrance to Yosemite National Park. Elevation 1,600. Stay limit 14 days. Open all year.

## 647 Jerseydale

**Location:** 13 miles northeast of Mariposa
**GPS:** 37.5456 / -119.8387
**Sites:** 10 sites, including 2 for RVs
**Facilities:** Tables, fire rings, drinking water, vault toilets
**Fee per night:** None
**Management:** Sierra National Forest, (559) 877-2218
**Activities:** None
**Finding the campground:** From Mariposa, drive 4 miles north on CA 140. Turn right (east) onto Triangle Road and drive 6 miles. Turn left (north) onto Jerseydale Road and drive 3 miles.
**About the campground:** Jerseydale is best used as an overflow camp for Yosemite National Park, whose main entrance is 24 miles to the east, or as a base from which to fish the South Fork of the Merced, 6 miles to the north. Elevation 3,700 feet. Stay limit 14 days. Open May through November.

## 648 Summerdale

**Location:** 15 miles north of Oakhurst
**GPS:** 37.4869 / -119.6330
**Sites:** Sites for tents and RVs up to 30 feet long
**Facilities:** Tables, fire rings, drinking water, vault toilets
**Fee per night:** $$; reservations: (877) 444-6777 or recreation.gov
**Management:** Sierra National Forest, (559) 877-2218
**Activities:** Fishing, swimming
**Finding the campground:** From Oakhurst, drive 15 miles north on CA 41.
**About the campground:** An attractive location, with campsites spread along Big Creek, a tributary of the South Fork of the Merced. Summerdale is 1 mile from the south entrance of Yosemite National Park and 2 miles from the Mariposa Grove of giant sequoia trees. Elevation 5,000 feet. Stay limit 14 days. Open May through September.

## 649 Nelder Grove

**Location:** 11 miles north of Oakhurst
**GPS:** 37.4311 / -119.5821
**Sites:** 7 sites for tents; 3 sites for RVs
**Facilities:** Tables, fire rings, vault toilets; no drinking water
**Fee per night:** None
**Management:** Sierra National Forest, (559) 877-2218
**Activities:** Hiking
**Finding the campground:** From Oakhurst, drive 4 miles north on CA 41. Turn right onto Sky Ranch Road and drive 4.5 miles. Turn left onto FR 6S47Y and drive 2 miles.
**About the campground:** Campsites are within Nelder Grove, which contains 106 mature giant sequoia trees, including the Bull Buck Tree. The sequoias are interspersed with second-growth pine, fir, and cedar. Trails lead through the grove, which also has an interpretive display and a

small museum. The campground is 15 miles from the south entrance to Yosemite National Park. Elevation 5,400 feet. Stay limit 14 days. Open May through September.

## 650 **Soquel**

**Location:** 10 miles north of Oakhurst
**GPS:** 37.4075 / -119.5628
**Sites:** 11 sites for tents and RVs up to 23 feet long
**Facilities:** Tables, fire rings, vault toilets; no drinking water
**Fee per night:** $$, double site: $$$$; reservations: (877) 444-6777 or recreation.gov
**Management:** California Land Management, (559) 877-2218
**Activities:** Fishing
**Finding the campground:** From Oakhurst, drive 4 miles north on CA 41. Turn right onto Sky Ranch Road and drive 5 miles. Turn right onto FR 6S40 and drive 1 mile.
**About the campground:** Situated on the North Fork of Willow Creek, Soquel is 19 miles from the south entrance to Yosemite. Elevation 5,400 feet. Stay limit 14 days. Open June through October.

## 651 **Greys Mountain**

**Location:** 11 miles north of Oakhurst
**GPS:** 37.3977 / -119.5646
**Sites:** 26 sites for tents and RVs up to 23 feet long
**Facilities:** Tables, fire rings, vault toilets; no drinking water
**Fee per night:** $$, double site: $$$$
**Management:** Sierra National Forest, (559) 877-2218
**Activities:** Fishing
**Finding the campground:** From Oakhurst, drive 4 miles north on CA 41. Turn right onto Sky Ranch Road and drive 5 miles. Turn right onto FR 6S40 and drive 2 miles.
**About the campground:** Situated on the North Fork of Willow Creek, Greys Mountain is 20 miles from the south entrance to Yosemite. Elevation 5,260 feet. Stay limit 14 days. Open May through October.

## 652 **Kelty Meadow**

**Location:** 11 miles north of Oakhurst
**GPS:** 37.4388 / -119.5429
**Sites:** 12 sites for tents and RVs up to 23 feet long
**Facilities:** Tables, fire rings, vault toilets, hitching posts and stock water for horses; no drinking water
**Fee per night:** $$, double site: $$$$; reservations: (877) 444-6777 or recreation.gov
**Management:** California Land Management, (650) 322-1181
**Activities:** Horseback riding
**Finding the campground:** From Oakhurst, drive 4 miles north on CA 41. Turn right onto Sky Ranch Road and drive 8 miles.
**About the campground:** Kelty Meadow is used primarily by equestrians and as an overflow for Yosemite, 17 miles to the north. Elevation 5,800 feet. Stay limit 14 days. Open June through October.

## 653 **Fresno Dome**

**Location:** 14 miles north of Oakhurst
**GPS:** 37.4544 / -119.5505
**Sites:** 15 sites for tents and RVs up to 23 feet long
**Facilities:** Tables, fire rings, vault toilets; no drinking water
**Fee per night:** $$, double site: $$$$
**Management:** Sierra National Forest, (559) 877-2218
**Activities:** Hiking, fishing
**Finding the campground:** From Oakhurst, drive 4 miles north on CA 41. Turn right onto Sky Ranch Road and drive 8.5 miles. Turn left onto FR 6S07 and drive 1.5 miles.
**About the campground:** Situated in a pretty meadow adjacent to Willow Creek, the campground has an old-fashioned wishing well at its center. An easy 0.5-mile trail leads to the top of Fresno Dome (7,540 feet). The south entrance to Yosemite is 18 miles to the north. Elevation 6,400 feet. Stay limit 14 days. Open May through October.

## 654 **Big Sandy**

**Location:** 17 miles north of Oakhurst
**GPS:** 37.4683 / -119.5819
**Sites:** 18 sites for tents; 4 sites for RVs up to 20 feet long
**Facilities:** Tables, fire rings, vault toilets; no drinking water
**Fee per night:** $$
**Management:** Sierra National Forest, (559) 877-2218
**Activities:** Fishing
**Finding the campground:** From Oakhurst, drive 4 miles north on CA 41. Turn right onto Sky Ranch Road and drive 8.5 miles. Turn left onto FR 6S07 and drive 4.5 miles.
**About the campground:** Located on the bank of Big Creek, 21 miles north of the south entrance to Yosemite. Elevation 5,800 feet. Stay limit 14 days. Open June through November.

## 655 **Forks (Bass Lake)**

**Location:** 6 miles east of Oakhurst
**GPS:** 37.3126 / -119.5701
**Sites:** 27 sites for tents; plus 6 sites for tents and RVs up to 35 feet long
**Facilities:** Tables, grills, drinking water, flush toilets, showers, boat ramp, restaurant
**Fee per night:** $$, double site: $$$$; reservations: (877) 444-6777 or recreation.gov
**Management:** California Land Management, (650) 322-1181
**Activities:** Hiking, swimming, fishing, boating, waterskiing
**Finding the campground:** From Oakhurst, drive 6 miles east on CR 426.
**About the campground:** Bass Lake is 4 miles long and about 0.5 mile wide and is located in a scenic, canyon-like setting. The lake is well stocked annually with rainbow trout and kokanee fingerlings. Catches also include bass, crappie, bluegill, and catfish. The campground is on the northwest shore of the lake. A trail leads from the campground to Goat Mountain Lookout. Group camping on Bass Lake is also available at Crane Valley Group Camp and Recreation Point Camp. Elevation 3,400 feet. Stay limit 14 days. Open May through September.

# 656 Lupine-Cedar Bluffs (Bass Lake)

**Location:** 8 miles east of Oakhurst
**GPS:** 37.3095 / -119.5472
**Sites:** 113 sites for tents and RVs up to 40 feet, including double sites
**Facilities:** Tables, grills, drinking water, flush toilets; boat ramp nearby
**Fee per night:** $$–$$$$; reservations: (877) 444-6777 or recreation.gov
**Management:** Sierra National Forest, (559) 877-2218
**Activities:** Hiking, swimming, fishing, boating, waterskiing
**Finding the campground:** From Oakhurst, drive 6 miles east on CR 426. Turn right onto CR 222 and drive 1.5 miles.
**About the campground:** Lupine is quieter and set further back from the lake than Cedar Bluff, and each site offers more privacy. Both are under tall Ponderosa pines. See Forks Campground (655) for lake and area information.

# 657 Spring Cove (Bass Lake)

**Location:** 9 miles east of Oakhurst
**GPS:** 37.3017 / -119.5414
**Sites:** 63 sites for tents; 10 for RVs up to 31 feet long
**Facilities:** Tables, grills, drinking water, flush toilets; boat ramp nearby
**Fee per night:** $$–$$$$; reservations: (877) 444-6777 or recreation.gov
**Management:** Sierra National Forest, (559) 877-2218
**Activities:** Hiking, swimming, fishing, boating, waterskiing
**Finding the campground:** From Oakhurst, drive 6 miles east on CR 426. Turn right onto CR 222 and drive 2.5 miles.
**About the campground:** Across the street from Bass Lake in a grove of oak, pine, and cedar trees. See Forks Campground (655) for lake and area information.

# 658 Wishon Point (Bass Lake)

**Location:** 10 miles east of Oakhurst
**GPS:** 37.2974 / -119.5346
**Sites:** 31 sites for tents and RVs, including some double family sites
**Facilities:** Tables, grills, drinking water, flush toilets, boat ramp
**Fee per night:** $$–$$$$; reservations: (877) 444-6777 or recreation.gov
**Management:** Sierra National Forest, (559) 877-2218
**Activities:** Hiking, swimming, fishing, boating, waterskiing
**Finding the campground:** From Oakhurst, drive 6 miles east on CR 426. Turn right onto CR 222 and drive 3.5 miles.
**About the campground:** Across the street from Bass Lake. Sites are shaded by manzanita, oak, pine, and cedar and quite private. A few sites have lake views. See Forks Campground (655) for lake and area information.

## 659 **Chilkoot**

**Location:** 13 miles northeast of Oakhurst
**GPS:** 37.3674 / -119.5374
**Sites:** 9 sites for tents and RVs up to 30 feet long
**Facilities:** Tables, fire rings, vault toilets; no drinking water
**Fee per night:** $$–$$$$; reservations: (877) 444-6777 or recreation.gov
**Management:** Sierra National Forest, (559) 877-2218
**Activities:** Fishing
**Finding the campground:** From Oakhurst, drive 3.5 miles north on CA 41. Turn right (east) onto CR 222 and drive 5.5 miles to the town of Bass Lake. Turn left (north) onto Beasore Road (FR 7) and drive 4 miles.
**About the campground:** Situated on the bank of Chilkoot Creek near its juncture with North Fork Willow Creek, the campground is best used as an overflow for Bass Lake (4 miles south) or Yosemite (south entrance 20 miles). Elevation 4,600 feet. Stay limit 14 days. Open May through September.

## 660 **Gaggs Camp**

**Location:** 22 miles northeast of Oakhurst
**GPS:** 37.3615 / -119.4707
**Sites:** 11 sites for tents and RVs up to 19 feet long
**Facilities:** Tables, fire rings, vault toilets; no drinking water
**Fee per night:** $$–$$$$
**Management:** Sierra National Forest, (559) 877-2218
**Activities:** Fishing
**Finding the campground:** From Oakhurst, drive 3.5 miles north on CA 41. Turn right (east) onto CR 222 and drive 5.5 miles to the town of Bass Lake. Turn left (north) onto Beasore Road (FR 7) and drive 8 miles. Then make a hard right turn onto FR 6S42 (Central Camp Road) and drive 4.5 miles. The road is gravel, narrow, and winding.
**About the campground:** Situated near Sand Creek, Gaggs Camp has little to recommend it except solitude. Some nearby meadows do offer pleasant walking. Elevation 5,700 feet. Stay limit 14 days. Open June through October.

## 661 **Whiskers**

**Location:** 25 miles east of Oakhurst
**GPS:** 37.3346 / -119.4911
**Sites:** 5 sites for tents; 3 sites for RVs
**Facilities:** Tables, fire rings, vault toilets; no drinking water
**Fee per night:** $$–$$$$
**Management:** Sierra National Forest, (559) 877-2218
**Activities:** Fishing
**Finding the campground:** From Oakhurst, drive 3.5 miles north on CA 41. Turn right (east) onto CR 222 and drive 5.5 miles to the town of Bass Lake. Turn left (north) onto Beasore Road (FR 7)

and drive 8 miles. Then make a hard right turn onto FR 6S42 (Central Camp Road) and drive 7.5 miles. The road is gravel, narrow, and winding.

**About the campground:** A small stream is nearby, but there is little else to recommend camping here. A good place to escape the crowds around Bass Lake. Elevation 5,300 feet. Stay limit 14 days. Open June through October.

## 662 Upper Chiquito

**Location:** 27 miles northeast of Oakhurst
**GPS:** 37.5023 / -119.4088
**Sites:** 20 sites for tents and RVs up to 23 feet long
**Facilities:** Tables, fire rings, vault toilets; no drinking water
**Fee per night:** None
**Management:** Sierra National Forest, (559) 877-2218
**Activities:** Hiking
**Finding the campground:** From Oakhurst, drive 3.5 miles north on CA 41. Turn right (east) onto CR 222 and drive 5.5 miles to the town of Bass Lake. Turn left (north) onto Beasore Road (FR 7) and drive 18 miles.

**About the campground:** Situated on the bank of Chiquito Creek. A trail northwest of the campground leads over Chiquito Pass into Yosemite National Park (2.5 miles), connecting to several park trails. The park's south entrance is 33 miles by vehicle. Elevation 6,800 feet. Stay limit 14 days. Open June through September.

## 663 Clover Meadow

**Location:** 36 miles northeast of Oakhurst
**GPS:** 37.5282 / -119.2808
**Sites:** 7 sites for tents and RVs up to 19 feet long
**Facilities:** Tables, fire rings, drinking water, vault toilets
**Fee per night:** None
**Management:** Sierra National Forest, (559) 877-2218
**Activities:** Hiking
**Finding the campground:** From Oakhurst, drive 3.5 miles north on CA 41. Turn right (east) onto CR 222 and drive 5.5 miles to the town of Bass Lake. Turn left (north) onto Beasore Road (FR 7) and drive 25 miles. Then turn left onto FR 4S60 and drive 1.5 miles. The campground is next to the Clover Meadow Ranger Station.

**About the campground:** At the edge of Clover Meadow. Trails lead west from the campground to several lakes and north into the Ansel Adams Wilderness. Elevation 7,000 feet. Stay limit 14 days. Open June through September.

## 664 Granite Creek

**Location:** 37 miles northeast of Oakhurst
**GPS:** 37.5408 / -119.2687
**Sites:** 15 tent sites; 5 RV sites
**Facilities:** Tables, fire rings, vault toilets; no drinking water

**Fee per night:** None
**Management:** Sierra National Forest, (559) 877-2218
**Activities:** Hiking, fishing, swimming
**Finding the campground:** From Oakhurst, drive 3.5 miles north on CA 41. Turn right (east) onto CR 222 and drive 5.5 miles to the town of Bass Lake. Turn left (north) onto Beasore Road (FR 7) and drive 25 miles. Then turn left onto FR 4S60 and drive 3 miles.
**About the campground:** Adjacent to raucous Granite Creek. Trails lead west from the campground to several different lakes and north and east into the Ansel Adams Wilderness. Elevation 7,000 feet. Stay limit 14 days. Open June through September.

## 665 **Whisky Falls**

**Location:** 10 miles northeast of North Fork
**GPS:** 37.2864 / -119.4418
**Sites:** 14 sites for tents and RVs
**Facilities:** Tables, fire rings, vault toilets; no drinking water
**Fee per night:** None
**Management:** Sierra National Forest, (559) 877-2218
**Activities:** Fishing
**Finding the campground:** From North Fork (south of Bass Lake), drive 3 miles east on CR 233. Turn left onto FR 8S09 and proceed 6 miles. Turn right onto FR 8S70 and drive 1 mile.
**About the campground:** Located in cool forest alongside Whisky Creek. A short walk 0.15 mile upstream leads to pretty Whisky Falls. Elevation 5,800 feet. Stay limit 14 days. Open May through September.

## 666 **Fish Creek**

**Location:** 18 miles east of North Fork
**GPS:** 37.2600 / -119.3532
**Sites:** 7 sites for tents and RVs up to 20 feet long
**Facilities:** Tables, fire rings, vault toilets; no drinking water
**Fee per night:** $$–$$$$; reservations: (877) 444-6777 or recreation.gov
**Management:** Sierra National Forest, (559) 877-2218
**Activities:** Hiking, fishing
**Finding the campground:** From North Fork, drive east and then south 3 miles on CR 225. Turn left onto Minarets Road (FR 81) and drive 15 miles.
**About the campground:** Situated on the bank of a small creek containing small wild trout. A trail from the campground leads 6 miles north to Mammoth Pool. Elevation 4,600 feet. Stay limit 14 days. Open April through October.

## 667 **Rock Creek**

**Location:** 21 miles northeast of North Fork
**GPS:** 37.2915 / -119.3615
**Sites:** 18 sites for tents and RVs up to 32 feet long
**Facilities:** Tables, fire rings, drinking water, vault toilets

**Fee per night:** $$–$$$$; reservations: (877) 444-6777 or recreation.gov
**Management:** Sierra National Forest, (559) 877-2218
**Activities:** Hiking, fishing, swimming
**Finding the campground:** From North Fork, drive east and then south 3 miles on CR 225. Turn left onto Minarets Road (FR 81) and drive 18 miles.
**About the campground:** Situated on the bank of Rock Creek, which provides good swimming in spring and early summer, as well as fishing for small wild trout. A dirt road leads southeast from the campground and connects to a trail to Mammoth Pool. Elevation 4,300 feet. Stay limit 14 days. Open April through October.

## 668 Soda Springs

**Location:** 31 miles northeast of North Fork
**GPS:** 37.3819 / -119.3892
**Sites:** 18 sites for tents and RVs up to 23 feet long
**Facilities:** Tables, fire rings, vault toilets; no drinking water
**Fee per night:** $$–$$$$
**Management:** Sierra National Forest, (559) 877-2218
**Activities:** Fishing, swimming
**Finding the campground:** From North Fork, drive east and then south 3 miles on CR 225. Turn left onto Minarets Road (FR 81) and drive 28 miles.
**About the campground:** Situated on the bank of Chiquito Creek, which provides swimming in spring and early summer, as well as fishing for small wild trout. The campground also serves as an overflow for Mammoth Pool, 7 miles to the southeast. Elevation 4,400 feet. Stay limit 14 days. Open April through October.

## 669 Lower Chiquito

**Location:** 36 miles northeast of North Fork
**GPS:** 37.4131 / -119.3844
**Sites:** 7 sites for tents and RVs up to 25 feet long
**Facilities:** Tables, fire rings, vault toilets; no drinking water
**Fee per night:** $$, double site: $$$$
**Management:** Sierra National Forest, (559) 877-2218
**Activities:** Fishing, swimming
**Finding the campground:** From North Fork, drive east and then south 3 miles on CR 225. Turn left onto Minarets Road (FR 81) and drive 29 miles. Turn left onto FR 6S71 and drive 3.5 miles.
**About the campground:** Situated on the bank of Chiquito Creek, which provides swimming in spring and early summer, as well as fishing for small wild trout. The campground also serves as an overflow for Mammoth Pool, 9 miles southeast. Elevation 4,900 feet. Stay limit 14 days. Open May through September.

## 670 Placer

**Location:** 35 miles northeast of North Fork
**GPS:** 37.3704 / -119.3619

**Sites:** 8 sites for tents and trailers up to 30 feet
**Facilities:** Tables, fire rings, vault toilets; no drinking water
**Fee per night:** $$, double site: $$$$
**Management:** Sierra National Forest, (559) 877-2218
**Activities:** Fishing
**Finding the campground:** From North Fork, drive east and then south 3 miles on CR 225. Turn left onto Minarets Road (FR 81) and drive 31 miles. Turn left onto Mammoth Pool Road (FR 6S71) and drive 0.7 mile.
**About the campground:** Situated on the bank of Chiquito Creek, which provides spring and summer swimming, as well as fishing for small wild trout. The campground also serves as an overflow for Mammoth Pool, 3 miles southeast. RVs are not recommended. Elevation 4,060 feet. Stay limit 14 days. Open April through September.

## 671 Sweet Water

**Location:** 36 miles northeast of North Fork
**GPS:** 37.3645 / -119.3516
**Sites:** 7 sites for tents; 5 sites for RVs up to 17 feet long
**Facilities:** Tables, fire rings, vault toilets; no drinking water
**Fee per night:** $$, double site: $$$$; reservations: (877) 444-6777 or recreation.gov
**Management:** California Land Management, (559) 877-2218
**Activities:** Fishing, swimming
**Finding the campground:** From North Fork, drive east and then south 3 miles on CR 225. Turn left onto Minarets Road (FR 81) and drive 31 miles. Turn left onto Mammoth Pool Road (FR 6S71) and drive 1.5 miles.
**About the campground:** Situated on the bank of Chiquito Creek, which provides spring and summer swimming, as well as fishing for small wild trout. The campground also serves as an overflow for Mammoth Pool, 2 miles south. Elevation 3,800 feet. Stay limit 14 days. Open May through October.

## 672 Mammoth Pool

**Location:** 38 miles northeast of North Fork
**GPS:** 37.3442 / -119.3333
**Sites:** 18 sites for tents; 30 sites for tents or RVs, including 5 multi-family sites
**Facilities:** Tables, fire rings, vault toilets; no drinking water; boat ramp and grocery store nearby
**Fee per night:** $$, double site: $$$$; reservations: (877) 444-6777 or recreation.gov
**Management:** Sierra National Forest, (559) 877-2218
**Activities:** Fishing, swimming, boating, waterskiing, hiking
**Finding the campground:** From North Fork, drive east and then south 3 miles on CR 225. Turn left onto Minarets Road (FR 81) and drive 31 miles. Turn left onto Mammoth Pool Road (FR 6S71) then drive 4 miles.
**About the campground:** The campground is near Mammoth Pool Reservoir, a steep-sided lake in the San Joaquin River gorge. It is 5 miles long and about 0.75 mile at its widest point. The lake is subject to heavy drawdowns of water in late summer and fall and is closed to boating and fishing May 1 to June 16. A trail leads north from the campground into the Ansel Adams Wilderness and south to Fish Creek. Elevation 3,500 feet. Stay limit 14 days. Open April through October.

## Yosemite National Park

### 673 Little Jackass

**Location:** 37 miles northeast of North Fork

**GPS:** 37.3997 / -119.3361

**Sites:** 5 sites for tents and RVs

**Facilities:** Tables, fire rings, vault toilets; no drinking water

**Fee per night:** None

**Management:** Sierra National Forest, (559) 877-2218

**Activities:** Fishing.

**Finding the campground:** From North Fork, drive east and then south 3 miles on CR 225. Turn left onto Minarets Road (FR 81) and drive 33 miles. Turn right onto FR 6S22 and drive 0.5 mile.

**About the campground:** Located on the bank of the West Fork of Jackass Creek, the campground can be used as overflow for Mammoth Pool, 6 miles to the south. Elevation 4,800 feet. Stay limit 14 days. Open May through October.

*Half Dome, a rare geological phenomenon, may well be the most recognizable feature in all of Yosemite National Park.*

## YOSEMITE NATIONAL PARK

"No temple wrought with hands can compare to Yosemite," wrote John Muir, the famed Western naturalist whose efforts led to the establishment of the park in 1890. This magnificent park encompasses 750,000 acres and offers so much that it would take a lifetime to experience it all.

The scenic highlight is Yosemite Valley, home to numerous natural icons including Half Dome, El Capitan, and Yosemite Falls. Nearly as sublime is the alpine splendor of the Tuolumne Meadows area, with its granite domes, lush meadows, and jagged skyline of majestic peaks. Nearby, the Grand Canyon of the Tuolumne is a spectacular slice of backcountry boasting grand cliffs and another impressive array of waterfalls. The tragically flooded Hetch Hetchy Valley retains much of its beauty and is a testimony to the need to preserve special places. Historic Wawona, at the southern end of Yosemite, offers rich history and natural beauty, highlighted by the Mariposa Grove of giant sequoias.

Visitors to Yosemite are nearly as diverse as the park itself. Families, backpackers, bohemians, RVers, and even socialites all rub elbows in the park, enjoying a wide array of amenities. The park has a reputation for being crowded, and this is at times deserved, though the grandeur of the landscape overcomes this. Whether you're scaling a granite wall, hiking the trails, or riding the free shuttle bus, the overwhelming beauty of Yosemite is the great equalizer.

Campgrounds are often full, and in summer the valley roads require patience. Fortunately, campers need not add their cars and RVs (maximum 40 feet) to the crush. A free shuttle bus service connects the campgrounds with most valley attractions, including Yosemite Village (visitor center, store, post office, museum, restaurants), Housekeeping Camp (showers, laundry), the famous tent cabins and hotel, Yosemite Falls, and various trailheads.

Premier hikes from the valley include Upper Yosemite Falls (7.2 miles round-trip, elevation gain 2,700 feet), Four-Mile-Trail to Glacier Point (3,200-foot elevation gain), top of Vernal Fall and Nevada Fall (3 miles and 7 miles round-trip, respectively, with trailheads within walking distance of the campgrounds), and a cable-assisted climb of Half Dome (17 miles round-trip, 4,800-foot elevation gain). A great way to climb Half Dome is to combine a horseback trip to the base of the dome with the climb. For information, call Yosemite Valley Stables at (209) 372-8348. For another world-class hike, take the bus to Glacier Point and hike down the magnificently scenic Panorama Trail to the valley floor (8.5 miles, descending 3,200 feet via Illilouette, Nevada, and Vernal Falls).

## 674 Lower Pines (Yosemite National Park, Yosemite Valley)

**Location:** East end of Yosemite Valley
**GPS:** 37.7392 / -119.5656
**Sites:** 75 sites for tents and RVs up to 40 feet long; double sites; 2 group sites
**Facilities:** Tables, grills/fire rings, drinking water, flush toilets, bear-proof food lockers; dump station at Upper Pines Campground (675).
**Fee per night:** $$, double and group sites: $$$; reservations: (877) 444-6777 or recreation.gov
**Management:** Yosemite National Park, (209) 372-0200
**Activities:** Hiking, fishing, swimming, rafting, cycling, horseback riding
**Finding the campground:** Enter Yosemite Valley from CA 120, CA 140, or CA 41. Follow Southside Drive (one-way into the valley) and signs for "Yosemite Valley Destinations" and "Pines Campgrounds."
**About the campground:** As the name indicates, the campsites are situated along several loops in a forest of tall pines. Elevation 4,000 feet. Stay limit 7 days. Open March through October. No pets allowed.

## 675 Upper Pines (Yosemite National Park, Yosemite Valley)

**Location:** East end of Yosemite Valley
**GPS:** 37.7392 / -119.5656
**Sites:** 238 sites for tents and RVs up to 35 feet long
**Facilities:** Tables, grills/fire rings, drinking water, flush toilets, bear-proof food lockers, dump station
**Fee per night:** $$; reservations: (877) 444-6777 or recreation.gov
**Management:** Yosemite National Park, (209) 372-0200
**Activities:** Hiking, fishing, swimming, rafting, cycling, horseback riding
**Finding the campground:** Enter Yosemite Valley from CA 120, CA 140, or CA 41. Follow Southside Drive (one-way into the valley) and signs for "Yosemite Valley Destinations" and "Pines Campgrounds."
**About the campground:** The setting is similar to Lower Pines (674), but the campground is much larger and thus more spread out. Upper Pines is the closest campground to the trail system leading to Vernal and Nevada Falls, Half Dome, and the Panorama Trail to Glacier Point. Elevation 4,000 feet. Stay limit 7 days. Open March through October.

## 676 North Pines (Yosemite National Park, Yosemite Valley)

**Location:** East end of Yosemite Valley
**GPS:** 37.7399 / -119.5643
**Sites:** 8 sites for tents and RVs up to 40 feet long
**Facilities:** Tables, grills/fire rings, drinking water, flush toilets, bear-proof food lockers; dump station at Upper Pines Campground (675)
**Fee per night:** $$; reservations: (877) 444-6777 or recreation.gov
**Management:** Yosemite National Park, (209) 372-0200
**Activities:** Hiking, fishing, swimming, rafting, cycling, horseback riding

**Finding the campground:** Enter Yosemite Valley from CA 120, CA 140, or CA 41. Follow Southside Drive (one-way into the valley) and signs for "Yosemite Valley Destinations" and "Pines Campgrounds."

**About the campground:** See Lower Pines (674) and Upper Pines (675) Campgrounds for area information. Elevation 4,000 feet. Stay limit 7 days. Open March through October.

## 677 Camp 4 Walk-in (Yosemite National Park, Yosemite Valley)

**Location:** 1 mile west of Yosemite Village
**GPS:** 37.7421 / -119.6011
**Sites:** 35 sites for tents
**Facilities:** Tables, grills, drinking water, flush toilets
**Fee per night:** $ per person
**Management:** Yosemite National Park, (209) 372-0200
**Activities:** Hiking, swimming, fishing
**Finding the campground:** From Yosemite Village, drive west 1 mile, just past Yosemite Lodge.
**About the campground:** Although technically a walk-in campground, Camp 4's campsites begin within 50 feet of its parking lot, making it an option for tent campers who find other valley campgrounds full or who do not have reservations at one of them. Sites are rented on a "per-person basis," meaning that 6 people will be placed in each campsite, regardless of the number of people in your own party. A rock climber's mecca, Camp 4 (also known as Sunnyside) often fills before 9 a.m. daily May through September. The Upper Yosemite Falls Trailhead begins at the campground, and Lower Yosemite Falls is within easy walking distance. Elevation 4,000 feet. Stay limit 7 days May 1 through September 15; 30 days the rest of the year. Open all year. No pets allowed.

## 678 Tuolumne Meadows (Yosemite National Park)

**Location:** 7 miles west of Tioga Pass entrance (east entrance)
**GPS:** 37.8724 / -119.3588
**Sites:** 34 sites for tents and RVs up to 35 feet long; 7 group sites for up to 30 people each; 4 equestrian sites for up to 6 people each
**Facilities:** Tables, grills, drinking water, flush toilets, dump station, store, gas station, restaurant; showers at Tuolumne Lodge, 0.5 mile away
**Fee per night:** $$, equestrian sites: $$$, group sites: $$$$; reservations: (877) 444-6777 or recreation.gov
**Management:** Yosemite National Park, (209) 372-0200
**Activities:** Hiking, swimming, fishing, horseback riding
**Finding the campground:** From the Tioga Pass entrance, drive west 7 miles on CA 120 (Tioga Pass Road).
**About the campground:** Tuolumne Meadows is a beautiful spot in the Yosemite high country. Surrounding peaks, such as Unicorn and Cathedral, make a perfect frame for the green meadows and the small streams that flow through them, feeding into the Tuolumne River. The campground is shaded by a forest of medium-size mixed pines, and it is laid out in several loops. Many attractive day hikes are possible from the campground, including a climb to the top of Lembert Dome

(9,450 feet, 3 miles round-trip); a hike to Dog Lake (3.5 miles); a hike to Elizabeth Lake (4.5 miles); and an easy, scenic 1.5-mile stroll around the meadow to Soda Springs and Parsons Lodge. No pets are allowed in the horse camp. Elevation 8,600 feet. Stay limit 14 days. Open mid-June through late September.

## 679 Porcupine Flat (Yosemite National Park)

**Location:** 21 miles west of Tioga Pass entrance (east entrance)
**GPS:** 37.8073 / -119.5648
**Sites:** 52 sites for tents, including limited space for RVs up to 40 feet long
**Facilities:** Tables, grills, vault toilets; no drinking water
**Fee per night:** $
**Management:** Yosemite National Park, (209) 372-0200
**Activities:** Hiking
**Finding the campground:** From the Tioga Pass entrance, drive west 21 miles on CA 120.
**About the campground:** RVs only have access to the front section of the campground. A trail leads east from the campground, connecting to another trail leading to North Dome, which overlooks Yosemite Valley (6 miles one-way). Elevation 8,100 feet. Stay limit 14 days. Open July through early September.

## 680 Yosemite Creek (Yosemite National Park)

**Location:** 35 miles north of Yosemite Village
**GPS:** 37.8263 / -119.5975
**Sites:** 75 sites for tents or small RVs
**Facilities:** Tables, grills, pit toilets; no drinking water
**Fee per night:** $
**Management:** Yosemite National Park, (209) 372-0200
**Activities:** Hiking, fishing
**Finding the campground:** From Yosemite Village, drive west on Northside Drive for 6 miles. Bear right at a fork onto Big Oak Flat Road and drive 9 miles to the intersection with CA 120 (Tioga Pass Road). Continue on Tioga Pass Road for 15 miles; turn right at the Yosemite Creek access road and drive 5 miles. The access road is winding, steep, and narrow and not suitable for large RVs or trailers.
**About the campground:** A trail leads south from the campground to the top of Upper Yosemite Falls and to the summit of El Capitan. Elevation 7,660 feet. Stay limit 14 days. Open from July through early September.

## 681 White Wolf (Yosemite National Park)

**Location:** 30 miles north of Yosemite Village
**GPS:** 37.8702 / -119.6487
**Sites:** 74 sites for tents and RVs up to 27 feet
**Facilities:** Tables, grills, drinking water, flush toilets
**Fee per night:** $
**Management:** Yosemite National Park, (209) 372-0200

**Activities:** Hiking, fishing
**Finding the campground:** From Yosemite Village, drive west on Northside Drive for 6 miles. Bear right at a fork onto Big Oak Flat Road and drive 9 miles to the intersection with CA 120 (Tioga Pass Road). Continue on Tioga Pass Road for 14 miles; turn left onto the campground access road and drive 1 mile.
**About the campground:** Trails from the campground lead east to Lukens Lake (4 miles) and north to Harden Lake. Elevation 8,000 feet. Stay limit 14 days. Open July through early September.

## 682 Tamarack Flat (Yosemite National Park)

**Location:** 21 miles west of Yosemite Village
**GPS:** 37.7528 / -119.7376
**Sites:** 52 sites for tents or small RVs
**Facilities:** Tables, grills, pit toilets; no drinking water
**Fee per night:** $
**Management:** Yosemite National Park, (209) 372-0200
**Activities:** Hiking
**Finding the campground:** From Yosemite Village, drive west on Northside Drive for 6 miles. Bear right at a fork onto Big Oak Flat Road and drive 9 miles to the intersection with CA 120 (Tioga Pass Road). Continue on Tioga Pass Road for 3 miles; turn left onto the campground access road and drive 3 miles. The dirt access road to the campground is not suitable for large RVs or trailers.
**About the campground:** A trail leads north from the campground to Aspen Valley and east to the summit of El Capitan. Elevation 6,300 feet. Stay limit 14 days. Open June through early September. No pets allowed.

## 683 Crane Flat (Yosemite National Park)

**Location:** 16 miles west of Yosemite Village
**GPS:** 37.7515 / -119.8003
**Sites:** 166 sites for tents and RVs up to 35 feet long
**Facilities:** Tables, grills, drinking water, flush toilets
**Fee per night:** $$; reservations (required) recreation.gov
**Management:** Yosemite National Park, (209) 372-0200
**Activities:** Hiking
**Finding the campground:** From Yosemite Village, drive west on Northside Drive for 6 miles. Bear right at a fork onto Big Oak Flat Road and drive 10 miles.
**About the campground:** The campground is within a few minutes drive of Merced Grove and Tuolumne Grove, both of which contain giant old-growth sequoia trees. It is an easy drive into Yosemite Valley from here. Elevation 6,200 feet. Stay limit 14 days. Open July through October.

## 684 Hodgdon Meadow (Yosemite National Park)

**Location:** 22 miles northwest of Yosemite Valley
**GPS:** 37.8000 / -119.8669
**Sites:** 105 sites for tents and RVs up to 35 feet long; 4 group sites for up to 30 people each
**Facilities:** Tables, grills, drinking water, flush toilets

**Fee per night:** $$, group sites: $$$$; reservations: (877) 444-6777 or recreation.gov
**Management:** Yosemite National Park, (209) 372-0200
**Activities:** None
**Finding the campground:** From Yosemite Village, drive west on Northside Drive for 6 miles. Bear right at a fork onto Big Oak Flat Road and drive 16 miles.
**About the campground:** Sites are close and rather small, but being off the beaten path, Hogden tends to be less crowded than other campgrounds in Yosemite. The adjacent meadow is green and very pretty. Elevation 4,872 feet. Stay limit 14 days May through September; 30 days the rest of the year. Open all year.

## 685 Bridalveil Creek (Yosemite National Park)

**Location:** 23 miles south of Yosemite Village
**GPS:** 37.6690 / -119.6243
**Sites:** 110 sites for tents and RVs up to 35 feet long; several group sites for tents only (up to 30 people each); several equestrian sites (up to 6 people and 2 horses each)
**Facilities:** Tables, grills, drinking water, flush toilets
**Fee per night:** $$, group sites: $$$$, equestrian sites: $$$; reservations: (877) 444-6777 or recreation.gov
**Management:** Yosemite National Park, (209) 372-0200
**Activities:** Hiking, fishing, horseback riding
**Finding the campground:** From Yosemite Village, drive west on Northside Drive for 5 miles. Turn left onto CA 41 and drive 9 miles. Turn left onto Glacier Point Road and drive 9 miles.
**About the campground:** Situated in a wooded grove along Bridalveil Creek. Several excellent trails are located within walking distance of the campground. McGurk Meadow Trail begins 0.2 mile west of the campground turnoff and leads 2 miles downhill to an attractive meadow and an old cabin that belonged to one of the original Yosemite pioneers. The Ostrander Lake Trail (12.7 miles round-trip) begins 1.3 miles east of the campground turnoff and leads to a beautiful alpine lake, offering views of Mount Starr King, the Yosemite Valley domes, and the peaks of the Clark Range en route. The Mono Meadow Trail (3 miles round-trip) provides magnificent views of Half Dome, the Clark Range, and Mount Starr King from the eastern end of the meadow. It begins 2.5 miles east of the campground turnoff.

Six miles east of the campground is the parking lot for the 2.2-mile round-trip to the top of Sentinel Dome, with its panoramic view over the park. From the same parking area, a 2.2-mile trail leads to the spectacular cliffs and fissures of Taft Point. This campground is also the closest one to the magnificent overlook at Glacier Point (6 miles northeast). Elevation 7,200 feet. Stay limit 14 days. Open July through September.

## 686 Wawona (Yosemite National Park)

**Location:** 25 miles southwest of Yosemite Village
**GPS:** 37.5448 / -119.6725
**Sites:** 93 sites for tents and RVs up to 35 feet long; 1 group site for up to 30 people; 4 equestrian sites for up to 6 people each

**Facilities:** Tables, fire grills/rings, drinking water, flush toilets, dump station; store, post office, gas station, and nine-hole golf course at Wawona, 0.5 mile from the campground

**Fee per night:** $$, group sites: $$$$; reservations: (877) 444-6777 or recreation.gov

**Management:** Yosemite National Park, (209) 372-0200

**Activities:** Hiking, swimming, fishing, horseback riding

**Finding the campground:** From Yosemite Village, drive west on Northside Drive for 5 miles. Turn left onto CA 41 and drive 20 miles.

**About the campground:** Spread out laterally in several loops along the banks of the South Fork of the Merced River, the campground provides swimming holes and fishing sites at many campsites. The Mariposa Grove of giant sequoia trees can be reached by a 6-mile trail from Wawona, by car, or by a free shuttle bus, which leaves from the post office. The grove contains many mature trees, including the Grizzly Giant, estimated to be more than 2,700 years old, and a tunnel tree, with a passage cut through its base.

A fine hike, little known among the more famous (and crowded) waterfall hikes, is the trail to Chilnaulna Falls. From Wawona, this scenic route gradually climbs 2,400 feet in 4.2 miles. A lovely basin is formed by the upper falls, with water flowing through five small, attractive pools before plunging over the main falls. Elevation 4,000 feet. Stay limit 14 days May through September; 30 days the rest of the year. Open all year.

## OVERFLOW CAMPING NEAR YOSEMITE NATIONAL PARK

Every year, thousands of campers are turned away from Yosemite campgrounds because they are full, especially during the summer months and on holiday weekends. The best way to avoid this disappointment is to travel during off-peak periods, reserve campground space when possible, and arrive at campgrounds early in the day. For those who find themselves without a space inside the park itself, the following campgrounds are within a reasonable driving distance. These are described in this book. There are a few privately owned and primitive sites as well.

- Big Oak Flat and Hetch Hetchy entrances: Dimond O, Sweetwater, Lost Claim, The Pines, Moore Creek
- Arch Rock entrance (El Portal): Merced River Recreation Area
- South entrance (Wawona): Summerdale, Big Sandy, Fresno Dome, Soquel, Greys Mountain, Nelder Grove, Crane Flat, Forks, Lupine–Cedar Bluffs, Spring Cove, Wishon Point
- East entrance (Tioga Pass): Tioga Lake, Ellery Lake, Junction, Saddlebag Lake, Big Bend, and Lower Lee Vining

# Mammoth Lakes Basin

Most of the undeveloped land in this area lies within the Inyo National Forest and in two of its wilderness areas: Ansel Adams and John Muir. Central to the area is the community of Mammoth Lakes, one of California's major summer and winter outdoor playgrounds. Mammoth Mountain, which towers over the town, hosts skiers in winter and hikers and mountain bikers from spring through fall. Devils Postpile National Monument and Rainbow Falls are two of the attractions of Reds Meadow, west of the town. Jewel-like lakes at the base of snowcapped mountains beckon swimmers, anglers, and boaters.

The Lee Vining Canyon Scenic Byway leads to the east entrance of Yosemite National Park, the highest vehicle crossing of the Sierra Nevada. Beginning at US 395 about 0.5 mile south of Lee Vining, the route climbs 12 miles through spectacular Lee Vining Canyon to Tioga Pass (9,945 feet). Only the artificial border of the national park separates the upper portions of the canyon and its beautiful alpine lakes from the geologically similar Yosemite high country it adjoins. The first nine campgrounds that follow are often considered part of greater eastern Yosemite area and make good alternatives for day trips into the Yosemite Valley, as well as offering a base for exploring the Mammoth Lakes Basin.

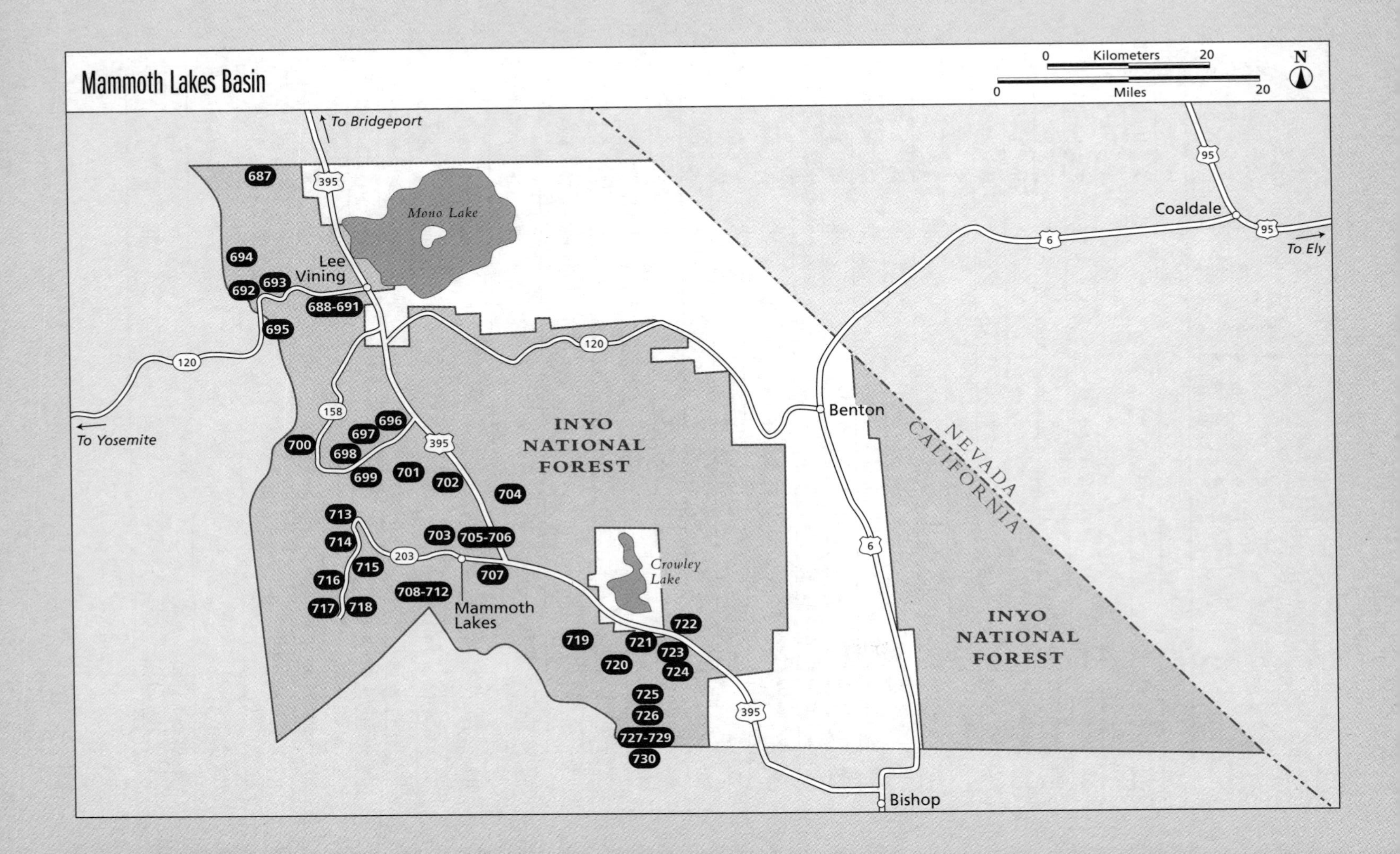
Mammoth Lakes Basin
0
Kilometers
20
0
Miles
20
N
To Bridgeport
To Yosemite
To Ely
Mono Lake
Lee Vining
Coaldale
Benton
Bishop
Mammoth Lakes
Crowley Lake
INYO NATIONAL FOREST
INYO NATIONAL FOREST
NEVADA
CALIFORNIA
395
120
158
203
6
95
687
688-691
692
693
694
695
696
697
698
699
700
701
702
703
704
705-706
707
708-712
713
714
715
716
717
718
719
720
721
722
723
724
725
726
727-729
730

| | Name | Group Sites | RV Sites | Max. RV Length | Hookups | Toilets | Showers | Drinking Water | Dump Station | Pets | Wheelchair | Recreation | Fee(s) | Season | Can Reserve |
|---|---|---|---|---|---|---|---|---|---|---|---|---|---|---|---|
| | **MAMMOTH LAKES AREA** | | | | | | | | | | | | | | |
| 687 | Lundy Canyon | | * | 23 | | V | | | | * | | HFB | $ | May-Oct | |
| 688 | Lower Lee Vining (Tioga Pass) | | * | | | VC | | | | * | | F | $ | May-Oct | |
| 689 | Moraine (Tioga Pass) | | * | | | P | | | | * | | F | $ | May-Oct | |
| 690 | Aspen Grove (Tioga Pass) | | * | | | P | | | | * | | F | $ | May-Oct | |
| 691 | Big Bend (Tioga Pass) | | * | | | V | | * | | * | * | F | $$ | Apr-Oct | |
| 692 | Ellery Lake (Tioga Pass) | | * | | | F | | * | | * | * | F | $$ | Jun-Oct | |
| 693 | Junction (Tioga Pass) | | * | | | V | | | | * | | F | $ | Jun-Oct | |
| 694 | Saddlebag Lake (Tioga Pass) | * | * | | | V | | * | | * | * | HFBL | $$ | Jun-Oct | |
| 695 | Tioga Lake (Tioga Pass) | | * | | | V | | * | | * | * | F | $$ | Jun-Oct | |
| 696 | Oh! Ridge (June Lake Loop) | | * | 40 | | F | | * | | * | | SF | $$ | Apr-Oct | * |
| 697 | June Lake (June Lake Loop) | | * | 23 | | F | | * | | * | | SFBHL | $$ | Apr-Oct | * |
| 698 | Gull Lake (June Lake Loop) | | * | 30 | | F | | * | | * | | SFBHL | $$ | Apr-Oct | * |
| 699 | Reversed Creek (June Lake Loop) | | * | 45 | | F | | * | | * | | F | $$ | May-Oct | * |
| 700 | Silver Lake (June Lake Loop) | | * | 35 | | F | | * | | * | | FBHR | $$ | Apr-Oct | * |
| 701 | Hartley Springs | | * | | | V | | | | * | | H | None | June-Sept | |
| 702 | Glass Creek | | * | | | V | | | | * | | HF | None | May-Oct | |
| 703 | Deadman | | * | | | V | | | | * | | F | None | June-Oct | |
| 704 | Big Springs | | * | | | V | | | | * | | F | None | Apr-Oct | |
| 705 | New Shady Rest (Mammoth Lakes) | | * | 38 | | F | | * | * | * | | HRO | $$ | Apr-Oct | * |
| 706 | Old Shady Rest (Mammoth Lakes) | | * | 45 | | F | | * | * | * | | HR | $$ | June-Sept | * |
| 707 | Sherwin Creek (Mammoth Lakes) | | * | | | F | | * | * | * | | HOR | $$ | May-Sept | * |
| 708 | Twin Lakes (Mammoth Lakes) | | * | 45 | | F | | * | | * | * | HFBSRL | $$ | June-Oct | * |
| 709 | Pine City (Mammoth Lakes) | | * | 36 | | F | | * | | * | * | HR | $$ | June-Sept | * |
| 710 | Coldwater (Mammoth Lakes) | | * | 40 | | F | | * | | * | | HFR | $$ | June-Sept | * |
| 711 | Lake George (Mammoth Lakes) | | * | 23 | | F | | * | | * | | HFBRL | $$ | June-Sept | * |
| 712 | Lake Mary (Mammoth Lakes) | | * | 30 | | F | | * | | * | | FSBRL | $$ | June-Sept | * |
| 713 | Agnew Meadows (Reds Meadow) | * | * | 30 | | V | | * | | * | | HFR | $$ | June-Oct | * |
| 714 | Upper Soda Springs (Reds Meadow) | | * | small | | V | | * | | * | | HFR | $$ | June-Sept | |
| 715 | Pumice Flat (Reds Meadow) | | * | | | F | | * | | * | | HFR | $$ | June-Sept | |
| 716 | Minaret Falls (Reds Meadow) | | * | | | V | | * | | * | | HFR | $$ | June-Sept | |

| | Name | Group Sites | RV Sites | Max. RV Length | Hookups | Toilets | Showers | Drinking Water | Dump Station | Pets | Wheelchair | Recreation | Fee(s) | Season | Can Reserve |
|---|---|---|---|---|---|---|---|---|---|---|---|---|---|---|---|
| 717 | Devils Postpile | | * | | | F | | * | | * | | HFR | $$ | June-snowfall | |
| 718 | Reds Meadow | | * | 30 | | F | * | * | | * | | HR | $$ | June-Oct | |
| 719 | Convict Lake | | * | | | F | * | * | | * | | FBHL | $$ | Apr-Oct | * |
| 720 | McGee Creek | | * | 23 | | FV | * | * | | * | * | HFR | $$ | Apr-Sept | * |
| 721 | Crowley Lake | | * | | | P | | * | | * | | FBS | $ | Apr-Oct | |
| 722 | Tuff | | * | 45 | | V | | * | | * | | | $$ | Apr-Oct | * |
| 723 | French Camp | | * | 23 | | F | | * | * | * | | F | $$ | Apr-Oct | * |
| 724 | Holiday | | * | 23 | | V | | * | | * | | F | $$ | Year-round | |
| 725 | Iris Meadow | | * | 26 | | F | | * | | * | | F | $$ | June-Oct | |
| 726 | Big Meadow | | * | 23 | | F | | * | * | * | | FHR | $$ | June-Oct | |
| 727 | East Fork | | * | 40 | | F | | * | | * | | F | $$ | May-Sept | * |
| 728 | Pine Grove | | * | 23 | | V | | * | | * | | F | $$ | May-Oct | |
| 729 | Upper Pine Grove | | * | 23 | | V | | * | | * | * | FR | $$ | May-Oct | |
| 730 | Rock Creek Lake | * | * | 23 | | V | | * | | * | | FHR | $$-$$$$ | May-Oct | * |

Toilets: F=flush V=vault P=pit C=chemical; Fee: $=Under $20 $$=$20-$29 $$$=$30-$39 $$$$ $40 or more; Recreation: H=hiking S=swimming F=fishing B=boating L=boat launch O=off-highway driving R=horseback riding, M=mountain biking
Hookups: W=water E=electric S=sewer

## 687 Lundy Canyon

**Location:** 12 miles northwest of Lee Vining
**GPS:** 38.0344402 / -119.208661
**Sites:** 36 sites for tents and RVs up to 23 feet long
**Facilities:** Vault toilets, boat launch; no drinking water
**Fee per night:** $
**Management:** Mono County Building and Parks Department, (760) 932-5440
**Activities:** Hiking, fishing, boating
**Finding the campground:** From Lee Vining, drive north 7 miles on US 395. Turn left (west) onto Lundy Lake Road and drive 5 miles.
**About the campground:** Situated on Lundy Creek near Lundy Lake, which is well stocked annually with rainbow trout and brown trout fingerlings. Lundy Lake is also famous for large Alpers trout. A trail leads southwest from the campground to a series of small lakes in the Hoover Wilderness and to Saddlebag Lake (694). Elevation 7,800 feet. Open May through October.

*A beaver pond in Lundy Canyon, not far from the campground. Photo by Bubba Seuss*

## 688 Lower Lee Vining (Tioga Pass)

**Location:** 3 miles west of the town of Lee Vining
**GPS:** 37.9319 / -119.1541
**Sites:** 5 sites for tents and RVs
**Facilities:** Tables, some stone fire rings, vault and portable toilets; no drinking water
**Fee per night:** $
**Management:** Inyo National Forest, (760) 924-5500
**Activities:** Fishing
**Finding the campground:** From Lee Vining, drive south on US 395 for 0.5 mile. Turn right onto CA 120 and drive 2.5 miles.
**About the campground:** Five campgrounds are spread closely along 2 miles of Lee Vining Creek, a beautiful stream with good fishing for rainbow trout. Campsites are in everything from large open fields to wooded areas, with some located right on the banks of the stream. The campgrounds are named Lower Lee Vining, Moraine [689], Aspen Grove [690], Big Bend [691] and two others overflow areas Cattleguard, and Boulder. They provide a base for exploring Mono Lake and Basin, located within 5 miles of the Mono Basin Scenic Area Visitor Center and about 15 miles from the South Tufa and Navy Beach tufa viewing areas. The campgrounds also serve as an overflow area for Yosemite National Park, 8 miles to the west. Elevation 7,300 feet. Stay limit 14 days. Open May through October.

## 689 Moraine (Tioga Pass)

**Location:** 4 miles west of Lee Vining
**GPS:** 37.9306 / -119.1614

## TIOGA PASS

The highest pass in California and the Sierra Nevada, at 9,943 feet Tioga Pass is the gateway to Yosemite from the east. Just south of the pass along the highway is picturesque Dana Meadows. Several small lakes can be accessed from backcountry trailheads here. Other trails lead to Gaylor Lakes and the summit of Mount Dana. The pass is named for the Tioga Mine, which was once the hope of forty-niners from New York. From the Iroquois and Mohawk, *Tioga* means roughly "where it forks."

**Sites:** 25 sites for tents and RVs
**Facilities:** Tables, some stone fire rings, pit toilets; no drinking water
**Fee per night:** $
**Management:** Inyo National Forest, (760) 924-5500
**Activities:** Fishing
**Finding the campground:** From Lee Vining, drive south on US 395 for 0.5 mile. Turn right onto CA 120 and drive 3 miles. Turn left onto Poole Power Plant Road, then turn left again. The road dead-ends at the campground, in about 200 yards.
**About the campground:** See Lower Lee Vining Campground (688) for area information.

# 690 Aspen Grove (Tioga Pass)

**Location:** 6 miles west of Lee Vining
**GPS:** 37.9392 / -119.1855
**Sites:** 45 sites for tents and RVs
**Facilities:** Tables, some stone fire rings, drinking water, pit toilets
**Fee per night:** $
**Management:** Inyo National Forest, (760) 924-5500
**Activities:** Fishing
**Finding the campground:** From Lee Vining, drive south on US 395 for 0.5 mile. Turn right onto CA 120 and drive 4 miles. Turn left and then right; follow the gravel road for 1.7 miles.
**About the campground:** Located on an attractive section of Lee Vining Creek (see Lower Lee Vining Campground, 688). Many campsites are right on the banks of the stream, among both tall pines and smaller aspens, affording both heavily wooded and more-open sites. The campground also serves as an overflow area for Yosemite National Park, 8 miles to the west. Elevation 8,000 feet. Stay limit 14 days. Open May through October.

# 691 Big Bend (Tioga Pass)

**Location:** 7 miles west of Lee Vining
**GPS:** 37.9450 / -119.2009
**Sites:** 17 sites for tents and RVs up to feet long
**Facilities:** Tables, fire rings, drinking water, vault toilets

**Fee per night:** $$
**Management:** California Land Management, (650) 322-1181
**Activities:** Fishing
**Finding the campground:** From Lee Vining, drive south on US 395 for 0.5 mile. Turn right onto CA 120 and drive 4 miles. Turn left and then right; follow the gravel road for 2.7 miles.
**About the campground:** A heavily shaded campground with some smaller sites on the banks of Lee Vining Creek. Fishing is similar to Aspen Grove Campground (690). The campground also serves as an overflow area for Yosemite National Park, 8 miles to the west. Elevation 7,800 feet. Stay limit 14 days. Open mid-April through mid-October.

## 692 Ellery Lake (Tioga Pass)

**Location:** 10 miles west of Lee Vining
**GPS:** 37.9385 / -119.2443
**Sites:** 12 sites for tents and RVs
**Facilities:** Tables, fire rings, drinking water, flush toilets
**Fee per night:** $$
**Management:** California Land Management, (650) 322-1181
**Activities:** Fishing
**Finding the campground:** From Lee Vining, drive south on US 395 for 0.5 mile. Turn right onto CA 120 and drive 9 miles.
**About the campground:** Situated in a dramatic setting on the shore of a beautiful blue alpine lake, the campground is only 2 miles east of the western entrance to Yosemite. It is an excellent alternative to camping in the park at Tuolumne Meadows. The lake is stocked annually with rainbow trout. Elevation 9,500 feet. Stay limit 14 days. Open June through mid-October.

## 693 Junction (Tioga Pass)

**Location:** 10 miles west of Lee Vining
**GPS:** 37.9384 / -119.2510
**Sites:** 13 sites for tents and RVs
**Facilities:** Tables, fire rings, vault toilets; no drinking water
**Fee per night:** $
**Management:** California Land Management, (650) 322-1181
**Activities:** Fishing
**Finding the campground:** From Lee Vining, drive south on US 395 for 0.5 mile. Turn right onto CA 120 and drive 9 miles. Across the highway from Ellery Lake Campground (692).
**About the campground:** Junction shares with Ellery Lake Campground (692) a dramatic setting and easy accessibility to Yosemite National Park. Elevation 9,600 feet. Stay limit 14 days. Open June through October.

## 694 Saddlebag Lake (Tioga Pass)

**Location:** 12 miles west of Lee Vining
**GPS:** 37.9657 / -119.2713
**Sites:** 20 sites for tents and RVs; 1 group site for up to 40 people

**Facilities:** Tables, fire rings, drinking water, vault toilets, store, boat ramp and rentals
**Fee per night:** $$
**Management:** California Land Management, (650) 322-1181
**Activities:** Hiking, fishing, boating
**Finding the campground:** From Lee Vining, drive south on US 395 for 0.5 mile. Turn right on CA 120 and drive 9 miles. Turn right (north) onto FR 04 and drive 2 miles.
**About the campground:** Saddlebag Lake is the highest lake accessible by car in California. It occupies a spectacular if stark setting well above tree line. The campground is within 0.25 mile of the lakeshore. The lake is well stocked annually with rainbow trout. A 4-mile trail circles the lake, another leads northwest to a series of smaller lakes, and a third leads north and then west to Lundy Canyon and Lundy Lake. The western entrance to Yosemite is 4 miles to the south. Elevation 10,087 feet. Stay limit 14 days. Open June through October.

## 695 Tioga Lake (Tioga Pass)

**Location:** 11 miles west of Lee Vining
**GPS:** 37.9280 / -119.2551
**Sites:** 13 sites for tents and RVs
**Facilities:** Tables, fire rings, drinking water, vault toilets
**Fee per night:** $$
**Management:** California Land Management, (650) 322-1181
**Activities:** Fishing
**Finding the campground:** From Lee Vining, drive south on US 395 for 0.5 mile. Turn right (west) onto CA 120 and drive 10 miles.
**About the campground:** Situated in a spectacular setting beside a beautiful alpine lake, which is stocked annually with rainbow trout. The campground is an excellent alternative to Yosemite's Tuolumne Campground, and the park's eastern entrance is only 1 mile south. Elevation 9,700 feet. Stay limit 14 days. Open June through mid-October.

## 696 Oh! Ridge (June Lake Loop)

**Location:** 17 miles northwest of the community of Mammoth Lakes
**GPS:** 37.7978 / -119.0731
**Sites:** 14 sites for tents and RVs up to 40 feet long
**Facilities:** Tables, fire rings, drinking water, flush toilets, playground; boat ramp 2 miles south
**Fee per night:** $$; reservations (877) 444-6777 or recreation.gov
**Management:** California Land Management, (650) 322-1181
**Activities:** Swimming, fishing
**Finding the campground:** From Mammoth Lakes, drive northwest 15 miles on US 395. Turn left (west) onto CA 158 (June Lake Loop) and drive 1.2 miles. Turn right (north) onto Oh! Ridge Road and drive 0.5 mile.
**About the campground:** The June Lake Loop Road (CA 158) traverses a beautiful horseshoe-shaped glacial canyon with streams, waterfalls, forests, alpine meadows, and high desert. Spectacular mountain scenery greets you at almost every turn in the road. There are four lakes along the loop, with public campgrounds on three of them and a private campground on the fourth (Grant Lake).

The exclamation point in Oh! Ridge is well deserved. Overlooking June Lake and the snow-capped peaks of the Sierra Nevada beyond, this campground has one of the most magnificent views of any in this book, and many campsites are located to take advantage of it. There is no direct access to the lake, but June Lake Beach is less than 0.5 mile away. Elevation 7,600 feet. Stay limit 14 days. Open April through October.

## 697 June Lake (June Lake Loop)

**Location:** 17 miles northwest of the community of Mammoth Lakes
**GPS:** 37.7819 / -119.0739
**Sites:** 28 sites for tents and RVs up to about 23 feet long
**Facilities:** Tables, fire rings, drinking water, flush toilets, boat ramp
**Fee per night:** $$; reservations: (877) 444-6777 or recreation.gov
**Management:** California Land Management, (650) 322-1181
**Activities:** Swimming, fishing, boating, hiking
**Finding the campground:** From Mammoth Lakes, drive northwest 15 miles on US 395. Turn left (west) onto CA 158 (June Lake Loop) and drive 2 miles.
**About the campground:** Although the campground is directly on the lake, the water is not visible from most campsites; nor are the surrounding mountains. Campers seeking a view should camp at Oh! Ridge Campground (696). June Lake is heavily stocked annually with rainbow trout. A trail leads southwest from the campground to tiny Yost Lake and onto Glass Creek Meadow. See the Oh! Ridge Campground listing for more area information. Elevation 7,600 feet. Stay limit 14 days. Open April through October.

## 698 Gull Lake (June Lake Loop)

**Location:** 18 miles northwest of the community of Mammoth Lakes
**GPS:** 37.7724 / -119.0835
**Sites:** 11 sites for tents and RVs up to 30 feet long
**Facilities:** Tables, fire rings, drinking water, flush toilets, boat ramp
**Fee per night:** $$; reservations: (877) 444-6777 or recreation.gov
**Management:** California Land Management, (650) 322-1181
**Activities:** Swimming, fishing, boating, hiking
**Finding the campground:** From Mammoth Lakes, drive northwest 15 miles on US 395. Turn left (west) onto CA 158 (June Lake Loop) and drive 3 miles.
**About the campground:** For its small size (a little over 60 acres), Gull Lake is heavily stocked with fish—more than 35,000 catchable-size rainbow trout and 10,000 cutthroat trout fingerlings annually. A trail leads west 2 miles from the campground to Silver Lake and north 3 miles to Reversed Peak (9,473 feet). See Oh! Ridge Campground (696) for area information. Elevation 7,600 feet. Stay limit 14 days. Open April through October.

## 699 Reversed Creek (June Lake Loop)

**Location:** 18 miles northwest of the community of Mammoth Lakes
**GPS:** 37.7712 / -119.0833
**Sites:** 17 sites for tents and RVs up to 45 feet long

**Facilities:** Tables, fire rings, drinking water, flush toilets; boat ramp at June Lake, 1 mile north
**Fee per night:** $$; reservations: (877) 444-6777 or recreation.gov
**Management:** California Land Management, (650) 322-1181
**Activities:** Fishing
**Finding the campground:** From Mammoth Lakes, drive northwest 15 miles on US 395. Turn left (west) onto CA 158 (June Lake Loop) and drive 3 miles. The campground is across the highway from Gull Lake Campground (698).
**About the campground:** Being the only stream in the area flowing toward rather than away from the mountains gave Reversed Creek its name. Situated across the highway from Gull Lake in a stand of tall pines, the campground is the most shaded and heavily wooded of those along June Lake Loop. Reversed Creek is stocked annually with a modest number of rainbow trout. See Oh! Ridge Campground (696) for more area information. Elevation 7,600 feet. Stay limit 14 days. Open May through October.

## 700 Silver Lake (June Lake Loop)

**Location:** 21 miles northwest of the community of Mammoth Lakes
**GPS:** 37.7831 / -119.1265
**Sites:** 63 sites for tents and RVs up to 35 feet
**Facilities:** Tables, fire rings, drinking water, flush toilets, boat ramp
**Fee per night:** $$; reservations: (877) 444-6777 or recreation.gov
**Management:** California Land Management, (650) 322-1181
**Activities:** Fishing, boating, hiking, horseback riding
**Finding the campground:** From Mammoth Lakes, drive northwest 15 miles on US 395. Turn left (west) onto CA 158 (June Lake Loop) and drive 6 miles.
**About the campground:** Located at the north end of Silver Lake, the campground occupies an open field with great views of the surrounding mountains. Only a few sites are near the water's edge, but all enjoy the view. If the campground is full, a large private campground is located across the highway. The lake is heavily stocked annually with rainbow trout. A trail leads from the south end of the lake to Agnew Lake (1 mile) and then divides into two trails (one east, one south), each leading to a different series of lakes in the Ansel Adams Wilderness. Elevation 7,200 feet. Stay limit 14 days. Open April through October.

## 701 Hartley Springs

**Location:** 13 miles northwest of the community of Mammoth Lakes
**GPS:** 37.7694 / -119.0370
**Sites:** 25 sites for tents and RVs
**Facilities:** Tables, fire rings, vault toilets; no drinking water
**Fee per night:** None
**Management:** Inyo National Forest, (760) 924-5500
**Activities:** Hiking
**Finding the campground:** From Mammoth Lakes, drive northwest 11 miles on US 395. Turn left (west) onto FR 2S10 and drive 1 mile. Turn right onto FR 2S48 and drive about 1 mile.
**About the campground:** Situated 2 miles north of Obsidian Dome, a volcanic "glass" flow of interest because of its unusual formation. Elevation 8,400 feet. Stay limit 14 days. Open June through September.

## 702 Glass Creek

**Location:** 10 miles northwest of the community of Mammoth Lakes
**GPS:** 37.7517 / -118.9878
**Sites:** 66 sites for tents and RVs
**Facilities:** Tables, fire rings, vault toilets; no drinking water
**Fee per night:** None
**Management:** Inyo National Forest, (760) 924-5500
**Activities:** Hiking, fishing
**Finding the campground:** From Mammoth Lakes, drive northwest 9 miles on US 395. Turn left (west) onto Glass Creek Road and drive about 1 mile. It may be necessary to drive past this turn-off to find an authorized U-turn area to gain access to the west side of US 395.
**About the campground:** A trail from the campground leads west along Glass Creek and the southern edge of Obsidian Dome, a volcanic "glass" flow of unusual formation. Fishing in Glass Creek usually results in mediocre catches of small trout; the stream is only minimally stocked. Elevation 7,600 feet. Stay limit 21 days. Open May through October.

## 703 Deadman

**Location:** 10 miles northwest of Mammoth Lakes
**GPS:** 37.7219 / -119.0081
**Sites:** 30 sites for tents and RVs
**Facilities:** Tables, fire rings, vault toilets; no drinking water
**Fee per night:** None
**Management:** Inyo National Forest, (760) 924-5500
**Activities:** Fishing
**Finding the campground:** From Mammoth Lakes, drive northwest 8 miles on US 395. Turn left (west) onto Deadman Creek Road (FR 2S05) and drive about 2 miles. The campground is adjacent to Obsidian Flat Group Camp.
**About the campground:** Situated on Deadman Creek, where catches of small rainbow and native trout are possible. The sites are divided between upper and lower sections, located across the road from each other. Both are adjacent to the creek. The campground is located next to the Obsidian Flat Group Camp, which has 1 site. Elevation 7,800 feet. Stay limit 14 days. Open June through October.

## 704 Big Springs

**Location:** 9 miles north of Mammoth Lakes
**GPS:** 37.7476 / -118.9389
**Sites:** 26 sites for tents and RVs
**Facilities:** Tables, fire rings, vault toilets; no drinking water
**Fee per night:** None
**Management:** Inyo National Forest, (760) 924-5500
**Activities:** Fishing
**Finding the campground:** From Mammoth Lakes, drive northwest 7 miles on US 395. Turn right (northeast) onto Owens River Road and drive about 2 miles. Bear left at the fork and drive 0.25 mile.

**About the campground:** Situated on Deadman Creek, where catches of small rainbow and native trout are possible. Elevation 7,00 feet. Stay limit 21 days. Open April through October.

## 705 New Shady Rest (Mammoth Lakes)

**Location:** In the town of Mammoth Lakes
**GPS:** 37.6470 / -118.9637
**Sites:** 92 sites for tents and RVs up to 38 feet
**Facilities:** Tables, fire rings, drinking water, flush toilets, dump station, playground
**Fee per night:** $$; reservations: (877) 444-6777 or recreation.gov
**Management:** California Land Management, (650) 322-1181
**Activities:** Hiking, horseback riding, biking, OHV driving
**Finding the campground:** Heading west on CA 203 in Mammoth Lakes, turn right immediately after passing the USDA Forest Service visitor center.
**About the campground:** Situated in an attractive Jeffrey pine forest within the town of Mammoth Lakes, New Shady Rest is best suited as a base for exploring the Mammoth Basin area and for overnighting when the lakeside campgrounds are full. It is within easy walking distance of the forest service visitor center and of restaurants and shopping facilities in town. Hiking, biking, and OHV trails are nearby. Horses may be rented at an adjacent riding stable. Some overflow camping is available in the adjacent Pine Glen group campground. Elevation 7,800 feet. Stay limit 14 days. Open April through October. Some sites remain open in winter for tent camping only.

## 706 Old Shady Rest (Mammoth Lakes)

**Location:** In the town of Mammoth Lakes
**GPS:** 37.6470 / -118.9637
**Sites:** 61 sites for tents and RVs up to 45 feet
**Facilities:** Tables, fire rings, drinking water, flush toilets, dump station, playground
**Fee per night:** $$; reservations: (877) 444-6777 or recreation.gov
**Management:** California Land Management, (650) 322-1181
**Activities:** Hiking, horseback riding
**Finding the campground:** Heading west on CA 203 in Mammoth Lakes, turn right immediately after passing the USDA Forest Service visitor center.
**About the campground:** Situated in the shade of a mature Jeffery pine forest. See New Shady Rest (705) for area information. Stay limit 14 days. Open June through September.

## 707 Sherwin Creek (Mammoth Lakes)

**Location:** 3 miles southeast of the town of Mammoth Lakes
**GPS:** 37.6290 / -118.9378
**Sites:** 85 sites for tents and RVs
**Facilities:** Tables, fire rings, drinking water, flush toilets, dump station, playground
**Fee per night:** $$; reservations: (877) 444-6777 or www.recreation.gov
**Management:** Inyo National Forest, (760) 873-2400
**Activities:** Hiking, OHV driving, horseback riding nearby

**Finding the campground:** From the USDA Forest Service visitor center in Mammoth Lakes, take CA 203 west for 0.3 mile. Turn left (south) onto Old Mammoth Road and drive 1 mile. Bear left onto FR 4S08 and drive 2 miles.

**About the campground:** Situated in an open pine forest on Sherwin Creek. A mile-long road from the campground leads to a trail that rises steeply to Sherwin Lakes (2 miles) and continues on to Valentine Lake (5 miles). Sherwin Lakes provide good fishing. A motocross track is located 1 mile southwest of camp. Elevation 7,600 feet. Stay limit 21 days. Open mid-May through mid-September.

## 708 Twin Lakes (Mammoth Lakes)

**Location:** 3 miles southwest of the town of Mammoth Lakes
**GPS:** 37.6170 / -119.0028
**Sites:** 92 sites for tents and RVs up to 45 feet long
**Facilities:** Tables, fire rings, drinking water, flush toilets, boat ramp, store
**Fee per night:** $$; reservations: (877) 444-6777 or recreation.gov
**Management:** California Land Management, (650) 322-1181
**Activities:** Hiking, fishing, boating, swimming, horseback riding
**Finding the campground:** From the USDA Forest Service visitor center in Mammoth Lakes, take CA 203 west for 1 mile. Bear left (southwest) onto Lake Mary Road and drive 2.3 miles.
**About the campground:** The campground is divided into two sections, one on the east shore and the other on the west shore of the lakes. The setting of the lakes is beautiful and is enhanced by Twin Falls, which spills into the upper lake from Lake Mamie. Many campsites are on the water, with great views of Twin Falls and the surrounding mountains. Twin Lakes are well stocked annually with rainbow trout, and both are heavily fished by anglers in boats and float tubes.

A trail leads northeast from the campground, past sites of historic interest, to Panorama Dome (1.5-mile loop via Valley View Point), which provides excellent views of the surrounding area. The Mammoth Mountain Summit Trail leads northwest from campsite 30 of the west loop of the campground. It reaches the peak in 4 miles, with an elevation gain of 2,500 feet. Mammoth Rock Trail, an equestrian and hiker trail, begins about 0.5 mile east of the campground on Old Mammoth Road (3 miles one way). Mammoth Pack Station is nearby for horse rental and equestrian tours. Elevation 8,760 feet. Stay limit 7 days. Open June through October.

## 709 Pine City (Mammoth Lakes)

**Location:** 5 miles south of Mammoth Lakes
**GPS:** 37.6042 / -119.0002
**Sites:** 10 sites for tents and RVs up to 36 feet
**Facilities:** Tables, fire rings, drinking water, flush toilets
**Fee per night:** $$; reservations: (877) 444-6777 or recreation.gov
**Management:** California Land Management, (650) 322-1181
**Activities:** Hiking, horseback riding
**Finding the campground:** From the USDA Forest Service visitor center in Mammoth Lakes, take CA 203 west for 1 mile. Bear left (southwest) onto Lake Mary Road and drive 3.2 miles. Bear left onto FR 4S09 and drive 0.3 mile.

**About the campground:** Situated in a pine forest across the road from Lake Mary, the campground has no direct lake access. Mammoth Pack Station is nearby for horse rental and equestrian tours. Elevation 8,900 feet. Stay limit 14 days. Open mid-June to mid-September.

## 710 Coldwater (Mammoth Lakes)

**Location:** 5 miles south of Mammoth Lakes.
**GPS:** 37.5995 / -118.9967
**Sites:** 77 sites for tents and RVs up to 40 feet long
**Facilities:** Tables, fire rings, drinking water, flush toilets
**Fee per night:** $$; reservations: (877) 444-6777 or recreation.gov
**Management:** Inyo National Forest, (760) 873-2400
**Activities:** Hiking, fishing, horseback riding
**Finding the campground:** From the USDA Forest Service visitor center in Mammoth Lakes, take CA 203 west for 1 mile. Bear left (southwest) onto Lake Mary Road and drive 3.2 miles. Bear left onto FR 4S09 and drive 0.5 mile. Then turn left onto FR 4S25 and drive 0.3 mile.
**About the campground:** Situated on Coldwater Creek, 0.3 mile from Lake Mary. There is no view of the lake or direct access. A trail from the campground leads to Emerald Lake (0.75 mile) and Sky Meadows (2 miles); both trails offer fine views of the surrounding Sierra peaks. Mammoth Pack Station is nearby for horse rental and equestrian tours. Elevation 8,900 feet. Stay limit 14 days. Open mid-June to mid-September.

## 711 Lake George (Mammoth Lakes)

**Location:** 6 miles southwest of the town of Mammoth Lakes
**GPS:** 37.6052 / -119.0091
**Sites:** 15 sites for tents and RVs up to 23 feet long
**Facilities:** Tables, fire rings, drinking water, flush toilets, boat ramp
**Fee per night:** $$; reservations: (877) 444-6777 or recreation.gov
**Management:** California Land Management, (650) 322-1181
**Activities:** Hiking, fishing, swimming, boating, horseback riding
**Finding the campground:** From the USDA Forest Service visitor center in Mammoth Lakes, take CA 203 west for 1 mile. Bear left (southwest) onto Lake Mary Road and drive 3.2 miles. Bear left onto FR 4S09 and drive 1.5 miles.
**About the campground:** The lake is in a marvelously scenic setting in a deep rock basin at the base of 10,377-foot Crystal Crag. From the campground there is direct access to the lake, which is well stocked annually with rainbow trout. The Barrett Lake/T.J. Lake Trail, a 1-mile round-trip from the campground, affords a maximum display of mountain scenery for minimum effort. The Crystal Lake/Mammoth Crest Trail (6 miles round-trip) provides even more spectacular scenery. Mammoth Pack Station is nearby for horse rental and equestrian tours. Elevation 9,000 feet. Stay limit 7 days. Open mid-June through mid-September.

## 712 Lake Mary (Mammoth Lakes)

**Location:** 6 miles south of the town of Mammoth Lakes
**GPS:** 37.6071 / -119.0066

**Sites:** 48 sites for tents and RVs up to 30 feet long
**Facilities:** Tables, fire rings, drinking water, flush toilets, boat launch and rentals, pier
**Fee per night:** $$; reservations: (877) 444-6777 or recreation.gov
**Management:** California Land Management, (650) 322-1181
**Activities:** Fishing, swimming, boating, horseback riding
**Finding the campground:** From the USDA Forest Service visitor center in Mammoth Lakes, take CA 203 west for 1 mile. Bear left (southwest) onto Lake Mary Road and drive 3.2 miles. Bear left onto FR 4S09 and drive 1.5 miles.
**About the campground:** Lake Mary was selected by *Sunset* magazine as one of the 100 best campgrounds in the western United States. The campsites are on a rise overlooking the lake and offer direct access to the water. Scenery at the lakeside is beautiful. The lake is heavily stocked annually with rainbow trout, and fishing is usually good from a trolling boat and fair from shore. Mammoth Pack Station is nearby for horse rental and equestrian tours. Elevation 8,900 feet. Stay limit 14 days. Open June through September.

## 713 Agnew Meadows (Reds Meadow)

**Location:** 10 miles northwest of the town of Mammoth Lakes
**GPS:** 37.6812 / -119.0807
**Sites:** 17 sites for tents and small RVs up to 30 feet long; 4 group sites
**Facilities:** Tables, fire rings, drinking water, vault toilets
**Fee per night:** $$; reservations (group sites only): (877) 444-6777 or recreation.gov
**Management:** California Land Management, (650) 322-1181
**Activities:** Hiking, fishing, horseback riding

*On the trail to Shadow Lake from Reds Meadow. Photo by Bubba Seuss*

**Finding the campground:** From the USDA Forest Service visitor center in Mammoth Lakes, drive west on CA 203 for 6 miles to the Reds Meadow entrance station. Check in and request a permit to use the road for camping purposes. Continue on what is now Minaret Summit Road for about 3 miles, descending on a paved but narrow and sometimes one-way route. Turn right onto the campground entry road and drive 0.5 mile. It is a narrow, single lane.
**About the campground:** Situated along the bank of a feeder stream of the Middle Fork of the San Joaquin River, which provides good fishing for small trout. The Pacific Crest National Scenic Trail passes the campground, offering a fine hike along the river to Soda Springs (3 miles), Devils Postpile (7 miles), Reds Meadow (9 miles), and Rainbow Falls (10 miles). In summer you can make the return trip on the park shuttle bus. You can also take the trail northward to Emerald and Thousand Island Lakes (6 miles), two beautiful spots in the shadow of two of the Minaret peaks. A pack station is located near the beginning of the campground entry road. Elevation 8,400 feet. Stay limit 14 days. Open June through October.

## 714 Upper Soda Springs (Reds Meadow)

**Location:** 11 miles west of the town of Mammoth Lakes
**GPS:** 37.6513 / -119.0743
**Sites:** 28 sites for tents and small RVs
**Facilities:** Tables, fire rings, drinking water, vault toilets
**Fee per night:** $$
**Management:** California Land Management, (650) 322-1181
**Activities:** Hiking, fishing, horseback riding
**Finding the campground:** Take US 395 to CA 203. Head west to and through the town of Mammoth Lakes. At the 2nd traffic light, turn right onto Minaret and continue up the mountain past Mammoth Mountain Main Lodge and Minaret Vista Station to campground.
**About the campground:** An overflow campground situated near the bank of the Middle Fork of the San Joaquin River, at a point where the Pacific Crest National Scenic Trail crosses the river (see Agnew Meadows Campground, 713). The river is stocked annually with trout from a place near the campground. Swimming is permitted at Starkweather Lake, about 1 mile north. A pack station is 2 miles north for horse rental and equestrian tours. Elevation 7,700 feet. Stay limit 14 days. Open June through September.

## 715 Pumice Flat (Reds Meadow)

**Location:** 12 miles west of the town of Mammoth Lakes
**GPS:** 37.6492 / -119.0739
**Sites:** 17 sites for tents and RVs; 4 group sites
**Facilities:** Tables, fire rings, drinking water, flush toilets
**Fee per night:** $$; reservations (group sites only): (877) 444-6777 or recreation.gov
**Management:** California Land Management, (650) 322-1181
**Activities:** Hiking, fishing, horseback riding
**Finding the campground:** From the USDA Forest Service visitor center in Mammoth Lakes, drive west on CA 203 for 6 miles to the Reds Meadow entrance station. Check in and request a permit to use the road for camping purposes. Continue on what is now Minaret Summit Road for about 6

miles, descending on a paved but narrow and sometimes one-way route to the valley floor and the campground.

**About the campground:** See Agnew Meadows Campground (713) for fishing information. The campground is adjacent to the San Joaquin River. Swimming is permitted in Starkweather Lake, about 1 mile north, and at Sotcher Lake, about 2 miles south. A pack station is located at Reds Meadow, about 2 miles south. Elevation 7,700 feet. Stay limit 14 days. Open June through September.

## 716 Minaret Falls (Reds Meadow)

**Location:** 14 miles west of the town of Mammoth Lakes
**GPS:** 37.6388 / -119.0771
**Sites:** 27 sites for tents and RVs
**Facilities:** Tables, fire rings, drinking water, vault toilets
**Fee per night:** $$
**Management:** California Land Management, (650) 322-1181
**Activities:** Hiking, fishing, horseback riding
**Finding the campground:** From the USDA Forest Service visitor center in Mammoth Lakes, drive west on CA 203 for 6 miles to the Reds Meadow entrance station. Check in and request a permit to use the road for camping purposes. Continue on what is now Minaret Summit Road for about 7 miles, descending on a paved but narrow and sometimes one-way route to the valley floor. Turn right onto the campground access road and drive 0.5 mile.
**About the campground:** Situated in a beautiful setting, with Minaret Falls just across the San Joaquin River. A 1-mile-long trail leads from the campground to Devils Postpile. See Agnew Meadows Campground (713) for fishing information. Swimming is permitted in Sotcher Lake, about 1 mile south. A pack station is located at Reds Meadow, about 2 miles south. Elevation 7,600 feet. Stay limit 14 days. Open June through September.

## 717 Devils Postpile

**Location:** 14 miles west of the town of Mammoth Lakes
**GPS:** 37.6388 / -119.0771
**Sites:** 20 sites for tents and RVs
**Facilities:** Tables, fire rings, drinking water, flush toilets
**Fee per night:** $$
**Management:** Devils Postpile National Monument, (760) 934-2289
**Activities:** Hiking, fishing, horseback riding
**Finding the campground:** From the USDA Forest Service visitor center in Mammoth Lakes, drive west on CA 203 for 6 miles to the Reds Meadow entrance station. Check in and request a permit to use the road for camping purposes. Continue on what is now Minaret Summit Road for about 8 miles, descending on a paved but narrow and sometimes one-way route to the valley floor to the campground.
**About the campground:** Devils Postpile is an unusual columnar-jointed basalt, formed when lava erupting from the river valley cooled and cracked into post-like columns. The campground is near the bank of the Middle Fork of the San Joaquin River, about 0.5 mile north of the actual "postpile"

on an easy trail. The same trail continues for 2.5 more miles to Rainbow Falls. Swimming is permitted in Sotcher Lake, about 1 mile south. A pack station is located at Reds Meadow, about 2 miles south. The combined Pacific Crest/John Muir Trail passes through the monument, offering hiking opportunities north and south. Elevation 7,600 feet. Stay limit 14 days. Open June 26 until snowfall.

## 718 **Reds Meadow**

**Location:** 15 miles west of the town of Mammoth Lakes
**GPS:** 37.6201 / -119.0766
**Sites:** 52 sites for tents and RVs up to 30 feet long
**Facilities:** Tables, fire rings, drinking water, flush toilets, hot springs showers and tubs
**Fee per night:** $$
**Management:** California Land Management, (650) 322-1181
**Activities:** Hiking, horseback riding
**Finding the campground:** From the USDA Forest Service visitor center in Mammoth Lakes, drive west on CA 203 for 6 miles to the Reds Meadow entrance station. Check in and request a permit to use the road for camping purposes. Continue on what is now Minaret Summit Road for about 9 miles, descending on a paved but narrow and sometimes one-way route to the valley floor to the campground.
**About the campground:** Situated in a sloping meadow dotted with trees. Trails lead from the campground to Devils Postpile (1 mile), Sotcher Lake (0.5 mile), and Red Cones (6.5-mile loop), a series of small, volcanically formed cinder cones. Swimming is permitted at Sotcher Lake; horse rentals and equestrian tours are available at Reds Meadow Pack Station. Elevation 7,600 feet. Stay limit 14 days. Open June through October.

## 719 **Convict Lake**

**Location:** 9 miles southeast of the town of Mammoth Lakes
**GPS:** 37.5926 / -118.8500
**Sites:** 85 sites for tents and RVs
**Facilities:** Tables, fire rings and grills, drinking water, flush toilets, dump station, boat ramp and rentals
**Fee per night:** $$; reservations: (800) 444-7275 or reserveamerica.com
**Management:** Inyo National Forest, (760) 873-2538
**Activities:** Fishing, boating, hiking
**Finding the campground:** From Mammoth Lakes, drive east on CA 203 for 3 miles. Turn right onto US 395 and drive 4 miles. Turn right onto FR 07 and drive 2 miles.
**About the campground:** Convict Lake has one of the most spectacular settings in the Sierra Nevada. The sheer sides of Mount Morrison and Laurel Mountain plunge directly down to the shoreline. The campsites are not directly on the lake, but they enjoy the full mountain panorama from open sites in a brush-and-grass field. The lake is heavily stocked with rainbow trout annually. A 2-mile trail circles the lake and also leads through Convict Creek Canyon to Mildred Lake (5 miles) and Lake Dorothy (6 miles). Elevation 7,600 feet. Stay limit 7 days. Open April through October.

## 720 McGee Creek

**Location:** 13 miles southeast of the town of Mammoth Lakes
**GPS:** 37.5654 / -118.7855
**Sites:** 28 sites for tents and RVs up to 23 feet long
**Facilities:** Tables, fire rings, drinking water, flush and vault toilets
**Fee per night:** $$; reservations: (800) 444-7275 or reserveamerica.com
**Management:** Inyo National Forest, (760) 873-2538
**Activities:** Hiking, fishing, horseback riding
**Finding the campground:** From Mammoth Lakes, drive east on CA 203 for 3 miles. Turn right onto US 395 and drive 7 miles southeast. Turn right onto the frontage road paralleling the freeway and drive 1.5 miles. Turn right onto McGee Creek Road and drive 1.5 miles.
**About the campground:** Situated in an attractive meadow adjacent to McGee Creek, which is stocked annually with rainbow trout. From the steep road leading to the campground, you get great views of the Sierra Nevada and Owen Valley. Sites are paved and level. There are no large trees, but ramadas shade the picnic tables. A hiker and equestrian trail about 1 mile southwest of the campground leads to Horsetail Falls and several small lakes. Elevation 7,600 feet. Stay limit 14 days. Open April through September.

## 721 Crowley Lake

**Location:** 13 miles southeast of the town of Mammoth Lakes
**GPS:** 37.5718 / -118.7709
**Sites:** 47 sites for tents and RVs; group parking area
**Facilities:** Tables, fire rings, pit toilets, drinking water
**Fee per night:** $
**Management:** Bureau of Land Management, (760) 872-5008
**Activities:** Fishing, boating, swimming at Crowley Lake (3 miles away)
**Finding the campground:** From Mammoth Lakes, drive east 3 miles on CA 203. Turn right onto US 395 and drive 7 miles southeast. Turn right onto the frontage road paralleling the freeway and drive 2.5 miles.
**About the campground:** This campground is located in open high-desert country, where there are no trees and the wind can often be strong. The area looks out over Crowley Lake, about 3 miles away. There is a boat ramp at South Landing. The lake is stocked annually with 40,000 rainbow trout and more than 300,000 Eagle Lake and rainbow fingerlings. Sacramento perch are also stocked. Elevation 7,000 feet. Stay limit 14 days. Open April through October.

## 722 Tuff

**Location:** 15 miles southeast of Mammoth Lakes
**GPS:** 37.5630 / -118.6718
**Sites:** 34 sites for tents and RVs up to 45 feet long
**Facilities:** Tables, fire rings, drinking water, vault toilets
**Fee per night:** $$; reservations: (877) 444-6777 or recreation.gov
**Management:** Inyo National Forest, (760) 873-2538

**Activities:** None at campground; fishing, boating, and swimming at Crowley Lake, 4 miles west
**Finding the campground:** From the intersection of CA 203 and US 395 (the Mammoth Lakes exit), drive east 15 miles on US 395.
**About the campground:** Campsites are organized in three separate loops along a small but attractive stocked trout stream. Tuff can be used as a base for those wanting to fish at Crowley Lake or explore the nearby Owens River Gorge. Elevation 7,000 feet. Stay limit 21 days. Open April through October.

## 723 French Camp

**Location:** 18 miles southeast of the town of Mammoth Lakes
**GPS:** 37.5568 / -118.6781
**Sites:** 86 sites for tents and RVs up to 23 feet long
**Facilities:** Tables, fire rings, drinking water, flush toilets, dump station
**Fee per night:** $$; reservations: (877) 444-6777 or recreation.gov
**Management:** Inyo National Forest, (760) 873-2538
**Activities:** Fishing
**Finding the campground:** From Mammoth Lakes, drive 3 miles east on CA 203. Turn right onto US 395 and drive 14.5 miles southeast. Turn right (south) at Tom's Place exit onto Rock Creek Road (FR 12) and drive 0.25 mile.
**About the campground:** Situated on Rock Creek near the entrance to Rock Creek Canyon, the campground is used as a base for activities at Crowley Lake, 3 miles to the northwest. The creek offers fair fishing for small trout. Elevation 7,500 feet. Stay limit 21 days. Open April through October.

## 724 Holiday

**Location:** 18 miles southeast of the town of Mammoth Lakes
**GPS:** 37.5506 / -118.6794
**Sites:** 35 sites for tents and RVs up to 23 feet long
**Facilities:** Tables, fire rings, drinking water, vault toilets
**Fee per night:** $$
**Management:** Inyo National Forest, (760) 873-2538
**Activities:** Fishing
**Finding the campground:** From Mammoth Lakes, drive 3 miles east on CA 203. Turn right onto US 395 and drive 14.5 miles southeast. Turn right (south) at the Tom's Place exit onto Rock Creek Road (FR 12) and drive 0.5 mile.
**About the campground:** Situated near the entrance to Rock Creek Canyon. Elevation 7,500 feet. Stay limit 14 days. Open all year. The campground serves as an overflow area and is open as needed.

## 725 Iris Meadow

**Location:** 21 miles southeast of Mammoth Lakes
**GPS:** 37.5192 / -118.7107
**Sites:** 14 sites for tents and RVs up to 26 feet long

**Facilities:** Tables, fire rings, drinking water, flush toilets
**Fee per night:** $$
**Management:** Inyo National Forest, (760) 873-2538
**Activities:** Fishing
**Finding the campground:** From Mammoth Lakes, drive 3 miles east on CA 203. Turn right onto US 395 and drive 14.5 miles southeast. Turn right (south) at Tom's Place exit onto Rock Creek Road (FR 12) and drive 3.75 miles.
**About the campground:** Situated on Rock Creek, with fishing for small trout. Just downstream is the Aspen Group Camp. Elevation 8,300 feet. Stay limit days. Open June through October.

## 726 Big Meadow

**Location:** 22 miles southeast of the town of Mammoth Lakes
**GPS:** 37.5119 / -118.7129
**Sites:** 11 sites for tents and RVs up to 23 feet long
**Facilities:** Tables, fire rings, drinking water, flush toilets, dump station
**Fee per night:** $$
**Management:** Inyo National Forest, (760) 873-2538
**Activities:** Fishing, hiking, horseback riding
**Finding the campground:** From Mammoth Lakes, drive 3 miles east on CA 203. Turn right onto US 395 and drive 14.5 miles southeast. Turn right (south) at Tom's Place exit onto Rock Creek Road (FR 12) and drive 4.75 miles.
**About the campground:** Situated on Rock Creek, with fishing for small trout. Elevation 8,600 feet. Stay limit 7 days. Open June through October.

## 727 East Fork

**Location:** 24 miles southeast of the town of Mammoth Lakes
**GPS:** 37.4926 / -118.7194
**Sites:** 133 sites for tents and RVs up to 40 feet long
**Facilities:** Tables, fire rings, drinking water, flush toilets
**Fee per night:** $$; reservations: (800) 444-7275 or reserveamerica.com
**Management:** Inyo National Forest, (760) 873-2538
**Activities:** Fishing
**Finding the campground:** From Mammoth Lakes, drive 3 miles east on CA 203. Turn right onto US 395 and drive 14.5 miles southeast. Turn right (south) at Tom's Place exit onto Rock Creek Road (FR 12) and drive 6.75 miles.
**About the campground:** Situated on Rock Creek, with fishing for small trout. Hiking nearby in the John Muir Wilderness. The nearby Palisades Group Camp accepts overflow campers. Elevation 9,000 feet. Stay limit 14 days. Open May through September.

## 728 Pine Grove

**Location:** 25 miles southeast of the town of Mammoth Lakes
**GPS:** 37.4705 / -118.7250
**Sites:** 11 sites for tents and RVs up to 23 feet long

**Facilities:** Tables, fire rings, drinking water, vault toilets
**Fee per night:** $$
**Management:** Inyo National Forest, (760) 873-2538
**Activities:** Fishing
**Finding the campground:** From Mammoth Lakes, drive 3 miles east on CA 203. Turn right onto US 395 and drive 14.5 miles southeast. Turn right (south) at Tom's Place exit onto Rock Creek Road (FR 12) and drive 7.75 miles.
**About the campground:** Situated on Rock Creek, with fishing for small trout. A pack station is nearby offering horse rentals and trips. Hiking nearby in the John Muir Wilderness. Elevation 9,300 feet. Stay limit 7 days. Open May through October.

## 729 Upper Pine Grove

**Location:** 26 miles southeast of the town of Mammoth Lakes
**GPS:** 37.4692 / -118.7260
**Sites:** 8 sites for tents and RVs up to 23 feet long
**Facilities:** Tables, fire rings, drinking water, vault toilets
**Fee per night:** $$
**Management:** Inyo National Forest, (760) 873-2538
**Activities:** Fishing, horseback riding
**Finding the campground:** From Mammoth Lakes, drive 3 miles east on CA 203. Turn right onto US 395 and drive 14.5 miles southeast. Turn right (south) at Tom's Place exit onto Rock Creek Road (FR 12) and drive about 8 miles.
**About the campground:** Situated on Rock Creek, with fishing for small trout. A pack station is nearby offering horse rentals and trips. Hiking nearby in the John Muir Wilderness. Elevation 9,400 feet. Stay limit 7 days. Open May through October.

## 730 Rock Creek Lake

**Location:** 28 miles southeast of the town of Mammoth Lakes
**GPS:** 37.4567 / -118.7353
**Sites:** 28 sites; 1 group site for tents and RVs up to 23 feet long
**Facilities:** Tables, fire rings, drinking water, vault toilets
**Fee per night:** $$–$$$$; reservations: (877) 444-6777 or recreation.gov
**Management:** Inyo National Forest, (760) 873-2538
**Activities:** Fishing, hiking, horseback riding
**Finding the campground:** From Mammoth Lakes, drive 3 miles east on CA 203. Turn right onto US 395 and drive 14.5 miles southeast. Turn right (south) at Tom's Place exit onto Rock Creek Road (FR 12) and drive about 10 miles.
**About the campground:** The campground is situated on small but beautiful Rock Creek Lake, which is well stocked annually with rainbow trout. A trail leads north from the campground to Hilton Creek Lakes; another trail 1.5 miles south of the camp leads to Little Lakes Valley, which holds more than a dozen small lakes amid a spectacular alpine basin. A nearby pack station offers horse rentals and trips. Elevation 9,700 feet. Stay limit 7 days. Open May through October.

# About the Author

**Linda Parker Hamilton** is a full-time writer who loves to explore creativity and the outdoors with her family and friends. When not bundled up enjoying morning song birds and morning coffee brewed on a campstove, she lives in Oakland, California. She is the author of FalconGuides *Best Hikes Near San Francisco*, *Hiking the San Francisco Bay Area*, and *Camping Activity Book for Families: The Kid-Tested Guide to Fun in the Outdoors*.